# COUNSELING ACROSS CULTURES

## Sixth Edition

# Elder Wisdom

*An elder Lakota was teaching his grandchildren about life. He said to them, "A fight is going on inside me . . . it is a terrible fight and it is between two wolves.*

*"One wolf represents fear, anger, envy, sorrow, regret, greed, arrogance, self-pity, guilt, resentment, inferiority, lies, false pride, superiority, and ego.*

*"The other stands for joy, peace, love, hope, sharing, serenity, humility, kindness, benevolence, friendship, empathy, generosity, truth, compassion, and faith.*

*"This same fight is going on inside you, and inside every other person, too."*

*The grandchildren thought about it for a minute, and then one child asked her grandfather, "Which wolf will win?"*

*The Elder replied simply, "The one you feed."*


*The Western conception of the person as a bounded, unique, more or less integrated motivational and cognitive universe, a dynamic center of awareness, emotion, judgment, and action, organized into a distinctive whole and set contrastively—both against other such wholes and against social and natural background—is however incorrigible it may seem to us, a rather peculiar idea within the context of the world's cultures. (p. 34)*

*Geertz, C. (1973).* The interpretation of cultures: Selected essays. *New York: Basic Books.*


*The first peace, which is the most important, is that which comes within the souls of men when they realize their relationship, their oneness, with the universe and all its Powers, and when they realize that at the center of the universe dwells Wakan-Tanka, and that this center is everywhere, it is within each of us. This is the real Peace, and the others are but reflections of this.*

*The second peace is that which is made between two individuals, and the third is that which is made between two nations. But above all you should understand that there can never be peace between nations until there is first known that true peace which . . . is within the souls of men. (p. 198)*

*Black Elk, in Neihardt, J. G. (1961).* Black Elk speaks: Being the life story of the holy man of the Oglala Sioux. *Lincoln: University of Nebraska Press.*

# COUNSELING ACROSS CULTURES

## Sixth Edition

**Paul B. Pedersen**
*Syracuse University (Emeritus); University of Hawaii (Visiting)*

**Juris G. Draguns**
*Pennsylvania State University*

**Walter J. Lonner**
*Western Washington University*

**Joseph E. Trimble**
*Western Washington University*

Editors

**SAGE** Publications
Los Angeles • London • New Delhi • Singapore

*For information:*

 Sage Publications, Inc.
2455 Teller Road
Thousand Oaks,
California 91320
E-mail: order@sagepub.com

Sage Publications India Pvt. Ltd.
B 1/I 1 Mohan Cooperative Industrial Area
Mathura Road, New Delhi
India 110 044

Sage Publications Ltd.
1 Oliver's Yard
55 City Road
London EC1Y 1SP
United Kingdom

Sage Publications Asia-Pacific Pte. Ltd.
33 Pekin Street #02-01
Far East Square
Singapore 048763

Printed in the United States of America.

*Library of Congress Cataloging-in-Publication Data*

Counseling across cultures / edited by Paul B. Pedersen . . . [et al.]. — 6th ed.
    p. cm.
Includes bibliographical references and index.
ISBN 978-1-4129-2739-0 (pbk.)
    1. Cross-cultural counseling. 2. Psychiatry, Transcultural. I. Pedersen, Paul, 1936–

BF636.7.C76C68 2008
616.89′14—dc22                          2007002084

This book is printed on acid-free paper.

09  10  11  10  9  8  7  6  5  4  3  2

| | |
|---|---|
| *Acquiring Editor:* | Kassie Graves |
| *Editorial Assistant:* | Veronica Novak |
| *Project Editor:* | Astrid Virding |
| *Copyeditor:* | Gillian Dickens |
| *Typesetter:* | C&M Digitals (P) Ltd. |
| *Indexer:* | Juniee Oneida |
| *Proofreader:* | Dennis W. Webb |
| *Cover Designer:* | Candice Harman |
| *Marketing Manager:* | Carmel Withers |

# Contents

# Foreword

The idea of culture is as old as humankind. It is a way of life that one generation of human beings passes to the next. Adult members of a community not only nourish and protect fragile newcomers, but they also teach them how to survive in and adjust to the world. During the Roman Empire, the Latin *cultura* referred to the cultivation of crops. Since then, the word *culture* has acquired many other meanings. For example, today it is used to refer to (a) the raising, improvement, or development of some plant, animal, or product; (b) the growth of bacteria or other micro-organisms in a specially prepared nourishing substance; (c) improvement, refinement, or development by study or training; and (d) the training and refinement of the mind, emotions, manners, taste, and the like. In general, social scientists conceive of culture as a complex whole that includes knowledge, beliefs, art, architecture, language, morals, laws, customs, and other capabilities and habits acquired by members of a society.

Culture is a requirement for human existence. Neonates enter the world unable to walk, talk, or eat solid food. They cannot survive without the love, care, and nourishment of their parents and the larger community into which they are born. As they mature, they acquire the language and way of life of their native group. Inseparable from the people already on the scene when they arrive, they become group dependent. They need the group, and the group needs them. Grown-ups protect and teach the young. Once grown up themselves, they protect and care for their elders. Each generation enhances the knowledge about the human group and invents objects and procedures designed to facilitate their existence. Culture evolves to meet needs of the time.

There is not just one culture to which people adjust. They are at the center of and influenced by five interactive cultures. First, there is a universal culture that is biologically based. As members of a single species, humans worldwide engage in similar necessary and predictable behaviors in order to meet a multitude of survival needs. Homo sapiens must find food, shelter, and a source of water. Endowed with the sex drive, they produce, nourish, protect, and socialize children in a family context. Since species-specific culture is universal, it enables humans to identify with their confrères across cultures.

Second, individuals must adjust to the local ecological conditions that support their existence and that of thousands of other living organisms. In establishing an existential relationship with their environment, they develop the ability to live with and use to their advantage available flora and fauna. Moreover, humans learn to relate to elements of nature such as the temperature, humidity, sources of water, and natural occurrences. These and their attitudes toward them affect how they exploit the natural abundance that can be used to support their existence. Of course, the existential challenge differs from one geographical area to another. Humankind can live almost anywhere in the world, so long as they know how to relate to their environment. The specific nature of the relationship is the ecological culture.

Third, a national culture derives from the fact that a group of people shares the same territory, heritage, language, and economic system and exemplifies an allegiance to a way of life that they hold dear. Although outsiders may join the society, they must fit into the culture already in place. Immigrants acculturate to the host culture in order to benefit from being a part of it.

The national culture is an interactive network of subsystems. Each subordinate unit provides goods and services to inhabitants of the society. The counseling profession is one of the subsystems. Formally established in 1952, today it has evolved into an association consisting of more than 60,000 members, organized into 19 divisions, 56 branches, and 4 regions in the United States, Europe, Latin America, Puerto Rico, the Virgin Islands, and the Philippines. Affiliates of the American Counseling Association have developed a psychotherapeutic culture. It consists of educational and licensure requirements, laws, a code of ethics, theories, techniques, and other counselor and client behaviors recognized, accepted, understood, and sanctioned by society at large.

Fourth, people may be culturally unique in their own country because of the peculiarity of the region in which they are socialized. In many nations, it is observed that regions differ from the others in terms of language, religion, crops grown, dress, customs, and in other ways. In large countries, climate zones influence how people negotiate their environment. In other cases, proximity to the borders of neighboring countries contributes to a blending of cultures along the territorial boundaries. Regional cultural differences are often caused by military conquests, political annexations, and immigration.

Fifth, individuals usually adjust to the way of life of the racio-ethnic group into which they are born and socialized. In general, large racial and ethnic communities exist apart from the dominant racial and cultural community. Separatism is likely to be a reality in countries in which minorities are denied equal opportunity or feel rejected by their dominant group compatriots. On the other hand, some may choose voluntarily to live in their own communities in order to keep vibrant their native culture. Regardless of the reason for racial and ethnic separation, the results are the same. A racio-ethnic culture usually remains intact and is transmitted from one generation to the next so long as minorities remain isolated from the mainstream culture.

However, in the middle of the 20th century, African Americans protested loudly their perceived "inferiority" and shunting aside in the social order. It was out of protests for inclusion as equal participants in society that the civil rights movement developed under the leadership of Dr. Martin Luther King Jr. and others. The demands for change in the society at large soon resonated in the counseling profession. A caucus of African American counselors attending the American Personnel and Guidance Association (now the American Counseling Association [ACA]) in Las Vegas, Nevada, in 1969, demanded at a meeting of the association's governing body that the ACA recognize the specific needs of American minority group clients. The leadership of the body was shocked, annoyed, and frustrated because "everybody knows that counseling is counseling," the prevailing view of mainstream counselor educators at the time. Although many academicians articulated that position, they at the same time often referred to African Americans as being culturally deprived, disadvantaged, or otherwise deficient.

As a result of the demands of the Black Caucus in Las Vegas, an office of Non-White Concerns was established at the association's national headquarters. Out of the activities of that office emerged the Association for Non-White Concerns in Personnel and Guidance (now the Association for Multicultural Counseling and Development [AMCD]), chartered as a division of the ACA in 1972. The AMCD strives (a) to enhance the awareness of human development and counseling needs of racial and ethnically diverse groups, (b) to sensitize professionals to racial and ethnic differences, (c) to advance the knowledge base of multicultural counseling through theory development and research, and (d) and to consult with others to advance multicultural issues across the counseling profession.

Since the 1970s, counselors and other psychotherapeutic professionals throughout the world now recognize the importance of culture in counseling. In the United States, culture continues to be defined and redefined. It is no longer just a way of life impressed on the individual by biological, ecological, national, regional, and racio-ethnic forces that are passed on to future generations. It now also includes the way of life of any group that deviates from a perceived cultural norm. Many clients deviating from social standards in terms of sexual orientation, psychophysical challenges, gender, and age declare themselves to be culturally different and demand that they be viewed as such by counselors. Their demands are now reflected in current psychotherapeutic literature.

Since the first use of the Latin word *cultura* to refer to growing crops in ancient Rome, culture continues to acquire other connotations. Even so, they all tend to communicate the idea that there is an interactive relationship between individuals and their environments. The environments are natural, social, personal, and spiritual. Humans establish a *modus vivendi* with them. The living arrangement constitutes the culture of Homo sapiens. They are basic to existence. Until about 50 years ago, culture was primarily associated with sociology and anthropology. However, during the push for equality initiated by Blacks in the United States, it was redefined. African Americans and others who perceived themselves to be outsiders in their own country rejected the cultural norms of mainstream America. The prevailing norms included racist attitudes and practices that were legally sanctioned. Therefore, they refused to accept many of them and began to express their view of other people and conditions that affected their existence. Although in the past, most of them had never considered the concept of culture, they began to understand it and apply it to their lives and enterprises. As an important institution in the society, the counseling profession became involved in the social revolution. Today, culture and its relationship to counseling has become a large literature.

A complex of diversified subsystems, culture remains difficult to define. It often seems to be a cauldron of entangled ideas and contradictions. For example, public schools are now integrated throughout the United States. Yet, churches remain largely segregated. Since the 1960s, African Americans have sought inclusion in the American society as equal participants. However, there is today an increase in all-Black ideologies, associations, and facilities. The number of advocates of Black psychology and Afrocentrism continues to grow. On many mainstream college campuses, Black students live in all-Black housing units and congregate in racially exclusive sections of student unions. On one hand, African American counselors wanted their mainstream confrères to recognize the unique needs of Black clients. On the other, they created a separate minority division in the American Counseling Association, instead of proposing that counselors in all divisions in the association address issues related to counseling minorities.

In counselor education and research, contradictions also exist. In the 1960s, African American counselor educators wanted to help majority-group counselors to become aware of the specific needs of minority-group clients. In the first decade of the 21st century, most of them have attempted to achieve this goal by stereotyping minorities. That is, in general, professors lecture about the general characteristics of racial and ethnic groups and discuss their implications for counseling. The same is often the case in cross-cultural counseling research. Usually, researchers design research in which they compare racio-ethnic groups. For example, they compare most often groups that they designate as Hispanic, Asian, European, or African American. Little or no attention is given to the country of origin of the subjects, degree of acculturation, or the social class of the participants. Such omissions tend to call into question the value of much of the research. Indeed, cross-cultural counseling seems to be at the crossroads of an important and innovative movement.

Although cross-cultural counseling has a long history, there is still a lot to learn about it. This book, the sixth edition of *Counseling Across Cultures,* is a godsend, just as were the first five editions. The editors deserve appreciation and recognition for introducing the ideas of creative scholars to the profession. The contributors are all original thinkers. They each bring a specific perspective on the exciting, global, and challenging field that means so much to people in a shrinking world, in which inhabitants move daily from one country to another. Their chapters inform educators, counselors, clients, and the public at large. *Counseling Across Cultures* remains a classic in the counseling profession. The ideas expressed in it should help all therapeutic professionals to evaluate the place of culture in their work and to become more effective counseling all clients.

*Clemmont E. Vontress, PhD*
Professor Emeritus of Counseling
George Washington University

# Introduction to the Sixth Edition

## Learning From Our "Culture Teachers"

Capture the visual image of a thousand persons sitting around you. People that you have chosen, or have chosen you, over a lifetime from friends, enemies, heroes, heroines, mentors, family members, and fantasy figures that influenced you in sometimes subtle but often profound ways. As these "culture teachers" talk with one another and sometimes include you in their conversations, they provide a vivid and concrete image of "multiculturalism." Many if not all our decisions are controlled or at least influenced by imagined conversations with our culture teachers. They broadly define the cultural context in which we live through ethnographic, demographic, status-oriented, and personal affiliations. All behaviors are learned and displayed in specific cultural contexts.

Therefore, accurate assessment, meaningful understanding, and appropriate interventions require that we learn more about our own cultural context and the culture teachers who shape our lives. To ignore our culture teachers is tantamount to driving down a busy highway and taking our hands off the steering wheel!

Since the first edition of *Counseling Across Cultures* was published in 1976, thousands of publications and research projects have increased our understanding of these culture teachers. Many of these sources are listed in the reference sections of this book. We owe a great debt to these culture teachers for the wisdom we have gained from them. As recently as 1973, when we presented a symposium at the American Psychological Association on "Counseling Across Cultures" and subsequently planned the first edition of this book, the term *multiculturalism* was largely unknown to counseling professionals. The University of Hawaii Press agreed to publish our book, provided we waived royalties. The book went through five printings the first year and then through three more editions in 1981, 1989, and 1996. The fifth edition was published by Sage in 2002, followed by the current sixth edition and illustrating the growing popularity of counseling across cultures.

The culture-centered or multicultural perspective provides us with at least 12 uniquely valuable outcomes:

1. Accuracy: because all behaviors are learned and displayed in a cultural context

2. Common ground: because the basic values in which we believe are expressed through different behaviors across cultures

3. Identity: because we learn who we are from the thousands of culture teachers in our lives

4. Health: because our socio-ecosystems require a diversified gene pool

5. Protection: because psychology has been culturally encapsulated through much of its history, and we need to identify our own biases to protect ourselves from failure

6. Survival: because the best preparation for life in the global village is to learn from persons who are culturally different from ourselves

7. Social justice: because history documents the injustices that result when a monocultural, dominant group is allowed to define the rules of living for everyone

8. Right thinking: because not only the content of our thinking is culturally biased but the linear thinking process itself also requires modification when thinking about nonlinear alternatives

9. Learning: because effective learning that results in change is also likely to result in culture shock

10. Spirituality: because it can be expected that we all experience the same Ultimate Reality in different ways

11. Political stability: because some form of cultural pluralism is the only alternative to either anarchy or oppression

12. Competence: because multiculturalism is generic to a genuine and realistic understanding of human behavior in all counseling and communication

Over and above these 12 points, culturally informed counseling can be likened to a bridge that helps transcend the gulf or the chasm of differences in practices, expectations, and modes of communication that separate persons whose backgrounds and outlooks have been molded by their respective cultures.

The present edition includes many new authors and offers ideas that have emerged since the appearance of the preceding edition in 2002. This edition is divided into five parts, which increases the number of topics while streamlining chapter lengths to fit with academic class assignments. Each part features an introduction that contains discussion questions for each chapter. Each chapter identifies primary and secondary objectives and includes conclusions, as well as a "critical incident" to illustrate key points of the chapter at the case level. We concede that not all of these incidents are critical in the strict sense of the term. They do, however, make abstract concepts concrete and exemplify, often in a vivid way, the interface between culture and counseling. Over and above this feature, authors in the present edition have been liberal with instances and vignettes of culturally distinctive ways of presenting personal dilemmas, seeking relief from distress, and, in the optimal case, reducing suffering and resolving quandaries and problems of living. On the theoretical plane, the authors of these chapters have contributed several explicit models of culturally sensitive intervention in a variety of contexts. Moreover, the results of several major multinational research projects have been brought to bear upon the current multicultural counseling enterprise. In this manner, contributors to this volume have endeavored to narrow the gap between basic cross-cultural research findings and culturally appropriate intervention at the case level.

A Web site is available that includes discussion questions, multiple-choice test items, simulations, classroom activities, additional readings, and information to supplement each chapter as well as other teaching/learning resources. Sample syllabi for teaching classes while using this edition have also been prepared, and plans for evaluating classes and opportunities for direct Internet contact between the authors, editors, and users of this edition have been developed. Increased emphasis is placed on global issues in this edition, not only because more counselors are likely to work outside of the United States and Canada, or their own societies, but also because modes of interventions developed beyond North America are increasingly relevant in the domestic context. Many of the authors have written on the basis of their international experience, and several live and work outside the United States.

Part I provides a foundation for the rest of the book. Chapter 1 on ethics, competence, and professional issues demonstrates the generic value of a multicultural perspective and the negative consequences of a monocultural orientation. Chapter 2 demonstrates that the same behavior can have different meanings across cultures and that, conversely, different behaviors within a specific culture may have the same meaning. Chapter 3 provides guidance on appraisal and assessment strategies in multicultural contexts. Chapter 4 outlines considerations for investigating competencies in cross-cultural counseling. Chapter 5 examines the self-concept and identity development, particularly in African American communities.

Part II surveys a sampling of the ethnocultural contexts in which counseling occurs. Chapter 6 provides guidance for working in the Native American Indian context. Chapter 7 suggests strategies for working with Asian and/or Asian American clients. Chapter 8 describes the distinctive features relevant to counseling in Latino/a settings. Chapter 9 introduces the needs and presenting problems of Arab and Muslim clients and proposes a number of culturally appropriate treatment approaches. This marks the first time that *Counseling Across Cultures* has committed a chapter to this segment of the world's population. Chapter 10 describes issues involving counseling persons of Black African ancestry.

Part III reviews demographic factors, statuses, and affiliations that often become culturally salient. Both differences between and within groups are examined. Chapter 11 explores gender issues from service providers' and recipients' points of view. Chapter 12 focuses on the unique dynamics of lesbian and gay communities and represents a topic not covered in earlier editions. Chapter 13 addresses the problems that are encountered by individuals who are marginalized in some way. Chapter 14 examines age as a social category in interaction with ethnicity and its relationship with counseling. Chapter 15 is devoted to the operation and dynamics of counseling in schools.

Part IV contains four chapters that feature a wide range of problems encountered by individuals who find themselves in other cultures or in nature-made or human-made disasters. Chapter 16 surveys numerous concerns and problems facing international students. Chapter 17 breaks new ground in describing research about acculturation and adaptation processes when individuals encounter other cultures, usually for the first time. Chapter 18 deals with the increasingly prominent problems of refugees and migrants. Chapter 19 tackles the novel challenge of providing counseling to survivors and sometimes witnesses of major disasters in diverse cultural contexts.

Part V contains five chapters that feature a variety of contexts in which culturally informed counseling increasingly occurs. The common denominator among these chapters features problems and perspectives that most people encounter every day. Chapter 20 addresses the importance of religion and spirituality as counseling resources. Chapter 21 highlights the prominence of health issues that are managed through a combination of clinically based and culturally isomorphic strategies. Chapter 22 provides a new perspective on cultural confrontation supplementing and enriching cultural empathy. Chapter 23 examines the role of counseling individuals and their loved ones who are living with alcohol and drug abuse. Chapter 24 is a new chapter concerned with the role of family across cultures in research, assessment, and intervention.

Although this edition introduces a great many new topics and approaches, it also reaffirms the relevance of major contributions from earlier editions. In the fourth edition of *Counseling Across*

*Cultures,* David Sue and Norman Sundberg contributed an important chapter on "Research and Research Hypotheses About Effectiveness in Intercultural Counseling." It contained 15 research hypotheses that are as relevant now as they were then. They are reproduced as follows:

1. Entry into the counseling system is affected by cultural conceptualization of mental disorders and by the socialization of help-seeking behavior.

2. The more similar the expectations of the intercultural client and counselor in regard to the goals and process of counseling, the more effective the counseling will be.

3. Of special importance in intercultural counseling effectiveness is the degree of congruence between the counselor and client in their orientations in philosophical values and views toward dependency, authority, power, openness of communication, and other special relationships inherent in counseling.

4. The more the aims and desires of the client can be appropriately simplified and formulated as objective behavior or information (such as university course requirements or specific tasks), the more effective the intercultural counseling will be.

5. Culture-sensitive empathy and rapport are important in establishing a working alliance between the counselor and the culturally different client.

6. Effectiveness is enhanced by the counselor's general sensitivity to communications, both verbal and nonverbal. The more personal and emotionally laden the counseling becomes, the more the client will rely on words and concepts learned early in life, and the more helpful it will be for the counselor to be knowledgeable about socialization and communication styles in the client's culture.

7. The less familiar the client is with the counseling process, the more the counselor or the counseling program will need to instruct the client in what counseling is and in the role of the client.

8. Culture-specific modes of counseling will be found that work more effectively with certain cultural and ethnic groups than others.

9. Ethnic similarity between counselor and client increases the probability of a positive outcome.

10. Within-group differences on variables such as acculturation and stage of racial identity may influence receptivity to counseling.

11. Credibility can be enhanced through acknowledgment of cultural factors in cross-cultural encounters.

12. In general, women respond more positively than men to Western-style counseling.

13. Persons who act with intentionality have a sense of capability and can generate alternative behaviors in a given situation to approach a problem from different vantage points.

14. Identity-related characteristics of White counselors can influence their reaction to ethnic minority clients.

15. Despite great differences in cultural contexts in language and the implicit theory of the counseling process, a majority of the important elements of intercultural counseling are common across cultures and clients.

The infusion of multiculturalism in the theory and practice of counseling is a long process that requires the understanding of "new rules." Clients in counseling and psychotherapy come from a multitude of cultures and ethnicities, each with their own unique assortment of culture teachers.

The imposition of a one-size-fits-all approach to counseling is no longer acceptable for clients who represent a substantial number of diverse cultural contexts. The counselor who thinks there are only two people involved in the transactions—the client and the counselor—is already in great difficulty.

In addressing these wide-ranging and key issues, we seek to articulate in this volume the positive contributions that can be realized when multicultural awareness is incorporated into the training of counselors. Properly understood and applied, this awareness of our culture teachers will make the work of counselors easier rather than harder, more satisfying rather than frustrating, and more efficient rather than clumsy and cumbersome.

## ACKNOWLEDGMENTS

SAGE Publications gratefully acknowledges the following reviewers:

Charlene M. Alexander, Ball State University; Greg Bolich, Webster University–Greenville; Linda G. Castillo, Texas A&M University; Suzanne Degges-White, Purdue University–Calumet; Jane Fried, Central Connecticut State University; Harvey Hoyo, National University; Heesoon Jun, Evergreen State College; Carol A. Langelier, Rivier College; Aneneosa A. G. Okocha, University of Wisconsin–Whitewater; Jeanne M. Slattery, Clarion University of Pennsylvania; and Leo Wilton, University of New York at Binghamton

*Paul B. Pedersen*
*Juris G. Draguns*
*Walter J. Lonner*
*Joseph E. Trimble*

To the many scholars who have influenced our thinking about the complexities in, and rewards of, counseling across cultures—wonderfully represented by C. Gilbert Wrenn, Otto Klineberg, Wolfgang M. Pfeiffer, and Anthony J. Marsella.

# PART I

## Basic Issues in Cross-Cultural Counseling

1

These five chapters provide a foundation for counseling across cultures. The first chapter begins by connecting ethics, competence, and professional behavior and showing the generic relevance of a multicultural perspective. The primary objective is to demonstrate the generic relevance of multiculturalism to ethics, competence, and professional behavior. As you read this chapter, keep the following questions in mind:

Can you identify an example of cultural bias and explain the consequences of that bias?

Can you select one of the many competencies and explain its generic importance?

How do you solve the "ethical dilemma" facing multicultural counselors?

To what extent is multiculturalism becoming a "fourth force" in counseling?

What are the most important positive consequences of a multicultural perspective?

The second chapter raises controversies in the field of counseling. The primary objective is to describe the universal and cultural components of the counseling experience—disentangling the humanly universal from the culturally distinctive—while providing services to people in multicultural contexts. In the search for universal truth, counselors have sometimes supported the status quo. Multicultural counselors have frequently rebelled against that conformity. In the search for cultural patterns that connect people with one another, the measures of similarity and difference may be artifacts of our own cultural perspective. In the search for worldview or globalization, are we doing more harm than good? In our search for empathy, whose guidelines for relationships are most relevant? In the search for excellence, can we become too dependent on technology? As you read this chapter, keep the following questions in mind:

To what extent do multicultural counselors uphold the status quo, and what are the consequences?

In what specific ways would cultural patterns affect the style, technique, and atmosphere of counseling?

What are the potential problems facing counselors that are brought about by globalization?

How do you adapt your definitions of empathy and relationships across cultures?

What is the relative importance of a counselor's technical skill, experience, sensitivity, and knowledge in counseling across cultures?

The third chapter reviews strategies for appraisal and assessment across cultures. The primary objective is to present an overview of contemporary issues and problems associated with the appraisal and assessment in a multicultural context. The chapter provides resources that will increase one's competence in culturally sensitive assessment and appraisal. The reader is guided toward selecting appropriate assessment and appraisal strategies. As you read this chapter, keep the following questions in mind:

Do you think the construct of "intelligence" can be measured accurately enough across cultures to be useful in multicultural counseling?

Are psychological measures of objective phenomena, such as levels of emotion, stress, and satisfaction, the only valid and reliable measures?

Can a counselor be effective if he or she does not speak the client's native language?

How can a counselor measure the effectiveness of counseling with clients from a decidedly different cultural or ethnic group?

Do you believe people are more similar than they are different, regardless of culture?

The fourth chapter reviews guidelines for research competence. The primary objective is to sensitize readers in the challenges of conducting cross-cultural counseling research and to provide general guidelines for promoting culturally relevant and ethically vigilant research. Research marks our advances in understanding multicultural counseling and is therefore of particular importance. The same biases and encapsulation that frustrate counselors are also relevant to those doing research on multicultural counseling. As you read this chapter, keep the following questions in mind:

How ethically vigilant were the researchers when you were a participant, and were they helpful in providing prebriefing, debriefing, and follow-up?

When you conducted research, how much attention did you give to the culturally sensitive care of participants, and what could you have done to be more ethically appropriate?

Which 3 of the 32 specific research competencies mentioned in this chapter are most important?

Can you evaluate your level of competence as a multicultural counseling researcher, and what are three things you can do to increase that competence?

In Chapter 5, through an intriguing and enticing title, "The Big Picture: Theorizing Self-Concept Structure and Construal," William E. Cross Jr. and Tuere Binta Cross challenge readers to consider the structure of the self-concept or the range of meanings and interpretations accorded self-construal and what this means for cross-cultural counseling. The authors demonstrate that while personality and individuality are very much present in all cultures, a peculiar form of individualism tends to be a marker of Western societies. Nonetheless, Cross and Cross argue that people are more alike than different at the level of self-concept structure across all ethnocultural populations. They arrive at this conclusion by suggesting that one should cease equating self-esteem with individualism and group esteem with collectivism. They go on to recommend that self-esteem and group esteem be viewed as different sources of psychological strength and, when combined, the result is a person who has multiple personality strengths. To set the discussion in motion and stimulate our thoughts, they ask us to consider if group identity dynamics play a negligible role in the everyday psychology of *individualists* and whether personality and individuality play a minor role in the everyday psychology of *collectivists*. The chapter also focuses on the implication of the thesis for identity development and formation and how it influences self and other perceptions. More important, though, the authors ask us to consider how attachment processes are linked to the formation of group identity and feelings of group belonging and what all of this means for delivering and providing counseling services.

Additional material to supplement the text will be available on the Web site for the sixth edition of *Counseling Across Cultures*. It is important for the reader of this book to be well prepared by carefully reading the first four foundation chapters. That investment of time will pay off as you read the chapters in the following parts of this book.

# CHAPTER 1

# Ethics, Competence, and Professional Issues in Cross-Cultural Counseling

Paul B. Pedersen

---

*Primary Objective*

- To demonstrate the generic relevance of multiculturalism to professional excellence in counseling

*Secondary Objectives*

- To describe examples of culturally defined bias in counseling
- To define competencies of multicultural awareness
- To discuss the ethical dilemma facing multicultural counselors
- To explore how multiculturalism is becoming a "fourth force" in psychology

---

CULTURE CONTROLS OUR LIVES AND DEFINES REALITY FOR EACH OF US, WITH OR WITHOUT OUR permission and/or intentional awareness. A "culture-centered" approach to counseling recognizes culture as central and not marginal, fundamental and not exotic, for all appropriate counseling interventions. While mental health problems are similar across cultures, the complex classification of the appropriate helping responses across cultures has given rise to a global variety of counseling styles that are complex and ever changing. The increase of urbanized, modernized, and industrialized societies and the corresponding breakdown of family and village support systems have heightened the need for a global variety of counseling styles in the search for solutions to global social problems. This chapter examines the ethical and professional foundations for culture-centered counseling.

All behaviors are learned and displayed in a cultural context. Behaviors can be measured more accurately, personal identity becomes more clearly defined, the consequences of problems are better understood, and counseling interviews become more meaningful in their cultural context. That cultural context is defined broadly to include ethnographic, demographic, status, and affiliation variables. Culture-centered interventions depend on an inclusive definition of culture as well as a broad definition of the counseling process. The search for models that tolerate the complexity of broadly defined multicultural contexts and methods has become a primary emphasis in culture-centered counseling and research. For a more comprehensive discussion of ethical research with ethnocultural populations, see Trimble and Fisher (2006a).

## EVIDENCE OF CULTURAL BIAS IN COUNSELING

The presence of cultural bias in counseling psychology requires, first, that all research studies address external validity issues for the populations being researched; second, that different research approaches be matched as appropriate to each population; and, third, that the psychological implications of a population's ethnocultural belief system be considered in making comparisons across cultures: "The lack of internal validity does not allow causal inferences to be made without some degree of convincingness or credibility. The lack of external validity may render findings meaningless with the actual population of interest" (S. Sue, 1999, p. 1072). The greater the emphasis on internal validity, the more research will be dominated by a majority culture bias.

The Euro-American or Western psychological study of cultures assumed that there was a fixed state of mind, whose observation was obscured by cultural distortions and that related cultural behaviors to some universal definition of normative behavior described in counseling and psychological textbooks. A contrasting anthropological perspective assumed that cultural differences were clues to divergent attitudes, values, or perspectives that differentiated one culture from another, based on a culture-specific viewpoint. Anthropologists have tended to take a relativist position when classifying and interpreting behaviors across cultures (Geertz, 1973). Psychologists, by contrast, have linked social characteristics and psychological phenomena with minimum attention to cultural differences (Bernal, Trimble, Burlew, & Leong, 2002). When counselors have applied the same interpretation to the same behavior regardless of the cultural context, cultural bias has been the consequence. While there is clear evidence of cultural bias in American psychology, much of it is unintentionally done by people who see themselves as moral, just, and fair-minded professionals. Ridley (2005) points out that unintentional racists may be well intentioned, and they are likely to deny their racism. Toporek, Gerstein, Fouad, Roysircar, and Israel (2006) provide an excellent discussion of the implications of cultural bias for social justice issues.

Lewis-Fernandez and Kleinman (1994) have identified three culture-bound assumptions about mental health and illness based on North American values. The first assumption is the egocentricity of the self. The second assumption is the mind-body dualism, which divides psychopathology into organic disorders and psychological problems. The third assumption is the view of culture as an arbitrary superimposition on the otherwise "knowable biological reality." Miller (1999) also looks at the norm of self-interest as it has influenced the applications of psychology: "It is proposed that a norm exists in Western cultures that specifies self-interest both is and ought to be a powerful determinant of behavior. This norm influences people's actions and opinions as well as the accounts they give for their actions and opinions" (p. 1053).

Counseling and therapy have a history of protecting the status quo against change, at least as perceived by minority cultures, through what has come to be called "scientific racism" (D. W. Sue &

Sue, 2003). Counseling psychology has been slow to respond to evidence of cultural bias. Sampson (1993) suggests that psychology and counseling have at best accommodated add-on eclectic strategies in response to culturally different movements and special interest groups without fundamentally transforming conventional frameworks of understanding. Houser, Domokos-Cheng Ham, Wilczenski, and Ham (2006) point out the shameless neglect of "ethics" as a professional discipline of study and a further neglect of ethical decision making in non-Western cultures in the professional literature on counseling and ethics. Fowers and Davidov (2006) link the "multicultural movement" to classical writings about ethics in the philosophy literature, contrasting "virtue ethics" with merely following the rules.

There are alternatives to conventional Western therapy. Moodley and West (2005) suggest how alternative traditional healing practices can be integrated into counseling. Torrey (1986) cites numerous examples where healing approaches have been mobilized by healers and through spirits. Sheikh and Sheikh (1989) describe the breakdown of the Western "dualistic-materialistic paradigm" by a conceptual revolution in which a non-Western holistic perspective is gaining importance. Specifically, they maintain that "Western medicine has tended to look upon the body as a sort of machine that can be treated in total isolation from the mind, but even before the major paradigm shifts, it was becoming clear that this mechanical approach was simply not working. This was especially apparent in areas where psychosomatic linkages were showing that the mind does have a major impact upon bodily functions" (p. v.).

Approximately one third of the people in the United States, half of those in Europe, and 80% of people worldwide regularly use some kind of complementary or alternative health treatment, frequently originating in non-Western cultures (Micozzi, 1996). There are many reasons why alternative therapies have become more popular recently. Alternative therapies are typically less expensive, insurance companies are increasingly recognizing them for third-party payments, reverse technology transfer has become more popular, and the patient is more directly involved as a participant in healing. Alternative therapies are also less invasive, more low-tech in their application, and more gentle and natural, and they rely on self-healing capabilities and value subjective relationship aspects of the therapy process.

The psychological study of altered states of consciousness has been suppressed by a behavioral bias against internal, intangible, inaccessible mental states that do not lend themselves to experimental research (Ward, 1989). However, in recent years, the medical model has been increasingly challenged by psychosocial approaches. Walsh (1989) describes how Eastern and Western approaches actually complement one another rather than compete with one another. By defining counseling interventions broadly according to their helping functions, we develop a more inclusive framework that reflects the cultural diversity and complexity of each client's cultural context and thus avoid cultural encapsulation. Zyphur (2006) provides a condensed explanation of how "race" and racism, having no biological basis in scientific research, have continued to be such potent constructs in their political impact.

Wrenn (1962) first introduced the concept of cultural encapsulation. This perspective assumes five basic identifying features. First, reality is defined according to one set of cultural assumptions. Second, people become insensitive to cultural variations among individuals and assume their own view is the only right one. Third, assumptions are not dependent on reasonable proof or rational consistency but are believed true, regardless of evidence to the contrary. Fourth, solutions are sought in technique-oriented strategies and quick or simple remedies. Fifth, everyone is judged from the viewpoint of one's self-reference criteria without regard for the other person's separate cultural context. There is evidence that the profession of counseling is even more encapsulated now than it was when Wrenn wrote his original article (Albee, 1994; Wrenn, 1985).

More examples of cultural encapsulation are evident in the counseling literature wherever the following assumptions are presumed to be true (Pedersen, 2000). (1) All persons are measured according to the same hypothetical "normal" standard of behavior, irrespective of their culturally different contexts. (2) Individualism is presumed to be more appropriate in all settings than a collectivist perspective. (3) Professional boundaries are narrowly defined, and interdisciplinary cooperation is discouraged. (4) Psychological health is described primarily in a "low-context" rather than a "high-context" perspective. (5) Dependency is always considered to be an undesirable or even neurotic condition. (6) The person's support system is not normally considered relevant in analyzing the person's psychological health. (7) Only linear-based "cause-effect" thinking is accepted as scientific and appropriate. (8) The individual is expected to adjust to fit the system, even when the system is wrong. (9) The historical roots of a person's background are disregarded or minimalized. (10) The counselor presumes herself or himself to be already free of racism and cultural bias. Ponterotto, Utsey, and Pedersen (2006) take on the enormous task of "preventing prejudice," which transcends all cultural boundaries in our society by combining all community resources in a coordinated effort, hoping to reduce our need for encapsulation. This difficult but not impossible task can no longer be ignored.

Perhaps the most urgent example of cultural encapsulation requiring our attention is the bias in tests and measures used by counselors. Paniagua (2001) reviews the problems of diagnosis in a multicultural context with particular emphasis on the accurate and appropriate use of the *Diagnostic and Statistical Manual of Mental Disorders* (*DSM-IV*) with a series of case examples. The search for culture-free or culture-fair tests has failed. A culture-free or culture-fair test would need to demonstrate content, semantic, technical, criterion, and conceptual equivalence across cultures. This does not necessarily mean that those tests and measures cannot or should not be used. The skilled counselor must be trained to interpret data from culturally biased tests in ways appropriate to the client's cultural context (Paniagua, 2001) rather than throwing out tests.

## DEFINING "MULTICULTURAL AWARENESS" COMPETENCIES

The multicultural competences were derived from a failure of professional ethical guidelines to maintain high levels of professional activity in counseling. Delgado-Romero (2003) describes how the issues of multicultural competency incorporate both obligatory behavior and aspirational goals for culture-centered counseling. Much of the recent literature on multicultural competencies has focused on the importance of awareness, knowledge, and skill. This three-stage developmental sequence of multicultural competency begins first with "awareness" of culturally learned assumptions, second on "knowledge" about culturally relevant facts, and third on "skill" for culturally appropriate interventions. These competencies are based on work by D. W. Sue et al. (1982); D. W. Sue, Arredondo, and McDavis (1992); Arredondo et al. (1996); Pope-Davis and Coleman (1997); and D. W. Sue et al. (1998). Dunn, Smith, and Montoya (2006) provide an excellent review of how competencies are measured with suggestions for future research.

Multicultural training programs that lack a balance of awareness, knowledge, and skill can fail for three reasons. Some programs overemphasize "awareness" objectives almost exclusively, making participants painfully aware of their own inadequacies or the inequities around them. Trainees who overdose on awareness are frustrated because they do not know what to do with their new awareness in the absence of knowledge and skill. Some programs overemphasize the exclusive importance of factual knowledge and information through lectures, readings, and information. Without awareness, the trainee cannot see the relevance of that information or how the information could be used with skill. Some programs overemphasize skill objectives without regard for the foundations of awareness and knowledge. These participants will never know if they are making things better or worse. All three components of awareness, knowledge, and skill are required for a balanced perspective of competence. The multicultural competencies enhance ethical thinking or "ethical reasoning" (Ford, 2006) as an alternative to blind "rule following."

Pedersen (2000) describes a framework for individuals or groups to increase their competence through a four-step training program. The first step in developing multicultural competence is a needs assessment of awareness, knowledge, and skill. Assessing the level of awareness requires the ability to accurately judge a situation both from one's own and the other's cultural viewpoint. Becoming aware of the assumptions being made about the other culture is a good example of awareness. If awareness helps the trainee ask right questions, then knowledge helps get the right answer to those questions. Increased knowledge and information will clarify the alternatives and reduce the ambiguity of a situation. Learning the language of another culture is a good example of how increased knowledge is important. Assessing the level of skill is the third stage of needs assessment. This involves measuring what the trainee can already do. If awareness and knowledge are lacking, the trainee will have a difficult time becoming skillful. If awareness is lacking, then wrong assumptions are likely, and if knowledge is lacking, then proper understanding is at risk.

The second stage of developing multicultural competence is to identify specific objectives at the awareness, knowledge, and skill levels. An awareness objective changes the person's attitudes, opinions, and personal perspectives about a topic. The primary need may be to help a group discover its own stereotypical attitudes and opinions. In identifying objectives for increasing knowledge, the focus is on increasing the amount of accurate information available. The student can then test his or her new assumptions against the reality of these facts and data so that increased knowledge will also increase the student's awareness. In identifying objectives for increasing skill, the focus is on abilities indicating what the student can now do with the previously gathered awareness and knowledge. If awareness has been neglected, the student may build his or her plan on wrong assumptions. If knowledge has been neglected, the student may describe the culture inaccurately.

Techniques to stimulate awareness might include experiential exercises such as role plays, role reversals, simulations, field trips, critical incidents, bilingual observation, field placements, question asking, discussions, and other direct immersion experiences. Teaching awareness usually relies more on experiential exercises that directly challenge the person's assumptions. Techniques to stimulate increased knowledge frequently rely on books, lectures, or classroom techniques. Guided self-study is a practical approach, as is a panel discussion with members of all cultures participating. Techniques to stimulate increased skill frequently rely on modeling and demonstrations of a particular behavior or activity (Pedersen, 2005). Supervision becomes especially important in learning skills in the other culture. The opportunity to practice new skills and behaviors will lead to increased multicultural competencies. The last step of the training sequence is to evaluate whether the persons have met the stated objectives regarding awareness, knowledge, and skill competencies. This may include "formative" evaluation regarding the stated objectives in the short term, and it may include "summative" evaluation, which determines where those stated objectives were appropriate in the long term. Evaluation methods range from informal discussions in the hallway to self-assessment or supervisor assessments of changes.

Pope-Davis and Dings (1995) provide the best discussion of the research validating these multicultural competencies. Four different measures have been developed to assess competencies of multicultural awareness, knowledge, and skill. The Cross-Cultural Counseling Inventory-Revised

(CCCI-R), by LaFromboise, Coleman, and Hernandez (1991), directs a supervisor to rate the counselor on 20 Likert scale items. The CCCI-R aims to measure knowledge more than awareness. The Multicultural Awareness-Knowledge-Skill Survey (D'Andrea, Daniels, & Heck, 1991) includes three 20-item scales to measure awareness, knowledge, and skills that are useful for evaluating students in multicultural courses organized around the awareness, knowledge, and skill framework. The Multicultural Counseling Awareness Scale-B, described by Ponterotto, Reiger, Barrett, and Sparks (1994), includes two subscales: a 14-item awareness scale and a 28-item knowledge/skills scale, with some evidence that the subscales measure different factors. The Multicultural Counseling Inventory (MCI), by Sodowsky, Taffe, Gutkin, and Wise (1994), contains four factors: skills (11 items), awareness (10 items), knowledge (11 items), and counseling relationship (8 items). The advantage of the MCI is that it includes the relationship factor, and the items describe behaviors rather than attitudes. The multicultural competencies depend on having a culture-centered theory as their foundation. The ultimate multicultural theory is based on a contextual understanding of psychology. As stated by Segall, Dasen, Berry, and Poortinga (1990), "There may well come a time when we will no longer speak of cross-cultural psychology as such. The basic premise of this field—that to understand human behavior, we must study it in its socio-cultural context—may become so widely accepted that all psychology will be inherently cultural" (p. 352). We have not, however, yet reached that stage of development.

A culture-centered perspective that developed from the awareness-knowledge-skill framework was a list of propositions about "multicultural theory" (MCT) (D. W. Sue, Ivey, & Pedersen, 1996). These six propositions demonstrate the fundamental importance of a culture-centered perspective:

1. Each Western or non-Western theory represents a different worldview.

2. The complex totality of interrelationships in the client-counselor experiences and the dynamic changing context must be the focus of counseling, however inconvenient that may become.

3. A counselor's or client's racial/cultural identity will influence how problems are defined and dictate or define appropriate counseling goals or processes.

4. The ultimate goal of a culture-centered approach is to expand the repertoire of helping responses available to counselors.

5. Conventional roles of counseling are only some of the many alternative helping roles available from a variety of cultural contexts.

6. MCT emphasizes the importance of expanding personal, family, group, and organizational consciousness in a contextual orientation.

As these MCT propositions are tested in practice, they will raise new questions about ethical guidelines that are more meaningful to multicultural contexts. Gielen (1994) provides examples of these questions. Under what circumstances and in which culturally circumscribed situations does a given psychological theory or methodology provide valid explanations for the origin and maintenance of behavior? What are the cultural boundary conditions potentially limiting the generalizability of psychological theories and methodologies? Which psychological phenomena are culturally robust in character, and which phenomena appear only under specified cultural conditions? Ethical guidelines and professional competencies are linked together in the multicultural perspective, and occasionally, the ethical and professional duties seem to be in conflict.

# THE ETHICAL DILEMMA OF A MULTICULTURAL COUNSELOR

The ethical dilemma of multicultural counselors occurs when the counselor is forced to choose between doing the right thing ethically and bending the professional ethical guidelines, on one hand, or following the professional ethical guidelines and disregarding the client's cultural context, on the other (Pedersen & Marsella, 1982). This dilemma has been highlighted in a trend toward ethical consciousness in culture-centered counseling resulting from demographic changes favoring minority groups, increased visibility of ethnic minorities, pressure by civil rights and human rights groups worldwide, and the economic incentives to attract minority clients (Casas, 1984). Specific examples of dual relationships, unintentional cultural bias, client welfare, bartering for services, fostering dependencies, boundaries of competence, and other potential dilemmas involving the American Counseling Association (ACA), the American Psychological Association (APA), and the National Association of Social Workers ethical codes are available in Pack-Brown and Williams (2003). All professional associations face the same challenges. Codes of ethics for the 16 largest counseling organizations are provided by Thomson Higher Education (2007) for comparison. The Web sites for all relevant professional counseling guidelines are available in Ivey and Ivey (2003).

Ridley, Liddle, Hill, and Li (2001) explain how the dilemma results from oversimplification of complexity in the existing professional guidelines. The universal "moral" issues are confused with the situational "ethical" rules, the provider's own ethical perspective is frequently unclear, and the decision-making process is typically confusing. They provide an ethical decision-making model based on stages and process, providing clarity to the "goodness of fit" among all parties in ethical decision making by contextualizing general ethical principles. The general ethical perspectives include absolutism, where the decision is made according to absolute principles; relativism, where the decision is made according to the conventional rules; consequentialism, where the decision is based on good or bad consequences; and intentionalism, where the decision is made according to the good or bad intentions of the doer.

Rather than focus on external force to impose ethical directives, Trimble and Fisher (2006b) focus on internal resources such as "trust" and "respect" as necessary conditions for a "goodness of fit" between the interests of providers, consumers, and the community. The emphasis is not on virtuous acts but on virtuous persons. Goodness is not just something we do but something we are. "It is the virtuous person that creates good acts, not good acts that add up to a virtuous person" (Boeree, 1999, p. 5). Trimble and Mohatt (2006) go on to describe prudence, integrity, respectfulness, benevolence, trustworthiness, and reverence as our ethical guidelines. Without these inner resources as a foundation, the enforcement of ethical behavior is likely to fail. This becomes a dilemma when the external forces recommend an action different from virtue-driven inner resources, which may often happen in a multicultural context. This perspective makes the task of ethical decision making especially difficult in a multicultural context. Both parties may share a belief in the same virtues but disagree on the appropriate behavior to express those virtues. In such a case, the beliefs and values need to be understood separately from the culturally learned behaviors used to express those beliefs and values in each particular cultural context. If two people share the same beliefs and values, there may be common ground for discussion and mediation, even though their behaviors are very different.

Herlihy and Corey (1996) distinguish between mandatory ethics, which means functioning according to minimum legal standards, and aspirational ethics, which means to function at a higher standard in accordance with the spirit behind the literal meaning of the code. In this way, fundamental values are identified while recognizing that different cultures may express those values through their own different culturally learned behaviors. Jordan and Meara (1990) distinguished between principle ethics—which focus on rational, objective, universal, and impartial principles mandating actions and choices—and virtue ethics, which focus on the counselor's motives, intentions, character, and ethical consciousness that recognize the need to interpret principles differently in each cultural context. Houser et al. (2006) present a hermeneutic framework to demonstrate the importance of contextual issues in ethical decision making. Ford (2006) likewise believes that ethical issues in counseling should be more grounded in the context of philosophical approaches to thinking about ethics as an alternative to abstract, code-based legalistic discussions about ethical issues.

The danger of any ethical code is that it might enforce the moral standards of the group in power (Opotow, 1990). A fair and just code of ethics needs to do more than reflect the cultural values of those who wrote the code. Kitchner (1984) described four of the basic moral principles that provide a foundation for the ethical code of counselors as autonomy, beneficence, nonmaleficence, and fairness. These four principles are presumed to be universally valued regardless of the cultural context. Autonomy refers to client's freedom for self-determination. Beneficence refers to actions that promote the growth and development of the client. Nonmaleficence means refraining from hurting clients. Justice or fairness refers to equal treatment of all people. While all clients and counselors may believe in these four psychological principles, this chapter takes the view that these general principles are defined differently in each cultural context (Pedersen, 1995).

Toporek and Williams (2006) examined ethics documents by professional organizations to explore their potential to guide counselors toward social justice in their decisions and found a need for clearer guidance. "For counseling psychology to truly demonstrate a commitment to positive social change, ethical codes and guidelines should reflect the issues inherent in this work. Related professions, organizations and specializations that have historically centralized social justice should be considered as resources in the pursuit of more relevant guidelines" (p. 32).

Welfel (2006) identifies specific limitations and oversimplifications in professional codes of ethics and aspects of multicultural ethical decisions not yet addressed by those codes. "Its central theme is that ethics requires counselors to break free from cultural encapsulation and develop a set of competencies and commitments for productive work with diverse populations" (p. 223). Defenders of the APA ethical code assert that the problem is not with the principles but with their interpretation. If the problem is not the principles but their appropriate application in practice, then this should be stated in the standard on education and training. This pattern implies a "one-size-fits-all" perspective of psychology in general and counseling in particular.

Corey, Corey, and Callanan (2007) point out that all of the contemporary therapeutic models need to recognize the cultural contexts in which behaviors are learned and displayed. Each therapy—and each ethical code—will reflect the values of its cultural context. This statement seems to imply that each Western-based code of ethics is based on a preference for individualism rather than collectivism as the preferred worldview. Individualism applies to societies in which everyone is expected to look after themselves, whereas collectivism applies to societies in which people are integrated into cohesive groups and/or relationships that protect the members of the group in exchange for their loyalty. A comprehensive code of ethics needs to respect the values of both individualistic and collectivistic cultural contexts. If that is not possible, the code of ethics at least needs to make its dependence on individualistic values explicit for the benefit of those who do not share the assumption about the importance of the individual over the group. Corey et al. describe a useful test of multicultural effectiveness in making ethical decisions. "When counselors are overly self-conscious about their ability to work with diverse client populations, they may become too analytical about what they say and do. Counselors who are afraid to face the differences between themselves and their clients, who refuse to accept the reality of those differences, who perceive such differences as problematic, or who are uncomfortable working out these differences are likely to fail" (p. 136).

Kendler (1993) described the dilemma facing the profession. "Natural science psychology, to be successful, must abandon two seductive myths: (1) Psychology is able to identify ethical principles that should guide humankind and (2) the logical gap between is and ought can be bridged by empirical evidence" (p. 1052). On the other hand, psychology can help identify the culturally different empirical consequences of different policy choices and thereby help counselors make better-informed decisions.

The tendency of contemporary professional ethical guidelines for counselors is to emphasize the responsibility of individual counselors for "following the rules" laid out in the ethical guidelines rather than teach the counselor to "think ethically." The differences between the cultural context in which the APA and ACA ethical codes were developed and the multicultural contexts where they are being applied create a serious discrepancy. This discrepancy has resulted in patterns of implicit cultural bias that may require the counselor to choose between being ethical, on one hand, or following the codes, on the other.

## MULTICULTURALISM AS A "FOURTH FORCE"

The field of counseling psychology has been a monocultural science, even though it was born in Central Europe and has spread throughout much of both the Western and non-Western world (Pedersen, 1998). There are contemporary global changes that are having increased influence in psychology, demonstrating the positive consequence of a culture-centered perspective. First, the ratio of non-American to American psychological researchers is gradually but steadily increasing (Rosenzweig, 1992), suggesting that psychology is growing faster outside than inside the United States. Second, all fields are becoming more global in their focus as a result of technological innovations. Third, there is a multicultural movement, particularly in the social sciences, that has raised sensitivity to cultural variables. Fourth, the topic of cultural and multicultural issues is becoming more widely accepted in psychology. Fifth, there is a reexamination of cultural bias in psychology so that instead of assuming values and beliefs, there is more emphasis on discovering each population's unique explanation of their behavior and meaning.

Psychology has been an "imported discipline" for most of the world's cultures that have adopted and transferred Western psychology's theories and problems to a quite different cultural milieu. Kagitcibasi (1996) points out the limitations for psychology as an imported discipline. She argues:

> What is common in the ideographic, hermeneutic, emic, indigenous, relativist, cultural approaches is an emphasis on the uniqueness of concepts in each cultural context, because they derive their meanings from these contexts. There is also a stress on the variability and the uniqueness of the individual case (person, culture, etc.) that requires its study from within and in its own right, defying comparison. In contrast, the nomothetic, positivist, etic, universalist, cross-cultural approaches study the "typical" not the unique. The emphasis is on the underlying similarities that render comparison possible. (p. 11)

A balanced perspective needs to consider both similarities and differences at the same time.

Wrightsman (1992) describes best the need to look outside the envelope for new approaches to management of social problems. He points out that we are living in a time when the conventional wisdom about human nature and the nature of society is under attack. Technology has run amok; many now question our ability to bring technology under manageable control. Bureaucracy—a social structure originally established to provide for personal growth—now stifles human development and generates a philosophy that human nature is lazy, irresponsible and extrinsically motivated. The communal movement has challenged a pessimistic drift in our society. Through study of the movement's assumptions, aims, procedures and outcomes, we may gain an understanding of the future of philosophies of human nature. (p. 293)

We are only beginning to understand the ways that psychology has been changed in the past two decades (Mahoney & Patterson, 1992) in what has come to be called a paradigm shift. The underlying assumptions about psychology are moving from a monocultural to a multicultural basis with profound consequences for counseling. The old rules of psychology focused on dissonance reduction by providing simple explanations of human behavior. The new rules focus on the tolerance of ambiguity and accept complexity as a necessary feature of human behavior.

Smith, Harre, and Van Langenhove (1995) contrast the new with the old paradigms. The new paradigms emphasize (1) understanding and describing a context more than just measuring variables, (2) predicting consequences more than finding causation, (3) social significance more than statistical significance, (4) language and discourse more than numerical reductionism, (5) holistic perspectives more than atomistic trivia, (6) complex interacting particulars more than simplistic universals, and (7) subjectively derived interpretations more than objectively imposed meanings. The new rules accept greater complexity as necessary to psychological interpretations and provide a flexible alternative more appropriate across cultures than the traditionally rigid perspective.

Transpersonal psychology (Tart, 1975) was the first branch of psychology to claim a "fourth force" status based on the spiritual revolution in modern society. Since that time, many of the principles of transpersonal psychology have been subsumed into the larger and more diffuse multicultural movement. Mahoney and Patterson (1992) describe the new paradigm as a "cognitive" revolution with an interdisciplinary perspective in which human behavior is described as reciprocal and interactive rather than linear and unidirectional. Wrightsman (1992) describes the new paradigm as beginning with George Kelly's personal construct theory based on collectivistic and non-Western indigenous psychologies. Smith et al. (1995) describe the new perspective of psychology as advocating tolerance of ambiguity rather than dissonance reduction, multidimensional reality rather than unidimensionalism, the validity of subjective as well as objective proof, and the recognition of cultural bias by the dominant culture in the applications of psychology (Rosenzweig, 1992).

Because a culture-centered perspective is complicated, it makes research, teaching, and direct service more inconvenient, which has caused cultural differences to be overlooked or viewed negatively. The monocultural perspective of psychology has served the purposes of a dominant culture in many specific ways. Counseling in particular has often been guilty of protecting the status quo system against change. With the increase in political activism, affirmative action, and articulate special interest groups, the cultural biases of conventional psychology have been illuminated (D. W. Sue & Sue, 2003). This will ultimately increase the accurate, meaningful, and appropriate competence of psychologists, but this will only occur after the painful process of reexamining our underlying culturally biased assumptions.

Thompson, Ellis, and Wildavsky (1990) described "cultural theory" as providing the basis of a new perspective, dimension, or force in psychology and counseling. They argue that

social science is steeped in dualism: culture and structure, change and stability, dynamics and statics, methodological individualism and collectivism, voluntarism and determinism, nature and nurture, macro and micro, materialism and idealism, facts and values, objectivity and subjectivity, rationality and irrationality, and so forth. Although sometimes useful as analytic distinctions, these dualisms often have the unfortunate result of obscuring extensive interdependencies between phenomena. Too often social scientists create needless controversies by seizing upon one side of a dualism and proclaiming it the more important. Cultural theory shows that there is no need to choose between, for instance, collectivism, values and social relations or change and stability. Indeed, we argue there is a need not to. (p. 21)

In discussing these sources of resistance, Stanley Sue (1998) pointed out the tendency to misrepresent or misunderstand the notion of multiculturalism and the dangers of that misunderstanding. Labels—such as *multiculturalism*—tend to oversimplify complicated relationships, and to that extent, they are dangerous. The sixth edition of *Counseling Across Cultures* has attempted to call attention to the ways in which a multicultural perspective is better able to address the complicated and dynamic cultural context in which psychology is practiced than the alternative monocultural models. Whether or not multiculturalism emerges as a fourth force in psychology and/or counseling psychology at a level of magnitude equivalent to that of psychodynamic, behavioral, and humanistic theories of culture, it will continue to provide a valuable metaphor for understanding ourselves and others. It is no longer possible for psychologists to ignore their own cultural context or the cultural context of their clients.

# CONCLUSION

Until the multicultural perspective is understood as having positive consequences toward making psychology more rather than less relevant and increasing rather than decreasing the quality of psychology, little real change is likely to occur. This chapter demonstrates the importance of culture centeredness to professional issues of culture-centered counseling and the relationship of professional competencies to ethical obligations. Pedersen (1997) summarizes more than a dozen positive "up-side" advantages of making culture central to counseling as follows:

1. Recognizing that all behavior is learned and displayed in a cultural context makes possible accurate assessment, meaningful understanding, and appropriate interventions relative to that cultural context. Interpreting behavior out of context is likely to result in misattribution.

2. People who express similar positive expectations or values through different culturally learned behaviors share the "common ground" that allows them to disagree in their behaviors while sharing the same ultimate positive value. Not everyone who smiles at you is your friend, and not everyone who shouts at you is your enemy.

3. By recognizing the thousands of "culture teachers" each of us has internalized from friends, enemies, relatives, heroes, heroines, and fantasies, we can better understand the sources of our identity. As we encounter problems, we are likely to imagine how one or another culture teacher might respond.

4. Just as a healthy ecosystem requires a diversity in the gene pool, so a healthy society requires a diversity of cultural perspectives for its psychological health. By considering many different perspectives in problem solving, we are less likely to overlook the right answer.

5. Recognizing our natural tendency to encapsulate ourselves, cultural diversity protects us from imposing our self-reference criteria inappropriately by challenging our assumption. We see the dangers of a one-size-fits-all psychological perspective.

6. Contact with different cultures provides opportunities to rehearse adaptive functioning skills that will help us survive in the diversified global village of the future. By learning to work with those different from ourselves, we can develop the facility for our own survival.

7. Social justice and moral development require the contrasting cultural perspectives of multiculturalism to prevent any one dominant group from holding the standards of justice hostage. Every social system that has imposed the exclusive will of the dominant culture as the measure of just and moral behavior has ended up being condemned by history.

8. By looking at both cultural similarities and differences at the same time, according to a quantum metaphor, it becomes possible to identify nonlinear alternatives to rigidly absolutist thinking. It is not just the content of our thinking but the very process of thinking itself that can become culturally encapsulated.

9. We are able to continue our learning curve to match the rapid social changes around us by understanding all education as examples of culture shock. Education is a journey through many different cultures.

10. Spiritual completeness requires that we complement our own understanding of Ultimate Reality with the different understandings others have in order to increase our spiritual completeness. All trails do indeed lead to the top of the mountain.

11. The untried political alternative of cultural pluralism provides the only alternative to absolutism, on one hand, and anarchy, on the other. Our survival in the future will depend on our ability to work with culturally different people.

12. A culture-centered perspective will strengthen the relevance and applicability of psychology by more adequately reflecting the complex and dynamic reality in which we all live. The multicultural perspective resembles the fourth dimension of time as it complements our understanding of three-dimensional space.

This chapter has reviewed the importance of professional, ethical, and competency issues as the foundation argument for taking a culture-centered perspective. The chapter further suggests that a paradigm shift is occurring in counseling psychology toward giving more attention to multiculturalism. Kuhn (1970) expressed the belief that a major paradigm shift will occur when scientific theories cannot adequately account for ideas, concepts, or data and when some new competing perspective better accommodates these data.

Counseling has become a powerful force for psychological change through culture-centered counseling. The primary professional issue for counseling is rooted in the understanding of "self." Western counseling and psychology have promoted the "separated" self as the healthy prototype across cultures, making counseling and psychology part of the problem through an emphasis on selfishness and lack of commitment to the group rather than part of the solution. Elements of analytical reductionism in psychology and counseling seem to be moving toward a more holistic, culturally inclusive, and integrative approach that recognizes how people from all populations are both similar and different at the same time.

## CRITICAL INCIDENT

### The Unintentional Violation

A well-known leader in the field of counselor education was accused by a student of violating her rights and disregarding her cultural values. The student's complaint was sent to the ethics committee of the professional counseling association for action.

The student complained that she was being required to self-disclose more of her personal feelings and activities in class than was comfortable for her. She felt that she was being pressured by the teacher and by her peers to talk about herself in a way she might only disclose to her own family under extreme conditions. These things were just never discussed in her home culture. Moreover, she had not been warned ahead of time that this embarrassing situation was likely to occur in her class. The class was a required one for her, so withdrawing from the class would mean sacrificing all the time and money she and her family had invested in her education. This was not an option for her. She had talked with her teachers but did not feel her concerns were being taken seriously enough. Her only choice was to file a formal complaint with the ethics committee.

The teacher's position was that he had been teaching this required counseling class for many years without any complaints from other students and that he was not requiring anything from her that he did not require from these other students. The ethics guidelines required him to treat all students alike, regardless of their ethnocultural background. He was sorry to hear that the class experiences had been embarrassing to the student, but he did not feel he could give her any special privilege that he could not give to any of the other students. Favoring this one student would not be fair to the other students and would deprive this student of the opportunity to learn essential insights about counseling through self-disclosure and feedback. He felt he had an ethical obligation to the complaining student and to all his other students to maintain his standards of excellence. From the student's viewpoint, the cultural differences between herself and other students in her classes were important and needed to be respected.

The incident occurred in the ethics committee meeting, where the accused teacher was well known and respected but the rights of the student were also respected. The ethical infraction was certainly not intentional, and a certain degree of self-disclosure is required in counselor education classes. After considering the rights and responsibilities of both the student and the teacher, the committee decided against the teacher for not forewarning his students that a high degree of self-disclosure might be required in this course. While self-disclosure would be easy and natural for students from some cultures, it would be very painful for students from other cultures. The teacher was instructed to include a warning in his syllabus for future courses indicating that a high degree of self-disclosure may be required.

## DISCUSSION QUESTIONS

1. To what extent does the course syllabus function as a legal contract?

2. Should all students enrolled in counselor education classes be expected to accept the norms of the majority culture?

3. Should the teacher modify his course to fit the needs of each and every culture represented by all the different students in his class?

4. Should the student be expected to bring her problem to the teacher directly, however embarrassing that might be, before complaining to others?

5. What are the likely consequences for the student and for the teacher?

# REFERENCES

Albee, G. W. (1994). The sins of the fathers: Sexism, racism and ethnocentrism in psychology. *International Psychologist, 35*(1), 22.

Arredondo, P., Toprek, R., Brown, S. P., Jones, J., Locke, D. C., Sanchez, J., et al. (1996). Operationalization of the multicultural counseling competencies. *Journal of Multicultural Counseling and Development, 24,* 42–78.

Bernal, G., Trimble, J., Burlew, K., & Leong, F. (Eds.). (2002). *Handbook of racial and ethnic minority psychology.* Thousand Oaks, CA: Sage.

Boeree, C. G. (1999). *Ethics.* Retrieved March 14, 2005, from http://www.ship.edu/cgboree/ethics.html

Casas, J. J. (1984). Policy training and research in counseling psychology: The racial/ethnic minority perspective. In S. Brown & R. Lent (Eds.), *Handbook of counseling psychology* (pp. 785–831). New York: John Wiley.

Corey, G., Corey, M. S., & Callanan, P. (2007). *Issues and ethics in the helping professions.* Belmont, CA: Thomson Brooks/Cole.

D'Andrea, M., Daniels, J., & Heck, R. (1991). Evaluating the impact of multicultural training. *Journal of Counseling and Development, 70,* 143–150.

Delgado-Romero, E. A. (2003). Ethics and multicultural counseling competencies. In D. B. Pope-Davis, H. L. K. Coleman, W. M. Liu, & R. L. Toporek (Eds.), *Handbook of multicultural competencies in counseling and psychology* (pp. 313–329). Thousand Oaks, CA: Sage.

Dunn, T. W., Smith, T. B., & Montoya, J. A. (2006). Multicultural competency instrumentation: A review and analysis of reliability generalization. *Journal of Counseling and Development, 84,* 471–482.

Ford, G. G. (2006). *Ethical reasoning for mental health professionals.* Thousand Oaks, CA: Sage.

Fowers, B. J., & Davidov, B. J. (2006). The virtue of multiculturalism: Personal transformation, character, and openness to the other. *American Psychologist, 61*(6), 581–594.

Geertz, C. (1973). *The interpretation of cultures.* New York: Basic Books.

Gielen, U. P. (1994). American mainstream psychology and its relationship to international and cross-cultural psychology. In A. I. Communian & U. P. Gielen (Eds.), *Advancing psychology and its applications: International perspectives* (pp. 26–40). Milan, Italy: Franco Angeli.

Herlihy, B., & Corey, G. (1996). *ACA ethical standards casebook* (5th ed.). Alexandria, VA: American Counseling Association.

Houser, R., Wilczenski, F. L., & Ham, M. A. (2006). *Culturally relevant ethical decision-making in counseling.* Thousand Oaks, CA: Sage.

Ivey, A. E., & Ivey, M. B. (2003). *Intentional interviewing and counseling.* Pacific Grove, CA: Thomson Brooks/Cole.

Jordan, A. E., & Meara, N. M. (1990). Ethics and the professional practice of psychologists: The role of virtues and principles. *Professional Psychology: Research and Practice, 21,* 107–114.

Kagitcibasi, C. (1996). *Family and human development across cultures.* Mahwah, NJ: Lawrence Erlbaum.

Kendler, H. H. (1993). Psychology and the ethics of social policy. *American Psychologist, 48,* 1046–1053.

Kitchner, K. S. (1984). Intuition, critical evaluation and ethical principles: The foundation for ethical decisions in counseling psychology. *The Counseling Psychologist, 12,* 43–55.

Kuhn, T. S. (1970). *The structure of scientific revolutions* (2nd ed.). Chicago: University of Chicago Press.

LaFromboise, T. D., Coleman, H. L. K., & Hernandez, A. (1991). Development and factor structure of the cross-cultural inventory-revised. *Professional Psychology: Research and Practice, 22,* 380–388.

Lewis-Fernandez, R., & Kleinman, A. (1994). Culture, personality and psychopathology. *Journal of Abnormal Psychology, 103,* 67–71.

Mahoney, M. J., & Patterson, K. M. (1992). Changing theories of changes: Recent developments in counseling. In S. D. Brown & R. W. Lent (Eds.), *Handbook of counseling and psychology* (2nd ed., pp. 665–689). New York: John Wiley.

Micozzi, M. S. (1996). *Fundamentals of complementary and alternative medicine.* New York: Churchill Livingstone.

Miller, D. T. (1999). The norm of self interest. *American Psychologist, 54*(12), 1053–1060.

Moodley, R., & West, W. (2005). *Integrating traditional healing practices into counseling and psychotherapy.* Thousand Oaks, CA: Sage.

Opotow, S. (1990). Moral exclusion and injustice: An introduction. *Journal of Social Issues, 46,* 1–20.

Pack-Brown, S. P., & Williams, C. B. (2003). *Ethics in a multicultural context.* Thousand Oaks, CA: Sage.

Paniagua, F. A. (2001). *Diagnosis in a multicultural context: A casebook for mental health professionals.* Thousand Oaks, CA: Sage.

Pedersen, P. (1995). Culture-centered ethical guidelines for counselors. In J. Ponterotto, J. M. Casas, L. A. Suzuki, & C. M. Alexander (Eds.), *Handbook of multicultural counseling and therapy.* Thousand Oaks, CA: Sage.

Pedersen, P. (1997). Recent trends in cultural theories. *Applied and Preventive Psychology, 6,* 221–231.

Pedersen, P. (1998). *Multiculturalism as a fourth force.* Philadelphia: Brunner/Mazel.

Pedersen, P. (2000). *Handbook for developing multicultural awareness* (3rd ed.). Alexandria, VA: American Counseling Association.

Pedersen, P. (2005). *110 experiences for multicultural learning.* Washington, DC: American Psychological Association Press.

Pedersen, P., & Marsella, A. J. (1982). The ethical crisis for cross-cultural counseling and therapy. *Professional Psychology, 13,* 492–500.

Ponterotto, J. G., Reiger, B. P., Barrett, A., & Sparks, R. (1994). Assessing multicultural counseling competence: A review of instrumentation. *Journal of Counseling and Development, 72,* 316–322.

Ponterotto, J. G., Utsey, S. O., & Pedersen, P. B. (2006). *Preventing prejudice: A guide for counselors, educators and parent* (2nd ed.). Thousand Oaks, CA: Sage.

Pope-Davis, D., & Coleman, H. (1997). *Multicultural counseling competencies.* Thousand Oaks, CA: Sage.

Pope-Davis, D. B., & Dings, J. G. (1995). The assessment of multicultural counseling competencies. In J. G. Ponterotto, J. M. Casas, L. A. Suzuki, & C. M. Alexander (Eds.), *Handbook of multicultural counseling* (pp. 287–311). Thousand Oaks, CA: Sage.

Ridley, C. (2005). *Overcoming unintentional racism in counseling and therapy: A practitioner's guide to intentional intervention* (2nd ed.). Thousand Oaks, CA: Sage.

Ridley, C., Liddle, M. C., Hill, C. L., & Li, L. C. (2001). Ethical decision making in multicultural counseling. In J. G. Ponterotto, J. M. Casas, L. A. Suzuki, & C. M. Alexander (Eds.), *Handbook of multicultural counseling* (2nd ed., pp. 165–188). Thousand Oaks, CA: Sage.

Rosenzweig, M. R. (1992). Psychological science around the world. *American Psychologist, 39,* 877–884.

Sampson, E. E. (1993). Identity politics: Challenges to psychology's understanding. *American Psychologist, 48*(12), 1219–1230.

Segall, M. H., Dasen, P. R., Berry, J. W., & Poortinga, Y. H. (1990). *Human behavior in global perspective: An introduction to cross-cultural psychology.* New York: Pergamon.

Sheikh, A., & Sheikh, K. S. (1989). *Eastern and Western approaches to healing: Ancient wisdom and modern knowledge.* New York: John Wiley.

Smith, J. A., Harre, R., & Van Langenhove, L. (1995). *Rethinking psychology.* London: Sage.

Sodowsky, G. R., Taffe, R. C., Gutkin T. B., & Wise, L. I. (1994). Development of the Multicultural Counseling Inventory: A self-report measure of multicultural competencies. *Journal of Counseling Psychology, 41,* 137–148.

Sue, D. W., Arredondo, & McDavis R. J. (1992). Multicultural counseling competencies and standards: A call to the profession. *Journal of Counseling and Development, 70,* 477–486.

Sue, D. W., Bernier, J. E., Durran, A., Feinberg, L., Pedersen, P., Smith, C. J., et al. (1982). Cross-cultural counseling competencies. *The Counseling Psychologist, 19*(2), 45–52.

Sue, D. W., Carter, R. T., Casas, J. M., Fouad, N. A., Ivey, A. E., Jensen, M., et al. (1998). *Multicultural counseling competencies.* Thousand Oaks, CA: Sage.

Sue, D. W., Ivey, A. E., & Pedersen, P. B. (1996). *Multicultural counseling theory.* Belmont, CA: Brooks/Cole.

Sue, D. W., & Sue, D. (2003). *Counseling the culturally different: Theory and practice* (4th ed.). New York: John Wiley.

Sue, S. (1998). In search of cultural competencies in psychology and counseling. *American Psychologist, 53,* 440–448.

Sue, S. (1999). Science, ethnicity and bias: Where have we gone wrong? *American Psychologist, 54*(12), 1070–1077.

Tart, C. T. (1975). Some assumptions of orthodox, Western psychology. In C. T. Tart (Ed.), *Transpersonal psychologies* (pp. 59–112). New York: Harper & Row.

Thompson, M., Ellis, R., & Wildavsky, A. (1990). *Cultural theory.* San Francisco: Westview.

Thomson Higher Education. (2007). *Codes of ethics for the helping professions.* Belmont, CA: Thomson Brooks/Cole.

Toporek, R. L., Gerstein, L. H., Fouad, N. A., Roysircar, G., & Israel, T. (2006). *Handbook for social justice in counseling psychology.* Thousand Oaks, CA: Sage.

Toporek, R. L., & Williams, R. A. (2006). Ethics and professional issues related to the practice of social justice in counseling psychology. In R. L. Toporek, L. H. Gerstein, N. A. Fouad, G. Roysircar, & T. Israel (Eds.), *Handbook for social justice in counseling psychology* (pp. 17–34). Thousand Oaks, CA: Sage.

Torrey, E. F. (1986). *Witchdoctors and psychiatrists: The common roots of psychotherapy and its future.* New York: Harper & Row.

Trimble, J. E., & Fisher, C. B. (2006a). *The handbook of ethical research with ethnocultural populations and communities.* Thousand Oaks, CA: Sage.

Trimble, J. E., & Fisher, C. B. (2006b). Introduction: Our shared journey: Lessons from the past to the future. In J. E. Trimble & C. B. Fisher (Eds.), *The handbook of ethical research with ethnocultural populations and communities* (pp. xv–xxix). Thousand Oaks, CA: Sage.

Trimble, J. E., & Mohatt, G. V. (2006). Coda: The virtuous and responsible researcher in another culture. In J. E. Trimble & C. B. Fisher (Eds.), *The handbook of ethical research with ethnocultural populations and communities* (pp. 325–334). Thousand Oaks, CA: Sage.

Walsh, R. (1989). Toward a synthesis of Eastern and Western psychologies. In A. Sheikh & K. S. Sheikh (Eds.), *Eastern and Western approaches to healing* (pp. 542–555). New York: John Wiley.

Ward, C. (1989). *Altered stages of consciousness and mental health.* Newbury Park, CA: Sage.

Welfel, E. R. (2006). *Ethics in counseling and psychotherapy.* Belmont, CA: Thomson Brooks/Cole.

Wrenn, C. G. (1962). The culturally encapsulated counselor. *Harvard Educational Review, 32,* 444–449.

Wrenn, C. G. (1985). Afterword: The culturally encapsulated counselor revisited. In P. Pedersen (Ed.), *Handbook of cross-cultural counseling and therapy* (pp. 323–330). Westport, CT: Greenwood.

Wrightsman, L. S. (1992). *Assumptions about human nature: Implications for researchers and practitioners.* Newbury Park, CA: Sage.

Zyphur, M. J. (2006). On the complexity of race. *American Psychologist, 61*(2), 179–180.

CHAPTER

2

# Universal and Cultural Threads in Counseling Individuals

Juris G. Draguns

## Primary Objective

- To describe the universal and cultural components of the counseling experience, especially in providing counseling services to persons of a distinctive cultural background, and to disentangle its humanly universal and culturally distinctive threads

## Secondary Objectives

- To spell out implications relevant to counseling practice that can be derived from cross-cultural clinical experience, research findings, and conceptual formulations
- To narrow the gulf between practice and research by suggesting needed topics of investigation, formulating hypotheses, and encouraging the exploration of new avenues of study

COUNSELING PROCEEDS BETWEEN INDIVIDUALS YET IS EMBEDDED IN DISTINCTIVE SOCIOCULTURAL milieus. Invariably, there is a cultural component in all counseling. Counseling and related human services such as psychotherapy and guidance can be construed as progressions in which culture is an invisible but crucial participant (Draguns, 1975). Counseling alleviates distress, facilitates adaptive coping, and promotes more effective problem solving and decision making. All of these objectives are attained by means of procedures that are at least partially sociocultural in their ends and necessarily interpersonal in their means. Encounter and dialogue are the cardinal features of counseling. These transactions between two or more human beings occur as social learning takes place, symbols are communicated, and implicit assumptions are shared, all of which are mediated by culture.

The objective of this chapter is to disentangle these threads of humanly universal and culturally particular influence. The chapter is focused on the counseling services provided to the ethnoculturally distinctive segments of the population of North America. However, cultural diversity, at one time the hallmark of such "New World" societies as those of the United States and Canada, has come to be the rule in the developed countries around the world. In fact, it is culturally homogeneous nations, such as Japan, Korea, and Iceland, that are exceptional in light of this global trend.

Moreover, multiple cultural threads impinge on the experience of individuals of ethnically mixed ancestry who identify themselves as generically American. Not infrequently, these themes are brought to the fore in the counseling process. In the optimal case, they coalesce and form part of an individual's complex multicultural identity. Often, however, such integration does not come about, and the jarring strands remain to be fused, sometimes with the help of counseling. Proceeding from this recognition, Pedersen (1999) has promoted multiculturalism as the fourth force in counseling, on par with psychodynamic, cognitive behavioral, and humanistic schools of thought. The challenge, which this book attempts to address, is to make the multicultural framework applicable and relevant for all counseling interventions. Its overriding goal is the incorporation of all of the person's cultural facets into a multifaceted unique self.

This chapter's specific objectives are similar, though less ambitious. It aims to convey empirically based information about counseling across cultures, present issues and dilemmas that confront cross-cultural counseling, and open new vistas for future exploration. A concerted attempt will be made to make this information relevant to the day-to-day operations of practicing counselors and counseling students. Preliminary to tackling these objectives, extended descriptions of both culture and counseling must be presented.

## CULTURE AND COUNSELING: THEIR CHARACTERISTICS AND SCOPE
### Culture: A Broad and Elusive Concept

Most readers start out with an intuitive understanding of the terms *culture* and *counseling*. Both of these words are part and parcel of the active daily vocabulary of members of all helping professions. Yet, these two concepts have somewhat fuzzy boundaries and an elusive core. Herskovits (1948) proposed a classic, pithy definition of culture that is widely known and frequently quoted: "Culture is the man-made part of the environment" (p. 17). More recently, Marsella (1988) identified the psychological attributes of culture as follows:

> Shared learned behavior which is transmitted from one generation to another for purposes of individual and societal growth, adjustment, and adaptation: culture is represented externally as artifacts, roles, and institutions, and is represented internally as values, beliefs, attitudes, epistemology, consciousness, and biological functioning. (pp. 8–9)

In a similar fashion, Hofstede (1991) equated culture with "software of the mind" (p. 5), and Brislin (2000) construed culture as enabling people to fill in blanks in their percepts and impressions on the basis of socially shared and accumulated knowledge. The concept of subjective culture, introduced and systematically investigated by Triandis (1972), is also consonant with Marsella's (1988) definition. This "culture in our heads" is composed of the shared information, rules of inference, and other cognitions that are part and parcel of our personal reality. Its components are formed and absorbed in the process of socialization, unobtrusively and implicitly. They do not need to be actively taught or effortfully acquired. Subjective culture encompasses perceptions, expectations, and cognitions that appear to be intuitively self-evident. As such, subjective culture is like the air we breathe; we become aware of it only when we are deprived of it. Such a state may occur when human beings are removed from their accustomed habitat and are confronted with a situation where their rules of living no longer apply. Under these circumstances, many experience culture shock (Oberg, 1958), characterized by disorientation and attendant helplessness.

As described, the concept of culture is applicable to populations that are geographically removed and linguistically separate. Often, cultures are equated with nations. In this manner, we speak of Japanese, Turkish, or Finnish cultures. The term *culture* is, however, also generally extended to the ethnically and/or racially distinct components of the population of Canada and the United States. Thus, we refer to African Americans, Chinese Canadians, Mexican Americans, and American Indians or Native Americans. Cultural differences impinge on the person around the world and around the block. Ever increasingly, cultural diversity and the challenges that it poses are becoming important features of human interaction in the new millennium, in North America and around the world.

In culturally diverse environments, an additional problem must be faced. Individuals in Canada, the United States, and other pluralistic cultures often participate both within their ethnically distinctive milieu and the mainstream sociocultural setting. Thus, multiculturalism exists not only on the social arena but on the intrapsychic level as well. In providing counseling services, it is vital to ascertain the client's relationship to the generic or dominant culture and to his or her ethnically distinctive cultural heritage. Aponte and Johnson (2000) have proposed an explicit model that traces these two threads of social influence, with particular emphasis on the expression and communication of personal distress. To this end, it is important to acquire information about the person's acculturation and his or her identity. Acculturation has to do with the extent and nature of conforming to the dominant culture and incorporating it into actions, beliefs, attitudes, values, and feelings. Identity determines the degree of retention of the threads of one's ancestral, ethnic, or racial background and their absorption into one's self-concept. These processes are elucidated in Ward's chapter (Chap. 17, this volume).

## COUNSELING: DIVERSE AND MULTIFACETED

The essence of counseling is difficult to capture. Counseling can be construed to encompass the sum total of professional techniques and interventions that are designed to help in the resolution of human problems. Pedersen (1977) proposed three essential components of counseling: the counselee, the problem, and the counselor. Moreover, counseling unfolds over time. The problem is often brought up in spurts, the bond between the counselor and the counselee tends to evolve fitfully, and the effect of counseling interventions may only progressively emerge. Typically, though not invariably, counselees embark on the counseling process in a state of incongruity (Rogers, 1957). Frequently, they experience distress and suffering (Prince, 1980). In the optimal case, counseling leads to the resolution of problems, elimination of distress, establishment or restoration of the equilibrium between the person and his or her family and community, and enhancement of personal efficacy and quality of life. A great many counseling experiences fall short of attaining these ambitious goals.

Approaches for attaining counseling objectives vary over a wide spectrum across individual counselors, theoretical orientations, and—last but not least—cultures. Counseling shades off into guidance that more prominently features providing authentic information relevant to academic, career, and personal decisions (Herr, 1985). There is also overlap between counseling and psychotherapy, which is focused on symptom removal, adaptive changes in behavior and personality, improved interpersonal functioning, and more effective coping. The boundary between counseling and psychotherapy is not sharp, and quite often a professional practices both, under either or both labels. Counselors typically aspire to modifying specific personal or social problems. Psychotherapists' objectives tend to be more global and may extend to reorganizing the person's adaptive resources. In this chapter, the term *counseling* will be used to encompass the entire range of helpful interventions, from guidance through psychotherapy.

## COUNSELING AND CULTURE IN CONTACT: EARLY ORIGINS AND TRADITIONAL PRACTICES

Historically, counseling is rooted in American culture. From its early beginnings in the United States, it has spread in all directions and is now practiced in all regions of the globe (Deen, 1985; Lowenstein, 1985; Samuda & Wolfgang, 1985). In particular, the counseling enterprise has been greatly influenced by such American values as optimism, individualism, egalitarianism, glorification of social mobility, and encouragement of personal change. Respect for a counselee's self-determination has been a core ingredient of the American counseling ethos. The counselee is to be empowered to chart her or his optimal course of action, and this goal is most likely to be achieved in the presence of a sympathetic, but not meddlesome, helper. For several generations, American counselors have been taught to respect the individuality of their clients. Their training, however, did not accord explicit recognition of their clients' culturally based needs and expectations. No doubt some counselors intuitively recognized the importance of their counselees' culturally mediated experience. Others, however, proceeded in a culturally encapsulated manner (Wrenn, 1962, 1985), oblivious to the heterogeneity of outlooks within their clientele and to the consequences of a culturally restrictive orientation. Thus, misunderstandings would ensue. Some counselors found their culturally different clients unmotivated, resistant, and unprepared to benefit from self-understanding or insight. Many culturally atypical clients saw their counselors as remote, cold, and unresponsive and found their questions and comments baffling or irrelevant. Early termination was common. Implicitly, it was assumed that the counselor and counselee had to share a framework of expectations that corresponded to the counselor's underlying theory. Little latitude was accorded for negotiating differences between the divergent conceptions that clients and counselors brought to their encounter.

## THE UNIVERSALITY OF INDIVIDUALISM: A QUESTIONABLE ASSUMPTION

In a critical analysis of premises and practices of American counseling, Katz (1985) singled out the pivotal role of individualism. Among them is the tacit assumption that the person is the primary target of intervention and that he or she is responsible for his or her present circumstances. In the counseling process, the individual must be helped to exercise mastery over her or his own environment. Independence and autonomy are prized, while personal problems are construed as intrapsychic and are often traced to the person's formative experience in childhood and adolescence. An active orientation is espoused in helping counselees cope with their problems of living. Counseling is viewed as work that requires expenditure of energy and effort. Passivity is decried and interdependence underemphasized. These North American cultural values may be foisted on groups that traditionally hold to different philosophies of life, and autonomy tends to be unquestioningly and unconditionally promoted. Yet, as Dwairy and Van Sickle (1996) and Dwairy (Chap. 9, this volume) point out, in Arab and other societies, these individualistic goals may often be rejected. These authors concede that such interventions may alleviate clients' distress and promote their well-being. However, Dwairy and Van Sickle maintain that this benefit, in some cases, may be achieved at the cost of exacerbating the conflict between the counselee and his or her family and community and may thereby generate new sources of frustration and distress.

Culturally sensitive counselors urge a greater awareness of the assumptions on which mainstream American culture rests. They advocate an open-ended and flexible counseling process that encourages counselees to set their own goals proceeding from their culturally mediated outlook, coupled in some cases with the recognition of the need to come to terms with the expectations of the mainstream culture.

# BEYOND ENCAPSULATION: ACCOMMODATING CULTURE IN COUNSELING

Several investigators have endeavored to bridge the cultural gulf by accommodating cultural practices and services. Nwachuku and Ivey (1991) introduced innovative conceptual analyses of cultural values and practices that are embodied in traditional healing and therapeutic services. They have proceeded to incorporate these elements into modern counseling interventions. This effort was animated by the willingness to learn from other cultures and by the respect for their experience, a theme that has also been emphasized by Nathan (1994), a psychoanalyst in Paris with a clientele of African sojourners and immigrants. To provide services on these clients' own cultural terms, Nathan urged therapists to respect their clients' culturally molded beliefs, even if they should appear bizarre or magical. Nathan's open and receptive orientation is consonant with the recent upsurge of interest in traditional healing practices.

In some instances, these interventions have been combined with more comprehensive intervention programs. Jilek (2004) succeeded in blending traditional Salish Indian rituals into a series of treatments designed to counteract depression among alienated young men. Through the pooled efforts of traditional shamans and modern psychiatrists, depressive and other symptoms were markedly reduced. Koss-Chioino (2000) pursued the same objective in her study of alternative ethnomedical healing among Hispanics and African Americans. She envisaged investigating the effectiveness of these practices, manualizing them, and eventually incorporating them into culturally fitting and scientifically validated interventions. These efforts have coalesced with the appearance of searching analyses (e.g., Krippner, 2002) and encyclopedic compendia (Moodley & West, 2005) on traditional healing practices and on their relevance for the psychotherapy and counseling enterprise. Through creative transformation and adaptation, these ministrations have the potential of enriching modern counselors' repertoire of techniques and broadening their outlooks.

Proceeding in the opposite direction, cross-cultural counselors have sought to identify the obstacles that stand in the way of adopting effective counseling procedures across ethnocultural lines. Cultures may vary in the amount of self-disclosure that they are prepared to encourage or tolerate, and they may restrict the settings in which such self-disclosure is deemed to be appropriate. Admission of negative characteristics may in some cases clash with the cultural standards of self-presentation. There may also be cultural norms prescribing rapid and directive intervention, perhaps even prior to interviewing, inquiry, or systematic observation. Oftentimes, what the client expects and what the counselor is prepared to offer operate at cross-purposes. Pfeiffer (1996) has described a recurrent clash of expectations between Turkish migrant patients and their German psychiatrists. Clients tended to seek direct, immediate, and authoritative relief while clinicians insisted on extensive exploration and protracted dialogue. Patients expressed their distress through somatic channels, yet their physicians appeared to be more interested in subjective experiences. Clinicians promoted one-on-one interaction, while clients wanted participation and involvement of their family and elders, even in psychotherapy or counseling sessions.

The most elaborate proposal for bridging the culture gulf in planning and delivering counseling services has been formulated by Higginbotham (1984). He proposed accommodating culture through a process of exploration and negotiations, to be undertaken prior to initiating mental health services in a new locale. Local needs and expectations as well as apprehensions, misgivings, and insecurities need to be ascertained and taken into account before introducing services. Culture accommodation was first applied in Southeast Asia. It is, however, also relevant to multicultural American settings. Thus, Rogler, Malgady, Costantino, and Blumenthal (1987) attempted to meet the expectations of their Hispanic clientele in New York by making interventions more compatible with the preexisting and traditional Hispanic helping practices. Culture can also be accommodated informally in individual intervention, through pretreatment negotiations. This occurs whenever a gap is bridged between a distraught but hopeful client in an unfamiliar setting and a culturally perceptive and empathetic counselor who is willing to modify his or her modus operandi.

## An Emerging Consensus

What are the practical implications of the increasing cultural awareness that has permeated the counseling field? First, interventions may need to be modified if they are to be effective with a culturally distinctive clientele. Second, complications in the counseling process must be anticipated whenever the cultural gulf between the counselor and the counselee is increased, especially if such a disparity remains unrecognized. Third, counseling techniques should be adapted or accommodated to the culturally mediated modes of self-presentation and communication of distress. Fourth, there is ample evidence (Draguns, 2000; Draguns & Tanaka-Matsumi, 2003) that complaints, presenting problems, and reported patterns of distress differ across cultural and ethnic lines. Fifth, norms and expectations, especially those pertaining to coping with stress, are also subject to cultural variation. Aponte and Johnson (2000) have identified ethnocultural identity and acculturation as pivotal components that moderate both the experience and presentation of distress and the utilization of and response to treatment services, including counseling.

## CULTURAL UNIVERSALS IN COUNSELING

Inevitably, writings on counseling and culture are slanted toward differences. This should not overshadow the importance of culturally universal features in counseling experience. Across space and time, distraught individuals have sought and received solace and guidance, often from specialized and experienced individuals in their midst. Culturally universal features in these transactions are more readily apparent in the counseling ethos than in specific interventions. As Marsella (2005) has pointed out, such ministrations provide general relief by instilling hope, reducing uncertainty, facilitating resocialization, and lowering the levels of anxiety, guilt, and shame. Prince (1980) presciently proposed that effective psychotherapeutic intervention sparks the mobilization of endorphins and the strengthening of the immune system, a daring suggestion that recent breakthroughs in neuropsychology have made more plausible (Grawe, 2004). The weight and explicitness of verbal communication vary across cultures, as does the content and style of interventions. These contrasts should not overshadow the common features that are deeply embedded in all helping encounters.

# THE SELF IN CULTURE AND IN COUNSELING
## The Self: Its Conceptual Origins and Cultural Variations

In the past two decades, the self has reemerged as a pivotal and unifying construct in a number of domains of psychology. In particular, variations of the self across cultures have been noted and conceptualized. These developments are germane to the application and modification of counseling across cultures. The self as a concept remains elusive and is exceedingly difficult to pin down. The classical definition by William James (1891/1952) is elegantly phrased but may be too inclusive: "*In its widest possible sense, however, a man's Self is the sum total of all that he* CAN *call his*" (p. 188). Note that the self is construed as property or possession and that its boundaries extend beyond the person. More restrictively and specifically, Rogers (1951) described the self-concept as "an organized configuration of perceptions of the self which are admissible to awareness. It is composed of such elements as the perceptions of one's characteristics and abilities; the percepts and concepts of self in relation to others and the environment; the value qualities which are perceived as associated with experiences and objects; and goals and ideas which are perceived as having positive or negative valence" (p. 136).

Cross-cultural psychologists would say that both of these definitions bear the marks of their time and place. As Chang (1988) put it, the individualistic self described in the above two definitions sets the person apart from other people. Such a conception of the self is prevalent in Western Europe and North America. By contrast, in more sociocentric milieus such as those of China, Japan, and Korea, the self connects a person to his or her family, companions, peers, and community. An individualistic self erects walls; a sociocentric self builds bridges. Chang's conception of the self is shared and elaborated by a host of other theorists. Proceeding from a variety of perspectives (Kimura, 1995; Landrine, 1992; Markus & Kitayama, 1991; Roland, 1988; Triandis, 1989, 1995), all of these formulations posit two contrasting selves: crystallized, explicit, and differentiated at the individualistic end of the continuum and relatively malleable and situation bound at the sociocentric extreme. Moreover, sociocentric selves are primarily based on bonds, allegiances, and commitments to persons, families, and communities; individualistic selves are marked by the unique attributes harbored by and within the person. The selves of specific persons are anchored between these two reference points.

As yet, normative information on the distribution of individualistic and sociocentric selves in Canada and the United States is lacking. The hypothesis that the selves of Asian Americans, African Americans, and Hispanics are less individualistic and encapsulated than those of "mainstream" Caucasian Americans is plausible but unproven. The challenge to counselors is to keep this possibility in mind in working with their clients. At the same time, they should guard against imputing sociocentric or individualistic selves mechanically, automatically, or stereotypically on the basis of their clients' ethnic background and identity.

# HOFSTEDE'S FACTORIALLY BASED CULTURAL DIMENSIONS: INDIVIDUALISM-COLLECTIVISM

In one of the largest psychological studies ever conducted, both in the numbers of countries represented and those of participants, Geert Hofstede (1980), an industrial psychologist with an engineering background in The Netherlands, was able to identify four statistically independent factors that accounted for intercountry differences in work-related values. In the ensuing decades, Hofstede's findings sparked worldwide interdisciplinary research on the correlates of these four dimensions and their implications. The yield of this effort was reviewed and interpreted by Hofstede (2001). Are Hofstede's dimensions relevant to cross-cultural counseling? To explore this possibility, these factors must now be briefly described.

Of the four factors, the bipolar axis of individualism-collectivism has generated the greatest amount of research and theoretical interest. In Hofstede's (1991) words, "Individualism pertains to societies in which ties between individuals are loose; everyone is expected to look after himself or herself and his or her immediate family. Collectivism pertains to societies in which people from birth onward are integrated into strong, cohesive ingroups, which throughout the people's lifetime continue to protect them in exchange for unquestioning loyalty" (p. 51). Across nations, the United States leads the pack and holds the highest rank in individualism. In light of Katz's (1985) assertions on the importance of individualism in American counseling, this finding is hardly surprising. United States is closely followed by Australia, Great Britain, Canada, The Netherlands, and New Zealand. East Asian, Middle Eastern, most Latin American, and several Mediterranean cultures cluster toward the collectivistic end of the continuum.

By now, individualism-collectivism has emerged as the most intensively investigated construct in cross-cultural psychology. In addition to research directly inspired by Hofstede, Triandis (1995) has independently pursued a systematic program of studies for more than 30 years. According to Triandis, collectivism possesses a number of advantages in social interaction within small groups, such as work teams and families. Individualists, however, hold the edge in impersonal social settings, such as corporations and governmental hierarchies. However, they are more likely to experience alienation and loneliness than are collectivists. On the other side of the ledger, some people in collectivistic societies feel stifled by social pressures and obligations and have a sense of being thwarted in the realization of their personal aspirations. Triandis concluded that "we need societies that would do well both in the citizen-authorities and person-to-person fronts, that provide both freedom and security, that have something for their most competent members but also for the majority of their members" (p. 187). This reasoning also applies to counseling. Individualistic clients may be encouraged to become aware of their suppressed affiliative strivings, and collectivists may be helped to work toward the realization of their personal aspirations that they had habitually submerged or overlooked.

## THE OTHER HOFSTEDE DIMENSIONS: POWER DISTANCE, UNCERTAINTY AVOIDANCE, MASCULINITY/FEMININITY, AND LONG-TERM VERSUS SHORT-TERM ORIENTATION

Individualism-collectivism was not the only cultural construct to emerge from Hofstede's (1980) mammoth multinational study. On the basis of multistage application of elaborate multivariate techniques, Hofstede was able to identify and label three more cultural dimensions: power distance, uncertainty avoidance, and masculinity/femininity.

As defined by Hofstede (1991), *power distance* refers to "the extent to which the less powerful members of institutions and organizations within a culture expect that power is distributed unequally" (p. 28). Compared with the other nations included in the Hofstede comparison, the United States and Canada are adjacent in this characteristic, and both are well below the median. Countries ranked high in power distance include Malaysia, Guatemala, Panama, Philippines, Mexico, Venezuela, and several Arab nations, while Israel and Scandinavian countries are located at the low end of the continuum.

*Uncertainty Avoidance.* This describes "the extent to which people within a culture are made nervous by situations which they perceive as unstructured, unclear, or unpredictable, situations which they therefore try to avoid by maintaining strict codes of behaviour and a belief in absolute truths" (Hofstede, 1986, p. 308). Around the world, Greece, Portugal, Guatemala, and Uruguay are at the high end of the continuum on this characteristic, and Hong Kong, Sweden, Denmark, Jamaica, and Singapore are at the low end. Canada and the United States hold adjacent ranks in the lowest quadrant of distribution.

According to Hofstede (1980), "*Masculinity* pertains to societies in which gender roles are clearly distinct (i.e., men are supposed to be assertive, tough and focused on material success whereas women are supposed to be modest, tender and concerned with the quality of life); *femininity* pertains to societies in which social gender roles overlap (i.e., both men and women are supposed to be modest, tender, and concerned with the quality of life)" (pp. 82–83). Internationally, high masculinity is exemplified by Japan, Austria, Venezuela, and Italy and femininity by Costa Rica, Denmark, The Netherlands, Norway, and Sweden. United States is moderately high in masculinity, and Canada is several ranks lower.

Another axis of cross-cultural appraisal was incorporated into Hofstede's (2001) system after the completion of his worldwide multivariate research project. It was developed in a very different manner. Instead of relying on factor analysis, researchers (Chinese Culture Connection, 1987) selected items for this scale proceeding from tenets of Confucian philosophy. The resulting scale tapped the search for personal virtue and achievement while accepting the social order as constant and virtually immutable. Not surprisingly, in a subsequent comparison of 23 countries, East Asian samples, from China, Hong Kong, Taiwan, Japan, and South Korea, obtained the highest scores, in contrast to the rather heterogeneous group of Canada, Philippines, Nigeria, and Pakistan, all of which were at the low end of the distribution. United States placed only slightly higher than the above four countries. Originally called Confucian dynamism, this dimension has been renamed by Hofstede (2001) as *long-term versus short-term orientation.*

## HOFSTEDE'S DIMENSIONS IN THE SELF AND IN COUNSELING

Hofstede's research was conducted in a multinational corporate setting. How far does its relevance extend beyond organizational psychology, and what are its outer limits? Let us address this question by conjecturally mapping the path from socialization through the formation of the self to the specification of fitting modes of counseling experience for each of Hofstede's five dimensions. In regard to the self, such predictions have already been advanced for the continuum from individualistic and collectivistic cultures.

In relation to childhood experience, it can be hypothesized that socialization in individualistic settings is demanding and is focused on the formation of a relatively small number of intense and lifelong relationships. In contrast, socialization in collectivistic cultures is thought to revolve around multiple relationships that may be less intense and exclusive. In relation to high power distance, socialization is thought to be fostered by forceful and possibly even harsh means; socialization procedures are hypothesized to be more lenient in low power distance cultures. In respect to uncertainty avoidance, socialization would enhance opportunities for exploration at the low levels of this cultural dimension. High uncertainty avoidance would be characterized by purposeful, concerted preparation for school, work, and other domains of activity. In masculine cultures, accent would be placed on pragmatism and efficiency, while feminine cultures would endeavor to foster sensitivity, self-expression, and creativity. Finally, long-term socialization would encourage conformity and self-control, and short-range orientation would place value on self-fulfillment and freedom.

In reference to the self, Draguns (2004) formulated the following four hypotheses:

1.   High power distance would promote the development of a highly differentiated and clearly bounded self with emphasis on personal and social status; low power distance would foster a relatively permeable self, with greater value accorded to personal relationships.

2.   In high uncertainty-avoidance cultures, consistency and explicitness of self-experience would be prized; in low uncertainty-avoidance cultures, greater inconsistency within the self would be tolerated, and self-experience would be less explicitly and elaborately articulated.

3.   Masculine cultures would value a self that is efficient and pragmatic; feminine cultures would promote an altruistic and sensitive self.

4.   Long-term orientation would place emphasis on self-restraint; short-term orientation would put a premium on self-assertion.

Extending these considerations to the counseling situation, it is predicted that counseling in individualistic settings would be focused on intrapsychic factors and would aim at increasing insight; emphasis in collectivist settings would be on promoting social harmony and enhancing relationships. With high power distance would come valuation of the counselor's expertise, status, and credentials; informality, egalitarianism, and authenticity would be valued as counselor qualities in low power distance milieus. Social distance and power distance would go hand in hand. High-uncertainty avoidance is expected to bring with it an emphasis on the scientifically demonstrated effectiveness of interventions, comprehensive and rigorous legal and administrative control of counseling services, and biological or behavioral conceptualizations over psychodynamic or experiential ones. At the low extreme on this variable, multiplicity of approaches would not only be accepted but celebrated, subjective, intuitive, and artistic; explanations would get a ready hearing, and novel and controversial interventions would have no trouble acquiring adherents. Masculine cultures would promote responsibility, conformity, and expertise in coming to terms with the occupational and economic imperatives. In feminine cultures, self-development and self-expression would be cultivated, along with sensitivity, caring, and compassion. Counselors in masculine societies would strive to make their clients more competent; in feminine societies, their counterparts would endeavor to promote personal fulfillment. Counseling for long-term orientation would concentrate on biological explanations, behavioral techniques, harmonious social interaction, and self-subordination; short-term orientation would accord greater importance to subjective experience, promotion of self-understanding, interpersonal and psychodynamic explanations, and self-assertion.

## FROM EXPECTATIONS TO EVIDENCE: FIRST STEPS

The above formulations have not yet been subjected to much research scrutiny. As Hall (2001) noted, empirically supported interventions have rarely been tested for their efficacy in various culturally distinctive populations, and culturally sensitive treatment approaches have only recently begun to be rigorously and systematically investigated. Illustrative in this respect is a study by Snider (2003), who explicitly examined the hypotheses about individualism-collectivism and power distance advanced earlier in this chapter. Chinese students studying in Australia were found to prefer more directive counselor interventions based on their expertise than their Australian and American counterparts studying in their respective countries. Snider concluded that individualism was the predominant orientation among Americans, egalitarianism among Australians, and acceptance of authority among Chinese. Joo (1998) also reported that the demeanor of Korean psychotherapists differed from American and European colleagues in a manner predictable from the knowledge of Korean culture, which emphasizes social harmony and avoidance of personal confrontation. These leads are promising and deserve to be further pursued by the gamut of methods from well-documented case studies approximating the features of investigations with an *N* of 1 to, eventually and ambitiously, a worldwide comparison of national meta-analyses of outcome and process studies.

## Toward Integrating Universal, Cultural, and Individual Threads in Counseling

Leong (1996) has reminded us of Kluckhohn and Murray's (1950) dictum that each person is in some respects like all other persons, in some respects like some other persons, and in some respects like no other person. The interplay of universal, cultural, and individual components of counseling continues to be a challenge on the clinical, research, and theoretical planes. Leong has responded to this challenge by proposing a comprehensive tripartite model of counseling and psychotherapy. It cautions counselors against imputations of homogeneity or similarity among members of various outgroups. At the same time, Leong's model emphasizes complementarity, which calls for a differentiated and fitting response to the needs that the counselees bring to the counseling encounter. Moreover, culture matters in different ways and to different degrees across individuals, and this awareness should be maintained throughout counseling. The inherent complexity of counseling transactions should be kept in mind, and counselors should guard against oversimplifications. Finally, counselors should be careful lest they perceive clients in terms of categories, view them from one limited perspective, and engage in automatic behavior in counseling situations. Leong's argument is exceedingly complex and subtle and defies being reproduced within the confines of this chapter. It is possible, however, to spell out a series of suggestions based on Leong's tenets that may be useful for working counselors:

1. Do not assume that the problems of a culturally distinctive client are necessarily related to or centered on his or her cultural experience or background.

2. Be prepared to switch from a cultural to universal or individual level, and vice versa, as the client's situation and needs may require.

3. The extent and nature of the person's relationship to his or her culture or cultures constitute an important area of consideration and inquiry and should be kept in mind throughout the entire counseling experience.

4. Complementarity involves empathy, sensitivity, and responsiveness to the client on the basis of the recognition of the differences of counselors' and counselees' roles; it also entails the mobilization of a counselor's expertise and skill in order to respond effectively and fittingly to the client's experienced distress.

5. Counseling represents human interaction at its most subtle and sensitive, and there is no room in counseling for reducing the inherent complexity.

6. Maximal flexibility, spontaneity, openness to experience, and authenticity are called for during all counseling experience.

7. Counselors should never limit themselves to a single perspective or commit themselves irrevocably to an explanation or hypothesis.

8. Remember at all times that each person is unique, yet similar in specific respects to a great many other humans, and that she or he is like all human beings in both biological and existential characteristics.

9. Be aware of the client's multiple facets, but do not lose sight of the fact that he or she is a whole and integrated human being.

## CONCLUSIONS

Within the span of 30 years, counseling across cultures has come a long way. As an area of study and application, it was initiated with the reports of a few experienced practitioners, coupled with the awareness of the complexities of the tasks involved and spiked with an ample dosage of warnings about the methodological and conceptual pitfalls to be encountered. Today, cross-cultural counseling rests on a solid empirical foundation (Griner & Smith, 2006), and its relevance and effectiveness are widely recognized and generally acknowledged. We know that empathy promotes counseling objectives, and stereotyping impedes their attainment. Empathic communication is a powerful counseling tool, provided that it is couched in a culturally fitting and meaningful manner. Confounding difference with disturbance is a pernicious peril, which, it is hoped, the enterprise of culturally sensitive counseling has contributed to reduce. Specific counseling techniques are cross-culturally less robust than counseling's ethos and its less tangible but no less real atmospheric components. Across cultures, counselors often provide opportunities for affective self-expression in a culturally congenial and personally safe context. However, a host of unanswered questions remain. Above all, what works with whom with what effect? The incorporation of ethnocultural variables into major funded research is well past due, as is the simultaneous pursuit of research objectives related to counseling across national and cultural lines. Yet, on two points, substantial agreement has been achieved: Counseling produces beneficial results across an impressive variety of populations, and ethnocultural and national differences matter in the delivery of counseling services. A lot of work remains to be done before we can fill the blanks between these two established points of reference.

## CRITICAL INCIDENT

Viktor is a 66-year-old man who presented himself for psychological services with depression and anxiety, in the form of insomnia, loss of appetite, and agitation, accompanied by insecurity, pessimism, and discouragement. Viktor was born in Western Ukraine and immigrated to the United States 7 years ago.

His parents, who were landless peasants before 1939, were first awarded a small plot of land by the Soviet authorities and then forced to join a collective farm. After a brief period as independent subsistence farmers, they were again agricultural laborers, poorly paid and overworked. Viktor's earliest recollections are of "not having enough to eat," and his diet during the first 10 years of life consisted mostly of bread, potatoes, and cabbage. Although Viktor's family was not arrested or persecuted, some of their neighbors were, and Viktor recalls that a knock on the door late at night sent the adults of the household into a state of nervousness, since that is when secret police were making arrests. After completing 5 years of schooling, well before the official school-leaving age, Viktor went to work full-time. Compulsory service in the Soviet Army followed. Surprisingly, it was a good experience, and Viktor was discharged with the rank of corporal. Paradoxically, however, this is when he converted to Evangelical Christianity. Throughout the ensuing decades, he was ridiculed, humiliated, and ostracized, as well as threatened with unemployment, arrest, and deportation. He was banished from Ukraine to Kazakhstan in Central Asia, where harassment continued until the collapse of the Soviet Union. Fired from jobs, denied raises and promotions, and shunned by many of his coworkers, Viktor persevered through hard work, ingenuity, and adaptability. Yet, a conflict ensued. As a Christian, he felt obliged to profess his faith openly and even publicly; as a provider for his wife, whom he had married early, and his five children, he was reluctant to jeopardize their safety and livelihood. Thus, he walked on a tightrope, yet reproached himself for doing so. Admitted to the United States and reunited with his children who had immigrated before him, he at first enjoyed the lack of pressure and insecurity. He even learned enough English to pass the naturalization examination. Inexplicably, however, disruptive symptoms appeared and intensified. Medication was to no avail, and physically, Viktor's health continued to be good. Psychotherapy was initiated in Russian, in which both Viktor and therapist are fluent.

In the first session, the therapist embarked on a focused symptom-centered approach to provide rapid relief from distress. A global, simplified muscular relaxation procedure was introduced to reduce anxiety and tension. Depression was targeted by means of cognitive restructuring of personal experiences and antidepressive self-statements, and paradoxical intention was initiated to counter insomnia. At the same time, empathy was communicated, and Viktor was assured that the therapist not only shared his distress and anguish but also understood the context in which they occurred. Viktor's strengths—his hard work, adaptability to circumstances, stable and lifelong relationships to his family, commitment to his beliefs and values, and ability to acquire new skills, including perfect Russian and a smattering of English—were recognized and verbally reinforced.

Viktor reported significant symptom reduction by the second session. "Nervousness" declined immediately and then disappeared. In rapid succession, insomnia, lack of appetite, pessimistic cognitions, and depressive affect followed suit. No trace of treatment resistance was detected. More gradually, Viktor started feeling better about himself, became less critical and dogmatic about the people and practices of his Russian Evangelical congregation, and related to his children and grandchildren in a more carefree, playful, and pleasant fashion. His self-perception shifted from victim to agent, who had survived, prevailed, and asserted himself against all odds. After 4 months of therapy, he proposed termination. His last words before leaving were, "I have never felt so free and easy in my life."

## Discussion

Within Leong's (1996) tripartite model, presented in this chapter, behavioral and cognitive interventions were aimed at universal aspects of Viktor's distress. Tension and anxiety are noxious everywhere, as are vegetative and affective symptoms of depression. Relaxation therapy and cognitive restructuring work across cultures and languages. Yet, it is doubtful that these procedures alone would have achieved a therapeutic effect. Cognitive and affective aspects of empathy, embedded in the cultural reality that the therapist knew and understood, probably played a role in making Viktor receptive to interventions. Remarkably, this brief therapy experience bypassed Leong's third level of intervention, based on unique individuality. Viktor may have reserved these subjective and intimate experiences for his private prayer or shared them with his pastor. Not prying into Viktor's private domain may have made universalistic interventions more acceptable, informed as they were by empathetic respect for his suffering at a specific time and place and his triumph over it.

1.  Viktor's behavior and his thoughts and feelings were changed in psychotherapy, but his insight or self-understanding was not increased. Can counseling with him be considered successful and complete?

2.  Why did Viktor feel depressed at the beginning of therapy? What, in your view, was the basic reason for his distress?

3.  Do you agree or disagree with therapist's decision not to delve into Viktor's private life and personal experience, and why?

# REFERENCES

Aponte, J. F., & Johnson, L. R. (2000). The impact of culture on intervention and treatment of ethnic populations. In J. F. Aponte & J. Wohl (Eds.), *Psychological intervention and clinical diversity* (2nd ed., pp. 18–39). Boston: Allyn &.Bacon.

Brislin, R. W. (2000). *Understanding culture's influence on behavior.* Fort Worth, TX: Harcourt, Brace, & World.

Chang, S. C. (1988). The nature of the self: A transcultural view. Part I: Theoretical aspects. *Transcultural Psychiatric Research Review, 25*(3), 169–204.

Chinese Culture Connection. (1987). Chinese values and the search for culture-free dimensions of culture. *Journal of Cross-Cultural Psychology, 18,* 143–164.

Deen, N. (1985). Cross-cultural counseling from a West European perspective. In P. B. Pedersen (Ed.), *Handbook of cross-cultural counseling and therapy* (pp. 45–54). Westport, CT: Greenwood.

Draguns, J. G. (1975). Resocialization into culture: The complexities of taking a worldwide view of psychotherapy. In R. W. Brislin, S. Bochner, & W. J. Lonner (Eds.), *Cross-cultural perspectives on learning* (pp. 273–289). Beverly Hills, CA: Sage.

Draguns, J. G. (2000). Psychopathology and ethnicity. In J. F. Aponte & J. Wohl (Eds.), *Psychological intervention and cultural diversity* (pp. 40–58). Boston: Allyn & Bacon.

Draguns, J. G. (2004). From speculation through description to investigation: A prospective glimpse at cultural research in psychotherapy. In U. P. Gielen, J. Fish, & J. G. Draguns (Eds.), *Handbook of culture, psychotherapy, and healing* (pp. 369–388). Mahwah, NJ: Lawrence Erlbaum.

Draguns, J. G., & Tanaka-Matsumi, J. (2003). Assessment of psychopathology across and within cultures: Issues and findings. *Behaviour Research and Therapy, 43,* 755–766.

Dwairy, M., & Van Sickle, T. D. (1996). Western psychotherapy in traditional Arabic societies. *Clinical Psychology Review, 16,* 231–239.

Grawe, K. (2004). *Neuropsychotherapie* [Neuropsychotherapy]. Goettingen, Germany: Hogrefe.

Griner, D., & Smith, T. B. (2006) Culturally adapted mental health interventions: A meta-analytical review. *Psychotherapy: Theory, Research, Practice, Training, 45,* 531–548.

Hall, G. C. N. (2001). Psychotherapy research with ethnic minorities: Empirical, ethical, and conceptual issues. *Journal of Consulting and Clinical Psychology, 69,* 502–510.

Herr, E. L. (1985). International approaches to career counseling and guidance. In P. B. Pedersen (Ed.), *Handbook of cross-cultural counseling and therapy* (pp. 3–10). Westport, CT: Greenwood.

Herskovits, M. (1948). *Man and his works.* New York: Knopf.

Higginbotham, H. N. (1984). *Third World challenge to psychiatry: Culture accommodation and mental health care.* Honolulu: University Press of Hawaii.

Hofstede, G. (1980). *Culture's consequences: International differences in work related values.* Beverly Hills, CA: Sage.

Hofstede, G. (1986). Cultural differences in teaching and learning. *International Journal of Intercultural Relations, 10,* 301–320.

Hofstede, G. (1991). *Culture and organizations: The software of the mind.* London: McGraw-Hill.

Hofstede, G. (2001). *Culture's consequences: Comparing values, behaviors, institutions, and organizations across nations.* Thousand Oaks, CA: Sage.

James, W. (1952). *The principles of psychology.* Chicago: Encyclopedia Britannica. (Original work published 1891)

Jilek, W. G. (2004). The therapeutic aspects of Salish spirit dance ceremonials. In U. P. Gielen., J. Fish, & J. G. Draguns (Eds.), *Handbook of culture, psychotherapy, and healing* (pp. 151–160). Mahwah, NJ: Lawrence Erlbaum.

Joo, E. (1998). Psychotherapeutic relationship in Korea compared to Western countries. *Korean Journal of Clinical Psychology, 17,* 39–54.

Katz, J. H. (1985). The sociopolitical nature of counseling. *The Counseling Psychologist, 13,* 615–624.

Kimura, B. (1995). *Zwischen Mensch und Mensch* [Between one human being and another] (H. Weinhendl, Trans.). Darmstadt, Germany: Akademische Verlagsanstalt.

Kluckhohn, C., & Murray, H. A. (1950). Personality formation: The determinants. In C. Kluckhohn & H. A. Murray (Eds.), *Personality in nature, society, and culture* (pp. 35–48). New York: Knopf.

Koss-Chioino, J. D. (2000). Traditional and folk approaches among ethnic minorities. In J. F. Aponte & J. Wohl (Eds.), *Psychological intervention and cultural diversity* (2nd ed., pp. 149–166). Boston: Allyn & Bacon.

Krippner, R. (2002). Conflicting perspectives on shamans and shamanism: Points and counterpoints. *American Psychologist, 57,* 962–978.

Landrine, H. (1992). Clinical implications of cultural differences: The referential versus the indexical self. *Clinical Psychology Review, 12,* 401–415.

Leong, F. T. L. (1996). Toward an integrative model for cross-cultural counseling and psychotherapy. *Applied and Preventive Psychology, 5,* 189–209.

Lowenstein, L. F. (1985). Cross-cultural research in relation to counseling in Great Britain. In P. B. Pedersen (Ed.), *Handbook of cross-cultural counseling and therapy* (pp. 37–44). Westport, CT: Greenwood.

Markus, H. M., & Kitayama, S. (1991). Culture and the self: Implications for cognition, emotion, and motivation. *Psychological Review, 98,* 224–253.

Marsella, A. J. (1988). Cross-cultural research on serious mental disorders: Issues and findings. *Acta Psychiatrica Scandinavica Supplement, 344,* 7–22.

Marsella, A. J. (2005, November 5). Rethinking the 'talking cures' in the global era. Retrieved from www.psych info.com.critiques

Moodley, R., & West, W. (Eds.). (2005). *Integrating traditional healing practices into counseling and psychotherapy.* Thousand Oaks, CA: Sage.

Nathan, T. (1994). *L'influence qui guérit* [The healing influence]. Paris: Odile Jacob.

Nwachuku, U. T., & Ivey, A. E. (1991). Culture specific counseling: An alternative training model. *Journal of Counseling and Development, 70,* 106–115.

Oberg, K. (1958). *Culture shock and the problem of adjustment to new cultural environments.* Washington, DC: U.S. Department of State, Foreign Service Institute.

Pedersen, P. B. (1977). The triad model of cross-cultural training. *Personnel and Guidance Journal, 56,* 480–484.

Pedersen, P. B. (1999). Culture-centered interventions as the fourth dimension in psychology. In P. B. Pedersen (Ed.), *Multiculturalism as a fourth force* (pp. 3–18). Philadelphia: Brunner/Mazel.

Pfeiffer, W. M. (1996). Kulturpsychiatrische Aspekte der Migration [Cultural psychiatric aspects of migration]. In E. Koch, M. Ozek, & W. M. Pfeiffer (Eds.), *Psychologie und Pathologie der Migration* (pp. 17–30). Freiburg/Breisgau, Germany: Lambertus.

Prince, R. H. (1980). Variations in psychotherapeutic procedures. In H. C. Triandis & J. G. Draguns (Eds.), *Handbook of cross-cultural psychology: Vol. 6. Psychopathology* (pp. 291–350). Boston: Allyn & Bacon.

Rogers, C. R. (1951). *Client-centered therapy.* Boston: Houghton Mifflin.

Rogers, C. R. (1957). The necessary and sufficient conditions of therapeutic personality change. *Journal of Consulting Psychology, 21,* 95–103.

Rogler, L. H., Malgady, R. G., Costantino, G., & Blumenthal, R. (1987). What do culturally sensitive services mean? The case of Hispanics. *American Psychologist, 42,* 565–570.

Roland, A. (1988). *In search of self in India and Japan.* Princeton, NJ: Princeton University Press.

Samuda, R., & Wolfgang, A. (Eds.). (1985). *Cross-cultural counseling.* Toronto: Hogrefe.

Snider, C. D. (2003). *Exploring the relationship between individualism-collectivism and attitude toward counseling among ethnic Chinese, Australian, and American university students.* Unpublished doctoral dissertation, Murdoch University, Perth, Australia.

Triandis, H. C. (1972). *Subjective culture.* New York: John Wiley.

Triandis, H. C. (1989). The self and social behavior in differing cultural contexts. *Psychological Review, 96,* 506–520.

Triandis, H. C. (1995). *Individualism and collectivism.* Boulder, CO: Westview.

Wrenn, C. G. (1962). The culturally encapsulated counselor. *Harvard Educational Review, 32,* 444–449.

Wrenn, E. G. (1985). Afterword: The culturally encapsulated counselor revisited. In P. B. Pedersen (Ed.), *Handbook of cross-cultural counseling and therapy* (pp. 323–330). Westport, CT: Greenwood.

CHAPTER

3

# Appraisal and Assessment in Cross-Cultural Counseling

Walter J. Lonner and Farah A. Ibrahim

---

## Primary Objective

- To present a general overview of contemporary issues and problems associated with the appraisal and assessment of individuals whose cultural or ethnic origins are different from that of the counselor or others in the helping professions

## Secondary Objectives

- To provide counselors and other professionals with relevant resources considered to be useful in increasing one's competence in the area of culture-sensitive assessment and appraisal in cross-cultural counseling
- To assist in the process of selecting appropriate assessment and appraisal strategies leading to effective and culture-specific diagnosis and counseling or treatment options

---

ASSESSING AND APPRAISING INDIVIDUALS FROM A BROAD SPECTRUM OF CULTURES AND ETHNIC groups, especially in today's global economy, has drawn much attention from clinicians and counselors. A significant part of this interest has involved ongoing challenges and difficulties with a number of conceptual and methodological concerns at both theoretical and applied levels. These challenges and difficulties include the identification, assessment, and/or measurement of culture-related variables thought to be important in the process of professional intervention. These variables are found in the diagnosis and treatment of individuals in clinical and counseling encounters, as well as in the evaluation of the outcomes of this process.

The ways in which these important matters are approached and resolved will greatly influence effective culturally appropriate appraisal and assessment. Many books, journal articles, monographs, conference presentations, college courses, training programs, and other academic and practical efforts have focused on possible solutions. The goal in these efforts is to understand the nature of intercultural competence (Lonner & Hayes, 2004) and to become increasingly "culturally competent" (Sternberg & Grigorenko, 2004) in professional interactions. There is a central point in this process. It is to bring together people who are, on one hand, culturally or ethnically different (the "clients" or recipients of skills and knowledge) and, on the other hand, psychologists, nurses, physicians, social workers, educators, and others in the helping professions (the "providers" and "appliers" of the requisite skills and knowledge) who are themselves culturally and ethnically diverse. Counselors and therapists should be acutely aware of the responsibility they have in the proper delivery of their services (Draguns, 1998).

## PROFESSIONAL INTERVENTIONS WITH "THE OTHER"

The Swiss cultural psychologist Ernest Boesch recently wrote a brief essay titled "The Enigmatic Other." In it, Boesch (see Lonner & Hayes, 2007, chap. 14) expressed a frank, unsettling, and career-long feeling of incompetence to "deal reasonably, in rational scientific terms, with the problem of 'the other.'" An astute multilingual observer of human behavior in various cultural contexts, one would think that this active 90-year-old, who was trained in part by Jean Piaget and psychoanalyzed by one of Sigmund Freud's closest disciples, would have utmost confidence in his ability to understand other people. Yet, based on years of experience, he has concluded that the seal of secrecy that encloses "the other" is secure and is forever to be an enigma. Each person, Boesch maintains, is always somewhat encapsulated in his or her unique world of thoughts, emotions, reflections, and behaviors, all shaped by culture. The enigma can be considerably compounded when "the other" is from a cultural or ethnic group different from one's own, thereby presenting a second—and quite possibly the most challenging—level of difficulty in professional interactions.

Boesch, of course, was not the first psychologist—nor will he be the last—to admit to a certain amount of bafflement or unease when rummaging around the private world of hopes, fears, disappointments, traumas, interpersonal relationships, marriage and family problems, and mental difficulties of the many people with whom he or she has interacts professionally. Indeed, a common problem when attempting to assess, appraise, or diagnose other people is the imperfections we all experience, both as humans and applied practitioners. Humans are complex and frequently guarded in what they disclose to others, even in professional settings. Unraveling these complexities and nurturing a working relationship are constant challenges, even to highly competent practitioners.

## THE CULTURAL ISOMORPHISM OF HUMAN ASSESSMENT AND APPRAISAL

All else being equal, the most effective counseling takes place in settings that are culturally isomorphic. This means that there is a high degree of equality in experiences that the client and counselor bring to the professional encounter. High isomorphism guarantees that individuals in such relationships will generally be "on the same page." This will be enhanced because those in the relationship will have learned the same language, will have been socialized in the same country or culture, and will have shared a "common fate" in the same social, cultural, and political milieu in which the counseling relationship takes place. Either explicitly or implicitly, all of the authors who have written chapters for this book agree with this rather simple and commonsense assertion. Another assumption made by all of the chapter authors is that "the other" often presents unusual challenges because there is a certain level or degree of "culturally nonisomorphic" interaction taking place; in some cases, the non-isomorphism may reach epic and even tragic proportions. In this sense, *all* professional interactions involve the appraisal or assessment of "the other" in his or her unique and enigmatic form that is exquisitely shaped by culture.

In previous editions of *Counseling Across Cultures,* we approached this area of concern by asking a number of questions and by giving examples of shared perspectives. For instance, in the fifth edition, we began the assessment and appraisal chapter by using a framework provided in a popular book, *The Spirit Catches You and You Fall Down* (Fadiman, 1997). The book is structured around the problems that a Hmong child experienced in her adopted United States and the clash of two medical systems—essentially two "worldviews"—in their attempts to explain the child's behavior.

This fascinating case challenged the efficacy of both systems. It served as a showcase for what some have called Arthur Kleinman's (1992) much-heralded "Eight Questions":

1. What do you call the problem?

2. What do you think has caused the problem?

3. Why do you think it started when it did?

4. What do you think the sickness does? How does it work?

5. How severe is the sickness? Will it have a short or long course?

6. What kind of treatment do you think the patient should receive? What are the most important results you hope the patient will receive from this treatment?

7. What are the chief problems the sickness has caused?

8. What do you fear most about the sickness?

These questions emerged in the context of "exotic" ethnopsychiatric conditions and anthropological perspectives. Not many professional mental health workers in the Western world routinely confront the problems faced by an unacculturated Hmong child. Kleinman, after all, has spent a career in ethnopsychiatry and medical anthropology. His model for cultural assessment likewise was designed to cover all facets of a client's cultural experience (Kleinman, 1992). Also containing eight points, the model will be useful in any professional interaction where cultural differences may be relevant. On the other hand, the eight questions can be modified slightly for use in various relatively modern and Western counseling settings rather than in specific ethnopsychiatric circumstances. Words such as *patient* and *sickness* can be replaced by *client* and *psychological condition,* thus making the eight questions appropriate for use in virtually all settings in multicultural counseling. Perhaps accurate answers to these questions could be used as criteria for successful appraisal and assessment in *any* counseling setting, regardless of how culturally isomorphic the setting happens to be.

# THE TWO PRIMARY DIMENSIONS OF ASSESSMENT AND APPRAISAL: QUALITATIVE AND QUANTITATIVE

While not suggesting that the world of psychological assessment is neatly dichotomized, we assert that two general perspectives in this area are worthwhile places to begin a discussion of assessment procedures. These perspectives are usually called qualitative (or idiographic) and quantitative (or nomothetic) and can create a great divide in defending which approach is better (Draguns, 1996; Draguns & Tanaka-Matsumi, 2003; Ponterotto, Gretchen, & Chauhan, 2001). Historically, this dichotomy was the centerpiece in Meehl's (1954) classic little book, *Clinical Versus Statistical Prediction.* Meehl noted that both approaches have had strong supporters and outspoken opponents. For instance, the clinical (qualitative) method has been described as rich, contextual, sensitive, open-minded, deep, genuine, insightful, flexible, and meaningful. It has also been pejoratively described as mystical, hazy, unverifiable, sloppy, crude, primitive, and intuitive. On the other hand, the statistical (quantitative) approach has been described by its adherents as communicable, testable, reliable, rigorous, precise, and empirical. Its detractors use such adjectives as mechanical, forced, superficial, rigid, pseudoscientific, and blind.

Historical and scientific posturing aside, psychology as a field is moving toward mixed methods in research and evaluation. Similarly, assessment and appraisal usually involve both perspectives. Furthermore, the guidelines for practice by the American Psychiatric Association (2000), the American Psychological Association (2002), and the American Counseling Association (2005) all emphasize that in working with culturally different clients, cultural impressionistic approaches are very important to identify the norm group of the client, so that quantitative assessments can be conducted ethically. Effective assessment involving individuals from other cultures or ethnic groups can only be accomplished *after* the person(s) doing the assessment has accumulated significant knowledge about the history, customs, and modes of interaction of the group or groups in question. Much of the remainder of this chapter is oriented around these dimensions and the issues that have doggedly followed them.

## The Qualitative Dimension

Qualitative assessment, of course, relies heavily on idiographic, informal, impressionistic, and often unstructured procedures or approaches. This dimension almost completely eschews traditional psychometrics and techniques that tend to "reduce" people to standard scores, percentiles, personality profiles, or points on a Likert-type scale. The qualitative approach includes the assessment of what may well be the most important phenomenon to understand: the client's view of the world. Koltko-Rivera (2004) describes worldviews as "sets of beliefs and assumptions that describe reality" (p. 3). A person's worldview ( *Weltanschauung* ) encompasses a wide range of topics, including morality, appropriate social behavior, political stances, ethics, and even the nature of the universe. A person's worldview, which he or she has overlearned by being socialized and enculturated in a specific culture for many or most of his or her formative years, is the main source of his or her intimate contact with and assumptions about the world. A *worldview,* arguably identical to the concept of culture (as the term is generally used in this book), is richly imbued with "meaningfulness," "purposefulness," and symbols (see Boesch, 1991; Lonner & Hayes, 2007) that can only be understood in specific cultural contexts. For everyone, the objective, subjective, and symbolic meanings we ascribe to people, places, and things are mediated in exquisite ways in all cultures (see Boesch, 2006; Lonner & Hayes, 2007, chap. 15).

Yet, while the person is socialized and enculturated in one specific culture during a certain time, he or she does not necessarily represent a pristine example of *everyone* in that particular culture. The person, in other words, is unique. On the other hand, it is highly likely the worldviews of most people from a given culture will be more similar than different. Recent research on "social axioms" supports the view that there is widespread agreement among people in a given culture regarding how the world "works." Conceptually similar to the measurement of "cultural syndromes" (Triandis, 1996) or the popular mode of "dimensionalizing" cultures via work-related values (Hofstede, 1980, 2001, 2006), social axioms (Bond et al., 2004; Leung et al., 2002) represent an intriguing new way to assess a person's view of the world. Leung et al. (2002) defined social axioms as "generalized beliefs about oneself, the social and physical environment, or the spiritual world, and are in the form of an assertion about the relationship between two entities or concepts" (p. 289). Detailed, multicultural factor analysis unearthed a quintet of social axioms: *cynicism*—a negative view of human nature, that life produces unhappiness; *social complexity*—a belief in multiple ways of doing things; *reward for application*— a belief that hard work and careful planning will lead to positive outcomes; *spirituality (or religiousness)*— a belief in a supreme being and the positive functions of religious practice; and *fate control*—a belief that life events are predetermined and that people can influence the outcomes.

Counselors and mental health professionals may conduct a worldview assessment with clients by using the Scale to Assess World View©, a social-psychological instrument (Ibrahim & Kahn, 1984, 1987; Ibrahim & Owen, 1994). Along with understanding the client's worldview, it is important to contextualize this knowledge with information on the client's cultural identity. Cultural identity can be assessed using a qualitative approach by using the Cultural Identity Check List© (Ibrahim, 1990, 1993, 1999, 2003). A critical point in understanding the "other" is self-knowledge of one's own worldview and cultural identity. Most recommendations for cultural competence require that this knowledge is taught and accumulated as a part of the educational and training process in becoming a professional counselor or an applied psychologist.

The qualitative dimension includes the notion, shared by many culture-oriented psychologists, that the person and the culture in which he or she lives are "co-constructed." They literally define each other. Constructivist assessment, such as that recommended by Neimeyer (1993) and Raskin (2002), have a number of features, including (1) an emphasis on "local" (emic) as opposed to "universal" (etic) meanings and beliefs shared by individuals in a circumscribed culture, (2) nonreliance on unchanging patterns of constructing meaning, (3) a fluidity in the production of social and personal processes, and (4) increased emphasis placed on the flexible and unfixed viability or pragmatic utility of applications.

In an excellent discussion of the qualitative-quantitative distinction, Carr, Marsella, and Purcell (2002) assert that in recent years, interest in the use of qualitative research methods has increased. The key ideas shared by those who tend to favor the former include a strong desire to preserve and study life in its true context, to examine the essence and nature of things, and to understand the dynamics of phenomena in their natural and nonmanipulated settings. The views of cultural psychologist Michael Cole are consistent with constructivist and qualitative assessment. Cole (1996) asserts, for example, that the analysis of everyday life events, the fact that individuals are "active agents in their own development," and that "mediated action in a context" are, among other factors, quite important. Cultural psychologists and constructivists in general tend to reject, as Cole puts it, "cause-effect, stimulus-response, explanatory science in favor of a science that emphasizes the emergent nature of mind in activity and that acknowledges a central role for interpretation in its explanatory framework" (p. 104). He also endorses drawing on "methodologies from the humanities as well as from the social and biological sciences" (p. 104). Thus, cultural psychologists such as Cole (see also J. G. Miller, 1997; Shweder, 1991; Wertsch, 1991) are far more likely to use qualitative methods than are their cross-cultural colleagues. The phenomenological nature of the human being and the belief that there are "multiple realities" rather than a uniform and completely objective and well-ordered world are other themes in qualitative approaches in general (Denzin & Lincoln, 1994) and also in research methodology (J. Smith, 2003).

## The Quantitative Dimension

Quantitative methodology in psychological research continues to be, in the opinion of many, the "gold standard" in terms of advancing psychology as a science. Guided by logical positivism and the belief and trust in the kind of "objectivity" or "universalism" that will transcend situations (including cultures), nomological approaches tend to be favored by most psychologists, whether or not their focus is on culture or ethnicity. A preference for objective data over idiographic "interpretation," standardization in both method and scoring, and efficiency of administering and interpreting tests and scales over on-the-spot constructivist approaches tend to be some of the hallmarks of this dimension in assessment and appraisal.

## Methodological Culture-Centered Concerns in Quantitative Research

While books such as Drummond and Jones (2006) cover important topics such as legal and ethical issues in testing, ability and intelligence tests, and the procedures of testing, few standard books in the area cover problems and issues associated with clients whose behavior has been calibrated in other cultures. Numerous problems have been associated with appropriate, fair, and useful employment of the many tests, inventories, scales, and other data-gathering devices designed to assess and appraise clients from various cultural and ethnic groups who are candidates for professional intervention. Psychologists who favor the use of such widely used devices as the NEO Personality Inventory—Revised (NEO-PI-R) or five-factor model (McCrae & Allik, 2002), the Minnesota Multiphasic Personality Inventory (MMPI; Butcher, 1996), various values scales, and so forth (see Dana, 2005) have been especially careful to address methodological problems of such multi-item scales and inventories when extended to other cultures. The most important methodological concerns tend to center on equivalence and bias. We will summarize several areas where these issues must be carefully considered.

*Conceptual (or Construct) Equivalence.* It should never be assumed that concepts or psychological constructs have exactly equivalent meanings in different cultures or ethnic groups. Many diagnostic categories, syndromes, or adjectives used to describe people do not carry well or transfer across cultures so that their meanings are exactly equivalent. Among scores of other definitions of culture, Hofstede (2001) says that "culture is the collective programming of the mind that distinguishes the members of one group or category of people from others" (p. 9). This means that every culture, either explicitly or implicitly, teaches its citizens to process concepts and constructs quite differently from members of other cultures. One of the counselor's tasks is to try and understand why and how this takes place differentially and to assess and appraise people accordingly. For instance, cultures that are highly individualistic tend to foster autonomy and independence among its citizens. The concept of dependency, therefore, when manifested by a client socialized in the Western world, will likely be viewed as "weak" or as harboring an "adjustment problem." On the other hand, in cultures that do not nudge people toward autonomy and independence, dependency and conformity may be the norm. Before a counselor uses a data-gathering device for individuals from other cultures or ethnic groups, he or she should consider the extent to which the counselor's definition of important concepts, both intrapersonal and interpersonal, matches those of the client. In other words, *cultural validity* should be established. Unfortunately, there is no objective "checklist" to guide the counselor in establishing such validity. However, most tests and scales designed or adapted for use in cross-cultural research have a significant body of research to guide the professional counselor. A search of the literature will usually pay off. Dana (2005), for instance, provides an excellent overview of multicultural assessment.

*Linguistic Equivalence, or Translation Equivalence.* Somewhat similar to conceptual equivalence, this area concerns all aspects of the language used in assessment devices. Psychologists who plan to make comparisons across cultures, as well as others who simply want to render a test or scale usable in other cultures, often spend a great deal of time translating the devices to be used. Back-translation is an almost obligatory procedure to ascertain the equivalence of scales. Brislin (1986) remains an important source of information about the procedures used in back-translation.

*Measurement Unit Equivalence.* As Marsella (1987) has noted, virtually everyone in the Western world is exposed to rating scales, attitude questionnaires, true-false ratings, and other efforts to quantify a broad range of what we experience in everyday life. Such measurement is so commonplace that we may almost miss them if people ceased to use them. Moreover, it is usually assumed that people will readily rate themselves and others and indeed have the ability to be self-reflective, with little or no regard for the person's right to privacy or concerns about how culture has influenced the tendency to disclose oneself to strangers or counselors. Van de Vijver and Leung (1997) give a cogent example of this problem by using two different scales to measure temperature—the Kelvin and Celsius scales. If used for two groups, the measurement unit would be identical. However, the *origins* of the scales are not. As van de Vijver and Leung explain it, "By subtracting 273 from the temperatures in Celsius, these will be converted into degrees Kelvin. Unfortunately, we hardly ever know the offset of scales in cross-cultural research" (p. 8). Suppose, for example, that a scale to measure anxiety was developed in Canada and was subsequently translated and administered to people in Japan. The original (Canadian) scale may contain a number of implicit and explicit references to the Canadian culture. These references will put Japanese respondents at a disadvantage. As a consequence, wrote van de Vijver and Leung, "the (supposedly) interval-level scores in each group do not constitute comparability at the ratio level" (p. 8).

*Scalar Equivalence, or Full-Score Comparability.* This type of equivalence can be achieved only with methods or scales that used the same ratio scale in each cultural group. Van de Vijver and Leung (1997) use the measurement of body length or weight (using any standard measure in either case).

## BIAS IN ASSESSMENT AND APPRAISAL

A large number of unwanted "nuisance" factors can threaten the validity and therefore usefulness of assessment devices when used with other cultural and ethnic groups. *Bias* is the general term used when considering such threats. van de Vijver and Leung (1997) offer that there are three types of bias: construct, method, and item.

*Construct bias* can occur, for example, when definitions of a construct across cultures do not completely overlap or when there is poor sampling of all relevant behaviors (such as in short questionnaires or scales). *Method bias* is a potential problem when (1) those who take a test are unequally familiar with the items; (2) a client may be subject to various types of response bias, such as acquiescence (e.g., agreeing with nearly everything) or extreme (responding only to endpoints of a continuum); (3) the person giving the test has differential effects on the participant; or (4) the samples are incomparable. And *item bias* occurs when one or more items are poorly translated or when there is complex wording in items.

A wealth of detailed information about the use of tests across cultures is readily available. The source we recommend is the International Test Commission (ITC). In 1999, the ITC formally adapted guidelines for test usage. In the same year, the European Federation of Professional Associations' Task Force on Tests and Testing endorsed the guidelines. Copies of the current guidelines can be obtained from the ITC Web site (http://www.intestcom.org).

## THE RANGE OF APPLICATIONS AND RESEARCH IN CROSS-CULTURAL ASSESSMENT AND APPRAISAL

Professional counselors in psychological or educational environments are well advised to understand the basic problems and issues in this area of intervention and service. Generally, the nature of their work will require an understanding of how problems and issues arise when using common tests and inventories discussed in Western-based texts in psychological assessment. Regardless of the device in question, they can all be considered against a backdrop of the methodological pitfalls and concerns summarized above.

## NEUROPSYCHOLOGICAL ASSESSMENT AND CULTURE

Another domain of assessment that merits consideration by the counselor, however, is *neuropsychological assessment.* Many individuals in need of some kind of professional psychological help are foreign born, are not fluent in English (or the dominant language where the professional encounter is taking place), are possibly victims of human-made or natural disasters or of physical or mental abuse, and may be severely malnourished. Because of these and other significant problems, the professional counselor would be wise to become somewhat familiar with the nature and scope of neuropsychological assessment. In this area of assessment, Nell (2000) clearly summarizes the reverberating general problem in cross-cultural psychoneurological assessment—a problem that presents a different kind of urgency:

> If mind, like brain, is one, and therefore unitary in all humans, the neuropsychological assessment founded on human universals will work equally well in London, New York, or the subsistence farming villages of South Africa and Brazil. If mind is many, however, and the ways in which people think and solve problems are determined by the interaction of their genetic endowment and the material conditions of their culture, then identical tests may make geniuses of average people in one culture and imbeciles of equally average people in another. (Nell, 2000, p. 13)

Currently, there are more than 500 tests available to the clinical psychoneurologist. In our opinion, it would be easy to dispose of the "universalist" argument in the use of any of these devices. We are certain that *some* cultural differences would be found in the employment of *all* of these tests. However, finding differences is not that important.

What is important to determine is if the differences are based on solid methodology and, if they are, *why* the differences exist.

Because culture or ethnicity may mask neuropsychological conditions, the professional counselor would be wise to become familiar with the current literature in this area. An important source of information is the *Handbook of Cross-Cultural Neuropsychology* (Fletcher-Janzen, Strickland, & Reynolds, 2000). The Web site of the National Academy of Neuropsychology (http://www.nanon line.org) is also an excellent source of information in this area of potential assessment of individuals from other lands.

## MODELS OF CROSS-CULTURAL APPRAISAL AND ASSESSMENT IN COUNSELING

Several models and approaches have been proposed to conduct an appraisal or an assessment within the context of cross-cultural counseling. These approaches have evolved over the past 30 years. They have developed within the context of cross-cultural or multicultural counseling. Essentially, this represents the collective thinking of researchers who were concerned about the ethics of appraisal and assessment within counseling and about cultural malpractice (Dana, 1998). Prior to a discussion of specific models, it is imperative that we accept that cross-cultural assessment requires a strong conceptual foundation that we have presented to address the complex and dynamic nature of culture (Lepez, 2002). Guanipa (2002) recommends the following characteristics as critical for the assessment and counseling process to be a success: flexibility, creativity, and respect. Furthermore, she notes that counselors who see normality in multicultural identities and have a sense of altruism, sensitivity, and cultural awareness have the best outcomes.

The earliest framework was presented by Kleinman (see above), where he posed his "eight questions" to guide the process of appraisal and assessment in counseling. These questions and his model (Kleinman, 1992) were developed to understand the client's explanatory rationale for the "problem" in both physical and mental health. This approach was quite revolutionary for the times because it included the client in the problem-solving process, and it focused on understanding what the client believed was the genesis of the problem, what function it was serving in the client's context, and how it could be treated. This model has provided the framework for ethical cross-cultural diagnosis and assessment such as the cultural formulation of the client's problem espoused by the American Psychiatric Association (1994, 2000). Castillo (1997) expanded on Kleinman's questions to include client and the context as the central component in the assessment and diagnosis process.

Ibrahim, Ohnishi, and Wilson (1994) presented a model of assessment and appraisal that expanded on the cultural dimension to understand the client. They proposed that simply asking questions about culture and what the problem means to the client will not make the answer apparent. One needs the tools to dissect and understand the cultural context and the client's unique place within the culture and its implications for appropriate assessment and intervention in a cross-cultural counseling encounter. This model puts the client's worldview and cultural identity at the core.

Worldview, as noted earlier, pertains to the client's beliefs, values, and assumptions that are developed within a cultural context and is the result of the socialization process; it is influenced by ethnicity, gender, religion and/or spirituality, familial values and behavior, regional and national values, and so on (Ibrahim, 2003; also see the brief discussion of social axioms above). Ibrahim and Kahn (1987) provide a reliable and valid instrument to assess worldview—that is, the Scale to Assess Worldview© (Ibrahim & Kahn, 1984; Ibrahim & Owen, 1994; Ibrahim, Roysircar-Sodowsky, & Ohnishi, 2001). Ibrahim (1993) recommends placing the client's worldview within the client's cultural identity. Cultural identity can be appraised by using the Cultural Identity Check List© (Ibrahim, 1990). This checklist helps the counselor and the client identify the significant influences in the client's life that have shaped his or her worldview and philosophy of life. It incorporates gender identity, ethnicity, culture, religion, developmental stage, languages spoken, acculturation level to own and primary culture, place in the family, socioeconomic status of the client and that of his or her parents, impact of living environment (urban, suburban, and rural), and ability and disability status.

The above are all key variables in cross-cultural assessment. Their purpose is to help establish that some semblance of a *shared worldview* is created between the assessor and the assessed. Ibrahim (1993, 1999) contends that each of these dimensions represents a cultural context, and this shapes and molds the client's conception of all he or she has experienced. This model provides an approach that helps clarify the client's cultural identity and worldview to assess the impact of the problem that the client faces. It also helps clarify what is normal and abnormal for that cultural context, reducing the fear of misdiagnosis and cultural malpractice. The counselor must make some key decisions in planning his or her assessment strategy when using this model. The decisions pertain to identifying the most salient features for the client that must be assessed before an intervention can be conducted. For example, if the client is an immigrant but has lived in the United States since age 25 and is currently 56 years old, the most salient factors are cultural identity, worldview, acculturation, and linguistic status (Ibrahim, 2003). Determining the key variables will depend on several factors, such as the issues that the client is facing relevant to his or her core values and culture. This would require worldview and cultural identity assessment. This assessment will reveal additional information that will dictate what other assessments to conduct. In the above example, if the person has lived nearly half or more of his or her life in the United States, acculturation level to mainstream culture and commitment to culture of origin must be concretely assessed to determine which values are most salient to the client-acquired or home culture. If the person speaks other languages, this will also influence his or her philosophy of life, as indicated by Maruyama (1999) and Ibrahim (1999). Furthermore, if the person is having significant difficulty speaking in English, the case should be referred because the counselor's ability to speak in the client's language is either nonexistent or very limited. This model and each of the others mentioned below require significant decision making on key variables to be assessed. We recommend that prior to any assessment, a counselor should become familiar with the literature, arts, and everyday life of the cultural group on which he or she plans to conduct assessments.

Dana (1993, 2005) has developed an ethnically sensitive model called the multicultural assessment-intervention process (MAIP). This model incorporates a process whereby therapists must make frequent and careful selections from among traditional and appropriate psychometric devices. Using the MAIP, the therapist does the following: (a) assesses the client's cultural identity; (b) assesses the client's level of acculturation; (c) provides a "culture-specific service delivery style" in which he or she phrases questions in accordance with cultural "etiquette"; (d) uses the client's language (or preferred language), if possible; (e) selects assessment devices or modes that are culturally appropriate to the client or that the client prefers; and (f) uses culture-specific strategies in informing the client about the results of assessment. Dana (2005) reports that the MAIP was identified by Ponterotto et al. (2001) as Dana's six-step cultural assessment model. He further notes that Morris (2000) expanded his model to propose a hybrid model for African Americans that combines the MAIP with Helms's (1990) racial identity development process.

Ridley, Li, and Hill (1998) propose a model they call the multicultural assessment procedure (MAP), which focuses on the incorporation of the client's culture in the assessment decision-making process. In addition, they emphasize the role of cognitive flexibility in clinical judgment and practice, as well as the role of language in assessments. The main goal of this model is to enhance the cultural competence of psychologists and other mental health professionals in multicultural and cross-cultural assessments. Constantine (1998) notes that one of the biggest strengths of this model is that it actively engages the client in the assessment process. This can help to short-circuit misunderstandings or culturally biased judgments by helping therapists engage their clients and get an accurate sense of the clients' issues and symptoms.

## THE LEVELS OF ANALYSIS PROBLEM IN USING DIMENSIONS AND CATEGORIES IN ASSESSMENT

This problem primarily includes the errant assumption that the highest level of abstraction (e.g., the whole country or culture) translates directly to the lowest level of abstraction (the individual and his or her specific behaviors). It is tempting, as P. B. Smith (2004) cautioned, to "test the plausibility of hypotheses by thinking about how the variables of interest [at the country level] relate at the individual level of analysis" (p. 9). Doing so is to commit what Hofstede (2001) has called the "ecological fallacy," for there is no logical reason why relationships between any two variables at one level of analysis should be the same at another level of analysis (Hofstede, 1980). In professional counseling, it may be tempting to inch toward committing an ecological fallacy. Doing so, however, may be tantamount to exhibiting bias or letting prejudice creep into the process. A special section of the January 2004 issue (vol. 35, pp. 3–96) of the *Journal of Cross-Cultural Psychology* addresses the level of analysis problem and the problems and challenges it presents.

## ASSESSING THE COUNSELING AND PSYCHOTHERAPY PROCESS

One dimension of assessment has little to do with either qualitative or quantitative measures of the type discussed up to this point. However, it can employ both standardized and nonstandardized instruments and tools. This is assessment of the process of counseling and psychotherapy and the outcomes achieved. Unfortunately, this domain has generated much theory, but actual research in it is still lacking. For counseling interventions to be effective, one of the most significant issues we confront is appropriate diagnosis and intervention (Draguns & Tanaka-Matsumi, 2003). The fourth edition of the *Diagnostic and Statistical Manual of Mental Disorders* (*DSM-IV*) introduced the notion of a cultural formulation of the client's identity, the cultural meaning of the problem, and "how" the problem could be resolved in a specific cultural context (American Psychiatric Association, 1994, 2000; Castillo, 1997). Since context is highly relevant in cross-cultural encounters, it must be assessed from a cultural perspective and understood prior to diagnosis (Draguns & Tanaka-Matsumi, 2003).

The counseling and psychotherapy process also requires that the therapist understand and match the client's verbal and nonverbal behaviors (Ibrahim, 1993, 1999, 2003; Ivey, 1994; Ivey, Ivey, & Simek-Downing, 1997; Sue & Sue, 1999). It also calls for both parties in the therapeutic dyad to understand one's own, as well as the other's, worldview (Grieger & Ponterotto, 1995; Ibrahim, 1993, 2003; Ibrahim et al., 2001; Ponterrotto et al., 2001; Sue & Sue, 1999). Furthermore, for an appropriate process to occur (one that is consistent with the client's cultural assumptions), it is important that both parties have a clear understanding of their cultural and gender identities, sociopolitical histories, acculturation levels, linguistic concerns, and the potential impacts of these elements on the therapeutic process (Santiago-Riviera, 1995). Unless all the cultural variables noted above are addressed, the most significant dimension in counseling and psychotherapy (i.e., power) will be overlooked (Pinderhughes, 1989). Several cultural assessments or appraisals must take place before the therapist can determine whether the process is appropriate for the therapeutic dyad (Dana, 1993, 1998, 2005; Ibrahim et al., 1994; Sedlacek, 1994). A positive movement has started in applied psychology, evidenced by some publications that address teaching competencies in cross-cultural and multicultural assessment that will lead to an effective process and outcome in counseling and psychotherapy (Hansen, 2002; Lepez, 2002).

Therapists must take many significant steps before the counseling process is established. Sue and Sue (1999) and Ibrahim (1984) have both maintained that the client's worldview must be clarified before an intervention can be put into place. Sue and Sue consider worldview from two psychological dimensions: locus of control (Rotter, 1966) and locus of responsibility. Ibrahim (1984, 1999, 2003) considers the client's worldview to be composed of beliefs, values, and assumptions that influence decisions and choices the client makes. Along with worldview, Sue and Sue (1999) maintain that the counselor must know and understand the sociopolitical history of the client's cultural group. Furthermore, McGoldrick, Giordano, and Garcia-Preto (2005) and Portes and Rumbaut (1990) assert that the impact of how a specific group has been received and integrated into the U.S. context affects people from that group for several generations. Considering the history of difficult race and cultural relations in the United States, this does not bode well for interactions between dominant group therapists and nondominant group members. Harmon et al. (2005) present two methods for enhancing outcome and preventing treatment failure in psychotherapy. The first involves providing therapists with a decision tree and several assessment measures. The second method involves providing clients with feedback on their progress throughout the course of treatment.

Ridley et al. (1998) proposed a comprehensive model of psychological assessment that is relevant to multicultural or cross-cultural clinician-client relationships. This model incorporates nearly all the recommendations to date in the literature into a framework that describes specific procedures that therapists must follow when making diagnostic decisions. It encourages practitioners to take a scientific stance in the counseling process when assessing client issues (Arbona, 1998; Spengler, Strohmer, Dixon, & Shivy, 1995). The model protects the counselor from making biased and distorted decisions, a risk that is inherent in any evaluation procedure. Ridley et al. also make a valuable point concerning the need for therapists to validate their clients' beliefs when they are working with culturally oppressed and marginalized clients. However, this should not be taken to imply uncritical acceptance of unhealthy coping mechanisms. They further recommend that counselors help clients differentiate between healthy and unhealthy expressions of values and beliefs in specific situations while at the same time affirming the clients' worldviews.

Ibrahim et al. (1994, 2001) maintain that the experience of nondominance (i.e., exclusion and rejection from the dominant group) can result in a condition that approximates posttraumatic stress disorder (PTSD). Specific to race, it is now possible for practitioners to assess the extent of race-related stress using a validated and reliable instrument, the Index of Race-Related Stress (Utsey & Ponterotto, 1996). Westermeyer (1988) makes several recommendations for the training of counselors and therapists to provide care for clients with PTSD across cultures. His focus is on cross-cultural encounters, specifically involving refugees; he also explores the bias inherent in Western counseling theory and practice and proposes methods to overcome it. In addition, T. W. Miller, Kraus, Kamenchenko, and Krasnienski (1993) argue that the impact of PTSD over time and its duration are critical dimensions that must be understood.

Stress-related disorders remain highest among nondominant group members and women in the American workplace, just as they do for a majority of all other facets of the population (Hatfield, 1990; Kieta & Jones, 1990). Although it is generally accepted that veterans of the armed forces and war refugees may suffer from PTSD, the view that nondominant status can lead to PTSD is more controversial. However, the text revision of the *DSM-IV* (*DSM-IV-TR;* American Psychiatric Association, 2000) defines a perspective that has been the battle cry for most cross-cultural theorists and researchers in mental health—that is, studying the individual's context (Arbona, 1998; Constantine, 1998; Draguns

& Tanaka-Matsumi, 2003; Ridley et al., 1998). PTSD as a disorder for nondominant group members in most societies, veterans, and/or refugees is environmentally induced and maintained. Assessing clients from these populations for PTSD is critical for practitioners prior to a counseling intervention. This will assist in identifying the nature of the problem as external rather than internal and can significantly affect the counseling process and outcome.

## OTHER CONTEMPORARY CONCERNS IN ASSESSMENT AND APPRAISAL ACROSS CULTURES

This section provides an overview of some contemporary approaches, problems, and issues in assessment and appraisal across cultures. In this section, we may want to make sure that we at least mention a good sampling of the ways in which authors of recent texts in the area have discussed important issues and perspectives.

### Linguistic Concerns

Mason (2005) echoes what most strongly believe: that the assessment of individuals from culturally diverse groups is complicated. This reality exists because the cultural meanings and associations, as well as the specific nuances of a term, differ from culture to culture and also may not be easily conveyed from one language to another (Mason, 2005; McDowell, 1992). Stewart and Bennett (1991) assert that since cultural experiences shape mental images, this affects the meaning ascribed to worldview. The ultimate effect of cultural socialization affects the way one processes information cognitively (Triandis, 1996). Language emerges as a significant variable, and there is agreement among theorists and researchers that language proficiency is the single most important factor in test performance (McDowell, 1992; Triandis, 1996). Testing procedures and interpretations also need to incorporate a recognition of sociopolitical and economic factors of those who are taking the tests. Olmedo (1981) and Oquendo (1996) address these concerns and note that linguistic differences also affect test taking. Furthermore, they both raise concerns regarding lack of research on how bilingualism, knowledge of two or more different languages, and competency in language acquisition vary, and bilingualism does not signify that the person comprehends the test items as a native, monolingual individual from a specific culture. Language competency and acculturation differences make it difficult to assess what was really understood by the test taker (Mason, 2005).

### Differential Definition of Assessment

There is an ongoing debate in the assessment field regarding the measurement of traits that are biologically based and universal to the human species, as well as traits that are culturally determined and specific to different contexts. Rossier (2004) and Watson, Duarte, and Glavin (2005) both conclude that theoretically based instruments from a specific culture cannot be used across cultures. Duarte (2004) recommends that to look for cultural equivalence is an outdated concept and proposes that ecological validity is a more useful concept than culture itself. This "implies that to assess behavior in a particular culture, test development should be based on *situation sampling* (defining the relevant and observable aspects of a . . . *construct*), *function sampling* (refining test items in terms of how they could be operationalized within a specific cultural context), and the identification of differential variables and context information (e.g., patterns of cultural or subcultural rewards)" (Watson et al., 2005, p. 30).

Another major concern addressed by Watson et al. (2005) pertains to the ubiquitous topic of conceptual/construct equivalence (an overview of which was presented earlier) and why this should precede issues of translation, such as linguistic, scale, and normative equivalence. The authors warned researchers regarding equating linguistic equivalence of test items as representing equivalence with the construct dimensions of the original career measure. They noted that the use of psychological tests in most countries followed a reverse order where conceptual/construct equivalence becomes a post hoc psychometric activity. In essence, construct equivalence equates cultural specificity. The authors warn against adapting and translating a country- or culture-specific measure for use in other countries. This practice leaves the profession vulnerable to a host of questions and concerns regarding the instrument (i.e., a test that is ready for use in a different country, in a different language, and for a different culture). The literature now recommends that cultural validation and specificity should focus on test developers and users, and the test development process should consider cultural factors in the earliest stages of test development (Duarte, 2004). This brings us to Leong's (1996) recommendation for cultural specificity in test construction that encourages starting with the culture in question and building an instrument relevant to the culture, rather than trying to fit an instrument developed in another culture in a new setting.

## SUMMARY AND CONCLUSIONS

The fair and accurate assessment and appraisal of clients who have been socialized in cultures that differ from that of the counselor present a number of potentially formidable problems. Regardless of culture of origin, ethnic identity, and other dimensions of human diversity that contribute to a person's identity, the usual psychometric concerns such as validity, reliability, practicality, and ethical treatment of clients are involved in *all* psychological assessment. Added to these concerns are specific, culture-related considerations regarding appropriateness, meaningfulness, and equivalence of numerous constructs, syndromes, and psychological dimensions that counselors and clinicians use in their attempts to understand their clients.

In this chapter, we surveyed the key issues and problems in cross-cultural assessment and appraisal that will always be present in some form. Those in the helping professions have a wealth of information to use in their interactions with clients from different cultures; we have identified and referenced a number of these sources and encourage readers to consult them for more details. Different organizations such as the American Psychological Association, the American Counseling Association, the National Academy of Neuropsychology, and the International Test Commission are useful sources of other information concerning the proper and ethical appraisal, assessment, and evaluation of clients who may be disadvantaged. The major source of this disadvantage is a scarcity of information about culturally diverse clients and the factors that may influence their performance on the immense variety of psychological devices that have been developed to help professionals understand them. Professionals must be constantly vigilant of these interactions and of all the methodological and conceptual factors that contribute to how one must be understood and respected, regardless of culture of origin or the nature of their ethnic identity.

### CRITICAL INCIDENT

Ronaldo is a 22-year-old immigrant from Peru. He came to Montreal with his parents and four older sisters when he was 15. When he was 18, he moved to Buffalo, New York, with two of his sisters and their husbands. He dropped out of school, and for about a year, he was employed as a carpenter's helper. His coworkers were all Spanish-speaking immigrants from Peru, Chile, and Paraguay. They have retained their cultural identity but have learned enough English to get by reasonably well. Still, Ronaldo and his family, together with four other people from South American countries, live in adjoining houses and share much of their financially challenged lives. Ronaldo's parents and his other two sisters travel to Buffalo frequently to visit. When they meet, only Spanish is spoken.

Ronaldo is both extremely shy and energetic. He wants to go back to school, perhaps enrolling in a program sponsored by a local community college. It is possible that within 2 years, he could be admitted as a freshman at a local 4-year college. He knows, however, that his shyness is a serious problem. He also has no clear academic goals. His primary motive is to "better himself" and find a respectable career. Thus, taking the advice of some acquaintances, he arranged to take a large battery of tests and inventories designed to assess his intelligence, academic potential, personality, interests, and even his learning styles. The testing took place over a 2-week interval and was an exhausting experience because he never had such assessment before. The experience, in fact, depressed Ronaldo to such an extent that he started to make other plans.

When the results came back, both the person assigned to interpret the results (a young woman with a master's degree in college personnel administration) and Ronaldo himself were surprised. The scores showed no clear pattern of results, and in many cases, various indices designed to give information about the validity of the scores strongly suggested retesting. This depressed Rolando even further. He decided to forego testing and application procedures and instead looked into an offer to become an apprentice in a local potato chip company.

If you were asked to intervene in this matter in an effort to help determine what went wrong, which of the following would you choose as the most plausible reason for this unfortunate situation and why?

1. It appears that Ronaldo, experiencing the demands of higher education for the first time, realized that further formal education was not for him.

2. Rolando was ill advised to subject himself to such extensive testing without first discussing the nature of psychological assessment with an expert. He could have benefited from some sort of "coaching" or preparation experience.

3. The surprising results showing no clear pattern of results strongly suggests that most or perhaps all of the assessment devices were not appropriate for Ronaldo.

4. The results suggest that Ronaldo may have one or more learning disorders and should therefore be tested to eliminate, or to confirm, this possibility.

Discuss the plausibility of each of the above explanations, each of which contains some reasonable bits of information. Realizing there is no totally correct answer, which one do you think is the most defensible?

## DISCUSSION QUESTIONS

1. Discuss what this critical incident tells us about the range of appraisal and assessment problems facing immigrants to the United States or perhaps in any country in the world where immigration exists.

2. Choose any section or subheading of Chapter 3 and discuss how it relates to key factors in this critical incident.

3. Like other critical incidents in this book, the one involving Ronaldo is extremely brief. Discuss two or three aspects of the incident that you think would merit further exploration in the area of assessment and appraisal.

4. Suppose that instead of Ronaldo, a single male 22 years of age, the main character was Rosalie, age 45 and the unmarried mother of four teenagers. Discuss how the cultural dynamics of the critical incident would change, especially with respect to how assessment and appraisal were approached.

# REFERENCES

American Counseling Association. (2005). *Code of ethics.* Alexandria, VA: Author.

American Psychiatric Association. (1994). *Diagnostic and statistical manual of mental disorders* (4th ed.). Washington, DC: Author.

American Psychiatric Association. (2000). *Diagnostic and statistical manual of mental disorders—text revision.* Washington, DC: Author.

American Psychological Association. (2002). *Guidelines for multicultural education, training, research, practice and organizational change.* Washington, DC: Author.

Arbona, C. (1998). Psychological assessment: Multicultural or universal? *The Counseling Psychologist, 26,* 911–922.

Boesch, E. E. (1991). *Symbolic action theory and cultural psychology.* Bern: Verlag Huber.

Boesch, E. E. (2006). A meditation on message and meaning. In J. Straub, D. Weidemann, C. Kölbl, & B. Zielke (Eds.), *Pursuit of meaning* (pp. 59–82). Brunswick, NJ: Rutgers University Press.

Bond, M. H., Xavier, P., Cabecinhas, R., Kwok, L., Al, A., & Kwok-Kit, T., et al. (2004). Culture-level dimensions of social axioms and their correlates across 41 cultures. *Journal of Cross-Cultural Psychology, 35,* 548–570.

Brislin, R. W. (1986). The wording and translation of research instruments. In W. J. Lonner & J. W. Berry (Eds.), *Field methods in cross-cultural research* (pp. 1337–1364). Newbury Park, CA: Sage.

Butcher, J. N. (1996). *International adaptations for the MMPI-2.* Minneapolis: University of Minnesota Press.

Carr, S. C., Marsella, A. J., & Purcell, I. P. (2002). Researching intercultural relations: Towards a middle way? *Asian Psychologist, 3*(1), 58–64.

Castillo, R. J. (1997). *Culture and mental illness.* Pacific Grove, CA: Brooks/Cole.

Cole, M. (1996). *Cultural psychology: A once and future discipline.* Cambridge, MA: Belknap-Harvard.

Constantine, M. G. (1998). Developing competence in multicultural assessment: Implications for counseling psychology training and practice. *The Counseling Psychologist, 26,* 922–1000.

Dana, R. H. (1993). *Multicultural assessment perspectives for professional psychology.* Boston: Allyn & Bacon.

Dana, R. H. (1998). *Understanding cultural identity in intervention assessment.* Thousand Oaks, CA: Sage.

Dana, R. H. (2005). *Multicultural assessment: Principles, applications, and examples.* Mahwah, NJ: Lawrence Erlbaum.

Denzin, N. K., & Lincoln, Y. K. (1994). *Handbook of qualitative research.* Thousand Oaks, CA: Sage.

Draguns, J. G. (1996). Multicultural and cross-cultural assessment of psychological disorder: Dilemmas and decisions. In G. R. Sodowsky & J. Impara (Eds.), *Multicultural assessment in counseling and psychology* (Buros-Nebraska Symposium on Measurement and Testing, 9, pp. 37–84). Lincoln, NE: Buros Institute of Mental Measurement.

Draguns, J. G. (1998). Transcultural psychology and the delivery of clinical psychological services. In S. Cullari (Ed.), *Foundations of clinical psychology* (pp. 375–402). Boston: Allyn & Bacon.

Draguns, J. G., & Tanaka-Matsumi, J. (2003). Assessment of psychopathology across and within cultures: Issues and findings. *Behavior Therapy and Research, 41,* 755–776.

Drummond, R. J., & Jones, K. D. (2006). *Assessment procedures for counselors and helping professionals* (6th ed.). Englewood Cliffs, NJ: Prentice Hall.

Duarte, M. (2004, June). *Assessment and cultural niches: Adaptation of psychological instruments and the global (research) village.* Symposium conducted at a joint meeting of the International Association for Educational and Vocational Guidance and the National Career Development Association, San Francisco.

Fadiman, A. (1997). *The spirit catches you and you fall down: A Hmong child, her American doctors, and the collision of two cultures.* New York: Farrar, Straus & Giroux.

Fletcher-Janzen, E., Strickland, T. L., & Reynolds, C. R. (2000). *Handbook of cross-cultural neuropsychology.* New York: Springer.

Guanipa, C. (2002). Important considerations in the counseling process of immigrant Venezuelan families. *American Journal of Family Therapy, 30,* 427–438.

Grieger, I., & Ponterotto, J. G. (1995). A framework for assessment in multicultural counseling. In J. G. Ponterotto, J. M. Casas, L. A. Suzuki, & C. M. Alexander (Eds.), *Handbook of multicultural counseling* (pp. 357–374). Thousand Oaks, CA: Sage.

Hansen, N. D. (2002). Teaching cultural sensitivity in psychological assessment: A modular approach used in distance education. *Journal of Personality Assessment, 79*(2), 200–206.

Harmon, C., Hawkins, E. J., Lambert, M. J., Slade, K., Whipple, J. L., & Wainright, F. (2005). Improving outcomes for poorly responding clients: The use of clinical support tools and feedback to clients. *Journal of Clinical Psychology, 61*(2), 175–185.

Hatfield, M. O. (1990). Stress and the American worker. *American Psychologist, 45,* 1162–1164.

Helms, J. E. (1990). An overview of Black racial identity theory. In J. Helms (Ed.), *Black and White racial identity: Theory, research, and practice* (pp. 9–47). New York: Greenwood.

Hofstede, G. (1980). *Culture's consequences: International differences in work-related values.* Beverly Hills, CA: Sage.

Hofstede, G. (2001). *Culture's consequences* (2nd ed.). Thousand Oaks, CA: Sage.

Hofstede, G. (2006). Dimensionalizing cultures. In W. J. Lonner, D. L. Dinnel, & S. A. Hayes (Eds.), *Online readings in psychology and culture.* Bellingham: Western Washington University, Center for Cross-Cultural Research. Retrieved from http://www.ac.wwu.edu/~culture/contents_complete.htm

Ibrahim, F. A. (1984). Cross-cultural counseling and psychotherapy: An existential-psychological perspective. *International Journal for the Advancement of Counseling, 7,* 159–169.

Ibrahim, F. A. (1990). *Cultural Identity Check List*©. Unpublished document, Storrs, CT.

Ibrahim, F. A. (1993). Existential world view theory: Transcultural counseling. In J. McFadden (Ed.), *Transcultural counseling: Bilateral and international perspectives* (pp. 23–58). Alexandria, VA: ACA Press.

Ibrahim, F. A. (1999). Transcultural counseling: Existential world view theory and cultural identity: Transcultural applications. In J. McFadden (Ed.), *Trancultural counseling* (2nd ed., pp. 23–57). Alexandria, VA: ACA Press.

Ibrahim, F. A. (2003). Existential worldview counseling theory: Inception to applications. In F. D. Harper & J. McFadden (Eds.), *Culture and counseling: New approaches* (pp. 196–208). Boston: Allyn & Bacon.

Ibrahim, F. A., & Kahn, H. (1984). *Scale to Assess World View*©. Unpublished document, Storrs, CT.

Ibrahim, F. A., & Kahn, H. (1987). Assessment of world views. *Psychological Reports, 60,* 163–176.

Ibrahim, F. A., Ohnishi, H., & Wilson, R. (1994). Career counseling in a pluralistic society. *Journal of Career Assessment, 2,* 276–288.

Ibrahim, F. A., & Owen, S. V. (1994). Factor analytic structure of the Scale to Assess World View©. *Current Psychology, 13,* 201–209.

Ibrahim, F. A., Roysircar-Sodowsky, G. R., & Ohnishi, H. (2001). World view: Recent developments and future trends. In J. G. Ponterotto, M. Casas, L. Suzuki, & C. Alexander (Eds.), *Handbook of multicultural counseling* (2nd ed., pp. 425–456). Thousand Oaks, CA: Sage.

Ivey, A. E. (1994). *Intentional interviewing and counseling: Facilitating client development in a multicultural world* (3rd ed.). Pacific Grove, CA: Brooks/Cole.

Ivey, A. E., Ivey, M. B., & Simek-Downing, L. (1997). *Counseling and psychotherapy: A multicultural perspective* (4th ed.). Boston: Allyn & Bacon.

Kieta, G. P., & Jones, J. M. (1990). Reducing adverse reactions to stress in the workplace. *American Psychologist, 45,* 1137–1141.

Kleinman, A. (1992). How culture is important for DSM-IV. In J. E. Mezzich, A. Kleinman, H. Fabrega, B. Good, G. Johnson-Powell, K. M. Lin, et al. (Eds.), *Cultural proposals for DSM-IV* (pp. 7–28). Pittsburgh, PA: University of Pittsburgh Press.

Koltko-Rivera, M. E. (2004). The psychology of worldviews. *Review of General Psychology, 8,* 3–58.

Leong, F. T. L. (1996). Career interventions and assessment in a multicultural world. In R. Feller & G. R. Walz (Eds.), *Career development in turbulent times: Exploring work, learning and careers* (pp. 275–283). Greensboro, NC: ERIC/CASS.

Lepez, S. R. (2002). Teaching culturally-informed psychological assessment: Conceptual issues and demonstrations. *Journal of Personality Assessment, 79,* 226–232.

Leung, K., Bond, M. H., Reimel de Carrasquel, S., Munoz, C., Hernandez, M., Murukami, F., et al. (2002). Social axioms: The search for universal dimensions of general beliefs about how the world functions. *Journal of Cross-Cultural Psychology, 33,* 286–302.

Lonner, W. J., & Hayes, S. A. (2004). Understanding the cognitive and social aspects of intercultural competence. In R. J. Sternberg & E. L. Grigorenko (Eds.), *Culture and competence: Contexts of life success.* Washington, DC: American Psychological Association.

Lonner, W. J., & Hayes, S. A. (2007). *Discovering cultural psychology: A profile and selected readings of Ernest E. Boesch.* Charlotte, NC: Information Age Publishing, Inc.

Marsella, A. J. (1987). The measurement of depressive experience and disorder across cultures. In A. J. Marsella, R. M. A. Hirshfield, & M. M. Katz (Eds.), *The measurement of depression* (pp. 376–379). New York: Guilford.

Maruyama, M. (1999). Self-heterogenization and cultural milieu selection: Two new directions in counseling. In P. B. Pedersen (Ed.), *Multiculturalism as a fourth force* (pp. 37–60). Philadelphia: Brunner/Mazel.

Mason, T. C. (2005). Cross-cultural instrument translation: Assessment, translation, and statistical applications. *American Annals of the Deaf, 150,* 67–72.

McCrae, R., & Allik, J. (Eds.). (2002). *The five-factor model of personality across cultures.* New York: Kluwer Academic/Plenum.

McDowell, C. (1992). Standardized tests and program evaluation: Inappropriate measures in critical times. *New Directions for Program Evaluation, 53,* 45–54.

McGoldrick, M., Giordano, J., & Garcia-Preto, N. (2005). *Ethnicity and family therapy* (3rd ed.). New York: Guilford.

Meehl, P. E. (1954). *Clinical versus statistic prediction.* Minneapolis: University of Minnesota Press.

Miller, J. G. (1997). Theoretical issues in cultural psychology. In J. W. Berry, Y. H. Poortinga, & J. Pandey (Eds.), *Handbook of cross-cultural psychology: Vol. 1. Theory and method* (2nd ed.). Boston: Allyn & Bacon.

Miller, T. W., Kraus, R. F., Kamenchenko, P., & Krasnienski, A. (1993). Posttraumatic stress disorder in U.S. and Russians veterans. *Hospital and Community Psychiatry, 44,* 585–587.

Morris, E. F. (2000). Assessment practices with African Americans: Combining standard assessment measures within an Africentric orientation. In R. H. Dana (Ed.), *Handbook of cross-cultural and multicultural personality assessment* (pp. 573–603). Mahwah, NJ: Lawrence Erlbaum.

Neimeyer, G. J. (Ed.). (1993). *Constructivist assessment: A casebook.* Newbury Park, CA: Sage.

Nell, V. (2000). *Cross-cultural neuropsychological assessment: Theory and practice.* Mahwah, NJ: Lawrence Erlbaum.

Olmedo, E. L. (1981). Testing linguistic minorities. *American Psychologist, 36,* 1078–1085.

Oquendo, M. A. (1996). Psychiatric evaluation and psychotherapy in the patient's second language. *Psychiatric Services, 47,* 614–618.

Pinderhughes, E. (1989). *Understanding race, ethnicity, and power: The key to efficacy in clinical practice.* New York: Free Press.

Ponterotto, J. G., Gretchen, D., & Chauhan, R. V. (2001). Cultural identity and multicultural assessment: Quantitative and qualitative tools for the clinician. In L. A. Suzuki, J. G. Ponterotto, & A. P. Meller (Eds.), *Handbook of multicultural competencies in counseling and psychology* (pp. 191–210). Thousand Oaks, CA: Sage.

Portes, A., & Rumbaut, R. G. (1990). *Immigrant America.* Berkeley: University of California Press.

Raskin, J. D. (2002). Constructivism in psychology: Personal construct psychology, radical constructivism, and social constructionism. In J. D. Raskin & S. K. Bridges (Eds.), *Studies in meaning: Exploring constructivist psychology* (pp. 1–25). New York: Pace University Press.

Ridley, C. R., Li, L. C., & Hill, C. L. (1998). Multicultural assessment: Reexamination, reconceptualization, and practical applications. *The Counseling Psychologist, 26,* 827–910.

Rossier, J. (2004, June). *An analysis of the cross-cultural equivalence of some frequently used personality inventories.* Symposium conducted at a joint meeting of the International Association for Educational and Vocational Guidance and the National Career Development Association, San Francisco.

Rotter, J. B. (1966). Generalized expectancies for internal versus external locus of control of reinforcement. *Psychological Monographs, 80*(1, Whole no. 609).

Santiago-Riviera, A. L. (1995). Developing a culturally-sensitive treatment modality for bilingual Spanish speaking clients: Incorporating language and culture in counseling. *Journal of Counseling and Development, 74,* 12–17.

Sedlacek, W. E. (1994). Issues in advancing diversity through assessment. *Journal of Counseling and Development, 72,* 549–553.

Shweder, R. A. (Ed.). (1991). *Thinking through cultures: Expeditions in cultural psychology.* Cambridge, MA: Harvard University Press.

Smith, J. (2003). *Qualitative psychology: A practical guide to research methods.* Thousand Oaks, CA: Sage.

Smith, P. B. (2004). Nations, cultures, and individuals: New perspectives and old dilemmas. *Journal of Cross-Cultural Psychology, 35,* 6–12.

Spengler, P. M., Strohmer, D. C., Dixon, D. N., & Shivy, V. A. (1995). A scientist-practitioner model of psychological assessment: Implications for training, practice, and research. *The Counseling Psychologist, 23,* 506–534.

Sternberg, R. J., & Grigorenko, E. L. (2004). *Culture and competence: Contexts of life success.* Washington, DC: American Psychological Association.

Stewart, E. C., & Bennett, M. J. (1991). *American cultural patterns.* Yarmouth, ME: Intercultural Press.

Sue, D. W., & Sue, D. (1999). *Counseling the culturally different* (3rd ed.). New York: John Wiley.

Triandis, H. C. (1996). The psychological measurement of cultural syndromes. *American Psychologist, 51,* 407–413.

Utsey, S. O., & Ponterotto, J. G. (1996). Development and validation of the Index of Race-Related Stress (IRRS). *Journal of Counseling, 43,* 490–501.

van de Vijver, F. J. R., & Leung, K. (1997). *Methods and data analysis for cross-cultural research.* Thousand Oaks, CA: Sage.

Watson, M., Duarte, M. E., & Glavin, K. (2005). Cross-cultural perspectives on career assessment. *The Career Development Quarterly, 54,* 30–35.

Wertsch, J. V. (1991). *Voices of the mind: A sociocultural approach to mediated action.* Cambridge, MA: Harvard University Press.

Westermeyer, J. (1988). Cross-cultural care for PTSD: Research, training and service needs for the future. *Journal of Traumatic Stress, 2,* 515–536.

# Guidelines and Competencies for Cross-Cultural Counseling Research

Joseph G. Ponterotto and Ingrid Grieger

---

*Primary Objective*

- To sensitize readers to the challenges of conducting cross-cultural counseling research and to provide general guidelines for promoting culturally relevant and ethically vigilant research

*Secondary Objective*

- To introduce 32 specific cross-cultural research competencies to guide counseling researchers in their empirical work across cultures

---

*We are all connected: To each other, to the land, to our ancestors, and to our children and all the children to come. That is powerful medicine that, rather than being viewed as "noise in the data," can inform, clarify, and strengthen our work as culturally competent and culturally grounded psychologists and scientists.*

Mohatt and Thomas (2006, p. 112)

THE ABOVE QUOTE, SPOKEN BY TLINGIT RESEARCHER LISA R. THOMAS TO HER COLLEAGUE GERALD V. MOHATT, captures well the researcher-community interconnectedness that we advocate in this chapter. Through a deep and respectful connection with the community under study, researchers will be better able to elucidate the worldview of the people they hope to understand, which is, in part, the goal of cross-cultural research (Mohatt & Thomas, 2006). It is only through a deep understanding of the worldview of a group or community that mental health professionals will be better equipped to contribute to the community's mental health assessment and intervention programs. Intimate contact with the community under study in all phases of research enhances the credibility of the findings within the community (Mohatt & Thomas, 2006) and facilitates the external validity of the study as perceived by the global psychological research community (S. Sue, 1999).

## CHAPTER PURPOSE AND FOCUS

The purpose of this chapter is to offer a set of guidelines and competencies for conducting (as well as reading and understanding) cross-cultural counseling research. The research competencies we advocate extend the well-established multicultural counseling practice competencies advocated by D. W. Sue et al. (1998) and are endorsed by multiple divisions within both the American Psychological Association (APA) and the American Counseling Association (ACA). Furthermore, our general guidelines and specific competencies are consistent with research guidelines recently put forth by the American Psychological Association (2003) in its "Guidelines on Multicultural Education, Training, Research, Practice, and Organizational Change for Psychologists."

Our competencies are organized along six more general guidelines for research: researcher self-awareness, knowledge of the history of research cross-culturally, community consultation and responsibility, ethical research practice, and philosophy of science knowledge with quantitative and qualitative research considerations. Within these six general guidelines are embedded 32 specific cross-cultural research competencies for counselors. These competencies are relevant to counseling researchers working in diverse communities within their own country, as well as to counselors conducting research abroad. Before presenting these competencies, we begin with our definition of cross-cultural research.

## DEFINING CROSS-CULTURAL RESEARCH

We believe that all counseling and mental health research is, to some degree, cross-cultural, in that it is highly unlikely that the researcher and her or his participants represent precisely the same cultural matrix. A cultural matrix is broad and represents a myriad of cultural variables, for example, race, gender, ethnicity, sexual orientation, nationality, socioeconomic status, religion, region of neighborhood of origin, age, individual and collective history of trauma, level of acculturation or racial identity, and/or disabilities. Therefore, the degree of cultural difference in worldview between researcher and participants may vary along a continuum from some similarities and some differences to many differences and few similarities.

A position we present in this chapter is that the greater the degree of potential cultural differences between the researcher and her or his research participants, the higher the degree of ethical care and community collaboration necessary to conduct culturally competent empirical research. An implication of the foregoing statement is that the less we know about our prospective research participants, the more we need to spend time in their communities to gain the trust of community representatives.

# INDIVIDUAL COMPETENCIES FOR THE CROSS-CULTURAL COUNSELING RESEARCHER

In this section, we present specific cross-cultural competencies that researchers may use as a guide in the conduct of their research. As noted above, these research competencies are intended to supplement the D. W. Sue et al. (1998) competencies, not to replace them. Whereas the Sue et al. competencies have a *practice* focus (i.e., intervention on the individual and systemic levels), the competencies to follow have a *research* focus. These sets of competencies, taken together, will serve as a strong foundation for the cross-cultural counseling researcher. Below we list and discuss 32 specific research competencies that are organized along six major guidelines; they may also be found in Table 4.1.

---

**TABLE 4.1**    Individual Competencies for the Multicultural Counseling Researcher

**The Multicultural Counseling Researcher**

**Guideline I: Researcher Self-Awareness as a Cultural Being**

1. is acutely aware of the transmitted values in her or his own socialization, upbringing, and scientific training; has explored in-depth his or her own racial, ethnic, and cultural biases; and has gotten in touch with and worked through her or his own experiences as a perpetrator and/or target of prejudice.

2. notes and records personal emotional and cognitive reactions to research projects before, during, and after the research study; processes these reactions with a cultural mentor.

**Guideline II: Knowledge of Past Psychological and Health Research in Diverse Communities**

3. has excellent command of the history of psychological research with racial/ethnic/cultural minority groups inside and outside the United States (e.g., racial/ethnic minority groups, lower socioeconomic groups, gay/lesbian groups, aboriginal peoples in Australia, Jews throughout the world, etc.).

4. has studied research ethics from a multicultural perspective and can cite and discuss negligence in past research studies; is familiar with potential and likely ethical issues and dilemmas in the conduct of both quantitative and qualitative research; actively monitors and receives consultation on ethics before, during, and after the study.

5. understands the origins and is aware of and empathic toward the attitudes and potential "resistance to being studied" present in some participant pools; this resistance may be particularly acute with regards to academics, particularly those of European descent working in racial/ethnic/cultural minority communities throughout the United States or with U.S. counseling researchers working abroad.

**Guideline III: Community Consultation and Responsibility**

6. frames research questions within parameters set by the larger community.

7. consults with members of the community in all phases of research—framing appropriate research questions, general design, implementation, analysis, results, interpretation, community follow-up, and so on.

8. includes community members as consultants to or members of a research team; includes community members as coauthors of the final report whenever possible.

9. submits the project proposal for review to a human participants review board (often called institutional review boards or IRBs) within their institutional base (e.g., university, hospital, clinic, government agency) *and to* another specially formed human participants and community impact review board composed of community representatives and elders/leaders.

*(Continued)*

**TABLE 4.1**    (Continued)

10. spends *at least* as much time learning about and visiting the community under study as in actually conducting the study.

11. works diligently to learn the language represented in the community.

12. asks independent scholars and community members representing the group under study to react and comment on result interpretation; seeks their advice on sharing results with participants and on how to use the research results to directly benefit the community in as timely a manner as is possible.

**Guideline IV: Ethical Research Practice**

13. plans all phases of the research program in close collaboration with community representatives.

14. is sensitive to appropriate procedures for accessing the population and has a cultural guide throughout the process.

15. fully briefs and explores with study's participants the purpose, rationale, methods, and implications of the proposed study.

16. makes all attempts to avoid deception in research; if minor deception is deemed absolutely necessary, checks deception procedures (including full risk/benefit assessment and briefing and debriefing plans) with community leaders/elders.

17. works diligently to directly benefit the studied community in all research endeavors; the researcher "gives back" to the community in a tangible and pragmatic way.

**Guidelines V and VI: Knowledge of Philosophy of Science and Research Paradigms, With Bi-Methodological Competence in Quantitative and Qualitative Methods**

18. has studied the philosophical roots regarding the nature (ontology, epistemology, axiology, rhetorical structure, and methods) of science and has "bi-methodological" competence in positivist/postpositivist (natural science) and constructivist (human science) approaches to human inquiry.

**Guideline V: Quantitative Research Considerations**

19. is well versed in quantitative methods and designs, including experimental, archival, analog, and survey research.

20. understands the construct of *cultural validity* in quantitative research.

21. is sensitive to sampling issues and is careful not to stereotype racial/ethnic/cultural groups as monolithic in between-group designs.

22. comprehensively describes participant samples in written reports.

23. understands the potential negative implications of "random sampling" in some collectivist communities.

24. is careful to consider within-group variables when researching racial/ethnic/cultural groups; such intracultural independent variables include collectivism/individualism, loss of face, cultural mistrust, acculturation, language preferences, racial identity, ethnic identity, religion, U.S.-based education level, education level abroad, occupation, geographic region, and so on.

25. in studies of survey or instrument format, is careful to select (or design) measures that have documented score validity and reliability with previous samples representing the population under study.

26. for instruments initially developed and normed for one population (e.g., English-speaking European Americans), includes careful translation procedures and tests of cultural equivalency before using them with a second population (e.g., African Americans, Native American populations, international populations).

27. in studies using psychological instruments, is careful to test both the reliability (e.g., internal consistency using coefficient alpha) and validity (e.g., concurrent validity, factorial validity) of the measures with *each* sample.

Our suggested research competencies stem from our own experiences in cross-cultural counseling research, from a review of literature, and from our consultation with multicultural elders as well as with other multicultural counseling researchers and research-study participants. Each of the competencies is consonant with and reflects aspects of the multicultural counseling practice competencies of D. W. Sue et al. (1998). The list is not exhaustive, and we are likely to have missed some important research considerations. Therefore, the competencies should be viewed as evolving, and their intent is to stimulate conscious consideration of the many ethical, process, and design factors that need to be taken into account when engaged in cross-cultural counseling research. Each competency listed in this chapter should be preceded with the sentence stem "The cross-culturally competent researcher…."

# Guideline I: Researcher Self-Awareness as a Cultural Being

1. is acutely aware of the transmitted values in her or his own socialization, upbringing, and scientific training; has explored in-depth his or her own racial, ethnic, and cultural biases; and has gotten in touch with and worked through her or his own experiences as a perpetrator and/or target of prejudice.

2. notes and records personal emotional and cognitive reactions to research projects before, during, and after the research study; processes these reactions with a cultural mentor.

These two competencies focus on the researcher's own self-awareness of cultural values, beliefs, biases, and so forth. Clearly, one who is ethnocentric and bound to a culturally encapsulated worldview will be handicapped as a cross-cultural researcher (APA, 2003). In fact, such a counselor is likely to do more harm than good in her or his research endeavors.

Trimble and Mohatt (2006) emphasized the important notions of virtue ethics and the virtuous researcher. Culturally sensitive and meaningful research begins within the researcher, not within an established research design. Boeree (1999, p. 5) noted that "it is a virtuous person that creates good acts, not good acts that that add up to a virtuous person" (cited in Trimble & Mohatt, 2006, p. 327). The virtuous researcher is self-reflective, is self-regulatory, and constantly seeks cultural consultation (Meara & Day, 2003; Joseph E. Trimble, personal communication, March 29, 2006).

Counseling researchers, whether they be graduate students or seasoned scholars, should be attuned to their own values, biases, and expectations, as well as their own role as oppressors or oppressed, during all phases of research. Because it is easy (and perhaps more comfortable) to lose sight of one's own biases and uncomfortable history with regard to prejudice, counselors are urged to work on collaborative, cross-cultural research teams, in which team members can help monitor each other's guiding value systems, including nonconscious biases and cultural assumptions. Importantly, all research teams should include representatives of the community under study (see APA, 2003; Trimble & Fisher, 2006a).

We have also found it very helpful to have research team members keep ongoing logs or journals in which they note their emotional and cognitive reactions to events as they take place during the research process. Although reflective journals or research diaries are often associated with qualitative research methods (Morrow, 2005; Ponterotto & Grieger, 2007), we advocate their use in *all* research. Researcher reactions might include summaries of interactions with participants (for example, noting how someone responded to a particular interview or survey question), as well as summaries of the research more generally, such as noting ideas for gaining greater trust in the community under study. It is helpful for researchers to periodically share journal entries with other team members and cultural mentors for processing and reflection. Furthermore, at various points during the empirical investigation, researchers can discuss evolving findings with members of the participant samples. When and how this dialogue takes place is dependent on the particular investigation. We have much more to say about this later.

## Guideline II: Knowledge of Past Psychological and Health Research in Diverse Communities

3. has excellent command of the history of psychological research with racial/ethnic/cultural minority groups inside and outside the United States (e.g., racial/ethnic minority groups, lower socioeconomic groups, gay/lesbian groups, aboriginal peoples in Australia, Jews throughout the world, etc.).

4. has studied research ethics from a multicultural perspective and can cite and discuss negligence in past research studies; is familiar with potential and likely ethical issues and dilemmas in the conduct of both quantitative and qualitative research; actively monitors and receives consultation on ethics before, during, and after the study.

5. understands the origins and is aware of and empathic toward the attitudes and potential "resistance to being studied" present in some participant pools; this resistance may be particularly acute with regard to academics, particularly those of European descent working in racial/ethnic/cultural minority communities throughout the United States or with U.S. counseling researchers working abroad.

These three competencies focus on the critical responsibility of the researcher to have basic knowledge of the history of psychological and health research with racial/ethnic/cultural minority groups. High levels of awareness regarding past abuse of the research process with less empowered groups may attenuate (but will not eliminate) the incidence of mistreatment of research participants and misrepresentation of the life experiences and worldviews of culturally diverse communities in North America and abroad (APA, 2003). The horrific "medical experiments" of Nazi physicians in the concentration camps during World War II, as well as the inexcusable Tuskegee Syphilis Study of untreated syphilis among African American men from 1932 to 1972 conducted by the U.S. Public Health Service in Alabama, are two of the more well-known examples of research communities' abuse (Trimble & Fisher, 2006b; Wallace, 2006).

More recent informed consent and related ethical violations were noted in the case of 52 Havasupai tribal members who filed a $25 million suit against a major research university in the Southwest. It is alleged that from 1990 to 1994, blood samples were drawn from these tribal members for the stated purpose of studying correlates of diabetes. However, according to the suit, tribal members later learned that the blood samples had been used for other purposes not agreed to during consent procedures, namely, to examine the incidence of schizophrenia and inbreeding and to study human migration patterns (see comprehensive overview in Trimble & Fisher, 2006b).

Clearly, knowledge and ownership of our profession's contribution to the abuse of research participants on an individual and community level is a prerequisite to cross-cultural research competence. In addition to a history of more blatant ethical violations in research on vulnerable communities, researchers have also been neglectful in more subtle ways through portraying minority communities as "culturally deficient" or "culturally deprived." This bias has been reflected in the misapplication of Eurocentric and U.S.-centric norms and theories of psychology, inappropriate use and interpretation of research instruments conceptually anchored in such theories, and the past practice of incorporating "White control groups" in interethnic studies, in which the White sample occupied the "normal" comparison group (APA, 2003; Ponterotto, Utsey, & Pedersen, 2006; D. W. Sue & Sue, 2003; S. Sue, 1999).

Understanding the history of research in minority communities will also sensitize researchers to the potential resistance of participants to outside researchers asking about very personal and private psychological and health issues. These issues are covered in depth in the recent edited contribution by Trimble and Fisher (2006a) on ethical research with ethnocultural communities (see particularly Trimble & Fisher, 2006b; Wallace, 2006).

# Guideline III: Community Consultation and Responsibility

6. frames research questions within parameters set by the larger community.

7. consults with members of the community in all phases of research—framing appropriate research questions, general design, implementation, analysis, results, interpretation, community follow-up, and so on.

8. includes community members as consultants to or members of a research team; includes community members as coauthors of the final report whenever possible.

9. submits the project proposal for review to a human participants review board (often called institutional review boards or IRBs) within their institutional base (e.g., university, hospital, clinic, government agency) *and to* another specially formed human participants and community impact review board composed of community representatives and elders/leaders.

10. spends *at least* as much time learning about and visiting the community under study as in actually conducting the study.

11. works diligently to learn the language represented in the community.

12. asks independent scholars and community members representing the group under study to react and comment on result interpretation; seeks their advice on sharing results with participants and on how to use the research results to directly benefit the community in as timely a manner as is possible.

These seven competencies emphasize the need to conceptualize, conduct, interpret, and disseminate research with the support, guidance, and vision of the communities under study, rather than operating within a detached scholarly vacuum (APA, 2003; Trimble & Fisher, 2006a). Similarly, Trimble and Mohatt (2006) advocate a "relational methodology" when working with ethnocultural communities. Specifically, they emphasize the importance of establishing trust through developing authentic and deep relationships with host communities. These authors note that nurturing relationships

> means spending precious time visiting with people at social functions such as community gatherings, celebrations, ceremonies, local school events, and related activities. It means spending time with community leaders such as elected officials and elders, as well as visiting with parents of school-aged youth as well as the youth themselves. It means being willing to engage in long conversations that have nothing at all to do with one's research interest. (Trimble & Mohatt, 2006, p. 331)

Furthermore, in a published dialogue with his colleague, Lisa Thomas, Gerald Mohatt suggests that researchers and community collaborators "build a critical set of feedback loops" that facilitate the constant questioning and interpretations of research results as they come in, whether they arrive through surveys, psychological instruments, or interview questions (Mohatt & Thomas, 2006, p. 112).

Groundbreaking research that significantly benefits multicultural communities is often conducted by scholars who represent the culture, life experiences, and language of the target community and who work in close collaboration with community elders. Strong research can also be conducted by "outsiders" to the community, if the researchers expend an effort to honor the community by giving their time to the community and living within it, sometimes for many years.

A role model for us in this regard is Dr. Gerald V. Mohatt, a European American psychologist who has spent much of his life living and working among Native communities in South Dakota and Alaska. Through his commitment to and respect for these Native communities, he has earned their acceptance and trust. Poignantly, he associates developing deep trust with the host community as similar to developing a kinship relationship with its members (Mohatt & Thomas, 2006).

Another important component of Dr. Mohatt's demonstration of honor and respect for his host culture involved learning to speak Lakota, the western dialect of the Sioux Nation. He notes that learning the language of the host community assists in understanding the worldview and epistemology of its members.

## Guideline IV: Ethical Research Practice

13. plans all phases of the research program in close collaboration with community representatives.

14. is sensitive to appropriate procedures for accessing the population and has a cultural guide throughout the process.

15. fully briefs and explores with study's participants the purpose, rationale, methods, and implications of the proposed study.

16. makes all attempts to avoid deception in research; if minor deception is deemed absolutely necessary, checks deception procedures (including full risk/benefit assessment and briefing and debriefing plans) with community leaders/elders.

17. works diligently to directly benefit the studied community in all research endeavors; the researcher "gives back" to the community in a tangible and pragmatic way.

Although ethical issues undergird all 32 competencies introduced in this chapter, we highlight five specific ethical considerations in this section. Chief among these is the researcher's responsibility to avoid harm to and deception of the community and to bring the benefits of the research directly to the community in a tangible way (Casas, Pavelski, Furlong, & Zanglis, 2001; Ponterotto & Casas, 1991). The research ethics discussed in this section complement and are anchored in established multicultural guidelines advocated in practice-based ethical decision-making models (Ridley, Liddle, Hill, & Li, 2001) and systems of care (Casas et al., 2001).

Fisher and Ragsdale (2006) advocate "goodness-of-fit" ethics for multicultural research, in which researchers and participants act as co-learners during the research enterprise. The goodness-of-fit framework conceptualizes participant protection and respect in light of the research context and the specific characteristics of the participant population. These authors suggest that in planning a research program, investigators should ask themselves the following three questions:

(a) What are the special life circumstances that render participants more susceptible to research risk? (b) Which aspects of the research design, implementation, or dissemination may create or exacerbate research risk? and (c) How can research and ethical procedures be fitted to participant characteristics to reduce vulnerability? (Fisher & Ragsdale, 2006, p. 6)

Mohatt and Thomas (2006) operationalize the goodness-of-fit models of Fisher and Ragsdale (2006) and Ridley et al. (2001) well in their "People Awakening Project." This mixed-method study included 101 life history interviews of Alaska Natives who were lifetime alcohol abstainers, were non-problem drinkers, or had been sober for 5 or more years. Phase two of the study was quantitative and involved the careful construction of instruments to assess protective and recovery variables that appeared to emerge from the life story interviews. Mohatt and Thomas present four ethically based research questions that guided their research program and that can serve as a guide for cross-cultural counseling research more generally:

1. "Does a common ground exist? Is the issue defined and understood similarly by the researcher and the community of population targeted for the study?" (p. 98).

2. "Do we share the same goals for each step of the research process?" (p. 100)

3. "Are the proposed methodologies not only 'scientifically sound,' but culturally appropriate, relevant, and respectful? Are the measurement instruments asking the appropriate questions? Are these questions and the responses given by the participants understood similarly by both the researchers and the participants?" (p. 104)

4. "What is our responsibility for dissemination of the research results, not just in peer-reviewed journals but also in venues that stakeholders and our participants will utilize?" (p. 107)

# Guidelines V and VI: Knowledge of Philosophy of Science and Research Paradigms, With Bi-Methodological Competence in Quantitative and Qualitative Methods

18.  has studied the philosophical roots regarding the nature (ontology, epistemology, axiology, rhetorical structure, and methods) of science and has "bi-methodological" competence in positivist/postpositivist (natural science) and constructivist (human science) approaches to human inquiry.

Guidelines V and VI focus on the need to develop multicultural research competency across contrasting research paradigms—namely, postpositivism and constructivism—and inquiry methods, specifically quantitative and qualitative approaches (APA, 2003; Ponterotto, 2005b). The majority of research in counseling has been anchored in postpositivism and has used quantitative methods (Ponterotto, 2005a; Ponterotto & Grieger, 2007). We believe that qualitative research methods, often anchored in constructivism, hold great promise for cross-cultural researchers, and we advocate increased usage of these methods (see also Morrow, Rakhsha, & Castaneda, 2001; Ponterotto, Costa, & Werner-Lin, 2002; S. Sue, 1999).

Both qualitative and quantitative methods have inherent strengths and limitations in terms of advancing science, and both approaches have and can be used to oppress, misrepresent, and stereotype various cultural groups. From a cross-cultural research perspective, both quantitative and qualitative approaches present distinct challenges that warrant careful consideration by the counseling researcher. We are also of the opinion that a competent cross-cultural researcher has strong skills in *both* quantitative and qualitative methods and can select research approaches based on the research question under consideration and the needs of the community under study (Ponterotto & Grieger, 1999).

## Guideline V: Quantitative Research Considerations

19.  is well versed in quantitative methods and designs, including experimental, archival, analog, and survey research.

20.  understands the construct of cultural validity in quantitative research.

21.  is sensitive to sampling issues and is careful not to stereotype racial/ethnic/cultural groups as monolithic in between-group designs.

22.  comprehensively describes participant samples in written reports.

23.  understands the potential negative implications of "random sampling" in some collectivist communities.

24.  is careful to consider within-group variables when researching racial/ethnic/cultural groups; such intracultural independent variables include collectivism/individualism, loss of face, cultural mistrust, acculturation, language preferences, racial identity, ethnic identity, religion, U.S.-based education level, education level abroad, occupation, geographic region, and so on.

25.  in studies of survey or instrument format, is careful to select (or design) measures that have documented score validity and reliability with previous samples representing the population under study.

26. for instruments initially developed and normed for one population (e.g., English-speaking European Americans), includes careful translation procedures and tests of cultural equivalency before using them with a second population (e.g., African Americans, Native American populations, international populations).

27. in studies using psychological instruments, is careful to test both the score reliability (e.g., internal consistency using coefficient alpha) and validity (e.g., concurrent validity, factorial validity) of the measures with *each* sample.

Quantitative designs that have been popular in the multicultural literature include survey, experimental, analog, and archival (Ponterotto & Casas, 1991). Regardless of the chosen design, researchers should assess the cultural validity of their research program. Cultural validity has been defined as

> the authentic *representation* of the cultural nature of the research in terms of how constructs are operationalized, participants are recruited, hypotheses are formulated, study procedures are adapted, responses are analyzed, and results are interpreted for a particular group as well as the *usefulness* of the research for its instructional utility in educating readers about the cultural groups being investigated, its practical utility in yielding practice as well as theoretical implications about the cultural group, and its service utility in "giving back" to the community in important ways. (Quintana, Troyano, & Taylor, 2001, p. 617)

In their major contribution to quantitative research methods, Quintana et al. (2001) specify ways to improve cultural validity in the areas of planning a study, using measurement instruments, recruiting participants, analyzing data, and interpreting results. We present a few samples from the Quintana et al. contribution in Table 4.2.

| **TABLE 4.2** | Sample Steps to Enhance Cultural Validity Across Stages of the Research Process |
| --- | --- |
| Planning Phase | Consult with cultural communities to help formulate research questions and methodology. |
| | Translate demographic characteristics (e.g., racial status) into psychological characteristics (e.g., experience of stigmatization). |
| Measurement Instruments | Adapt ethnocentric instruments by decontextualizing and recontextualizing for cultural group. |
| | Pilot test instruments on sample of target population. |
| Participant Recruitment | Make recruitment procedures congruent with cultural group. |
| | Recruit sample that the community itself believes represents the target population. |
| Data Analysis | Evaluate cultural hypotheses as well as rival hypotheses. |
| | Investigate moderator effects of cultural variables. |
| Result Interpretation | Engage participants in meaningful way during interpretation process. |
| | Individualize procedures and reports of results for participants and give back to community through service ideas related to research. |

SOURCE: Extracted directly from Quintana, Troyano, and Taylor (2001, pp. 621–623, 625–626). Table adapted with permission of Sage Publications.

Quantitative researchers should take care to comprehensively describe their samples in the Method sections of their reports. For readers to assess the generalizability of study results, adequate detail with regard to sample descriptors is necessary. S. Sue (1999) is quite critical of published cross-cultural research in that Sample sections of reports are often limited to basic demographics of the participants, neglecting important participant characteristics that would enhance the external validity of the findings. Good sample descriptions include basic demographics, for example, male and female percentages, age breakdowns, geographic considerations, socioeconomic characteristics, religious affiliations, racial and specific ethnic affiliations, length of time living or attending school in the United States (i.e., generation status), and nondemographic characteristics, such as previous experience with the counseling process, level of acculturation or racial identity, and so forth. The more detail and preciseness in describing one's sample, the better able the reader is to assess result generalizability.

Random sampling is considered the sine qua non for quantitative research, in that only from a fully random sample can one reliably generalize results to the population in question. However, random sampling, in some communities where its constituents operate more from a collectivist worldview, would create concerns. Reflecting on his work with Native populations in South Dakota and Alaska, Gerald Mohatt, in his published dialogue with colleague Lisa Thomas, notes the following:

> I believe that random sampling procedures violate a fundamental principle of every indigenous group with whom I have ever worked. It assumes that a statistical or mathematical relationship rationale should determine whom we talk to or with whom we intervene. It is exclusive rather than inclusive (that is, it selects only a certain number of participants rather than invites everyone to participate). (Mohatt & Thomas, 2006, p. 110)

Mohatt and Thomas (2006) suggest that sampling in Native communities should strive to invite all members to participate or, when this is not possible, to consult with elders to selectively sample community representatives who most clearly illustrate the psychological concept or construct under study.

Other competencies in this section focus on careful use of psychological instrumentation in research. For example, many research instruments, by their very nature of presenting multiple items to the participants in a paper-and-pencil format, tend to isolate behaviors, cognitions, and emotions in an effort to quantify and measure them. In discussing this issue, Mohatt and Thomas (2006, p. 109) note that many Native people believe "in the connectedness of life" and, therefore, would not be comfortable isolating cognitions, emotions, or behaviors with the goal of measuring, manipulating, and interpreting them.

When research instruments or measures are used, researchers should take great care to assess the cultural relevance of the construct under study to the population of interest. Researchers should be aware of whether the measurement device, if developed within Western psychological constructs and the English language, has undergone appropriate translation procedures and tests of construct equivalence (Lonner & Ibrahim, Chap. 3, this volume; Merenda, 2006; Quintana et al., 2001; van de Vijver & Hambleton, 1996).

## Guideline VI: Qualitative Research Considerations

28.  is well versed in qualitative research methods, including participant observation, life story and oral history, in-depth individual interviewing, and focus group interviewing.

29.  is particularly sensitive to the impact on participants and communities in highly researcher-involved interactions such as in participant observation and in-depth interviewing.

30. in describing samples in reports, is careful to provide adequate descriptions without compromising the anonymity of participants in small samples.

31. carefully monitors interviewing procedures and is clear on the distinction between qualitative interviewing and therapy; is careful not to fall into the therapist role.

32. is particularly sensitive to the impact of terminating (withdrawing from) the interactive researcher role—for example, the impact on the interviewees when the lengthy, highly revealing interviews end or the impact on the site (community) when the participant observation ends.

Throughout this chapter, we have emphasized the need to work collaboratively with culturally diverse communities. Qualitative research methods, particularly those emanating from the constructivist research paradigm, in which multiple realities (worldviews) are acknowledged and where researchers and participants interact closely to co-construct descriptions of "lived experiences" appear to offer unlimited potential for cross-cultural research. Ponterotto (2005a) recently reviewed some particular advantages of qualitative research with diverse communities. First, by entering the community and showing respect for participants' worldview and life experiences, researchers achieve close, intimate contact with community members, which serves to help them suspend and challenge preexisting expectations and come to understand the experiences of participants. Second, qualitative researchers often see themselves as co-investigators, rather than "experts," thus facilitating mutual understanding and equal distribution of power. Such a stance gives voice to often silenced cultural groups and attenuates the chance of marginalizing study participants.

Balancing the clear advantages of qualitative research, these methods introduce particular research challenges. First, since most counselors and psychologists were trained in the postpositivist research paradigm, which posits one true reality, a goal for research of prediction and explanation, and a detached researcher-participant stance, learning constructivist qualitative methods involves a shift of research worldview (Ponterotto, 2005a, 2005b; Ponterotto & Grieger, 2007) and years of additional training. Second, the intensity and extent of interaction between researchers and participants common to constructivist qualitative methods, such as in participant observation and in-depth long interviews, necessitate vigilant ethical care as we develop "kinship relationships" (Mohatt & Thomas, 2006, p. 112) with our participants and then leave the communities under study to head back to campus. Finally, forms of in-depth interviewing are deeply personal and intense, and counseling researchers have to carefully monitor the fine line between such interviews and the counseling process itself (see Sciarra, 1999). Furthermore, follow-up contact with research participants, sometimes for many years, is critical given the bond that has been formed with participants through such highly involved and personal research procedures.

## CONCLUSION

We believe the delineation of specific research competencies presented in this chapter will facilitate the conduct of culturally sensitive and relevant research both domestically and internationally. Furthermore, we believe the competencies have equal applicability to the novice researcher and to the seasoned cross-cultural expert. As noted at the start of this chapter, the research competencies introduced here are evolving and require ongoing scrutiny, revision, and expansion. Certainly, for the cross-cultural researcher, developing and maintaining cross-cultural research competence in a rapidly changing demographic and sociopolitical world is an ongoing process. There will never be a point when the researcher has reached full cross-cultural competence and, therefore, need not attend to continuing self-scrutiny and professional development.

Dr. John Casalingua is a second-year assistant professor in the counseling psychology program at a university in New York City. Dr. Casalingua received his undergraduate degree in psychology and a doctoral degree in counseling psychology from prestigious universities in California, where he spent his entire life, until moving to New York City 2 years ago. During graduate training, Dr. Casalingua received strong quantitative research training and has already published in the area of multicultural health counseling. Dr. Casalingua is a third-generation Mexican American who, though quite acculturated to the "American culture," still maintains ties with his Mexican ancestry and has some fluency in the Spanish language ("enough to get by," he states).

Dr. Casalingua has conceptualized his next research project, in which he hopes to investigate what he perceives as a high teen pregnancy rate among some Hispanic subgroups in various New York City neighborhoods. He is concerned with the high teen pregnancy in these communities, and he hopes to conduct a survey using a large random sample of Hispanic teenage young women from these neighborhoods. Given that his university has long-established ties with many community and mental health agencies in the city, Dr. Casalingua hopes to work through these centers to collect his random data. His survey will consist of paper-and-pencil instruments that assess sexual risk-taking attitudes and behavior, alcohol and substance use, self-esteem, and individual assertiveness scales. Planning to employ a regression model, Dr. Casalingua hypothesizes that those teenage women who exhibit high self-esteem, high assertiveness, and low levels of substance use will report less risky sexual attitudes and behaviors. Dr. Casalingua's research plan receives approval from his university's institutional review board (IRB).

## DISCUSSION QUESTIONS

First, we commend Dr. Casalingua for his commitment to researching underserved populations on a topic of great importance. However, given the guidelines and competencies posited in this chapter, we offer the following questions we would hope Dr. Casalingua and his research team would consider further.

1. Dr. Casalingua is a third-generation Mexican American, with some fluency in the Spanish language. However, what is his familiarity with other Hispanic subgroups that he would likely be sampling in New York City, such as Puerto Rican and Dominican Americans? Does he have a member on his research team who knows these groups well and represents them personally? Does he have a member in his research team who is bilingual?

2. Dr. Casalingua, who is male, plans to study a very personal and sensitive topic with teenage women. How will he be received by the female community? Does he have women who represent the various Hispanic subgroups on the research team?

3. Though receiving university IRB approval, there is no indication that Dr. Casalingua's research plan was presented to and reviewed by a *community-based* human participant review board. Does Dr. Casalingua intend to present his research plan to a community-based review board?

4. Dr. Casalingua has chosen to attempt random sampling and quantitative measures for his study. Is this sampling plan the most appropriate for this community? Have the instruments been translated into Spanish and validated for cultural equivalence for the sample groups? Are the constructs on which the instruments are based (e.g., self-esteem, individual assertiveness) appropriate for community members who may have more collectivist values? Is Dr. Casalingua knowledgeable about the salient values of the communities that he is studying?

5. Is a quantitative study the best way to access the worldview and life experiences of these young women? Could sensitive, culturally contextualized long interviews or focus groups be better matched to study this sensitive topic (see Sciarra & Ponterotto, 1998)?

6. There is no sense from the case description that Dr. Casalingua is working closely with community representatives and elders in planning, designing, conducting, and following up with the study. Does Dr. Casalingua intend to spend time with community members in order to form collaborative relationships with them?

7. How does Dr. Casalingua plan to ensure that no harm will accrue to community members as a result of his investigation? How does Dr. Casalingua plan to give back to the community that has participated in his study?

Our analysis raises many questions about Dr. Casalingua's research plan. If these questions are not addressed at a formative stage of the study, the investigation is likely to be flawed. Within the seven points or questions we raised, there are many critical decision points. For example, in Point 3, in which the research plan is reviewed positively by the university's IRB, there is a danger of Dr. Casalingua being led to believe that his plan and design is most appropriate. However, without also having the proposal reviewed by a mixed-gender community-based group from the locale of the study, the chances of the investigation framing questions appropriately and leading to fruitful findings are severely limited.

# REFERENCES

American Psychological Association (APA). (2003). Guidelines on multicultural education, training, research, practice, and organizational change for psychologists. *American Psychologist, 58,* 377–402.

Boeree, C. G. (1999). *Ethics.* Retrieved March 14, 2005, from www.ship.edu/~cgboeree/ethics.html

Casas, J. M., Pavelski, R., Furlong, J. M., & Zanglis, I. (2001). Advent of systems of care: Practice and research perspectives and policy implications. In J. G. Ponterotto, J. M. Casas, L. A. Suzuki, & C. M. Alexander (Eds.), *Handbook of multicultural counseling* (2nd ed., pp. 189–221). Thousand Oaks, CA: Sage.

Fisher, C. B., & Ragsdale, K. (2006). Goodness-of-fit ethics for multicultural research. In J. E. Trimble & C. B. Fisher (Eds.), *The handbook of ethical research with ethnocultural populations & communities* (pp. 3–25). Thousand Oaks, CA: Sage.

Meara, N. M., & Day, J. D. (2003). Possibilities and challenges for academic psychology: Uncertain science, interpretive conversation, and virtuous community. *American Behavioral Scientist, 47*(4), 459–478.

Merenda, P. F. (2006). An overview of adapting educational and psychological assessment instruments: Past and present. *Psychological Reports, 99,* 307–314.

Mohatt, G. V., & Thomas, L. R. (2006). "I wonder, why would you do it that way?" Ethical dilemmas in doing participatory research with Alaska Native communities. In J. E. Trimble & C. B. Fisher (Eds.), *The handbook of ethical research with ethnocultural populations & communities* (pp. 93–115). Thousand Oaks, CA: Sage.

Morrow, S. L. (2005). Quality and trustworthiness in qualitative research in counseling psychology. *Journal of Counseling Psychology, 52,* 250–260.

Morrow, S. L., Rakhsha, G., & Castaneda, C. L. (2001). Qualitative research methods for multicultural counseling. In J. G. Ponterotto, J. M. Casas, L. A. Suzuki, & C. M. Alexander (Eds.), *Handbook of multicultural counseling* (2nd ed., pp. 575–603). Thousand Oaks, CA: Sage.

Ponterotto, J. G. (2005a). Integrating qualitative research requirements into professional psychology training programs in North America: Rationale and curriculum model. *Qualitative Research in Psychology, 2,* 97–116.

Ponterotto, J. G. (2005b). Qualitative research in counseling psychology: A primer on research paradigms and philosophy of science. *Journal of Counseling Psychology, 52,* 126–136.

Ponterotto, J. G., & Casas, J. M. (1991). *Handbook of racial/ethnic minority counseling research.* Springfield, IL: Charles C Thomas.

Ponterotto, J. G., Costa, C. I., & Werner-Lin, A. (2002). Research perspectives in cross-cultural counseling. In P. B. Pedersen, J. G. Draguns, W. J. Lonner, & J. E. Trimble (Eds.), *Counseling across cultures* (5th ed., pp. 395–420). Thousand Oaks, CA: Sage.

Ponterotto, J. G., & Grieger, I. (1999). Merging qualitative and quantitative perspectives in a research identity. In M. Kopala & L. A. Suzuki (Eds.), *Using qualitative methods in psychology* (pp. 49–62). Thousand Oaks, CA: Sage.

Ponterotto, J. G., & Grieger, I. (2007). Effectively communicating qualitative research. *The Counseling Psychologist, 35,* 404–430.

Ponterotto, J. G., Utsey, S. O., & Pedersen, P. B. (2006). *Preventing prejudice: A guide for counselors, educators, and parents* (2nd ed.). Thousand Oaks, CA: Sage.

Quintana, S. M., Troyano, N., & Taylor, G. (2001). Cultural validity and inherent challenges in quantitative methods for multicultural research. In J. G. Ponterotto, J. M. Casas, L. A. Suzuki, & C. M. Alexander (Eds.), *Handbook of multicultural counseling* (2nd ed., pp. 604–630). Thousand Oaks, CA: Sage.

Ridley, C. R., Liddle, M. C., Hill, C. L., & Li, L. C. (2001). Ethical decision making in multicultural counseling. In J. G. Ponterotto, J. M. Casas, L. A. Suzuki, & C. M. Alexander (Eds.), *Handbook of multicultural counseling* (2nd ed., pp. 604–630). Thousand Oaks, CA: Sage.

Sciarra, D. T. (1999). The role of the qualitative researcher. In M. Kopala & L. A. Suzuki (Eds.), *Using qualitative methods in psychology* (pp. 37–48). Thousand Oaks, CA: Sage.

Sciarra, D. T., & Ponterotto, J. G. (1998). Adolescent motherhood among low-income urban Hispanics: Familial considerations of mother-daughter dyads. *Qualitative Health Research, 8,* 751–763.

Sue, D. W., Carter, R. T., Casas, J. M., Fouad, N. A., Ivey, A. E., Jensen, M., et al. (1998). *Multicultural counseling competencies: Individual and organizational development.* Thousand Oaks, CA: Sage.

Sue, D. W., & Sue, D. (2003). *Counseling the culturally diverse: Theory and practice* (4th ed.). New York: John Wiley.

Sue, S. (1999). Science, ethnicity, and bias: Where have we gone wrong? *American Psychologist, 54,* 1070–1077.

Trimble, J. E., & Fisher, C. B. (Eds.). (2006a). *The handbook of ethical research with ethnocultural populations & communities.* Thousand Oaks, CA: Sage.

Trimble, J. E., & Fisher, C. B. (2006b). Our shared journey: Lessons from the past to protect the future. In J. E. Trimble & C. B. Fisher (Eds.), *The handbook of ethical research with ethnocultural populations & communities* (pp. xv–xxix). Thousand Oaks, CA: Sage.

Trimble, J. E., & Mohatt, G. V. (2006). Coda: The virtuous and responsible researcher in another culture. In J. E. Trimble & C. B. Fisher (Eds.), *The handbook of ethical research with ethnocultural populations & communities* (pp. 325–334). Thousand Oaks, CA: Sage.

van de Vijver, F., & Hambleton, R. K. (1996). Translating tests: Some practical guidelines. *European Psychologist, 1,* 89–99.

Wallace, S. A. (2006). Addressing health disparities through relational ethics: An approach to increasing African American participation in biomedical and health research. In J. E. Trimble & C. B. Fisher (Eds.), *The handbook of ethical research with ethnocultural populations & communities* (pp. 67–75). Thousand Oaks, CA: Sage.

# The Big Picture

## Theorizing Self-Concept Structure and Construal

### William E. Cross Jr. and Tuere Binta Cross

---

*Primary Objective*

- To present a holistic perspective of the self-concept for use in counseling, therapeutic interventions, and research with minority, marginalized, and cross-cultural populations

*Secondary Objectives*

- To differentiate self-concept structure from construal of the self by exploring two key components of the self: personal identity and group identity
- To make the connection between child development, personality development, and the emergence, during adolescence, of group identity dynamics
- To show that the psychological definitions of individuality and personality are distinct from philosophical notions of individualism

---

THIS CHAPTER STRESSES THE IMPORTANCE OF THE BIG PICTURE IN THEORIZING THE SELF. WE BEGIN AND end with the proposition that whether one is engaged in a discussion of the structure of the self or the range of meanings and interpretations accorded the self (construal), the self-concept consists of personal identity (PI) and group identity (GI) components. We offer a counternarrative to those who truncate the self by exaggerating the significance of either self-esteem or collective-esteem, and we favor a holistic approach in research and counseling psychology, especially when the research participants or counseling clients are members of targeted racial/cultural groups. We take on the important distinction to be made between self-concept structure and self-concept construal. Fusing elements of developmental psychology, ego psychology, object relations theory, psychoanalytic theory, activity theory, social identity theory, and reference group theory, we trace the development of the self-concept from infancy through early adulthood, showing the distinctiveness and interconnectedness of PI and GI. We view this bifurcated structure to be invariant across cultures. In explicating our thesis, we differentiate between personality, individuality, and individualism to show that while personality and individuality are very much present in all cultures, individualism (a particular form of individuality) tends to be a marker of Western societies.

Theory and research on self-concept structure seek to isolate elements and dynamics that are universal and thus applicable to an analysis of the self across cultures (Mischel & Morf, 2003; Rosenberg, 1979; Schmitt & Allik, 2005). On the other hand, theory and research on self-construal explicate the interpretations and meanings accorded the self from one culture to another. The construal discourse is centered less on structure and more on the way cultures differ in the interpretation of the person-society relationship (Markus & Kitayama, 1991). Construal theorists argue that in the West, a philosophy of individualism permeates self-orientations, while in the East, a more interdependent or collectivist philosophy guides self-orientations.

In this chapter, we concern ourselves with the conflation of structural and construal arguments, especially with regard to self-concept profiles thought to be prototypical of the Western-Self as contrasted with the Eastern-Self. For example, does the prototype of a collectivist translate into high scores on group esteem (GI) and low scores on self-esteem (PI)? Likewise, does the prototype of an individualist translate into high scores on self-esteem (PI) and low scores on group esteem (GI)? Furthermore, do group identity dynamics play a negligible role in the everyday psychology of individualists, and conversely, do personality and individuality play a minor role in the everyday psychology of collectivists? We offer a different interpretation and suggest that people are more alike than different at the level of self-concept structure—even across cultures. A self-concept profile, juxtaposing moderate to high levels of self-esteem with moderate to high levels of group esteem, may be more commonplace than previously thought possible, especially in light of differential West-East profiles predicted by self-construal theory.

To arrive at this conclusion, one must stop equating self-esteem with individualism and group esteem with collectivism. Instead, PI and GI should be viewed as different types of psychological strength, and when combined, the result is a person who has various personality strengths (self-esteem has been shown to be associated with a wide range of positive personality strengths) and a moderate to high sense of social purpose (group esteem is linked to ideology, intentionality, and resolve). In a collectivist society, people with high self-esteem and other positive personality traits and dynamics may provide vitality, agency, creativity, and resiliency to the enactment of everyday activities and tasks, as guided by the society's social agenda. However, when the individual is asked to reflect on what it means (construal) to be a part of the society, he or she may "silence" his or her personality and spotlight the group's worldview and the joint activities that give him or her a sense of social grounding. In response to questions of construal and despite having moderate to high self-esteem, the individual's focus becomes the activities and beliefs for which his or her "personality" and personal actions are seen to be in the service of. In this sense, self-esteem can be seen to facilitate the enactment of either collectivity ("my strength is for the people and our community") or individualism ("my strength benefits me"). Cultural difference may reside more in purpose, intention, ideology, philosophy, and meaning making and less so in the specific PI and GI characteristics people bring to the everyday enactment of culture and identity (Strauss & Cross, 2005).

In turning to the West, we think the profile of positive PI combined with positive GI is also commonplace; however, we will try to show that at the level of self-construal, Westerners do the opposite of people from the East and silence not their individuality and personality but their need for group esteem, interdependency, and interconnectedness (Kohut, 1984). That aspects of the self are silenced is not the same as making them disappear, and we will attempt to argue that PI and GI components of the self-concept play a major role in all cultures.

## A UNIVERSAL UNFOLDING OF THE SELF: INDIVIDUATION AND ATTACHMENT

Much of the debate on the relative importance of PI and GI for individuals living in either individualist or collectivist societies tends to be premised on studies conducted with adolescents, college students, and adults. At times, the tenor of the debate suggests that a fully developed self-concept may evidence the dominance of one component over the other (PI or GI dominance), so much so that one or the other component is of limited developmental significance. If one anchors the discourse in child development, the divide between the two constructs shrinks, because, while in later life the distinctions to be made between the two components are real, the early development of each component that takes place during infancy and early childhood is sequentially intertwined (Kohut, 1984; Winnicott, 1987). The either/or quality of the self-esteem versus group esteem debate must make room for the possibility that, independent of cultural context, the structure of the self for all human beings reveals not one but *both* personal and group identity dynamics and that PI development precedes GI development (Mahler, Pine, & Bergman, 1975).

## SEPARATION-INDIVIDUATION, INDIVIDUALITY, AND PERSONALITY

D. W. Winnicott's (1987, p. 88) famous statement—"There is no such thing as a baby, there is the baby and someone"—reflected his belief that the sense of self evolves from the baby-mother or child-caretaker relationship (Roland, 1996, p. 11). According to Winnicott, newborn babies have little sense of personal self (PI), let alone awareness of membership in a particular group (GI), and the psychological building blocks the baby uses to construct the self are derived in large measure from daily, persistent, and sustained interactions with the mother. Newborns and infants are dependent on their mothers and other primary caretakers for fulfillment of basic physiological and psychological needs. The symbiotic relationship triggers a developmental process that results in the scaffolding of the self.

For the newly born, sensations and experiences have no borders. The infant is unable to determine where the psychological and physical contours of the self begin and end and when sensations signal the presence of another human being or nearby object. Emerging from the womb, able to feel and experience sensations, the infant has limited insight, given the nearly complete absence of a developed social perspective. The process infants go through to comprehend that their physicality and psychology are distinct from others is called separation-individuation (Mahler et al., 1975). Not to be confused with notions of individualism, individuation maps movement from a sense of self that is diaphanous and without borders to one where the integrity of people and outline of inanimate objects becomes comprehensible to the infant.

We take the position that differentiation and emergence of a conscious sense of self or social perspective are universal. Outside of severe physiological or psychological malformation, every infant, regardless of cultural context, learns to differentiate the self from the people and objects that make up the human ecology within which the infant is nested (Bronfenbrenner, 1979). The sense of self that is born out of this process is more akin to personal identity than group identity. To underscore our point, let us take the case of Danjuma, a 2-day-old infant born in rural Nigeria whose mother's name is Lantana. As the mother cradles Danjuma, she talks to the infant about her African name, makes frequent reference to the village people, walks over to the window, and describes to the infant all the things the villagers are doing just outside their home. The baby seems to be hungry so Lantana places her breast to the infant's lips while singing an African lullaby. Now let's shift the focus to the baby. Danjuma cannot comprehend her mother's African language and singing, nor can she process the discrete behaviors and bits of conversation of the people just outside the window. But Danjuma feels Lantana's arms, fingers, and warm body; is soothed by the tone of her voice and singing; and is agitated by an internal sensation of hunger that soon loses its grip, as milk from Lantana's breast is sucked into her mouth and flows wonderfully down her throat.

A fundamental marker of development is an infant's ability to differentiate between me and not-me perceptions. That is, what is Danjuma's body, her sense of hunger, her sense of pleasure, her sense of vision as compared to the touch, feel, and actions that are the properties of her mother—Lantana—and the other "not-me" aspects of the situation. Although an infant is literally a separate physical entity, the perception and comprehension of one's separateness—that there are physical and psychological boundaries between me and others—is a developmental process driven by experience and learning. What emerges first is a rudimentary personal identity that is not to be confused with any notion of individualism; it is the realization that one is alive, that one is a human being among other humans, that one's sense of personhood is a frame of reference for comprehending one's surroundings and the people and things that make up one's human ecology (Winnicott, 1987).

## FROM INDIVIDUATION TO INDIVIDUALITY AND PERSONALITY

With age, development, the acquisition of language, increased cognitive sophistication, and increasing self-agency, what began as the infant's primal sense of self evolves by late adolescence into stable though not fixed psychological traits. The configuration of these traits and patterns of self-expression is what is meant by individuality or personality. Over and above the debates pitting self-esteem and group esteem is the reality that within all cultures—Western and Eastern alike—are individuals with diverse personalities reflective of their unique individuality. Individuality is the logical outcome of individuation.

Individuality is not confined to the human experience and is very much a part of the discourse in comparative psychology, pointing to its evolutionary origins and survivalist functions. Studies involving chimpanzees, orangutans, and gorillas readily yield evidence concerning stylistic and personality differentiation that facilitate problem solving related to the finding of food, location of shelter, mate selection, intracolony/intercolony power struggles, and infant care (Boesch & Boesch-Achermann, 2000; de Waal, 2005; Mitchell, 2003; see http://www.npi.ucla.edu/center/primate/). Among humans, personality differentiation helps explain, in part, the variability with which different people approach everyday problems and challenges, increasing the chances for the discovery of new and better solutions and thus survival. Personality variability is not the same as individualism. Much of the tension between the self-esteem versus collective esteem camps is centered on the confusion between individuality and individualism, and while the concepts are related, they are not one in the same. Individuality is universal, but individualism is not.

Imagine we are conducting a study of a collectivist community in Africa, where we observe people at play and work. Whether the focus is on children, adolescents, or adults, we observe the modal ways people perform across both contexts. Eventually, our notes reveal that different individuals perform similar tasks with considerable variability. Over time, we are able to predict, for example, that shy African males will tend to approach work and play differently from African males who are gregarious and more comfortable in various social settings. Such observations of individuality or personality difference—not individualism—could surely be replicated in any collectivist culture.

We suggest that personality variability is ubiquitous. Within each culture, some members fare better than others in fulfilling various social roles. Patterns of success and failure can often be attributed to the personality characteristics members bring to the activity or responsibility. Personality has powerful explanatory value—regardless of the cultural context—and to mention individuality and collectivism in the same breath is *not* a contradiction. Individualism is but one expression of personality, while individuality captures the full range of ways people within any culture demonstrate personality variability. Consequently, separation-individuation and personality help us to comprehend personality variability within any given culture.

In summary, separation-individuation is the developmental pathway that culminates in individuality and personality. An infant starts with self-awareness that is borderless and, through the separation-individuation process, constructs a sense of self that has physical boundaries and psychological integrity. During childhood and preadolescence, individuality emerges, and by late adolescence and early adulthood, individuality has been molded into a distinct personality or the PI component of the self. In this chapter, separation-individuation, individuality, and personality are processes and categories subsumed under the component of the self-concept we are calling personal identity or PI.

## PERSONAL IDENTITY MATRIX AND SELF-ESTEEM

In cross-cultural counseling as well as research on minority identity, PI or the personality component of the self-concept is often framed by self-esteem (Rosenberg, 1979; Twenge & Crocker, 2002). For this reason, it becomes easy to equate and thus confuse self-esteem with PI, thereby losing sight of the fact that the PI domain is multidimensional. The discourse on personality makes reference to clusters if not hundreds of personality traits and factors in addition to syndromes, profile, patterns, and so on. Advocates of the Big Five model have tried to bring order to the myriad of factors linked to personality by arguing that the latent structure of most personality analyses reveals a five-factor solution. However, work in the applied fields of clinical or counseling psychology and psychiatric social work lends itself to a more elaborate conceptualization of personality, and the Big Five model is too constraining when conducting therapy. Clients present stories that wrap around every conceivable personality construct and mode of personality expression, and whether the plethora of factors presented might be reducible to only five, as suggested by the Big Five theory, is beside the point when operating in a therapeutic context.

As a reminder that PI extends far beyond self-esteem, let us conceptualize and label the totality of PI as the PI matrix. Conceptualizing the totality of PI as a matrix helps remind us that, beyond self-esteem, a comprehensive discussion of individuality or personality would extend to positive (affection, creativity, compassion, resiliency, and so on) as well as negative (anger, anxiety, obsession, self-loathing, and so on) traits and tendencies. In a clinical setting, therapists (hopefully) greet new clients with a certain degree of wonderment, as they listen and learn how, out of the matrix of possibilities, the person has configured a unique personality.

## UNCONSCIOUS DIMENSIONS OF PI

While there is considerable controversy in cross-cultural circles about the universality of Sigmund Freud's explication of the unconscious, there is little disputing that the concept of the unconscious is, in fact, a universal phenomenon (Roland, 1996). Our purpose here is not to resolve how best to theorize the unconscious but to affirm that any holistic concept of the self must take into account that unconscious factors play a role in the dynamics of the PI matrix. Psychiatrists, artists, and those in between make comprehensive use of conscious and unconscious levels of the PI matrix in their work. For instance, a novelist might start with a depiction of what a character is doing at any particular moment, show how the person construes her or his behavior (conscious insight), and then, using various devices, reveal the deep structure or unconscious drives that are propelling the fictional person's psychology. On the other hand, a great deal of the state-of-the-art research on minority personality that is conducted by social-psychologists or social-experimental psychologists employs a single factor to operationalize personality: self-esteem (Schmitt & Allik, 2005) or some related construct such as self-enhancement (Sedikides, Gaertner, & Vevea, 2005).

When the first author of this chapter teaches an Africana studies course on the psychology of African Americans, students in the seminar are first asked to read excerpts from plays by August Wilson, novels by Zora Neale Hurston, or biographies by David Levering Lewis. After digesting such rich, multilayered, and complex depictions of Black personalities, the students then read samplings of recent psychological research on Black personality. The students are generally stunned at how simplistic the psychological discourse on Black personality can be. In short, capturing the PI component of the self-concept requires demarcating not only its multitrait structure but also its conscious and unconscious dynamics as well.

## ATTACHMENT AND THE ORIGINS OF THE COLLECTIVE COMPONENT OF THE SELF

Intertwined with childhood individuation of the self and the evolution of object relations (interpersonal relationships) are attachment dynamics (Ainsworth & Bowlby, 1991; Bretherton, 1992). The phenomenon of attachment is critical to our analysis of the self because attachment dynamics between mother and child lay the psychological foundation for an individual to achieve, during other phases in development (preadolescence, adolescence, and early adulthood), a sense of belonging, community focus, and social group attachment. Seen in this light, attachment makes possible the experience of collective esteem and collective or group identity (GI), the second key component of the self.

The propensity of an infant to attach to its mother is central to the infant's survival and is probably innate (Cassidy, 1999). Research has documented that appearing between birth and the first year of infancy are these discrete and randomly expressed behaviors: crying, sucking, smiling, clinging, and following. These behaviors undergird the symbiotic relationship between mother and child. Over time and with experience, the random behaviors give way to various attachment styles (Cassidy, 1999).

Although the overall attachment phenomenon is universal, attachment styles are subject to cultural influence. An infant born in Japan, where closeness is valued above separation and adults normally adopt an interdependent self-orientation, may manifest a secure attachment differently than a baby parented in a culture such as the United States (van IJzendoorn & Sagi, 1999). U.S. society values individualism, and most of its inhabitants adopt an independent self-orientation; thus in the West, mothers reward their infants for separating (Markus & Kitayama, 1991). This suggests that attachment behaviors are flexible and adaptive, and thus it makes sense that infants in various places within various sociocultural contexts would be equipped with the ability to pick and choose from a constellation of attachment behaviors according to the appropriate cultural norm (Heine, Kitayama, & Lehman, 2001; van IJzendoorn & Sagi, 1999).

## ATTACHMENT AND THE ADULT NEED TO BELONG

Over the past 20 years, research has shown that the quality of one's attachment experience during infancy and childhood is foundational to the quality of one's later relationships (friendships, romantic relationships, etc.) (Weaver & de Waal, 2003). Here, we want to underscore another legacy of attachment, which is the lifelong need to feel one belongs to, is connected to, and is part of a larger whole. This has led to theorizing and research on cultural attachment, shared attachment, and attachment to one's group (Shaver & Mikulincer, 2006). The attachment process is fundamental to understanding the evolution of belonging, obligation, and shared community.

In the discourse on Western identity, individualism is presented as antithetical to collectivism and interdependence. However, we want to show that although collectivism may not be a marker of Western societies, all human beings, including persons socialized in the West, need to have a sense of collective belonging and connectedness that has origins in the attachment process (Kohut, 1984). That is, group identity and group esteem play a major role in the structure of the self for persons from Western as well as Eastern cultures (Shaver & Mikulincer, 2006). The notion that Westernization leads to the lessening of one's need for belongingness and connectedness was tested in recent research by Yip and Cross (2004) and found wanting.

Yip and Cross (2004) divided a group of college-aged Chinese American youth into those who (1) evidenced a strong ingroup nationalistic or Chinese ethnic identity, versus another group who (2) showed a dualistic or bicultural identity in which being American and being Chinese were accorded equally high importance, and (3) a third group that evidenced signs of assimilation in that their sense of being American was accorded high salience while their sense of being Chinese was low. The three groups could not be differentiated on the basis of scores on well-being and self-esteem, yet only those who exhibited a sense of being Chinese or bicultural scored high on a measure of ethnic-group identity (Multi-Ethnic Identity Measure [MEIM]). The fact that the more assimilated group scored low on the MEIM (ethnicity) but equally high on well-being and self-esteem seemed to go against social identity theory, which predicts a positive—not an inverse—relationship between the two outcomes.

Yip and Cross (2004) saw things differently. They predicted that in expressing a low sense of being Chinese and a high sense of being American, this third group should, as was found, score low on ethnic identity. On the other hand, this group might be expected to score as high as any group on a generic measure of group identity that was sensitive to whatever group identity dynamics might be operating across the three groups, inclusive of an assimilated and highly Americanized form of group identity. The measure used was the original version of the Luhtanen & Crocker Collective Self-Esteem (Luhtanen & Crocker, 1992) measure, a measure that can be administered to any group, including Whites, as the wording of the individual items operationalizes a generic conceptualization of group identity. On this measure, all three groups scored at the same level. The nationalistically inclined and biculturally oriented Chinese youth scored high on collective self-esteem, and the fact that they also scored equally high on the MEIM was interpreted to mean that their group identity was informed by a strong sense of ethnicity.

The more assimilated and American-focused group, on the other hand, showed signs of an equally well-developed and positive group identity, but their low scores on ethnicity meant that their sense of belonging and connectedness was not framed by ethnicity. Thus, consistent with the notion that people who shows signs of positive mental health should also show evidence of positive group identity, the findings from the Yip and Cross (2004) study point to the following possibility: Most if not all human beings need a sense of positive self-regard (PI level of analysis) as well as a sense of group connectedness (GI level of analysis); however, how the individual person derives a sense of belonging and connectedness may extend beyond the identity choices explored in most research or, in the case of the frame of reference of a counselor, beyond the identity choices the counselor thinks the client should be according salience.

Working with a predominantly African American population consisting of more than 300 college students, Vandiver, Worrell, Cross, and Fhagen-Smith (2002) looked for personality and well-being differences between Blacks holding either of two types of collective identity (Afrocentric and multi-cultural) as compared to a third group that disassociated from notions of Black identity and affirmed instead an American-individualist identity. The findings revealed slight but basically inconsequential differences between the groups with regard to level of self-esteem, well-being, and outcomes captured by a measure of the Big Five personality structure. Additional research examining the same three identity stances found among African American college students (Jones, 2005), as well as a more mixed sample of college students and community participants (Foster, 2004), again showed that, after various interactions were taken into account, all three identity frames were equally efficacious in the achievement of well-being and positive self-esteem. More important for the points being raised here, the holders of American-individualist attitudes showed signs of thinking like a group in that they were more likely to blame Blacks themselves for various social problems, hold conservative political attitudes about racial matters, and express the attitude that race should be accorded limited salience. In addition, they perceive and experience less race-related stress in their daily lives as compared to Blacks holding Afrocentric and multicultural identity perspectives.

We think these studies, along with findings from the Yip and Cross (2004) study, are suggestive of the fact that high scores on American-individualist measures of identity, particularly when found among minority populations, reveal the dissociation from notions of group identity based on race and minority status. They are rejecting as important social identity categories closely linked to the discourse on popular notions of group identity that the society generally uses to "categorize" them. In rejecting their socially ascribed identity, one might mistakenly conclude that they are without a "group identity," but as we have tried to show, their ascribed identity has been replaced by interdependencies linked to other groups. The GI component of their self-concept is just as important and, dare we say, central as the GI component found among minority group members whose expression of GI is more in line with the popular culture's discourse on group identity. The nonconforming minority group members do, in fact, have a group identity, but it is based on something other their socially ascribed category.

## CONSCIOUS AND UNCONSCIOUS GROUP IDENTITY DYNAMICS

We generally do not think of the group identity component of the self-concept as operating on both conscious and unconscious levels. However, in a modern context, the mesh of ideas and cultures is so thick that people may not be aware of the origins of their ideas and beliefs (Roland, 1996). Whites, for example, live together; marry each other; create predominantly White neighborhoods and communities; configure high schools, colleges, and churches that are almost completely White in membership; and create powerful organizations such as the Federalist Society, the membership of which is overwhelmingly White and male. Yet when one introduces the issue of racial identity, Whites often have difficulty comprehending that race plays anything but a minor role in their everyday lives. In fact, critical race theory (CRT; Crenshaw, Gotanda, Peller, & Thomas, 1995) emerged because Whites do not see that laws and social arrangements make affirmative action for middle-class and wealthy whites an everyday privilege, much to the disadvantage of those who are not White middle class or wealthy.

## GI MATRIX

The possibility of unconscious GI dynamics aside, the psychological discourse on group identity tends to turn on the ability of research participants to state, with some degree of certitude, that they are conscious of their group identity, especially if it involves a social ascription (Tajfel, 1981). Going a step further, the tendency of researchers and commentators to center the discourse on group identity around ascription and (minority) cultural factors causes many to overlook the fact that the GI component of the self-concept is no less a matrix than is PI. Increasingly, optimal psychological functioning is associated with multiple affiliations, multiple alliances, and multiple group connections. Each person is a matrix of group identities—even if in the enactment of self-construal, only one or a few identities are accorded high salience.

## STRUCTURE AND CONSTRUAL OF THE SELF

Arguing for a universal two-factor structure of the self might at first appear to put us at odds with the discourse found within cross-cultural psychology that Western and Eastern societies differ in the way the self is construed. However, while not definitive, the evidence is compelling that societies are inclined to divergent psychologies, one based on individualism (the West) and the other collectivism (the East). We began our discourse with a structural analysis because we think structure and construal, although overlapping, are not one in the same.

To begin, the study of the structure of the self does not depend on self-perceived information, while self-construal does. Furthermore, researching structure does not require that there be evidence of low or high levels of either PI or GI in a person's profile for we are arguing that in the analysis of anyone's self-concept, there will be evidence of the existence of both structural components. The point is not the degree to which each is present but that both are always present to some degree. Theory and research on self-construal reinforce categorical interpretations, but the study of the structure of the self literally requires one to think in configurative terms. Theorizing and researching construal of the self places a premium on self-insight, self-report, and a phenomenological self-analysis of what aspects of the self the person's culture favors. In some ways, self-construal is not necessarily concerned with structure; it is asking, "Beyond structure, how does a culture teach and socialize its members to perceive the self?" "What tasks, values, everyday experiences, etc., define what an analysis of the self is?"

Some have gone to the extreme and concluded that in certain cultures, the individual self (PI) does not really exist, meaning that it is possible for psychological functioning to be based solely on a collective sense of self (Akbar, 1989; Baldwin & Bell, 1985; Nobles, 1991). This, of course, is unlikely. Separation-individuation precedes collectivity because, until one understands what self means, one cannot comprehend what other(s) means. Given that various traits reflective of individuality can be found across cultures, the assessment of, say, self-esteem is likely a weak marker for separating persons into collectivistic versus individualistic categories. Self-esteem in and of itself does not define individualism. It is simply a characteristic of normal development and is an extension of the separation-individuation process triggered shortly after birth.

There is a degree of denial inherent in self-construal, at least at the extremes. If one accepts the argument that, at the level of structure, all human beings operate with a two-factor self-concept, then extreme forms of construal—whether oriented toward individualism or collectivism—reflect degrees of denial or repression. This may be taking things too far; however, we have been privy to debates and discussions wherein collectivism is equated with low self-esteem. But why should low self-esteem be a marker of high collective esteem? A person living in a collectivist society whose childhood produced strong and positive separation-individuation and strong and positive attachment may evidence personal strength that helps him or her excel at living and contributing to a collectivist philosophy of life. The idea that a group is strong to the degree that its individual members are weak is problematic. Likewise, the idea that a person who affirms his or her individualism will always show low levels of group identity or group esteem is equally problematic. Members of Western cultures espouse individualism, but a close examination of their culture show the existence of a multitude of group identities (i.e., religious affiliations, political parties, social groups, and various other social class distinctions that belie any notion of pure individualism). If collectivist self-construal underplays separation-individuation and individuality, then construal that is slanted toward individualism exaggerates the role of the individual while blocking out the dynamics of group esteem and GI.

## Summary of Our Theoretical Discourse on Self-Concept

At the structural level, the self-concept has no less than two components, and each evolves from separation-individuation and attachment processes activated at birth. Although infants are more hardwired than once imagined, the bulk of the research on self, personality, and group identity suggests that infants have no preset, organized schema for organizing and acting on their perceptions and felt sensations. An infant must literally learn to construct and sustain psychological boundaries that differentiate the self from others, inclusive of one's mother or key caretaker(s). The boundaries of the self are prerequisite to all other psychological schemas, and over time, self-development evolves into a complex sense of individuality generally referenced as personality. Personality is multidimensional, and for reasons of predisposition and environment, human beings who reach adolescence and adulthood tend to evidence considerable personality variation. In the discourse on self-concept, individuality and personality are often referenced as personal identity or PI, and to capture its multidimensionality, we referenced the PI component of the self-concept as the PI matrix. For various historical reasons, the PI matrix has too often been equated with self-esteem, delaying recognition that it is an extraordinarily complex, multidimensional construct.

The second important process emerging during infancy is the attachment phenomenon (AP). AP lays the psychological foundation for the emerging human being's capacity to eventually feel connected to individuals as well as groups of people. The need to have fulfilled and nourished throughout one's life a sense of connection, belonging, and affiliation is foundational to the second component of the self-concept, group identity or GI. Although the discourse on group identity treats it in singular fashion, we have stressed that most human beings—and this is especially true of people living in metropolitan communities across the globe—have multiple groups that frame their overall group identity, and to capture such multiplicity, we fashioned the label GI matrix.

In addition to issues of multidimensionality, we also stressed that each domain is subject to unconscious dynamics, a factor not foreign to personality research but more prominently discussed within the circles of applied psychology, such as the likely audience for the current volume.

We examined the contradictions that emerge when approaching the self-concept from a perspective of construal as compared to structure. We argued that the two-dimensional structure of the self-concept is universal and is revealed independently of cultural context. Construal, on the other hand, is very context sensitive because construal research tries to unearth not the structure of identity but the way a person has been socialized on what aspect of the self is favored, from one culture to another. Self-concept construal is more akin to the study of worldview, philosophy, and politics than psychology per se.

Much of the construal discourse is driven by hypothetical differences in the way the self is construed in the West as compared to the East. In the face of assertions about collectivity and individualism, we have argued that there is structural constancy of the self and that, to a certain extent, the construal discourse is subject to a categorical and thus flawed analysis of the self. The construal of the self as collectivistic tends to dismiss (silence) the role of individuality in the structural dynamics of the self, while notions of individualism make the opposite mistake and underplay, if not deny, the role of belonging, connection, community mindedness, and the need for affiliation in the lives of people living in so-called individualistic cultures. That is, the role and importance of group esteem to the psychological dynamics of persons affirming an individualistic identity has been underestimated, just as the role of personality and individuality has been understudied and undertheorized in the discourse on collective identity.

# CONCLUSIONS AND IMPLICATIONS
## PI and GI Assets

The major implication of our analysis is the need to adjust the understanding of self-esteem (PI) and group (GI) esteem from that of competing to complementary psychological assets. In a collectivist context, moderate to high self-esteem coupled with moderate to high group esteem may translate into a potent combination of personal efficacy and commitment to the group that helps the person enact, in joint ventures with others, the group's social vision. In the same context, another person who combines low self-esteem, depression, and high group esteem will bring less energy and confidence to the same tasks and activities, even though at the level of ideology or worldview, there is little that separates the two people. In effect, personal strength is not antithetical to an ideology of collectivism because many of the activities required in sustaining most societies require personal competence, tenacity, or calmness under pressure, to mention but a few personal traits. The idea that self-esteem is an offshoot of individualism is to confuse individuation and personality with a particular worldview. From our perspective, personal strength, positive perceptions of one's personhood, and an abundance of personal efficacy explain rather than contradict the psychological dynamics found within a collective-oriented community.

Such an analytic scheme would seem to have limited application to situations involving individualism, where group esteem, in particular, appears to fall out of the equation. However, group esteem dynamics make a strong showing among persons dedicated to a philosophy of individualism, even though at the level of ideology, one discovers that group identity, group esteem, and feelings of group belonging are typically silenced, downplayed, and, to some extent, denied. The Western self-made person may be a myth to the extent that the true story uncovers the minimizing of a lifelong series of interdependent relationships, which allowed the person to achieve a sense of singularity, and ends by showing how the person's continued need for social attachment, belongingness, and social connectedness is silenced to create the illusion of self-contentment derived from one's devices, trophies, and head games.

## Activity Theory and the Role of Culture

Given that a structural analysis of the self reveals people to be more alike than different, in that they evidence advanced development of both the PI and GI components of the self, then it stands to reason that something other than generic structures accounts for identity variability, especially when trying to address identity variation linked to cross-cultural differences. We will use activity theory (AT) to frame the cultural implications of our model because, in addition to making possible a succinct discussion of culture, it provides a way of avoiding an essentialist and static depiction of cultural dynamics (Gjerde, 2004).

Born in the aftermath of the Russian Revolution and a search for a new theory of psychology that integrated with Marxist thought, AT attempts to explain the unity of consciousness and action, where action is defined as everyday activities (Vygotsky, 1962, 1978). Perhaps the central tenet of AT is that *you are what you do.* From this straightforward assertion, AT balloons into a multilayered theory of culture: (1) You are what you do, and what you do was taught to you by others; (2) in teaching an activity, the teacher is passing down what she or he was taught about the activity by someone else from an earlier generation; (3) the cornerstone of culture is the passing down from one generation to the next "ways of doing" everyday activities; (4) books, museums, and the study of history are in large measure the formal codification and study of how a society/culture conducts war and peace (political science), designs and constructs edifices (architecture and engineering), prepares foods (culinary arts), conducts commerce (business), captures the human spirit (humanities, arts, and literature), and so on; and (5) implicitly and explicitly, one also learns the meaning and purpose for an activity, and thus ideology is the meaning making associated with whatever it is one is learning and doing. As formulated in AT, culture is never static because the sociocultural, socioeconomic, and sociohistorical circumstances (revolution, migration, war, natural disasters) cause some teachers and learners to make changes in what is taught and learned; consequently, curiosity, creativity, and necessity cause change, ranging from the barely consequential to radical (Stetsenko, 2005).

With this broader understanding of activity, we can return to the following question: How does AT help one comprehend that people from different cultures who otherwise reflect very similar PI and GI profiles nevertheless experience reality differently, such that at the level of self-construal, one person will depict herself or himself primarily in GI characteristics and another in PI dynamics? If, as suggested by AT, you are what you do and the meaning of what you do is framed by the society's ideology, then "doing" in a society guided by a collective orientation creates a consciousness of self that spotlights (1) the activity itself and not the attributes of the doer per se, (2) the collective objectives of the doing, and (3) a sense of self that is concerned with the discovery and invention of ways to refine and improve the activity not for reasons of self-gratification or personal glory but to participate in making things better for the group (Stetsenko, 2005; Stetsenko & Arievitch, 2004). Under such conditions, high self-esteem (Schmitt & Allik, 2005) or the related trait self-enhancement (Sedikides et al., 2005) need not be equated with individualism.

When the cultural context shifts to an emphasis on the reification of the individual person, even though that person's action might reflect his or her personal connections and interdependencies, the ideology or meaning-making system the person uses to interpret the activity spotlights the singularity of the self. Under the conditions of individualism, the connection between consciousness and activity continues to be important, but the interpretation changes and the purposes of the activity are seen in a personal light. In short, two people from two different cultures will experience high self-esteem differently, as determined by whether one is operating in an individualist- or collectivist-oriented society.

## Implications for Cross-Cultural Counseling

For clinical settings and applications, we favor the approach voiced by the distinguished cross-cultural psychoanalyst, Alan Roland (1988, 1996). Roland argues for a tripartite self-concept structure by adding a spiritual dimension; however, here we confine the analysis to his use of PI and GI information in the therapeutic process. Roland is comfortable discussing the PI and GI psychodynamics of a client, regardless of cultural origin. He meticulously maps the person's subjective sense of self, not as evidence of misplaced individualism but as the product of the separation and individuation process along with ego development. Because he is an analyst, he also maps the person's unconscious reality, but that labyrinth of underground psychological currents is best left for another discussion. What we find so fascinating about his work is his use of what we will call intentionality and function. Roland (1988, 1996) takes for granted that to the extent the person's socialization into a culture's frame of reference has been successful, the PI information about the client reveals the personality strengths the person brings to whichever ideology governs her or his worldview.

Personality strength can be present in either Western or Eastern contexts; what separates individuals are their intentions. In the East, most people see themselves in the service of the group's larger agenda, and they depict happiness as the alignment between their subjective being and the group's agenda. In seeing themselves as functioning at the individual level for the greater good and intentions of the larger group, individualism becomes a minor theme, even in the face of evidence that the person's personality profile reveals evidence of high self-esteem.

In Roland's cases (1988, 1996), GI information (along with PI information) is readily collected for clients from the West. Their interdependencies, social attachments, and multiple group identity dynamics are unearthed and given voice in the therapeutic process. The pressure felt by Western clients to silence these interdependencies under the weight of the larger society's idealization of the self-made person is a recurring theme in Roland's work. Again, it is the framework of intentionality (what ideology is the client trying to enact?) and functionality (how functional does the client perceive herself or himself to be?) that allows Roland to bridge the client's PI and GI information.

## RESEARCH IMPLICATIONS AND CONCLUDING REMARKS

We argue that data on self-construal are very useful in isolating the way cultures overlap or diverge in the meaning(s) accorded the self. However, information on self-construal should not be confused with the direct assessment of the more general and universal dynamics of the self. Likewise, researching the generic structures of the self can be misleading if one is actually more concerned with self-construal because similar levels of PI and GI strengths may be present in individuals from either Western or Eastern contexts. Generic measures of self-esteem should not be confused with specific measures of individualism, and generic measures of group identity should not be confused with culture-specific measures of collectivity. From our vantage point, the study by Yip and Cross (2004) models the type of study that needs to be replicated. In using independent measures of generic dynamics (self-esteem, group esteem, and a range of other well-being traits) and independent measures of culture-specific identity dynamics (ethnic identity, racial identity, etc.), they were able to show that Chinese participants who were assimilated and American focused evidenced similar levels of positive well-being and self-esteem as those Chinese participants who favored a more collectivist identity that was either Chinese-ethnic or biculturally focused. Although positive PI and GI dynamics were present in all groups, the ideological category into which a person fell predicted the cultural activities he or she was more likely to initiate and participate in, with Chinese-ethnic and bicultural participants showing more involvement in Chinese-oriented activities than Chinese participants who were more American inclined. In the face of similarity across the generic aspects of their self-concepts, it was intent and ideology that formed the basis for predicting the level of (Chinese) community involvement.

## CRITICAL INCIDENT

The Counseling Center at Carter University provides counseling for 10,163 undergraduates and 2,204 graduate students. The student body is very diverse, with heavy representation from the Asian American, African American, and Latina/Latino communities. The Counseling Center also houses the training and research arm of the university's renowned doctoral program in cross-cultural counseling. The intake process incorporates a modest battery of psychological measures that assess generic self-esteem, generic collective esteem, the Big Five personality traits, young-adult attachment styles, and individualism-collectivism propensities. Part of the intake interview and elements of the first two sessions explore the client's self-construal, value system, and worldview. At the termination of a case, the counselor summarizes her or his impression of the client's (1) problem and eventual level of resolution, (2) self-construal, (3) worldview classification (individualist oriented versus collective oriented), (3) personality strengths and weaknesses, and (4) level of social support and important interdependencies. As part of their training, students are encouraged to work in teams and to develop projects that "mine" the intake data. Recently the second-year class of doctoral students did a statistical analysis of 40 cases (split evenly across the individualism and collectivism orientations) and conducted detailed case studies of 5 clients from each worldview category (total of 10 case studies). At the presentation before the faculty, a heated debate erupted, as part of the study group claimed it was rather easy to confirm the *worldview and self-construal* differences between most clients, but other students argued that from the perspective of *self-concept structure,* the clients were more alike than different. At the end of this chapter, you should be able to explain how each perspective has merit, depending on what data are used to construct a client's profile.

### Debriefing and Resolution

Recall that some of the graduate students used individualism-collectivism scores combined with qualitative data on values and worldviews to cluster clients into one of two categories: (1) individualist oriented and (2) collectivist oriented. These students did not check the personality information but assumed such data would complement the worldview classifications. A second group of students also categorized the clients (individualism and collectivism), and the interrater reliability for the two groups of students was high (85% agreement). However, this second group went further and also created PI and GI profiles. To their surprise, clients from both categories (individualists and collectivists) showed evidence of strong PI and positive GI development. At the level of self-concept structure, individualists and collectivists were more alike than different. The two groups of students joined together to unravel the riddle they created and confirmed that both the I-oriented and we-oriented clients evidenced moderate to strong personality development (positive self-esteem, positive attachment styles, positive trait development) and moderate to strong group identity development (positive group esteem, positive social support, and key interdependencies). However, at the level of construal, the individualism group depicted a life in which they (as individuals) held center stage and tended to silence the role of social support and interdependencies. Although assessed to have high self-esteem, strong personality qualities, and generally positive attachment styles, the construal narratives for the we-oriented clients silenced or dimmed the spotlight on the self and highlighted, instead, activities and concerns that linked them to the group that dominated their GI matrix. At the level of *self-concept structure,* both groups showed advanced development of both PI and GI characteristics, while their *construal of self* and social agendas placed them miles apart.

## DISCUSSION QUESTIONS

1. Define the two key components of the self-concept.

2. How does a discussion of self-concept structure differ from a discussion of self-concept construal?

3. What is the connection between the process of individuation and the unfolding of personality?

4. How are attachment processes linked to the formation of group identity and feelings of group belonging?

5. What role does individuality play in the survival patterns for humans, monkeys, and chimps?

# REFERENCES

Ainsworth, M., & Bowlby, J. (1991). An ethological approach to personality development. *American Psychologist, 46*(4), 333–341.

Akbar, N. (1989). *Chains of psychological slavery.* Jersey City, NJ: New Mind Productions.

Baldwin, J. A., & Bell, Y. R. (1985). The African self-consciousness scale: An Africentric personality questionnaire. *Western Journal of Black Studies, 9*(2), 61–68.

Boesch, C., & Boesch-Achermann, H. (2000). *The chimpanzees of the Tai Forest: Behavioral ecology and evolution.* New York: Oxford University Press.

Bretherton, I. (1992). The origins of attachment theory: John Bowlby & Mary Ainsworth. *Developmental Psychology, 28*(5), 759–775.

Bronfenbrenner, U. (1979). *The ecology of human development.* Cambridge, MA: Harvard University Press.

Cassidy, J. (1999). The nature of the child's ties. In J. Cassidy & P. Shaver (Eds.), *Handbook of attachment: Theory, research, and clinical applications* (pp. 3–20). New York: Guilford.

Crenshaw, K., Gotanda, N., Peller, G., & Thomas, K. (1995). *Critical race theory.* New York: The New Press.

de Waal, F. (2005). *Our inner ape: Power, sex, violence, kindness, and the evolution of human nature.* New York: Penguin.

Foster, K. (2004). *The relationship between well being, attitudinal and behavioral factors across three black identity orientations.* Unpublished dissertation, Graduate Center–CUNY.

Gjerde, P. F. (2004). Culture, power, and experience: Toward a person-centered cultural psychology. *Human Development, 47,* 138–157.

Heine, S. J., Kitayama, S., & Lehman, D. R. (2001). Cultural differences in self-evaluation: Japanese readily accept negative self-relevant information. *Journal of Cross-Cultural Psychology, 32,* 434–443.

Jones, H. L. (2005). *Experiencing, appraising, and coping with race-related stress: Black women living in New York City.* Unpublished dissertation, Graduate Center–CUNY.

Kohut, H. (1984). *How does analysis cure?* Chicago: University of Chicago Press.

Luhtanen, R., & Crocker, J. (1992). A collective self-esteem scale: Self-evaluation of one's social identity. *Personality and Social Psychology Bulletin, 18*(3), 302–318.

Mahler, M. S., Pine, F., & Bergman, A. (1975). *The psychological birth of the human infant: Symbiosis and individuation.* New York: Basic Books.

Markus, H., & Kitayama, S. (1991). Culture and the self: Implications for cognition, emotion, and motivation. *Psychological Review, 98*(2), 224–253.

Mischel, W., & Morf, C. C. (2003). The self as a psycho-social dynamic processing system: A meta-perspective on a century of the self in psychology. In M. R. Leary & J. P. Tangney (Eds.), *Handbook of self and identity* (pp. 15–46). New York: Guilford.

Mitchell, R. W. (2003). Subjectivity and self-recognition in animals. In M. R. Leary & J. P. Tangney (Eds.), *Handbook of self and identity* (pp. 567–593). New York: Guilford.

Nobles, W. (1991). Extended self-concept: Rethinking the so-called Negro self-concept. In R. L. Jones (Ed.), *Black psychology* (2nd ed., pp. 99–105). New York: Harper & Row.

Roland, A. (1988). *In search of self in India and Japan: Towards a cross-cultural psychology.* Princeton, NJ: Princeton University Press.

Roland, A. (1996). *Cultural pluralism and psychoanalysis: The Asian and North American experience.* New York: Routledge.

Rosenberg, M. (1979). *Conceiving the self.* New York: Basic Books.

Schmitt, D. P., & Allik, J. (2005). Simultaneous administration of the Rosenberg self-esteem scale in 53 nations: Exploring the universal and culture-specific features of global self-esteem. *Journal of Personality and Social Psychology, 89,* 623–642.

Sedikides, C., Gaertner, L., & Vevea, J. L. (2005). Pancultural self-enhancement reloaded: A meta-analytic reply to Heine (2005). *Journal of Personality and Social Psychology, 89,* 539–551.

Shaver, P. R., & Mikulincer, M. (2006). Attachment theory, individual psychodynamics, and relationship functioning. In A. L. Vangelisti & D. Perlman (Eds.), *The Cambridge handbook of personal relationships* (pp. 251–272). New York: Cambridge University Press.

Stetsenko, A. (2005). Activity theory as object-related: Resolving the dichotomy of individual and collective planes of activity. *Mind, Culture, and Activity, 12*(1), 70–88.

Stetsenko, A., & Arievitch, I. M. (2004). The self in cultural-historical activity theory: Reclaiming the unity of social and individual dimensions of human development. *Theory & Psychology, 14*(4), 475–503.

Strauss, L. C., & Cross, W. E., Jr. (2005). Transacting Black identity: A two-week daily diary study. In G. Downey, J. S. Eccles, & C. M. Chatman (Eds.), *Navigating the future: Social identity, coping, and life tasks* (pp. 67–95). New York: Russell Sage.

Tajfel, H. (1981). *Human groups and social categories: Studies in social psychology.* Cambridge, UK: Cambridge University Press.

Twenge, J. M., & Crocker, J. (2002). Race and self-esteem: Meta-analysis comparing Whites, Blacks, Hispanics, Asians, and Native Americans and comment on Gray-Little & Hafdahl (2000). *Psychological Bulletin, 128,* 371–408.

van IJzendoorn, M., & Sagi, A. (1999). Cross-cultural patterns of attachment: Universal and contextual dimensions. In J. Cassidy & P. Shaver (Eds.), *Handbook of attachment: Theory, research, and clinical applications* (pp. 713–734). New York: Guilford.

Vandiver, B. J., Worrell, F., Cross, W. E., Jr., & Fhagen-Smith, P. (2002). Validating the cross racial identity scale. *Journal of Counseling Psychology, 49,* 71–85.

Vygotsky, L. S. (1962). *Thought and language.* Cambridge: MIT Press.

Vygotsky, L. S. (1978). *Mind in society.* Cambridge, MA: Harvard University Press.

Weaver, A., & de Waal, F. (2003). An index of relationship quality based on attachment theory. *Journal of Comparative Psychology, 116*(1), 93–106.

Winnicott, D. W. (1987). *The child, the family and the outside world.* Reading, MA: Addison-Wesley.

Yip, T., & Cross, W. E., Jr. (2004). A daily diary study of mental health and community involvement outcomes for three Chinese American social identities. *Cultural Diversity and Ethnic Minority Psychology, 10,* 394–408.

# PART II

## Counseling in Ethnocultural Contexts

The focus of the five chapters in Part II is an acknowledgment of the substantial contributions to the multicultural perspective made by Arabs and Muslims, Asian Americans, Hispanics, and Native American Indians, the ethnocultural groups featured in this section. Most of the early and contemporary writings in the field of multiculturalism have approached ethnicity from the perspective that these groups are members of ethnocultural *minority* groups. The very term *minority,* however, has become divisive and contentious because of the implicit stigma sometimes associated with it and the fact that these groups are increasing in numbers beyond that of what was once considered the *majority* population. In earlier writings in the multicultural field of psychology, these groups were written about through use of a broad *ethnic gloss* where attention was given to the groups as though they were homogeneous entities; they are not since there may well be more heterogeneity within these groups than within North America's *majority* Euro-American population. Perhaps at one time, that approach was necessary to draw general attention to a group's ethnic and cultural differences. However and fortunately, the entire field of multicultural and cross-cultural counseling has matured to such an extent that scholarly attention must now focus on the between- and within-group variations of ethnocultural populations and the challenges they present for counselors and clinicians. The authors of the five chapters in Part II take that position and more as they lay out the psychological and sociocultural intricacies of their respective populations to illustrate the increasing contemporary challenges faced by the groups and how counselors and clinicians can respond to them in an efficacious style and comportment. Moreover, the reader will be challenged to consider conventional self and identity conceptualizations and how they pertain to people from distinctive ethnocultural populations; a deep, thorough exploration of the self-construct has profound implications for delivering counseling services to people who straddle multiple ethnic identities. The following five questions serve as a constructive and summative way to introduce the chapters in this section:

1. How adequately do conventional psychodynamic, humanistic, and behavioral approaches relate to cross-cultural considerations in providing counseling services for ethnocultural populations?

2. How does the concept of *principled cultural sensitivity* influence and guide the conduct of research and the delivery of counseling services in traditional ethnocultural communities?

3. What are the influences of *historical trauma* and *delayed grieving* and their effects on providing counseling services to oppressed and exploited populations?

4. How do degrees of client *acculturative status, ethnic identification,* and *self-esteem* or *sense of self-worth* influence a counselor's approach to providing counseling services for the groups discussed in this section?

5. What evidence exists for the influence of *cultural encapsulation* in understanding and effectively working with clients from unique ethnocultural populations?

Indeed, some of questions pertain to other topics and themes covered in this sixth edition of *Counseling Across Cultures.* Moreover, there is a good chance many readers have experienced some or all of the circumstances and problems embedded in the questions as well as those posed for the other sections of this book. Perhaps the discussion presented in the forthcoming chapters can help them come to the realization that others acknowledge and avow their experiences and that there are effective and constructive ways for dealing with them. Now let's turn to a summary of the topics and themes covered in the five chapters in this part of the book.

In Chapter 6, Joseph E. Trimble and John Gonzalez survey the problems, issues, and perspectives associated with the counseling of Native American Indians. They focus on the recommendations and observations of numerous counselors and other scholars and practitioners concerning the multitude of topics covered in this rapidly growing field. In an extensive section on demographics and ethnic identities, Trimble and Gonzalez provide useful background for counselors who want to work effectively with North America's indigenous populations. They include information concerning historical trauma, delayed grieving, and the historical and contemporary factors that contribute to these troubling psychosocial problems occurring among many Indians and other Native peoples. Other topics of specific interest include acculturation, diagnostic problems, values, trust, client ethnic matching, and use of traditional approaches in providing counselor services to these populations. One of the main questions the authors pose, given the content and emphasis of their chapter, is as follows: If one were unfamiliar with Native American Indian communities, how would one go about preparing a counseling approach that would resonate with the *lifeways* and *thoughtways* of an Indian or Native community of interest?

The topic and theme presented in Chapter 7 focus on client and therapist variables in providing counseling and clinical services for Asian Americans. Frederick T. L. Leong, Szu-Hui Lee, and Doris Chang review and summarize the growing body of literature on the rapidly growing Asian population in the United States, paying special attention to acculturation and ethnic identity issues of interest to counselors working with Asian American clients. The authors emphasizes that the cultural socialization of many Asian Americans has contributed to the importance of an interpersonal orientation that values interdependence, conformity, emotional self-restraint, humility, and respect for authority. Given this observation, the authors contend that it is not surprising that Asian Americans expect their counselors to play the role of an authority figure that provides structured guidance in problem solving; many conventionally trained counselors are reluctant to use this style regardless of what the ethnic origin of the client may be. One of the questions asked in this chapter is, Why do Asian Americans still not use professional services at rates proportionate to their percentage of the U.S. population?

Chapter 8, titled "¡Adelante! Counseling the Latina/o From Guiding Theory to Practice," written by J. Manuel Casas, Jason Duque Raley, and Melba J. T. Vasquez, invites the reader to assess counseling with Latina/o clients, who constitute the fastest growing population in the United States according to the 2000 U.S. decennial census. Within the framework of an interesting and inclusive road map, including a four-part counselor-client framework, the authors provide a detailed description of the multitude of factors that contribute to the provision of counseling services to this burgeoning and broadly defined ethnocultural population. The authors add an important situational dimension to their framework that takes the process of providing counseling beyond examining client-counselor relationships; the reader may want to spend considerable time examining the intricacies of Figure 8.4 to get a deeper sense of their concept. Casas and his coauthors also pay specific attention to language problems and the degree of emotional expressiveness within this heterogeneous group. They clearly identify commonalities among otherwise diverse Latina/o groups to guide counselors through the process of selecting culturally effective counseling strategies. One of the more important cross-cultural counseling questions the authors raise is the following: What makes self-reflection on the part of the counselor an important aspect of counseling with Latina/o clients?

Chapter 9 gives attention to the complex theme of providing counseling services to Arab and Muslim clients. The author, Marwan Dwairy, introduces the reader to the culturally unique lifeways and thoughtways of an ethnocultural population that has not received much attention in the multicultural psychological field until recently. The reader will learn that in general, Arab and the Muslim worlds share the *ethos* of tribal collectivism and Islamic values but are also influenced by their exposure to Western culture. The social system in both worlds tends to be collective and authoritarian:

The individual is very submissive to family and norms, and a patriarchal and hierarchical authority rules the family. In the collective, group-centered orientation, typically Arab/Muslim youth do not become psychologically individuated from their families. Their personality continues to be collective and directed by external norms and values rather than by internal structures and processes of personality. The ethos and value orientation greatly influences the dynamics that occur within conventional counseling sessions. For example, Dwairy points out that it is difficult for Arab children to criticize their parents in a conversation with a foreigner, such as a counselor, and they typically emphasize that the intentions of their parents were good. A number of questions are raised by the content of this chapter. The reader should consider the important cross-cultural counseling question the author raises, specifically the following: Why are Arab/Muslim parent traditions and values more important for decision making than their children's feelings?

In Chapter 10, Ivory Achebe Toldson emphasizes that the principal problem when working with Black clients is that few conventional counseling approaches offer a recipe for healing all persons of African descent because the ethnoculture is not homogeneous. If counselors attempt to fit Black people into an all-encompassing ethnocultural category, then no matter what counseling approach is used, it will miss the varied and deep cultural differences that exist within the population. Use of Eurocentric paradigms to classify and diagnose clients of African descent can lead to judgmental errors that can erode the client's confidence in the mental health system. Toldson indicates that people of African descent tend to de-emphasize classification systems and guidelines; instead, they highlight relativity and rhythm, especially the rhythm that ebbs and flows and the counseling session. Toldson maintains that effective counseling for Black people requires recognizing group identity and collective responsibility within Black culture and accepting spiritual forces as meaningful phenomena in the life realm and decision-making processes. Counselors can use African ethos by recognizing the client's family, church, social/civic organizations, associations, friends, fraternal and sorority societies, and/or sociopolitical organizations as sources of influence and healing.

The following question for discussion will help prepare the reader for this chapter: Why is it that several treatment outcomes must be considered within the context of current research on ethnocultural populations and mental health? Consider that (1) many ethnocultural people tend to be overdiagnosed with psychosis and underdiagnosed with depression, (2) certain ethnocultural people are more likely to be prescribed psychotropic medication than other populations, and (3) many ethnocultural people have difficulty trusting conventional academic-developed treatment practitioners.

# Cultural Considerations and Perspectives for Providing Psychological Counseling for Native American Indians

Joseph E. Trimble and John Gonzalez

### Primary Objective

- To identify and describe the essential sociocultural factors that lead to effective counseling strategies for prospective Native American Indian clients

### Secondary Objectives

- To describe counselor characteristics that have been demonstrated to be effective in the counseling of North American Indians
- To present a framework designed to guide counselors in making culturally resonant choices when counseling North American Indians

*Traveling along the straight path requires constant struggle and vigilance. It is not a clear and linear process but rather is filled with ambiguity, confusion, and temptation, leading to wrong turns on the way to understanding. Specific behaviors may be necessary to stay on the path, and along it, one may pass though specific stages. But, since the path presents a way of being, it is not so much an exact prescription or chronology as a guide for the way life should be lived. Critical to this way of being are fundamental values and attitudes needed to find and stay on the path, typically including respect, humility, love, sharing, and service.*

Katz, Biesele, and St. Denis (1997, p. 143)

BELIEF IN THE "STRAIGHT PATH," A WAY OF LIVING THE IDEAL LIFE ESPOUSED BY FIJIANS, IS A LIFEWAY COMMON TO MOST if not all of the world's cultures (Katz, 1993). In North America, this way of life is often symbolized by a circle but contains the same meaning. The Dine (Navajo) emphasize harmony and beauty in relationships and connections with others and nature (Benally, 1987); for the Lakota, one can choose to follow the Red Road or the Black Road, each of which presents unique challenges for the proper way to live (McGaa, 1992; Mohatt & Eagle Elk, 2000); for the Inupiat Inuit, *ahregah,* or "well-being," is a state of being in which one experiences a healthy body, inner harmony, and "a good feeling within" oneself (Reimer, 1999, p. 6; see also Napoleon, 1996); and for the Ojibwe, the Seven Council Fires of Life mark significant transitions through life stages (Katz et al., 1997). Locust (1985) points out that "Native American Indians believe that each individual chooses to make himself well or to make himself unwell. If one stays in harmony, keeps all the tribal laws and the sacred laws, one's spirit will be so strong that negativity will be unable to affect it. Once harmony is broken, however, the spiritual self is weakened and one becomes vulnerable to physical illness, mental and /or emotional upsets, and the disharmony projected by others" (p. 4). This "path" or "way of living" provides the individual with traditionally grounded directions and guidelines for living a life free of emotional turmoil, confusion, animosity, unhappiness, poor health, and conflict-ridden interpersonal and intergroup relations. There are many reasons why one may "stray" from the circle, which will be highlighted below; ultimately, though, our goal is to provide assistance for the individual to once again find the "straight path" or way back to the circle.

It is safe to assume that all American Indian and Alaska Native tribes and villages developed and maintained sophisticated and elaborate systems or collections of principles, rules, or regulations that guided individuals along the straight path.[1] Healing practices also were well established to assist individuals who strayed from the straight path. Shamans or healers were delegated or inherited by birthright the responsibility to conduct healing ceremonies, and healing traditions were handed down from one generation to the next following highly regulated rites of transmission and passage. Healing practices as well as the specifics concerning the "ways of living" no doubt varied considerably from one tribe or village to another. Moreover, many of these practices likely changed over the centuries because of the exchanges of procedures, rituals, and ceremonies generated by contact with other groups and new insights gained by healers through personal and spiritual experiences. Traditional "ways of living" continue to be endorsed and practiced by most North American Indians and Alaska Natives, although some vary considerably from the ways they were practiced and carried out centuries ago.

For contemporary observers to assume or claim that mental health healing practices are new to Indians and Natives would be presumptuous. In one form or another, healing those who stray from the straight path has always been a part of the holistic fabric of the lifeways and thoughtways of indigenous peoples. The majority of American Indians and Alaska Natives know something about contemporary versions of these practices. However, not all Indians or Natives choose or have the opportunity to participate in them, owing to a number of factors, including orthodox religious convictions marked by conformity to doctrines or practices held as right or true by some authority, standard, or tradition or distrust of traditional healers and their practices. Other factors could include the geographic distance of traditional healers from their home villages or communities or lack of access to traditional healers, especially in urban settings. Finally, there may be a lack of awareness of the presence and effectiveness of traditional practices and/or confusion concerning the choice between traditional healing and use of mental health counselors and clinicians. Certainly, the reasons vary from one individual to another. For those who choose not to seek the services of traditional healers, the only available alternative is to seek the assistance of professionals in conventional mental health fields; that choice, too, can be compounded by numerous factors, including distrust, misunderstanding, apprehension, and the real possibility that mental health practitioners may be insensitive to the cultural backgrounds, worldviews, and historical experiences of Indian and Native clients. The main issues for these clients are concerns that their "presenting problems" may be distorted by the results of psychological tests that are incongruent with their cultural worldviews and that professionals may arrive at clinical diagnoses grounded in psychological theories that do not value and consider culturally unique perspectives.

For many Indian and Native clients, interpersonal and interethnic problems can emerge when counselors' lack of experience and knowledge, deeply held stereotypes, unwitting racist attitudes, and preconceived notions interfere with the counseling relationship and thwart counseling effectiveness. Yet, there is ample evidence that by using particular techniques, counselors can promote client trust and improve the counselor-client relationship, both in general and with American Indian and Alaska Native clients specifically. Matters relating to trust and other counseling considerations form the basis of this chapter; in the pages that follow, we provide information aimed at helping to stimulate effective cross-cultural contacts between mental health counselors and Native American Indians.

## PROVIDING COUNSELING SERVICES TO NATIVE AMERICAN INDIANS

Often there is a wide range of individual differences among members of any cultural group. This is particularly true for Indians who follow tribal lifeways and those who marginally identify with their indigenous culture. The concept of acculturation provides a useful context for understanding this and suggests different paths that ethnic minority individuals and groups may follow when functioning in a majority dominant context. In its simplest form, there are four options that minority group members have: integration, in which Native people maintain their culture of origin and adopt those of the majority so that they function biculturally; assimilation, in which they primarily function according to the lifeways of the majority culture; separation, in which they maintain their culture of origin, with very little adoption of the majority culture; and marginalization, in which they may not strongly maintain their culture of origin or adopt the ways of the majority (Berry, 1980, 2002). Given these differences, how can a counselor provide effective and culturally resonant mental health services to members of these populations? Is there a common set of procedures and strategies available that are known to be effective? What does a conventionally trained counselor need to know about facilitating positive relationships with Indian clients? While some counselors have been successful in helping Native clients, many others have not. Counselors may be unsuccessful in working with Native clients for a number of different reasons, many of which we discuss below. Among the possibilities are the following: The counselor may lack basic knowledge about the client's ethnic and historical backgrounds, the client may be driven away by the professional's counseling style, the client may sense that his or her worldview is not valued, the client may feel uncomfortable talking openly with a stranger, or the ethnic background of the counselor may create client apprehension. In the following section, we present a summary review of numerous journal articles, chapters, and writings that is organized around central counseling-related

*Handwritten margin notes:*

Assimilation maintain culture of origin + adopt majority culture to live biculturally

Separation maintain culture of origin w/o adoption of majority

Marginalization may not strongly maintain culture of origin or adopt the ways of the majority themes: the nature of Indian communities, counselor characteristics, client characteristics, values, counseling styles, and the role and influence of traditional healing practices in the provision of mental health services.

Knowledge about the nature and history of Indian and Native communities is essential to counseling effectiveness (Herring, 1992; Koverola, 1992; LaFromboise, Berman, & Sohi, 1994). The "newcomer," "outsider," "stranger," or "White" who asks questions without making preliminary contacts or seeking previous agreements and approvals will be greeted by closed doors and, most likely, uncooperative and suspicious attitudes (Trimble & Hayes, 1984). It may well take a counselor considerable time to gather sufficient knowledge of the community and to gain an understanding of the counselor's role as perceived by the residents. In the course of that undertaking, mutual awareness can develop and, along with it, trust, an essential component for all human relations. A critical factor affecting this trust building centers on trauma because of historical and contemporary intergroup relations between Natives and Whites.

# HISTORICAL TRAUMA AND UNRESOLVED GRIEF

Mental health counselors must be keenly aware that many Indian and Native communities continue to experience various degrees of individual and community trauma as a consequence of European contact, a "wound to the soul of Native American people that is felt in agonizing proportions to this day" (Duran & Duran, 1995, p. 27). This cumulative trauma has been fueled by centuries of incurable diseases, massacres, forced relocation, unemployment, economic despair, poverty, forced removal of children to boarding schools, abuse, racism, loss of traditional lands, unscrupulous land mongering, betrayal, broken treaties—the list goes on. In Canada and the United States, government and church educational systems contributed to Indian and Native student loneliness; fear; physical, sexual, and psychological abuse; malnutrition; and forced labor (Millar, 1996). Chrisjohn and Young (1997) charge in their moving and insightful book, *The Circle Game: Shadows and Substance in the Indian Residential School Experience in Canada,* that the history of abuses created by the boarding and mission school experience lingers to this day and thus has created a "residential-school syndrome" that strongly contributes to unresolved grief among former students (for a review of *The Circle Game,* see Darou, 1998).

Brave Heart and DeBruyn (1998), LaDue (1994), and Duran and Duran (1995) all maintain that postcolonial "historical and intergenerational trauma" has left a long trail of unresolved grief and a "soul wound" in Indian and Native communities that contributes to high levels of social and individual problems such as alcoholism, suicide, homicide, domestic violence, child abuse, and negative career ideation. Adding support to this observation is Duran's (1999) finding that more than 58% of the Indian clients at a Native American health center were experiencing anxiety disorders. Moreover, Duran maintains that anxiety may be at the heart of most Indian and Native mental health and social problems.

Duran and Duran (1995) emphasize that counselors must acknowledge the legitimacy of Native ways of knowing and must attempt to understand intergenerational and cultural trauma from a Native worldview. To understand some of the issues facing contemporary Indians and Natives and their communities, counselors must also acknowledge the profound influence of unresolved historical grief within the context of Indian and Native worldviews. When counselors attempt to comprehend the experiences of Native communities through the use of conventional psychological and psychiatric diagnostic approaches, they not only disavow the grief and trauma of Indians' and Natives' experiences, but they also introduce a cultural bias that is incongruent and disrespectful. It is important to consider how conceptualizations of time and history may differ between Native and Western culture. For many Native cultures, the past, present, and future are viewed as being unified and continuous, whereas in Western culture, the meaning of time and history does not hold that same continuity. For example, in the Ojibwe language, the word *time, ishise,* is a verb and acts upon us, whereas time in the English language is a noun and is seen as something we possess.

Historical trauma and unresolved grief are, in part, reactions to cultural loss and involuntary change. Although culture as a construct has multiple meanings, it represents the essential lifeways and thoughtways of ethnic and national enclaves; in its elementary form, culture provides meaning, structure, and direction. For trauma and grief experiences, culture serves a psychological function by providing a buffer against terror (Salzman, 2001). If an indigenous community's lifeways and thoughtways are under assault, community members will turn to their rituals, ceremonies, and healers to restore balance, fend off destruction, and protect traditions. However, when traditional lifeways and thoughtways are suppressed, stolen, or lost, trauma may be irresolvable and subsequently may be passed along from one generation to the next.

In response to the existence of historical trauma and unresolved grief, "cultural recovery movements are occurring among indigenous people throughout the world to reconstruct a world of meaning to act in . . . and to recover ceremonies and rituals that address life's problems" (Salzman, 2001, p. 173). For example, to illustrate how tribal rituals promote a sense of community and continuity for troubled individuals, Brave Heart and DeBruyn (1998) and Duran, Duran, Brave Heart, and Yellow Horse-Davis (1998) describe the effectiveness of a tradition-based psychoeducational intervention intended to resolve historical trauma and grief. Results from this 4-day group experience point to positive and long-term changes that assist individuals in dealing with racism, grief contexts, and the resolution of grief. Similar "cultural recovery" programs are being offered in various parts of North America, as are Native-sponsored conferences devoted to the topic of cultural recovery. Morrissette (1994) has called for more focused clinical and counseling attention on the parenting struggles of those Natives who have experienced "residential-school syndrome." The growing interest in resolving historical trauma has captured the attention and interest of numerous indigenous groups. Along with this interest, the value of culture and all it represents is being elevated to higher levels of significance as community voices gain influence and power. As Salzman (2001) points out, "Empowering political movements tend to accompany cultural recovery movements and [thus] should be supported by mental health and social workers" (p. 173).

Thus, cultural recovery movements are increasingly viewed as effective responses to the existence of historical trauma and unresolved grief among indigenous peoples throughout the world.

## COUNSELOR CHARACTERISTICS AND CONSIDERATIONS

At the outset, counselors must examine their motives for wanting to work in Indian and Native mental health settings and specifically with Indians and Natives from varied tribal backgrounds with varying degrees of Native identity (Koverola, 1992). Helms and Cook (1999) put it succinctly: "How can counselors resolve the different manners in which counselors and clients conceptualize mental health problems if the counselors and clients come from different culture-related life experiences?" They add, "To the extent that the therapists' and clients' socialization histories in either the racial or cultural domains of life have been incongruent, then one would expect differences in the ways in which therapists and clients conceptualize the problem for which help is sought, as well as what they consider to be appropriate 'treatment' for the problem" (p. 7). Ignoring or camouflaging these differences eventually leads to inadequate counseling and often to early client termination.

Certain critics of the cross-cultural counseling process believe that counselors must abandon conventional styles and wisdom to be effective in working with clients who come from cultures different from the counselors' own. We believe that such an approach is not only ill conceived but foolish. Conventional counselors may possess generic personal characteristics that promote positive relationships with any clients, regardless of their cultural backgrounds. In fact, many conventional providers of mental health services share healing characteristics similar to those of shamans, spirit healers, and medicine people. Providers of traditional helping services in Indian communities most likely exemplify empathy, genuineness, availability, respect, warmth, congruence, and concreteness, characteristics that are likely to be effective in any therapeutic treatment setting, regardless of the provider's theoretical orientation or counseling style. Effective counseling with Indians begins when a counselor carefully internalizes and uses these basic characteristics in counseling settings (see Morse, Young, & Swartz, 1991).

Continuing with this theme, Reimer (1999, p. 60) collected information from Inupiat members of an Alaska Native village concerning the characteristics they found desirable in a healer. Her respondents indicated that a healer is (a) virtuous, kind, respectful, trustworthy, friendly, gentle, loving, clean, giving, helpful, not a gossip, and not one who wallows in self-pity; (b) strong physically, mentally, spiritually, personally, socially, and emotionally; (c) one who works well with others by becoming familiar with people in the community; (d) one who has good communication skills, achieved by taking time to talk, visit, and listen; (e) respected because of his or her knowledge, disciplined in thought and action, wise and understanding, and willing to share knowledge by teaching and serving as an inspiration; (f) substance free; (g) one who knows and follows the culture; and (h) one who has faith and a strong relationship with the Creator. Thus, counselors do not need to abandon their conventional counseling styles but instead must show a willingness to pay attention to what Indian and Native clients value in respected healers. Moreover, having the ability to suspend disbelief is helpful for counselors working with Native clients—that is, counselors need to be willing to listen to and hear whatever clients may say without judging the credibility of the belief systems associated with healing ceremonies, Indian medicine, and spiritual quests.

The critical lesson is to not make assumptions or rush into a treatment plan before listening to the client. This is further highlighted in a qualitative study by Yurkovich, Clairmont, and Grandbois (2002), who found that the clinician's ability to be culturally responsive varied and was dependent on an awareness of his or her own personal culture and the diversity within and between American Indian cultures. For example, some of the mental health providers were themselves Native and therefore perceived the client as Native and automatically assumed they were providing culturally responsive care. Another group of providers (Native and non-Native) acknowledged potential differences in cultural background based on their own but only provided culturally relevant care if the client requested it. Finally, a third group of providers fully acknowledged cultural differences and actively assessed the client's preferred treatment approach. Although some of the Native mental health providers were not of the same tribal affiliation as the clients, they still perceived the client as similar to them and seemed to ignore the diversity that exists within Native cultures. This highlights several issues discussed above. A counselor working with Indian clients needs to become aware of the client's individual as well as collective cultural background while examining any preconceptions, biases, and attitudes they may have about "Indians." The counselor also needs to examine and be aware of their own cultural background and how that influences the client-therapist relationship. This gets at the core of what it takes to become a "cross-cultural" counselor and clinician.

Bransford (1982) points out that counselors' perceived expertise, attractiveness, and avowed respect for Indian clients' culture are likely to improve counseling effectiveness by contributing to rapport building. Counselors must also be comfortable with silence and must maintain tolerance for what may appear to be ambiguity. Indian clients may listen very carefully to counselors' statements without giving any immediate response, as they take some time to think through what has been said. This does not mean that these clients are noncompliant or slow; rather, such behavior indicates that they are giving the discussion a great deal of thought. Thus, counselors working with Indian and Native clients should take care to observe their clients' nonverbal behavior. Counselors must have the cognitive flexibility to allow clients to engage in thought processes at their own pace; such flexibility is enhanced by counselors' awareness of culture-based differences in dyadic relationships (Herring, 1999; Lockhart, 1981). Similar ideas about a counselor being aware of his or her own beliefs about culture and spirituality were also expressed by Olsen (2003), who interviewed Natives about cultural and spiritual loss. She stressed that understanding the histories of Native people with a particular emphasis on the losses indigenous peoples have endured will ultimately provide the basis for the therapeutic relationship.

A number of authors, both Indian and non-Indian, have argued that counselors of Indian ancestry are more likely to be effective with Indian clients than are non-Indian counselors (Darou, 1987; Dauphinais, Dauphinais, & Rowe, 1981; M. Johnson & Lashley, 1989; Lowrey, 1983; Uhlemann, Lee, & France, 1988). Bennett and BigFoot-Sipes (1991) note that Indian clients might actually prefer counselors whom they perceive as having attitudes and values similar to theirs, instead of counselors who are necessarily of the same ethnicity. Indian clients who are involved in their cultural heritage, however, have much stronger preferences for Indian counselors than do those who are not so involved or who do not identify strongly with their Indian heritage (M. Johnson & Lashley, 1989).

Providing counseling services to Indian and Native clients requires careful thought and planning. Part of that planning should involve an assessment of the biases and myths that have been perpetrated about non-Indian counselors within the Native community from which clients will be drawn. Such biases and myths vary from one community to the next; hence, counselors would be wise to examine these at all levels (Peregoy, 1999). Informal ethnographic interviews with community members represent one way to gather information on these biases while at the same time building trust and rapport. In conducting such a survey, non-Indian counselors are likely to discover that community members believe, among other things, that (a) "outsiders" tend to interpret behavior and emotions in terms of norms and expectations not shared by the tribal community, and (b) counselors will attempt to convert Indians to a "better" culture or try to get them to act and think according to the outsiders' worldview (Anderson & Ellis, 1995).

Counselors also should consider carefully a number of other important factors, such as their own awareness of and sensitivity to Native family structures, clients' language preferences, cultural and community conflicts, the barriers to the provision of counseling services perceived by community members, cultural factors that influence the establishment of a client-counselor relationship, clients' acculturation/deculturation and bicultural competencies and orientations, and the presence and influence of traditional forms of healing and how these interface with conventional counseling approaches (Brucker & Perry, 1998; Herring, 1997). Many of these are client factors, some of which will be addressed in the following sections. A final consideration to note before moving on is that counselors must engage in inner self-assessment and evaluation and be prepared to adjust their own values, beliefs, and practices accordingly to accommodate the bicultural or cultural expectations and perspectives of their Indian or Native clients (Matheson, 1986).

## CLIENT CHARACTERISTICS AND CONSIDERATIONS

The degree of cultural and psychological diversity existing among Indian clients is likely to present a multitude of challenges for any counselor (Lee, 1997; Sage, 1997). Degree of acculturation, physical appearance, and lifestyle preferences vary considerably. M. Garrett and Pichette (2000) note that counselors must assess each individual client's degree of acculturation and not rely solely on the limited information provided by physical appearances. In addition, they suggest that Indian clients' differing degrees of acculturation are influenced by such factors as the history of mistrust created by government policies toward Native peoples. Degree of acculturation may influence how a particular client responds to a typical counseling session. Some researchers have observed that clients who come from traditional backgrounds are not likely to maintain direct eye contact, will avoid personalizing and disclosing troubled thoughts, and may act shy in the presence of non-Indian counselors (Attneave, 1985). Very traditional clients might tell counselors that "Indian doctors" have tended to their problems and that they have no need for any advice or consultation. Clients whose acculturation leans more toward mainstream U.S. culture may understand counseling goals and procedures and have a good idea of what is expected of them as clients.

The counseling situation, especially for a traditional Native client, can be a unique experience and thus is likely to elicit concern and wariness (McCormick, 1996). Often these emotions may be accompanied by a hint of hostility that springs from both knowledge of historical events and the Indian client's personal experiences. Many Indians and Natives have had personal experiences with White culture that have left them suspicious of anyone who is offering help. Indian schools, in particular, have been the source of many negative experiences (Duran & Duran, 1995). The only effective way a counselor can respond to client wariness, concern, and hostility is with a great deal of patience; the counselor must wait for trust to develop. A counselor in this situation may often feel that the client is testing him or her; in fact, this is probably accurate. The client may gradually become more self-disclosing, and only when he or she senses that his or her experiences are being heard and respected will full disclosure likely occur. Although such reluctance to disclose has been cast as a cross-cultural issue, it occurs with many non-Indian clients as well; it is best resolved through use of competent counseling skills and approaches (see Marsiglia, Cross, & Mitchell-Enos, 1998).

Blue and Blue (1983) note that many Indians might react to stressful conditions by merely waiting out the circumstances. Because many traditional Indians place importance on living in harmony with their environment, they quite naturally expect the environment to offer solutions. Hence, an individual may appear to be depressed and withdrawn but may actually be waiting for something to happen. In this situation, Blue and Blue emphasize, passivity is a sign not of hopelessness but of hopefulness (p. 20). Other tribe-specific normative styles of behavior that Indians might invoke to deal with stressful and problematic life events are yet to be identified. Some expressed behaviors may be similar to what many mental health professionals view as psychopathological symptoms. Clinical and counseling intervention in these instances would be not only disruptive but also futile because the seemingly "exotic behaviors" are actually expressive forms of self-treatment and healing. Counselors should consult with knowledgeable community members so that they can learn appropriate ways to identify these forms of self-healing and should respect them in their context and the manner in which they are expressed.

## VALUE DIFFERENCES

Clients who come from cultures that are different from the counselor's own may subscribe to values and beliefs that are distinctly different from those of the counselor (Herring, 1999; Trimble, 1981). Their values may be mediated by their degree of acculturation—that is, the degree to which they identify with their Indianness and their tribal or village orientation. At a general level, a few authors suggest that a majority of traditional Indians and Natives share a common set of beliefs and values that emphasize harmony, personal spiritual power, and use of traditional medicine; these beliefs often clash with conventional approaches to healing (M. Garrett, 1999; Locust, 1995). At a more specific level, Browne (1995) notes that the First Nations peoples of Canada place a strong value on respect and on the inherent worth, uniqueness, and dignity of the individual.

Value conflicts may emerge for Indians who leave reservations to live in cities or towns. Typically, urban Indians have a strong tendency to want to retain their "Indianness" even as they struggle through daily contact with non-Indian lifeways and thoughtways (Witko, 2006). Because of this, an urban Indian typology has emerged that emphasizes the internalization of values typical of Indians in general, thus resulting in what Thornton (1996) describes as a population of "'new' Native Americans." Invariably, these values are elaborations, with modifications, of typical tribal values and are characterized by pan-Indian ideologies.

Value orientation conflicts do not necessarily occur when Indians relocate to urban areas. Affiliation, maintenance of traditional ceremonials, and opportunities to visit ancestral homes may reinforce the retention of traditional values. "Stayers," those who remain in the cities, can retain tribal-based values if their expectations for goal attainment are realized (Graves & Arsdale, 1966). Put another way, if an Indian voluntarily leaves his or her rural or reservation home for the city and experiences a sense of achieving his or her goals there (e.g., finding a suitable significant other, landing a respectable job and being successful at it), it is less likely that his or her values will change substantially. Presumably, those who stay in cities are willing to learn and internalize additional values and behaviors that will assist them in adapting to their new lifestyle. In contrast, "leavers" may recognize that, overall, their culturally rooted lifestyle preferences are not appropriate for city life; thus, rather than change their perspective, they leave. Even those who stay in nonreservation environments may express a strong need to return periodically to their homes for what can be referred to as a regrounding or a reinfusion of cultural strength. Such individuals may express a strong need to participate in traditional ceremonial events, to visit with relatives and friends, to eat traditional foods, and, as one Indian graduate student recently put it, "to see a lot of brown faces around me." Many Indians and Natives exhibit a pattern of movement back and forth from the city to the reservation, often for extended periods of time that may even necessitate changes in employment. This pattern has often been interpreted as a way of avoiding stressful life events and, in that sense, has been seen as a negative behavioral response. Although this is always a possibility and must be assessed as part of the counseling process, it is also very likely that this type of mobility is adaptive.

Thus, it is essential to examine value differences when working with Native clients. Through a clarification and analysis of client values, both counselor and client may discover that a value prompts the client's initial difficulty. A client's perceived inability to acknowledge, respond to, and deal with the value conflict may contribute to feelings of inadequacy, anxiety, and low self-worth. Recognition of value differences, however, should not be the only concern of counselors working with Indian clients; they must also consider the strength and degree of endorsement of principal value preferences.

## COUNSELING APPROACHES AND TECHNIQUES

Given the information and recommendations we have presented thus far, what counseling styles or theoretical orientations are most effective and useful with Indian clients? Unfortunately, we can make no simple, straightforward recommendation. On one hand, if a counselor shows evidence of being warm and empathic, establishes trust and rapport, shows respect for the client's cultural values and beliefs, and expresses flexibility in meeting the client's expectations, then it would make sense that any counseling style should work. Once these basic criteria are met, one particular style is worth noting. Dauphinais et al. (1981) and LaFromboise, Trimble, and Mohatt (1990) strongly recommend the exclusive use of a directive style, and they present empirical data to back up their recommendation. LaFromboise, Dauphinais, and Rowe (1980, p. 15) also state that available evidence indicates that the Rogerian or nondirective style might be counterproductive in counseling work with members of most American ethnic minority groups. This position matches with clinical experience: The directive style seems to be more effective because many Indian clients, especially more culturally traditional ones, are likely to be reticent and taciturn during the early stages of counseling, if not throughout the entire course of treatment. Quite often, traditional Indian clients are very reluctant to seek conventional counseling because they may perceive the experience as intolerable and inconsistent with their understanding of a helping relationship. At that point, they may feel very helpless and burdened. It is significant to note that traditional Native clients' initial expectation of the counseling experience may be that it will offer an opportunity to obtain advice from Elders (those with greater wisdom and knowledge). For this reason, by beginning with brief, directive therapy, counselors may be more apt to meet such clients' expectations concerning the helping relationship.

Given that clients' problems are often situational and contextual, Trimble and Hayes (1984) recommend that non-Indian counselors of American Indians attempt to understand the cultural contexts in which their clients' problems are embedded. Familial patterns, peer group relationships, and community relationships are a few of the ecological processes that counselors need to understand and incorporate into their intervention plan (Trimble & LaFromboise, 1985). Family counseling thus is an approach that makes a good deal of sense. Attneave (1969, 1977), McWhirter and Ryan (1991), and C. Johnson and Johnson (1998) recommend that counselors and therapists account for the social and network characteristics of Indian families and involve clients' kin in the counseling process. Napoli and Gonzalez-Santin (2001) describe an intensive home-based wellness model of care for families living on the reservation. They describe a four-phase model that seeks input and assistance not only from nuclear family members but also from extended family and community members. While this approach can certainly apply to non-Indian families and communities, a counselor would greatly benefit from acknowledging this cultural factor when working with Indian clients.

The use of counseling strategies and techniques that resonate with Indian traditions and customs can be effective. Herring (1994) recommends that counselors use humor, especially in the forms of storytelling, story reading, puppetry, and games. M. Garrett, Garrett, Toress-Rivera, Wilbur, and Roberts-Wilbur (2005) provide a brief discussion of humor in Native cultures and offer recommendations for incorporating humor into counseling sessions with Native clients. Others note the importance of art for Indian clients and its role in promoting well-being and healing (Appleton & Dykeman, 1996; Dufrene & Coleman, 1994). Humor and art are very much a part of many traditional healing practices. Thus, these recommendations make good sense because they tie counseling procedures to the clients' traditions and customs.

The majority of recommendations proffered by the writers cited above and others tend to be based on a view of Indian clients taken together; that is, they make no distinctions based on individual Indians' unique psychological conditions and physical characteristics. Degree of ethnic identity and acculturation, residential situation, and tribal background are but a few of the areas that counselors must account for in determining suitable counseling techniques. In addition to these client descriptors, counselors also must consider gender, sexual orientation, disability, and history of sexual and physical abuse. Black Bear (1988) draws attention to the special case of counseling with Indian women, whose situations often include child care and family responsibilities, as well as additional layers of oppression. For example, in researching Native ethnic identity, Gonzalez and Bennett (2000) found that Native women reported feeling less valued by mainstream society than their male counterparts. This is highlighted by Malone (2000), who discusses the importance of counselors integrating feminist theory with multicultural counseling perspectives when working with Indian and Native women, in large part because these clients' presenting problems have as much to do with gender issues as with cultural ones (see Portman & Garrett, 2005). Mangelson-Stander's (2000) work with samples of Indian women in recovery from personal trauma amplifies this recommendation. Mangelson-Stander also found differences between urban and reservation women in their participation in traditional spiritual practices, activities provided by recovery centers, and the value of family members providing care for the women's children while they were in recovery.

Finally, Indian clients with alcohol and drug abuse problems also may require unique attention (Moran & Reaman, 2002; Oetting & Beauvais, 1990; Trimble, 1984, 1992; Trimble & Beauvais, 2000). Intervention and treatment techniques that follow the recommendations made earlier in this chapter may be effective in many cases, but because of the complexity of the problem of substance abuse among Native populations, treatment effectiveness may be compromised. An example of the unique attention this problem may require is that substance abuse counselors may need to develop a respect and appreciation for the spirituality that is strongly entrenched in indigenous communities. Research has shown that infusing spirituality in alcohol recovery programs for Natives, coupled with a multicultural counseling perspective, can enhance outcome effectiveness (M. Garrett & Carroll, 2000; Hazel & Mohatt, 2001; Navarro, Wilson, Berger, & Taylor, 1997; Noe, Fleming, & Manson, 2003).

# TRADITIONAL HEALING PERSPECTIVES AND CONSIDERATIONS

Recently, considerable discussion has taken place concerning counseling paradigm shifts and the manner in which counseling and mental health services are offered to Indian and Native individuals and communities (Herring, 1999; Pedersen, 1999). Rather than focusing exclusively on how to use and/or adapt Western perspectives of healing, many are describing and proposing models of healing from a Native American Indian perspective (M. Garrett, Garrett, & Brotherton, 2001; Lewis, Duran, & Woodis, 1999; Tafoya, 1989; Thomason, 1991). A few authors have recommended that counselors establish working relationships with traditional healers. Such collaboration with an indigenous healing system can take several forms: The counselor may (a) support the viability of traditional healing as an effective treatment system, (b) actively refer clients to indigenous healers, or (c) actively work together with indigenous healers. Increasingly, numerous examples have been proposed concerning the worth of introducing Indian and Native beliefs and ceremonies within the conventional counseling setting (Dufrene & Coleman, 1992; M. Garrett et al., 2001; Gray, 1984; Heilbron & Guttman, 2000; Roberts, Harper, Tuttle-Eagle Bull, & Heideman-Provost, 1998; Tafoya, 1989). In general, the recommendations and examples follow the wisdom and advice offered by LaFromboise et al. (1990) concerning the importance of blending culturally unique and conventional psychological interventions to advance the goal of Native American Indian empowerment.

A few counselors working with Indian and Native clients have incorporated spirituality in counseling sessions and have achieved a modicum of success. J. Garrett and Garrett (1998) describe the use of the "sacred circle" and its related symbolism in an "inner/outer circle" form of group therapy and how the Native perspective can facilitate client progress. Using a variant of process-oriented training that is grounded in spirituality, Lewis et al. (1999) have found that the technique can allow therapists to enter into a non-Western-based reality with their clients, thus enhancing their sensitivity to and respect for Native worldviews. Heilbron and Guttman (2000) used a traditional aboriginal "healing circle" with nonaboriginal and First Nations women who were survivors of child sexual abuse and found that both groups responded favorably to the approach. Moreover, Tafoya (1989) advocates the use of a traditional Sahaptin legend as a paradigm for the way many Indians and Natives view the core elements of family therapy—specifically, relationships, responsibilities, learning, and teaching. He recommends that counselors working with Indians and Natives recognize and value the significance of the circle as a model for relationships; he also suggests that counselors avoid the use of direct, confrontational questioning; respect individual clients' life choices; and strive to achieve rapport with clients by openly expressing respect for culturally different worldviews.

Simms (1999) describes the use of a blended counseling approach that combined an integrated relational behavioral-cognitive strategy with traditional healing approaches, including talking circles, sweats, and participation in cultural forums. The client that Simms describes was experiencing cultural identity, self-confidence, and academic problems that could not be resolved through the use of a straightforward conventional counseling technique. Similarly, McDonald and Gonzalez (in press) describe the weaving of cognitive-behavioral therapy with traditional Lakota healing practices for a veteran experiencing posttraumatic stress disorder. Here again, there were cultural circumstances related to war and battle that necessitated the inclusion of Native ways of knowing and healing. The use of sweat lodges and talking circles as means for promoting client participation and retention is receiving some attention in the multicultural counseling literature (M. Garrett & Osborne, 1995). Specifically, Colmant and Merta (1999) describe the effectiveness of incorporating a sweat lodge ceremony in the treatment of Navajo youth who were diagnosed with behavioral disruptive disorders. They show how the ceremony has considerable overlap with conventional forms of group therapy and thus merits consideration in the treatment of Native youth.

Although incorporating traditional spiritual and healing methods such as the sweat lodge and talking circles can facilitate counselor effectiveness, client retention, and progress under controlled circumstances, decisions to use such techniques must be made with a strong degree of caution. LaDue (1994) strongly recommends that non-Indian counselors abstain from participating in and using such practices, asserting that they should not promote or condone the stealing and inappropriate use of Native spiritual activities. Doing so may invoke ethical considerations, as Native spiritual activities and practices are the sole responsibility of recognized and respected Native healers and Elders. Indeed, there is currently high interest in spirituality worldwide, and part of this growing interest involves the exploitation and appropriation of traditional Indian and Native ceremonies without the consent of indigenous healers. Matheson (1986) maintains that non-Native individuals who use traditional Native American Indian spiritual healing practices are under mistaken, even dangerous impressions and, as a consequence, are showing grave disrespect for the indigenous origins, contexts, and practices of these traditions by Native peoples. If the essence of a counseling relationship is built on trust, rapport, and respect, then the exploitation and appropriation of indigenous traditional healing ceremonies and practices for use in counseling sessions will undoubtedly undermine a counselor's efforts to gain acceptance from the Indian community and the client. These last points are not meant to discourage the non-Native counselor from exploring and learning about Native ways of knowing and healing. Instead, they are meant to bring us full circle to how we began this chapter with a discussion of historical trauma and spiritual loss that many Native communities have experienced.

## SUMMARY OF LITERATURE FINDINGS AND RECOMMENDATIONS

Throughout the literature on the topic of counseling with Indian clients, one theme surfaces repeatedly: Counselors of Indian clients must be adaptive and flexible in their personal orientations and in their use of conventional counseling techniques. To achieve a comfortable level of flexibility, Herring

(1999) proposes that counselors should adopt a "synergetic orientation" to assist them in establishing a "culturally affirmative environment" (pp. 55, 58). His recommendations include the following:

> 1) address openly the issue of dissimilar ethnic relationships rather than pretending that no differences exist; 2) schedule appointments to allow for flexibility in ending the session; 3) be open to allowing the extended family to participate in the session; 4) allow time for trust to develop before focusing on problems; 5) respect the uses of silence; 6) demonstrate honor and respect for the [client's] culture(s); and 7) maintain the highest level of confidentiality. (pp. 55–56)

Herring's suggestions reflect the sentiments and recommendations of many observers concerning the conduct of research in Indian and Native communities (Darou, Kurtness, & Hum, 2000; Darou, 1998; Trimble & Fisher, 2005) and are in keeping with what Trickett, Watts, and Birman (1994) refer to as "principled cultured sensitivity."

Counselors' commitment to understanding the cultural contexts and unique cultural characteristics of their clients also is essential. This often requires counselors to extend their efforts beyond what is typical. Salzman (2001, pp. 189–190) recommends that counselors respect culture as a necessary psychological defense and design interventions accordingly, promote interventions emphasizing meaning construction at the community level and support the collective (community) and individual construction of meaning that sustains adaptive action, support and assist individuals and communities in the identification of standards and values within the cultural worldview they identify with that promote adaptive action in current realities, and support and assist communities in cultural recovery through collaborative content analysis of traditional stories.

A final theme that arises is the need for counselors to assess the Native client's acculturation and ethnic identity levels (preferably during the early intake sessions). An Indian client's responsiveness to counseling is not necessarily a function of where he or she was born and reared. Rather, it would appear that a client's acculturation and the degree and intensity of his or her Indian identity are potent contributors to that client's receptivity to counseling in a conventional sense. Like many other members of ethnic minority groups and other culturally distinct people in North America, Indians express the full range of acculturation. Many, regardless of age, are traditional and Native oriented; others are transitional in the sense that they reflect an understanding and appreciation of culture-specific folkways yet recognize the need to adopt the values and beliefs of the dominant, mainstream culture. Others, whether because of geographic isolation from their ancestral homes or personal choice, to some degree have internalized the lifeways and thoughtways of modern society.

Although a counselor's sensitivity to the client's degree of acculturation will facilitate the counseling process, the dynamics surrounding acculturation also may create therapeutic issues. For some individuals who are otherwise healthy, the conflicts surrounding movement between cultures may be what bring them into counseling, and the counselor must be prepared to assist with these conflicts. These issues become more salient for Indian people who are living in urban or other non-reservation environments.

## CONCLUSION

Just as we have provided tenable suggestions for promoting counselor effectiveness in various sections of this chapter, the material we have presented also points to the gaps that exist in our understanding of what works best given the heterogeneity of Indian and Native populations. The presence of these gaps serves as a reminder of the need for careful documentation of the intervention strategies that appear to be effective for counselors and clinicians working with Indian and Native clients.

These gaps also suggest the need for more carefully controlled research that is inherently sensitive to the cultural orientation of Indians and Natives and their respective communities. A blend of case study documentation and empirical findings can only lead to the improvement of the delivery of mental health services to North America's indigenous populations.

# NOTE

1.   Throughout this chapter, we use different terms to refer to the indigenous peoples of North America; these terms include *American Indians, Alaska Natives, First Nations Peoples, Native American Indians, Native Americans, Indians,* and *Natives.* We use the briefest of these terms frequently for ease of reading and to make the best use of our limited space. Although all these terms have historical and sociopolitical value, in fact the indigenous peoples of the Americas generally prefer to be referred to by the names of their tribes or village affiliations.

## CRITICAL INCIDENT

### Working in Indian Country

Kevin Running Bird is a 17-year-old male living in a large urban city in the upper Midwest. He was referred to an Indian Health Service (IHS) clinic for an evaluation and possible counseling by the school guidance counselor because of recent trouble with school attendance and poor schoolwork. It was reported that many of the non-Native teachers were concerned about changes in Kevin's appearance and behavior. Kevin had cut his hair during the summer and was reportedly displaying a loss of interest in school subjects and activities that he once excelled at such as class participation and sports.

The IHS clinic only has one psychologist, Dr. Iam Newsome, who is just off internship and is working at the clinic as part of a service obligation to pay back his federal student loans. In looking at the school records, Dr. Newsome learns that Kevin had previous psychoeducational testing done 3 years ago and immediately decided to schedule him for follow-up testing with the Wechsler Adult Intelligence Scale (WAIS) and the Woodcock Johnson Battery. Without scheduling an initial intake interview, Dr. Newsome met with Kevin for testing. After the testing, Dr. Newsome provided a report that Kevin has a learning disorder and recommending he be placed in a remedial class. Dr. Newsome indicated his conclusions were based on a number of findings from testing, such as the discrepancy between Kevin's Verbal IQ score of 85 and Performance IQ score of 110 on the WAIS, below-average percentiles on the Woodcock Johnson reading and comprehension subtests, and Kevin's overall poor test-taking skills, lack of eye contact, and low motivation, which he interpreted as poor comprehension.

Upon receiving the report, the school guidance counselor decided to follow up with Dr. Newsome because the findings did not resemble the same young man that he had come to know. The guidance counselor did not agree with the diagnosis because Kevin has always been a good student and felt that his recent trouble at school was the result of many recent factors in Kevin's life. The school counselor strongly encouraged Dr. Newsome to meet with Kevin again and provided Dr. Newsome with more background information. After many attempts and missed appointments, Dr. Newsome was able to meet with Kevin several times over a 2-month period. Dr. Newsome learned that Kevin indeed had many recent significant events in his life. He learned that Kevin's aunt, whom he was very close to, passed away over the summer. Furthermore, Kevin was an only child, and his mother had passed away at a young age, so he became very close to this aunt and his cousins from this family. Kevin had cut his long hair as a sign of mourning and grieving his aunt. Kevin further informed Dr. Newsome that as part of his culture, he had gone on a vision quest back on his reservation and was struggling with the vision he had received. Kevin indicated that his grandfather was a traditional healer for his people, and during his fasting, Kevin was given a vision that he possesses a similar gift. This was part of the reason Kevin started losing interest in school and school activities because he felt they were not as important now if he were to follow in his grandfather's steps, and he was struggling with which direction to take in his life. During the sessions with Kevin, Dr. Newsome struggled with understanding Kevin's dilemma and kept insisting that Kevin should forget about this vision and go to college instead.

## DISCUSSION QUESTIONS

1. What are some alternate ways that Dr. Newsome could have approached this client to improve the relationship and communication?

2. Do you agree with the learning disorder diagnosis based on the IQ scores? What issues in cross-cultural assessment should you consider when interpreting test scores?

3. What about Kevin's ambivalence about school, academics, and following his grandfather? How would you approach these issues with Kevin?

4. What are some alternative therapy methods to approach in working with Kevin, and would they be helpful? For example, bringing in family members and collaborating with Native Elders and Healers.

# REFERENCES

Appleton, V., & Dykeman, C. (1996). Using art in group counseling with Native American youth. *Journal for Specialists in Group Work, 21,* 224–231.

Anderson, M., & Ellis, R. (1995). On the reservation. In N. Vacc & S. DeVaney (Eds.), *Experiencing and counseling multicultural and diverse populations* (pp. 179–197). Muncie, IN: Accelerated Development.

Attneave, C. L. (1969). Therapy in tribal settings and urban network intervention. *Family Process, 8,* 192–210.

Attneave, C. L. (1977). The wasted strength of American Indian families. In S. Unger (Ed.), *The destruction of American Indian families* (pp. 29–33). New York: Association on American Indian Affairs.

Attneave, C. L. (1985). Practical counseling with American Indian and Alaska Native clients. In P. B. Pedersen (Ed.), *Handbook of cross-cultural counseling and therapy* (pp. 135–140). Westport, CT: Greenwood.

Benally, H. (1987). "Dine bo'ohoo'aah bindii'a": Navajo philosophy of learning. *Dine Bi'ina' Journal, 1,* 23–31.

Bennett, S., & BigFoot-Sipes, D. (1991). American Indian and White college students' preferences for counselor characteristics. *Journal of Counseling Psychology, 38,* 440–445.

Berry, J. W. (1980). Acculturation as varieties of adaptation. In A. Padilla (Ed.), *Acculturation: Theory, models, and findings* (pp. 9–25). Boulder, CO: Westview.

Berry, J. W. (2002). Conceptual approaches to acculturation. In K. M. Chun, P. B. Organista, & G. Marin (Eds.), *Acculturation: Advances in theory, measurement, and applied research* (pp. 17–37). Washington, DC: American Psychological Association.

Black Bear, T. (1988). Native American clients. In A. Horton & J. Williamson (Eds.), *Abuse and religion: When praying isn't enough* (pp. 135–136). Lexington, MA: Lexington Books.

Blue, A., & Blue, M. (1983). The trail of stress. *White Cloud Journal, 3*(1), 15–22.

Bransford, J. (1982). To be or not to be: Counseling with American Indian clients. *Journal of American Indian Education, 21*(3), 18–21.

Brave Heart, M. Y. H., & DeBruyn, L. (1998). The American Indian Holocaust: Healing unresolved grief. *American Indian and Alaska Native Mental Health Research, 8*(2), 56–78.

Browne, A. (1995). The meaning of respect: A First Nations perspective. *Canadian Journal of Nursing Research, 27*(4), 95–109.

Brucker, P., & Perry, B. (1998). American Indians: Presenting concerns and considerations for family therapists. *American Journal of Family Therapy, 26,* 307–319.

Chrisjohn, R., & Young, S. (1997). *The circle game: Shadows and substance in the Indian residential school experience in Canada.* Penticton, British Columbia: Theytus.

Colmant, S., & Merta, R. (1999). Using the sweat lodge ceremony as group therapy for Navajo youth. *Journal for Specialists in Group Work, 24,* 55–73.

Darou, W. G. (1987). Counseling and the northern Native. *Canadian Journal of Counselling, 21,* 33–41.

Darou, W. G. (1998). *The circle game: Shadows and substance in the Indian residential school experience in Canada:* A review. *Journal of Cross-Cultural Psychology, 29,* 766–767.

Darou, W. G., Kurtness, J., & Hum, A. (2000). The impact of conducting research with a First Nation. *Canadian Journal of Counselling, 34,* 43–54.

Dauphinais, P., Dauphinais, L., & Rowe, W. (1981). Effects of race and communication style on Indian perception of counselor effectiveness. *Counselor Education and Supervision, 21*(1), 72–80.

Dufrene, P., & Coleman, V. (1992). Counseling Native Americans: Guidelines for group process. *Journal for Specialists in Group Work, 17,* 229–234.

Dufrene, P., & Coleman, V. (1994). Art and healing for Native American Indians. *Journal of Multicultural Counseling and Development, 22,* 145–152.

Duran, E. (1999). *Aniongwea Native American health center: Original people.* San Francisco: Fast Forward.

Duran, E., & Duran, B. (1995). *Native American postcolonial psychology.* Albany: State University of New York Press.

Duran, E., Duran, B., Brave Heart, M. Y. H., & Yellow Horse-Davis, S. (1998). Healing the American Indian soul wound. In Y. Danieli (Ed.), *International handbook of multigenerational legacies of trauma* (pp. 341–354). New York: Plenum.

Garrett, J., & Garrett, M. (1998). The path of good medicine: Understanding and counseling Native American Indians. In D. R. Atkinson, G. Morten, & D. W. Sue (Eds.), *Counseling American minorities* (5th ed., pp. 183–192). New York: McGraw-Hill.

Garrett, M. (1999). Understanding the "medicine" of Native American traditional values: An integrative review. *Counseling and Values, 43*(2), 84–98.

Garrett, M., & Carroll, J. (2000). Mending the broken circle: Treatment of substance dependence among Native Americans. *Journal of Counseling and Development, 78,* 379–388.

Garrett, M., Garrett, J., & Brotherton, D. (2001). Inner circle/outer circle: A group technique based on Native American healing circles. *Journal for Specialists in Group Work, 26,* 17–30.

Garrett, M., Garrett, J. T., Toress-Rivera, E., Wilbur, M., & Roberts-Wilbur, J. (2005). Laughing it up: Native American humor as spiritual tradition. *Journal of Multicultural Counseling and Development, 33*(4), 194–204.

Garrett, M., & Osborne, W. (1995). The Native American sweat lodge as a metaphor for group work. *Journal for Specialists in Group Work, 20,* 33–39.

Garrett, M., & Pichette, E. (2000). Red as an apple: Native American acculturation and counseling with or without reservation. *Journal of Counseling and Development, 78,* 3–13.

Gonzalez, J., & Bennett, R. (2000, February). *Self—Identity in the indigenous peoples of North America: Factor structure and correlates.* Poster session presented at the 1st annual meeting of the Society for Personality and Social Psychology, Nashville, TN.

Graves, T. D., & Arsdale, M. V. (1966). Values, expectations and relocation: The Navajo migrant to Denver. *Human Organization, 25,* 300–307.

Gray, L. (1984). Healing among Native American Indians. *PSI-Research, 3,* 141–149.

Hazel, K. L., & Mohatt, G. V. (2001). Cultural and spiritual coping in sobriety: Informing substance abuse prevention for Alaska Native communities. *Journal of Community Psychology, 29*(5), 541–562.

Heilbron, C., & Guttman, M. (2000). Traditional healing methods with First Nations women in group counseling. *Canadian Journal of Counselling, 34,* 3–13.

Helms, J., & Cook, D. (1999). *Using race and culture in counseling and psychotherapy: Theory and practice.* Boston: Allyn & Bacon.

Herring, R. D. (1992). Seeking a new paradigm: Counseling Native Americans. *Journal of Multicultural Counseling and Development, 20,* 35–43.

Herring, R. D. (1994). The clown or contrary figure as a counseling intervention strategy with Native American Indian clients. *Journal of Multicultural Counseling and Development, 22,* 153–164.

Herring, R. D. (1997). Counseling indigenous American youth. In C. C. Lee (Ed.), *Multicultural issues in counseling: New approaches to diversity* (2nd ed., pp. 53–70). Alexandria, VA: American Counseling Association.

Herring, R. D. (1999). *Counseling with Native American Indians and Alaska Natives: Strategies for helping professionals.* Thousand Oaks, CA: Sage.

Johnson, C., & Johnson, D. (1998). Working with Native American families. *New Directions for Mental Health Services, 77,* 89–96.

Johnson, M., & Lashley, K. (1989). Influence of Native Americans' cultural commitment on preferences for counselor ethnicity and expectations about counseling. *Journal of Multicultural Counseling and Development, 17,* 115–122.

Katz, R. (1993). *The straight path: A story of healing and transformation in Fiji.* Reading, MA: Addison-Wesley.

Katz, R., Biesele, M., & St. Denis, V. (1997). *Healing makes our hearts happy.* Rochester, VT: Inner Traditions.

Koverola, C. (1992). Counseling aboriginal people of North America. *Journal of Psychology and Christianity, 11,* 345–357.

LaDue, R. (1994). Coyote returns: Twenty sweats does not an Indian expert make. *Women and Therapy, 5*(1), 93–111.

LaFromboise, T., Berman, J., & Sohi, B. (1994). American Indian women. In L. Comas-Diaz & B. Greene (Eds.), *Women of color: Integrating ethnic and gender identities in psychotherapy* (pp. 30–71). New York: Guilford.

LaFromboise, T., Dauphinais, P., & Rowe, W. (1980). Indian students' perceptions of positive helper attributes. *Journal of American Indian Education, 19,* 11–16.

LaFromboise, T., Trimble, J. E., & Mohatt, G. (1990). Counseling intervention and American Indian tradition: An integrative approach. *Counseling Psychologist, 18,* 628–654.

Lee, S. (1997). Communication styles of Wind River Native American clients and the therapeutic approaches of their clinicians. *Smith College Studies in Social Work, 68*(1), 57–81.

Lewis, E., Duran, E., & Woodis, W. (1999). Psychotherapy in the American Indian population. *Psychiatric Annals, 29,* 477–479.

Lockhart, B. (1981). Historic distrust and the counseling of American Indians and Alaskan Natives. *White Cloud Journal, 2*(3), 31–43.

Locust, C. (1985). *American Indian beliefs concerning health and wellness* (Native American Research and Training Monograph). Tucson: University of Arizona Press.

Locust, C. (1995). The impact of differing belief systems between Native Americans and their rehabilitation service providers. *Rehabilitation Education, 9,* 205–215.

Lowrey, L. (1983). Bridging a culture in counseling. *Journal of Applied Rehabilitation Counseling, 14,* 69–73.

Malone, J. (2000). Working with aboriginal women: Applying feminist therapy in a multicultural counseling context. *Canadian Journal of Counseling, 34,* 33–42.

Mangelson-Stander, E. (2000). Strategies for survival though healing among Native American women: An urban case study. *Dissertation Abstracts International, 61*(2-A), 780.

Marsiglia, F., Cross, S., & Mitchell-Enos, V. (1998). Culturally grounded group work with adolescent American Indian students. *Social Work With Groups, 21*(1–2), 89–102.

Matheson, L. (1986). If you are not an Indian, how do you treat an Indian? In H. P. Lefley & P. B. Pedersen (Eds.), *Cross-cultural training for mental health professionals* (pp. 115–130). Springfield, IL: Charles C Thomas.

McCormick, R. (1996). Culturally appropriate means and ends of counseling as described by the First Nations people of British Columbia. *International Journal for the Advancement of Counseling, 18*(3), 163–172.

McDonald, J. D., & Gonzalez, J. (in press). Cognitive-behavior therapy with American Indians. In P. A. Hays & G. Y. Iwamasa (Eds.), *Cognitive-behavior therapy with culturally diverse people.* Washington, DC: American Psychological Association.

McGaa, E. (1992). *Rainbow tribe: Ordinary people journeying on the red road.* San Francisco: Harper.

McWhirter, J., & Ryan, C. (1991). Counseling the Navajo: Cultural understanding. *Journal of Multicultural Counseling and Development, 19,* 74–82.

Millar, J. (1996). *Shingwauk's vision: A history of Native residential schools.* Toronto: University of Toronto Press.

Mohatt, G., & Eagle Elk, J. (2000). *The price of a gift: A Lakota healer's story.* Lincoln: University of Nebraska Press.

Moran, J. R., & Reaman, J. A. (2002). Critical issues for substance abuse prevention targeting American Indian youth. *Journal of Primary Prevention, 22*(3), 201–233.

Morrissette, P. (1994). The holocaust of First Nation people: Residual effects on parenting and treatment implications. *Contemporary Family Therapy, 16,* 381–392.

Morse, J., Young, D., & Swartz, L. (1991). Cree Indian healing practices and Western health care: A comparative analysis. *Social Science and Medicine, 32,* 1361–1366.

Napoleon, H. (1996). *Yuuyaraq: The way of the human being.* Fairbanks: University of Alaska, Native Knowledge Network.

Napoli, M., & Gonzalez-Santin, E. (2001). Intensive home-based and wellness services to Native American families living on reservations: A model. *Families in Society: The Journal of Contemporary Human Services, 82*(3), 315–324.

Navarro, J., Wilson, S., Berger, L., & Taylor, T. (1997). Substance abuse and spirituality: A program for Native American students. *American Journal of Health Behavior, 21*(1), 3–11.

Noe, T., Fleming, C., & Manson, S. (2003). Healthy Nations: Reducing substance abuse in American Indian and Alaska Native communities. *Journal of Psychoactive Drugs, 35*(1), 15–25.

Oetting, E. R., & Beauvais, F. (1990). Adolescent drug use: Findings of national and local surveys. *Journal of Consulting and Clinical Psychology, 58,* 385–394.

Olsen, M. J. (2003). Counselor understanding of Native American spiritual loss. *Counseling and Values, 47,* 109–117.

Pedersen, P. B. (Ed.). (1999). *Multiculturalism as a fourth force.* Philadelphia: Brunner/Mazel.

Peregoy, J. (1999). Revisiting transcultural counseling with American Indians and Alaskan Natives: Issues for consideration. In J. McFadden (Ed.), *Transcultural counseling* (2nd ed., pp. 137–170). Alexandria, VA: American Counseling Association.

Portman, T. A., & Garrett, M. T. (2005). Beloved women: Nurturing the sacred fire of leadership from an American Indian perspective. *Journal of Counseling and Development, 83*(3), 284–291.

Reimer, C. S. (1999). *Counseling the Inupiat Eskimo.* Westport, CT: Greenwood.

Roberts, R., Harper, R., Tuttle-Eagle Bull, D., & Heideman-Provost, L. (1998). The Native American medicine wheel and individual psychology. *Journal of Individual Psychology, 54,* 135–145.

Sage, G. (1997). Counseling American Indian clients. In C. C. Lee (Ed.), *Multicultural issues in counseling: New approaches to diversity* (2nd ed., pp. 35–52). Alexandria, VA: American Counseling Association.

Salzman, M. (2001). Cultural trauma and recovery: Perspectives from terror management theory. *Trauma, Violence, & Abuse, 2,* 172–191.

Simms, W. (1999). The Native American Indian client: A tale of two cultures. In Y. Jenkins (Ed.), *Diversity in college settings: Directives for helping professionals* (pp. 21–35). New York: Routledge.

Tafoya, T. (1989). Circles and cedar: Native Americans and family therapy. *Journal of Psychotherapy and the Family, 6*(1–2), 71–98.

Thomason, T. (1991). Counseling Native Americans: An introduction for non-Native American counselors. *Journal of Counseling and Development, 69,* 321–327.

Thornton, R. (1996). Tribal membership requirements and the demography of "old" and "new" Native Americans. In G. Sandefur, R. Rindfuss, & B. Cohen (Eds.), *Changing numbers, changing needs: American Indian demography and public health* (pp. 103–112). Washington, DC: National Academy Press.

Trickett, E., Watts, R., & Birman, D. (1994). *Human diversity: Perspectives on people in context.* San Francisco: Jossey-Bass.

Trimble, J. E. (1981). Value differentials and their importance in counseling American Indians. In P. B. Pedersen, J. G. Draguns, W. J. Lonner, & J. E. Trimble (Eds.), *Counseling across cultures* (Rev. ed., pp. 203–226). Honolulu: University of Hawaii Press.

Trimble, J. E. (1984). Drug abuse prevention research needs among American Indians and Alaskan Natives. *White Cloud Journal, 3*(3), 22–34.

Trimble, J. E. (1992). A cognitive-behavioral approach to drug abuse prevention and intervention with American Indian youth. In L. A. Vargas & J. D. Koss (Eds.), *Working with culture: Psychotherapeutic interventions with ethnic minority children and adolescents* (pp. 246–275). San Francisco, CA: Jossey-Bass.

Trimble, J. E., & Beauvais, F. (Eds.). (2000). *Health promotion and substance abuse prevention among American Indians and Alaska Natives: Issues in cultural competence* (CSAP Cultural Competence Series, No. 9). Rockville, MD: U.S. Department of Health and Human Services, Substance Abuse and Mental Services Administration, Center for Substance Abuse Prevention, and Office of Minority Health, Health Resources and Service Administration, Bureau of Primary Health.

Trimble, J. E., & Fisher, C. B. (Eds.). (2005). *The handbook of ethical research with ethnocultural populations and communities.* Thousand Oaks, CA: Sage.

Trimble, J. E., & Hayes, S. A. (1984). Mental health intervention in the psychological contexts of American Indian communities. In W. A. O'Connor & B. Lubin (Eds.), *Ecological models: Applications to clinical and community mental health* (pp. 293–321). New York: John Wiley.

Trimble, J. E., & LaFromboise, T. (1985). American Indians and the counseling process: Culture, adaptation, and style. In P. B. Pedersen (Ed.), *Handbook of cross-cultural counseling and therapy* (pp. 127–134). Westport, CT: Greenwood.

Uhlemann, M., Lee, D., & France, H. (1988). Counselor ethnic differences and perceived counseling effectiveness. *International Journal for the Advancement of Counseling, 11,* 247–253.

Witko, T. (2006). *Mental health care for urban Indians: Clinical insight from Native practitioners and culturally responsive cognitive-behavioral therapy: Assessment, practice, and supervision.* Washington DC: American Psychological Association.

Yurkovich, E. E., Clairmont, J., & Grandbois, D. (2002). Mental health care providers' perception of giving culturally responsive care to American Indians. *Perspectives in Psychiatric Care, 38*(4), 147–156.

# Counseling Asian Americans

## Client and Therapist Variables

Frederick T. L. Leong, Szu-Hui Lee, and Doris Chang

---

### Primary Objective

- To inform the reader about some cultural factors related to client and therapist variables that may play a significant role in providing effective counseling for Asian American clients

### Secondary Objectives

- To expand and update the literature review provided by Leong (1986) in his earlier review of the literature
- To contribute to the process of bridging the existing knowledge base from research to clinical practice

---

WITH THE GROWING DIVERSITY IN THE UNITED STATES, IT IS INEVITABLE THAT MENTAL HEALTH service providers will increasingly encounter clients with diverse cultural backgrounds who may also present with clinical issues that are different from the mainstream culture. It is important for service providers to increase their levels of cultural awareness and competency in working with a diverse clientele. The development of cross-cultural counseling is a continual process, and the purpose of the present chapter is to contribute to that process through updating and bridging the knowledge base from research to clinical practice.

In 1986, Leong provided a comprehensive review of the literature related to counseling Asian Americans that covered client and therapist variables as well as counseling process and outcome variables. Since the Leong (1986) review of literature, the field has seen an increase of research efforts with focused attention on Asian Americans. Three noticeable research trends emerged: (1) research on specific Asian ethnic groups, (2) research on specific psychological issues (e.g., severe psychopathology) as it relates to Asian Americans, and (3) international research comparing Asian Americans in the United States and Asian in other nations. These trends are appropriate toward deeper understanding of how to best meet the needs of Asian Americans, especially given the heterogeneity within this population. Due to space limitations, the current review will only cover client and therapist variables as they relate to counseling Asian Americans. For an updated review of counseling process and outcome variables concerning Asian Americans, please see the chapter by Leong, Chang, and Lee (2007) in the second edition of the *Handbook of Asian American Psychology*. While the term *Asian Americans* will be used throughout this chapter, the authors acknowledge that this general term encompasses many Asian ethnic subgroups, and the information provided may not always be generalizable across all Asian ethnic groups and all Asian individuals. The use of this broad term is primarily due to the space limitations of this survey chapter but also mirrors limitations of current research literature. Research findings on specific Asian ethnic subgroups will be incorporated throughout the chapter to enhance applicability of information to clinical practice.

## CLIENT VARIABLES

It is important to consider the cultural lens from which Asian Americans view themselves and the world. Understanding the personality characteristics and worldviews of Asian Americans from the cultural perspective is critical for an accurate understanding and assessment of how Asian Americans may respond to counseling and psychotherapy.

## Personality Characteristics Within the Cultural Context

Asian Americans exhibit distinct personality characteristics that are often different from European American and other racial ethnic minority groups. Not only are their characteristics influenced by their heritage culture, but the characteristics also resulted from interactions of those cultures with the cultures of the Western society (D. Sue, 1998). The Asian American worldview emphasizes humility, modesty, treating oneself strictly while treating others more leniently, obligation to family, conformity, obedience, and subordination to authority. Other factors that contextualize the cultural context of Asian Americans include familial relations, interpersonal harmony versus honesty emphasis, role hierarchy versus egalitarianism, and self-restraint versus self-disclosure (W. W. Chien & Banerjee, 2002). See Table 7.1 for summary of elements of the Asian American worldview. Asian Americans' tendency to exhibit lower levels of verbal and emotional expressiveness than do Euro-Americans, for example, can be accounted for by the cultural context as described. Recognizing and understanding the cultural context of these characteristics would enhance appreciation for why Asian Americans may respond to psychotherapy differently than those with different worldviews.

With a worldview that emphasizes role hierarchy and respect for authority, Asian Americans often exhibit greater respect for counselors than do Euro-Americans, whose worldview places less emphasis on deference based on role hierarchy (D. W. Sue & Kirk, 1973). Asian Americans have shown strong preference for a counselor who is an authority but is not authoritarian (Exum & Lau, 1988). For example, Chinese Americans were found to more likely expect counselors to make decisions for them and to provide immediate solutions (Mau & Jepsen, 1990). Research shows that not only do Asian

| TABLE 7.1 | Selected Elements of the Asian American Worldview |
|---|---|

Humility

Interpersonal harmony

Obligation to family

Self-restraint

Conformity, obedience, and subordination to authority

Body and mind as unitary

Role hierarchy

Americans prefer structured situations and immediate solutions to problems, but they also prefer directive counseling styles because they exhibit lower tolerance for ambiguity than Euro-Americans. Given this, Asian Americans are likely to find difficulty with the Western model of counseling and psychotherapy, which is filled with ambiguity by design and typically conducted as an unstructured process. Asian clients tend to prefer crisis-oriented, brief, and solution-oriented approaches rather than insight and growth-oriented approaches (Berg & Jaya, 1993). For Asian Americans, who tend to be less tolerant of ambiguity, the mismatch with insight-oriented psychotherapy may account for the early termination and the underutilization rates that exist.

Without interpretation through the appropriate cultural lens, researchers and counselors are vulnerable to making false assumptions and inappropriate comparisons across populations. More specifically, Western worldview and perspective ought not to be used as the normative to interpret characteristics and behaviors of Asian Americans. Without accounting for the Asian cultural context, any differences of Asian Americans compared to Euro-Americans might potentially be viewed with negative and deficit connotations. For example, Asian values of reserve, restraint of strong feelings, and subtleness in approaching problems may come into conflict with Western counselors and counselors who expect their clients to exhibit openness, psychological mindedness, and assertiveness. A counselor may assume that the person is repressed, inhibited, or shy rather than simply exhibiting characteristics aligned with his or her culture (S. Sue, 1981).

Erroneous conclusions made about Asian Americans by interpreting their personality characteristic with the Euro-American culture as the normative are also found in the arena of career counseling. For example, Asian Americans historically report significantly higher parental career expectations and parental involvement in the career decision-making process than Euro-Americans (Castro & Rice, 2003). When making career decisions, Asian Americans are more likely to be influenced by their families and cultural values than Euro-Americans (Tang, 2002). From an Asian cultural perspective, however, involving family is aligned with the cultural norms and values. However, from a Western perspective, the inclusion of parental expectations and wishes may be interpreted as being immature and maladaptive. In a study by Hardin, Leong, and Osipow (2001), the career decision-making measures used indicated that Asian Americans exhibit less mature career choice attitudes than European Americans. As the authors noted, the results might not have been accurate indicators of maturity because the measures designed to measure maturity in career decision making were biased toward the cultural norms and expectations of the Western culture. Again, it is important to consider the worldview of Asian Americans and use their cultural worldview as the normative measuring rubric rather than a biased measure from another worldview.

The complexity of how cultural values affect the lives of Asian Americans is being explored continuously. Research suggests that gender and racial identity have influenced the cultural value held by Asian Americans (Yeh, Carter, & Pieterse, 2004). A strong preference for distinct cultural value orientations could reflect both traditional Asian and European American cultural values. The unique personality characteristics of Asian American women (True, 1990) and Asian American men (D. Sue, 2001) have also been an area of much literature and research focus. Factors such as socialization of gender roles, societal pressures, acculturation, and traditional Asian cultural values have been explored for how they relate to the personality development of Asian American women and men. For example, for traditionally oriented Asian American males, reframing and discussing culture conflicts can help resolve issues of living up to cultural expectations. For acculturated Asian American males, a more didactic presentation that includes a discussion of Asian males in American society might be a better first step than introspective techniques in the consciousness-raising process. Understanding the unique characteristics of the two sexes provides context for which psychologists can provide therapeutic assistance.

## Emotion of Shame—Loss of Face

Emotions are important in understanding human behaviors because they provide energy for and guide behaviors. Shame and shaming are the mechanisms that traditionally help reinforce societal expectations and proper behavior in Asian culture. The fear of losing face can be a powerful motivational force to conform to family and societal expectations. Losing face and the resulting shame are especially salient for Asian American clients because loss of face is often a dominant interpersonal dynamic in Asian social relations, particularly when the relationship involves seeking help for personal issues (Zane & Yeh, 2002). In Asian American culture, the emotion of shame and the experience of "losing face" involve not only the exposure of the individuals' actions for all to see but also the withdrawal of the family's, community's, or society's confidence and support. Feelings of shame are painful for individuals of collectivistic cultures (e.g., Asian cultures) because of the social consequences (Yeh & Huang, 1996). The web of obligation and fear of shame are frequently crucial parts of the lives of East Asian and Asian Americans who seek or are referred for treatment. These feelings can affect their behavior and perceptions of the world and their presentation of material in therapy. It can envelop the relationship with the therapist in ways that the therapist does not understand unless he or she is familiar with the cultural relevancy of shame of the particular Asian American groups.

## Language

Many investigators have identified language as an important client variable to attend to when counseling Asian Americans (C. P. Chien & Yamamoto, 1982). There are several ways in which language may serve as a barrier to effective cross-cultural counseling. Language barriers could also lead to misinterpretations and false assumptions. For example, bilingual backgrounds could result in Asian Americans being perceived as uncooperative, sullen, and negative (D. W. Sue & Sue, 1972). Asian Americans who speak little or no English may be misunderstood by their counselors. The use of dialects or nonstandard English may interfere with the effective exchange of information or even stimulate bias on the part of the therapist. Given these language barriers, Asian Americans may attempt to communicate their concerns nonverbally, which in turn could be misinterpreted by the counselor (Tseng & McDermott, 1975). The use of interpreters with non-English-speaking Asian clients could result in interpreted-related distortions (Marcos, 1979).

Problems with intercultural communication are not limited to the use of different languages but are also due to differences in thought patterns, values, and communication styles (Chan, 1992). Communication styles of Asian Americans are significantly different from Euro-Americans. Asian Americans tend to communicate in a high-context style with context as the primary channel for communication. Direct and specific references to the meaning of the message are not given. Receivers are expected to rely on their knowledge and appreciation for nonverbal cues and other subtle affects for interpreting message meaning. The Euro-American culture tends to focus on communication through a low-context style, where words are the primary channel for communication. Direct, precise, and clear information is delivered verbally. Receivers can expect to simply take that which is said at face value. The high-context communication style can be seen as an elaborate, subtle, and complex form of interpersonal communication.

The high-context communication style enables Asian Americans to avoid causing shame or loss of face to themselves and others to maintain harmonious relations. In fact, any form of direct confrontation and verbal assertiveness might be considered rude and disrespectful. The use of direct eye contact is limited because direct eye contact may imply hostility and aggression and be taken as a rude gesture. Mental health service providers must be aware and sensitive to these communication style differences to prevent cross-cultural misunderstandings. An individual's preferential communication style (high or low context) could influence how he or she perceives others who use the opposite style. Those who prefer high-context communication may perceive those who use low context to be too direct, insensitive to context, and minimally communicative. Those who use a low-context communication style may, in turn, perceive the high-context communicators as indirect, lacking in verbal skills, and even untrustworthy. Cultural awareness and accommodation for the different communication styles would positively affect the therapy process and therapeutic alliance between the therapist and the client.

## Family

The role that the family plays in Asian American culture is considered to be another important client variable. Many social scientists have continually emphasized that the family plays a central role in the mental health of Asian Americans. While Asian families may emphasize connectedness within family members, Western norms prioritize separateness and clear boundaries in relationships, individuality, and autonomy (Tamura & Lau, 1992). Mental health service providers should note that the preferred direction of change may be better toward a process of integration, rather than a process of differentiation. Within the Asian American cultural context, family constancy, equilibrium, duty, obligation, and appearance of harmonious relations are important factors.

Family dynamics and related factors that should also be considered when working with Asian Americans include immigration history, adaptation experiences, cultural values, and generational differences due to differences in acculturation experience (e.g., B. S. K. Kim, Brenner, Liang, & Asay, 2003; J. M. Kim, 2003). More specifically, immigrant families may face difficulties with social isolation, adjustment difficulties, and cultural and language barriers. Issues such as language and cultural barriers may contribute to the parent-child conflicts within immigrant families. Family organization, roles and functioning, and cultural values across generations are also important to explore within Asian American families. Studies have shown that for Asian Americans, their immediate and extended family are important loci of identity formation, social learning, support, and role development. Asian culture also places higher value on males, which could result in a disproportionate share of power within the family (Cimmarusti, 1996). Finally, parenting styles received may also explain personality development and life experiences of Asian Americans (Lim & Lim, 2004). H. Kim and Chung (2003) found that authoritative parenting behaviors were most common in Korean American families, followed by authoritarian behaviors, then permissive behaviors. Authoritative parenting styles and the number of years lived in the United States were also predictive of higher academic competence. Authoritarian and permissive parenting styles were predictive of lower self-reliance, whereas number of years lived in the United States was related to higher self-reliance. As with any populations, families not only have the potential of facilitating mental health but could also serve as potential mental health stressors. It is important to note that not all families are alike, and clinicians should expect much variation among them.

## Acculturation

Acculturation is used here to represent the degree to which Asian Americans are identified with and integrated into the Euro-American majority culture. Acculturation involves a minority individual's behavioral, cultural, and social adaptations that take place because of contact between the individual's ethnic society and the Euro-Americans' dominant society. One consistent consequence of this pattern of acculturation has been the experience of culture conflicts by Asian Americans. As the later generations of Asian Americans became exposed to Western influence via the schools, mass media, and their peers, they began to experience situations of culture conflict (S. Sue, 1981). For example, Connor (1974) found that there are significant generational differences among Japanese Americans due to acculturation experiences. Behaviors and values of the later generations were much more similar to those of Euro-Americans than those of their own parents or grandparents. Fong (1973) has also identified a similar process of internalization of Western norms and values among younger Chinese Americans (fifth generation vs. first generation). Caught between the Western standards and the traditional cultural values of their parents, Asian Americans may experience stress related to these culture conflicts generated by the acculturation process as well as interpersonal conflicts. Based on their clinical experience with Asian Americans, D. W. Sue and Sue (1972) have developed a conceptual scheme for understanding how Asian Americans adjust to these conflicts. They observed that Asian Americans tended to exhibit three distinct ways of resolving the culture conflicts experienced. First, *the traditionalist* is one who remains loyal to his or her own ethnic group by retaining traditional Asian values and living up to expectations of the family. Second, *the marginal person* is one who becomes overly Westernized by rejecting traditional Asian values and whose pride and self-worth are defined by the ability to acculturate into Euro-American society. The third way of resolving cultural conflict is the *Asian American,* who is rebelling against parental authority and at the same time is attempting to integrate his or her bicultural elements into a new identity by reconciling viable aspects of his or her heritage with the present situation. One way that Asian Americans attempt to resolve the cultural conflicts generated by the acculturation process is by developing a sense of ethnic identity to their heritage culture (Cheryan & Tsai, 2007).

An Asian American's level of acculturation may influence his or her response to both therapy process and outcome. There is a wide consensus grounded by data that there is a significant relationship between levels of acculturation and attitudes toward seeking professional psychological help (Gim, Atkinson, & Whiteley, 1990). The more acculturated individuals tend to be more likely to seek professional psychological help, while the less acculturated individuals tend to exhibit a higher likelihood of seeking help from community elders, religious leaders, student organizations, and church groups (Solberg, Choi, Ritsma, & Jolly, 1994). Individuals who are most acculturated are most likely to recognize the need for professional psychological help because they are most tolerant of the stigmas often associated with seeking psychological assistance (Atkinson & Gim, 1989). Finally, studies involving self-reported symptoms have found that along with age and cultural adjustment difficulties, acculturation is significantly predictive of effects on mental health symptoms (Yeh, 2003). That is, acculturation is negatively related to self-reported symptoms. For example, acculturation had been found to be positively related to job satisfaction and negatively related to occupational strain on Asian Americans. It is important for clinicians to be cognizant of the impact of acculturation and provide services that would address the impact of acculturation whenever appropriate.

## Counseling Expectations

The counseling expectations and conceptions of the mental health of Asian Americans are an important client variable that has been examined empirically. When effects of Asian students' cultural conceptions of mental health on the expectations of counseling are examined, Asians generally tend to view counseling as a directive, paternalistic, and authoritarian process (Arkoff, Thaver, & Elkind, 1966). Consequently, Asian Americans are more likely to expect the counselor to provide advice and recommend a specific course of action. Tan (1967) surveyed Asian foreign students and Euro-American students in the United States and found that all of the Asian groups considered counseling primarily as an advice- and information-giving process by an experienced person. In a study of counseling expectation, Chinese students reported more expectations for directiveness, empathy, and nurturance from counselors than Euro-American students. The same group of Chinese students also expected more expertise from the counselor and believed that clients should possess lower levels of responsibility, openness, and motivation. The findings from these studies of counseling expectations seem quite consistent even though separate measures were used.

## Help-Seeking Attitudes

Asian Americans historically have exhibited patterns of underutilization of health services. Barriers that have been identified to explain the low utilization rates of Asian Americans include cognitive (e.g., stigmas), affective (e.g., shame), value orientation (e.g., collectivistic nature), and physical barriers (e.g., access to resources) (Leong & Lau, 2001). Furthermore, in some cultures, there is not a cultural analogy to psychological therapy; therefore, utilization of mental health services may not be viewed as a treatment option. To account for the lack of understanding of psychological services and stigmas attached to service utilization, recent studies have begun to explore ways in which one may appropriately explain mental illness to Asian Americans (Yep, 2000). Stigmas and lack of understanding can account for the low frequencies of self-referrals inasmuch that studies have shown that Asian Americans are more likely than Euro-Americans to be referred by friends and through health and social service agencies (Akutsu, Snowden, & Organista, 1996). Preferred use of traditional Asian healing practices can also account for underutilization of professional psychological services. Recent research efforts have been placed on exploring the indigenous healing methods used within Asian communities.

Levels of acculturation can also influence the attitudes held by Asian Americans toward mental health services (Zhang & Dixon, 2003). Studies show that Asian Americans with high acculturation levels are more willing to seek help than those less acculturated. In one study, across three Asian ethnic groups (Chinese, Japanese, and Korean), the most acculturated individuals were more likely to recognize the need for professional psychological help, more tolerant of stigmas, and more open to discuss problems with a psychologist than individuals who were not acculturated (Atkinson & Gim, 1989).

Studies also show that gender can influence one's willingness to seek psychological services (Gim et al., 1990). More specifically, Asian American women exhibit greater willingness to see a counselor than do Asian American men. To account for service underutilization and premature termination among Asian Americans, mental health providers must recognize the influences of the Asian cultural context on cultural values, attitudes, beliefs, and the help-seeking behaviors that result. Finally, service providers should also be open to explore vulnerabilities of ethnocentrism and cultural uniformity myths that may hinder their full appreciation of the worldview of their ethnically different clients.

## Experiences of Psychological Distress and Coping Mechanisms

Asian Americans, just as any other racial/ethnic group, are not immune to mental health issues (Takeuchi, Mokuau, & Chun, 1992). The prevalence of mental health problems among Asian Americans is noteworthy despite the stereotype of being the "model minority." Much literature and research attention has been devoted to understanding and describing the unique mental health needs and experiences of Asian Americans. The cultural context helps us to understand the experiences and the expression of symptoms of distress. For Asian Americans, there may be a tendency to replace psychological symptoms with somatic ones (Kleinman & Sung, 1979). This tendency to somaticize complaints may extend beyond the diagnostic interview to influence the therapy process itself. Failure to recognize this client characteristic among Asian Americans may result in both diagnostic and therapeutic errors.

The worldview of Asian Americans is further contextualized by understanding their ethnic identity. Asian Americans' experience with racism and discrimination should also be taken into consideration in the therapy process. This is especially true for Euro-American counselors and counselors who may be inadvertently associated with this negative cultural experience by Asian American clients. Furthermore, some immigration experiences also have served as a source of mental health problems as Asian Americans have sought to adjust to living within the United States (Cheung, 1980). Acculturative stress, for example, is the direct result of the acculturation adaptation process for first-generation immigrants, and bicultural stress is a response to the pulls of maintaining ethnic ties in second and later generations and has significant predictive effects on mental health symptoms (Yeh, 2003). Examining within-group differences of immigration status (e.g., international, permanent residents, and naturalized citizens) while accounting for immigration history should be considered, as it further contextualizes the life experiences of the individual Asian American client.

While some studies have found that Asian Americans in general may have less of a need for psychological and social support than Euro-Americans (Wellisch et al., 1999), others have found that Asian American adolescents specifically have a higher level of depressive symptomatology, withdrawn behavior, and social problems than Euro-American adolescents (Chang, 2001). More specifically, some studies have found that foreign-born Asian American college students experienced greater levels of intrapersonal and interpersonal distress when compared to U.S.-born Asian Americans and Euro-Americans (Abe & Zane, 1990). While stressors such as racism can exacerbate difficulties with cultural adjustments, it has been found that social support, including friends, family, and even international student offices, can all provide buffering effects (Chen, Mallingckrodt, & Mobley, 2002). It is well documented that social support is an instrumental tool for coping among many Asian Americans.

How Asian Americans tend to cope with psychological distress can best be understood through the lens of their cultural worldview. Asian Americans have tended to endorse coping sources and practices that emphasize talking with familial and social relations rather than professionals such as counselors and doctors. More specifically, among the ethnic groups examined in one study (i.e., Chinese, Korean, Filipino, and Indian), Korean Americans were fond to be more likely to cope with problems by engaging in religious activities (Yeh & Wang, 2000). Other studies have found that Japanese Americans were more likely than Euro-Americans to attribute mental illness to social causes and preferred to seek help from family members and/or friends (Narikiyo & Kameoka, 1992). Finally, indigenous coping resources are also used by Asian Americans. For example, the use of traditional folk healers, spiritual identifications, and religious practices such as Buddhism are primary resources for support among Asian American communities.

## THERAPIST VARIABLES

As with client variables, the literature on how therapist variables affect therapy with Asian Americans has been characterized by only a handful of empirical studies. Data suggest that the most preferred therapist characteristics include having similar attitudes, having a similar personality, having more education, and being older than the clients (Atkinson, Wampold, Lowe, Mathews, & Ahn, 1998). Counselors who are culturally responsive are also rated by Asian clients to be more expert, attractive, and trustworthy than those counselors who are not culturally responsive (Zhang & Dixon, 2003). Although not definitive, some studies indicate that cultural differences between therapist and client may result in less effective treatment. These barriers to effective psychotherapy may result from a series of therapist variables such as the therapist's prejudice or cultural bias, training bias, and the therapist's lack of both intercultural skills and culture-specific knowledge about Asian Americans.

## Counselors' Bias

Counselors' bias toward Asian Americans and other ethnic minorities comes from at least two sources: their own cultural and personal backgrounds and their professional training. Beginning with counselors' cultural background, the personal characteristics of most counselors may be in contrast to those of Asian Americans. The cultural bias of counselors toward minority and lower-class groups may also operate against Asian Americans. In a study examining this particular source of bias, the degree of cultural stereotyping among practicing counselors was explored using structured interviews (Bloombaum, Yamamoto, & James, 1968). The results indicated that counselors' attitudes toward Mexican Americans, African Americans, Chinese Americans, Japanese Americans, and Jews reflected the similar degree of cultural stereotyping usually found in the general population. The tendency for counselors to fall prey to cultural stereotyping when working with ethnic minorities is cause for concern. At present, there are some empirical data on the degree to which a counselor's lack of culture-specific knowledge about Asian Americans may act as a barrier to effective counseling, and it has been cited as a potential source of problems (C. P. Chien & Yamamoto, 1982). For example, assuming homogeneity among Asians Americans and stereotyping the clients can compromise the therapeutic process and therapeutic alliance (Berg & Miller, 1992). Counselors should emphasize the importance of being culturally aware and sensitive by attending to influences of their own cultural biases and stereotyping tendencies.

The effect of ethnic identity and identity attribution may also account for some other biases on the part of the therapist. In one study, the effects of client-counselor ethnic match on visitation and counselor evaluation of Asian patients' Global Assessment of Function (GAF) were examined. Results showed that ethnically matched clients attained more positive GAF evaluations and attended more clinic visits than did nonethnically matched patients (Gamst, Dana, Der-Karabetian, & Kramer, 2001). In a similar study, it was found that ethnically matched counselors judged Asian American clients to have higher mental health functioning than did mismatched counselors, even when variables such as age and gender were controlled. Again, counselors need to attend to the potential influences of these cultural biases and vulnerabilities.

Clinicians' lack of intercultural skills and cultural-specific knowledge can also result in Asian American patients not receiving the necessary care. Due to Asian traditions of viewing the body and mind as unitary rather than dualistic, patients tend to focus more on physical discomforts than emotional symptoms, leading to an overrepresentation of somatic complaints. Clinicians may fail to make the connection between the physical symptoms and their potential emotional and psychological sources. In a study that examined the degree to which primary care physicians recognize psychiatric distress among an ethnically diverse primary care sample, the results were cause for concern. While 41.6% of the Asian patients exhibited depressive symptoms indicative of psychiatric distress, only 23.6% of the patients were identified as being distressed by the physicians (Chung et al., 2003). Similarly, Asian Americans' self-reported levels of anxiety and depression are often underestimated by their Euro-American counterparts. The discrepancy of distress levels reported and rated can certainly affect the recognition of distress and service delivery (Okazaki, 2002). Finally, misdiagnosis frequently occurs due to lack of precise correspondence between cultural experiences of distress, the existence of culture-bound syndromes, and established diagnostic measures and categories. All of these issues deem changes in the field of psychology and highlight the need for appropriate resources for clinicians. One example of how the field is taking steps toward greater cultural validity is the emphasis on the cross-cultural applicability of the *Diagnostic and Statistical Manuals of Mental Disorders* (*DSMs*). The recent fourth edition of the *DSM* (*DSM-IV*), published by the American Psychiatric Association (1994), now emphasizes cross-cultural applicability. The *DSM-IV* provides methods to classify culture-bound syndromes within the diagnostic system. The inclusion of culture in the multiaxial assessment and multidimensional classification system is certainly a right step toward enhancing cross-cultural counseling effectiveness.

The professional training received by counselors can be another source of bias in working with Asian Americans. Most counselors are trained with Western models of psychotherapy. Certain characteristics and assumptions inherent in the Western models may conflict with the cultural background of Asian Americans. Such conflicts can become barriers to effective cross-cultural counseling (S. Sue, 1977). The major characteristics of Western models include (1) language variables such as the use of Standard English, (2) class-bound values such as strict adherence to time schedule and unstructured approach to problems, and (3) culture-bound values such as emphasis on the individual (as opposed to the group or family) and verbal and emotional expressiveness. In light of some of the Asian American characteristics already reviewed (e.g., intolerance of ambiguity), counselors using a Western approach with Asian American clients may run into a considerable amount of resistance (Tseng & McDermott, 1975).

Given that social and cultural variables affect Asian Americans' help-seeking behaviors, experiences of distress, manifestation of symptoms, and therapeutic process and outcome, it is important that training curriculum place emphasis on these variables. Without incorporation of these cultural variables, clinicians would be limited in their ability to implement their learning into care of diverse populations such as their Asian American clients (Lu, Du, Gaw, & Lin, 2002). In essence, training bias tends to operate in the form of using traditional psychotherapeutic procedures acquired from Western-model-based training with culturally different clients without first evaluating if those procedures would be culturally appropriate. One of the notable themes found in the literature is the need to examine the applicability of Western psychotherapy for racial/ethnic diverse groups. There appears to be a consensus that some psychotherapeutic concepts and practices do not fit the needs of racial/ethnic groups (Tseng, 2004). Recent focus has been on the modification of the practice of culturally relevant psychotherapy to meet the needs of racial and ethnic individuals.

# Cultural Competency and Appropriateness of Treatment

For Asian Americans, appropriateness of psychotherapy approaches is influenced by the issues relevant to the Asian cultural context. See Table 7.2 for summary key factors to consider when working with Asian American clients as discussed throughout this chapter. Given the role family plays in the lives of Asian Americans, a large body of literature has focused on how to apply Western family therapy approaches to work with Asian American families (Chao, 2002). Proper respect for the family structure and hierarchy, for example, is said to be crucial when working with Asian families. Clinicians ought to be sensitive to the cultural norm of placing family needs over individual needs as well as the need for facilitation of "saving face" throughout the therapeutic process (E. Y. K. Kim, Bean, & Harper, 2004). Bae and Kung (2000) proposed a five-stage model (i.e., reparation, engagement, psychoeducation, family sessions, and ending) for working with Asian American patients with schizophrenia and their families. The model accounts for the value orientations and cultural characteristics of Asian Americans. Tien and Olson (2003) proposed that when working with Asian American families, service providers should understand a family's Confucian-based philosophical/cultural stance.

**TABLE 7.2**  Key Factors to Consider When Working With Asian American Clients

Adherence to Asian cultural values

Acculturation level

Immigration experience

High-context communication style

Family dynamics and interdependence

Shame proneness

Use of traditional healing methods

Another culturally appropriate approach to psychotherapy includes the "Pa Sook" model of counseling Thai families. *Pa Sook* means well-being, wholeness, peacefulness, and happiness in the Thai language. Such an approach incorporates the traditional cultural values with selected therapeutic constructs to create a foundation for a culturally relevant therapeutic approach (Pinyuchon, Gray, & House, 2003). The *Santo Niño* healing method has been noted in the literature as a traditional healing method followed by many Filipinos and Filipino Americans (Lin, Demonteverde, & Nuccio, 1990). The healing approach consists of a prayer session led by a healer. The focus of synergism between religious healing and modern medicine, as well as the need for service providers to acknowledge indigenous health beliefs, is emphasized. Another example of synergism between religious healing and modern medicine is the Sikh model of the person, suffering, and healing. The Sikh model integrates traditional South Asian healing resources with a Western approach to counseling (Sandhu, 2004). Since Asian Americans' collective notion of the self includes large influences of the family and culture, crisis work with Asian Americans, for example, requires very different treatment strategies than those used in work with Western clients, whose notion of the self is far more individualistic. These examples of cultural-based psychotherapy models signify the critical and necessary movement toward providing culturally appropriate, competent, and valid mental health services.

# SUMMARY AND CONCLUSIONS

As an update to Leong's (1986) review of the literature on counseling Asian Americans, the current chapter highlights the culturally relevant client and therapist variables that shape the counseling relationship. A growing body of psychological research on Asian Americans has demonstrated the ways in which clients' subjective experiences and expressions of distress, openness to formal mental health services, expectations of their provider, therapeutic goals, and interpersonal and communication styles are shaped by culture and context. Specifically, the cultural socialization of many Asian Americans has contributed to the salience of an interpersonal orientation that values interdependence, conformity, emotional self-restraint, humility, and respect for authority. Against this backdrop, it is not surprising that studies have shown that Asian Americans expect their counselors to play the role of an authority figure that provides structured guidance in problem solving. However, individual differences are also important to acknowledge, particularly with regard to how Asian Americans reconcile the conflicting norms and values of their cultures of origin and that of mainstream U.S. society. Individuals who are more culturally identified with Western norms and values may be more responsive to mainstream helping approaches, whereas more traditionally oriented individuals may require culturally modified approaches. Regardless, the literature suggests that the tensions inherent in resolving different cultural expectations may affect the majority of Asian Americans who often find themselves straddling two (or more) different cultural worlds, often within their own families.

As highlighted in the present chapter, the worldview of a traditional Asian American client may differ quite dramatically from that of a Euro-American therapist or a therapist of color who has been trained primarily in Western models of psychotherapy. The greater the cultural distance between client and therapist, the greater the potential for inaccurate assessment of the presenting problem and difficulties in establishing a strong working relationship. These interpersonal barriers are thought to contribute to the tendency of Asian Americans to underutilize mental health services and to prematurely terminate treatment once it is initiated. Specifically, counselors' lack of culture-specific knowledge and susceptibility to popular ethnic stereotypes has been linked to inaccurate assessment and misdiagnosis.

Because many Asian Americans are hesitant to seek formal mental health services, the individual who does find himself or herself in the counselor's office may be particularly sensitive to therapists' failure to meet their help-seeking expectations. By now, there is convergent evidence that Asian Americans as a whole tend to favor more structured and problem-focused interventions over more unstructured, exploratory approaches. The good news is that modifications of mainstream therapeutic approaches as well as culturally grounded interventions are being developed to complement traditional Asian American clients' cultural values and illness constructs. Therapists working with predominantly with Asian clients may seek training in newly developed, culturally grounded approaches that respect the hierarchical structure of traditional Asian families and integrate religious healing rituals with psychological interventions.

Therapists who are sensitive to the acculturative stressors faced by recent immigrants and their children may also achieve greater credibility due to their ability to empathize and recommend specific coping strategies. In addition, awareness of the cultural roots of traits such as modesty, conformity, and emotional self-control may minimize the risk of overpathologization and improve therapists' ability to connect with their Asian clients.

Finally, given space limitations, the present chapter restricted its coverage to the recent literature on client and therapist variables affecting Asian Americans in counseling and therapy. Readers interested in a review of research studies of the therapy process and outcome involving Asian Americans are referred to Leong et al. (2007).

# Future Directions

Despite the rapid growth of research in Asian American mental health to include children and families, college students, and community members, more research is needed to more fully capture the cultural diversity of the Asian American community. As discussed, the field is showing favorable signs of representing the complexity of the Asian American identity by exploring how racial and ethnic identity, generational status, and gender interact to shape mental health and mental health care. However, an increasing number of investigators are now examining how status variables such as sexual orientation, religion, and social class also contribute to Asian Americans' sense of well-being and help-seeking behavior. Another exciting development is that the field is also now moving beyond studies of individual-level acculturation to capturing the processes by which families and communities change as a result of exposure to diverse cultural systems. This is an important new research area given the bidirectional nature of acculturation; immigration flows are dramatically changing the social and cultural landscape of American society just as immigrants themselves are changed in the resettlement process. Finally, in light of recent efforts to develop clinical training models that are flexible enough to address the needs of diverse client populations, empirical studies are needed to examine the effects of such curricula on therapists' ability to effectively meet the needs of their Asian American clients.

## CRITICAL INCIDENT

### Failing a Course

Simon Ho is a 19-year-old Chinese American sophomore attending a midwestern university. He has a good academic record with a 3.25 grade point average, but he is having difficulty understanding various concepts in his advanced chemistry class. With a big exam approaching, Simon is not only increasingly worried but is also experiencing headaches and stomach troubles. Fearing the possibility of failing the exam and disappointing his family, Simon decided to seek assistance from his chemistry professor. Upon seeking assistance from his chemistry professor, he is greeted happily and courteously. His professor spent over an hour reviewing some of the material with him. From this review with his professor, Simon felt a bit more confident about his understanding of the concepts. Unfortunately, Simon received a D on the exam. Disappointed by his poor performance, he begins to skip class to avoid his professor and never seeks his professor's assistance again.

## DISCUSSION QUESTIONS

1. Why did Simon not ask his professor for further assistance or guidance? Choose the best answer:
   a. Simon thought that the professor would have written on the test that it was necessary to see him, if he really cared.
   b. Simon felt that chemistry was no longer important in his life.
   c. Simon was too ashamed to see his professor again.
   d. Simon was upset with his professor for not reviewing the necessary material with him.

2. How might Simon's cultural context help to explain the headaches and stomach troubles he experienced? *psychosomatic symptoms*

3. What other cultural factors could also account for Simon's experience?

# REFERENCES

Abe, J. S., & Zane, N. W. (1990). Psychological maladjustment among Asian and White American college students: Controlling for confounds. *Journal of Counseling Psychology, 37*(4), 437–444.

Akutsu, P. D., Snowden, L. R., & Organista, K. C. (1996). Referral patterns in ethnic-specific and mainstream programs for ethnic minorities and Whites. *Journal of Counseling Psychology, 43*(1), 56–64.

American Psychiatric Association. (1994). *Diagnostic and statistical manual of mental disorders* (4th ed.). Washington, DC: Author.

Arkoff, A., Thaver, F., & Elkind, L. (1966). Mental health and counseling ideas of Asian and American students. *Journal of Counseling Psychology, 13*(2), 219–223.

Atkinson, D. R., & Gim, R. H. (1989). Asian-American cultural identity and attitudes toward mental health services. *Journal of Counseling Psychology, 36*(2), 209–212.

Atkinson, D. R., Wampold, B. E., Lowe, S. M., Matthews, L., & Ahn, H. (1998). Asian American preferences for counselor characteristics: Application of the Bradley-Terry-Luce model to paired comparison data. *Counseling Psychologist, 26*(1), 101–123.

Bae, S. W., & Kung, W. W. M. (2000). Family intervention for Asian Americans with a schizophrenic patient in the family. *American Journal of Orthopsychiatry, 70*(4), 532–541.

Berg, I. K., & Jaya, A. (1993). Different and same: Family therapy with Asian-American families. *Journal of Marital and Family Therapy, 19*(1), 31–38.

Berg, I. K., & Miller, S. D. (1992). Working with Asian American clients: One person at a time. *Families in Society, 73*(6), 356–363.

Bloombaum, M., Yamamoto, J., & James, Q. (1968). Cultural stereotyping among psychocounselors. *Journal of Consulting and Clinical Psychology, 32*(1), 99.

Castro, J. R., & Rice, K. G. (2003). Perfectionism and ethnicity: Implications for depressive symptoms and self-reported academic achievement. *Cultural Diversity and Ethnic Minority Psychology, 9*(1), 64–78.

Chan, S. (1992). Families with Asian roots. In E. W. Lynch & M. J. Hanson (Eds.), *Developing cross-cultural competence* (pp. 181–257). Baltimore: Paul H. Brookes.

Chang, E. C. (2001). Cultural influences on optimism and pessimism: Differences in Western and Eastern construals of the self. In E. C. Chang (Ed.), *Optimism & pessimism: Implications for theory, research, and practice* (pp. 257–280). Washington, DC: American Psychological Association.

Chao, C. M. (2002). The central role of culture: Working with Asian children and families. In F. W. Kaslow (Ed.), *Comprehensive handbook of psychotherapy: Interpersonal/humanistic/existential* (Vol. 3, pp. 35–58). New York: John Wiley.

Chen, H. J., Mallinckrodt, B., & Mobley, M. (2002). Attachment patterns of East Asian international students and sources of perceived social support as moderators of the impact of U.S. racism and cultural distress. *Asian Journal of Counseling, 9*(1–2), 27–48.

Cheryan, S., & Tsai, J. (2007). Ethnic identity. In F. T. L. Leong, A. Inman, A. Ebreo, L. Yang, L. Kinoshita, & M. Fu (Eds.), *Handbook of Asian American psychology* (2nd ed., pp. 125–139). Thousand Oaks, CA: Sage.

Cheung, F. K. (1980). The mental health status of Asian Americans. *Clinical Psychologist, 34*(1), 23–24.

Chien, C. P., & Yamamoto, J. (1982). Asian-American and Pacific-Islander patients. In F. X. Acosta, J. Yamamoto, & L. A. Evans (Eds.), *Effective psychotherapy for low-income and minority patients* (pp. 117–145). New York: Plenum.

Chien, W. W., & Banerjee L. (2002). Caught between cultures: The young Asian American in therapy. In E. Davis Russell (Ed.), *The California School of Professional Psychology handbook of multicultural education, research, intervention, and training* (pp. 210–220). San Francisco: Jossey-Bass.

Chung, H., Teresi, J., Guarnaccia, P., Meyers, B., Holmes, D., Bobrowitz, T., et al. (2003). Depressive symptoms and psychiatric distress in low income Asian and Latino primary care patients: Prevalence and recognition. *Community Mental Health Journal, 39*(1), 33–46.

Cimmarusti, R. A. (1996). Exploring aspects of Filipino-American families. *Journal of Marital and Family Therapy, 22*(2), 205–217.

Connor, J. W. (1974). Acculturation and family continuities in three generations of Japanese-Americans. *Journal of Marriage and the Family, 36,* 159–165.

Exum, H. A., & Lau, E. Y. (1988). Counseling style preference of Chinese college students. *Journal of Multicultural Counseling and Development, 16*(2), 84–92.

Fong, S. L. M. (1973). Assimilation and changing social roles of Chinese-Americans. *Journal of Social Issues, 29,* 115–127.

Gamst, G., Dana, R. H., Der-Karabetian, A., & Kramer, T. (2001). Asian American mental health clients: Effects of ethnic match and age on global assessment and visitation. *Journal of Mental Health Counseling, 23*(1), 57–71.

Gim, R. H., Atkinson, D. R., & Whiteley, S. (1990). Asian-American acculturation, severity of concerns, and willingness to see a counselor. *Journal of Counseling Psychology, 37*(3), 281–285.

Hardin, E. E., Leong, F. T. L., & Osipow, S. H. (2001). Cultural relativity in the conceptualization of career maturity. *Journal of Vocational Behavior, 58*(1), 36–52.

Kim, B. S. K., Brenner, B. R., Liang, C. T. H., & Asay, P. A. (2003). A qualitative study of adaptation experiences of 1.5-generation Asian Americans. *Cultural Diversity and Ethnic Minority Psychology, 9*(2), 156–170.

Kim, E. Y. K., Bean, R. A., & Harper, J. M. (2004). Do general treatment guidelines for Asian American families have applications to specific ethnic groups? The case of culturally-competent therapy with Korean Americans. *Journal of Marital and Family Therapy, 30*(3), 359–372.

Kim, H., & Chung, R. H. (2003). Relationship of recalled parenting style to self-perception in Korean American college students. *Journal of Genetic Psychology, 164*(4), 481–492.

Kim, J. M. (2003). Structural family therapy and its implications for the Asian American family. *Family Journal Counseling and Therapy for Couples and Families, 11*(4), 388–392.

Kleinman, A., & Sung, L. H. (1979). Why do indigenous practitioners successfully heal? *Social Science & Medicine, 13B*(1), 7–26.

Leong, F. T. L. (1986). Counseling and psychotherapy with Asian-Americans: Review of the literature. *Journal of Counseling Psychology, 33*(2), 196–206.

Leong, F. T. L., Chang, D., & Lee, S. H. (2007). Counseling and psychotherapy with Asian Americans: Process and outcomes. In F. T. L. Leong, A. Inman, A. Ebreo, L. Yang, L. Kinoshita, & M. Fu (Eds.), *Handbook of Asian American psychology* (2nd ed., pp. 429–447). Thousand Oaks, CA: Sage.

Leong, F. T. L., & Lau, A. S. L. (2001). Barriers to providing effective mental health services to Asian Americans. *Mental Health Services Research, 3*(4), 201–214.

Lim, S. L., & Lim, B. K. (2004). Parenting style and child outcomes in Chinese and immigrant Chinese families: Current findings and cross-cultural considerations in conceptualization and research. *Marriage and Family Review, 35*(3–4), 21–43.

Lin, K. M., Demonteverde, L., & Nuccio, I. (1990). Religion, healing, and mental health among Filipino Americans. *International Journal of Mental Health, 19*(3), 40–44.

Lu, F. G., Du, N., Gaw, A., & Lin, K. M. (2002). A psychiatric residency curriculum about Asian-American issues. *Academic Psychiatry, 26*(4), 225–236.

Marcos, L. R. (1979). Effects of interpreters on the evaluation of psychopathology in non-English-speaking patients. *American Journal of Psychiatry, 136*(2), 171–174.

Mau, W. C., & Jepson, D. A. (1990). Help-seeking perceptions and behaviors: A comparison of Chinese and American graduate students. *Journal of Multicultural Counseling and Development, 18*(2), 9–104.

Narikiyo, T. A., & Kameoka, V. A. (1992). Attributions of mental illness and judgments about help seeking among Japanese-American and White American students. *Journal of Counseling Psychology, 39*(3), 363–369.

Okazaki, S. (2002). Self-other agreement on affective distress scales in Asian Americans and White Americans. *Journal of Counseling Psychology, 49*(4), 428–437.

Pinyuchon, M., Gray, L. A., & House, R. M. (2003). The Pa Sook model of counseling Thai families: A culturally mindful approach. *Journal of Family Psychotherapy, 14*(3), 67–93.

Sandhu, J. S. (2004). The Sikh model of the person, suffering, and healing: Implications for counselors. *International Journal for the Advancement of Counseling, 26*(1), 33–46.

Solberg, V. S., Choi, K. H., Ritsma, S., & Jolly, A. (1994). Asian-American college students: It is time to reach out. *Journal of College Student Development, 35*(4), 296–301.

Sue, D. (1998). The interplay of sociocultural factors on the psychological development of Asians in America. In G. Morten & D. R. Atkinson (Eds.), *Counseling American minorities* (5th ed., pp. 205–213). New York: McGraw-Hill.

Sue, D. (2001). Asian American masculinity and therapy: The concept of masculinity in Asian American males. In G. E. Good & G. R. Brooks (Eds.), *The new handbook of psychotherapy and counseling with men: A comprehensive guide to settings, problems, and treatment approaches* (Vols. 1 & 2, pp. 780–795). San Francisco: Jossey-Bass.

Sue, D. W., & Kirk, B. A. (1973). Differential characteristics of Japanese-American and Chinese-American college students. *Journal of Counseling Psychology, 20*(2), 142–148.

Sue, D. W., & Sue, S. (1972). Counseling Chinese-Americans. *Personnel & Guidance Journal, 50,* 637–644.

Sue, S. (1977). Psychological theory and implications for Asian Americans. *Personnel & Guidance Journal, 55*(7), 381–389.

Sue, S. (1981). Programmatic issues in the training of Asian-American psychologists. *Journal of Community Psychology, 9*(4), 293–297.

Takeuchi, D. T., Mokuau, N., & Chun, C. A. (1992). Mental health services for Asian Americans and Pacific Islanders. *Journal of Mental Health Administration, 19*(3), 237–245.

Tamura, T., & Lau, A. (1992). Connectedness versus separateness: Applicability of family therapy to Japanese families. *Family Process, 31*(4), 319–340.

Tan, H. (1967). Intercultural study of counseling expectancies. *Journal of Counseling Psychology, 14*(2), 122–130.

Tang, M. (2002). A comparison of Asian American, Caucasian American, and Chinese college students: An initial report. *Journal of Multicultural Counseling and Development, 30*(2), 124–134.

Tien, L., & Olson, K. (2003). Confucian past conflicted present: Working with Asian American families. In T. J. Goodrich, L. B. Silverstein, & B. Louise (Eds.), *Feminist family therapy: Empowerment in social context* (pp. 135–145). Washington, DC: American Psychological Association.

True, R. H. (1990). Psychotherapeutic issues with Asian American women. *Sex Roles, 22*(7–8), 477–486.

Tseng, W. S. (2004). Culture and psychotherapy: Asian perspectives. *Journal of Mental Health, 13*(2), 151–161.

Tseng, W. S., & McDermott, J. F. (1975). Psychotherapy: Historical roots, universal elements, and cultural variations. *American Journal of Psychiatry, 132*(4), 378–384.

Wellisch, D., Kagawa-Singer, M., Reid, S. L., Lin, Y. J., Nishikawa-Lee, S., & Wellisch, M. (1999). An exploratory study of social support: A cross-cultural comparison of Chinese-, Japanese-, and Anglo-American breast cancer patients. *Psycho Oncology, 8*(3), 207–219.

Yeh, C., & Huang, K. (1996). The collectivistic nature of ethnic identity development among Asian-American college students. *Adolescence, 31*(123), 645–661.

Yeh, C., & Wang, Y. W. (2000). Asian American coping attitudes, sources, and practices: Implications for indigenous counseling strategies. *Journal of College Student Development, 41*(1), 94–103.

Yeh, C. J. (2003). Age, acculturation, cultural adjustment, and mental health symptoms of Chinese, Korean, and Japanese immigrant youths. *Cultural Diversity and Ethnic Minority Psychology, 9*(1), 34–48.

Yeh, C. J., Carter, R. T., & Pieterse, A. L. (2004). Cultural values and racial identity attitudes among Asian American students: An exploratory investigation. *Counseling and Values, 48*(2), 82–95.

Yep, G. A. (2000). Explaining illness to Asian and Pacific Islander Americans: Culture, communication, and boundary regulation. In B. B. Whaley (Ed.), *Explaining illness: Research, theory, and strategies* (pp. 283–297). Mahwah, NJ: Lawrence Erlbaum.

Zane, N., & Yeh, M. (2002). The use of culturally-based variables in assessment: Studies on loss of face. In K. S. Kurasaki, S. Okazaki, & S. Sue (Eds.), *Asian American mental health: Assessment theories and methods* (pp. 123–138). New York: Kluwer Academic/Plenum.

Zhang, N., & Dixon, D. N. (2003). Acculturation and attitudes of Asian international students toward seeking psychological help. *Journal of Multicultural Counseling and Development, 31*(3), 205–222.

CHAPTER 8

# ¡Adelante!

## Counseling the Latina/o From Guiding Theory to Practice

J. Manuel Casas, Jason Duque Raley, and Melba J. T. Vasquez

### Primary Objective

- To assist counselors and therapists in becoming more competent in their efforts to work with persons who are ethnically, racially, and/or culturally different from themselves, particularly those identified as Latina/o[1]

### Secondary Objectives

- To provide a demographic overview of the diverse Latina/o population in the United States
- To provide the outlines of a theoretical approach that would unify theories of person, environment, and the counseling situation
- To present a framework that counselors can use to direct and drive their work with Latina/o clients, including identifying likely sources of both friction and possibility

ETHNIC AND LINGUISTIC DIVERSITY IS A FACT OF LIFE IN THE UNITED STATES. ETHNIC MINORITY (I.E., NON-WHITE) persons represent 28.6% of the population, and counselors and therapists, whether nonminority or minority, are now more than ever confronted with having to work with persons who are culturally different from themselves. Faced with these facts, the counseling profession has demonstrated an increased commitment to multicultural issues and multicultural training.

This is most evident in the efforts to make individual differences and diversity an integral part of the training program accreditation process (Heppner, Casas, Carter, & Stone, 2000). Specifically, the American Psychological Association Council approved revised *Guidelines and Principles in Professional Psychology,* which called for training programs to make "systematic, coherent and long-term efforts to attract and retain students and faculty from differing ethnic, racial, and personal backgrounds . . . and implement a coherent plan to provide students with relevant knowledge and experience about the role of cultural and individual diversity in psychological phenomena and professional practice" (APA, Office of Program Consultation and Accreditation, 1996, p. 8). Although these efforts have paid off in a variety of ways, including increased multiculturally focused research and publications, there still exists a significant need to better prepare counselors to work with diverse multicultural individuals (see Casas, Pavelski, Furlong, & Zanglis, 2001; Ponterotto, Casas, Suzuki, & Alexander, 1995, 2001). With this in mind, this chapter is aimed at helping counselors and therapists become more competent in their efforts to understand and work with Latina/o clients. In the first section, we provide a demographic overview of Latinas/os in the United States, giving special attention to the diversity that exists within this population. We then outline a theoretical basis for understanding the challenges of counseling Latinas/os. A third section details a framework that counselors and therapists can use to direct and drive their work with Latina/o clients.

## ATTRIBUTES AND TRENDS FOR LATINAS/OS IN THE UNITED STATES

### General Attributes and Trends

According to the 2000 census, Latinas/os number 35.3 million, or almost 13% of the U.S. population (U.S. Bureau of the Census, 2001). A comparison of the statistics obtained in the 1990 census with those obtained in 2000 shows that Latinas/os are the fastest growing racial/ethnic group in the United States. During this 10-year period, the total U.S. population grew at a rate of 13.2%, while the Latina/o population grew at the much higher rate of 58% (U.S. Bureau of the Census, 2000c, 2001). Although this growth rate is impressive enough, it is worth remembering that census procedures may exclude many, if not most, undocumented Latinas/os. Even the most comprehensive statistics may significantly underestimate the true size of this population. Regardless of the accuracy of the census count, the trend is clear: The Latina/o population is growing rapidly and will likely continue to grow (U.S. Bureau of the Census, 2000a).

Besides the continuing flow of immigrants from Mexico, Central and South America, and the Caribbean, two other phenomena are largely expected to account for this growth: the relative youth of the U.S. Latina/o population in general and the prevalence of high birthrates among several Latina/o subgroups (e.g., Mexican American and Puerto Rican). The youth of this population is underscored by the fact that in 1999, Hispanics younger than age 21 represented 41.1% of the total Hispanic population. By comparison, only 27.6% of non-Hispanic Whites were younger than age 21 (U.S. Bureau of the Census, 2000b). The fertility rate of Latinas as a whole is 53% greater than the rate among non-Latinas.

### Educational and Economic Well-Being

Although their numbers are growing, Latinas/os remain among the least formally educated and least economically successful Americans. The number of Latinas/os graduating from high school has increased very little since 1970 (U.S. Department of Education, 2000), and Latinas/os continue to drop out of high school at rates that are higher than those of any other major group in the United States (Kaufman, Kwon, Klein, & Chapman, 2000). A substantial number of Latinas/os who drop out of school do so before high school, a distinction that may challenge the economic development of the Latina/o population. Needless to say, the low rates of high school completion also continue to hinder Latina/o progress toward college (Carter & Wilson, 1991).

Of course, the reality will always be more complex than such statistical correlations permit. For example, we know with certainty that the composition of the group we call "Latina/o" or "Hispanic" evolves in response to patterns of migration into and out of the United States. Recent research confirms that foreign-born youth are significant contributors to the nation's school dropout population. According to a Pew Hispanic Center analysis of data from the 2000 U.S. census, only 8% of the nation's teens are foreign born, but nearly 25% of teen school dropouts were born outside the United States (Fry, 2005).

Insofar as occupational, economic, and educational levels are symbols of status and power in the United States, we feel justified in our worry that the well-being, image, and identity of Latinas/os may be at considerable risk (McNeill et al., 2001). These facts and others argue for continued attention to the educational and economic experience of Latinas/os.

## Sociocultural Common Ground

Besides the common shared experience of Spanish as a heritage language, Latinas/os may also share the following: a close-knit sense of family within a hierarchical structure; *personalismo,* a very intense sense of privacy and protectiveness; a profound religious faith; a powerful notion of pride and regionalism; a strong sense of moral righteousness accompanied by a personal sense of guilt or shame; and a high degree of emotional expressiveness (Alarcón, 2001, p. 7–8). Although much more could be said about these and other characteristics, they are only briefly mentioned here for illustrative purposes. For more details regarding these characteristics, see Diaz-Loving and Draguns (1999). In line with the theoretical model presented herein that focuses on the uniqueness and complexity of culturally embedded individuals, readers are cautioned to avoid indiscriminately ascribing these characteristics to all Latinas/os.

Although some of these characteristics have been validated by means of contemporary, flexible, and complex research designs, others await such scrutiny (Diaz-Loving & Draguns, 1999).

## Diversity Within the Latina/o Population

Working from the perspective that the strength of the Hispanic population lies in its diversity, this section directs attention to selective variables that contribute to such diversity. To begin with, although the individuals who make up the Latina/o population in the United States share a strong sociocultural, linguistic, and historical background, the large group referred to as Latina/o is made up of diverse groups that are often defined along ethnic, national, or cultural lines. These include Mexican Americans, Puerto Ricans, and Cuban Americans, as well as persons with roots in one of the Central American (i.e., Guatemala, Honduras, Costa Rica, El Salvador, Nicaragua, Panama), South American (i.e., Colombia, Venezuela, Peru, Chile, Ecuador, Uruguay, Paraguay, Argentina), or Caribbean (e.g., Cuba, the Dominican Republic) countries.

Although the term *Latina/o* is meant to describe persons from any of the diverse groups noted above, most of the information on Latinas/os in the United States deals with the three largest single national groups within the U.S. Latina/o population: Mexican Americans, Puerto Ricans, and Cuban Americans. Latinas/os of Mexican origin are clearly the largest national subgroup, accounting for 66.1% of the total Hispanic population. They are followed by Central and South Americans, 14.5%; Puerto Ricans, 9.0%; Cubans, 4.0%; and "other Hispanics," who listed census identification labels such as *Spanish, Spanish American,* and *Latino,* 6.4% (this group includes many Latinas/os, probably of Mexican origin, from the Southwest, especially New Mexico).

Race may also be used by Latinas/os and others to distinguish among different persons and groups. It is important to understand that the Latina/o population is made up of persons who fall into many racial categories (Caucasian, Mongoloid, Negroid, or some combination); furthermore, each country may have its own customary ways of drawing or reinforcing racial categories. Race also has a major impact on the life experiences and stressors that Latinas/os encounter in the United States (e.g., the way that they are treated or accepted by non-Hispanic Whites, African Americans, etc.).

Latinas/os may also vary in other ways. These may include demographic variations (e.g., mean and median age, family size and composition, geographic distribution), variations in sociohistorical experience (e.g., length of time in the United States, impetus for immigration to the United States, experiences with racism), political and social experience (e.g., immigrant/citizen status, level of political participation), socioeconomic status (e.g., educational attainment, labor force participation, individual and family income), or sociopsychological matters (e.g., acculturation level, actual and perceived power and self-entitlement, and intragroup similarity and cohesion). It is important to note that as Latina/o individuals and groups vary according to these nonexclusive and frequently interacting variables, they concomitantly vary with respect to the level of vulnerability to social and psychological risks. Gender also appears to matter. Latinas have a higher proportion of school enrollment relative to Latinos. In fact, Latinas earn three of every five baccalaureate degrees awarded to Latinas/os in all fields (American Association for the Advancement of Science, 2000). However, Ginorio and Huston (2000) found that Latinas have higher high school dropout rates than do girls and young women in any other racial or ethnic group and are the least likely to earn a college degree. In comparison with other groups, there is some evidence that Latinas in general, and Mexican American women in particular, fare less well across diverse socioeconomic variables (Chacon, Cohen, Camarena, Gonzalez, & Strover, 1985).

Although the Latina/o population is growing at a much more rapid rate than its non-Hispanic White counterpart, not all of the Hispanic subgroups are growing at the same rate. For instance, between 1990 and 2000, the population growth was 54% for Mexicans, 30% for Cubans, and 15% for Puerto Ricans. During this same period, the subgroups designated as "other Hispanics" grew significantly (Ramirez, 2000).

Numbers of births increased 3% to 4% for Mexican, Cuban, and Puerto Rican women in 1998, but subgroup differences existed with respect to fertility rates. In 1998, the U.S. fertility rate was 65 births per 1,000 women ages 15 to 44 years. Mexican and Puerto Rican female subgroups had the highest fertility rates, 112.1 and 75.5, respectively; Cubans had the lowest fertility rate at 50.1, which, incidentally, is even lower than the fertility rate for non-Hispanic Whites (57.7) (Ventura, Martin, Curtin, Matthews, & Park, 2000).

## THEORY OF PERSON AND ENVIRONMENT

We now direct attention to a theory of the person and his or her environment, striving especially to represent the complexity of the environment and the interdependence of any person's multiple psychological contexts. Ezequiel A. Chavez (1901), considered to be the first Mexican psychologist, warned that not paying attention to culture "can only produce a distorted and misleading understanding of human conduct" (Diaz-Loving & Draguns, 1999, p. 104). With a self-conscious nod to Chavez, we strive to represent the ubiquitous influence of culture in our emerging theory of the person.

We are wary of treating the "environment" as if it were a collection of independent influences acting upon individuals. Nor should we look to the individual as an independent actor exerting his or her agency within or upon the environment. Instead, we ought to *begin* with the idea that any individual is embedded in a *life space* comprising an individual in interaction with the environment; the individual and the environment are interdependent and mutually constitutive.

This present thinking rests heavily on the foundations laid by Kurt Lewin (1935, 1936), whose field theory tells us that all psychological events are differentially and interactively dependent on both psychological states and environmental factors. Lewin's famous equation depicted in rough mathematical terms this idea of "life space" as a contention that individual behavior ($B$) is a function ($f$) of the individual person ($P$) in interaction with the his or her psychological environment ($E$), so $B = f (P, E)$. Lewin also depicted the ($P, E$) part of his equation as in Figure 8.1.

This ($P, E$) graphic is, for us, the minimal unit of analysis for understanding the psychology of any person, including Latina/o persons.

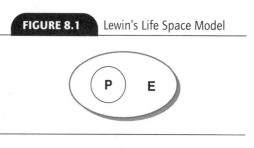

**FIGURE 8.1** Lewin's Life Space Model

The reality is, of course, always more complicated than formulas and figures can represent. Individuals live and grow within and across *multiple* environments. In describing his theory of the ecology of human development, Bronfenbrenner (1977) described the "progressive, mutual accommodation, throughout the life span, between a growing human organism and the environments in which it lives" (p. 514). Noting the self-evident fact that people interact with different environments over a life span and even over the course of a single day, Bronfenbrenner goes on to describe the various levels of systems and structures that make up these environments. These include a hierarchy of the following: the *microsystem,* consisting of the immediate physical setting and its collection of individual actors; the *mesosystem,* comprising the interrelations among settings; the *exosystem,* an extension of the mesosystem "embracing other specific social structures, both formal and informal . . . that impinge upon or encompass the [individual's] immediate settings"; and a *macrosystem,* which includes the overarching patterns of the culture or subculture (p. 515). Working from the foundation laid by Bronfenbrenner, we suggest that these various systems be understood as levels of *context,* preliminarily defined as follows:

a. *interpersonal* contexts, including both the number and quality of relationships, as well as the more immediate contexts built up of ongoing, emergent interactions;

b. *social* contexts, where individuals must manage their lives in multiple social systems (cf. Hartup, 1979, for a discussion of the interrelated peer, family, and school "social worlds" of children) and networks;

c. *institutional* contexts, including schools, local governments, and the maze of everyday bureaucracies; and

d. *economic* and *political* contexts, where one's place in the larger economic system and relative access to resources are deeply consequential.

The *interdependent relationships* among these contexts are more important than their independent influences on individual behavior and experience. While we may consider them separately in many phases of our research and practice, we must keep in mind that these contexts never, in fact, *exist* independently of each other.

Figure 8.2 offers one way of depicting this multiple, overlapping environments.

We hope to capture the following points in our graphic/visual representation. First, the individual person still rests at the center of the drawing, and he or she is always already embedded in a set of contexts. These contexts are as nested circles, all of which share a side. By presenting these circles as sharing a side, we intend to convey our understanding that contexts are mutually constituted, as parts of each other.

What about *culture?* We presume that any individual is continuously *situated in culture* (personal, local, global, etc.). This "cultural situatedness" of person and mind means that a person's individual history as a member of various ethnic, linguistic, national, class, or other groups always colors a person's experience within and across multiple contexts and, most important, the way those various contexts are interdependent. Where is culture in our picture?

Although the black-and-white illustration can never show it, culture would be much like the shifting color of the lines and figures—always present but never separable in any way from the whole.

For the purposes of this book and chapter, the theory we have outlined already requires elaboration: How might we think of these persons-in-environments within a *counseling* frame? A person experiences these environments in the dynamic ebb and flow of everyday life, in relations with other persons, and in practical efforts to get things done. Said another way, these person-environment relations are only ever *potential* and must be *activated* and *reconstructed* and *transformed* in real-life situations. Whichever person-environment relations or experiences are immediately relevant depend on the dynamic, unfolding situation in which the person finds himself or herself. The counseling session is one such situation. This constitutes a move away from an essentializing view of person/personality (e.g., "She is Latina and Latinas experience the world in such and such a way") to a *situated* view.

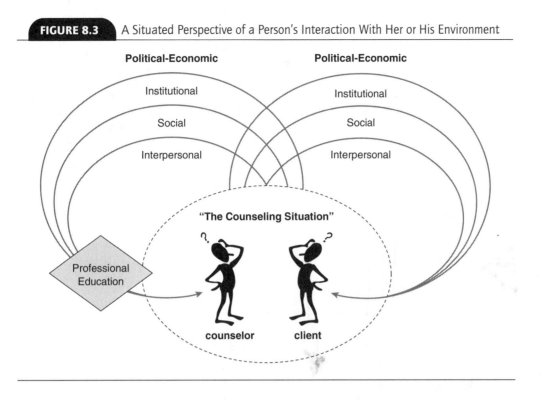

Before proceeding, one feature of the model graphic in Figure 8.3 deserves special notice: the mediating role of *professional education* in the counselor's orientation to the counseling situation. Later in this chapter, we discuss some specific, likely complications that may originate in a counselor's required professional education experience.

## A GUIDING FRAMEWORK FOR COUNSELING PRACTICE

The practice framework we offer here builds on the theoretical approach outlined above, describing in more concrete terms those particular concerns most likely to be relevant to cross-cultural counseling. The framework represents an evolution of thinking from the framework initially proposed by Casas and Vasquez (1989). Figure 8.4 depicts this framework.

We have placed "the counseling situation" at the upper center of the figure, borrowing intentionally from the theory outlined above. On the far-left and far-right sides of the figure, we list a small collection of "person-environment" factors that may influence or be activated in the given counseling situation. Their location at the far edges of the figure reflects our understanding that these person-environment factors are relatively distal to the actual counseling situation. These factors take shape in the counselor's and client's "orientation to the counseling situation." We locate these orientations closer to the situation, as they are relatively proximal.

For both counselor and client, "person-environment factors" and "orientation to the counseling situation" are uniquely and integrally related. The double-sided arrow near the top of these sections is designed to represent this relationship.

As a counselor...
I would establish...

**FIGURE 8.4**  A Framework for Approaching Cross-Cultural Counseling

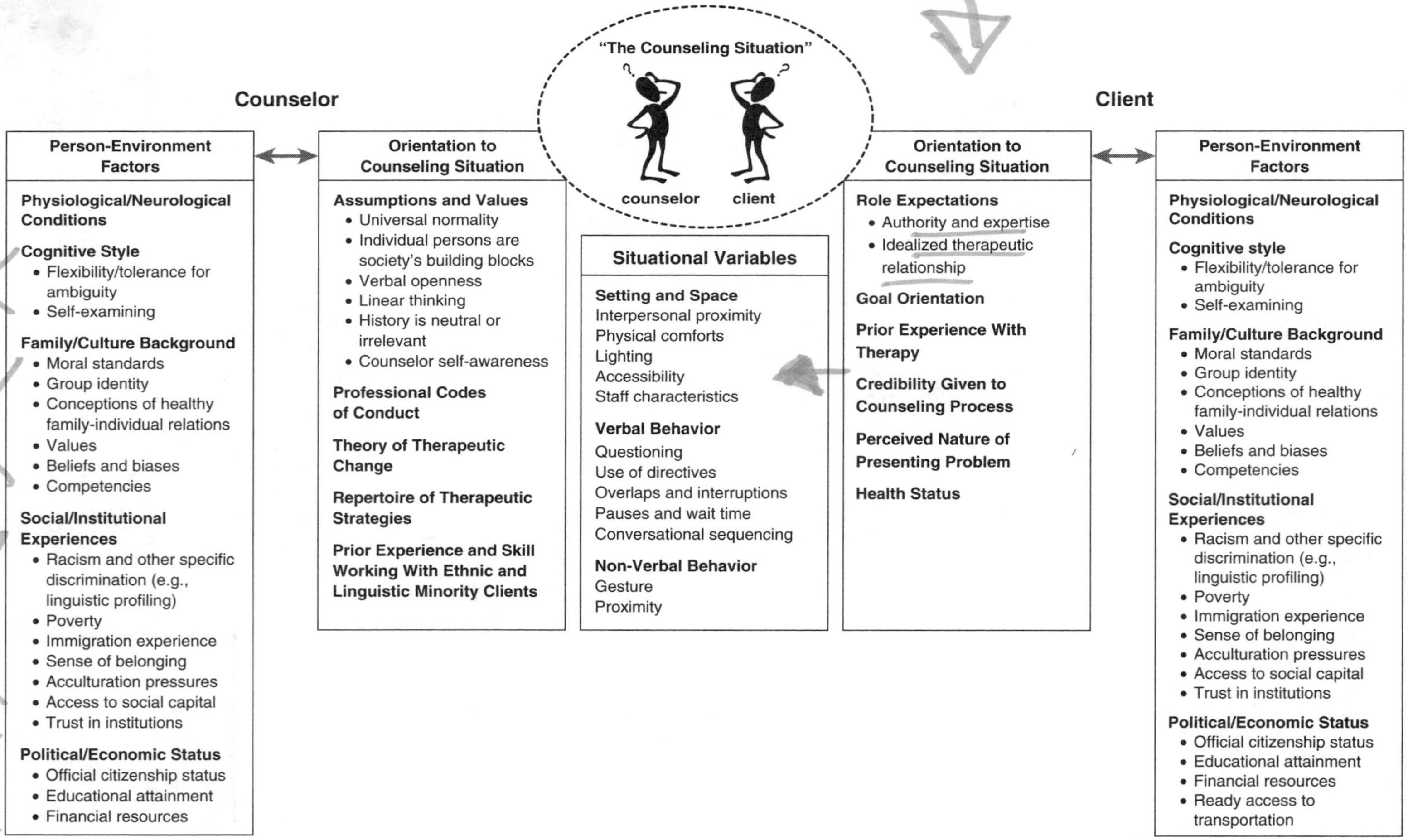

**Counselor**

**Person-Environment Factors**

**Physiological/Neurological Conditions**

**Cognitive Style**
- Flexibility/tolerance for ambiguity
- Self-examining

**Family/Culture Background**
- Moral standards
- Group identity
- Conceptions of healthy family-individual relations
- Values
- Beliefs and biases
- Competencies

**Social/Institutional Experiences**
- Racism and other specific discrimination (e.g., linguistic profiling)
- Poverty
- Immigration experience
- Sense of belonging
- Acculturation pressures
- Access to social capital
- Trust in institutions

**Political/Economic Status**
- Official citizenship status
- Educational attainment
- Financial resources

**Orientation to Counseling Situation**

**Assumptions and Values**
- Universal normality
- Individual persons are society's building blocks
- Verbal openness
- Linear thinking
- History is neutral or irrelevant
- Counselor self-awareness

**Professional Codes of Conduct**

**Theory of Therapeutic Change**

**Repertoire of Therapeutic Strategies**

**Prior Experience and Skill Working With Ethnic and Linguistic Minority Clients**

**"The Counseling Situation"**

counselor    client

**Situational Variables**

**Setting and Space**
- Interpersonal proximity
- Physical comforts
- Lighting
- Accessibility
- Staff characteristics

**Verbal Behavior**
- Questioning
- Use of directives
- Overlaps and interruptions
- Pauses and wait time
- Conversational sequencing

**Non-Verbal Behavior**
- Gesture
- Proximity

**Client**

**Orientation to Counseling Situation**

**Role Expectations**
- Authority and expertise
- Idealized therapeutic relationship

**Goal Orientation**

**Prior Experience With Therapy**

**Credibility Given to Counseling Process**

**Perceived Nature of Presenting Problem**

**Health Status**

**Person-Environment Factors**

**Physiological/Neurological Conditions**

**Cognitive style**
- Flexibility/tolerance for ambiguity
- Self-examining

**Family/Culture Background**
- Moral standards
- Group identity
- Conceptions of healthy family-individual relations
- Values
- Beliefs and biases
- Competencies

**Social/Institutional Experiences**
- Racism and other specific discrimination (e.g., linguistic profiling)
- Poverty
- Immigration experience
- Sense of belonging
- Acculturation pressures
- Access to social capital
- Trust in institutions

**Political/Economic Status**
- Official citizenship status
- Educational attainment
- Financial resources
- Ready access to transportation

Extending below the counseling situation, we have listed as "situational variables" a few of those variables that are undetermined until both counselor and client mutually construct the counseling situation. Although we have been tempted to characterize these variables as "matters within the counselor's control," we realize that *both* counselor *and* client have control over their own behavior. The point, in fact, is not who has control over these variables but that these variables remain *variables* throughout a counseling situation. That is, they *vary* in ways that are responsive to and constructive of the live, unfolding situation.

Although we are convinced of the general usefulness of the framework we propose, we have not provided an exhaustive list of all the person-environment factors that could be relevant to the counseling situation. Nor have we described in detail all the various orientations or identified all possible situational variables. We have only identified those factors and orientations that are most likely to be sources of both friction—positive or negative—and possibility in cross-cultural counseling.

In the sections that follow, we describe in greater detail the orientations of counselor and client as likely sources of friction (and of possibility) for cross-cultural counseling. It is in these descriptions that we draw out specific implications for the counseling of Latinas/os.

## The Counselor

Many counselors believe that theirs is an impartial helping profession in which practitioners relate to the essential humanity in each client (Korchin, 1980). In fact, the practice of counseling in the United States is anything but impartial (Pedersen, 1987; Sue & Sue, 1999). To effectively counsel Latina/o clients, counselors must first become aware of their own professional and personal experiences, orientations, and beliefs and biases that influence their interactions with clients from diverse backgrounds. A common set of values forms the core of the profession—values that may reflect a dominant, White, middle-class, even uniquely U.S. culture. These values are themselves neither good nor bad. But myopic, unquestioning adherence to such values can become problematic for a counselor working with a Latina/o client. Many Latinas/os from diverse backgrounds find these values at odds with their own thinking and experience. A counselor's interpretation of a client's behavior in terms of the counselor's own values rather than those of the client can lead to poor assessment and diagnosis, which can lead in turn to ineffective or even destructive intervention.

In the paragraphs that follow, we describe a few additional value-based sources of potential client-counselor friction rooted in the norms of typical contemporary professional training.

*What counts as "normal" is widely understood and universally accepted.* Many counselors learn to assume a more or less universal definition of "normal" behavior and, furthermore, that this definition is shared by everyone. This assumption can lead counselors to assume that describing a person's behavior as inherently "normal" is meaningful and implies a recognizable pattern of behaviors by the "normal" person. However, what is considered normal is better evaluated and understood within the context of that behavior, including the cultural background(s) of the persons involved, the time during which the behavior is being displayed and observed, and preceding and subsequent actions. Rather than ask if an observed belief or behavior is "normal," we ought to examine the circumstances of that belief or behavior so that we can determine how reasonable and sensible it is.

*Individuals are the building blocks of a society.* Contemporary U.S. culture makes a hero of the independent, self-sufficient person, deliberately freed from the limitations of family, community, and circumstance. Counselors who share this assumption have as a primary goal the development of the individual as an independent person. This assumption works to the detriment of many Latino/as who have learned to give greater importance to the external self, the "other-directed" and interdependent individual (e.g., cultures that put family or other designated social units above the individual), a self that is best understood through its contextual and historical linkages (Cushman, 1992; Pedersen, 1995).

Complementing the high value placed on individualism in traditional counseling theories and practice is the assumption that independence has value and dependence does not. Counselors who attempt to assess the appropriateness of relationships among and between Latina/o clients must consider other possibilities, including the positive health functions served by an individual's reliance on others (Niemann, 2001). More specifically, effective counselors of Latinas/os must understand the value of connecting, supporting, and cooperating within a group.

*Positive change requires verbal openness.* Prevalent among professional counselors is a tendency to equate cooperativeness in counseling and the likelihood of positive change with the client's willingness to be verbally open and direct. In fact, many, if not most, of the world's cultures view the revelation of intimate personal and family details to strangers as highly unacceptable (Sue & Sue, 1999). Although more empirical research is needed to verify the universality of the claim (Prieto, McNeill, Walls, & Gomez, 2001), many Latinas/os prefer to handle their problems discreetly, within the family or within other personal support systems.

*"Right" thinking is logically linear and causal.* Many counselors equate "right" or "good" thinking with linear thinking, where each cause has an effect and each effect a cause. Not all cultures encourage such a style of thinking. According to Pedersen (1987, 1995), some cultures routinely describe events independent of their relationship to any surrounding, preceding, or consequent events. With this in mind, counselors should strive to understand the way their clients *think,* the cultural bases for such thinking, and the relationships among thinking and the client's presenting problem.

*The individual person is the unit of change.* Many counselors understand their duty as changing individuals to better fit society rather than to change society to fit individuals (for details, see Cushman, 1992). Counseling interventions tend to focus on the individual and how the individual should take the initiative to change, regardless of the possibility that the individually experienced problem may have more to do with that person's environment (Sue & Sue, 1999). Latinas/os in the United States experience second-class citizenship, oppression, and discrimination to varying degrees (McNeill et al., 2001). Given the reality of many Latinas/os' sociohistorical experience, the effective counselor may need to assume nontraditional roles to actively validate and support Latina/o clients' efforts to change the environmental factors that prevent them from attaining their personal goals. The alternative may imply colluding with the unhealthy dynamics of oppression and "blaming the victim."

*History is irrelevant; what matters is now.* As Pedersen (1987) has observed, some counselors are most likely to focus on the immediate events that created crises in their clients' lives. When clients begin talking about their own histories or the histories of "their people," such counselors are likely to stop listening and wait for the clients to "catch up" to current events. For many Latinas/os, the past and the present interrelate in such a complex manner that it is impossible for anyone to understand a total individual without also understanding and appreciating his or her sociohistorical experience (McNeill et al., 2001).

*Counselors are aware of their own beliefs and biases.* Some believe that counselors are already aware of the assumptions built into their profession and, moreover, that they already possess all the information and skills necessary for dealing effectively with those assumptions. This is a dangerous and most often plainly false belief. The assumptions, as well as the values that generate them, are so implicit, so deeply rooted in the everyday life of mainstream, majority culture that they may often go unrecognized and unchallenged even by broad-minded and insightful psychologists. The consequences of these assumptions are reflected in institutionalized racism, ageism, sexism, and other forms of cultural bias (Niemann, 2001; Pedersen, 1987).

At this time, given the availability of research, the question is no longer *whether* counselors are personally and professionally encapsulated and biased but *to what degree* and *in what ways* (see Niemann, 2001). Each and every human—including professional counselors—is encapsulated by the values and beliefs of the society and ethnicity that nurtured him or her. An awareness of the profession's cultural encapsulation (Wrenn, 1962) and the negative impact of such encapsulation on the credibility and effectiveness of counselors with minority-group clients should serve as adequate impetus for self-examination by individual counselors and by the profession. Once we accept that axiom, we can turn our attention to generating and implementing professional training and development mechanisms that will help to free us from both personal and professional prejudice as well as enable us to see both the risk and resilience factors that are inherent among all cultural, ethnic, racial, and socioeconomic groups. With such freedom, we will be better situated to develop or identify those theoretically based approaches that may be most appropriate and effective for use with diverse Latino/a clients (see Casas, Vasquez, & Ruiz de Esparza, 2002).

## The Client

The client in a multicultural counseling situation is neither a blank slate nor anything like a "basic" individual person, same as other individuals, with one or more presenting problems. Evidence strongly suggests that an individual's genetic makeup, for example, may determine the likelihood that he or she will develop certain psychological disorders (e.g., depression, anxiety, alcoholism). More to the point of this chapter, every client brings with him or her social cultural characteristics and a trove of experiences in and with multiple, overlapping environments.

Latina/o clients are not solely products of their sociocultural backgrounds, nor are they the mere extrapolations of the statistically derived "average" Latina/o found in the literature. That said, just as there are specific sociohistorical factors that distinguish Latina/o subgroups, there are also unique sociohistorical life factors that differentiate Latinas/os regardless of subgroup. These life factors can play major risk or resilience roles in the psychosocial development and adjustment of each and every Latina/o, as they do for each member of the general population. Such life factors can be as mundane and "normal" as family size, birth order, childhood illnesses, family mobility, family deaths, authoritarian parenting, and family overprotectiveness; they can also be as dramatic and sociopolitically generated as racism, segregation, unequal opportunities for education, unequal access to health and social services, unfair employment (or unemployment) practices, and political disenfranchisement.

Indeed, the unique life experiences of members of ethnic minority groups in the United States have high potential for stressful psychological consequences. As early as 1985, Smith proposed a model of the life stress process for ethnic minorities, identifying the various types of life stresses that these individuals experience, such as outgroup status, social isolation, marginal social status, and status inconsistency. She formulated several hypotheses to describe the situation of members of ethnic minority groups as well as a model for counseling with members of ethnic minority groups. More recently, the U.S. Surgeon General's (1999) report on mental health has underscored this perspective. In the sections that follow, we describe a few of the person-environment factors that are especially relevant to counseling Latinas/os.

*Experience With Racism.* When the client is a member of an ethnic or linguistic minority group, she or he is likely to have had some personal experience with racism or other forms of discrimination. For Latinas/os in particular, experience with linguistic discrimination or "linguistic profiling" (Baugh, 2003) may be as common as discrimination on the basis of race or class. Personal experience is often but need not be firsthand experience; the stories a person hears from family and other minority group members can build a sense of an experienced history that includes shared—and therefore *personal*—instances of discrimination. Frequently, these experiences are formative for the client, carried forward as personal orientations to everyday encounters.

*Acculturation Pressures.* Acculturation is a major variable that contributes to the dynamic, ever-changing nature of the Latina/o population. In its original and still quite acceptable definition, acculturation refers to the phenomena that result when groups of individuals from different cultures come into continuous firsthand contact and experience subsequent changes in the original patterns of either or both groups (Redfield, Linton, & Herskovits, 1936). Although originally perceived from the perspective of the group, acculturation occurs both in groups and in individuals.

Recent studies have identified four facets of acculturation: (1) It is not simple and unidirectional; (2) its direction can be reversed; (3) its rate can be halted, slowed, or accelerated; and (4) it can have an orthogonal nature (Oetting & Beauvais, 1991). That is to say, identification with any culture, in this case an identifiable Latina/o culture, is essentially independent of identification with any other culture (e.g., the dominant culture in the United States). (For thorough coverage of the acculturation process from a psychological perspective, see Berry, 1990; Casas & Casas, 1994.)

First of all, a variety of factors determine the direction and rate of acculturation, as well as the pressures an individual person may experience as a result of acculturation processes. Among these are contextual changes in the racial or ethnic demographics of a community or region, proximity to their native homeland, prevailing sociopolitical attitudes and policies (e.g., segregation), economic conditions and practices (e.g., means and opportunities for improving employment and economic status), and access to high-quality, advanced education. According to Kurtines and Szapocznik (1996; Szapocznik & Kurtines, 1980), differentially available opportunities and the continued prevalence of traditionally prescribed gender roles cause acculturation rates to vary by generation and gender. The rate is faster for younger generations.

Acculturation pressure can be a risk factor when it occurs in an environment that lacks relevant support networks among family, teachers, friends, and counselors; it can and often does create conflict, stress, and loss of self-esteem as the individual struggles with an inevitable clash of values. When acculturation pressures confront especially strong ethnic identification, a person's mental health may be put at increased risk. In relation to resilience, other researchers contend that, with support from significant others, an individual's choice to maintain important aspects of his or her sociocultural background can create a "healthy, aware" individual who can function effectively across cultures and settings (see, e.g., Elliott, 2000).

*Role Expectations.* Every client enters the counseling situation with expectations about the roles she or he and the counselor might take up. These relations are often organized around questions of authority and trust. For many, the mere act of sitting down with a counselor involves handing over an uncomfortable level of authority for one's own well-being. Progress through one or more counseling sessions requires that the counselor and client establish (and consistently reestablish) trust. To the extent that Latinas/os from various backgrounds learn to value discretion in personal matters, Latinas/os may be especially disinclined to take their personal struggles public. The careful management of authority relations and the constant work to establish trust would be, in such cases, extraordinarily important.

*Credibility Given to the Counseling Process.* Latinas/os' general attitudes toward counseling and the credibility given to the counseling process remain largely unexplored in research on multicultural counseling. That said, anecdotal evidence from a broad spectrum of counselors and caregivers encourages, at least, a question about widely held skepticism about psychological treatment, including counseling, among Latinas/os. That a particular individual may carry this skepticism into the counseling situation is only one possibility. Whether or not a client is skeptical herself or himself, she or he may be having to deal with skepticism from a spouse or partner, family members, or friends.

## The Counseling Situation

The central category of our framework focuses on variables within the counseling situation itself. The way we conceive this category includes those behaviors and positionings that are most clearly in the direct control of *both* counselor *and* clients. Rather than prescribe an appropriate sequence of behaviors, organization of physical space, or proximity, we turn to Atkinson, Thompson, and Grant's (1993) description of the diverse roles that a counselor may assume in the counseling situation. Before doing so, the reader is cautioned that, given limitations on length, the focus here is on generic counseling roles and not on specific therapeutic theories and approaches. Should the reader want such information, refer to Casas et al. (2002).

Atkinson et al. (1993) proposed a three-dimensional model that focuses on the diverse roles that a counselor may have to assume when counseling these clients. Within the proposed model, Atkinson et al. suggest that in the process of selecting roles and strategies when working with racial/ethnic minority clients, counselors need to take into consideration three factors, each of which exists on a continuum: (1) client level of acculturation to the dominant society (high to low), (2) locus of problem etiology (external to internal), and (3) goals of helping (prevention, including education/development, to remediation). Just as the role itself is interactionally constituted, so is the client's particular location on any of these continua. That is, the extent to which acculturation pressures *matter,* the location of the problem and the specific goal for counseling may vary from one moment to the next and will certainly vary over the longer haul of multiple sessions. The point bears repeating: The appropriate counselor role may vary even within a single counseling session, as the counselor works with every available sense to decide how to think and act for the client's well-being.

Atkinson et al. (1993) identify eight therapist roles that intersect with each of the three continua extremes. More specifically, the therapist serves as the following:

1. *Adviser:* When the client is *low* in acculturation, the problem is *externally* located, and *prevention* is the goal of treatment.

2. *Advocate:* When the client is *low* in acculturation, the problem is *external* in nature, and the goal of treatment is *remediation.*

3. *Facilitator of indigenous support systems:* When the client is *low* in acculturation, the problem is *internal* in nature, and *prevention* is the goal of treatment.

4. *Facilitator of indigenous healing systems:* When the client is *low* in acculturation, the problem is *internal* in nature, and *remediation* is the treatment goal.

5. *Consultant:* When the client is *high* in acculturation, the problem is *external* in nature, and *prevention* is the treatment goal.

6. *Change agent:* When the client is *high* in acculturation, the problem is *external* in nature, and *remediation* is the goal of treatment.

7. *Counselor:* When the client is *high* in acculturation, the problem is *internal* in nature, and *prevention* is the primary goal of treatment.

8. *Psychotherapist:* When the client is *high* in acculturation, the problem is *internal* in nature, and *remediation* is the goal of therapy.

## CONCLUSION

Our chapter asserts the essential importance of counselors' cultural knowledge and awareness of the social, institutional, political, and economic experience of clients who are members of ethnic minority groups. If counselors understand the relevant cultural values, norms, and behaviors of their clients, as well as the unique stresses that they face, they may propose interpretations of their clients' behaviors that are different from those that might otherwise apply. Regardless of theoretical orientation, effective and ethical counselors must assess which aspects of their orientations may result in their colluding with the dynamics of oppression, such as blaming the victim by presenting certain interpretations of psychodynamic formulations.

In addition to culturally sensitive or modified approaches to counseling and therapy with Latinas/os, counselors must also employ other frameworks and perspectives beyond those traditionally used, many of which have been based on remedial models (i.e., treating the client after a specific problem has surfaced). Romano and Hage (2000) strongly assert the need for a much stronger emphasis on and commitment to the science and practice of prevention in counseling psychology. Preventive interventions forestall the onset of problems or needs through anticipation of the risks and challenges faced by persons across their multiple environments. To this end, we suggest the incorporation of such interventions for enhancing the quality of life of Latina/o groups. Following the outlines of the theory described in this chapter, preventive *environmental* interventions (Banning, 1980; Morrill, Oetting, & Hurst, 1974) designed for members of ethnic minority groups may be included. Examples include national, state, and local policies and laws that affect the mental health and general well-being of ethnic minority individuals.

A "business-as-usual" mentality will not work with Latinas/os or other minority clients. The challenges that such clients bring to counseling sessions demand careful ways of thinking that must be regularly refreshed by explorations into new theoretical, cross-national, and cross-disciplinary terrains (see Díaz-Guerrero, 1995) as well as by genuine contact with the dynamic, diverse "real world." We have provided a road map for such exploration, including the outline of a framework that identifies a range of possibly relevant variables. In the journeys that counselors may take with their clients, we have anticipated a few likely challenges and encouraged a preventive, resilience orientation.

## The Case of Liliana

In the section that follows, we present a counseling situation in order to outline some potential implications of our work for counselors' real-life practice. Although hypothetical, the situation draws on an actual case described in greater detail elsewhere (Raley, Casas, & Corral, 2004).

Twenty-four-year-old Liliana is voluntarily seeking counseling for "relationship issues." She has lived in California's Bay Area for most of the time since her family emigrated illegally from Mexico. Recently married, Liliana currently lives within a few miles of her mother and sisters. Liliana's family of origin is economically poor. She has met but does not have ongoing contact with her biological father, who is "somewhere in Mexico." Her mother and two older sisters are deeply committed to their Apostolic Christian church, but Liliana does not attend regularly. Liliana speaks reverently of her grandmother, though relations were tense for a time. Liliana and her grandmother were not speaking to each other at all because of the grandmother's rejection of Liliana's younger sister and brother. According to Liliana, her grandmother could not accept that their biological father was African American. Despite a very difficult time in public school, Liliana's experience at a small private high school propelled her to an Ivy League university. She left the university after her sophomore year to raise her own family. She is currently working for a successful technology firm as she completes a college degree.

Liliana's sense of humor engages both young people and adults, her penetrating insights guide conversations, and she is well liked by those who know her well. She continues to defy authority when she feels that it is unjustifiably imposed, is occasionally impatient with what she perceives to be the irrelevance of other people's emotions or reasoning, and sometimes balks at what she sees as unnecessary or unimportant work.

How might this chapter be useful to a counselor's efforts to improve Liliana's mental health? The framework offered here does not provide a script that Liliana's counselor might follow. In fact, the framework is designed to discourage a search for *solutions*, pointing instead to better *questions* to guide a counselor's practice. Some of these *guiding* questions might become *actual* questions that the counselor could ask Liliana. Others could guide a counselor's attention during their meetings, helping the counselor discern those important ecological factors, identify the particulars of Liliana's orientation to the counseling situation, and design and co-create a safe physical and social space. The following is a limited example of guiding questions, organized according to the broad categories of variables described in our framework.

## DISCUSSION QUESTIONS

### Person-Environment Factors

1. What sorts of experiences, if any, has Liliana had with racism and other kinds of discrimination? How have these contributed to the way Liliana sees herself and her lived world? How do race, language, class, gender, and so on matter to Liliana's beliefs?

2. What are Liliana's own conceptions and explanations of her economic situation and that of her family?

3. What is Liliana's "take" on her experience as an immigrant?

### Orientation to the Counseling Situation

4. Has Liliana been in counseling therapy before? What was the experience like? Have any of her family members been in therapy? For what reason, and with what perceived results?

5. What concerns does Liliana bring to the present counseling situation?

6. How, if at all, does the ethnic, racial, linguistic, or economic background of the counselor matter to Liliana's orientation to the counseling situation?

### Situational Variables

7. What is the most neutral arrangement of space and materials?

8. What are Liliana's observable responses (linguistic, behavioral, etc.) to the counseling situation, including especially the specific behaviors of the counselor?

9. Given what the counselor is learning about Liliana's environment and orientation, what roles might best meet Liliana's needs? And under what conditions might such roles usefully vary?

## NOTE

1. Realizing no consensus has emerged around the use of *Latina/o* or *Hispanic,* and understanding the advantages and disadvantages of any term, we have chosen to use the term *Latina/o* in this chapter. We will use terms other than *Latina/o* (e.g., *Hispanic, Mexican American*) when presenting and/or referencing the works of other writers and researchers. In addition, at several points in this chapter, we write of Latinas/os' likely experiences with "racism." We also use the terms *prejudice* and *discrimination.* We recognize that, for many Latinas/os, individual maltreatment and structural inequalities may have everything to do with race but may also extend to issues of language, national background, history, and socioeconomic and cultural-behavioral stereotypes. In any case, we use these terms more or less interchangeably, intending to capture an aspect of experience we find especially salient to the mental health of Latinas/os.

## REFERENCES

Alarcón, R. D. (2001). Hispanic psychiatry: From margin to mainstream. *Transcultural Psychiatry, 38*(1), 5–25.

American Association for the Advancement of Science. (2000). *Limited progress: The status of Hispanic Americans in science and engineering.* Retrieved May 20, 2005, from http://ehrweb.aaas.org/mge/Reports/Report2/Report2.html

American Psychological Association, Office of Program Consultation and Accreditation. (1996). *Guidelines and principles for accreditation of programs in professional psychology.* Washington, DC: Author.

Atkinson, D. R., Thompson, C. E., & Grant, S. K. (1993). A three-dimensional model for counseling racial/ethnic minorities. *The Counseling Psychologist, 21,* 257–277.

Banning, J. (1980). The campus ecology manager role. In U. Delworth & G. Hanson (Eds.), *Student services: A handbook for the profession* (pp. 209–227). San Francisco: Jossey-Bass.

Baugh, J. (2003). Linguistic profiling. In S. Makoni, G. Smitherman, A. F. Ball, & A. K. Spears (Eds.), *Black linguistics: Language, society, and politics in Africa and the Americas* (pp. 155–168). London: Routledge.

Berry, J. W. (1990). Psychology of acculturation: Understanding individuals moving between cultures. In R. W. Brislin (Ed.), *Applied cross-cultural psychology* (pp. 232–253). Newbury Park, CA: Sage.

Bronfenbrenner, U. (1977). Toward an experimental ecology of human development. *American Psychologist, 32,* 513–531.

Carter, D. J., & Wilson, R. (1991). *Minorities in higher education.* Washington, DC: American Council on Education.

Casas, J. M., & Casas, A. (1994). *Acculturation: Theory, models, and implications.* Santa Cruz, CA: Network.

Casas, J. M., Pavelski, R., Furlong, M. J., & Zanglis, I. (2001). Addressing the mental health needs of Latino youth with emotional and behavioral disorders: Practical perspectives and policy implications. *Harvard Journal of Hispanic Policy, 12,* 47–69.

Casas, J. M., & Vasquez, M. J. T. (1989). Counseling the Hispanic client: A theoretical and applied perspective. In P. B. Pedersen, J. G. Draguns, W. J. Lonner, & J. E. Trimble (Eds.), *Counseling across cultures* (3rd ed., pp. 153–175). Honolulu: University of Hawaii Press.

Casas, J. M., Vasquez, M. J. T., & Ruiz de Esparza, C. A. (2002). Counseling the Latina(o): A guiding framework for a diverse population. In P. B. Pedersen, J. G. Draguns, W. J. Lonner, & J. E. Trimble (Eds.), *Counseling across cultures* (5th ed., pp. 133–159). Thousand Oaks, CA; Sage.

Chacon, M., Cohen, E., Camarena, M., Gonzalez, J., & Strover, S. (1985). *Chicanas in California post-secondary education: A comparative study of barriers to program progress.* Stanford, CA: Center for Chicano Research.

Chavez, E. (1901). Ensayo sobre los rasgos distintivos de la personalidad como factor del carácter del mexicano [Essay on the distinctive personality traits as a factor of the character of the Mexican]. *Revista Positiva, 3,* 84–89.

Cushman, P. (1992). Psychotherapy to 1992: A historically situated interpretation. In D. K. Freedheim (Ed.), *History of psychotherapy: A century of change* (pp. 21–64). Washington, DC: American Psychological Association.

Díaz-Guerrero, R. (1995). Origins and development of Mexican ethnopsychology. *World Psychology, 1*(1), 49–67.

Diaz-Loving, R., & Draguns, J. G. (1999). Culture, meaning, and personality in Mexico and in the United States. In Y. Lee, C. R. McCauley, & J. G. Draguns (Eds.), *Personality and person perception across cultures* (pp. 103–126). Mahwah, NJ: Lawrence Erlbaum.

Elliott, K. A. G. (2000). *The relationship between acculturation, family functioning, and school performance of Mexican American adolescents.* Unpublished doctoral dissertation, University of California, Santa Barbara.

Fry, R. (2005). *The higher dropout rate of foreign-born teens: The role of schooling abroad.* Washington, DC: Pew Hispanic Center Reports. Retrieved June 15, 2006, from http://pewhispanic.org/reports/report.php?ReportID=5520

Ginorio, A., & Huston, M. (2000). ¡*Si, se puede!/Yes, we can: Latinas in school.* Washington, DC: American Association of University Women.

Hartup, W. W. (1979). The social worlds of childhood. *American Psychologist, 34,* 944–950.

Heppner, P., Casas, J. M., Carter, J., & Stone, G. (2000). The maturation of counseling psychology: Multifaceted perspectives from 1978–1998. In S. Brown & R. Lent (Eds.), *Handbook of counseling psychology* (3rd ed., pp. 3–49). New York: John Wiley.

Kaufman, P., Kwon, J. Y., Klein, S., & Chapman, C. D. (2000). *Dropout rates in the United States: 1998* (Statistical Analysis Report No. 2000022). Washington, DC: National Center for Education Statistics.

Korchin, S. J. (1980). Clinical psychology and minority problems. *American Psychologist, 35,* 262–269.

Kurtines, W. M., & Szapocznik, J. (1996). Family interaction patterns: Structural family therapy in contexts of cultural diversity. In E. D. Hibbs & P. L. S. Jensen (Eds.), *Psychosocial treatments for child and adolescent disorders: Empirically based strategies for clinical practice* (pp. 671–697). Washington, DC: American Psychological Association.

Lewin, K. (1935). *A dynamic theory of personality.* New York: McGraw-Hill.

Lewin, K. (1936). *Principles of topological psychology* (F. Heider & G. Heider, Trans). New York: McGraw-Hill.

McNeill, B. W., Prieto, L. R., Niemann, Y. F., Pizarro, M., Vera, E. M., & Gomez, S. P. (2001). Current directions in Chicana/o psychology. *The Counseling Psychologist, 29,* 5–17.

Morrill, W. H., Oetting, E. P., & Hurst, J. C. (1974). Dimensions of counselor functioning. *Personnel and Guidance Journal, 52,* 354–359.

Niemann, Y. F. (2001). Stereotypes about Chicanas and Chicanos: Implications for counseling. *The Counseling Psychologist, 29,* 55–90.

Oetting, E. R., & Beauvais, F. (1991). Orthogonal cultural identification theory: The cultural identification of minority adolescents. *International Journal of the Addictions, 25,* 655–685.

Pedersen, P. B. (1987). Ten frequent assumptions of cultural bias in counseling. *Journal of Multicultural Counseling and Development, 15,* 16–24.

Pedersen, P. B. (1995). Culture-centered ethical guidelines for counselors. In J. G. Ponterotto, J. M. Casas, L. A. Suzuki, & C. M. Alexander (Eds.), *Handbook of multicultural counseling* (pp. 34–49). Thousand Oaks, CA: Sage.

Ponterotto, J. G., Casas, J. M., Suzuki, L. A., & Alexander, C. M. (Eds.). (1995). *Handbook of multicultural counseling.* Thousand Oaks, CA: Sage.

Ponterotto, J. G., Casas, J. M., Suzuki, L. A., & Alexander, C. M. (Eds.). (2001). *Handbook of multicultural counseling* (2nd ed.). Thousand Oaks, CA: Sage.

Prieto, L. R., McNeill, B. W., Walls, R. G., & Gomez, S. P. (2001). Chicanas/os and mental health services: An overview of utilization, counselor preference, and assessment issues. *The Counseling Psychologist, 29,* 18–54.

Raley, J. D., Casas, J. M., & Corral, C. V. (2004). Quality de vida: "Browning" our understanding of quality of life. In R. J. Velasquez, L. M. Arellano, & B. W. McNeil (Eds.), *Handbook of Chicana/o psychology and mental health* (pp. 455–468). Mahwah, NJ: Lawrence Erlbaum.

Ramirez, R. (2000). *The Hispanic population in the United States: 1999* (Current Population Reports, Series P-20, No. 527). Washington, DC: Government Printing Office.

Redfield, R., Linton, R., & Herskovits, M. J. (1936). Memorandum for the study of acculturation. *American Anthropologist, 38,* 149–152.

Romano, J. L., & Hage, S. M. (2000). Prevention and counseling psychology: Revitalizing commitments for the 21st century. *The Counseling Psychologist, 22*(6), 733–763.

Smith, E. M. J. (1985). Ethnic minorities: Life stress, social support, and mental health issues. *The Counseling Psychologist, 13,* 537–580.

Sue, D. W., & Sue, D. (1999). *Counseling the culturally different: Theory and practice* (3rd ed.). New York: John Wiley.

Szapocznik, J., & Kurtines, W. (1980). Acculturation, biculturalism, and adjustment among Cuban-Americans. In A. M. Padilla (Ed.), *Recent advances in acculturation research: Theory, models, and some new findings* (pp. 914–931). Boulder, CO: Westview.

U.S. Bureau of the Census. (2000a). Census Bureau projects doubling of nation's population by 2100. *United States Department of Commerce News.* Retrieved from http://www.census.gov/press-release/www/2000/cb00–05 .html

U.S. Bureau of the Census. (2000b). *Hispanic population in the United States: March 1999* (Current Population Reports, Series P-20, No. 527). Washington, DC: Government Printing Office.

U.S. Bureau of the Census. (2000c). *Resident population estimates of the United States by sex, race, and Hispanic origin* (Table). Retrieved from http://www.census.gov/population/estimates/nation/intfile3–1.txt

U.S. Bureau of the Census. (2001). *Census 2000 redistricting (Public Law 94–171) summary file.* Retrieved from http://www.census.gov/home/en/pldata.html

U.S. Department of Education. (2000). *Key indicators of Hispanic student achievement: National goals and benchmarks for the next decade.* Retrieved from http://www.ed.gov/pubs/hispanicindicators/index.html

U.S. Surgeon General. (1999). *Mental health: A report of the surgeon general.* Washington, DC: Government Printing Office.

Ventura, S. J., Martin, J. A., Curtin, S. C., Matthews, T. J., & Park, M. M. (2000). Births: Final data for 1998. *National Vital Statistics Reports, 48*(3), 1– 100.

Wrenn, C. G. (1962). The culturally encapsulated counselor. *Harvard Educational Review, 32,* 444–449.

# Counseling Arab and Muslim Clients

Marwan Dwairy

---

### Primary Objective

- To help counselors understand the historical and cultural background needed to understand their Arab and/or Muslim (hereafter Arab/Muslim) clients

### Secondary Objectives

- To direct counselors to revise or modify psychological theories and practices related to development, personality, assessment, and mental health to fit Arab/Muslims
- To develop new assessment and intervention tools that are more suited to Arab/Muslims clients

---

A COUNSELOR WHO WORKS WITH ARAB/MUSLIM CLIENTS MAY NOTICE THAT THEY ARE LESS AUTONOMOUS than other, Western clients. The former tend to focus on external circumstances and have difficulty addressing internal and personal issues. Terms such as *self, self-actualization, ego, opinion,* and *feeling* have a collective meaning for them. They are preoccupied with duties, expectations and the approval of others, and family issues. In conversing with them, it is not easy to distinguish between the clients' personal needs, opinions, or attitudes and those of their families. While we need to be aware of these psychocultural features, we must also keep in mind the diversity that exists among Arab/Muslims, and these features may exist in one way or another among some other cultures as well (Gregg, 2005). Furthermore, Arab/Muslims have many characteristics and features in common with other cultures.

As an aid to understanding Arab/Muslim clients, knowledge of their historical and cultural background is necessary to counteract the misunderstandings and accusations Arab/Muslims have faced since the famous attack on September 11, 2001.

## ARAB/MUSLIM HISTORY AND CULTURE

Arabs are the descendants of Arabic tribes who lived in the deserts located in what are now known as the Saudi peninsula, Iraq, and Syria. In the early seventh century (AD 610), Islam emerged in Mecca and became the third and most recent of the world's great monotheistic religions. At this time, the prophet Mohammad began to exhort men and women to reform themselves morally and to submit to the will of God, as expressed in His revelations to him, which he and his adherents accepted as divine messages and were later embodied in a book, the Qur'an. Arabs today number about 285 million spread over 22 Arab countries in North Africa and the Middle East.

Islam has also been adopted by many non-Arab nations in the world. Muslims today number about 1.3 billion people worldwide. Although the majority of Arabs are Muslims, while also including Christian and Druze minorities, the majority of Muslims are not Arabs but rather Indonesians, Malaysians, Iranians, Turks, and so on. Despite this, the Arabic language and history remain central to Muslims since Islam was revealed to an Arab prophet, *Mohammad,* who was a member of the biggest Arab tribe, *Quraysh,* in an Arab city in Arabia, *Mecca,* and its holy book, the *Qur'an,* was written in Arabic (Dwairy, 2006).

The five fundamental tenets of Islam that are shared by all Islamic groups are as follows:

1. *Shahada:* The profession of faith ("There is no God but Allah, and Mohammad is His Prophet")

2. *Siyam:* Fasting in the holy month of Ramadan

3. *Salah:* Praying five times a day

4. *Zakah:* A tax that is devoted to providing financial help to the poor

5. *Haj:* The pilgrimage to Mecca

These tenets order Muslims to submit and pray to one God (Shahada, Salah, and Haj), to learn to control their instincts (Siyam), and to empathize with the poor and offer them help (Zakah). A true fundamentalist should adhere to and fulfill these five principles. Antagonism and hostility directed toward the West are far divorced from any true Islamic fundamental belief. On the contrary, Islam is very clear about the need to accept and respect other monotheistic religions, such as Christianity and Judaism.

Islam provides strict rules and laws (*Shari'aa*), based on the Qur'an and the Prophet's life (*Sunna*), according to which one's personal, familial, social, economic, and political life must be led. Therefore, Islam not only involves faith and prayer to God but also provides legislature pertaining to almost every issue in life. Islam is a social religion that suggests a balanced order in society. Basic to the teachings of Islam is finding legal ways to satisfy the sexual instincts and needs of men. Unlike Christianity, which tends to ignore or deny human sexuality, Islam specifically treats sexual issues and provides legal sexual vents for men (e.g., polygamy) and sexual control of women (e.g., veiling). Fortunately, among Islamic countries today, only Saudi Arabia enforces the veiling of women, and in many of them, such as Tunisia and Turkey, state laws prohibit veiling and polygamy.

For many decades, Arab/Muslims were acquainted with Westerners as occupiers and oppressors in Africa and Asia. Today, they know the West as supporting or condoning the Israeli occupation of

Palestinian land. Nevertheless, they are fascinated by Western technology and science. They consume Western products, and their scholars absorb Western theories and research findings. In the past few decades, Arab/Muslim societies have been aggressively pushed by the United States to adopt democratic and liberal political systems in their countries. These attempts are seen as threats to the Arab/Muslim societies' independence and to their collective character, as well as being hypocritical, because the human rights and liberty of people in these societies are abused by the West in the name of democracy, human rights, and, recently, the fight against terrorism. There is no doubt that the exposure to Westerners, through imperialism or through the media, sciences, and technology, has introduced new individualistic values that challenge the Arab/Muslim collective traditions. The attitude toward the West is therefore a mixture of rage and antagonism, on one hand, and identification and glorification, on the other. Arab/Muslim emigrants may vary in the proportion of their rage and resentment versus their identification with the West (Dwairy, 2006).

## AUTHORITARIAN AND COLLECTIVE CULTURE

The Arab and the Muslim worlds share the ethos of tribal collectivism and Islamic values but are also influenced by their exposure to Western culture. The social system in both the Arab and the Muslim world tends to be collective and authoritarian: The individual is very submissive to the family and norms; the family is ruled by a patriarchal hierarchical authority. Despite some progress in the past few decades, democratic values and political rights remain limited in most Arab/Muslim countries, and the citizens still rely for their survival on the family or tribe rather than on the state (United Nations Development Programme [UNDP], 2002). In the absence of a state system that provides the needs of the citizens, the individual and family continue to be interdependent. Individuals are dependent for their survival on their families, and family cohesion, economy, status, and reputation are in turn dependent on the individual's behavior and achievements. The individual is expected to serve the collective in order to receive the familial support needed for his or her survival. Most of the citizens in Arab/Muslim countries rely on their family more than on the state in matters related to child care, education, finding jobs, finding houses, protection, and so on.

In this social system, two polarized options are open to individuals: (1) to be submissive in order to gain vital collective support or (2) to relinquish the collective support in favor of self-fulfillment. Arab/Muslims are spread in terms of the choice that they make between these two poles and can be roughly divided into three societal categories: authoritarian/collectivists, mixed, and individualistic. The vast majority of Arab/Muslims are found in the first two categories. Few Arab/Muslims may be characterized as individualists; those who may were typically raised in educated middle-class families and have been exposed to Western culture. Of course, these categories are dynamic and contextual: An Arab person's orientation can be more collective in terms of one issue, such as family life, and less collective in terms of another, such as business issues.

For most Arab/Muslim individuals, choices in life are collective matters, and therefore almost all the major decisions in life are determined by the family. Decisions concerning clothing, social activity, career, marriage, housing, size of the family, and child rearing are made within the family context where the individual has only a minimal space for personal choice. Within this system, in which issues are determined by others, a person learns to be helpless as an individual, avoids personal initiative or challenges, and expects matters to be arranged by some external force. To maintain the cohesion of the collective system, authentic self-expression of feelings is not welcomed; instead, one is expected to express what others anticipate. This way of communication within the collective is directed by values of respect (*Ihtiram*), fulfilling social duties (*wajib*), and pleasing others and avoiding confrontations (*mosayara*). Emotional expressions on good or bad occasions, such as a marriage or death, are very much ruled by social norms.

Immigration to the West exposes and challenges all the cultural features mentioned above. Before and after emigration, a fundamental cultural revision and change takes place in the mind of the Arab/Muslim. The Western liberal individualistic life seems too permissive and therefore threatens traditional Arab/Muslim values concerning family, women, and child rearing. They want to be part of the Western society but are afraid of becoming enmeshed and losing their culture and identity. At some initial stage of emigration, Arab/Muslims become aware of and committed to certain cultural norms and values that had only a marginal position in their way of life before emigration. Many may find refuge in their culture of origin and, at some stage, become more fundamentalist than before. Many first-generation Arab/Muslim emigrants live in two polarized worlds and are torn between two conflicting cultures. Counselors are expected to facilitate these two contradictory goals: to adapt to Western society and to retain their culture.

To understand the Arab/Muslim client, counselors are recommended to revise their theoretical understanding of psychological development, assessment, psychopathology, and psychotherapy as it pertains to these clients.

## PSYCHOSOCIAL DEVELOPMENT

Western theories of development emphasize a separation-individuation process that normally ends in the individual developing an independent identity after adolescence. While they may use different terminology, all theories of development agree that normal development starts in full dependency and ends in full independency. Freud claimed that after the fifth year of life, children already possess, through a process of identification with the same-sex parent, an almost independent personality structure. After age 5, children unconsciously repeat and transfer their early relationship with their parents to the present interpersonal relationships (Freud, 1900, 1940/1964). Erikson (1950) saw that the formation of an independent ego identity is a necessary stage in the normal development of children. He described the stages that lead to autonomous ego identity: First, children attain basic trust (0–1 years), then seek autonomy (1–3 years) and move on toward initiation (3–6 years) and industry (6–12 years), until they achieve ego identity in late adolescence. Object-relation theories also focus on analyzing the process of separation-individuation in the first 3 years of life (Mahler, Bergman, & Pine, 1975) and its continuance into adolescence (Blos, 1967), until the individuation of the self is achieved.

Theories of development actually describe the ideal development in Western society. Accordingly, the adult mentally healthy person is independent, autonomous, individuated, internally controlled, and responsible for himself or herself, with an inner sense of self. In an individualistic society, dependency in an adult may be considered as a disorder (e.g., dependent personality disorder) or a sort of fixation. Conversely, in collective/authoritarian societies, where collective/authoritarian norms and values continue to be the major generators of behavior, assuming autonomy and independency is inappropriate. Adolescents and adults in such societies continue to be emotionally and socially dependent on their social environment.

Many studies found that an authoritarian or abusive socialization style is adopted toward Arab children (Achoui, 2003). Some reports indicated that physical and emotional abuse is a widespread style of parenting in Egypt (Saif El-Deen, 2001), Bahrain (Al-Mahroos, 2001), Kuwait (Qasem, Mustafa, Kazem, & Shah, 1998), Jordan (Al-Shqerat, & Al-Masri, 2001), and Morocco (Al-Kittani, 2000), especially among lower-class, uneducated parents and large or dysfunctional families. Some studies indicate that Arab children and youth are satisfied with authoritarian parenting (Hatab & Makki, 1978) and do not complain of the abusive-aggressive behavior of teachers (Dwairy, 1997b). Some other studies indicate that authoritarianism is not associated with any detriment to the mental health of Arab youth (Dwairy, 2004b; Dwairy & Menshar, 2006).

In a collective/authoritarian society that adopts authoritarian parenting styles, the separation-individuation process is not expected to be accomplished. Indeed, Timimi (1995) postulated that Arab youth do not experience identity crises in adolescence or achieve individual autonomy. This is because their identity is enmeshed in that of the family, to which they are always loyal. Arab adolescents are not expected to act out, become self-centered, or engage in nonconformist behavior (Racy, 1970).

When the ego identity of Arab-Palestinian adolescents was tested, it was found to be more "foreclosed" and "diffused" than that of the American youth. *Foreclosed* adolescents do not experience a crisis period but rather adopt commitments from others (usually parents) and accept them as their own without shaping, modifying, or testing them for personal fit. *Diffused* adolescents do not experience a need or desire to explore alternatives and/or deal with the question of their identity. The identity of male adolescents was more "foreclosed" than that of female adolescents (Dwairy, 2004a). The interconnectedness with their parents was of a higher level than that found among Western sample populations. Arab-Palestinian adolescents, for instance, displayed a higher level of emotional, financial, and functional interdependence with their parents. Female adolescents displayed a higher level of financial dependence on their parents than did males (Dwairy, 2004a). Among the Arab/Muslims in Israel, the ego identity of Bedouin adolescents was the most "foreclosed" by their parents.

Authoritarian parenting and psychological dependency are frequently misunderstood by Western counselors. Explaining these psychocultural features among Turkish families, Fisek and Kagitcibasi (1999) commented that authoritarianism should not be considered as oppression, emotional connectedness as enmeshment or fusion, or the collective familial self as constriction or developmental arrest. Western counselors and therapists who work with Arab/Muslim families should not consider psychosocial dependency as a fixation, immaturity, or transference from early childhood but rather as an appropriate and functional behavior that is based on correct reality testing and understanding of the controlling social reality in Arab/Muslim collective societies.

# PERSONALITY

The concept of personality emerged along with the development of individualism in the West. After the individual became an independent entity, personality theories arose to explain the internal dynamic that rules the individual's behavior. Most personality theories assume an intrapsychic construct (ego, self, trait, drives, or intelligence) and processes (conflicts, repression, self-actualization, or thinking) according to which behavior is explained (Dwairy, 2002). In most collective societies, where the personality does not become autonomous but rather continues to be other focused (Markus & Kitayama, 1998), norms, values, rules, and familial authority, rather than personality, explain the behavior of the individual. In these societies, such as the Arab/Muslim one, the concept of personality should go beyond the intrapsychic constructs and processes and encompass a social layer that works in conjunction with the intrapsychic layer in ruling the individual's behavior. It is worth emphasizing here that the intrapsychic structures are not independent but rather are ruled by the external social layer of personality.

The main dynamic in the personal life of the Arab/Muslim individual is in the interpersonal domain rather in the intrapsychic one. The source of oppression and repression is mainly external (social and familial control), and therefore the main conflict is intrafamilial (personal needs vs. family control) rather than intrapsychic. To contend with this kind of conflict, one needs social coping skills to manipulate the social controlling authority rather than defense mechanisms that manipulate the ego and superego.

Central to these social coping skills that prevail in Arab/Muslim societies is the *Mosayara* (or *Mojamala*) and *Istighaba*. Mosayara is to get along with others' needs and expectations by concealing one's feelings and attitudes. It is an essential value in Arab/Muslim societies that helps maintain the harmony within the family and society. Istighaba, on the other hand, allows feelings, attitudes, and needs that were not expressed because of the Mosayara to be expressed in the absence (*Ghiyab*) of the familial or the social authority. Socially unacceptable behavior is expressed in solitude away from the "eyes of the society" to avoid punishment or isolation. These are two complementary skills needed to cope within the collective Arab/Muslim society (Dwairy, 1997b, 1998).

In the collective personality, the individual's needs, thoughts, and values are confused with those of others. Furthermore, the individual's needs (id), thoughts, attitudes (ego), and values (superego) are mixed up together in one whole mind-body system with no strict distinction between each function. The meaning of the *mind* in the Arab/Muslim culture is confused with values rather than reasoning. Intelligent people are those who know the values and know how to judge behavior and events accordingly. Emotional distress is expressed physically in somatic complaints rather than in thoughts or emotions. Within a collective personality, the main distinct entities are the social layer of personality versus the private layer. The social layer is the component that is exposed to others and communicates with them according to the norms and values while using coping skills such as Mosayara. The private layer is the component that enables ventilation of unacceptable needs or expressions away from the scrutiny of social control, using coping skills such as Istighaba. Neither layer is independent but rather is or is not conveyed according to the presence or absence of the social external control. Thus, the collective personality, as compared to the individualistic one, tends to act contextually rather than consistently across social situations. Individual differences between Arab/Muslim people may be displayed in two main factors:

1. Domination of the social layer in relation to the private one: The more individuated the person, the less dominated by the social layer he or she is.

2. Social status: People behave differently according to their social roles, gender, age, and profession.

These two factors help explain and predict Arab/Muslim behavior more than do the intrapsychic components mentioned in the theories of personality (for further reading, see Dwairy, 2002).

## ASSESSMENT

Since the typical intrapsychic structures of personality, such as ego, self-concept, intelligence, conflict, and defense mechanisms, are collective rather than individual among Arab/Muslim clients, to understand a client's personality, the clinician needs to assess its other, more relevant components. The level of individuation is the main factor that should be assessed to understand whether the social or the private layer predominates and to know in what context each component is activated and how efficiently the client uses social skills. The conventional battery of tests that focuses on intrapsychic components of personality does not meet this need; therefore, alternative assessment tools should be developed that can assess the client's level of individuation, norms, values, and coping skills and the individual's need to be understood within the family context. The structured interview, such as the Person-in-Culture Interview (Berg-Cross & Chinen, 1995), is one example of interviews that should provide the therapist or counselor with the information required to understand the needs, attitudes, and values of the person as opposed to those of the family. Talking about a significant object (TASO) is another innovative technique that directs the client to talk about himself or herself through a significant object the client brings from his or her home. This technique is based on the assumption that people in traditional cultures are emotionally attached to their physical environment; therefore, talking about a significant item brought from their environment reveals significant memories and events pertaining to their lives and their families (see Dwairy, 1999, 2001).

## PSYCHOPATHOLOGY

Psychopathology, according to Western personality theories, is considered to be a *disorder* within the intrapsychic domain that causes suffering, impairment in functioning, somatic complaints, or detachment from reality (American Psychiatric Association, 1994). Arab/Muslims, whose personalities are rarely individuated, may display these symptoms because of a *disorder* within the individual-family relationship. Dysfunction of the social and private layers of personality and failure or misuse of social coping skills are the main causes of abnormality. For instance, an imbalance between Mosayara and social approval or the discovery of the Istighaba by the family may cause psycho-somato-social distress.

Since the individual and the family, the mind and the body, and reality and imagination are not distinguishable entities among most Arab/Muslims, a disorder is displayed in all of these domains in a diffused rather than stylistic way. Patterned disorders that are described in the fourth edition of the *Diagnostic and Statistical Manual of Mental Disorders* (*DSM-IV*) are not displayed clearly among Arab/Muslims. For instance, depression, which is considered in the West to be a mood disorder characterized by sad feelings, hopelessness, and helplessness, is manifested among Arab/Muslims in somatic complaints, frequently, with no feeling of sadness, hopelessness, and helplessness (Al-Issa, 1989; Baasher, 1962).

Many Arab/Muslims have a different concept of reality from that of Westerners. They consider visions and dreams to be the true reality rather than the physical one (Al-Issa, 1995; Dwairy, 1997a). On the basis of dreams and visions, they make crucial decisions in their lives. These differences in the concept of reality challenge *reality testing* as a criterion for mental disorder, as adopted by the Western nosology. These cultural differences are reflected in the diagnosis of schizophrenia, which is based on the identification of hallucinations and delusions. In the case of Arab/Muslims, the conventional *DSM-IV* nosology does not help to differentiate between cultural hallucinations or delusions and psychotic ones. The typical psychotic disorder among Arab/Muslims is acute, precipitated by familial or social distress, and polymorphic; it involves a large range of symptoms. Many recover mental health within a year, even without any medication, and typically have no family history of psychosis (Okasha, Seif El Dawla, Khalil, & Saad, 1993).

## PSYCHOTHERAPY AND COUNSELING

Almost all counseling and psychotherapeutic interventions (excluding behavior therapy) aim to restore the intrapsychic *order*, while revealing unconscious (typically forbidden) contents, and help the client to accomplish self-actualization. Because the common distresses of clients from collective cultures are related to intrafamilial disorder, counselors need to work on restoring this *order*. Working on revealing unconscious contents and helping the client to accomplish self-actualization, in many cases, can be counterproductive, in that it changes the client's behavior in a way that is usually not approved by the family and social environment. Assuming that the clients are typically the weakest members of the family, it seems unrealistic to expect that they will endure the conflicts with their family that would result from their expressing forbidden, and therefore repressed, feelings and drives and from their becoming assertive and self-actualized.

Before embarking on a therapeutic path that delves deep into the unconscious contents, counselors and therapists should assess the resources available to the client versus the power her or his social environment exerts on her or him. Level of individuation from the family, ego strength, and the strictness of the family are three major factors that should be assessed before any therapy takes place. On the basis of this assessment, counselors and therapist may decide whether to apply Western therapy that reveals unconscious contents and ends in self-actualization or to apply therapies that focus on problem solving and symptom reduction such as behavior therapy. The higher the level of the client's individuation, the stronger the ego; the greater the flexibility of the family, the more apposite it is for counselors to apply dynamic Western interventions. With clients who are un-individuated, have a weak ego, and live in strict and traditional families, counselors may adopt short-term and problem-focused intervention.

Counselors and psychotherapists who work with Arab/Muslim clients are encouraged to give special attention to understanding the relationship dynamics of the family (conflicts, coalitions, and force balances) and the status of the client within the family. Counselors who ignore the influence of the family and focus instead on personal issues may miss the point and make a client who is totally enmeshed in the family feel misunderstood. Therefore, assessment of the level of authoritarianism/collectivism of the client and the family is one of the first tasks of the counselor. Judgmental attitudes concerning the submission of the client to familial authority should be avoided. Counselors are encouraged to try to understand the rationale of this submission from within and to help the client find support and better coalitions within the family.

Counselors and psychotherapists should bear in mind that Islam prohibits renunciation of the Islamic faith. They should therefore avoid any confrontation with Islam and try to help their clients find new answers and ways to change within Islam. Fortunately, as a result of the long history of Islamic debate, one can find within this heritage many Qur'an verses, *hadith* directives, and proverbs that can be employed to facilitate therapeutic change. One major idea that may be employed, for instance, to make a strictly adherent client rethink his or her attitudes is to invoke the centrality of 'Aql (reason) in Islam. Thus, the therapist may remind a client of the Islamic teaching to use 'Aql. In psychological terms, activating the 'Aql means activating the client's ego to find compromises and realistic answers and revise and rethink his or her attitude (for more concrete ways to employ Islamic teachings in dealing with women's oppression, stress, and violence, see Dwairy, 2006).

The ambiguity toward the West may be manifested explicitly or implicitly in counseling with a Western counselor. It may be displayed in transference and countertransference processes. As collectivists, many Arab/Muslim clients may bring their Arab/Muslim culture to the counseling session and consider the Western counselor as a representative of all that the West means for the Arab/Muslim. The Arab/Muslim client may express submissiveness to the counselor not only as transference of the child-parent relationship but also as transference of the Arab/Muslim-West relationships. Expressions of anger and rage, on one hand, and inferiority feelings, shame, or fear of punishment, on the other, are other expected components of an Arab/Muslim's transference toward a Western counselor. For some Arab or Muslim clients, a therapist from the U.S., for example, may represent the entire U.S. régime and its attitude to the Arabic and Islamic nations. The transference may be expressed, for instance, in terms of *we* (the Arabs) and *you* (the entire U.S.). Therapists need not take any accusation against any specific Western country personally but rather help the client to differentiate between the therapist and any particular nation state. An inquiry such as, "When you say *you,* do you mean *we* the entire U.S. (for example) or me the therapist?" may help the Arabic client to be aware of the differences between Americans in general and the therapist as a particular person.

As collectivists, Arab/Muslim clients can be helped by a counselor who empathizes with their collective culture. Manifesting acceptance, tolerance, and unconditional positive regard toward the family and tradition on the part of the therapist may help these clients to trust and to relinquish anger or inferiority feelings. Empathy and acceptance that are limited to the individual client and do not encompass the family and culture do not suffice and, in some cases, may be counterproductive or threatening. Empathizing with the client while pushing her or him to cope assertively with her or his family may prematurely place the client in an irresolvable familial conflict.

Western counselors also need to be aware of their own countertransference toward Arab/Muslim clients and families. They need to be open to listen and learn about the client and family and divest themselves of any stereotypic notions and prejudices that they may have absorbed from the Western media. They may need to make a great conscious effort to avoid judging the client's and his or her family's behavior and attitudes according to Western norms and values.

Counselors may misunderstand the individual-family dependency of Arab/Muslim clients and misattribute it to immaturity of the self. Counselors are recommended to try to understand the rationale of this dependency and remember that freedom of choice and personal decision making is punishable, even among adults. This caution is crucial when the client is a female because disobedience may have fatal consequences for her.

Counselors who work with Arab/Muslim clients should bear in mind that the intrapsychic constructs such as self, ego, and superego are not independent constructs but rather are collective structures that include collective norms and values. Counselors are directed to give more attention to intrafamilial conflicts and coalitions than to intrapsychic processes within the individual client. Western counselors will find it difficult to understand the rationale of the authoritarian parenting style, not having experienced, as Arab/Muslims have, the vital individual-family interdependence that exists where state-provided care is absent. Counselors may easily find themselves opposing the authority of the Arab/Muslim families and employing therapeutic and legal means to create a liberal egalitarian order in the family. Imposing such Western values on Arab/Muslim families is, however, both unethical and counterproductive. Instead, counselors are encouraged to try to understand the rationale of the authoritarian system from within, to listen to the stresses and anxieties that the authoritarian parents experience, to express empathy with their conflicts, and to encourage and empower those progressive components in the parents' value system that may facilitate therapeutic changes. Counselors should remember that their role is to serve the needs of the client within his or her family and value system rather than to serve their own needs and values. Threatening familial authority may terminate the counseling process and leave the client to suffer the consequences.

## CULTURANALYSIS

Therapy should not be perceived as a tool with which to change the client's culture. Rather, therapists are advised to apply a within-culture therapy and exploit culture to facilitate therapeutic change. Within the Arab/Muslim culture, there are many contradictions. The therapist should identify subtle contradictions within the belief system of the client and employ cultural aspects that may facilitate change. Similarly to how a *psychoanalyst* analyzes the intrapsychic domain and brings conflicting aspects to the consciousness (e.g., aggression and guilt) to mobilize change, a *culturanalyst* analyses the client's belief system and brings contradicting aspects to the consciousness to mobilize a revision in attitudes and behavior. The assumption that underlies *culturanalysis* is that culture influences people's lives unconsciously. When therapists inquire and learn about the client's culture, they may find some unconscious aspects that are dissociated from other conscious attitudes with which a conflict exists. Once the therapist brings these aspects to the awareness of the client, the client starts to revise his or her conscious attitudes, and a significant change may be effected. Unlike the unconscious drives that are revealed through psychoanalysis, these intraculture conflicts are not supposed to be threatening because all aspects revealed are culturally and morally legitimized.

*Culturanalysis* can be understood in different theoretical perspectives. In the same way that a humanistic (Rogerian) therapist establishes an unconditional positive regard for and empathy with the *individual* to facilitate the expression of the authentic self, a *culturanalyst* establishes positive regard for and empathy with the *culture* and facilitates the recognition of more and more aspects of the culture that were denied and that may be employed to accomplish change. Alternatively, one can understand this process in terms of generating a cognitive dissonance within the client's belief system that necessitates change.

A "within-culture therapy" therapist needs to be open and incorporate several aspects of the culture in the therapy to create a new dynamic within the client's culture. Besides empathy, a thorough inquiry into the client's culture is needed to identify the cultural aspects that may be employed in therapy.

The case of 22-year-old Samer, who was a religious depressive client, is an example of within-culture therapy. As many depressives do, he was focusing on minor negative events in his life and denying many positive ones. He tried with no success to protect himself from negative events by praying more. When I confronted him with the notion that a truly religious Muslim man should appreciate the grace of God and asked him to examine whether he really appreciated that grace, he realized that he needed to focus on the positive events in his life. I could have tried to achieve this change through cognitive therapy, but exploiting his religious belief system made the change easier and stable. For more examples, readers are referred to Dwairy (2006, chap. 9).

## INDIRECT THERAPIES

Arab/Muslims, like members of many other cultures, have a different concept of reality than that of Westerners. The positivistic concept of reality in the West is associated with materialistic reality. Imagination, dreams, and visions are considered as a sort of detachment from reality. Reality testing is considered a major criterion of mental health, and hallucinations and delusions are the major criteria of psychosis (*DSM-IV*). Contrary to the Western concept of reality, many Arabs/Muslims appreciate dreams and visions and consider them to be indications of the true reality (Al-Issa, 1995). In addition, the Arabic language is very metaphoric (Hourani, 1983, 1991), and therefore many clients may express their problems through metaphors. These cultural characteristics raise the question for therapists whether to approach the imaginative and metaphoric conceptions of the client or to help her or him reach a positivistic conception. In this context, we suggest implementing metaphor therapy in the treatment of Arabs/Muslims as an indirect way of dealing with their repressed contents. This indirect therapy suits Arabs/Muslims since, as mentioned before, therapists treating unindividuated clients are advised to avoid helping the client to reveal unconscious contents or to reach self-actualization; by doing so, confrontations with the family may be triggered.

Since Arab/Muslim clients do not feel comfortable with addressing their family life directly, and because they primarily use a metaphoric language to express their distresses, therapists and counselors are encouraged to enter their metaphoric world and facilitate a metaphoric solution. When a client who is trying to say that her family does not understand her suffering expresses herself using a proverb such as "*Elli eidu belmay mesh methl elli eidu bennar*" (the one whose hand is in water is not like the one whose hand is in fire), the therapist can work on this metaphor without addressing the familial relationship directly.

Kopp (1995), in his three-stage metaphor therapy, first asks the client to select a metaphor that describes the problem in concrete terms; in the second stage, he asks the client to change the metaphor in such a way that it describes the solution of the problem; and at the end, the client is asked what she or he has learned from the metaphoric solution and what practical implications can be deduced from it that can be used to cope with the problems.

Bresler (1984) directs his patients who suffer from chronic pain to control it by controlling the images in their minds. First, he guides his clients to draw the pain, then to draw the state of no pain, and then to draw the pleasure state. Through these three drawings, the client processes the pain experience metaphorically. In the second stage, Bresler teaches the clients to control the images in their minds and to retain the pictures (images) of no pain and pleasure.

Let us return to our example about the feeling of a hand in water versus the feeling of a hand in fire. If this metaphor describes the problem, therapists may suggest that the client draw (or imagine) the metaphor and then create a new picture that describes the relief of finding a solution. Often, there is no need to discuss the solution directly, as Kopp (1995) suggests as the third stage of therapy. The fact that the client was involved in a metaphor-based solution influences his or her real experience. According to my model of metaphor therapy (Dwairy, 1997a), any manipulation or change in the metaphor level is transmitted to the biological, psychological, and social level through unconscious processes. Hence, metaphor therapy is a suitable intervention when the aim of the therapist is to avoid dealing directly with repressed contents. There are some other indirect therapies that may be applied and can be explained according to my model, such as guided imagery therapy, art therapy, and bibliotherapy (Dwairy & Abu Baker, 1992). In all these therapies, the client processes the problem and finds solutions or new coping strategies in a symbolic imaginative level, which influences the bio-psycho-social level of experience through unconscious processes that connect the two levels of experience. For more concerning my metaphor model of therapy, see Dwairy (2006, chap. 11).

## CONCLUSION

Arabs are the descendents of Arabic tribes who once lived in the deserts of the Saudi peninsula, Iraq, and Syria and today number about 285 million living in 22 Arab countries. The Islamic religion appeared in one of the main Arabic tribes in the seventh century and has now been adopted by 1.3 billion Arab and non-Arab people worldwide. The Arab and the Muslim worlds share the ethos of tribal collectivism and Islamic values but are also influenced by their exposure to Western culture. The social system in both worlds tends to be collective and authoritarian: The individual is very submissive to family and norms, and the family is ruled by a patriarchal hierarchical authority.

Within this collective system, Arab/Muslim youth do not become psychologically individuated from their families. Their personality continues to be collective and directed by external norms and values rather than by internal structures and processes of personality. The clinical picture of Arab/Muslim clients may differ from that described in the *DSM-IV.* Counselors are advised to be aware of the danger of dealing with unconscious, personal, and repressed contents in cases involving unindividuated clients. It is suggested that therapists consider helping them by indirect therapies such as metaphor therapy, guided imagery, art therapy, and bibliotherapy.

Sawsan, 17 years old, was brought by her father to counseling because in the past 2 months, she started to withdraw from family meetings and activity. She spent most of the time listening to music in her room. Lately, she has complained about a headache that lasts all day with no relief despite painkillers. The medical doctor told them that she may be passing through a stressful period and referred them to counseling. At the initial intake meeting with Sawsan and her father, the father dominated the conversation, and Sawsan approved his attitude. The father described her as a perfect girl who always met the parents' expectations in school and in social behavior. The change in her behavior made her seem "not her" as they knew her all the time. He tried to attribute this change to "bad friends" or "bad readings" that changed her so much. He tried to deny any stress and emphasized how much they love her and care for her needs. He said, "Nothing is missing in her life. We bought her every thing she wants. She couldn't be passing any stress."

Knowing that Arab girls do not dare express their feelings in front of their father (or parents), after I listen to the father (or parents), I typically ask him (or them) to allow a private conversation with the girl. At the beginning of the conversation with Sawsan, she continued in her father's line, describing how much they love and support her and denying any stress. Only after she felt that I understood that she has good parents was she ready to reveal a conflict that was raised lately concerning her need to study at a university located far from her village, which necessitated living in the student dorms. Her father rejected his daughter living away from the house far away from his immediate control. To compensate her, he brought her a new computer and suggested that she study at a local nearby college. She insisted that she wanted to learn at the university and tried to push until her father became angry and shouted at her, claiming that she is imitating some bad girls who sleep away from their homes. As she described this conflict, she continued to remove any accusation to her father and said, "He did this because he is worried about my future" and "He is right and I should understand this." The counseling process lasted for five meetings, during which I met the father three times in order to establish a good joining with his attitudes and worries and then revealed some contradictions within his belief system, as described in culturanalysis. After that, he agreed to allow his daughter to learn at another university, in a city where she could live with her uncle's family. After that, I met with the two and encouraged the daughter to explain her need to study at the university and to express her commitment to her family values, and I encouraged the father to express his care and worry to her and then to discuss with her the compromise that may be accepted by both of them. In a follow-up meeting, the two of them expressed satisfaction, and Sawsan returned to normal communication with the family with no headaches.

## Typical Issues

- Girls are typically *brought* by their parents and take a passive and submitting role in the first meeting, when their parents are present and dominate the conversation. ~~Believing physical symptoms/ailments~~

- Sawsan has expressed her distress passively (withdrawal) and somatically (headache).

- Arab/Muslim clients approach counseling and psychotherapy after they visit a medical doctor.

- Arab/Muslim parents typically are not sensitive and empathic to their children's emotional needs and do not understand their distress as long as the materialistic needs (computer) are supplied.

- For Arab/Muslim parents, traditions and values are more important for decision making than their children's feelings.

- Arab/Muslim parents tend to attribute bad behavior to external entities such as "bad friends or readings" or, at other times, to bad spirits.

- The behavior of Arab children in the presence of their parents (external control) is extremely different from that when they are away from external control. It is not that one behavior is real and the other is false; rather, the two behaviors represent two different real components in their personality.

- It is too difficult for Arab children to criticize their parents in a conversation with a foreigner, such as a counselor, and they typically emphasize that the intentions of their parents were good.

- The main conflict that should have been resolved was an intrafamilial rather than an intrapsychic one; therefore, counseling was focused on the family relationship to accomplish change in the relationship that fits the family belief system. Change was possible only after establishing a good joining with the father.

- Counseling with Arab/Muslim families does not change or confront the family culture or the family structure; rather, it helps to find better solutions within that culture.

## DISCUSSION QUESTIONS

1. What can you learn from this case about the characteristics of Arab/Muslim clients?

2. Can this case be understood in psychodynamic terms? According to the psychodynamic approach, was this treatment efficient?

3. Do you have any other culturally sensitive ideas that may help with this case?

# REFERENCES

Achoui, M. (2003). Taa'dib al atfal fi al wasat al a'ai'li: Waqea' wa ittijahat [Children disciplining within the family context: Reality and attitudes]. *Al tofoolah A Arabiah, 16*(4), 9–38.

Al-Issa, I. (1989). Psychiatry in Algeria. *Psychiatric Bulletin, 13,* 240–245.

Al-Issa, I. (1995). The illusion of reality or the reality of illusion: Hallucination and culture. *British Journal of Psychiatry, 166,* 368–373.

Al-Kittani, F. (2000). *Al ittijahat al walideyah fi al tanshia'a al ijtimaa'yah* [Parents' approaches in socialization]. Amman, Jordan: Dar Al Shorooq.

Al-Mahroos, F. (2001, October 20–22). Rasd thaherat sooa' al moa'amalah in Bahrain [Observation on abuse in Bahrain]. Abstract presented at the Conference on Child Abuse, Bahrain.

Al-Shqerat, M. A., & Al-Masri, A, N. (2001). Al isaa'a al laftheyah ded al atfal [Verbal abuse against children]. *Majallat Al Tofoolah Al Arabiah, 2*(7), 33–45.

American Psychiatric Association. (1994). *Diagnostic and statistical manual of mental disorders* (4th ed.). Washington, DC: Author.

American Psychiatric Association. (1997). *DSM IV sourcebook* (Vol. 3). Washington, DC: Author.

Baasher, T. (1962). Some aspects of the history of the treatment of mental disorders in the Sudan. *Sudan Medical Journal, 1,* 44.

Berg-Cross, L., & Chinen, R. T. (1995). Multicultural training models and person-in-culture interview. In J. G. Ponterotto, J. M. Casas, L. A. Suzuki, & C. M. Alexander (Eds.), *Handbook of multicultural counseling* (pp. 333–356). Thousand Oaks, CA: Sage.

Blos, P. (1967). The second individuation process of adolescence. *Psychoanalytic Studies of the Child, 22,* 162–186.

Bresler, D. (1984). Mind-controlled analgesia: The inner way to pain control. In A. A. Sheikh (Ed.), *Imagination and healing: Imagery and human development series* (pp. 211–230). New York: Baywood.

Dwairy, M. (1997a). A biopsychosocial model of metaphor therapy with holistic cultures. *Clinical Psychology Review, 17*(7), 719–732.

Dwairy, M. (1997b). *Personality, culture, and Arabic society.* Jerusalem: Al-Noor (in Arabic).

Dwairy, M. (1998). *Cross-cultural counseling: The Arab-Palestinian case.* New York: Haworth.

Dwairy, M. (Ed.). (1999). Cross-cultural psychotherapy [Special issue]. *Clinical Psychology Review, 19*(8).

Dwairy, M. (2001). Therapeutic use of the physical environment: Talking about a significant object. *Journal of Clinical Activities, Assignments & Handouts in Psychotherapy Practice: Innovations in Resources for Treatment and Intervention, 1*(1), 61–71.

Dwairy, M. (2002). Foundations of psychosocial dynamic personality theory of collective people. *Clinical Psychology Review, 22,* 343–360.

Dwairy, M. (2004a). Individuation among Bedouin versus urban Arab adolescents: National, ethnic and gender differences. *Cultural Diversity and Ethnic Minority Psychology, 10*(4), 340–350.

Dwairy, M. (2004b). Parenting styles and psychological adjustment of Arab adolescents. *Transcultural Psychiatry, 41*(2), 233–252.

Dwairy, M. (2006). *Counseling and psychotherapy with Arabs and Muslims: A culturally sensitive approach.* New York: Teachers College Press, Columbia University.

Dwairy, M., & Abu Baker, K. (1992). The use of stories in psychotherapy. *Al-Thaqafa, 1,* 34–37 (in Arabic).

Dwairy, M., & Menshar, K. E. (2006). Parenting style, individuation, and mental health of Egyptian adolescents. *Journal of Adolescence, 29,* 103–117.

Erikson, E. H. (1950). *Childhood and society.* New York: Norton.

Fisek, G. O., & Kagitcibasi, C. (1999). Multiculturalism and psychotherapy: The Turkish case. In P. B. Pedersen (Ed.), *Multiculturalism as a fourth force* (pp. 75–92). Philadelphia: Brunner/Mazel, Taylor & Francis Group.

Freud, S. (1900). *The interpretation of dreams* (Standard Edition, Vol. 4). New York: Macmillan.

Freud, S. (1964). An outline of psychoanalysis. In J. Strachey (Ed. & Trans.), *The standard edition of the complete psychological works of Sigmund Freud* (Vol. 23). London: Hogarth. (Original work published 1940)

Gregg, G. S. (2005). *The Middle East: A cultural psychology.* New York: Oxford University Press.

Hatab, Z., & Makki, A. (1978). *Al-solta el-abawia wal-shabab* [Parental authority and youth]. Beirut: Ma'had El-Inmaa' El-Arabi (in Arabic).

Hourani, A. (1983). *Arabic thoughts in the liberal age.* Cambridge, UK: Cambridge University Press.

Hourani, A. (1991). *A history of the Arab peoples.* New York: Warner.

Kopp, R. R. (1995). *Metaphor therapy: Using client-generated metaphors in psychotherapy.* New York: Brunner/Mazel.

Mahler, M., Bergman, A., & Pine, F. (1975). *The psychological birth of the infant: Symbiosis and individuation.* New York: Basic Books.

Markus, H. R., & Kitayama, S. (1998). The cultural psychology of personality. *Journal of Cross-Cultural Psychology, 29*(1), 63–87.

Okasha, A., Seif El Dawla, A., Khalil, A. H., & Saad, A. (1993). Presentation of acute psychosis in an Egyptian sample: A transcultural comparison. *Comprehensive Psychiatry, 34*(1), 4–9.

Qasem, F. S., Mustafa, A. A., Kazem, N. A., & Shah, N. M. (1998). Attitude of Kuwaiti parents toward physical punishment of children. *Child Abuse & Neglect, 22,* 1189–1202.

Racy, J. (1970). Psychiatry in Arab East. *Acta Psychiatrica Scandinavica, 221,* 160–171.

Saif El-Deen, A. (2001, October 20–22). *Sooa' al moa'amalah wa ihmal al atfal* [Abuse and neglect of children]. Abstract presented at the Conference on Child Abuse, Bahrain.

Timimi, S. B. (1995). Adolescence in immigrant Arab families. *Psychotherapy, 32,* 141–149.

United Nations Development Programme (UNDP). (2002). *Arab human development report 2002: Creating opportunity for future generations.* New York: Author.

# Counseling Persons of Black African Ancestry

Ivory Achebe Toldson

---

*Primary Objective*

- To teach counselors how to identify and accommodate the unique psychological traits and sociocultural background of persons of Black African ancestry

*Secondary Objectives*

- To describe psychological, cultural, and sociopolitical issues that counselors might consider before working with clients of Black African ancestry
- To propose enhanced practices and procedures for providing a more conducive counseling environment for African Americans and other clients of African descent

---

THE PURPOSE OF THIS CHAPTER IS TO HELP COUNSELORS AND OTHER MENTAL HEALTH PROFESSIONALS develop practices and procedures that appreciate Black people's common folkways and collective struggle. In North America and abroad, persons of Black African ancestry share behavioral patterns that evince their African origin, cultural adaptations to colonial autocracies (e.g., language and religion), and a collective struggle against racism and discrimination. The chapter emphasizes challenges counselors might face when working within traditional counseling settings, which often have values that are inconsistent with African cultural mores. Counseling solutions involve understanding, appreciating, and celebrating

Black culture; contextualizing mental health problems; promoting social advocacy and justice; and building on clients' strengths.

# COUNSELING PERSONS OF BLACK AFRICAN ANCESTRY: THE WAYS OF THE NONCOMMITTAL COUNSELOR

Envision a busy public mental health center servicing a poverty-stricken district in a major urban area. Medicaid recipients, wards of the state, court-ordered referrals, and others requiring public welfare or scrutiny comply with counselors, who comply with compliance officers, in a series of routine and spiritless encounters. Innovative counselors and inquisitive clients are perceived as insubordinate. Treatment plans are as mundane and recycled as the informed consent forms they follow, yet clients sign them with a blunted indifference. Expectations are low, relapse and recidivism are high, and the recipients are overwhelmingly overrepresented by poor persons of Black African ancestry.

The foregoing describes a real-life setting that was fictitiously depicted in a novel about an anxious young African American man's encounter with a community mental health center (I. A. Toldson, 2004b). After the young man revealed that he had nightmares about "demons" that represented actual people whom he wanted to "kill," the clinical director committed him under duty-to-warn guidelines. After being disrobed and restrained, the client conceded to the clinic's consternations by subduing his overt feelings of ire and suppressing his anger with psychotropic medication. His new docile demeanor pleased the clinical director and her staff but troubled one conscientious counselor. Covertly, the counselor preached Black empowerment to the defeated client and warned him that submitting to the will of the clinic was tantamount to submitting to oppression. In the end, the counselor's noncommittal intervention proved to be more effective for the Black client than the clinical manager's strict adherence to the status quo.

In many counseling settings, routine clinical practices and compliance standards often diminish the quality of care for Black clients. Some counselors report that they often alter standards and bend rules, not only to enhance Black clients' services but also to protect them from maltreatment (Williams, 2005). For example, one Black counselor reported that he instructs his Black adolescent clients to use the title of "Brother" instead of "Mr." when addressing him. Another counselor described the dissonance she felt when she frankly told her client to "just ignore that label . . . that's not who you really are," when referring to her client's treatment plan diagnosis. Yet another counselor encouraged her client to call out the name of a deceased loved one to keep his memory alive and not merely to "let go" of the past. Finally, a counselor admitted that he applauded his client's tough confrontation of her son's drug use. When used in traditional counseling settings, all of the above interventions may appear refractory and audacious, yet a body of literature supports their legitimacy for Black clients (Ayonrinde, 2003; Bhugra & Bhui, 1999; Brody et al., 2006; Harvey & Coleman, 1997; Herrick, 2006; Leavitt, 2003; Madsen & Leech, 2007; Reiser, 2003; I. A. Toldson & Toldson, 1999; Wills et al., 2007).

Notably, nothing heretofore stated should be casually considered a counseling strategy for African Americans or any other client of Black African ancestry. Throughout this chapter, I will resist the impulse to directly suggest counseling strategies and hope that readers will not intuit counseling methods that he or she will "try out" on a Black client. The literature is replete with novel techniques to address the unique counseling needs of persons of African descent—too many to reiterate in this chapter, but no less deserving of consideration.

Typically, however, counseling strategies are not the primary problem when working with Black clients. No counseling strategy offers a recipe for healing all persons of African descent. Several recent articles have warned against using a "cookie-cutter" approach to working with Black clients (Bowie, Cherry, & Wooding, 2005; Estrada, 2005; Respress & Lutfi, 2006; Taylor-Richardson, Heflinger, & Brown, 2006). Like a carpenter's tools, counseling strategies can be as effective, inept, or destructive as the person or organization using them. Helpers must be self-aware and able to use themselves as agents of change (Middleton et al., 2000). Moreover, the millions of Black people who exist are more different from one another than they are collectively different from other races (Artiles, Rueda, Salazar, & Higareda, 2005; de Valenzuela, Copeland, Huaqing Qi, & Park, 2006). In fact, the practice of force-fitting Black people into a category reflects a Eurocentric paradigm, which relies heavily on taxonomies to understand complex material (Leong & Wong, 2003).

Afrocentric approaches de-emphasize classification systems and guidelines and highlight relativity and rhythm (Cokley, 2005; Washington, Johnson, Jones, & Langs, 2007). In this view, counseling strategies are not rules that match a specific taxonomy of clients and their problems. Rather, the relative importance of a counselor's strategy depends on the rhythm and context of a session.

## HISTORY AND NOMENCLATURE

Persons of Black African ancestry live as citizens, foreign nationals, and indigenous populations on every continent as a result of immigration, colonialism, and slave trading. With an estimated population of 39.9 million, 13.8% of the total population, African Americans constitute the second largest non-White ethnic group in the United States (U.S. Census Bureau, 2003). Today, most Black people in the Americas are the progeny of victims of the transatlantic slave trade. From 1619 to 1863, millions of Africans were involuntarily relocated from various regions of West Africa to newly established European colonies in the Americas. Many different African ethnic groups, including the Congo, Yoruba, Wolof, and Ibo, were casualties of the transatlantic slave trade. The Black American population is the aggregate of these groups, consolidated into one race, bound by a common struggle against racial oppression and distinguished by cultural dualism (I. A. Toldson, 1999). Du Bois (1996) illustrated cultural dualism in his observation that the Black American has "two souls, two thoughts, two unreconciled strivings; two warring ideals in one dark body, whose dogged strength alone keeps it from being torn asunder" (p. 23).

Importantly, the historic legacy of Black people in the Western Hemisphere is not limited to slavery. The Olmec heads found along the Mexican Gulf Coast is striking evidence of African colonies in the Americas centuries before Columbus arrived in the Caribbean (Van Sertima, 2003). Black people were also responsible for establishing the world's first free Black republic and only the second independent nation in the Western Hemisphere, with the Haitian Revolution (Geggus, 2001). In the United States, almost 500,000 African Americans were free prior to the Civil War and were immensely instrumental in shaping U.S. policy throughout abolition and beyond. Post Civil War, African Americans influenced U.S. arts, agriculture, foods, textile, and language and invented technological necessities such as the traffic light and elevators, as well as parts necessary to build the automobile and personal computer. All of these contributions were necessary for the United States to become a world power in the 20th century.

Racism and oppression are forces that have shaped the experiences and development of Black people worldwide. Although European colonialists initially enslaved Black people because of their agricultural expertise and genetic resistance to diseases, they used racist propaganda to justify their inhumane practices (Loewen, 1996). During periods of slavery and the "Scramble for Africa," European institutions used pseudoscience and religion (e.g., the Hamitic myth[1]) to dehumanize Black people. The vestiges of racism and oppression survived centuries after propaganda campaigns ended and influence all human interactions, including counseling relationships.

Today, racism is perpetuated most profoundly through the educational system (Loewen, 1996). Loewen (1996) pointed out that students are taught to revere Columbus, who nearly committed genocide against the native population of the Dominican Republic, and Woodrow Wilson, who openly praised the Ku Klux Klan. Although many of these facts are not well known and purposefully disguised in history texts, children often leave traditional elementary and secondary education with the sense that, aside from a few isolated figures (e.g., Martin Luther King Jr. and Harriet Tubman), Black people had a relatively small role in the development of modern nations (May, Willis, & Loewen, 2003).

Contemporary literature on the health, economic, and social status of Black people, especially in the United States, is dismal. Evidence is often presented that suggests that African Americans have the highest incidence and mortality of any given mental or physical disorder, are more deeply affected by social ills, and generally have the lowest economic standing. While most of the statistics are accurately presented, rationales are usually baseless, and findings typically lack a sociohistorical context. In addition, studies on African Americans unfairly draw social comparisons to the social groups that historically benefited from their oppression. Rarely are African Americans compared to national groups with a similar age, history, and experience. For example, although the median income of African Americans is roughly 66% of the median income of Americans of European descent, the gross domestic production (GDP) of African Americans collectively is 2.5 times the GDP of Poland and 8 times the GDP of the Ukraine. African Americans' unemployment is about the same as Spain's (I. A. Toldson & Scott, 2006).

Historical distortions accompanying dismal statistics have resulted in many counselors perpetually using a deficit model when working with Black clients. The deficit model focuses on clients' problems, without exploring sociohistorical factors or institutional procedures. Persons of Black African ancestry have a distinguished history, are immeasurably resilient, and have developed sophisticated coping mechanisms throughout centuries of oppression. Appreciating and celebrating a client's legacy, contextualizing problems, and building on strengths instead of focusing on deficits are universally appreciated counseling strategies, which merit greater prudence when working with Black clients (Amatea, Smith-Adcock, & Villares, 2006).

## PSYCHOLOGICAL DEVELOPMENT

Historically, the quest for a bona fide cultural identity has been ubiquitous in the lives and experiences of persons of Black African ancestry (Cross, 1989; Du Bois, 1996). Throughout centuries of colonialism, slavery, and racial oppression, Black people emerged who rejected inferiority labels to advance a more positive image for their race. The legacies of Harriet Tubman, Nat Turner, and Nelson Mandela are exemplars of this phenomenon. While many Black psychologists interpret the successive stages and components of Black identity differently, the consensus maintains that the development of Black people is not embedded in mental illness or self-hate but is a natural disposition to oppose miseducation and internalize Black culture, heritage, and folkways. Essentially, three forces make up the identity of persons of Black African ancestry. Within each force, there are countless manifestations through Black persons' personality, psyche, and behavior:

1. Expressions of African consciousness

2. Resistance to racism and oppression

3. Adaptations to colonialism

# Expressions of African Consciousness

African consciousness embodies archetypal and ancestral wisdom in Black people's collective memory. Predisposition toward vital emotionalism, spontaneity, rhythm, naturalistic attitudes, physical movement, style, and creativity with the spoken word are cultural expressions that form the core of African consciousness. These characteristics interact to produce human behavior that registers images, sounds, aromas, and euphoria to the senses (Pasteur & Toldson, 1982; I. L. Toldson & Toldson, 2001).

Expressions of African consciousness heavily influence Black people's subjective worldview. As a construct, African consciousness helps persons of African descent to attain optimal self-concept, self-esteem, and self-image (Constantine, Myers, Kindaichi, & Moore, 2004). African consciousness is the archetypal background from which diasporic Africans must formulate answers to questions of identity. "Who am I? How do I see myself? Who defined my image, and was my image defined in a way to help me challenge, confront, and overcome adversity? Who do I come from? What can I do? What do I believe about my lineage and myself? Where am I going in life? And what does it mean when I become ill (sick, fail, transgress, addicted)?" (I. L. Toldson & Toldson, 2001, p. 405).

Black communities use elements of African consciousness to serve as a balance or counterpart to the mind and body (Cervantes & Parham, 2005). This balance secures harmony, proportion, and symmetry with nature, self, and others. Spirituality is the basic underlining or constituting entity of the African consciousness, embodying essential properties, attributes, and elements indispensable to their subjective worldview. The spirit is an immaterial, sentient part of Black persons, providing inward structure, dynamic drive, and creative responses to life encounters or demands. Recognition of the African consciousness, as well as the distinct way it manifests under various circumstances, is essential to African-centered therapeutic interventions.

Traditional Africans consider affliction illness to be both spiritual and physical (Mbiti, 1969) and healing as a function of every thought, emotion, and activity working toward achieving individual balance. This holistic perspective makes healing a collective undertaking. Accordingly, James-Myers (1988) argues that the view that reality is inseparably spiritual and material is essential to the African consciousness (Hatter & Ottens, 1998; Mphande & James-Myers, 1993; Tyehimba, 1998).

Contrarily, Western psychology emphasizes a material view of reality that focuses on awareness through the five senses. The Eurocentric perspective sees the world as an infinite number of discreetly different manifestations presenting as observable, material phenomena (Leong & Wong, 2003). Simply stated, while the Eurocentric paradigm might suggest, "Seeing is believing," the Afrocentric paradigm would suggest, "There is more than meets the eye."

Consistent with Afrocentric perspectives, many contemporary physicists and psychologists believe that a material conception of reality is outmoded (Cunliffe, 2006; Davis, 2005; Nelson, 2006). Spirit, in the African cosmos, rhythmically shapes things, ideals, animals, and human beings together in the representative whole of its essence (Cervantes & Parham, 2005; Constantine et al., 2004; Herrick, 2006; I. L. Toldson & Pasteur, 1972). When this rhythm is disturbed, the spirit is unsettled and manifests in the individual as anxiety, depression, or other mental or physical disorders (Blackett & Payne, 2005). Restoring this rhythm to achieve an integrative harmony within the self is the goal of African-centered approaches to therapy. These approaches form the backdrop to culturally appropriate therapeutic services delivered in the African American community (Vontress, 1991, 1999).

The absence of a "balanced focus" in modern-day medicine places many Black patients in an *etiological dilemma* with respect to acquired illnesses. Finch (1990) insists that among traditional African people, "Without the psycho-spiritual cure—without reestablishing this sensitive harmony—the medicinal cure is considered useless" (p. 129). Finch goes on to say that African medicine has baffled scholars because it completely integrates the "magico-spiritual" and "rational" elements. The spiritual aspect of healing has been discredited among the modern-day scientific-minded scholars. However, Finch explains that modern medicine acknowledges that 60% of illnesses treated by physicians have a psychological basis, and interventions quite often involve pharmacologically inactive drugs, or placebos.

## Resistance to Racism and Oppression

Kessler, Mickelson, and Williams (1999) conducted a telephone survey that explored the impact of racism on mental health. The study revealed that 50% of African Americans have experienced "major discrimination." In addition, major discrimination was associated with psychological distress. The authors concluded that racism and oppression adversely affect mental health and place African Americans at a greater risk for mental disorders such as depression and anxiety (Kessler et al., 1999).

Akbar (1991) asserted that racism and oppression is an aberration to the natural development of Black people. Therefore, when Black people exhibit "abnormal" behavior, psychological explanations should consider (1) whether the behavior is a product of an "alien-self" (i.e., an identity that has conformed to racism and behaves contrary to his or her true self-interest) or (2) whether the behavior, though anomalous, is perceived as necessary to survive under oppressive conditions (Akbar, 1991).

Thus, the influences of racism and oppression on the psychological development of Black people are twofold. First, racism and oppression contribute to behavioral responses that signal concern about survival, which can either increase psychological distress or promote unconventional survival mechanisms (Clark, Anderson, Clark, & Williams, 1999). In this view, Black people are not collectively injured by racism and oppression. Using basic ego defense mechanisms to illustrate, when responding to racism and oppression, some Black people might take a "middle-of-the-road" stance such as denial, intellectualization, or humor. A more harmful mechanism might be displacement, where a Black person will unconsciously redirect the resentment he or she feels for his or her oppressor to less threatening targets, such as that person's family and community. Contrarily, sublimation is a healthy and productive reaction to racism, which involves refocusing negative feelings into healthy outlets of expression, allowing for creative solutions to problems.

Beyond extrapolations from psychodynamic theory, several African-centered theories have emerged to explain the impact of racism and oppression on Black people's psychological functioning. *Cultural trauma*, for example, describes slavery, lynching, and legal discrimination beyond their past institutional manifestations and asserts that these experiences are embedded in the collective memory of present-day Black people (Alexander, 2004; Eyerman, 2001). The legacy of cultural trauma, according to Whaley (2006), is manifested in the destructive activities that occur in African American communities, including violence and substance abuse, which are also associated with symptoms of posttraumatic responses. *Posttraumatic slave syndrome* asserts that positive and negative adaptive behaviors survived throughout generations of Black people from the transatlantic slave trade and other atrocities (Leary, 2005). Leary (2005) suggests reinforcing adaptive behaviors and replacing maladaptive ones to promote healing among Black people.

Other models of racism and oppression focus on more contemporary manifestations of racism. *Invisibility syndrome*, for example, is a more subtle form of racism and White privilege that engenders race-related stress (Franklin & Boyd-Franklin, 2000; Franklin, Boyd-Franklin, & Kelly, 2006). Finally, the presence of *historical hostility*, resulting from slavery and discrimination, is reported to contribute to a "unique psychology" among African Americans that may result in tension and mistrust of non-Black counselors (Vontress & Epp, 1997).

The second consequence of racism and oppression is more directly related to postcolonial institutions, including organizations that provide counseling services (Fairchild, 1991; Fairchild, Yee, Wyatt, & Weizmann, 1995). Mental health in America has roots in racism and oppression. During slavery, mental health professionals diagnosed runaways with *Drapetomania,* meaning "flight from home mania" (Fernando, 2003). Black people who were content with subservience were considered mentally healthy. Similarly, Thomas and Sillen (1972) revealed that among the "startling facts from the census" published in the *American Journal of Insanity* (1851) was the fact that enslaved Black people experience lower levels of insanity than free Black people.

Today, the attitude that persons of Black African ancestry should have psychomotor restrictions continues to pervade mental health systems. African American patients are more frequently involuntarily committed to psychiatric hospitals and administered psychotropic drugs (F. Baker, 1988). In addition, persons of Black African ancestry continue to receive labels of borderline intellectual functioning and mental retardation on the basis of psychometric scales that were constructed based on a Eurocentric paradigm and normed primarily on persons of European descent (Hilliard, 1976, 1980).

Many conscious counselors are aware that current mental health systems are failing Black clients. In a counseling psychology doctoral class at an urban university, a professor asked his students in a Black psychology class to "raise your hand if you've ever oppressed your client." More than half of the students dejectedly raised their hands. With remarkable insight, the students realized that by simply following the rules of their employers, they were participating in less than optimal practices that contributed to their clients' oppression.

Ways in which counselors and other mental health professionals routinely oppress their clients include (1) using biased psychological tests to inform counseling decisions, (2) writing or endorsing reports that emphasize deficits, (3) endorsing the use of psychotropic medication to suppress culturally or developmentally appropriate behaviors, (4) using the majority culture as the basis for behavioral norms, and (5) adhering to diagnostic classification systems, without regard to cultural considerations.

## Adaptations to Colonialism

Persons of Black African ancestry have had to adapt to the language, customs, religious practices, educational pedagogy, economic philosophies, and geopolitical systems of European colonial tyrants (Loomba, 2005; Lyons & Pye, 2006; Valls, 2005). For centuries, European colonial empires extended their sovereignty over territory beyond their homeland, using Black African slave labor to cultivate the Americas and native Black Africans to build dependencies, trading posts, and plantation colonies. The colonizers imposed their sociocultural mores, religion, and language on Black people and adopted a corrupt set of values, including racism, ethnocentrism, and imperialism, which aimed to justify the means by which colonial settlements were established.

In the relatively recent history of Black people achieving equal rights under the law in the Americas (i.e., 1964) and sovereign nationhood in Africa (i.e., 1950s–1970s), Black people have adapted, mastered, and innovated traditional European systems. Black people have added words and dialects to European languages, established educational institutions based on Eurocentric pedagogy, and maintained financial institutions based on laissez-faire capitalism. A Eurocentric mind-set will lead many to assert that Black people are obliged to adapt, and adaptation should be effortless. In reality, adaptation is a cultural imposition to Black people worldwide. Imagine White Americans having to adapt to a system in which expressive oratory mastery was required for college admission, bartering was the primary method of exchange, and laws were determined by a counsel of elders.

In the postcolonial era, there have been many critiques of the impact of colonialism and whether colonialism exists today. Colonialism permanently changed the social-cultural, geographical, political, and economic landscape of the world. Persons of Black African ancestry in Africa and the Americas continue to live as second-class citizens, whereas generations-old businesses and banks that financed acts of genocide and other atrocities reap residual benefits from the legacy of colonialism.

Colonialism has implications for counseling practice and research on Black people. First, the psychological impact of colonialism and the survival of indigenous values among colonialized people influence counseling relationships. Second, cultural imperialism is a natural by-product of colonialism, leading many counselors to make assumptions about a client's traditions and values that are shaped by the majority culture. In addition to cultural imperialism, ethnocentrism, racism, White supremacy, and pseudo-scientific theories used to justify colonialism have lingered well past decolonialism and influence counseling research and practice.

*Conclusion.* Collectively, the three forces of Black people's psychological development embody the infinite diversity and the omnipotent potential of persons of Black African ancestry. It is the archetypal forces providing definition to their inner structures, mechanisms of endurance, dynamic drive, and ability to adapt to foreign environments. It represents the whole of Black people, illustrating past preeminence, assuring present perseverance, and ensuring future consummation.

# MENTAL HEALTH AND MENTAL HEALTH CARE
## Conceptualizing Mental Health Problems

Difficulties conceptualizing Black people's mental health problems typically arise from the tendency of mental health professionals to objectively deduce mental health problems and assume individual autonomy. Practitioners who rely on deductive assessment methods typically assemble discrete and specific data (e.g., age, duration of problem, and scores on psychometric assessments) to determine the probability that a client has a particular problem and predict associated behavioral outcomes. This diagnosis/prognosis approach implicitly suggests that problems originate and are perpetuated within each individual (Atkinson, Morten, & Sue, 1997), potentially undermining the complexity of Black people's mental health problems and resilience factors.

Nonlinear scientific approaches and ecological theory (e.g., Bronfenbrenner, 1979) have been used to more effectively explain the etiology and course of mental health challenges within the Black community. Some authors note that a competent assessment of Black problematic behavior should not be limited to a description of mental and emotional deficits or to observations of externalized abnormal behaviors (Hill, 2004; Kagawa-Singer, Katz, Taylor, & Venderryn, 1996; I. A. Toldson & Toldson, 1999). Instead, an accurate assessment should extend to describe inherent responses to social and environmental conditions, in which the so-called abnormal behavior might be a "normal" reaction. In other words, Black behavioral pathology is sometimes best explained as a consequence of dynamic ecological systems, rather than the result of intrapsychological deficits (I. A. Toldson & Toldson, 1999). Furthermore, nonlinear conceptions of mental health challenges will assert that a client's potential is more important than her or his position, and "possibility" is as real and material as probability when prognosticating the course of any given disorder.

On a basic level, when considering the mental health status of Black people, counselors must consider the universality of diagnoses, be aware of biases in mental health procedures, and be sensitive to diversity. Universality is the idea that disorders found in some cultures may manifest differently or be obsolete in other cultures (Lee, 2002). However, to achieve true authenticity in conceptualizing the mental health status of Black people, professionals must relate to their subject with the holism that is consistent with African-centered perspectives and its Western adaptations, such as existentialism (De Maynard, 2006; Epp, 1998) and positive psychology (Seligman, 2002).

Nontraditional approaches might require clinicians to grasp a client's mental health using insight and intuition, intellectual creativity, and abstract reasoning. This might sound absurdly irrational to a staunch adherent to the scientific method. However, in practice, using deductive logic to understand mental health often reduces the client to a blunder of fragmented inferences, rent asunder from the whole in which they belong. The mental health status of Black people should be viewed within the context of their history and nomenclature, as well as the complex set of forces that influence their cultural identity.

## Specific Mental Health Challenges

*Prevalence of Mental Health Disorders.* The Epidemiological Catchment Area (ECA) studies and the National Comorbidity Survey (NCS) have been used to assess the prevalence rate of mental health disorders across cultures. The ECA indicated that Black people have an overall higher prevalence of mental health disorders; however, when controlling for socioeconomic factors, most differences are statistically eliminated. Both the ECA and NCS found that African Americans are less likely to suffer from depression. The ECA indicated that African Americans are more likely to suffer from phobia than are Whites. Using several studies, the U.S. Department of Health and Human Services (U.S. DHHS, 2001) concluded that African Americans are overdiagnosed with schizophrenia and underdiagnosed with depression and anxiety (F. M. Baker & Bell, 1999; Borowsky et al., 2000; Neal-Barnett & Smith, 1997). Schizophrenia and affective disorders specifically are uniquely associated with forces that shape Black people's psychological development and must be carefully examined within a cultural context.

According to Fernando (2003), reports suggesting high rates of schizophrenia among African Americans began to appear in the 19th century (e.g., Babcock, 1895). By the mid-1900s, the over-diagnosis of schizophrenia was firmly established, while the diagnosis of bipolar disorders began to decline. Interestingly, British studies during the same time period revealed similar diagnostic trends, although reports of schizophrenic behavior in Africa were rare (Fernando, 2003). In 1973, Simon et al. conducted an examination of the excessive diagnosing of schizophrenia among Black people. Simon et al.'s findings revealed that the overrepresentation of Black people with schizophrenia was primarily due to diagnostic biases, rather than true differences in the population. Today, the excessive and inaccurate diagnosis of schizophrenia may be attributed to Black people's nonmaterial conception of reality, spirituality or religiosity, and/or "healthy paranoia," originally defined as a generalized reaction to racism, which is perceived as necessary for normal adaptive functioning in oppressive environments (Grier & Cobbs, 1968).

Racial biases that permeate mental health systems may also contribute to the underdiagnosis of depression. Fernando (2003) noted that in the past, the lower incidence of depression among African Americans has been attributed to frontal lobe idleness, which caused Black people to lack higher order emotional functions (Carothers, 1953) and resulted in a tendency for Black people to "respond to adversity with cheery denial" (Bebbington, Hurry, & Tennant, 1981, p. 51). These blatantly racist explanations are comparable to recent findings that clinicians tend to minimize emotional expressions by African Americans (Das, Olfson, McCurtis, & Weissman, 2006), which lead to less Black people being diagnosed with depression. Das et al. (2006) suggested that clinicians circumvent cultural influences by examining "somatic and neurovegetative symptoms rather than mood or cognitive symptoms" (p. 30). This approach undermines Black people's psychological functioning and implies that clinicians should ignore symptoms that they do not understand, rather than broaden their cultural lenses.

*Suicide.* Research on suicide within the African American community has recently increased. African Americans generally have lower suicide rates when compared to Caucasians, despite significant economic and social disparities within the Black community. Black women have the lowest suicide rate among all race/gender groups. However, recent analyses of suicide rates across cultures indicate that although older White men commit suicide more than all other older race/gender groups, the suicide rates among young White men and young Black men are the same (U.S. DHHS, 2001). The Centers for Disease Control and Prevention (1998) reported that between 1980 and 1995, the suicide rate among African Americans ages 10 to 14 increased at almost twice the rate of comparable White respondents. During a meeting, a former police chief and president of the National Organization of Black Law Enforcement Executives (NOBLE) described a trend that basically implied "police-assisted suicides," where young Black men would try to bait police officers into shooting them (C. Edwards, personal communication, 2005). This mainly occurred in impoverished areas with high rates of violence and police brutality.

*Exposure to Violence and Posttraumatic Stress.* African Americans are more likely to be victims of violent crimes than any other ethnic or racial group (Cooper Helfrich, 2000; U.S. Public Health Service, 2001). Citing Schwab-Stone et al. (1999), the U.S. DHHS (2001) noted that more than 40% of inner-city young people have witnessed someone being shot or stabbed (Schwab-Stone et al., 1999). According to Feldman (2006), while murder is the fifth leading cause of death for young White men, it is the number one cause of death among young Black men. In some areas of the country, a young Black male has a higher probability of being murdered than a soldier did in the Vietnam War (Feldman, 2006). Approximately one fourth of African American youth who had been exposed to violence fit the diagnostic criteria for posttraumatic stress disorder (Fitzpatrick & Boldizar, 1993).

*Vulnerable Segments of the Population.* Persons of Black African ancestry are susceptible to a variety of mental health problems because they are overrepresented in the most vulnerable segments of the population. Although only 13.8% of the U.S. population, African Americans comprise between 40% and 44% of the homeless population (U.S. DHHS, 2001), nearly half of state and federal inmates (Bureau of Justice Statistics, 1999), and 45% of children in state custody (U.S. DHHS, 2001). Mental health problems are commonly the antecedent and consequence of being exposed to any of the aforementioned social conditions. In addition, all of the above conditions are interrelated. For example, a child may enter state custody as a result of a parent's incarceration.

The mental health of younger African Americans is of particular concern. Currently, African Americans' representation in the juvenile justice system (30%) is twice their representation in the general population (Rozie-Battle, 2002). In addition, only half of Black students who start high school graduate within 4 years, compared to 75% of White students (Edney, 2004; Valentine, 2005). Research evidence suggests that the juvenile justice system and current educational policies fail to meet the basic educational and remedial needs of socially disadvantaged African American children. A recent study indicated that nationwide, most juvenile correctional facilities offer substandard educational accommodations to youth detainees (Gehring, 2005).

Consequently, African American adolescent detainees, incarcerated for even minor offenses, will exit the juvenile justice system with severe educational deficits (Morrison & Epps, 2002). Moreover, recent research findings challenge the utility of educational policies, such as the No Child Left Behind (NCLB) Act, for African American adolescents. The NCLB mandates that funnel resources into classroom instruction, prescribed by commercial "whole-school reform" packages, inherently neglect social and emotional factors that predict African American achievement (McMillian, 2003).

## Healing Practices and Experiences With Mental Health Treatment

Survey research suggests that persons of Black African ancestry prefer mental health healing practices that are consistent with African cultural mores. In accord with African consciousness, Black people are more likely to use prayer, faith, and spirituality to cope with personal difficulties (Constantine, Lewis, Conner, & Sanchez, 2000; Cooper-Patrick et al., 1997; Taylor, Ellison, Chatters, Levin, & Lincoln, 2000). In the Black community, religious figures serve a prominent role in providing counseling services for bereavement, marital problems, and personal adjustment issues (Levin & Taylor, 1998). The tradition of relying on religious leaders, such as Nat Turner, Elijah Muhammad, Malcolm X, and Martin Luther King Jr., to overcome adversity is well established within the Black community. Accordingly, in the United States, Black Americans have reported more religious involvement and more often seek comfort through spiritual activities when compared to White Americans (Taylor, Chatters, Jayakody, & Levin, 1996).

Black people's collectivist orientation is also evident in their healing preferences. Specifically, persons of Black African ancestry are more likely to rely on family and friends to cope with personal difficulty (Logan, 1996; Ruiz, 1990). The "brotherhood/sisterhood" concept among African Americans elevates family extensions to the status of core family members, and solutions to personal difficulties often involve meaningful exchange throughout the extended family. Sue's (1998) finding that African Americans prefer therapists of the same race or ethnicity likely reflects the collectivist orientation, in which Black people will disclose more readily when they feel a certain kinship with the caregiver. Thus, Black people in therapy may feel compelled to elevate the status of the clinician to an extended family member before actively engaging in the therapeutic process.

Naturalistic healing is another value that is evident in mental health healing practices among Black people. In a review of the literature, the U.S. DHHS (2001) found that African Americans prefer counseling to drug therapy and are more likely to have concerns about the side effects, effectiveness, and addiction potential of medications (Cooper-Patrick et al., 1997; Dwight-Johnson, Sherbourne, Liao, & Wells, 2000). Similarly, Das et al. (2006) observed that African Americans may have more stigmas related to taking medication and more likely to have spiritual values that are inconsistent with medication use. The U.S. DHHS also reported that African Americans tend to take an "active approach" (p. 28) to facing personal problems and are less likely than Whites to use any professional services to deal with mental health issues. In this view, Black people might prefer a process of healing that feels more natural, emphasizing normal adjustments to life transitions, and less intrusive or "technical" approaches, such as medication or a formal brand of therapy.

Conceivably, Black people's healing preferences have many inconsistencies with traditional mental health systems. For example, mental health providers may misconstrue staunch spirituality as hypereligiosity; often viewed as a symptom of psychosis. Furthermore, any semblance of "kinship" with caregivers deviates from ethical practice standards. Therefore, many mental health providers will likely resist a client's attempts to create a more personal tone to the treatment process. Research evidence suggests that inconsistencies between Black cultural mores and traditional mental health systems may lead to some disenchantment among Black clients. African Americans are less likely than Whites to use professional mental health services and more likely to rely on family, friends, and the extended community to deal with personal challenges (Sussman, Robins, & Earls, 1987; I. L. Toldson & Toldson, 2001). Sussman et al. (1987) revealed that almost 50% of African Americans are afraid of mental health services, compared to 20% of White Americans (U.S. DHHS, 2001). In addition to the cultural incompatibility associated with Black people's African consciousness, apparently, racism and oppression have contributed to disillusionment with mental health services among African Americans. LaVeist (2000) reported that 43% of African Americans, compared to 5% of Whites, experienced racism in a treatment setting.

## TOWARD AUTHENTICITY IN COUNSELING PERSONS OF BLACK AFRICAN ANCESTRY

*Community-Based Treatment.* Some progressive and comprehensive mental health treatment programs endorse rendering services in the clients' homes, schools, and communities (Bennett, 2006; Teicher, 2006; I. L. Toldson & Toldson, 2001). Community-based approaches could address Black people's reluctance to seek mental health care in traditional settings, reduce the ethnocentric biases among care providers, and help care providers to have a better context for clients' problems.

From an African-centered perspective, community-based interventions could represent a progressive step toward communalizing the mental health delivery process. Traditional African healers typically treat patients in the home and initiate informal and unstructured contact with the family. In addition, traditional West African healers often manipulate the environment to alter anxiety-arousing stimuli and encourage some acting out or abreaction to permit the patient to release feelings of angst (Swift & Asuni, 1975).

*Group Therapy.* Research suggests that group therapy is consistent with the African values of collectivism and communalism (Hopa, Simbayi, & Du Toit, 1998; Utsey, Howard, & Williams, 2003; Watlington & Murphy, 2006). The group combats the sense of isolation that Western individualism might engender. Yalom's (1995) idea of universality resembles the African notion of oneness of being. Creating this sense within the group requires culturally appropriate interventions and procedures.

*Rituals and Rites.* Based on Black expressive psychology theory, some research has provided cogent examples of integrating African ethos into clinical settings through rituals and rites of passages (I. A. Toldson & Toldson, 1999). Specific techniques suggested include having therapy group members dress alike on designated days, leading ritualistic unison recitation of important beliefs, creating ceremonies that emphasize group members' reliance on each other, and developing cohesive elements such as secret hand signals, passwords, and codes. Creating dance/drilling steps that embody the African propensity for psychomotor kinesthesia, combined with music and dramatic storytelling to express innermost and troubling feelings, is another example of recommendations they make.

*Social Justice and Advocacy.* Social and institutional policies often affect the scope, direction, and daily functioning of counselors who work with clients of Black African ancestry. Policies can directly transform professional practice by weakening the stability of vulnerable segments of society and manipulating social conditions associated with risk and resilience (Burnett, Oyemade-Bailey, & Toldson, 2006). Traditionally, helping professionals adjust and adapt to changing institutional policies and legislation, with little involvement or influence over legislative agendas. Because of the unique needs of Black people, stemming from a history of racism and oppression, effective counselors should gain the knowledge and tools they need to shape policy and influence legislative agendas to advocate for their clientele.

Being an effective counseling advocate might involve (1) learning how to identify and interpret legislative bills and policies affecting their clients, (2) understanding the formal and informal power structure of the legislature, (3) directly and indirectly communicating with law makers and influencing legislative agendas, and (4) using the legislative process to enhance social advocacy and promote social justice for clients.

## SUMMARY AND CONCLUSIONS

Accommodating Black people's history, common belief patterns, thoughts, and sociocultural customs enhances counseling services for clients of Black African ancestry. Mental health care providers who embrace the idea that an African identity can manifest in the psyches of their Black clients will be more effective in recognizing and addressing problem areas and resilience factors. Therefore, effective counseling for Black people requires recognizing group identity and collective responsibility within Black culture and accepting spiritual forces as meaningful phenomena in the life realm and decision-making processes. Counselors can use African ethos by recognizing the clients' family, church, social/civic, associations, friends, fraternal and sorority societies, and/or sociopolitical organizations as sources of influence and healing. Equally important, counselors should remain open to dialogue about the clients' faith and not view "magico-logical" thinking as pathology or naïveté. Simply stated, counselors are advised not to compete with God.

Conscientious providers also understand the sociopolitical forces that create barriers for Black clients and have the fortitude to advocate for social justice or be a "noncommittal counselor" when necessary. Differentiating between symptoms of acute stress and stress arising from sociopolitical powerlessness is an essential clinical skill of counselors who work with Black clients. In addition, using diagnostic labels such as schizophrenic, borderline personality, oppositional defiant, and conduct and attention deficit hyperactivity disorder (ADHD) to describe the mental health condition of Black people should be used with extreme caution. Mental states such as fear, attachment and loss, sadness, and identity role confusion are more useful for instilling hope and promoting healing. One question that might be helpful for a counselor to ask herself or himself is, "What is the opposite of the label I'm giving?" When the counselor can answer the question easily (e.g., the opposite of restlessness is calm), solutions are more lucid. Contrarily, when the question is difficult (e.g., the opposite of ADHD is . . .), a transient state may become endorsed as an enduring trait.

Overall, effective work with Black clients does not require a specific set of strategies. Rather, it requires adopting a worldview that appreciates a client's creative potential and an imaginative thought pattern that perceives the relativity and rhythm of a counseling experience. Relativity teaches counselors to work within a client's frame of reference and understand that his or her position in life is relative, rather than absolute. This concept is consistent with many emerging counseling perspectives, including existentialism and positive psychology. Using rhythm in counseling settings requires counselors to pick up on a certain "vibe" between the counselor and the client. In order to perceive the vibe, communication must be lucid, with unconditional positive regard, harmony, and altruistic responses. In other words, a counselor's cerebral understanding of the counseling craft and a client's sociocultural history must be combined with creative reasoning, compassion, faith, and spirit for advocacy.

Duce grew up in the Lower 9th Ward of New Orleans, Louisiana, in a rotting shotgun house with his mother and younger brother. An intellectually gifted teen, Duce prevailed academically in a community marred by drugs and poverty and received a scholarship to attend a historically Black university, located about 100 miles away from his community.

In college, Duce was a campus leader—a fiery orator and talented writer who chaired campus advocacy groups, spearheaded social justice rallies, and labored part-time at a halfway house for juvenile delinquents. He graduated with honors and accepted a scholarship to attend graduate school at a large flagship university in a rural mid-Atlantic college town.

Duce experienced some "culture shock" when he arrived at the university. He found the happy-go-lucky townies patronizing and fellow African American students scarce. Furthermore, his all-White thesis committee derided his thesis on Black men in the criminal justice system, calling it everything from "impractical" to "dangerous." Feeling isolated and misunderstood, Duce sought asylum in a trip to Brooklyn, New York, to visit a friend, only to become victim to a carjacking. The three Black men who carjacked him stole his car, with all digital and hard copies of his 67-page thesis in his trunk.

Beat and bitter, Duce took a leave of absence from school and returned to New Orleans to rewrite his thesis. However, when he returned home, he felt estranged from his community, his family, and his self. His family was struggling to rebuild their lives after losing their home to Hurricane Katrina, and his undergraduate college mentor died of prostate cancer. In addition, he had not emotionally resolved the irony and ill fate of losing his thesis to the type of Black men he wrote it to help. Duce began to battle with depression, bereavement, and anger. His only emotional and financial support came from his high school friend, who was a drug dealer. His friend purchased a new computer for him and gave him an opportunity to earn money by delivering narcotics to New Jersey.

Eventually, the FBI identified Duce as a suspect in the "war on drugs" and petitioned him to set up his best friend. Duce refused to "snitch," so the FBI turned him over to local authorities for a small amount of cocaine that he had in his possession. Although Duce never used cocaine, the public defender at the drug court convinced him to confess to "experimenting" to receive the full mercy of the court. The drug court judge gave him parole and mandated him to drug treatment.

In treatment, Duce was confrontational and verbally combative. He challenged the procedures at the clinic and insisted that he did not need treatment. A clinical manager construed some of Duce's gestures to be threatening. In addition, she found him to be extremely suspicious of others, and she considered his references to "demons attacking his spirit" to imply a state of psychosis. She recommended him to be evaluated by a psychiatrist, who prescribed Duce an "atypical antipsychotic" medication, commonly used to treat problems with anger. Duce reluctantly relented to the medication. After a week, he reported that the medication helped him sleep better. He continued to insist that he did not need drug counseling but conceded, "I have my fair share of problems, but right now, I'm just gonna put it in God's hands. . . . Only God can judge me."

## DISCUSSION QUESTIONS

1.  What are some of the psychological, cultural, and sociopolitical issues that a counselor might consider when working with Duce?

2.  Duce demonstrated many positive assets and resilience factors throughout his life. However, many of Duce's strengths appear masked in treatment by mistakes he made during a period of immense pain and

vulnerability. Discuss ways in which counselors can contextualize Duce's problems, and build on his strengths instead of focusing on his problems.

3. Racism and oppression may be involved in some of Duce's circumstances. Consider the following questions: (a) What was the cultural impact of Duce's graduate school experiences? (b) Why did the public defender think it was necessary for Duce to endorse drug use? (c) Would Duce have been perceived as threatening to the clinical manager if he was another race and/or gender?

4. What are several treatment outcomes that must be considered within the context of current research on Black people and mental health?

## NOTES

1. The Hamitic myth held that Black people descended from the biblical Ham—the "cursed" son of Noah. The Hamitic myth was used to promote Black inferiority worldwide and had particular consequences in the interethnic division preceding the genocide in Rwanda.

2. The critical incident is based on the main character of the novel by I. A. Toldson (2004a).

## REFERENCES

Akbar, N. (1991). Mental disorder among African Americans. In R. L. Jones (Ed.), *Black psychology* (Vol. 3, pp. 339–352). Berkeley, CA: Cobb & Henry.

Alexander, J. C. (2004). *Cultural trauma and collective identity.* Berkeley: University of California Press.

Amatea, E. S., Smith-Adcock, S., & Villares, E. (2006). From family deficit to family strength: Viewing families' contributions to children's learning from a family resilience perspective. *Professional School Counseling, 9*(3), 177–189.

Artiles, A. J., Rueda, R., Salazar, J. S. J., & Higareda, I. (2005). Within-group diversity in minority disproportionate representation: English language learners in urban school districts. *Exceptional Children, 71*(3), 283–300.

Atkinson, D. R., Morten, G., & Sue, D. W. (1997). *Counseling American minorities* (5th ed.). Dubuque, IA: McGraw-Hill.

Ayonrinde, O. (2003). Importance of cultural sensitivity in therapeutic transactions: Considerations for health-care providers. *Disease Management & Health Outcomes, 11*(4), 233–248.

Babcock, J. W. (1895). The colored insane. *Alienist and Neurologist, 16,* 423–447.

Baker, F. (1988). Afro-Americans. In I. Comas-Diaz & E. Griffith (Eds.), *Clinical guidelines in cross-cultural mental health* (pp. 151–181). New York: John Wiley.

Baker, F. M., & Bell, C. C. (1999). Issues in the psychiatric treatment of African Americans. *Psychiatric Services, 50,* 362–368.

Bebbington, P. E., Hurry, J. & Tennant, C. (1981). Psychiatric disorders in selected immigrant groups in Camberwell. *Social Psychiatry, 16,* 43–51.

Bennett, M. D., Jr. (2006). Cultural resources and school engagement among African American youths: The role of racial socialization and ethnic identity. *Children & Schools, 28*(4), 197–206.

Bhugra, D., & Bhui, K. (1999). Racism in psychiatry: Paradigm lost—paradigm regained. *International Review of Psychiatry, 11*(2/3), 236.

Blackett, P. S., & Payne, H. L. (2005). Health rhythms: A preliminary inquiry into group-drumming as experienced by participants on a structured day services programme for substance-misusers. *Drugs: Education, Prevention & Policy, 12*(6), 477–491.

Borowsky, S., Rubenstein, L. V., Meredith, L. S., Camp, P., Jackson-Triche, M., & Wells, K. B. (2000). Who is at risk of nondetection of mental health problems in primary care? *Journal of General Internal Medicine, 15*(6), 381–388.

Bowie, S. L., Cherry, D. J., & Wooding, L. H. (2005). African American MSW students: Personal influences on social work careers and factors in graduate school selection. *Social Work Education, 24*(2), 169–184.

Brody, G. H., McBride Murry, V., McNair, L., Brown, A. C., Molgaard, V., Spoth, R. L., et al. (2006). The Strong African American Families Program: Prevention of youths' high-risk behavior and a test of a model of change. *Journal of Family Psychology, 20*(1), 1–11.

Bronfenbrenner, U. (1979). *The ecology of human development: Experiments by nature and design.* Cambridge, MA: Harvard University Press.

Bureau of Justice Statistics. (1999). *The sourcebook of criminal justice statistics.* Washington, DC: Author.

Burnett, A. L., Oyemade-Bailey, U. J., & Toldson, M. (2006). *Blue ribbon commission on racial disparities in substance abuse policies.* Washington, DC: The National African American Drug Policy Coalition, Inc.

Carothers, J. C. (1953). *The African mind in health and disease: A study in ethnopsychiatry* (WHO Monograph Series No. 17). Geneva, Switzerland: World Health Organization.

Centers for Disease Control and Prevention. (1998). Suicide among Black youths—United States, 1980–1995. *Morbidity and Mortality Weekly Report, 47,* 193–195.

Cervantes, J. M., & Parham, T. A. (2005). Toward a meaningful spirituality for people of color: Lessons for the counseling practitioner. *Cultural Diversity & Ethnic Minority Psychology, 11*(1), 69–81.

Clark, R., Anderson, N., Clark, V., & Williams, D. (1999). Racism as a stressor for African Americans: A biopsychosocial model. *American Psychologist, 54*(1), 805–816.

Cokley, K. O. (2005). Racial(ized) identity, ethnic identity, and Afrocentric values: Conceptual and methodological challenges in understanding African American identity. *Journal of Counseling Psychology, 52*(4), 517–526.

Constantine, M. G., Lewis, E. L., Conner, L. C., & Sanchez, D. (2000). Addressing spiritual and religious issues in counseling African Americans: Implications for counselor training and practice. *Counseling and Values, 45*(1), 28.

Constantine, M. G., Myers, L. J., Kindaichi, M., & Moore, J. L., III. (2004). Exploring indigenous mental health practices: The roles of healers and helpers in promoting well-being in people of color. *Counseling and Values, 48*(2), 110–125.

Cooper Helfrich, L. D. (2000). *Children's exposure to community violence: Behavioral outcomes.* Doctoral dissertation, Wayne State University, Detroit, MI.

Cooper-Patrick, L., Powe, N. R., Jenckes, M. W., Gonzales, J. J., Levine, D. M., & Ford, D. E. (1997). Identification of patient attitudes and preferences regarding treatment of depression. *Journal of General Internal Medicine, 12,* 431–438.

Cross, W. E. (1989). Nigrescence: A nondiaphanous phenomenon. *Counseling Psychologist, 17*(2), 273–276.

Cunliffe, E. (2006). Without fear or favour? Trends and possibilities in the Canadian approach to expert human behaviour evidence. *International Journal of Evidence & Proof, 10*(4), 280–315.

Das, A. K., Olfson, M., McCurtis, H. L., Weissman, M. M. (2006). Depression in African Americans: Breaking barriers to detection and treatment. *Journal of Family Practice, 55*(1), 30–39.

Davis, A. (2005). Learning and the social nature of mental powers. *Educational Philosophy & Theory, 37*(5), 635–647.

De Maynard, V. A. (2006). Philosophy, 'race' and mental health: Another existential perspective. *Internet Journal of World Health & Societal Politics, 3*(1), 4.

de Valenzuela, J. S., Copeland, S. R., Huaqing Qi, C., & Park, M. (2006). Examining educational equity: Revisiting the disproportionate representation of minority students in special education. *Exceptional Children, 72*(4), 425–441.

Du Bois, W. E. B. (1996). *Souls of Black folks.* Grand Rapids, MI: Candace Press.

Dwight-Johnson, M., Sherbourne, C. D., Liao, D., & Wells, K. B. (2000). Treatment preferences among primary care patients. *Journal of General Internal Medicine, 15,* 527–534.

Edney, H. T. (2004). Black students still struggle in post-*Brown* era. *New York Amsterdam News, 95*(22), 37–38.

Epp, L. R. (1998). The courage to be an existential counselor: An interview of Clemmont E. Vontress. *Journal of Mental Health Counseling, 20,* 1.

Estrada, D. (2005). Multicultural conversations in supervision: The impact of the supervisor's racial/ethnic background. *Guidance & Counseling, 21*(1), 14–20.

Eyerman, R. (2001). *Cultural trauma: Slavery and the formation of African American identity.* Cambridge, UK: Cambridge University Press.

Fairchild, H. H. (1991). Scientific racism: The cloak of objectivity. *Journal of Social Issues, 47*(3), 101–115.

Fairchild, H. H., Yee, A. H., Wyatt, G. E., & Weizmann, F. M. (1995). Readdressing psychology's problems with race. *American Psychologist, 50*(1), 46–47.

Feldman, R. S. (2006). *Development across the life span* (4th ed.). Upper Saddle River, NJ: Pearson/Prentice Hall.

Fernando, S. (2003). *Cultural diversity, mental health and psychiatry: The struggle against racism.* New York: Brunner-Routledge.

Finch, C. (1990). *The African background to medical science: Essays on African history, science & civilizations.* London: Karnak House.

Fitzpatrick, K. M., & Boldizar, J. P. (1993). The prevalence and consequences of exposure to violence among African-American youth. *Journal of the American Academy of Child and Adolescent Psychiatry, 32,* 424–430.

Franklin, A. J., & Boyd-Franklin, N. (2000). Invisibility syndrome: A clinical model of the effects of racism on African-American males. *American Journal of Orthopsychiatry, 70*(1), 33.

Franklin, A. J., Boyd-Franklin, N., & Kelly, S. (2006). Racism and invisibility: Race-related stress, emotional abuse and psychological trauma for people of color. *Journal of Emotional Abuse, 6*(2/3), 9–30.

Geggus, D. P. (2001). *The impact of the Haitian Revolution in the Atlantic world.* Columbia: University of South Carolina Press.

Gehring, J. (2005). NCLB's mandates on delinquent youths get attention. *Education Week, 24*(43), 3.

Grier, W. H., & Cobbs, P. (1968). *Black rage.* New York: Basic Books.

Harvey, A. R., & Coleman, A. A. (1997). An Afrocentric program for African American males in the juvenile justice system. *Child Welfare, 76*(1), 197–211.

Hatter, D. Y., & Ottens, A. J. (1998). Afrocentric world view and Black students' adjustment to a predominantly White university: Does worldview matter? *College Student Journal, 32*(3), 472.

Herrick, K. E. (2006). Spirituality legitimized—almost. *Journal of Spirituality & Paranormal Studies, 29*(4), 227–236.

Hill, R. L. (2004). *An ecological view of the risk discourse in African-American adolescent identity development.* Doctoral dissertation, Syracuse University.

Hilliard, A. G. (1976). A review of Leon Kamin's *The science and politics of I.Q. Journal of Black Psychology, 2*(2), 64–74.

Hilliard, A. G. (1980). Cultural diversity and special education. *Exceptional Children, 46*(8), 584–588.

Hopa, M., Simbayi, L. C., & Du Toit, C. D. (1998). Perceptions on integration of traditional and Western healing in the new South Africa. *South African Journal of Psychology, 28*(1), 8.

James-Myers, L. (1988). *Understanding an Afrocentric worldview: Introduction to an optimal psychology.* Dubuque, IA: Kendall/Hunt.

Kagawa-Singer, M., Katz, P. A., Taylor, D. A., & Vanderryn, J. H. (Eds.). (1996). *Health issues for minority adolescents.* Lincoln: University of Nebraska Press.

Kessler, R. C., Mickelson, K. D., & Williams, D. R. (1999). The prevalence, distribution, and mental health correlates of perceived discrimination in the United States. *Journal of Health and Social Behavior, 40,* 208–230.

LaVeist, T. A. (2000). On the study of race, racism, and health: A shift from description to explanation. *International Journal of Health Services, 30,* 217–219.

Leary, J. D. (2005). *Post traumatic slave syndrome: America's legacy of enduring injury and healing.* Milwaukie, OR: Uptone Press.

Leavitt, R. L. (2003). Developing cultural competence in a multicultural world part II. *PT: Magazine of Physical Therapy, 11*(1), 56.

Lee, S. (2002). Socio-cultural and global health perspectives for the development of future psychiatric diagnostic systems. *Psychopathology, 35*(2), 152–157.

Leong, F. T., & Wong, P. T. (2003). Optimal human functioning from cross-cultural perspectives: Cultural competence as an organizing framework. In W. B. Walsh (Ed.), *Counseling psychology and optimal human functioning* (pp. 123–150). Mahwah, NJ: Lawrence Erlbaum.

Levin, J. S., & Taylor, R. J. (1998). Panel analyses of religious involvement and wellbeing in African Americans: Contemporaneous vs. longitudinal effects. *Journal for the Scientific Study of Religion, 37,* 695–709.

Loewen, J. W. (1996). *Lies my teacher told me: Everything your American history textbook got wrong.* New York: Simon & Schuster.

Logan, S. L. (Ed.). (1996). *The Black family: Strengths, self-help, and positive change.* Boulder, CO: Westview.

Loomba, A. (2005). *Colonialism/postcolonialism* (2nd ed.). London: Routledge.

Lyons, T., & Pye, G. (2006). *Africa on a global stage.* Trenton, NJ: Africa World Press.

Madsen, K., & Leech, P. (2007). *The ethics of labeling in mental health.* Jefferson, NC: McFarland & Co.

May, N., Willis, C., & Loewen, J. W. (2003). *We are the people: Voices from the other side of American history.* New York: Thunder's Mouth Press.

Mbiti, J. S. (1969). *African religions and philosophy.* New York: Praeger.

McMillian, M. (2003). Is No Child Left Behind 'wise schooling' for African American male students? *High School Journal, 87*(2), 25–33.

Middleton, R. A., Rollins, C. W., Sanderson, P. L., Leung, P., Harley, D. A., Ebener, D., et al. (2000). Endorsement of professional multicultural rehabilitation competencies and standards: A call to action. *Rehabilitation Counseling Bulletin, 43*(4), 219–240.

Morrison, H. R., & Epps, B. D. (2002). Warehousing or rehabilitation? Public schooling in the juvenile justice system. *Journal of Negro Education, 71*(3), 218.

Mphande, L., & James-Myers, L. (1993). Traditional African medicine and the optimal theory: Universal insights for health and healing. *Journal of Black Psychology, 19*(1), 25–47.

Neal-Barnett, A. M., & Smith, J. (1997). African Americans. In S. Friedman (Ed.), *Cultural issues in the treatment of anxiety* (pp. 154–174). New York: Guilford.

Nelson, J. M. (2006). Missed opportunities in dialogue between psychology and religion. *Journal of Psychology & Theology, 34*(3), 205–216.

Pasteur, A. B., & Toldson, I. L. (1982). *Roots of soul: The psychology of Black expressiveness: An unprecedented and intensive examination of Black folk expressions in the enrichment of life.* Garden City, NY: Anchor/Doubleday.

Reiser, M. (2003). Why should researchers care about culture? *Canadian Journal of Psychiatry, 48*(3), 154.

Respress, T., & Lutfi, G. (2006). Whole brain learning: The fine arts with students at risk. *Reclaiming Children & Youth, 15*(1), 24–31.

Rozie-Battle, J. L. (2002). African American teens and the neo-juvenile justice system. *Journal of Health & Social Policy, 15*(2), 69–79.

Ruiz, D. S. (1990). *Handbook of mental health and mental disorder among Black Americans.* New York: Greenwood.

Schwab-Stone, M., Chen, C., Greenberger, E., Silver, D., Lichtman, J., & Voyce, C. (1999). No safe haven II: The effects of violence exposure on urban youth. *Journal of the American Academy of Child and Adolescent Psychiatry, 38,* 359–367.

Seligman, M. E. P. (2002). *Authentic happiness: Using the new positive psychology to realize your potential for lasting fulfillment.* New York: Free Press.

Simon, R. J., Fleiss, J. L., Gurland, B. J., Stiller, P. R. & Sharpe, L. (1973) Depression and schizophrenia in hospitalized black and white mental patients. *Archives of General Psychiatry 28,* 509–512.

Sue, S. (1998). In search of cultural competence in psychotherapy and counseling. *American Psychologist, 53,* 440–448.

Sussman, L. K., Robins, L. N., & Earls, F. (1987). Treatment-seeking for depression by Black and White Americans. *Social Science and Medicine, 24,* 187–196.

Swift, C. R., & Asuni, T. (1975). *Mental health and disease in Africa: With special reference to Africa south of the Sahara.* Edinburgh, UK: Churchill Livingstone.

Taylor, R. J., Chatters, L. M., Jayakody, R., & Levin, J. S. (1996). Black and White differences in religious participation: A multisample comparison. *Journal for the Scientific Study of Religion, 35,* 403–410.

Taylor, R. J., Ellison, C. G., Chatters, L. M., Levin, J. S., & Lincoln, K. D. (2000). Mental health services in faith communities: The role of clergy in Black churches. *Social Work, 45*(1), 73.

Taylor-Richardson, K. D., Heflinger, C. A., & Brown, T. N. (2006). Experience of strain among types of caregivers responsible for children with serious emotional and behavioral disorders. *Journal of Emotional & Behavioral Disorders, 14*(3), 157–168.

Teicher, S. A. (2006). An African-centered success story. *Christian Science Monitor, 98*(135), 14–17.

Thomas, A., & Sillen, S. (1972). *Racism and psychiatry*. New York: Brunner/Mazel.

Toldson, I. A. (1999). Black American. In J. S. Mio, J. E. Trimble, P. Arredondo, H. E. Cheatham, & D. Sue (Eds.), *Key words in multicultural interventions*. Westport, CT: Greenwood.

Toldson, I. A. (Ed.). (2004a). *Black sheep: When the American dream becomes a Black man's nightmare.* Baton Rouge, LA: House of Songhay Commission for Positive Education.

Toldson, I. A. (2004b). Demons, zombies and ghosts. In I. A. Toldson (Ed.), *Black sheep: When the American dream becomes a Black man's nightmare.* Baton Rouge, LA: House of Songhay Commission for Positive Education.

Toldson, I. A., & Scott, E. L. (2006). *Poverty, race and policy: Strategic advancement of a family economic success agenda.* Washington, DC: Congressional Black Caucus Foundation.

Toldson, I. A., & Toldson, I. L. (1999). Esoteric group therapy: Counseling African American adolescent males with conduct disorder. *Journal of African American Men, 4*(3), 73.

Toldson, I. L., & Pasteur, A. B. (1972). Soul music: Techniques for therapeutic intervention. *Journal of Non-White Concerns in Personnel and Guidance, 1*(1), 31–39.

Toldson, I. L., & Toldson, I. A. (2001). Biomedical ethics: An African-centered psychological perspective. *Journal of Black Psychology, 27*(4), 401–423.

Tyehimba, K. A. (1998). The relationship between an Afrocentric world view and perceived psychological distress among African-Americans. *Dissertation Abstracts International: Section B: The Sciences & Engineering, 58*(8), 4476.

U.S. Census Bureau. (2003). *108th congressional district summary files census of population and housing, 2000.* Washington, DC: Author.

U.S. Department of Health and Human Services (DHHS). (2001). *Mental health: Culture, race, and ethnicity.* Rockville, MD: U.S. Department of Health and Human Services, Substance Abuse and Mental Health Services Administration, Center for Mental Health Services.

U.S. Public Health Service, Office of the Surgeon General. (2001). *Mental health: Culture, race, and ethnicity.* Washington, DC: U.S. Department of Health and Human Services.

Utsey, S. O., Howard, A., & Williams, O. (2003). Therapeutic group mentoring with African American male adolescents. *Journal of Mental Health Counseling, 25*(2), 126.

Valentine, V. L. (2005, December). Crisis in the classroom. *Crisis (The New),* p. 2.

Valls, A. (2005). *Race and racism in modern philosophy.* Ithaca, NY: Cornell University Press.

Van Sertima, I. (2003). *They came before Columbus: The African presence in ancient America.* New York: Random House Trade Paperbacks.

Vontress, C. E. (1991). Traditional healing in Africa: Implications for cross-cultural counseling. *Journal of Counseling & Development, 70*(1), 242–249.

Vontress, C. E. (1999). Interview with a traditional African healer. *Journal of Mental Health Counseling, 21,* 326.

Vontress, C. E., & Epp, L. R. (1997). Historical hostility in the African American client: Implications for counseling. *Journal of Multicultural Counseling & Development, 25*(3), 170–184.

Washington, G., Johnson, T., Jones, J., & Langs, S. (2007). African-American boys in relative care and a culturally centered group mentoring approach. *Social Work With Groups, 30*(1), 45–68.

Watlington, C. G., & Murphy, C. M. (2006). The roles of religion and spirituality among African American survivors of domestic violence. *Journal of Clinical Psychology, 62*(7), 837–857.

Whaley, A. L. (2006, April). *Cultural trauma, compound trauma, and posttraumatic growth: Relevant concepts for survivors of chattel slavery, Jim Crow racism, and Hurricane Katrina.* Paper presented at the 3rd Annual National Black Counseling Psychologist Conference, Howard University, Washington, DC.

Williams, O. (2005, April). *The Black student who sat by the door: Agents of social justice.* Paper presented at the 2nd Annual National Black Counseling Psychologist Conference, Howard University, Washington, DC.

Wills, T. A., Murry, V. M., Brody, G. H., Gibbons, F. X., Gerrard, M., Walker, C., et al. (2007). Ethnic pride and self-control related to protective and risk factors: Test of the theoretical model for the Strong African American Families Program. *Health Psychology, 26*(1), 50–59.

Yalom, I. D. (1995). *The theory and practice of group psychotherapy* (4th ed.). New York: Basic Books.

# PART III

## Counseling Broadly Defined Cultural Populations

The five chapters included in Part III cover an impressive and challenging array of topics and issues that involve what we are calling "broadly defined" populations. This descriptive term may sound a little bland and uncreative, but the interest value of these chapters compensates for the title. Considering the topics and the populations involved—gender, lesbian and gay clients, millions of people in a sizable number of "marginalized" groups, older people, and schoolchildren who may benefit greatly from counseling—the coverage is vast. These chapters can be considered as all-encompassing in some ways. At some time in our lives, the topics have been, are, or will be directly relevant for each of us. Consider, for instance, the following five questions that may be a simple but useful way to introduce the chapters:

- Have you ever been concerned how problems and issues concerning gender have seriously affected you or your loved ones at work, at play, or in school?

- Have concerns regarding lesbians and gays—for example, how they are perceived and their status in society—ever bothered you or those with whom you work?

- Have you ever felt so "marginalized" that you are or have been on the fringes of society for some reason (skin color, a chronic and disabling medical or mental condition, a member of a "lower class," body type or weight) that it has affected your sense of self-worth and well-being?

- Have you ever wondered how old people "make it" in a world that tends to be heavily youth oriented, or how you will react when you lose your spouse, your health, or your driver's license?

- When you were a very young student, did you receive counseling in schools by a qualified school counselor; if not, have you ever wished that you did?

The odds are very high that at least one of these questions hits you to the core. The odds are reasonably high that these questions are quite meaningful to you for one reason or another. The odds are also high that the questions transfer well across cultures. Because of this, we could easily classify these chapters as "generic" as well as broadly applicable.

Amy Harkins, Sunny Hansen, and Beth Gama, the authors of Chapter 11, have considerably updated their chapter on gender issues that was part of the fifth edition of *Counseling Across Cultures*. Extensive e-mail correspondence and a thorough search of the literature have paid off handsomely. Gender alone, or culture by itself, is difficult enough to tackle. When the two cross, as they often do, circumstances can create sparks and complications that counselors often face. Written in a highly personal and engaging manner and challenging the reader to think, Harkins, Hansen, and Gama have produced a remarkably readable and informed chapter.

Chapter 12 is a richly informative overview focusing on the culturally appropriate counseling of clients who are lesbian or gay or, more accurately when *being* lesbian or gay is the central issue. Mark Pope, the author of the chapter, writes with genuine authority on this topic. Among his achievements in counseling, he is past president of the Association for Gay, Lesbian, and Bisexual Issues in Counseling. His other interests dovetail with the numerous issues discussed in the chapter. We are pleased that this is the first time in the *Counseling Across Cultures* series that a chapter has been dedicated to lesbian and gay issues. As with gender, when sexual orientation intersects with culture and all that it does to shape the beliefs and attitudes of individuals, a variety of problems, conflicts, traditional beliefs and values, and misunderstandings will likely surface and cause a number of interpersonal and intrapersonal difficulties. Professional counselors need to be aware of the range of delicate phenomena that emerge in the area of sexual orientation.

What does it mean to be "marginalized" in any particular society, and what does this mean to the professional mental health worker? The authors of Chapter 13, Melanie Rodríguez, Charlea McNeal, and Ana Mari Cauce, as you shall realize, define marginalization in somewhat sociological terms: It is "a process by virtue of which individuals, groups, and communities are excluded from the center [of society] or relegated to the periphery or margins of 'a center' on the basis of some characteristic (e.g., race, ethnicity, class, gender, sexual orientation)" (p. 224). Such a definition naturally overlaps somewhat with other chapters in the book. However, it is convenient and enriching to focus on these broad conceptualizations. Devoting an entire chapter to issues involving the marginalized joins Chapter 11, which covers lesbian and gay issues, as first-time chapters for *Counseling Across Cultures.*

Carrie Hill and Susan Eklund extensively revised their chapter covering gerontological issues in counseling individuals from a large, and growing, group. Considering that millions of individuals who are "elderly" (a description that may vary by culture or ethnicity) are also marginalized, displaced, or refugees or victims of disasters (see Part IV), the likelihood of mental health workers coming into contact with them is dramatically increasing every year. As Hill and Eklund note, this "graying of the population"—in the United States, at least—as documented by demographic profiles means that there soon will be a strikingly disproportionate growth of ethnic minority members. It appears likely that there will be a very large need for mental health workers who are familiar with the special needs of older people. These special needs will be defined by such factors as language, beliefs, customs, health and family factors, and all of the other considerations that individuals who are in the twilight of their lives badly need.

The topical focus of the final chapter in Part III stands in stark contrast with the gerontological segment of a population. In Chapter 15, schoolchildren are the center of attention. Susanna A. Hayes and Arleen C. Lewis, both certified school counselors and part of a strong graduate program in school counseling, articulate exceptionally well the need for school counseling everywhere in the world. Hayes's 8-year experience working with children on the Colville Indian Reservation in the state of Washington adds a strong sense of authenticity to the chapter. Any nation's health and wealth—indeed, the health and wealth of the world—can be measured by the manner in which children are guided by caring professionals whose work puts them in daily contact with huge numbers of children who are in their formative years and are also vulnerable to so many disruptions and challenges in their young lives.

Taken together, the five chapters in Part III comprise an extremely important unit that includes hundreds of millions of people. The collective wisdom of the authors serves as a wise guide for counselors in many facets of professional counseling.

# CHAPTER 11

# Updating Gender Issues in Multicultural Counseling

Amy K. Harkins, Sunny S. Hansen, and Elizabeth M. P. Gama

---

*Primary Objective*

- To examine gender research, theory, and interventions from a multicultural counseling perspective

*Secondary Objective*

- To offer suggestions for counseling in a cultural and gender-aware manner

---

GENDER AND CULTURE INFORM AND INFLUENCE EACH OTHER IN A DYNAMIC RELATIONSHIP. What it means to be male or female, to be masculine or feminine, or to be nongendered or other gendered is defined by the cultural norms of a particular group at a particular point in time. Likewise, what we understand about cultural issues ranging from power dynamics to aspects of everyday living is shaped by a culture's understanding of gender. Of course, there are occasions when either the issues of gender or issues of culture become more visible or of greater salience than the other. Nonetheless, gender and culture coexist, imparting meaning and value upon the other.

Notice your personal reactions to the content contained in this chapter. Pay attention to when you agree or disagree with the text; when you learn something new, and when you feel angry, proud, or bored. The practice of staying aware of your internal experience will help identify topics that are ripe for exploration. By the end of this chapter, we hope you will increase your sensitivity to issues that exist at the intersection of gender with both cultural and global issues and that this increased sensitivity will ultimately contribute to greater awareness of your own gender and cultural identity, resulting in the desire to increase your knowledge of a client's gender-related worldview, and improve your skill in selecting appropriate therapeutic interventions that promote healing and wellness within your clinical practice (Arredondo et al., 1996).

## SETTING THE STAGE

Five years ago, in the previous edition of this textbook, we expressed our hunger for literature that explored the intersection of gender and culture in the helping fields (S. Hansen, Gama, & Harkins, 2002). Quality publications are now being produced. For example, Rabin (2005) collected narratives from helping professionals who discuss gender issues in global settings. Also, in *The Stories We Tell: The Lives and Friendship of Two Older Black Lesbians,* Hall and Fine (2005) provide an example of culture/gender-inclusive research that uses qualitative methodology and narrative analysis to learn about two women through the lens of positive marginality—a lens used to recognize the strength that lies in the margins of social contexts. They find that "triple minority status created strengths and skills rather than barriers and stumbling blocks" (p. 182). These two publications exemplify current qualitative and positively focused projects aimed at expanding the knowledge base at the intersection of gender and culture.

Affirmation of the importance of considering both gender and cultural issues has been supported by the Council of Representatives of the American Psychological Association (2004), which adopted the Resolution on Culture and Gender Awareness in International Psychology on July 28, 2004. Furthermore, the American Counseling Association (ACA, 2005) recently published the *ACA Code of Ethics,* which demonstrates a heightened attention to issues of cultural and social justice, including an expanded nondiscrimination policy. Of importance to this chapter, the ACA requires nondiscrimination based on gender, thereby encouraging equal treatment of men and women, as well as nondiscrimination based on gender identity, which encourages equal treatment of all persons, including persons who have unique gender expression. Initiatives such as these by professional governing bodies validate the need for systemic awareness of gender and cultural issues within our field.

## RESPECT FOR CULTURAL TRADITIONS AND MORAL DILEMMAS

One issue we believe to be very important to the reconceptualization of gender and multicultural counseling is the generalized idea that all culture-specific behaviors, belief systems, customs, values, and traditions are morally correct; therefore, counselors must respect them. The issue of moral relativism is certainly complex. Can people from one culture understand and judge with empathy, fairness, and validity the customs of another culture? Are moral principles universal or culture specific?

We believe that certain practices and their associated values, although traditional or common among certain cultural groups, are morally wrong. For example, we call attention to various forms of abuse to which girls and women are subjected, such as their sale for marriage or prostitution, male domination and consequent wife abuse, restriction of liberty, inhumane treatment and torture, and genital mutilation and clitoral circumcision. According to the UN Population Fund (2000), approximately 130 million girls and young women worldwide have undergone the painful and dangerous practice of female genital mutilation, and an additional 2 million are at risk each year.

The underlying assumptions that allow such practices to continue are that women are inferior, incompetent to make decisions and run their own lives, emotionally unstable, and that their sexuality is evil. Obviously, such assumptions can have devastating effects on anyone's perception of self. These assumptions represent absence of respect for human freedom and dignity. Furthermore, these are often situations in which the women themselves do not agree with the practices and in which they are unwilling victims of an unjust social order. The point is that cultural specificity is no guarantee that certain assumptions, traditions, or behaviors are right when judged in the light of larger human values. For further discussion, see the section on violence.

## DEFINITION OF GENDER

The distinction between what is male and female, masculine (M) and feminine (F), is solidly embedded in mainstream Western culture as well as many other cultures around the world. Why is it so common? What purpose does a focus on the difference between M and F serve? Who benefits? Who is hurt? What happens when a person or persons by choice or by circumstance violate the culturally defined roles of M or F? These are important questions to ponder.

Gender comprises many factors, including chromosomal sex, gonadal sex, hormonal sex, internal and external genital structures, and culturally learned factors of gender identity (Crooks & Baur, 1993). Although study of the former aspects of gender is important, gender identity is our primary concern and is the aspect of gender addressed when the word *gender* is used in this chapter.

*Gender is a social construction*

Children have no gender identity at birth. Gender is not naturally and inevitably determined by the shape of one's body. Rather, gender is a social construction, "learned and achieved at the interactional level, reified at the cultural level, and institutionally enforced via the family, law, religion, politics, economy, medicine, and the media" (Gagne, Tewksbury, & McGaughey, 1997, p. 479). Social experiences loaded with culturally shaped content regarding what ought to be male and female give people their gender and associate them with a world of men and a world of women. These worlds have distinctions and similarities. Each is a complex social system with specific norms, traditions, belief systems, and socialization procedures that constitute a culture of its own, and yet both belong to other cultural dimensions.

Gender differences are enculturated in young children through the process of differential socialization. On the basis of minimal biological differences in sex organs and hormones, as well as average size and weight, national and racial/ethnic cultures have subtle and subliminal ways of imposing their gender-role ideology. Weber (1998) asserts that in Western culture

> Dominant groups define race, gender, and sexuality as ranked dichotomies, where Whites, men, and heterosexuals are deemed superior. Dominant groups justify these hierarchies by claiming that the rankings are a part of the design of nature—not the design of those in power. Subordinate groups resist the binary categories, the rankings associated with them, and the biological rationales used to justify them. (p. 18)

Not all cultures define gender as dichotomies. Many cultures have an honored third classification for people who live outside M/F categories. Instead of being ignored or abused, the third-gendered person has held an equal or elevated status, valued for the diversity and innovation that resulted from a unique gendered experience. In Native America, for example, many tribes recognize a third gender, calling such persons "Two Spirits," believing that both the spirit of a man and a woman coexist within one body. Third-gendered persons can also be found with "the hijras of India, the kqoluaatmwols of the Sambia in Papua New Guinea, and the guevedoche of the Dominican Republic" (Eugenides, 2002, p. 495).

In a separate example, some contemporary Native American cultures, such as the Ojibway/Chippewa, divide gender into four categories based on traditional teachings of the medicine wheel (M. H. Bazinau Jr., personal communication, December 15, 2005). Adults of child-bearing age are divided into male and female, but children and elders are considered to be from additional gender categories. While the behavior of children and elders is still guided by culturally defined sex-based roles, the rigidity of male-female distinctions for behaviors is minimized during these developmental periods. These examples show that it is possible to think about gender in different ways. It is precisely because gender identity is socially defined and learned that we believe it is possible to unlearn, on both an individual and societal level, those designations that are limiting, maladaptive, or harmful.

## WHY THE FOCUS ON DIFFERENCE?
## A HISTORICAL PERSPECTIVE

There is no doubt that Western society is enamored by a "*differences hypothesis:* that males and females are, psychologically, vastly different" (Shibley Hyde, 2005, p. 581). The repeated message is that men and women are different, and these differences are stable and natural, a result of either evolution, divine plan, or perhaps both. The popularity of pop psychology books such as John Gray's (1992) *Men Are From Mars, Women Are From Venus* and Deborah Tannen's (1990) *You Just Don't Understand: Women and Men in Conversation* are evidence of the affinity for the differences hypothesis. When in time did the focus on differences begin? While disciplines such as history, religion, anthropology, and the like might recall periods and places where power dynamics were differently constructed and record contexts wherein the seeds of patriarchal systems of gender differences were sown, we will remain focused on the relatively short history of psychology. Within the field of psychology, support for difference-focused gender teachings was solidly established from the beginning. Sigmund Freud's model of psychosexual development hypothesized that males and females struggle with vastly different issues as a result of anatomy. While much of Freud's gender identity formation theories are antiquated, Freud's work still affects gender relations to this day—as evidenced by the high recognition value of "penis envy" and the "Oedipal complex." Ultimately, Freud's work resulted in the popularization of a system of human development that defined womanhood through the lens of deficit and manhood as being linked to management of sexual and aggressive impulses. Nearly 70 years after his death, even after many reputable challenges, Freud's gender-based theories, as well as those of many of his followers, contemporaries, or detractors, have yet to be fully retired from either professional or everyday conversation.

Jumping forward in time to the 1970s, feminist activity on a societal level in the United States provided the environmental support for empowered female psychology theorists to present another series of arguments against deficit-based models of femininity. For example, Nancy Chodorow (1974) challenged Freud's work while still using psychoanalytical theories as her foundation to present her own model of female and male identity formation. She noted the importance of connection and caring in the relational work of women as well as the influence of individuation and separation for men. The importance of this literature is that Chodorow did not view women as incomplete men but as having a unique and valuable set of attributes different from men.

In the 1980s, the gender debate flared in Western culture and American psychology. One of the most important discussions of gender in psychology occurred when Carol Gilligan (1982) reacted to the research and theories of Lawrence Kohlberg. Gilligan argued that Kohlberg's theory of moral development unfairly derogated females and elevated male scores on measures of ethical decision making.

Building on the work of Chodorow, Gilligan conceptualized male decision making as being guided by justice-based "morality of rights," while female decision making was guided by the principle of caring in a "morality of responsibility." Gilligan argued that a separate metric or ruler needed to be used to evaluate the different genders. Even though Gilligan's work has been criticized for not meeting rigorous scientific standards, and even though Kohlberg and his colleagues were able to produce research showing that females did not substantially differ from male subjects on his measures of moral development, the message about differences seemed to find an accepting audience in psychology and in mainstream Western society.

At their core, the work of Chodorow and Gilligan was designed to value that which is female and feminine. These ideas emerged during a cultural climate wherein women who wished to venture beyond the home environment or inner sphere of power needed to be become ultra-masculine to be successful in the outer sphere of influence. The work of feminist scholars did indeed succeed in reclaiming caring and nurturing qualities as positive ways of knowing and being in the world. Yet, there was a trap embedded in the new paradigm. Unfortunately, the message of difference central to the theories was co-opted and became the "favorite foundation for arguments that innate differences—not gender discrimination—are responsible for women's slow pace of advancement in the workplace" (Barnett & Rivers, 2004, p. 34). The underlying assumptions of these arguments are that because women are nurturing by nature, it would be too difficult for female business managers to be strong leaders, to drive hard for results, to manage performance with a firm hand, and ultimately to take strong and unpopular stands in occasions of firing employees or downsizing staff; therefore, it is unwise and risky to promote women to managerial positions. Furthermore, because it is their nature to be caretakers, women would prefer to stay home and take care of their children than work in economically rewarding careers. By comparison, men are rational decision makers, while women are emotional decision makers; therefore, women should not be encouraged to become judges, lawyers, presidents, CEOs, or police officers. Moreover, men are not naturally caring and should not be caretakers of children. Each of these statements severely limits the range of acceptable behaviors for an individual based on M-ness or F-ness. Certainly, Gilligan and other feminists of her time did not intend for their ideas to be used in this manner.

The fallacy of the assumptions that the so-called "masculine" characteristics are more desirable than the "feminine" characteristics for success in the business world is now shown by the many studies in the area of emotional intelligence and leadership success conducted by Goleman (1998, 2000). Basically, the studies show that the most competent and successful leaders are those who are able to combine the "masculine" characteristics of achievement motivation and drive with the "feminine" characteristics of empathy and affiliation, as well as self-awareness, flexibility, or optimism (Spreier, Fontaine, & Malloy, 2006).

## EVOLUTION-BASED ARGUMENTS OF DIFFERENCE

The existence of innate differences between genders is argued by Buss (1989), an evolutionary psychologist. According to Buss, evolution has resulted in different reproductive strategies for men and women in order to increase the survival of one's own genetic makeup. The conclusion of this logic is that it is to every man's evolutionary advantage to impregnate as many women as possible to increase the chances that his genes will survive into the next generation. Conversely, it is to a women's evolutionary advantage to ensnare a mature male mate who would be a reliable provider for her smaller number of offspring, enabling her to invest the enormous time and nurturance needed to raise children to reproductive age. Barnett and Rivers (2004) state that evolution-based theories are used to explain or, worse, validate a variety of assertions such as the following: Women are by nature coy and seek monogamous relationships; men aggressively seek many sex partners; women are less ambitious and less competitive and less successful at gathering resources than men; men prefer younger, fertile women; and men are not invested in their children. Consider the popularity of themes such as these in Hollywood movies, in prime-time television sitcoms, and on tabloid magazine covers.

In their book *Same Difference* (2004), Barnett and Rivers examine the evidence for and against the assertions of "Ultra Darwinists" (p. 71) and find all of them to be unsubstantiated. Their review of the literature includes cross-cultural studies of human behavior, field studies of primate behavior, laboratory studies of rats, and anthropological and archeological evidence. Ultra-Darwinist evolution theories do not withstand the scrutiny of good science. Even so, the ideas are "sexy" and superficially plausible, making them easily used to sell everything from cars to anti-aging cream.

The sad conclusion of the differences hypothesis is that men and women are from different planets, they cannot hope to have successful conversations across the gender divide, they are not able to understand why the other makes decisions the way that they do, and they have perfectly different goals for reproduction and relationships. It is imperative to ask why so many societies are invested in propagating the gender divide when this path seems so bleak.

## Science of Similarities

Over and over again, empirical research has shown that boys and girls, men and women have far more gender similarities than differences on a wide range of psychological domains. In a landmark review of the literature, Maccoby and Jacklin (1974) examined more than 2,000 studies of gender differences and found that many common beliefs about gender were not supported by the data. Maccoby and Jacklin concluded that no consistent evidence was found on the presumed differences between males and females in level of competitiveness, dominance, nurturance, suggestibility, sociability, activity level, self-esteem, compliance, analytic abilities, anxiety level, and achievement motivation. Maccoby and Jacklin only detected four areas of difference: verbal ability, visual-spatial ability, mathematical ability, and aggression. Unfortunately, the bulk of the attention for Maccoby and Jacklin's study was not on the overwhelming evidence *for* gender similarities but rather on those four domains where small differences were in evidence. The importance of the main message of similarities was generally overlooked. In fact, after Maccoby and Jacklin's study was published, there was a boom in research that attempted to further explore those areas wherein gender differences were detected.

In the past 20 years, the number of gender differences studies has accumulated to permit meta-analyses of the data. In 2005, Shibley Hyde gathered the major meta-analyses conducted on psychological gender differences to gain an even broader overview of the research findings and found that "78% of gender differences are small or close to zero" (p. 586). The largest effect size, where the greatest difference was detected, was in the measurement of motor performance, as in throwing velocity and distance. Imagine the investment of time and resources on gender differences research that has resulted in the conclusion that the average boy can throw a ball farther and faster than the average girl! Shibley Hyde reported that large but inconsistent gender differences have been found in studies of sexuality, while moderate but inconsistent differences are found in studies of aggression. Shibley Hyde argues that the inconsistent differences in these areas can be accounted for when developmental and contextual influences are examined in the design and the subject pool used in the original studies. Overall, research shows that the magnitude of gender differences often fluctuates across the life span and is highly influenced by contextual conditions, such as activation or de-emphasis of gender-based stereotypes during the time of measurement.

# Gender-Role Ideology and Stereotyping Across Cultures

While research shows males and females do not differ from each other all that much, there are strong forces that divide the sexes. Gender-role ideology varies somewhat across countries and is patterned after cultural factors. Usually, developed countries with larger numbers of women employed and in college have more egalitarian beliefs than less developed countries, in which women are seen from a more traditional perspective (Williams & Best, 1990). Despite this variation in normative beliefs about what women and men *should* be like, there is an impressive agreement across cultures about what women and men *are* like, leading some authors to suggest that gender stereotyping may be universal (Berry, Poortinga, Segall, & Dasen, 1992).

Despite linguistic, religious, economic, and social differences among the many countries of the world, the process of reproducing the ideology of male superiority from generation to generation and perpetuating inequality between the sexes has been remarkably successful. Perhaps the most extensive cross-cultural study in gender roles to date is the international investigation conducted by Williams and Best (1982). In their adult study, a total of 2,800 university students (from 28 countries) took a 300-item adjective checklist describing psychological characteristics of persons. Each respondent had to rate, for each adjective, whether it was more related to men or women in his or her country.

Although within-country results showed extensive differentiation in views about gender roles, there was an impressive consensus across countries. By more than two thirds of the respondents and at least 20 of the countries, some of the adjectives chosen to describe males were *active, adventurous, aggressive, ambitious, arrogant, assertive, clear-thinking, daring, logical, strong,* and *wise.* By the same criteria, some adjectives used to describe women were *affected, affectionate, attractive, dependent, emotional, fearful, sensitive, submissive, superstitious, talkative,* and *weak.* Note that many of the stereotypes associated with women have negative meanings, whereas those associated with men are more positive. In 1999, Williams, Satterwhite, and Best reanalyzed the data using the five-factor model and found that males were seen as having elevated scores on extraversion, conscientiousness, emotional stability, and openness to new experiences, while females were higher on agreeableness.

The remarkable similarity across cultures that Williams and Best (1982) found in the university student sample was also shown in a second study conducted with children in 24 countries and two age groups: 5 to 6 and 8 to 9 years old. The descriptions of male and female were quite similar to the stereotypes evidenced with the adult samples. By age 5, there was already gender stereotyping, and this increased at age 8, when children associated even more of the 32 items with males or females. Comparisons between countries showed greater similarity in the older age group, leading the authors to conclude that the 3 additional years of experience in their individual cultures had led to greater similarity rather than greater diversity—"a testament to the pancultural similarity in the traits ascribed to women and men" (p. 204).

The findings of Williams and Best (1982) are a good example of a series of studies with similar results about the stereotypes associated with males and with females. In general, the descriptions can be organized into two dimensions: competency-rationality-assertion and warmth-expressiveness, with men typically seen in the competency cluster of traits and women personifying warmth-expressiveness. Once again, masculine stereotypes are considered more desirable than feminine ones (Broverman, Vogel, Broverman, Clarkson, & Rosenkrantz, 1972). Breakwell (1990) called stereotypes "the fulcrum of the social belief system about gender differences" and stated that they persist because they serve the valuable purpose of "reify[ing] the gulf between the sexes" (p. 214).

The damaging effects of differential gender-role socialization and subsequent social-cultural pressure to conformity and sex discrimination on mental health are important to consider. The pressures to fulfill one's gender stereotype and the conflicts generated from diverse role models or discrepant perceptions between what one is and what one should be can certainly produce psychological distress. It has been suggested that many of the problems experienced by women stem from their acceptance of a lower status role stereotype and their conformity to that predetermined image. Similarly, men's problems often result from their lack of success in attaining the high-status, strong, competent, and self-confident male role. With failure, their self-image suffers, and they often deal with the problem in dysfunctional ways (Davenport & Yurich, 1991). Both O'Neil (1981) and Skovholt (1990) pointed out how men are limited by their socialization. O'Neil described a masculine mystique in Western cultures consisting of expectations of success and achievement that result in male gender-role strain, causing heart disease, emphysema, inability to express emotions, pressures to succeed in a career, and premature death. Skovholt also identified the restricted emotionality to which boys and men are exposed and what he called "the 180-degree role conflict," in which men are socialized for aggression, violence, and war and then are expected to do a complete reversal and be nurturing and loving husbands and fathers.

The research of Claude Steele (2003) and his colleagues illuminates the effect of stereotypes on performance in real-world settings. They began by looking at the underperformance of women in difficult math classes and the underperformance of African Americans in higher educational settings compared to classmates who were intellectually equal. They asked the following question—if two people are equally prepared for a challenging task, what is getting in the way for those who are performing below their ability? Using a brilliant series of experiments, they identified a factor they termed *stereotype threat*. As described by Steele, stereotype threat could "be felt by anyone who cared about a performance and yet knew that any faltering at it could cause them to be reduced to a negative group stereotype" (p. 316). The subtle activation of a negative stereotype consistently resulted in decreased performance on difficult tasks. Aronson (2002) has pursued these findings and is exploring ways in which strategies can be taught to minority and female students to reduce the negative impact of stereotype threat on academic achievement.

Barnett and Rivers (2004) counter the difference argument by asserting that "people behave differently in different situations . . . their behavior is often determined by how much power they have in a given situation, not their sex" (p. 36). Issues of power are so central to gender and culture issues that whenever you hear messages of difference, we challenge you to switch paradigms and consider issues of power. Ask the following questions. Who has more status or resources and who has less? Who is invested in maintaining the current power structure? What is the duration and origination of the current structure of power? What other models of power distribution could be used in this context? What factors would be necessary for the power structure to change?

## At the Intersection of Gender and Culture: Interventions, Education, and Advocacy Counseling Interventions

Because both cultural and gender stereotyping and discrimination have real-world consequences on the career aspirations and attainments of young women and men, programs have been developed to promote gender and cultural equity. Barbara Kerr and Sharon Kurpius (Kerr, Kurpius, & Harkins, 2005; Kurpius, Kerr, & Harkins, 2005) conducted a 10-year study of equity intervention research at Arizona State University, funded by the National Science Foundation. The program targeted talented, at-risk adolescent and young women who were excelling at math and science to encourage persistence into nontraditional careers, particularly in the fields of science, technology, engineering, and math (STEM). During a 2-day intervention, female students were welcomed into a "girl-friendly" learning environment, which acknowledged and respected their culturally unique life experiences, introduced them to vibrant mentors who embodied perseverance in the face of gender-restrictive obstacles, and engaged the young women in conversations about their current talents as well as their dreams and fears about the future. Girls who participated in this project showed improved educational and career self-efficacy, increased career information-seeking behaviors, and lower rates of high-risk behaviors. At follow-up, the women were persisting in education tracts that prepared them for STEM careers. The two-volume publication provides current literature as well as a detailed account of the interventions used to make such a positive impact on the career aspirations of talented, at-risk young women.

## Career and Systems Interventions

In the United States in the 1970s and 1980s, hundreds of programs were funded by federal and private agencies to address issues of sexism, stereotyping, and socialization of girls and boys in schools and colleges. One such program was BORN FREE (Build Options, Reassess Norms, Free Roles through Educational Equity), designed to reduce gender-role stereotyping and expand career options for males and females across the life span (L. S. Hansen, 1980). The program assumes the following: Stereotyping and socialization limit the options of both women and men, one sex cannot redefine its roles without affecting the other, and both genders need to be involved in addressing the issues. The program identified inhibitors and facilitators of career development at every stage of the educational ladder.

For the past 2 years, the extensive print and video training materials of BORN FREE have been updated and put on CD-ROM or DVDs, eventually to be available on a Web site. The revised materials will also have an international dimension with career, multicultural, and gender issues and the status of women and men discussed by indigenous authors from several countries around the world. The articles will include demographics, economics, social context, career guidance and counseling available, national policies related to gender role and multicultural issues, barriers to change, and the authors' own experience growing up or studying in the country. BORN FREE was one of the first projects to connect gender and career.

## Education and Advocacy for Expanded Concepts of Males and Masculinity

At the intersection of men and culture, it is possible to find high-quality readings that address issues such as Latino males' expression or rejection of the cultural construct of machismo, the changing role of mature African American men in urban communities, and many other topics. Lee Mun Wah's (1994) film *The Color of Fear*, which documents the conversation between eight North American men representing diverse cultural and racial backgrounds during a weekend retreat, is a very powerful teaching tool.

It is important to note that men's movements are also occurring outside of our professional community. Some groups are designed to explore the diversity within male identities, encouraging participants to press against restrictive stereotypes, and expand the range of behaviors that are possible for them. Others promote traditionally masculine gender roles for men. Certainly, a wide range of both quantitative and qualitative research studies could be generated concerning the impact of popular men's groups such as these.

## The "Boy Crisis"

An emerging body of literature has appeared in the United States charging that as girls have become more successful, boys are losing out. Some researchers claim that too many male children are falling behind in school. For example, more women than men are earning undergraduate college degrees, gaining access to previously limited studies in fields such as medicine, law, dentistry, and veterinary medicine. In schools, boys receive the majority of D and F grades; create 80% of discipline problems; represent 80% of high school dropouts, 70% of children with learning disabilities, and 80% of those with behavior disorders; are two and one half times more likely to have a special education disability; and are suspended and expelled from school two to three times more often than girls (Sax, 2006). It has been reported that similar trends are occurring in other developed countries such as Germany, France, and England.

Some call the "boy" problem an exaggerated backlash against the women's movement. Others suggest it is a race and class problem and that the problem, if it exists, is primarily in urban and rural schools. Rivers and Barnett (2006) suggest that single-sex classrooms are not the answer. They argue that much attention still needs to be given to the education of girls. "Obsessing about a boy crisis or thinking that American teachers are waging a war on boys won't help kids. What will help is recognizing that students are individuals, with many different skills and abilities. And that goes for both girls and boys" (Rivers & Barnett, 2006, p. AA1). See also Horne and Kiselica (1999) for programs for boys and adolescent males.

## Advocacy for Intersexuals, Transpeople, and Gender Benders

By asking questions of individuals who occupy the territory of gender identity that lie outside the M and F groupings, we have an opportunity to challenge our beliefs and assumptions about gender and expand our perception about what is possible for others and for ourselves. Autobiographies provide a data-rich means of entering into another's worldview. O'Keefe and Fox (2003) edited 26 chapters by gender-variant people, illustrating the rich diversity of sex and gender experience and expression. In addition, Leslie Feinberg (1998) has produced a body of work using personal experiences to fuel activism for political reform on issues ranging from health care to genital mutilation to queer rights.

Clinical guidance for therapists working with gender-diverse persons is now being addressed in books (i.e., Lev, 2004), and Web sites and conferences are growing in strength and number to promote clinical skills in individual, group, and couples/family therapy aimed at empowering transgender and gender queer clients. Furthermore, the Intersex Society of North America, founded in 1993, has been working to de-stigmatize intersex by openly educating and advocating for people who were born into bodies that have atypical reproductive features (www.isna.org).

Popular American culture has demonstrated an increasing interest in exploring nondominant gender expression storylines. Recent examples include the Pulitzer Prize–winning novel *Middlesex* (Eugenides, 2002), which follows the life narrative of a fictional intersexual child, raised as female, who ultimately identifies as a male, as well as the character Bree, played by Golden Globe Winner Felicity Huffman in the movie *TransAmerica* (Tucker, 2005), which gives a powerful portrayal of a preoperative, posthormone treatment, MTF (male to female) transsexual person.

While gender-bending stories are gaining exposure, the real-life experiences of gender-variant persons all too often include a pervasive pattern of discrimination and prejudice against persons who violate gender norms. Lombardi, Wilchins, Priesing, and Malouf (2001) conducted a survey of 402 transgender people and found that more than half had experienced some form of harassment within their lifetime, with a quarter experiencing a violent incident.

## Education and Advocacy Against Violence

Education and advocacy are central to any discourse on violence in relation to gender/cultural issues. Volumes of literature are linked with each of the following issues: violence of men against women, violence in domestic partnerships, violence in same-sex partnerships, violence against gender-variant people, violence on a global level, violence in different cultures at different points in time, victims' experience of violence, perpetrators' experience of violence, female genital mutilation, forced prostitution, human trafficking, rape, incest, child abuse, rape as a weapon of war, and activism against violence.

Links to statistics on violence against women are maintained on the V-Day Web site (http://www.vday.org/contents/violence/statistics). Sexual violence, as reported by the World Health Organization (WHO, 2002), "is a serious problem affecting millions of people worldwide. It is driven by many factors operating in a range of social, cultural and economic contexts. Its underlying purpose is frequently the expression of power and dominance over the person assaulted. It is also used to punish people for transgressing perceived social or moral codes." WHO further states that "sexual violence is more likely to occur where beliefs in male sexual entitlement are strong, where gender roles are rigid, and in countries with high rates of other types of violence" (p. 1).

Hautzinger (2003) published an essay based on her research involving male violence against women in Brazil. She argued that "men's prerogatives to dominance are increasingly being questioned on a global level, and this continues to shape attitudes and practices surrounding male violence" (p. 94). She asserts that violence was more symptomatic of men losing and women gaining power and control, resulting in what she terms *male insecurity*. She is interested in insecurity resulting from destabilization, especially those economic and social changes affecting gender roles that coincide with exacerbated occurrences of violence by men against women. She notes that there are generational differences in Brazil, where younger males are striving to construct definitions of masculinity that are more autonomous, so that control over women is not the reflection of strength of masculinity. She also emphasizes that domestic violence is not a universal response to the destabilization of traditional masculine gender roles, as seen in cultures that hold nonviolent resolution of conflict as a core value. She writes:

> Questioning of patriarchy and rapidly changing gender roles is the fruit of our work as feminists and profeminists. It is what we want. What we do not want is the violence. . . . Our challenge is how to support gender change, while uncoupling it from resulting in new rounds of contestatory violence. In meeting that challenge, I can think of no work more important than that of creating alternative, nonviolent, and non-domineering ways of being men. (p. 104)

Questions about violence often focus on male aggressors. There are some recent exceptions to this trend, however, and we are beginning to learn about the role of aggression in the lives of females. Richardson (2005) reviewed 30 years of research about female aggression and revealed findings that contradict the myth of female passivity. Early research in aggression was based on the assumption of female nonaggressiveness, a myth based in part on the research findings of Maccoby and Jacklin (1974). While the current findings do not suggest that females are as aggressive as males, research does show, however, that females are not "passive creatures"; rather, they are perpetrators as well as victims of aggression. "In the case of intimate violence, men and women are about equally likely to engage in acts of physical aggression, but that men are somewhat more likely to inflict injury" (p. 238).

According to the authors, "The most important outcome of this research was the realization of the need to consider direct and indirect aggression in the context of interactions between aggressors and targets" (p. 244).

The Convention on the Elimination of All Forms of Discrimination Against Women (CEDAW; United Nations, 2006a, 2006b) was an effort begun in the mid-1970s to codify a comprehensive international legal standard for women, sometimes referred to as the international bill of rights for women. CEDAW gives definitions of and expectations for equal treatment of women across the globe. By ratifying CEDAW, a country agrees to undertake a series of measures to end discrimination against women and be held accountable to the international community for those changes by submitting a regular report to the United Nations. Efforts to end discrimination in legal settings provide institutional power for those who wish to raise awareness of unjust actions against women and empower positive change. As of this writing, the United States of America is not a party to the CEDAW convention.

Issues of human trafficking and slavery are gaining exposure through the work of groups such as Human Rights Watch (2004). International standards set in Article 3(a), in the Protocol to Prevent, Suppress and Punish Trafficking in Persons, Especially Women and Children, supplementing the United Nations Convention Against Transnational Organized Crime, defines trafficking as follows:

> The recruitment, transportation, transfer, harboring or receipt of persons, by means of threat or use of force or other forms of coercions, of abduction, of fraud, of deceptions, of abuse of power or of position of vulnerability or of the giving or receiving of payments or benefits to achieve the consent of a person having control over another person, for the purpose of exploitation. Exploitation shall include, at a minimum, the exploitation of the prostitution of others or other forms of sexual exploitation, forced labor or services, slavery or practices similar to slavery, servitude or the removal of organs.

Finally, advocacy takes many forms. Eve Ensler, playwright of *The Vagina Monologues,* also founded V-Day—the global movement to end violence against women and girls. In 8 years and in 81 countries, V-Day has raised more than $30 million for local groups working to stop violence against women (V-Day, n.d.).

## A CALL FOR GENDER-AWARE MULTICULTURAL COUNSELING

We would like to offer the following guidelines for those in helping professions:

- Recognize that gender is socially constructed and based on presumed differences between women and men. Be careful about perpetuating stereotypes and maintaining the status quo through overemphasizing gender differences, thereby ignoring the importance of similarities across gender groups as well as within gender categories.

- Make use of historical contexts in attempting to understand diverse cultures and diverse constructions of gender.

- Help clients of all backgrounds to become more aware of their own racial/ethnic identities (including White racial identity), as well as their gender identities.

- Help clients of all backgrounds to assess their multiple identities, including exploration of both negative and positive aspects of these identities.

- Be aware of abusive traditions, their underlying ideological assumptions, and their social psychological implications for clients. Even with the understanding of how cultural traditions, values, attitudes, and beliefs are historically constructed, do not accept or recommend that clients submit to abusive practices in the name of cultural relativism. Even so, be extremely careful when challenging deeply accepted traditions, so as not to cause a breakdown in communication with clients or jeopardize clients' well-being.

- Identify, create, and employ techniques that are appropriate for use with clients from diverse populations. For example, using narrative and storytelling may help clients express, explore, and understand their heritage and strengths.

- Become an agent of change and try to reduce the barriers of racism, sexism, classism, and other "isms" that limit the full development of human beings. Be proactive in seeking to reduce violence against women, as well as against men and transgendered persons.

- Recognize that the scientist-practitioner model of training that characterizes most counselor training programs is not sufficient and needs to be expanded to include a third counseling role: one of advocate.

## CONCLUSION

In this chapter, we have covered a lot of ground in our effort to further expand thought, research, and practice on gender issues in multicultural counseling. Much of what we wrote in previous editions of this text continues to be valid today. Because change occurs slowly in the areas of culture and gender, we are encouraged by recent publication trends, as it appears that increasing attention is being paid to gender issues across cultures and that social activism, social justice, and advocacy are a central part of this movement.

## CRITICAL INCIDENT

Scenario 1: Ms. Silva is a 30-year-old married woman living in a low-income urban area in Brazil. She reluctantly sought community counseling services after a health clinic was unable to identify medical reasons for her headaches. Recent economic changes have resulted in fewer employment opportunities for Mr. Silva. The income Ms. Silva earns by laundering clothing in her home is not enough to support them. Last month, Ms. Silva decided to explore her options. She learned of a nanny position with a family who encourages her to complete high school at night. Later, she hopes to enroll in nursing classes. After details were gathered, Ms. Silva proudly presented her plan to her husband, expecting him to praise her initiative and share hopes of a brighter future. Instead, Mr. Silva expressed outrage at her making plans without consulting him. While he would allow her to attend school, he refused to permit her to work outside the home, not as a nanny or nurse. Ms. Silva was saddened by his reaction but accepted his decision because she has never disobeyed her husband in the 13 years they have been married, and she would not start now. The school application is due next week, but she has opted not to enroll. Meanwhile, the couple's debts continue to rise.

Scenario 2: Raj is a 17-year-old bilingual high school student living in a middle-class suburban area in the United States. He has been meeting with the college counselor in order to prepare university applications. Raj has lived in the United States for 10 years. He is comfortable with his American peers, as well as his extended family that tends to be closer to their Indian values. Soon, his parents plan to return to India, where they will enjoy a higher economic status as a result of their accomplishments as mechanical engineers. When daydreaming, Raj imagines blending Indian and American design elements to create a unique line of clothing and textiles. With his counselor's guidance, he has identified schools that offer degrees in textiles, fashion design, and marketing. His family was irate when he shared his ideas. They expect him to earn a degree in engineering or medicine. They will not finance any other academic path. Furthermore, his grandfather in India scolded him in a recent phone conversation for wanting a woman's job. Raj tells his counselor that he is confused and restless, unable to sleep or concentrate in class. He worries that he might fail an upcoming science exam, which will make matters worse.

## DISCUSSION QUESTIONS

These examples demonstrate conflicts at the intersection of gender and culture. Consider that both clients are exposed to media influences and interpersonal support systems that encourage contemporary values regarding the individual rights of women and men to economic advancement and flexible career choice. Also consider that both clients have important familial and cultural obligations.

1. What gender issues are raised?

2. What cultural issues are important to consider?

3. What would change if the client was a different gender? A different culture?

4. Who has more power, status, or resources in each situation?

5. What is the duration and origination of the current power structure?

6. Can the client relate an instance when a person challenged the current power structure?

7. Is the story theme one of tragedy or success?

8. Who is invested in maintaining the current power structure?

9. What factors might need to be in place for the power structure to change?

10. What strategies might the counselor use to ease the distress currently experienced by the client?

11. What might happen to the client's motivation to question the status quo if symptoms are reduced?

12. What strengths can the counselor identify in the client?

# REFERENCES

American Counseling Association. (2005). *ACA code of ethics*. Alexandria, VA: Author.

American Psychological Association. (2004, July 28). *Resolution on culture and gender awareness in international psychology*. Retrieved March 6, 2006, from http://www.apa.org/international/resolutiongender.html

Aronson, J. (2002). Stereotype threat: Contending and coping with unnerving expectations. In J. Aronson (Ed.), *Improving academic achievement: Impact of psychological factors on education* (pp. 279–301). San Diego: Academic Press.

Arredondo, P., Toporek, R., Brown, S., Jones, J., Locke, D. C., Sanchez, J., et al. (1996). *Operationalization of the multicultural counseling competencies*. Washington, DC: Association for Multicultural Counseling and Development.

Barnett, R., & Rivers, C. (2004). *Same difference: How gender myths are hurting our relationships, our children, and our jobs.* New York: Basic Books.

Berry, J. W., Poortinga, Y. H., Segall, M. H., & Dasen, P. R. (1992). *Cross-cultural psychology: Research and applications.* New York: Cambridge University Press.

Breakwell, G. M. (1990). Social beliefs about gender differences. In C. Fraser & G. Gaskell (Eds.), *The social psychological study of widespread beliefs* (pp. 210–225). Oxford, UK: Clarendon.

Broverman, I. K., Vogel, S. R., Broverman, D. M., Clarkson, F. E., & Rosenkrantz, P. S. (1972). Sex-role stereotypes: A current appraisal. *Journal of Social Issues, 28*(2), 59–78.

Buss, D. M. (1989). Sex differences in human mate preference: Evolutionary hypotheses tested in 37 cultures. *Behavioral and Brain Science, 12,* 1–49.

Chodorow, N. (1974). Family structure and feminine personality. In M. Z. Rosaldo & L. Lamphere (Eds.), *Women, culture and society* (pp. 43–66). Stanford, CA: Stanford University Press.

Crooks, R., & Baur, K. (1993). *Our sexuality* (5th ed.). Redwood City, CA: Benjamin/Cummings.

Davenport, D. S., & Yurich, J. M. (1991). Multicultural gender issues. *Journal of Counseling and Development, 70,* 64–71.

Eugenides, J. (2002). *Middlesex.* New York: Farrar, Straus & Giroux.

Feinberg, L. (1998). *Transliberation: Beyond pink or blue.* Boston: Beacon. Available at http://www.transgen derwarrior.org/writings/pinkblue/pinkbluehome.htm

Gagne, P., Tewksbury, R., & McGaughey, D. (1997). Coming out and crossing over: Identity formation and proclamation in a transgender community. *Gender & Society, 11,* 478–508.

Gilligan, C. (1982). *In a different voice: Psychological theory and women's development.* Cambridge, MA: Harvard University Press.

Goleman, D. (2000). *Leadership that gets results* (HBR OnPoint, no. 4487). Boston: Harvard Business School Publishing Corporation.

Goleman, D. (1998). *Working with emotional intelligence.* New York: Bantam.

Gray, J. (1992). *Men are from Mars, women are from Venus: A practical guide for improving communication and getting what you want in your relationships.* New York: HarperCollins.

Hall, R., & Fine, M. (2005). The stories we tell: The lives and friendship of two older Black lesbians. *Psychology of Women Quarterly, 29,* 177–187.

Hansen, L. S. (1980). *BORN FREE: Training packets to reduce career-related sex-role stereotyping.* Palo Alto, CA: American Institute for Research.

Hansen, S., Gama, E., & Harkins, A. (2002). Revisiting gender issues in multicultural counseling. In P. B. Pedersen, J. G. Draguns, W. J. Lonner, & J. E. Trimble (Eds.), *Counseling across cultures* (5th ed., pp. 163–184). Thousand Oaks, CA: Sage.

Hautzinger, S. (2003). Researching men's violence: Personal reflections on ethnographic data. *Men and Masculinities, 6*(1), 93–106.

Horne, A., & Kiselica, M. (Eds.). (1999). *Handbook of counseling boys and adolescent males.* Thousand Oaks, CA: Sage.

Human Rights Watch. (2004). *U.S.: Efforts to combat human trafficking and slavery.* Retrieved on December 28, 2005, from http://hrw.org/english/docs/2004/07/15/usdom9075_txt.htm

Kerr, B., Kurpius, S., & Harkins, A. (2005). *Handbook for counseling girls and women: Ten years of gender equity research at Arizona State University: Vol. 2. Talent development.* Mesa, AZ: Nueva Science Press.

Kurpius, S., Kerr, B., & Harkins, A. (2005). *Handbook for counseling girls and women: Ten years of gender equity research at Arizona State University: Vol. 1: Talent, risk and resiliency.* Mesa, AZ: Nueva Science Press.

Lev, A. I. (2004). *Transgender emergence: Therapeutic guidelines for working with gender-variant people and their families.* Binghamton, MA: Hawthorn.

Lombardi, E. L., Wilchins, D., Priesing, D., & Malouf, D. (2001). Gender violence: Transgender experiences with violence and discrimination. *Journal of Homosexuality, 42*(1), 89–101.

Maccoby, E. E., & Jacklin, C. N. (1974). *The psychology of sex differences.* Stanford, CA: Stanford University Press.

Mun Wah, L. (Producer/Director). (1994). *The color of fear* [Motion picture]. Oakland, CA: Stirfry Seminars. Available at www.stirfryseminars.com./pages/coloroffear.htm

O'Keefe, T., & Fox, K. (Eds.). (2003). *Finding the real me: True tales of sex and gender diversity.* San Francisco: Jossey-Bass.

O'Neil, J. (1981). Male sex role conflicts, sexism and masculinity: Psychological implications for men, women, and the counseling psychologist. *The Counseling Psychologist, 9,* 61–80.

Rabin, C. (Ed.). (2005). *Understanding gender and culture in the helping process: Practitioners' narratives from global perspectives.* Belmont, CA: Thomson/Wadsworth.

Richardson, D. S. (2005). The myth of female passivity: Thirty years of revelations about female aggression. *Psychology of Women Quarterly, 29,* 238–247.

Rivers, C., & Barnett, R. (2006, May 28). Others call the 'boy' problem an overblown backlash against the women's movement. *Minneapolis StarTribune,* p. AA1.

Sax, L. (2006, May 28). The trouble with boys. *Minneapolis StarTribune,* p. AA1.

Shibley Hyde, J. (2005). The gender similarities hypothesis. *American Psychologist, 60*(6), 581–592.

Skovholt, T. (1990). Career themes and counseling and psychotherapy with men. In D. Moore & F. Leagren (Eds.), *Problem-solving strategies and interventions for men in conflict* (pp. 39–53). Alexandria, VA: American Counseling Association.

Spreier, S., Fontaine, M., & Malloy, R. (2006). Leadership run amok: The destructive potential of overachievers. *Harvard Business Review, 84*(6), 72–82.

Steele, C. M. (2003). Through the back door to theory. *Psychological Inquiry 14*(3–4), 314–317.

Tannen, D. (1990). *You just don't understand: Women and men in conversation.* New York: HarperCollins.

Tucker, D. (Writer/Director). (2005). *TransAmerica* [Motion picture]. Solana Beach, CA: IFC Films. Web site at www.transamerica-movie.com

UN Population Fund. (2000). *The state of the world population 2000: Lives together, worlds apart: Men and women in a time of change.* New York: Author. Retrieved October 29, 2000, from http://www.unfpa.org/swp/swpmain.htm

United Nations. (2006a, April 5). Convention on the elimination of all forms of discrimination against women (CEDAW). *Country Report.* Retrieved May 16, 2006, from http://www.un.org/womenwatch/daw/cedaw/reports.htm

United Nations. (2006b, April 28). *Convention on the elimination of all forms of discrimination against women (CEDAW).* Retrieved May 16, 2006, from http://www.un.org/womenwatch/daw/cedaw/

V-Day. (n.d.). *Violence against women statistics.* Retrieved December 28, 2005, from http://www.vday.org/contents/violence/statistics

Weber, L. (1998). A conceptual framework for understanding race, class, gender, and sexuality. *Psychology of Women Quarterly, 22,* 13–32.

Williams, J. E., & Best, D. L. (1982). *Measuring sex stereotypes: A thirty nation study.* Beverly Hills, CA: Sage.

Williams, J. E., & Best, D. L. (1990). *Sex and psyche: Gender and self viewed cross-culturally.* Newbury Park, CA: Sage.

Williams, J. E., Satterwhite, R. C., & Best, D. L. (1999). Pancultural gender stereotypes revisited: The five factor model. *Sex Roles 40*(7–8), 513–525.

World Health Organization, Department of Injuries and Violence Prevention (2002, October 3). *World report on violence and health.* Retrieved December 18, 2005, from http://www.who.int/violence_injury_prevention

# Culturally Appropriate Counseling Considerations for Lesbian and Gay Clients

Mark Pope

---

## Primary Objective

- To identify and describe the essential social, cultural, and historical factors that lead to effective counseling strategies for prospective gay and lesbian clients

## Secondary Objectives

- To discuss multiple cultural identities and the intersection of lesbian and gay issues with race and ethnicity
- To describe gay and lesbian identity development and discuss its implications for effective counseling with lesbian and gay clients
- To present a framework designed to guide counselors in making culturally relevant choices when counseling lesbian and gay clients, organized around issues of counselor self-preparation, individual counseling, appropriate programs, and social advocacy

---

PROVIDING EFFECTIVE AND CULTURALLY APPROPRIATE COUNSELING TO GAY OR LESBIAN CLIENTS MAY appear, at first glance, to be largely the same as helping nongay or nonlesbian clients. One, therefore, might believe that "people are people" or the opposite even that "gays are perverse" and want to help

201

BIG Brother
BIG Sister

them find their way out of their sin. With the former position, information may be enough. With the latter, it is at best a more difficult task. It is hoped that this chapter will help ease one out of those positions so that one can become a more effective helper of lesbian, gay, bisexual, transgender, intersex, queer, or questioning people.

The primary intent of the chapter is to introduce the reader to the complexity of counseling with gay and lesbian persons along with all of their varied cultural and ethnic identities. For example, counseling with a gay man who is American Indian and HIV positive, is 65 years old, and lives in an urban center provides layer upon layer of complexity to that process (Croteau, Lark, Lidderdale, & Chung, 2005; Trimble, Stevenson, & Worell, 2003).

Issues and topics associated with multiple cultural identities and the intersection of lesbian and gay issues with race and ethnicity are central themes in this chapter. The social, cultural, and historical context of sexual orientation provides an important backdrop for the study of sexual minorities. In addition, emphasis is placed on gay and lesbian identity development as a critical component to understanding this most critical developmental process for all sexual minorities. In looking at practice interventions for working with this group, the chapter is organized around four themes: counselor self-preparation for working with gay and lesbian clients, individual counseling issues useful for working with gay and lesbian clients, programs useful to address the special issues that this group presents, and appropriate advocacy or social action interventions.

Providing counseling for individuals who are gay or lesbian is a complicated process that requires a person to have strong multicultural counseling competencies (Barret & Logan, 2002; Brown, 1989; Dworkin & Gutierrez, 1992; Greene, 1997; Hancock, 2000; Perez, DeBord, & Bieschke, 2000; Pope, 1995b; Pope et al., 2004; Pope & Barret, 2002; Pope & Chung, 2000). Three important seminal documents inform the competence of individuals who work with lesbian and gay people: the "Multicultural Counseling Competencies and Standards" (Sue, Arredondo, & McDavis, 1992); the Association for Gay, Lesbian, and Bisexual Issues in Counseling's (AGLBIC's) *Competencies in Counseling Gay, Lesbian, Bisexual, and Transgendered Clients* (Terndrup, Ritter, Barret, Logan, & Mate, 1997); and the American Psychological Association's (2000) *Guidelines for Psychotherapy With Lesbian, Gay, and Bisexual Clients.*

Thirty years ago, there was little research addressing counseling with lesbian and gay clients other than literature addressing such clients generally as "deviants" (Bell & Weinberg, 1978; M. S. Weinberg & Williams, 1974). The literature content is changing and evolving, and for mental health professionals who are seeking practical advice on how to provide such counseling services, there is now a growing body of literature to plumb for knowledge of how to intervene appropriately with lesbian and gay clients.

## SEXUAL ORIENTATION: SOCIAL, CULTURAL, AND HISTORICAL CONTEXT

The first step in the counseling process is to gain access to the information that will help one understand the social, cultural, and historical context in which lesbian women and gay men function. It is critical that one have an appreciation for this context as so much of what makes counseling lesbian and gay people different from counseling others is a direct result of this (Herdt, 1992; Pope, 1995b).

Mental health professionals who work with lesbian and gay clients must become aware of that culture to be truly helpful. Counselors should become aware of the sociopolitical issues, specific knowledge, necessary information, and institutional barriers that confront gay and lesbian clients who are seeking counseling. Counselors also must be aware of the history, language, rituals, traditions, and sense of community that define the gay and lesbian culture (Pope et al., 2004).

Many counselors may believe that they know that context, but everyone has a worldview that may or may not match up with that of any of their clients. So, we always start with a review of our information and our prejudices and try to move to more accurate information that will inform our practice.

## "Gay" or "Lesbian"

Let's start with terminology. *Gay* can be used broadly to include men or women who are sexually and/or affectionally attracted to members of their same gender. Some women identify as "gay," others as "lesbian," usually for political reasons. In the mental health literature, the term *lesbian women*, although redundant, is being used more and contrasted with *gay men*. In this chapter, *gay* will be used exclusively to refer to gay men and *lesbian* to refer to lesbian women. *Bisexual* is a term that refers to a person of one gender who is sexually attracted to individuals of both genders. *Transgender* refers to individuals who identify as one gender but have the physiology of the opposite gender. *Sexual minority* is an inclusive term that is appearing more in the professional literature to describe all the various aspects of sexuality and gender, including gay, lesbian, bisexual, transgender, intersex, queer, and questioning. *Queer,* while not generally used in this chapter, is a political statement of difference from the majority culture.

## Societal Barriers and Social Progress

Most industrialized societies are in transition on the issue of the acceptance of lesbian, gay, bisexual, and transgender people; in general, trends are moving in a positive direction. In the past several decades, the emergence of an identifiable lesbian and gay culture in most medium- to large-sized metropolitan areas in North America has dispelled the long-held negative stereotypes of gay men as effeminate and lesbian women as overly masculine (Herdt, 1992; Pope & Barret, 2002). Prior to that, if they did not live in large cities such as New York, San Francisco, Montreal, Toronto, Vancouver, and Boston where vital lesbian and gay culture thrives, gay men and lesbian women generally kept their sexual orientation a closely guarded secret. If there were social events with coworkers, many would bring opposite-sex "dates" that had been secured to help "cover" and guard their secret. Some even chose "safe" careers in the event they did decide to come out. Others carefully guarded their sexual orientation for fear that the promotions would be denied them if they were more "out." Fortunately, today, for many lesbians and gays, much of this is changing, as it is not unusual to hear casual conversations about the social and relationship aspects of gay and lesbian coworkers in the workplace. That too, however, would suggest that the special needs of gay men and lesbian women are changing.

Despite the increased visibility and acceptance, gay men and lesbian women continue to experience discrimination in various aspects of their lives: in the workplace, when buying homes, when trying to adopt a child, and when seeking a marriage license to solemnize their relationships. Just as African Americans, Asian Americans, Hispanic Americans, and American Indians and Alaska Natives continue to experience discrimination in various aspects of their lives (Bowman, 1993), lesbians and gay men do so as well. The failure of the U.S. Congress, for example, to pass laws to protect the lives and livelihoods of lesbian women and gay men attests to the lack of acceptance of their most basic human rights.

On the other side, local governments especially in urban areas and the judicial branch of government concerned with fairness instead of votes have begun to ensure those rights to lesbian, gay, bisexual, and even transgender citizens. On May 17, 2004, Massachusetts became the first state in the

United States to grant marriage licenses to same-sex couples (Human Rights Campaign, 2005). On June 26, 2003, in the most significant governmental ruling ever for lesbian and gay Americans' civil rights in *Lawrence v. Texas* (2003), the U.S. Supreme Court struck down Texas's sodomy law, which had criminalized oral and anal sex by consenting gay couples and was used widely to justify discrimination against lesbians and gay men. This effectively overturned all the remaining 13 state sodomy laws in the United States. Similar to *Plessy v. Ferguson; Brown v. Board of Education of Topeka, Kansas;* and *Roe v. Wade, Lawrence v. Texas* is a landmark judicial decision (Pope, 2006). It would appear that gays and lesbians have entered a new, contradictory era, where their sexual orientation may or may not be an issue. It all depends on the circumstances and the settings.

Lesbian and gay discrimination continues to exist, but there are major changes occurring in most industrialized societies, especially in the workplace. Many national and some international corporations are including sexual orientation in their nondiscrimination personnel policies, and many are providing domestic partner benefits. In 1995, in the United States, there were only 90 state and local governments that provided domestic partner benefits to their gay and lesbian employees. In 2004, there were 185 state and local governments that provided these benefits (Human Rights Campaign, 2005), with 2,867 different employers including sexual orientation in their nondiscrimination policies and 8,250 offering domestic partners benefits.

## Lesbian and Gay Culture Primer

There is a debate ongoing among multicultural counseling leaders and within the multicultural counseling community as to the scope of the definition of *multiculturalism* (Arredondo et al., 1992; Pedersen & Locke, 1999; Pope, 1995b, 2006). On one side of the debate are those who favor an inclusive definition of multiculturalism (including racial, ethnic, and sexual minorities), and on the other side are those who support an exclusive one (including only ethnic and racial minorities). The split centers on the inclusion of lesbians and gays as part of that definition.

Pope (1995a, 1995b) argued strongly for an inclusive definition of multiculturalism and that lesbians and gays must be a part of that definition. Locke (1990) stated that sexual orientation is an aspect of "diversity" but does not fit his definition of "culture." One should be reminded, though, that at a basic level, culture "denotes an historically transmitted pattern of meanings embodied in symbols, a system of inherited conceptions expressed in symbolic forms by means of which men communicate, perpetuate, and develop the knowledge about and attitudes toward life" (Geertz, 1978, p. 89). As with any discernible group, gay and lesbians fall within the general definition of what constitutes a cultural unit.

The defining characteristics of gay and lesbian culture are salient for counseling and thus include a number of common themes. The multicultural counseling skills that are required for dealing with racial and ethnic minorities also are important domains for including sexual minorities. Indeed, lesbians and gays constitute a cultural group. "Families" are "chosen" and are not always biological for gays and lesbians. Whether a cultural minority is "hidden" or "visible" is not the issue; gay and lesbian oppression, as well as the results of that oppression by the majority culture, is very real, having real effects on real people's lives, development, and career. And finally, identity formation tasks that racial and ethnic minorities must accomplish are very similar for sexual minorities. As the identity development stage is important, the processes of "coming out to self" versus "coming out to others," "passing" or hiding, and "coming out" to families have deep collectivist cultural traditions.

# Similarity in Cultural Counseling Skills

Pedersen (1988), Sue et al. (1992), Espin (1993), and Pope (1995b) have all discussed the role of the counselor in a multicultural society. An important role for counselors who provide counseling to cultural minority populations is to help reduce the stereotypes, discrimination, environmental barriers, and other forms of bias that typically impede the development of such groups. Furthermore, to counsel such individuals—that is, members of a cultural minority—counselors must have some familiarity with the culture of that minority. Counselors must be familiar with the gay and lesbian culture as well as the status of gays and lesbians within other cultural communities if they hope to adequately serve their clients from the gay and lesbian community.

The special needs of this cultural minority arise from the historic discrimination that has helped to define the gay and lesbian community and include the lack of civil rights, secret or semi-secret lives, oppression, rejection or ostracism by their family of origin, societal censure, lowered self-esteem due to internalized homophobia, fear and reality of physical violence, and being the object of campaigns of hatred and vilification by right-wing political groups and fundamentalist religious groups (Cooper, 1989; Fassinger, 1991).

# Cultural Minority in a Multicultural Society

Gay males and lesbians are surely a sexual minority numerically according to any measure that has been used (Bell & Weinberg, 1978; Kinsey, Pomeroy, & Martin, 1948; Kinsey, Pomeroy, Martin, & Gebhard, 1953).

They are also a psychological minority in the sense that lesbians and gay men were labeled as "diseased" by the psychological community until 1973 and the seventh printing of the third edition of the *Diagnostic and Statistical Manual of Mental Disorders* (American Psychiatric Association, 1980, p. 380). This change in definition was a result of a protracted professional discussion, which finally led to a membership vote on whether homosexuality *per se* was a mental disease (Bayer, 1981). Gays and lesbians, therefore, are certainly a minority created by the psychological community out of the prejudices of the majority culture (Pope, 1995b).

Are lesbians and gays, then, a "cultural" minority as well? Pope (1995b) argued forcefully for that position and status. Cultural minority status has been given to groups who are minorities within the majority culture and have their own geographic living areas, economic and social organizations, cultural traditions, and rituals. Furthermore, a *definition* of what constitutes a cultural minority must transcend national boundaries, although which specific groups meet the requirements of this definition may vary from country to country. For example, Chinese are a minority culture within the United States, even though they are numerically the majority in China, Singapore, Taiwan, Hong Kong, Macau, and substantial minorities within several other countries, including Malaysia, Vietnam, Thailand, Burma, and Cambodia.

Within almost all large cities in the United States and around the world, gay males and lesbians have developed geographic communities where large numbers live: Greenwich Village in New York, Castro Street in San Francisco, New Town in Chicago, West Hollywood in Los Angeles, and many others. Gay- and lesbian-owned businesses abound in these areas, catering to the special needs of this minority. In these communities, one finds bookstores such as the Oscar Wilde Memorial Bookshop and Judith's Room; clothing stores such as Leather Forever and All-American Boy; restaurants such as the Patio, Hot and Hunky Hamburgers, and Welcome Home; bars such as Twin Peaks, Girl-Spot,

Rawhide, Maud's, and the Eagle; and newspapers and other periodicals such as *The Advocate, OUT* magazine, San Francisco's *Bay Area Reporter,* Boston's *Gay Community News,* Washington, DC's *Washington Blade, Christopher Street,* St. Louis's *Vital Voice,* and *The Edge.* These resources for the gay and lesbian community are collected and distributed through international, national, and local directories such as *Spartacus Gay Guide,* the *Gayellow Pages,* and the *Gay Book.*

Each major religious denomination, political organization, and professional organization has a lesbian and gay caucus or group associated with it. The American Counseling Association has the Association for Gay, Lesbian, and Bisexual Issues in Counseling. The American Psychological Association has Division 44: The Society for the Psychological Study of Lesbian and Gay Issues. The American Medical Association has the Physicians for Human Rights. The Episcopalians have Integrity. The Catholics have Dignity. The Methodists have Affirmation. There is even a specific Protestant church having its origins in the lesbian and gay community, the Metropolitan Community Church. The Democrats have the Harvey Milk Democratic Club, Stonewall Democratic Clubs, and others. The Republicans have the Log Cabin Republican Clubs. There are Gay and Lesbian Sierrans in the Sierra Club, the Golden Gate Business Association for businesses, and High Tech Gays for individuals in high-technology industries. The newest addition to this panoply of cultural organizations is the employee clubs that many large corporations have encouraged, including Microsoft, Hewlett-Packard, IBM, Apple, United Airlines, and many more.

The rituals and traditions of lesbians and gays include those like most families—long-term relationships, marriages, raising children, the celebration of anniversaries—as well as the lesbian and gay marches/parades around the world to commemorate the Stonewall Riot in 1969 in New York City, the event that, for many historians, marks the beginning of the modern gay and lesbian rights movement (Altman, 1971).

The information on lesbian and gay culture is an important beginning to understand the context in which lesbian and gay individuals function. The culture plays an important role in the socialization of the person just discovering his or her sexual orientation or gender identity. It provides a safe place to go and figure out if you are lesbian and gay and, therefore, different from the majority of people, a place where one feels better about being different. This safe place is important to the next step—understanding gay and lesbian identity development.

## "Family" for Gays and Lesbians

One of the differences between gay and lesbian culture and the racial/ethnic cultures is the concept of family. "Coming out to others" is a unique process that differentiates lesbians and gay men from other minority cultures in that they are probably the only group where the family of origin has to be informed about their membership status. This presents a powerful cohesive experience for gay males and lesbians—a rite of passage. Conversely, it is the only group where the family of origin may also reject the person for his or her cultural minority status (Elliott, 1993).

During the "coming-out" process, individuals gather around them a group of other sexual minorities like them for support of their new cultural identity. This new "chosen" family is composed of gays and lesbians—most are older chronologically and most have been "out" for a much longer period of time—who mentor the person through the "coming-out" process and into the gay and lesbian culture. Sometimes, these individuals take on the roles as well as titles of the family of origin or biological family members. In one gay Filipino family, one older gay man took on the role of "mother" and was even referred to by that title. The process, however, is one of mentoring the younger person into his or her new identity and new culture. There may or may not be a sexual attraction or sexual relationship involved in these relationships.

## Gay and Lesbian Identity Development

Gay and lesbian identity development—or, as it is termed in the literature, "coming out"—is a critical process for anyone who is lesbian or gay. How individuals accomplish this process provides the foundation for the rest of their lives. Having a strong cultural identity is critical for psychological health. Coming out also is a very difficult developmental process that may not be completed well into an individual's adult years.

Coming out has been defined by Altman (1971) as

> the whole process whereby a person comes to identify himself/herself as homosexual, and recognizes his/her position as part of a stigmatized and semi-hidden minority. The development of a homosexual identity is a long process that usually begins during adolescence, though sometimes considerably later. Because of the fears and ignorance that surround our views of sex, children discover sexual feelings and behavior incompletely, and often accompanied by great pangs of guilt. [Many of us] manage to hide into our twenties a full realization that [we are] not like [them]. (pp. 15–16)

In traditional identity development models, individuals progress from initial awareness of attraction to and feelings for the same sex; then experiences of sex, followed by explorations of the gay and lesbian cultural community; then self-labeling as lesbian, gay, or bisexual; and finally the disclosure of one's identity to others. Cass (1979) was one of the first to offer an identity development model and specified the specific developmental stages that gays and lesbians must accomplish: (1) identity confusion (feeling different, inner turmoil), (2) identity comparison (bargaining and intellectualizing the feelings away), (3) identity tolerance (realization they probably are gay/lesbian), (4) identity acceptance (more culture contact, some disclosure), (5) identity pride (immersion in gay/lesbian culture, anger and outrage at dominant culture), and (6) identity synthesis (integration of gay/lesbian identity into total person). Identity foreclosure, where the person stops his or her coming-out process, can occur at any stage, or the individual can progress to the last stage with a fully integrated lesbian or gay cultural identity.

## "Coming Out to Self" Versus "Coming Out to Others"

The issue of coming out has been central for gay men and lesbian women who are seeking counseling. Furthermore, it is important for counselors to recognize that there are two different types of coming out. On one hand, coming out has been discussed as a developmental task for gay and lesbian individuals to successfully complete. This form of coming out involves a self-acceptance of the individual's own sexual orientation and might be better termed "coming out to self." On the other hand, coming out also has been discussed as disclosing to others. Such disclosure might be accomplished by verbal or written, private or public statements to other individuals. By this action, individuals inform other persons of their sexual orientation. This might be better termed "coming out to others."

Even if unstated, it is important for the counselor to recommend "coming out to others" as a topic for discussion as part of the counseling process. Issues to address in such a discussion include "how to," including conducting an environmental scan, and the "whys" associated with deciding to come out. Counselors can help their clients consider the advantages and disadvantages of coming out in the workplace or school. Counselors can provide clients with opportunities for behavioral rehearsals directed toward developing strategies for informing others.

It may be important to determine if one's fears of coming out to others are based on reality, on previous experiences, or on the person's own internalized homophobia (Pope & Barret, 2002). To determine this, an objective "environmental homophobia assessment" must be conducted. There are two parts to this process, in which the environment must be objectively observed and analyzed for actual clues: the general corporate/organizational climate (e.g., corporate/institutional antidiscrimination policy, gay/lesbian employees/student group, inclusionary or exclusionary language, such as only "wives and husbands" are invited to events) and the attitudes of the specific department, manager, or coworkers toward sexual orientation issues (e.g., types of jokes that are told and tolerated, newspaper articles on the bulletin boards). The findings of this assessment can help you determine when a workplace, school, or any institution is safer.

The Workplace Sexual Identity Management Measure (WSIMM) (Anderson, Croteau, Chung, & DiStefano, 2001) is a useful assessment tool to guide the coming-out process. Psychometric properties of the WSIMM were examined for a sample of 172 student affairs professionals. The authors reported that the WSIMM successfully assessed a continuum of strategies for coming out in the workplace. Such measures as this are important to aid lesbian and gay workers in assessing their work environment and exploring appropriate strategies for sexual orientation disclosure.

Coming out to others is a continuous process that has no end; gay males and lesbians must make this decision to "come out" any time they meet a new person in a new situation. Pope and Schecter (1992) have identified some different strategies that briefly include simply using the correct gender-specific pronouns when speaking of dates or love relationships, matter-of-fact statements of reality, or defiant announcements as a response to pejorative homophobic, racist, or sexist comments made in the workplace.

It is difficult to determine which cultural identity development process is most important. There is some research to suggest that the coming-out process for a gay/lesbian person may even be more important than his or her ethnic/racial identity development or even gender identity. For many sexual minorities, coming out is the most important event in their lives at that point in time and may be fraught with peril. Croghan (2001) discussed the special issues in coming out and forming a strong cultural identity. Croghan found that the special characteristics in the development of a cultural identity as a gay man included being more aware of the acquisition of his gay identity than male identity; having feelings leading to secrecy, withdrawal, self-loathing, and creation of false selves; and separating gay and nongay aspects of life in attempts to hide sexual orientation from others. These were all precursors to the internal resolution and development of a healthy cultural identity as a gay man.

Coming out is an important and necessary developmental task for anyone who is gay or lesbian. Unfortunately, there are also costs for not coming out. Pope (1995b) and Gonsiorek (1993) identified some inherent problems in delayed mastery of the developmental task of accepting one's sexual orientation (coming out to self) along with the concomitant development of appropriate dating and relationship strategies with same-sex partners. This may cause a "developmental domino effect" whereby the inadequate completion of a particular task causes the next important developmental task to be delayed, missed, or inadequately completed. These delayed or skipped developmental tasks may have long-term and pervasive effects for individuals who come out in their 30s, 40s, 50s, or even later.

## "Passing" or Hiding

Many gays and lesbians and some racial and ethnic minorities can "pass," but this is not a very effective method of creating a positive self-identity. In fact, "passing" behavior is antithetical to creating this positive self-identity. The consequences of passing include lower self-esteem (Berger, 1982) along with feelings of inferiority and the internalization of negative self-concepts (M. S. Weinberg & Williams, 1974). The cumulative effect of this devaluing of self and like-others is emotionally unhealthy (Fischer, 1972; Freedman, 1971; G. H. Weinberg, 1971).

For those minorities, in general, who can hide their membership and for sexual minorities, specifically, there are profound reasons to not hide from their family, friends, coworkers, and employers (Pope, 1995a). For lesbians and gays, these include their own individual mental health as well as three categories of other reasons: (1) personal reasons such as honesty, integration of their sexuality into every aspect of their life, recognition of who they are as a person, and support from those around them; (2) professional, political, and societal reasons such as providing a role model for other gay males and lesbians, desensitizing their coworkers and themselves toward the issue, and eliminating any fear of blackmail; and (3) practical reasons, so that their domestic partner can get benefits and come to events, as well as to prevent slips of the tongue and embarrassment when it inevitably slips out in everyday conversation with coworkers. The most important reason, however, is the full integration of every aspect of who the person is into one fully functioning human being.

Such an integrative approach is illustrated by this study of gay male flight attendants. Adams (1997) discussed how gay men's selection of jobs as flight attendants was a choice to integrate their cultural identity with their work identity. The participants in this study saw their movement into an occupation composed of a large group of gay men as extremely positive. They reported that three factors were most important for them: their hope of companionship with a large group of other gay men; an escape from family, a community, or a job that stifled being gay; and being safe. Adams found a positive relationship between working as a flight attendant and acculturation into the gay community, an increase in openness with others, and heightened self-esteem.

## Coming Out to Families Having Collectivist Cultural Traditions

Special attention also must be paid to the issue of coming out in families from cultures that do not readily accept same-sex sexual orientations. "There is not much qualitative difference between Asian and United States cultures in terms of traditional attitudes toward homosexuality, but the intensity of heterosexism and homophobia is much stronger in Asian cultures than in U.S. culture" (Chung & Katayama, 1998, p. 22). The strategies that are used in more collectivist cultures (such as Asian countries) are different from those employed in more individualist cultures (such as the United States) (Chan, 1997; Espin, 1993; Han, 2001; Pope, 1999; Pope & Chung, 2000; Pope, Rodriguez, & Chang, 1992). Newman and Muzzonigro (1993) studied differences between gay males in general who were raised in more traditional families and those raised in less traditional families. They reported that gay males from more traditional families felt more disapproval of their sexual orientation than gay males from less traditional families. Wooden, Kawasaki, and Mayeda (1983) addressed the issue of sexual identity development (coming out to self) in a sample of Japanese men and found that, although almost all of the sample had come out to their friends, only about half had disclosed their sexual orientation to their families. These issues must be addressed when providing counseling to lesbian women or gay men from such cultures, and strategies must be revised accordingly. Other authors have similarly addressed these issues for African Americans (Maguen, Floyd, Bakeman, & Armistead, 2002; Martinez & Sullivan, 1998; McLean, Marini, & Pope, 2003), Hispanic Americans (Espin, 1993; Fimbres, 2001; Merighi & Grimes, 2000), and Native Americans (Garrett & Barret, 2003; Morris & Rothblum, 1999; Piedmont, 1996).

Furthermore, issues of multiple identity and discrimination are complex and challenging. Martinez and Sullivan (1998) examined the complexity of gay/lesbian identity development in African American gay men and lesbian women. They identified three specific issues as adding the most complexity and as differentiating their identity development from most gay or lesbian identity development models: racial prejudice, limited acceptance by the African American community, and a lack of integration into the larger, White gay community. Van Puymbroeck (2002) found that the effects on individual development of ethnic or sexual minority status are not simply additive but interactive and that gender plays a defining role.

For the lesbian or gay person from a collectivist cultural tradition, issues of coming out are more complicated because of their increased focus on the extended family as decision maker. In that context, it may seem to the family that the gay/lesbian person is being the ultimate individualist and is, therefore, choosing to separate himself or herself from the family and their traditions. If their coming out is seen as an individual choice at the cost of the family good, the person may be cast out of his or her family—the ultimate punishment in a collectivist culture. On the other hand, if the coming out is seen as being based on more immutable factors (not choice) and not seen as separation from the family but as an integral part of and contribution to the family good, then the acceptance is more probable. For example, in the American Indian tradition, individuals who exhibited amodal gender/sexual behavior (sometimes referred to as *winkte* or *berdache* in some tribes) were still a part of the tribe and more accepted. The community roles of such individuals included children's caretaker (for males), medicine person, and even warrior (for females)—all considered important contributions.

Obviously, the mental health implications of all of this are very critical both at the individual and the systemic levels. In this situation, the counselor may take on the role of mediator where knowledge of the specific cultures (both lesbian/gay and traditional collectivist) is especially important to a successful outcome for both the individual and the family.

## COUNSELOR SELF-PREPARATION FOR WORKING WITH GAY AND LESBIAN CLIENTS

The first step for counselors who want to work with gay and lesbian clients is to take a personal inventory of the ways that often subtle or unconscious biases may influence the counseling process (Buhrke & Douce, 1991; Prince, 1997). Previous research studies have documented the mental health profession's poor treatment of all sexual minorities (Barret & Logan, 2002). Bias toward this oppressed minority will influence interventions that the individual counselor chooses to use. For example, Pope (1992) used the example of how heterosexually oriented counselors may have the idea that if they can help a young man become more masculine in his behaviors, he can change his sexual orientation and will not have to deal with all of the problems that being gay brings for him. Such counselors are simply trying to help, but these interventions are not research based, and although they may seem intuitively appropriate to some counselors, there is no research literature that (1) suggests that training in gender-appropriate behavior is a determinant of sexual orientation or (2) suggests that a same-sex sexual orientation is subject to change anymore than an opposite-sex orientation is (LeVay, 1996).

Living in communities that routinely discriminate against gay men and lesbian women, it is virtually impossible, however, to avoid internalizing negative stereotypes or attitudes about this sexual minority culture. Misinformation or misunderstanding will quickly be evident to sexual minority clients and may cause them to seek help elsewhere or not to get help at all. Counselors, however, must be familiar with gay and lesbian culture so they are credible and congruent in their attitudes. Attending workshops, reading the literature, and participating in lesbian and gay culture are effective ways to acquire knowledge about gay men and lesbian women and their culture. Former clients and friends who are gay men or lesbian women will be an invaluable source of information.

Counselors need explicit awareness of their own religious and spiritual nature and beliefs as their role in sexuality in almost all national and tribal cultures is important (Hancock, 2000). Counselors never impose their own belief system on their clients, but many lesbian and gay clients have been hurt deeply by religious organizations. Counselors do not have to study religion to have respect for the role that such beliefs play in many people's lives or to help clients discover gay-positive alternatives to a fundamentalist religious approach.

In particular, counselors who work with gay men and lesbian women must understand the process of developing a gay or lesbian cultural identity. Morgan and Brown (1991) found that age cannot be a predictor of lesbian or gay identity development as individuals discover their sexual orientation at a variety of ages, and counselors need to be aware of their clients' stage of gay/lesbian identity development as well as their other development issues to provide effective counseling.

Counselors also must develop their own strategies for handling contact with their gay and lesbian clients outside of the counseling session (Barret & Logan, 2002). The gay and lesbian community is a relatively small community, and similar to other cultural communities, counselors and clients may bump into each other at various community functions such as gay and lesbian pride events, at the local gay bar, or in a variety of nontherapeutic situations. Although such situations may be uncomfortable for the counselor or client, they may also be potentially beneficial (American Counseling Association, 2005). The counselor needs to have developed strategies and boundaries that are healthy and realistic for the good of the client and addressed such issues as part of the counseling process.

Finally, as has been noted previously, counselors must confront their own individual prejudice and bias toward lesbian and gay clients and culture. When and if they decide they cannot be gay and lesbian affirmative in their attitudes, they are ethically required to refer the client to a counselor who has such attitudes and experience with sexual minorities (Barret & Logan, 2002; Pope, Prince, & Mitchell, 2000; Pope & Tarvydas, 2006; Sanlo, 1998). The American Counseling Association and American Psychological Association both have well-defined ethical codes that offer guidance for individuals who work with clients around issues related to their sexual orientation (American Counseling Association, 2005; American Psychological Association, 2002).

## INDIVIDUAL COUNSELING INTERVENTIONS USEFUL FOR WORKING WITH GAY AND LESBIAN CLIENTS

Too much harm has been done to gays, lesbians, and those questioning their own sexual orientation by ill-trained, misinformed, or malicious mental health practitioners (Garnets, Hancock, Cochran, Goodchilds, & Peplau, 1991; Nystrom, 1997; Shidlo & Schroeder, 2002). Certain issues arise consistently because of the special needs of gays and lesbians. Coming out has been central for gay men and lesbian women who are seeking counseling, as has been previously discussed. Other prominent issues include discrimination, relationships, parenting, HIV, aging, substance abuse, internationalized homoprejudice, and psychological testing.

# Discrimination

Discrimination against individuals based on their race, ethnic origin, gender, (dis)ability, religion, political affiliation, or sexual orientation is an unpleasant fact in U.S. society and really most societies around the world (Goffman, 1963). Counselors who fail to recognize this and do not assist their clients in coping with this reality do a disservice to their clients. Issues of dual and multiple discrimination also must be addressed when providing counseling services. For example, lesbian women face at least two virulent forms of discrimination in U.S. society—sexism and heterosexism. If they are also a member of an ethnic or racial minority, older, or physically challenged, they may face daunting barriers to achieving their life goals, especially with their careers. Openly addressing these issues and preparing clients to cope with the more overt manifestations of racism, sexism, heterosexism, ableism, and ageism is an important and primary role of the counselor. As simple as it may seem, talking openly with clients about issues of employment or housing discrimination is very important. Even if clients are not the first to broach the subject, the issues ought to be discussed so that the client is aware of the counselor's sensitivity and knowledge in this area, which would, at the least, enhance the therapeutic alliance. When these issues are openly and fully discussed, such discussions lead to improved life decision making.

For example, Ford (1996) found that young lesbians in her sample sought jobs, communities, and employers in which they were less likely to experience discrimination and chose occupations in which they could disclose their sexual orientation. Terndrup (1998), in a study of gay male teachers, found that most of the participating teachers revealed their primary reliance on "implicitly out" identity management strategies to alleviate fears of discrimination, public accusation, job loss, and impaired credibility. Keeton (2002) found that both lesbian women and gay men participants listed sexual orientation discrimination among the top three most anticipated career-related barriers and expected a moderately high degree of hindrance if encountered. There were, however, important gender differences in three areas as lesbians also chose anticipation of sex discrimination, anticipation of conflict between children and career demands, and anticipation of being discouraged from choosing nontraditional careers.

# Relationships

Another important issue involves relationship counseling with same-sex couples. Such issues that might be explored are differences in HIV status, employment and/or economic status, substance use, religious preferences, childrearing practices, immigration status, sexual behavior, partner relocation for work, and many others. The issues are important ones for the male couple or female couple with no relationship experience and only few "out" same-sex couple role models.

Hetherington, Hillerbrand, and Ertinger (1989) highlighted the issues facing same-sex couples— how to present the relationship, how to introduce one's partner, whether to openly acknowledge the love relationship, and how to deal with social events. Belz (1993) discussed same-sex couple issues in the workplace, including geographic relocation when one partner's job is moved, lifestyle that one partner would want to maintain while employed, problems that one partner's job may cause for a partner who may not want to be as open about this orientation, when to tell people at work, and how to handle situations that may arise at work for which the partner must be involved.

# Parenting

Whether by previous opposite-gender marriage, adoption, foster parenting, or donor insemination, gays and lesbians are becoming parents. Estimates of the number of children living with gay and lesbian parents range between 6 and 14 million (Patterson & Chan, 1996). There are gay and lesbian parent groups who meet regularly in almost every major city in the United States.

Myths promoted by conservative religious groups include the following: (1) children raised by same-sex-oriented individuals are more likely to become gay/lesbian, and (2) children raised by same-sex-oriented individuals are more likely to be sexually abused by their parents. Neither of these is supported by evidence in the existing research literature.

In fact, the issue of the ability of gay and lesbian individuals to be biological parents, foster parents, and adoptive parents has been settled in the research literature (Flowers, Barrett, & Robinson, 2000). Research indicates that the adjustment, development, and psychological well-being of children are unrelated to parental sexual orientation, and the children of gay and lesbian parents are as likely as those of heterosexual parents to thrive. There is even some research to suggest that having two female parents is even better than opposite-sex parents or two male parents.

Every professional association that deals with the welfare of children, including the American Counseling Association, American Psychological Association, National Association of Social Workers, American Psychiatric Association, and American Academy of Pediatrics, has stated unequivocally that a parent's sexual orientation should not solely be used to disqualify a person from such roles.

## HIV

Educating the client about safe sex is a critical aspect of counseling gay men in particular but also lesbian women (Barret & Logan, 2002). Counselors who work with gay men will inevitably encounter clients who have HIV disease and managing the double stigma of HIV-positive status and being gay or the triple stigma of also being American Indian (for example). This adds immense complexity to client issues. "Counseling HIV-positive gay men brings up a number of issues, such as shame, anger, grief over the loss of health, confusion about how to manage safe-sex negotiation, and life planning that incorporates the realities of HIV treatment" (Barret & Logan, 2002, p. 81). Lesbians are much less likely to contract HIV disease, but lesbians should nonetheless be aware of safe sex precautions.

## Aging

Over the past three decades, several researchers (Adelman, 1987; Berger, 1996; Kelly, 1977; Kimmel, 1978; Pope, 1997; Pope & Schulz, 1990; Quam, 1993; Wierzalis, Barret, Pope, & Rankins, 2006) have begun to address aging within the gay and lesbian community. Gays and lesbians face aging issues similar to those of their heterosexual counterparts, but these issues are compounded by societal stigma, invisibility related to their sexual orientation, and general negative stereotypes and discrimination regarding aging.

Generations of lesbians and gays have gone into their years as older adults as longtime witnesses to and victims of prejudice and rejection. While the current atmosphere in many countries in which gay men and lesbians live today involves greater visibility, many came out in a climate of severe oppression and stigmatization. This new status imbues life with potential and promise for all sexual minorities as they seek intimacy and forge relationships. Now, cohorts of gay men and lesbian women are living more openly—many in intimate relationships—offering encouragement to earlier generations of their counterparts. The opportunity exists for a better quality of life for gay, lesbian, and bisexual individuals as they age because greater understanding of sexual behavior, intimacy, and relationships in later life continues to emerge. Nonetheless, many older gay men and lesbians struggle with the vestiges of stigma and shame that were so evident in their youth as well as the loss of many from their gay and lesbian family who have died from HIV or from other age-related diseases.

## Substance Abuse

Substance abuse is a common issue for gay men and lesbians for at least two reasons: The gay or lesbian bar is many times the most accessible community institution, and alcohol and drugs are socially common ways of coping with the stressors of stigma. Also, the "I was so drunk I don't remember a thing" approach to meeting sexual needs or coming out is common. Furthermore, access to treatment may be complicated due to these same issues. In larger cities, AA groups (and related organizations) and recovery centers that are gay only or gay positive are common (e.g., Steps Alano), and there are several national treatment centers with a specific gay and lesbian focus (Barret & Logan, 2002).

## Internalized Homoprejudice

Helping clients overcome internalized negative stereotypes or homoprejudice is another task of the counselor. It is important for the counselor to understand the concept of internalized homophobia for gay and lesbian clients as this may affect the client's life choices. Oppression oppresses even the mentally healthy and well-adjusted people in cultural minorities. Societal messages repeated over and over again about "evil, sick, and sinful" people may be believed and accepted at some conscious or unconscious level, and these messages permeate the U.S. dominant culture. Internalized homophobia, when it occurs, cannot be overcome easily.

It is important that counselors understand and appreciate the effect that these messages can and do have on their gay and lesbian clients as well as all cultural minorities in the United States. When the client is a sexual minority, a gender minority, and a racial or ethnic minority, these issues are intensified (Chung & Katayama, 1998; Keeton, 2002; Pope & Chung, 2000). Culturally appropriate self-esteem interventions (e.g., positive self-talk, reframing, forgiveness) can be used here to overcome these internalized negative stereotypes.

## Psychological Testing

Another aspect of providing counseling to lesbian women and gay men includes special procedures for using psychological tests with gay men and lesbian women (Belz, 1993; Chung & Harmon, 1994; Gonsiorek, 1993; Mobley & Slaney, 1996; Pope, 1992; Pope et al., 1992; Prince, 1997). Mental health professionals need to know what special procedures are required to get accurate results or to make accurate interpretations. Because personality inventories, career interest inventories, and card sorts are all important interventions in the repertoire of counselors, how these items are used with lesbian women and gay men is an important issue.

Pope (1992) identified and analyzed the use and misuse of specific subscales on five major psychological inventories used in counseling and personnel selection (Strong Interest Inventory, Myers-Briggs Type Indicator, Edwards Personal Preference Schedule, California Psychological Inventory, and Minnesota Multiphasic Personality Inventory). Using a case study methodology, Pope wove into the cases technical and psychometric data to illustrate how psychological tests have been misused with gay and lesbian clients. He identified the following issues: fear of identification/exposure of sexual orientation, especially in the highly sensitive personnel selection area; bias and prejudice (heterosexism) of the counselor; appropriate interpretation based on identification of the client response set; issues of sex-role and "sexual orientation" stereotyping (male feeling types and females thinking types); and generally the appropriate interpretation of psychological tests with a gay or lesbian client.

Chung and Harmon (1994) used the Self-Directed Search (SDS; Holland, 1995) and compared gay and heterosexual men of equivalent age, socioeconomic background, ethnicity, student status, and education and reported that gay men scored higher on Artistic and Social scales of the SDS and lower on the Realistic and Investigative scales. They concluded that gay men's aspirations were less traditional for men, yet their aspirations were not lower in status than those of the heterosexual men.

Using inventories and other assessment instruments with lesbian and gay clients presents a whole host of issues for counseling professionals. It becomes even more complex when confronted with the data on the use of such instruments with ethnic and racial minorities (Marsella & Leong, 1995). Counselors must approach the use and interpretation of such instruments with caution and with knowledge of how such instruments have been misused. Such instruments may have utility but must be used with great care.

## PROGRAMS USEFUL TO ADDRESS LESBIAN AND GAY ISSUES

Program interventions include interventions that are programmatic in scope and can be implemented in an agency or institution, such as a community center or college/university (D'Augelli, 1993). All of the recommended interventions in this area have one commonality: Each tries to create more options for the gay man or lesbian woman. The interventions recommended here include the following: support and encourage gay and lesbian professionals as role models for students; provide information on national lesbian and gay networks of professionals and community people such as the Association for Gay, Lesbian, and Bisexual Issues in Counseling (gay/lesbian/bisexual counselors in the American Counseling Association) and the Golden Gate Business Association (gay/lesbian chamber of commerce in San Francisco); share information on existing local gay/lesbian community resources; offer special programming such as talks by lesbian/gay professionals; and establish mentoring programs.

Other recommendations include having the counselor publish a list of "out" gay/lesbian individuals who would be available for informational interviews with clients and offer special programming to meet the career development needs of lesbian women and gay men, including special programming on (a) job fairs and (b) support groups.

Programmatic interventions in the workplace that could be implemented to assist gay and lesbian workers include mentoring programs, diversity workshops, and gay, lesbian, and bisexual affirmative policies such as nondiscrimination policies and domestic partners benefits (Kirby, 2002).

## APPROPRIATE ADVOCACY OR SOCIAL ACTION INTERVENTIONS

Advocacy or social action interventions include interventions that are focused on the external social environment of the client. Positive social advocacy for our gay and lesbian clients could include lobbying for the inclusion of sexual orientation in the nondiscrimination policies of local employers or picketing a speech made by an "ex-gay" who claims to have become a happy, fully functioning heterosexual. Some lesbian and gay clients will need basic information on the gay and lesbian community as well as the facts on sexual orientation discrimination.

There are many different types of advocacy that might be appropriate. Counselors should know and provide client information on the geographic location and the size of the gay and lesbian communities in their area. They could also have access to information on the employment policies and Equal Employment Opportunity statements of local businesses as well as information on local and federal antidiscrimination laws. They might also even provide assistance to aid their clients in avoiding arrest, such as if the local police has a propensity to raid certain bars or other local areas where gays and lesbians might meet. Counselors might also provide assistance to clients about how to construct affirming work environments as well as working to change employer-related statements or policies that discriminate.

It is imperative that counselors be gay and lesbian affirmative, going beyond the "do no harm" admonition to encompass a positive advocacy for gay and lesbian clients and their rights (Pope & Barret, 2002). Examples of such a positive advocacy include working to change employer-related statements or policies that discriminate, working toward changing the laws that criminalize certain sexual acts between two consenting adults, changing housing laws that do not allow two "unrelated" persons to live together, or working to stop police entrapment. Such laws are often used to prevent lesbian and gay couples and their children from renting a house or apartment or to deny employment to teachers, counselors, police officers, and other professionals.

Counselors have an opportunity to lobby law enforcement officials to stop entrapments as well as the unequal enforcement of laws. Such issues as these are also especially relevant for ethnic and racial minorities. Counselors must take an active, advocacy approach to working with lesbian or gay clients as well as all cultural minorities.

## MULTIPLE CULTURAL IDENTITIES: THE INTERSECTION OF SEXUAL ORIENTATION WITH OTHER CULTURES

Gay and lesbian people come in many different sizes, colors, and economic classes. Lesbian and gay culture includes special groups that cross racial, ethnic, and other culture boundaries. It sometimes takes a little hunting to find these groups, but they are there.

For women, such groups include Asian & Pacific Islanders Lesbian and Bisexual Women, Asian Lesbian and Bisexual Alliance (Asian lesbian and bisexual women), Older Asian Sisters In Solidarity (OASIS) (Asians and Pacific Islander lesbians and bisexual women 35 years and older in the San Francisco Bay Area), Black African American Dykes (African American lesbian women), United Lesbians of African Heritage (African American lesbian women), Amigas Latinas (lesbian and bisexual Latina women), Bridging the Gap Alliance (deaf/hard-of-hearing and hearing lesbians), Dykes Who Hike (hiking for/with/by lesbians), Back Country Bettys (social and outdoor activities for lesbians), and many others.

For men, such groups include Black and White Men Together (gay African American males), Men of All Colors Together, Pacific Friends (gay Asian males in the United States), Trikone (gay South Asian males), Long Yang Clubs (gay Asian males around the world), Gay Asian Pacific Alliance, Lavendar Godzilla (gay Asian males in San Francisco), Gay & Lesbian Latinos Unidos (gay and lesbian Latinos in Los Angeles), Rainbow Deaf Society (gay deaf men), Girth and Mirth Clubs (large gay men), and many others.

There is even a special group called "H.O.O.D.I.E.S."—a gay/lesbian/bisexual youth organization targeting youngsters age 25 and younger who are or have grown up gay in the "hoods" of the San Francisco Bay Area.

The basic education and training of most counselors, however, has not prepared them for dealing with clients who face daily oppression based on both sexual orientation and race/ethnicity (Greene, 1997). The issues are complex. Ethnic minority lesbians and gays may not turn to either of their cultural communities for fear of neither understanding fully the totality of their issues. Cultural identity formation becomes bifurcated and/or delayed, at least, depending on the other cultures represented within the individual. You cannot easily apply Cass's (1979) model of gay and lesbian identity development with a first-generation gay Japanese woman who came out at age 45.

The primary cultural consideration in doing counseling with gay men from nondominant cultures is to identify the stages associated with that individual's cultural identity development. Cultural identity development refers to all of the many cultures of which a person may be composed, including racial, ethnic, gender, socioeconomic status, geographic, and sexual orientation. These data are crucial in designing an effective treatment plan. For example, suppose a gay Filipino man who is seeing you for relationship issues is at the identity confusion stage (Cass's [1979] Stage 1, where previously accepted heterosexual identity is just beginning to be questioned) and coming from a collectivist culture (the Philippines) where decisions are made by the entire extended family. But if you, as a helping professional, are treating him as if he is at the identity acceptance stage (Cass's Stage 4: Gay or lesbian identity is accepted, and selective disclosure to others is begun), you may recommend certain behavioral options that your client would strongly resist, as you may be encouraging his individuality and independence to make the decisions all by himself.

There are other special considerations in counseling gays and lesbians that follow from variations in ethnicity, race, and other culture. For example, Pope and Chung (2000) discussed the cultural considerations in conducting psychotherapy with gay and lesbian Asian Americans. Gay and lesbian Asian and Pacific Islander Americans (APIAs) are, by their nature, a cultural hybrid—the dominant Asian/Pacific Islander culture mixed with the dominant American culture, stirred with the gay and lesbian cultures within both—and this mixture produces a new and challenging task for those who would provide counseling and psychotherapy services for this group. To appreciate lesbian and gay APIAs, it is important to understand their cultural roots, the acculturation process of immigrants in a new land, and their social status as a variant from the modal sexual orientation. Pope and Chung recommended that counselors look at the role of family, religion/philosophy, acculturation, and identity development in the lives of their gay Asian and Pacific Islander clients, as these four issues are what bind together all Asian cultures.

## SUMMARY

In this chapter, I have discussed the cultural context for counseling with gay and lesbian clients, especially focusing on the complexity of counseling clients with multiple cultural identities. I also looked at coming out—the identity development model for gays and lesbians—and recommended specific interventions directed at counselors themselves, at individual counseling activities, at counseling programs within institutions, and at advocacy or social/community action. Those interventions aimed at gay and lesbian counseling clients must either be learned during graduate school education or through continuing professional development at conferences or workshops.

Providing effective and culturally appropriate counseling services for lesbian and gay clients is not an easy task. It is fraught with personal and social issues, including internalized homophobia, social discrimination, and much more. The counselor who directly addresses these issues will find the path smoother and rewards greater for their clients who are seeking help with their lives.

## Culturally Appropriate Counseling
## With Lesbian and Gay Clients

Ben is a 36-year-old gay Cherokee American Indian male. He is originally from a small town in southeast Missouri. His parents were raised there after his grandparents escaped from the Trail of Tears death march that was intended to resettle peaceful Cherokee tribespeople from the Carolinas to Oklahoma after the U.S. government had stolen their lands. Ben is the youngest child of parents who are now in their late 60s. He attended a large state university in California on an American Indian scholarship and completed his undergraduate degree in social work. Ben has spent the past 10 years living in San Francisco, where he moved when he found out he was HIV seropositive. He has a fairly extensive network of friends and lives with his partner of 8 years. Ben has worked in a number of jobs in social welfare agencies but is currently unemployed because 6 months ago, he had become symptomatic with recurring pneumocystis. He is now taking a combination of medications that seem to have the pneumonia under control, and he is ready to go back to work.

Ben loves nature and being outdoors. He talks about how he used to sleep out in the backyard at his grandparents' house all by himself and stay awake all night listening to the insects and feeling the morning dew settle on his sleeping bag. It is his happiest childhood memory. He would love to return to Missouri to be with his parents and grandparents, but his AIDS complications and the required medical care along with his 8-year relationship have kept him in the city. Ben also loves his Cherokee heritage and is a prize-winning American Indian dancer at powwows all over the country. He competes in the "Fancy Dancer" category, which is a highly costumed dance characterized by intricate footwork and rapid spins. He has not participated in these competitions for 2 years due to his health. Also, his partner has a thriving legal practice, and Ben is aware of how difficult it is to move such a practice to another state.

A week ago, Ben's parents strongly requested that he return home to southeast Missouri. A local medicine person had a dream and saw a rooster being eaten by a large black snake. The medicine person interpreted that dream to mean that Ben was going to die if he did not return home where he could receive traditional Cherokee medicines and be cared for by his parents, grandparents, brothers, and sisters. There is no modern medical facility with specialists in HIV medicine within 200 miles.

Ben has spent the past 3 days on a vision quest to determine what he should do. He emerges from the smudging, fasting, and sweat lodges with a decision to return to Missouri and to stop taking all of his physician-prescribed medications. He knows that this is a decision to die, and he has accepted that. His partner is distraught and attempts to dissuade him from the decision, but Ben is certain that this is his right path.

### DISCUSSION QUESTIONS

1. Whose decision is it? The family's? Ben's? His partner's? The medicine person's?

2. Does this decision mean that the family is more important to Ben than his partner?

3. Who is right and who is wrong in this incident?

4. What would be the role of a counselor in this situation if Ben and his partner had decided to come in for counseling?

5. Should a person be allowed to commit suicide in this manner?

# REFERENCES

Adams, K. V. (1997). The impact of work on gay male identity among male flight attendants (Doctoral dissertation, Loyola University of Chicago, 1997). *Dissertation Abstracts International, 57–12,* 7754.

Adelman, M. (Ed.). (1987). *Long time passing: Lives of older lesbians.* Boston: Alyson Publications.

Altman, D. (1971). *Homosexual: Oppression and liberation.* New York: Avon.

American Counseling Association. (2005). *ACA code of ethics and standards of practice.* Alexandria, VA: Author.

American Psychological Association. (2000). *Guidelines for psychotherapy with lesbian, gay, and bisexual clients* [Adopted by the American Psychological Association Council of Representatives on February 26, 2000]. Washington, DC: Author.

American Psychological Association. (2002). Ethical principles of psychologists and code of conduct. *American Psychologist, 57,* 1060–1073.

American Psychiatric Association. (1980). *Diagnostic and statistical manual of mental disorders* (3rd ed.). In "Appendix C, Comparative listing of DSM-II and DSM-III," p. 380. Washington, DC: American Psychiatric Association.

Anderson, M. Z., Croteau, J. M., Chung, Y. B., & DiStefano, T. M. (2001). Developing an assessment of sexual identity management for lesbian and gay workers. *Journal of Career Assessment, 9,* 243–260.

Arredondo, P., Lee, C., Leong, F., Ponterotto, J., Redleaf, V., & Vontress, C. (1992, September). Valuing pluralism: Community building for the 21st century. In C. Lee (Chair), *Valuing pluralism.* A panel presented at the meeting of the Association for Counselor Education and Supervision, San Antonio, TX.

Barret, B., & Logan, C. (2002). *Counseling gay men and lesbians: A practice primer.* Belmont CA: Brooks/Cole.

Bayer, R. (1981). *Homosexuality and American psychiatry: The politics of diagnosis.* New York: Basic Books.

Bell, A. P., & Weinberg, M. S. (1978). *Homosexualities: A study of diversity among men and women.* London: Mitchell Beazley.

Belz, J. R. (1993). Sexual orientation as a factor in career development. *The Career Development Quarterly, 41,* 197–200.

Berger, R. (1982). *Gay and gray: The older homosexual man.* Boston: Alyson Publications.

Berger, R. M. (1996). *Gay and gray: the older homosexual man* (2nd ed.). Boston: Alyson Publications.

Bowman, S. L. (1993). Career intervention strategies for ethnic minorities. *Career Development Quarterly, 42,* 14–25.

Brown, L. (1989). Lesbians, gay men, and their families: Common clinical issues. *Journal of Gay and Lesbian Psychotherapy, 15,* 323–336.

Buhrke, R. A., & Douce, L. A. (1991). Training issues for counseling psychologists in working with lesbians and gay men. *The Counseling Psychologist, 19,* 216–234.

Cass, V. C. (1979). Homosexual identity formation: A theoretical model. *Journal of Homosexuality, 4,* 219–235.

Chan, C. (1997). Don't ask, don't tell, don't know: The formation of a homosexual identity and sexual express among Asian American lesbians. In B. Greene (Ed.), *Ethnic and cultural diversity among lesbians and gay men* (pp. 240–248). Thousand Oaks, CA: Sage.

Chung, Y. B., & Harmon, L. W. (1994). The career interests and aspirations of gay men: How sex-role orientation is related. *Journal of Vocational Behavior, 45,* 223–239.

Chung, Y. B., & Katayama, M. (1998). Ethnic and sexual identity development of Asian-American lesbian and gay adolescents. *Professional School Counseling, 1*(3), 21–25.

Cooper, C. (1989, April). Social oppressions experienced by gays and lesbians. In P. Griffin & J. Genasce (Eds.), *Strategies for addressing homophobia in physical education, sports, and dance* (pp. 212–223). Workshop presented at the annual convention of the American Alliance for Health, Physical Education, Recreation, and Dance, Boston.

Croghan, J. G. (2001). Mirrors of manhood: The formation of gay identity. *Dissertation Abstracts International, 62*(1–B), 574. (UMI No. AAI3002381)

Croteau, J., Lark, J., Lidderdale, M., & Chung, Y. B. (Eds.). (2005). *Deconstructing heterosexism in the counseling professions.* Thousand Oaks, CA: Sage.

D'Augelli, A. R. (1993). Preventing mental health problems among lesbian and gay college students. *Journal of Primary Prevention, 13*, 245–261.

Dworkin, S., & Gutierrez, F. (Eds.). (1992). *Counseling gay men and lesbians: Journey to the end of the rainbow.* Alexandria, VA: American Counseling Association.

Elliott, J. E. (1993). Career development with lesbian and gay clients. *Career Development Quarterly, 41*, 210–226.

Espin, O. (1993). Issues of identity in the psychology of Latina lesbians. In L. Garnets & D. Kimmel (Eds.), *Psychological perspectives on lesbian and gay male experiences* (pp. 348–363). New York: Columbia University Press.

Fassinger, R. E. (1991). The hidden minority: Issues and challenges in working with lesbian women and gay men. *The Counseling Psychologist, 19*, 157–176.

Fimbres, M. F. (2001). Case study of a gay Mexican American. *Journal of Gay & Lesbian Social Services, 12*, 93–101.

Fischer, P. (1972). *The gay mystique: The myth and reality of male homosexuality.* New York: Stein & Day.

Flowers, C., Barret, B., & Robinson, B. (2000). Research on gay parenting. In B. Barret & B. Robinson (Eds.), *Gay fathers.* San Francisco: Jossey-Bass.

Ford, H. W. (1996). The influence of sexual orientation on the early occupational choices of young lesbians using Astin's model of career choice and work behavior (Doctoral dissertation, University of San Francisco, 1996). *Dissertation Abstracts International, 57–12*, 5061.

Freedman, M. (1971). *Homosexuality and psychological functioning.* Belmont, CA: Brooks/Cole.

Garnets, L., Hancock, K., Cochran, S., Goodchilds, J., & Peplau, L. (1991). Issues in psychotherapy with lesbians and gay men: A survey of psychologists. *American Psychologist, 46*, 964–972.

Garrett, M. T., & Barret, B. (2003). Two spirit: Counseling Native American gay, lesbian, and bisexual people. *Journal of Multicultural Counseling and Development, 31*, 131–142.

Geertz, C. (1978). *The interpretation of cultures: Selected essays.* New York: Basic Books.

Goffman, E. (1963). *Stigma: Notes on the management of a spoiled identity.* Englewood Cliffs, NJ: Prentice Hall.

Gonsiorek, J. C. (1993). Threat, stress, and adjustment: Mental health and the workplace for gay and lesbian individuals. In L. Diamant (Ed.), *Homosexual issues in the workplace* (pp. 243–264). Washington, DC: Taylor & Francis.

Greene, B. (1997). Ethnic minority lesbians and gay men: Mental health and treatment issues. In B. Greene (Ed.), *Ethnic and cultural diversity among lesbians and gay men* (pp. 216–239). Thousand Oaks, CA: Sage.

Han, S.-H. (2001). Gay identity disclosure to parents by Asian American gay men. *Dissertation Abstracts International, 62*(1–A), 329. (UMI No. AAI3000394)

Hancock, K. A. (2000). Lesbian, gay, and bisexual lives: Basic issues in psychotherapy training and practice. In B. Greene & G. L. Croom (Eds.), *Education, research, and practice in lesbian, gay, bisexual, and transgendered psychology: A resource manual* (pp. 91–130). Thousand Oaks, CA: Sage.

Herdt, G. (Ed.). (1992). *Gay culture in America.* Boston: Beacon.

Hetherington, C., Hillerbrand, E., & Etringer, B. (1989). Career counseling with gay men: Issues and recommendations for research. *Journal of Counseling & Development, 67*, 452–454.

Holland, J. L. (1995). *Self-directed search.* Lutz, FL: Psychological Assessment Resources.

Human Rights Campaign. (2005). *The state of the workplace for lesbian, gay, bisexual, and transgender Americans—2004.* Retrieved January 15, 2006, from www.hrc.org

Keeton, M. D. (2002). Perceptions of career-related barriers among gay, lesbian, and bisexual individuals. *Dissertation Abstracts International, 63*(2–B), 1075. (Transaction Periodicals Consortium, Rutgers University)

Kelly, J. (1977). The aging male homosexual. *The Gerontologist, 17*, 328–332.

Kimmel, D. C. (1978). Adult development and aging: a gay perspective. *Journal of Social Issues, 34*, 113–130.

Kinsey, A. C., Pomeroy, W. B., & Martin, C. E. (1948). *Sexual behavior in the human male.* Philadelphia: W. B. Saunders.

Kinsey, A. C., Pomeroy, W. B., Martin, C. E., & Gebhard, P. H. (1953). *Sexual behavior in the human female.* Philadelphia: W. B. Saunders.

Kirby, K. M. (2002). Gay, lesbian, and bisexual employee issues in the workplace. In D. S. Sandhu (Ed.), *Counseling employees: A multifaceted approach* (pp. 169–184). Alexandria, VA: American Counseling Association.

Lawrence v. Texas, 539 U.S. 558 (2003).

LeVay, S. (1996). *Queer science: The use and abuse of research into homosexuality.* Cambridge: MIT Press.

Locke, D. C. (1990). A not so provincial view of multicultural counseling. *Counselor Education and Supervision, 30,* 18–25.

Maguen, S., Floyd, F. J., Bakeman, R., & Armistead, L. (2002). Developmental milestones and disclosure of sexual orientation among gay, lesbian, and bisexual youths. *Journal of Applied Developmental Psychology, 23,* 219–233.

Marsella, A. J., & Leong, F. T. L. (1995). Cross-cultural issues in personality and career assessment. *Journal of Career Assessment, 3,* 202–218.

Martinez, D. G., & Sullivan, S. C. (1998). African American gay men and lesbians: Examining the complexity of gay identity development. *Journal of Human Behavior in the Social Environment, 1,* 243–264.

McLean, R., Marini, I., & Pope, M. (2003). Racial identity and relationship satisfaction in African American gay men. *The Family Journal, 11,* 13–22.

Merighi, J. R., & Grimes, M. D. (2000). Coming out to families in a multicultural context. *Families in Society, 81,* 32–41.

Mobley, M., & Slaney, R. B. (1996). Holland's theory: Its relevance for lesbian women and gay men. *Journal of Vocational Behavior, 48,* 125–135.

Morgan, K. S., & Brown, L. S. (1991). Lesbian career development, work behavior, and vocational counseling. *The Counseling Psychologist, 19,* 273–291.

Morris, J. F., & Rothblum, E. D. (1999). Who fills out a "lesbian" questionnaire? The interrelationship of sexual orientation, years "out," disclosure of sexual orientation, sexual experience with women, and participation in the lesbian community. *Psychology of Women Quarterly, 23,* 537–557.

Newman, B. S., & Muzzonigro, P. G. (1993). The effects of traditional family values on the coming out process of gay male adolescents. *Adolescence, 28,* 213–226.

Nystrom, N. (1997, February). *Mental health experiences of gay men and lesbians.* Paper presented at the annual meeting of the American Association for the Advancement of Science, Houston, TX.

Patterson, C., & Chan, R. (1996). Problems in studying gay fathers. In M. E. Lamb (Ed.), *The role of the father in child development* (pp. 245–260). New York: John Wiley.

Pedersen, P. (1988). *A handbook for development of multicultural awareness.* Alexandria, VA: American Counseling Association.

Pedersen, P., & Locke, D. (1999). *Cultural and diversity issues in counseling.* Greensboro, NC: ERIC/CASS.

Perez, R. M., DeBord, K. A., & Bieschke, K. J. (Eds.). (2000). *Handbook of counseling and psychotherapy with lesbian, gay, and bisexual clients.* Washington, DC: American Psychological Association.

Piedmont, O. (1996). The veils of Arjuna: Androgyny in gay spirituality, East and West. *Dissertation Abstracts International, 57*(6–B), 4076. (UMI No. AAM9633907)

Pope, M. (1992). Bias in the interpretation of psychological tests. In S. Dworkin & F. Gutierrez (Eds.), *Counseling gay men and lesbians: Journey to the end of the rainbow* (pp. 277–291). Alexandria, VA: American Counseling Association.

Pope, M. (1995a). Career interventions for gay and lesbian clients: A synopsis of practice knowledge and research needs. *Career Development Quarterly, 44,* 191–203.

Pope, M. (1995b). The "salad bowl" is big enough for us all: An argument for the inclusion of lesbians and gays in any definition of multiculturalism. *Journal of Counseling & Development, 73,* 301–304.

Pope, M. (1997). Sexual issues for older lesbians and gays. *Topics in Geriatric Rehabilitation, 12*(4), 53–60.

Pope, M. (1999). Applications of group career counseling techniques in Asian cultures. *Journal for Multicultural Counseling and Development, 27,* 18–30.

Pope, M. (2006). *Professional counseling 101: Building a strong professional identity.* Alexandria, VA: American Counseling Association.

Pope, M., & Barret, B. (2002). Counseling gay men toward an integrated sexuality. In L. D. Burlew & D. Capuzzi (Eds.), *Sexuality counseling* (pp. 149–176). Hauppauge, NY: Nova Science.

Pope, M., Barret, B., Szymanski, D. M., Chung, Y. B., McLean, R., Singaravelu, H., et al. (2004). Culturally appropriate career counseling with gay and lesbian clients. *Career Development Quarterly, 53,* 158–177.

Pope, M., & Chung, Y. B. (2000). From bakla to tongzhi: Counseling and psychotherapy issues for gay and lesbian Asian and Pacific Islander Americans. In D. S. Sandhu (Ed.), *Asian and Pacific Islander Americans: Issues and concerns for counseling and psychotherapy* (pp. 283–300). Commack, NY: Nova Science.

Pope, M., Prince, J. P., & Mitchell, K. (2000). Responsible career counseling with lesbian and gay students. In D. A. Luzzo (Ed.), *Career counseling of college students: An empirical guide to strategies that work* (pp. 267–284). Washington, DC: American Psychological Association.

Pope, M., Rodriguez, S., & Chang, A. P. C. (1992, September). *Special issues in career development and planning for gay men.* Presented at the meeting of International Pacific Friends Societies, International Friendship Weekend 1992, San Francisco.

Pope, M., & Schecter, E. (1992, October). *Career strategies: Career suicide or career success.* Presented at the 2nd Annual Lesbian and Gay Workplace Issues Conference, Stanford, CA.

Pope, M., & Schulz, R. (1990). Sexual behavior and attitudes in midlife and aging homosexual males. *Journal of Homosexuality, 20* (3–4), 169–178.

Pope, M., & Tarvydas, V. M. (2006). Career counseling. In R. R. Cottone & V. M. Tarvydas (Eds.), *Ethical and professional issues in counseling* (2nd ed., pp. 289–331). Upper Saddle River, NJ: Merrill/Prentice Hall.

Prince, J. P. (1997). Assessment bias affecting lesbian, gay male and bisexual individuals. *Measurement and Evaluation in Counseling and Development, 30,* 82–87.

Quam, J. K. (1993, June/July). Gay and lesbian aging. *SEICUS Report,* pp. 14–22.

Sanlo, R. (Ed.). (1998). *Working with lesbian, gay, bisexual, and transgender college students: A handbook for faculty and administrators.* Westport, CT: Greenwood.

Shidlo, A., & Schroeder, M. (2002). Changing sexual orientation: A consumers' report. *Professional Psychology: Research and Practice, 33,* 249–259.

Sue, D. W., Arredondo, P., & McDavis, R. J. (1992). Multicultural counseling competencies and standards: A call to the profession. *Journal of Counseling & Development, 70,* 477–486.

Terndrup, A. I. (1998). Factors that influence career choice and development for gay male school teachers: A qualitative investigation (Doctoral dissertation, Oregon State University, 1998). *Dissertation Abstracts International, 59–12,* 4371.

Terndrup, A., Ritter, K., Barret, B., Logan, C., & Mate, R. (1997). *Competencies in counseling gay, lesbian, bisexual, and transgendered clients.* Retrieved January 15, 2004, from http://www.aglbic.org/competencies.html

Trimble, J. E., Stevenson, M. R., & Worell, J. P. (2003). *Toward an inclusive psychology: Infusing the introductory psychology textbook with diversity content.* Washington, DC: American Psychological Association.

Van Puymbroeck, C. M. (2002). Career development of lesbian, gay, and bisexual undergraduates: An exploratory study. *Dissertation Abstracts International, 62*(12–B), 5982. (UMI No. AAI335159)

Weinberg, G. H. (1971). *Society and the healthy homosexual.* New York: St. Martin's.

Weinberg, M. S., & Williams, C. J. (1974). *Male homosexuals.* New York: Oxford University Press.

Wierzalis, E. A., Barret, B., Pope, M., & Rankins, M. (2006). Gay and bisexual men and aging: Sex and intimacy. In D. Kimmel, T. Rose, & S. David (Eds.), *Lesbian, gay, bisexual, and transgender aging: Research and clinical perspectives* (pp. 91–109). New York: Columbia University Press.

Wooden, W. S., Kawasaki, S., & Mayeda, R. (1983). Lifestyles and identity maintenance among gay Japanese-American males. *Alternative Lifestyles, 5,* 236–243.

# Counseling With the Marginalized

Melanie M. Domenech Rodríguez, Charlea T. McNeal, and Ana Mari Cauce

## Primary Objective

- To broaden the conceptualization of marginalization to go beyond the limited range of groups that currently receive clinical/research attention and to inform ethical practice in order to contribute to the clinical competence of mental health practitioners working with marginalized populations

## Secondary Objectives

- To present an approach to counseling people from marginalized groups
- To highlight the particular flexibility needed when applying mainstream counseling techniques and skills to a population other than the one they were intended for

*Our survival depended on an ongoing public awareness of the separation between margin and center and an ongoing private acknowledgment that we were a necessary, vital part of that whole.*

bell hooks (2000, p. xvi)

BELL HOOKS (2000) WROTE IN HER INTRODUCTION TO *FEMINIST THEORY: FROM MARGIN TO CENTER* about the frustrating contrast of Black Americans' marginalized status and their critical importance to the broader U.S. community. By serving as the periphery of a given entity, the margin demarcates the boundary of that entity. Typically, researchers have focused their work on the "center," the means, the averages. Anything outside of the average tends to be considered unusual, aberrant, or abnormal. By doing so, scientists have participated in the creation and/or perpetuation of perceptions of what is average and what is not. For example, examining the mental health outcomes of ethnic minorities *in contrast to* those of Whites is commonplace practice. White is average; ethnic minority is not. More recently, mental health researchers have questioned this practice and called for research focusing on particular groups without contrasting outcomes to Whites (Bernal & Scharrón del Río, 2001; Cauce, Coronado, & Watson, 1998), thus challenging the notion that the unit of analysis is necessarily the broad general population of the United States and disengaging from the traditional conception that ethnic minorities are at the margin of the broader White culture or community.

## DEFINING THE MARGIN

*Marginalization* is defined in this chapter as the social process by virtue of which individuals, groups, or communities are excluded from the center (of society) or relegated to the periphery or margins of "a center" on the basis of some characteristic (e.g., race, ethnicity, class, gender, sexual orientation). Marginalization by definition is a dynamic concept that occurs *in relation*. For example, the mentally ill are at the margins of the broader community proceeding from which mental health is defined. Migrants are at the margins of the broader community into which they have migrated. The obese are at the margin of a group where there is a mean and standard deviation for weight set within a given geographical boundary. These examples underscore the importance of going beyond a statistical average to define marginalization; they exemplify the social contracts present in the dynamic of marginalization. Social expectations for behavior and beauty ideals in the United States are such that it is punishing to be overweight in the United States but often desirable to be underweight. This knowledge of cultural context is of critical importance in defining and understanding marginalization.

A context is created by the people who populate it. So, who defines the center and the margin? By government accounts, in 2004, a family of four (two children younger than age 18), with an annual family income of less than $19,157, was considered by the government to be poor (DeNavas-Walt, Proctor, & Lee, 2005). In an international arena, poverty has been defined as anyone living with earnings of less than $2 per day, or $530 per year (The World Bank, 2005). These definitions are set forth by institutions and can be quite irrelevant to the daily lives of individuals, who are more likely to define themselves in relation to others in a more tangible way (e.g., all of my neighbors have televisions sets and I don't, therefore I am less privileged). However, the definitions are relevant to individuals in very powerful ways, as is the case with government assistance programs that provide goods and/or services on the basis of these definitions. A mother who is enrolled in the Women, Infants, and Children (WIC) program will have access to goods that will affect how she sees herself, her family, and her community. Depending on the context, she may feel marginalized in relation to women who do not qualify for WIC because of higher earnings but less marginalized than a recent immigrant who is not receiving the needed assistance for fear of deportation.

An awareness of the definition of *margin* (whether self-generated or other generated) is critical in a counseling relationship for a variety of reasons: It places the person(s) and the relationship in a broader sociopolitical context, and it focuses on external sources of impact on the person(s). In addition, knowledge of context can present a first line of intervention in a counseling relationship. Indeed, the "Guidelines on Multicultural Education, Training, Research, Practice, and Organizational Change for Psychologists" (American Psychological Association [APA], 2003; Fouad & Arredondo, 2006) state the following:

Psychologists are in a position to provide leadership as agents of prosocial change, advocacy, and social justice, thereby promoting societal understanding, affirmation, and appreciation of multiculturalism against the damaging effects of individual, institutional, and societal racism, prejudice, and all forms of oppression based on stereotyping and discrimination. (p. 382)

Counselors are encouraged to be aware that the label itself ("the marginalized") serves the purpose of placing person(s) outside of mainstream. The label can be misused and/or misunderstood and become a tool for objectification and further marginalization. Arredondo (2002) warns that "marginalized group identity" can prematurely and erroneously pigeonhole individuals into groups with prescribed characteristics and an assumed group identity. She challenges us all to seek a more holistic understanding of individuals.

## LIVING AT THE MARGIN

Living at the margins places people in a unique situation. Two dynamics are critical to address in the context of the counseling relationship as it pertains to marginalization: how the persons see themselves and how they are perceived by others (e.g., Trimble, 2000). Specifically, does a person see himself or herself as marginalized? Do others, and which others, see her or him that way? Seeking answers to these questions can help tremendously to inform practice. For example, a middle-class, well-educated, professional African American female may be perceived by a counselor to be a member of marginalized group, by virtue of her "African American-ness," yet she may not perceive herself as marginalized at all. How does the counselor proceed? The next steps have serious practice, ethical, and social implications. If the counselor decides the client is marginalized and that the intervention should focus on creating more awareness of the marginalization (i.e., the client is in denial), the counselor could not only be pursuing an unfruitful course but also may be engaging in potentially unethical behavior (e.g., 2.01, Boundaries of Competence, APA, 2002).

The example serves as a reminder that people are members of many social groups and that the same person may be at the margin of one social group and may concurrently be in the "center" of another group. The intersection of identities leads to a separate set of questions: Which margins? And how relevant are they to the people who would be categorized? The same African American professional may feel more marginalized when placed in a context where the majority of African Americans have a low level of education (and may perceive her as "selling out" or "acting White"; Neal-Barnett, 2001; Ogbu, 1991) than in a professional setting where her peers have the same level of education and income but are seldom African American. The predominant stereotypes highlight certain group characteristics while rendering other segments of the population invisible (Jones, 2003). In the latter situation, the professional may feel more marginalized by her educational status than her race. An awareness of the intersection of identities as well as self- and other-perception of relative placement in (or out of) a marginalized group is critical in a counseling relationship.

## CHARACTERISTICS OF MARGINALIZATION FOR FURTHER CONSIDERATION

Marginalization—or the social, political, geographical, or psychological placement away from a center—places persons away from sources of privilege. Privilege is broadly defined to encompass material, instrumental, social, emotional, and otherwise important resources. The impact of marginalization will likely vary depending on the depth (e.g., lack of privilege results in loss of essential resources) and breadth (i.e., the cumulative effect of lacking privilege in multiple areas) of the

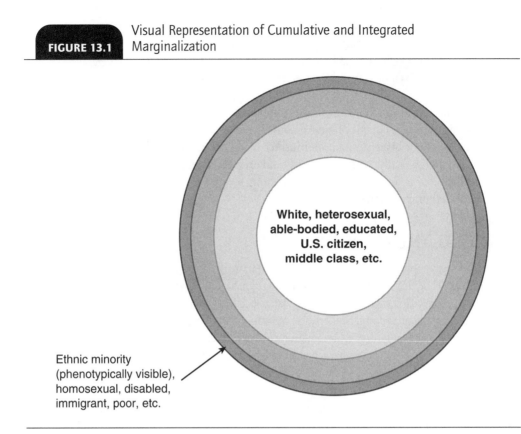

**FIGURE 13.1** Visual Representation of Cumulative and Integrated Marginalization

White, heterosexual, able-bodied, educated, U.S. citizen, middle class, etc.

Ethnic minority (phenotypically visible), homosexual, disabled, immigrant, poor, etc.

marginalization experienced. It is essential in a counseling relationship to have a thorough understanding of both depth and breadth of marginalization.

Related to the breadth and depth of the experience of marginalization is the visibility of the characteristics that signal marginalized status. For example, an American Indian man with strong indigenous physical features who is gay is a visible ethnic minority with a sexual orientation that may or may not be visible. In addition to visibility, the intersection of identities must be understood as cumulative and integrated (Arredondo et al., 1996; Lowe & Mascher, 2001), wherein individuals are marginalized the further away they are from the valued "center." Figure 13.1 depicts this relationship. Persons at the center or mainstream of a particular social group have the utmost privilege. With every move away from the center, layers of privilege are removed, and persons at the very edge of the margin (which becomes thinner or less populated at the edges) may be marginalized by people who are themselves marginalized by others.

The case in point below provides a framework with which to approach the counseling relationship. It requires acquiring important knowledge about the group, the counselor, and the available tools for engaging effectively in the counseling relationship. These general questions can guide the knowledge acquisition about the group: How is the group defined? What do we know about the group? What are specific challenges to counseling and/or the counseling relationship? What are other relevant challenges? Further questions guide knowledge acquisition about the counselor: What are my values and beliefs about this group? What is my privilege (especially in areas relevant to the marginalized group)? How do my skills and knowledge potentially apply (or not) to this group? Finally, acquiring tools requires counselor engagement with institutions and individuals outside of the agencies in which the counselor operates.

# CASE IN POINT: UNDOCUMENTED IMMIGRANTS

*How is the group defined? Who defines it?* Undocumented immigrants are persons who have entered the United States, bypassing the official routes and/or procedures to enter the country that would render them documented, or traceable, by the U.S. government. Undocumented immigrants may also have entered the country with the proper documentation and remained in the United States past the government's allotted time or may have received a visa and be engaging in activities not permitted by their visa (e.g., working full-time with a student visa). Other terms used to describe undocumented immigrants are *illegal aliens, migrant workers,* or simply *illegals* and/or *migrants.* Exceedingly pejorative terms, such as *wetback,* also continue to be used by important political and media figures (e.g., Carr, 2003), as well as open displays of hostility at the community level (such as a bumper sticker recently seen in Oregon that read, "This is Oregon, not Mexico"). Various visas generally fall into either nonimmigrant (e.g., visitors, students) or immigrant categories (e.g., lawful permanent residency or "green cards"). Undocumented status may be temporary, as for immigrants who are in the process of obtaining necessary documents, or it could be of a more permanent nature, as is the case for many low-wage and/or seasonal workers in the United States who would not qualify for a visa (called "inadmissibles"; Immigration and Naturalization Services [INS], 2006). In this particular case in point, the group—undocumented immigrants—is defined by the INS.

*What do we know about the group?* Undocumented immigrants are growing in numbers at rates that constantly exceed prior projections. In 1996, it was estimated that there were approximately 5 million undocumented immigrants living in the United States with an estimated growth of 275,000 per year. The U.S. Department of Homeland Security (USDHS) reported that 54% of those were of Mexican origin (USDHS, 1996). More recent estimates (INS, 2003) show that the number of undocumented immigrants rose to 7 million in the year 2000, 9.3 million in 2002 (Passel, Capps, & Fix, 2004), 10.3 million in 2004 (Passel, 2005), and 11.1 million in 2005 (Pew Hispanic Center, 2006). Each updated estimate far surpasses the predictions for growth made by the previous estimates. Many undocumented immigrants, especially persons of Mexican origin, migrate to the United States looking for work (Berk, Schur, Chavez, & Frankel, 2000; Passel et al., 2004) and are contributing to social programs such as Social Security (Porter, 2005, 2006).

Of the many undocumented immigrants that are in the United States, a sizable proportion is identified by the U.S government for deportation. In 2004, more than 1.2 million undocumented immigrants were identified by Border Patrol and processed (USDHS, 2006). While these persons hailed from many countries around the globe, the overwhelming majority of undocumented immigrants in the United States was of Mexican origin (92%) and identified for processing in the Southwest (98.2%). The vast majority of persons identified by Border Patrol chose to voluntarily return to their countries of origin. The statistics on the national origin of those identified for deportation (i.e., 92%) are striking in comparison to the relative number of immigrants from Mexico (i.e., 54%). These data are important in understanding the unique context of Mexican immigrants in comparison to immigrants from other countries.

The visibility of undocumented immigrants varies greatly. Geographically, undocumented immigrants are unevenly distributed in the United States, with 40% of the undocumented population estimated to reside in California in 1996 (USDHS, 1996). The same report reflected that 83% of the total undocumented population resided in seven states (California, Texas, New York, Florida, Illinois, New Jersey, and Arizona). A more recent report suggests that there has been significant dispersion in the past decade, and currently, approximately 68% of undocumented immigrants live in eight states (the same as prior plus North Carolina; Passel, 2005). Although specific statistics are not available for workforce participation of undocumented immigrants, the U.S. Department of Labor (2006) reported that 15%

of the labor force in 2005 was foreign born. Conversely, 97% of children of foreign-born parents have a parent who works (National Center for Children in Poverty [NCCP], 2005). These high employment rates, however, do not protect immigrants from living in poverty (NCCP, 2005).

*What are specific challenges to counseling and the counseling relationship?* The first major challenge is access to care. Undocumented immigrants are likely to face tremendous challenges in obtaining publicly funded health care services both because of policies creating barriers to access (Kullgren, 2003) and fear of identification as undocumented (Berk & Schur, 2001). Indeed, research shows that undocumented immigrants tend to underuse health services, especially preventive services (Chavez, Cornelius, & Jones, 1986). Families may find themselves in a very challenging position when seeking services is imperative, as in the case of children with chronic conditions (Rehm, 2003). Further complicating this matter, undocumented immigrants are significantly less likely to be insured than legal residents and native-born Americans or have a consistent health care provider (K. J. Marshall, Urrutia-Rojas, Mas, & Coggin, 2005; Prentice, Pebley, & Sastry, 2005).

In terms of mental health, research has found a significant relationship between undocumented status and poor mental health outcomes for different ethnic groups (Eisenman, Gelberg, Liu, & Shapiro, 2003; Law, Hutton, & Chan, 2003; G. N. Marshall, Schell, Elliott, Berthold, & Chun, 2005). These findings are often associated with prior exposure to violence, and mental health outcomes have been found to vary across national origin (Salgado de Snyder, Cervantes, & Padilla, 1990). The effects of violence affect adults as well as children. Children of immigrants are at high risk of exposure to violence. Jaycox and colleagues (2002) found that 32% and 16% of the children in their sample (ages 8–15) reported post-traumatic stress disorder (PTSD) and depressive symptoms, respectively, in the clinical range. These numbers are substantially higher than would be expected for a national sample.

Immigrants also have to deal with the negative attitudes toward them (Hovey, Rojas, Kain, & Magaña, 2000) and the negative climate that these attitudes create. Experience of discrimination or negative social climate may create difficulties for undocumented immigrants in disclosing information or forming a productive alliance with a counselor. Negative attitudes toward immigrants have been documented in the United States (e.g., Suro, 2005) and abroad (Fetzer, 2000). Nationally, Suro (2005) found negative attitudes towards migration across ethnic groups with the exception of Latinos, who had relatively positive attitudes. Internationally, Fetzer (2000) studied anti-immigration sentiment in the United States, France, and Germany. He tested the economic self-interest and cultural marginality theories. He found weak support for the economic self-interest theory, which suggests that anti-immigration attitudes would be directly tied to material self-interest. In contrast, Fetzer found strong evidence for the cultural marginality theory in all countries; this theory posits that experiencing marginality engenders sympathy or support for other marginalized groups, even outside one's own. The data showed that when controlling for other factors, belonging to an ethnic, racial, or religious minority group decreased anti-immigration sentiments, as did being female and being foreign born. Similar research found support for anti-immigration policies as tied to ingroup/outgroup biases (Lee & Ottai, 2002). These negative attitudes toward immigration policy and immigrants are a particular challenge because the variables implicated in creating change in attitudes would require targeting at a broad social level.

Another specific challenge for undocumented immigrants lies in the intersection between social and individual issues. For example, one study found that husbands of undocumented women in domestic violence situations use their legal status to control their behavior (Dutton, Orloff, & Aguilar Haas, 2000), highlighting the intersection between gender and documented status. Another author suggests that the intergenerational transmission of violence may begin for children and adolescents with the violence of the border crossing (Solís, 2003), potentially signaling a relationship between susceptibility to aggression and undocumented status. As an interesting example of abusive behavioral control exerted over undocumented immigrants by others, the first author (Rodríguez) recently read a post on a professional listserv involving a Latina woman who was lesbian and partnered. She was undocumented, and her family said she could not move out of the family house (to cohabitate with her partner); if she chose to move, they would report her to the authorities. In both of these situations, an individual's struggles are affected by broader social issues of power and legitimacy.

Overall, the literature shows that undocumented immigrants are vulnerable—both socially and instrumentally. In counseling, contextual information is critical to approach the counseling relationship. For example, a counselor who detects reluctance to disclose on the part of an undocumented immigrant could mis-attribute the behavior (e.g., the client doesn't like me, the client is being excessively guarded), or the counselor could better understand the behavior in context and attempt to create an environment that maximizes the possibility of establishing a positive, productive relationship. Information must be consumed with care so as not to create stereotypes or promote "glosses" (Trimble & Dickson, 2005), but rather to obtain a sense of the complexity of the group's circumstances and give the counselor a good indication of areas of assessment and potential intervention. However, information is one dimension of importance in the counseling relationship. In addition to the information gathered, clinician variables are of critical importance.

## CONTRASTING CASE IN POINT

Similar to other marginalized groups, the overweight and obese are beset with stigmatization and victim blaming (Friedman et al., 2005; Puhl & Brownell, 2001). There is a common belief that the overweight and obese are responsible for or are the cause of their medical condition, despite the documented underlying behavioral, psychological, psychosocial, and physical underpinnings of these medical conditions (Devlin, Yanovski, & Wilson, 2000; Puhl & Brownell, 2001). This misperception is also present among health care professionals, including physicians, nurses, dietitians, and mental health care practitioners (Harvey, Summerbell, Kirk, & Hill, 2002; Schwartz, O'Neal Chambliss, Brownell, Blair, & Billington, 2003). However, despite steadily increasing and substantial prevalence rates of overweight and obesity and far-reaching implications of these conditions, the overweight and obese receive relatively little attention as a marginalized group.

*How is the group defined? Who defines it? Overweight* and *obesity* are traditionally defined by health organizations such as the World Health Organization and the Centers for Disease Control and Prevention (CDC) as body mass index (BMI), which is weight in kilograms divided by height in meters squared. Recommendations identify a BMI of 25 to 29.9 as overweight and a BMI of 30 or greater as obesity among adults (CDC, 2006b). The CDC (2006a) presents guidelines for children using BMI-for-age charts. It specifies that children in the 85th to 94th percentiles are overweight, and those at the 95th percentile or above are obese.

*What do we know about the group?* According to data from the National Health and Nutrition Examination Survey (NHNES), the prevalence of overweight and obesity have reached epidemic proportions during the past 20 years, climbing from 23% to 32% (National Center for Health Statistics, 2004). Overweight and obesity is the fastest growing health concern globally, involving 1 billion people, at least 300 million of which are clinically obese (Allison, Fontaine, Manson, Stevens, & VanItallie, 1999). It is also the fastest growing health concern in the United States (Allison et al., 1999). Current estimates show 127 million overweight and 69 million obese adults (American Obesity Association, 2005). Overweight and obesity increase the risk of chronic diseases and health conditions, such as diabetes mellitus, cardiovascular disease, sleep apnea, respiratory problems, hypertension, certain forms of cancer (e.g., breast, colon, endometrial), menstrual abnormalities, impaired fertility, and increased pregnancy risks (U.S. Department of Health and Human Services [USDHHS], 2001b, 2001c). Overweight- and obese-related medical conditions overwhelm the national health care system, straining medical resources through greater rates of utilization and increased health care expenditures, and yield high costs of lost productivity (Fontaine & Bartlett, 2000). Most disturbing, obesity is responsible for 300,000 premature deaths per year (Allison et al., 1999; USDHHS, 2001b). Lying beneath the notable trends and associated medical costs of overweight and obesity are particular challenges that the overweight and obese face—challenges that have implications for clinicians who treat this population.

The rising trends in economic costs and health burdens of overweight and obesity reflect the range of obstacles or impediments to weight loss and management. Adverse side effects—especially weight gain—of treatment for other medical conditions promote noncompliance with treatment or premature discontinuation of weight loss efforts (Devlin et al., 2000). Moreover, necessary medical attention (e.g., advice, information) directed at short- and long-term weight management can be lacking (Kuppersmith, Smoot, Williams, & Cilburn, 2006). Outcomes such as these, as well as misperceptions about the cause of weight problems, can be discouraging, potentially influencing a reluctance to maintain or restart programs of treatment, low self-esteem, self-rejection, and negative body image (Friedman et al., 2005).

Psychiatric disorders figure prominently among the challenges of the overweight and obese, and this has important implications for mental health professionals. Overweight and obese individuals internalize related stigmas and hold antifat biases (Latner, Stunkard, & Wilson, 2005; Puhl & Brownell, 2001; Schwartz, Vartanian, Nosek, & Brownell, 2006). In addition, the prevalence of mood disorders, particularly those classified under Axis I and Axis II, among this population has been well documented (for a review of the literature, see Malhotra & McElroy, 2002; McElroy et al., 2004; Simon et al., 2006). Anxiety, depressive, and bipolar disorders are among the Axis I disorders that have strong documentation (McElroy et al., 2004; Simon et al., 2006). Empirical evidence also identifies suicide attempts and suicidal ideation as covariates of increased weight (Carpenter, Hasin, Allison, & Faith, 2000).

*What are specific challenges to counseling and the counseling relationship?* Erroneous beliefs about the responsibility of overweight and obesity cast doubt on these weight problems as serious medical conditions and give rise to stigmatizing attitudes, biases, and discrimination, even among health care professionals (Harvey et al., 2002; for a review, see Puhl & Brownell, 2001). For example, many health care professionals hold neutral to negative or pessimistic views about their ability to treat overweight and obese patients (Harvey & Hill, 2001; Harvey et al., 2002). These attitudes may collide with other biases or prejudices, for example, as when the client in counseling is both obese and African American. Ethnic minorities (especially African American women), women, and those with less education and lower income are disproportionately represented among the overweight and obese (Sarlio-Lahteenkorva, Silventoinen, & Lahelma, 2004; USDHHS, 2001b). Indeed, the intersection of gender, weight, and socioeconomic status has been referred to as a "triple threat" (Bowen, Tomayasu, & Cauce, 1991).

## THE PURPOSE OF COUNSELING

Before moving on to what to do in a counseling relationship, the purpose of the counseling relationship must be clear. The American Counseling Association (ACA) defines counseling as "the application of mental health, psychological, or human development principles, through cognitive, affective, behavioral or systematic intervention strategies, that address wellness, personal growth, or career development, as well as pathology" (ACA, 1997, p. 1). Similarly, Pipes and Davenport (1999) provide the following insight:

Presumably one of the characteristics of all human cultures is that within the culture, there are certain people, at certain times, who exhibit and/or report an undesirable (to them) state of affairs in terms of their perceptions, thoughts, behavior, or emotions, or some combination thereof. These may or may not be undesirable to others. Presumably, it is also a characteristic of each culture that certain processes, procedures, and structures are both made available to and at times imposed upon the individuals in order to deal with these perceived problems . . . one such process . . . [is] psychotherapy or counseling. (p. 4)

Both definitions include the notion of counseling as a relationship that serves to effect change in the lives of the client or person receiving the counseling services. What is of interest is that the definitions do not specify type, location, or duration of interventions, nor the point of intervention. Indeed, the ACA's (1997) definition does not even specify a client per se, lending flexibility to the application and definition of counseling. This flexibility is consistent with the APA (2003) guidelines, which call to action at the individual as well as social levels. The following counselor considerations are offered in the context of a call to flexible yet life-improving interventions.

## COUNSELOR CONSIDERATIONS

The "Guidelines on Multicultural Education, Training, Research, Practice, and Organizational Change for Psychologists" (APA, 2003) provide an excellent frame from which counselors can inform their practice of counseling the marginalized. Counselors who work with marginalized persons are urged to read and/or review the document in its entirety. For the purposes of this section on counselor considerations, Guideline 1 (psychologists as cultural beings) and Guideline 5 (application of culturally appropriate skills in practice) are discussed in detail. Ethical considerations are also discussed, especially in light of the particular difficulty of integrating theoretical/applied knowledge to a population for which it was not originally designed.

The first APA (2003) guideline states the following: "Psychologists are encouraged to recognize that, as cultural beings, they may hold attitudes and beliefs that can detrimentally influence their perceptions of and interactions with individuals who are ethnically and racially different from themselves" (p. 382). In the context of the case in point on undocumented immigrants, personal beliefs and values about immigration will likely affect the counseling relationship. In addition to perceptions of the "other" in a cultural frame, it is important for the counselor to examine him- or herself in a cultural context. Specifically, a personal awareness of the counselor's own privilege (see Rothenberg, 2002) as well as the cultural lenses of his or her professional knowledge (see Pfaffenberger, 2006) are essential to meet this first guideline (APA, 2003). Rothenberg (2002) writes, "White privilege is the other side of racism. Unless we name it, we are in danger of wallowing in guilt or moral outrage with no idea of how to move beyond them. It is often easier to deplore racism and its effects than to take responsibility for the privileges some of us receive as a result of it" (p. 1). Counselors are urged to turn attention to themselves as cultural beings and make the invisible (e.g., privilege derived from racism) visible. This is not only responsible professional action; it is an ethical mandate (e.g., C.2.a. Boundaries of Competence, ACA, 2005).

Couching personal exploration as an examination of privilege might be unpalatable to some counselors (as it is to many of the students in the authors' multicultural psychology courses). A counselor may consider using his or her own counseling skills in this process of exploration. Where a counselor feels attacked or negatively engaged by the language of "White privilege," reframing might be a powerful ally. An exploration of White privilege can also be understood as an exploration and challenge of cultural assumptions or cultural programming. Privilege may sound intentional, unearned, an accusation to be rebutted. Cultural programming is unintentional, covert, something to be challenged to achieve further professional and personal growth. Knowing the language of White privilege is important because many writings have been presented (and can only be found) using these key words.

The fifth APA (2003) guideline states the following: "Psychologists are encouraged to apply culturally appropriate skills in clinical and other applied psychological practices" (p. 390). The application of appropriate skills requires that the counselor be mindful of how previously learned skills are applied and not necessarily the development of an entirely new repertoire of skills (APA, 2003). For example, during parent training, the lead author (MDR) works with immigrant Latino/a families in teaching skills building, problem solving, positive involvement, effective discipline, and effective monitoring/supervision. The concepts remain the same (especially since there is cross-cultural evidence of their utility), but the presentation of the skills and the counseling relationship with parents is noticeably different from what it would be with White, middle-class parents (e.g., see Critical Incident). Indeed, there is accumulating evidence that empirically supported approaches to treatment work across ethnic groups (for a review, see Miranda et al., 2005). Miranda and colleagues further state that practitioners are constantly making these adaptations in their work, and thus the adaptation skills do not necessarily represent an entirely new repertoire of behavior on the part of the counselor.

Finally, an intimate knowledge of the professional counselor's ethics code (e.g., ACA, 2005; APA, 2003) is needed. When applying interventions flexibly and appropriately to the cultural context, counselors may find themselves having to examine their ethics code carefully with a special focus on understanding the rationale behind each code. For example, the APA (2003) code of ethics presents mandates for ethical delivery of psychological services but does not present a definition of therapy. Counselors who find themselves in unusual settings may be hard-pressed to understand the scope of what needs to be done to engage in the ethical delivery of services. It is likely that a full understanding is only obtained after beginning service delivery and working through potential problems as they arise. Resources are available to help counselors understand ethics codes beyond the written mandates (e.g., Fisher, 2003; Ford, 2006), and specific resources are available for understanding ethics applied to work in culturally diverse communities (e.g., Trimble & Fisher, 2006).

## CONCLUSIONS

The focus of this chapter is on "counseling with the marginalized." Rather than mandate or recommend a series of actions for counselors, a series of important issues is highlighted for those who provide counseling to people who are marginalized. For a thorough review on theories of multicultural counseling, please see Fuertes and Gretchen (2001). Because "the marginalized" can be broadly defined, it is important to have a clear definition (by self and others) of the group or groups, as well as knowledge about the group's context and the areas of challenge, especially those related to the counseling relationship. Knowledge alone does not suffice. We emphasize that it is the *approach* to the counseling relationship that is most important to successful outcomes. The challenge to counselors is to be flexible and to increase their self-awareness, especially as it pertains to privilege (or cultural programming). In counseling with the marginalized, counselors are pushed to not just practice their trade but to apply the knowledge they have received in settings for which it was not conceptualized (e.g., a cognitive-behavioral therapist who now runs groups with undocumented immigrants can use the technical skills but needs to do many other things to truly have a fruitful counseling relationship). Overall, the challenges are many but are easily surpassed by the rewards. A counselor who works with marginalized persons is indeed yielding the call to action for social justice (APA, 2003; Sue, 2005) by proving a service to groups that are often underserved (USDHHS, 2001a).

As part of a preventive intervention study, families participate in groups to promote the use of parenting practices that have been found to interrupt the development and/or escalation of behavior problems in children. The intervention is for Spanish-speaking parents of children between 5 and 9 years of age who are exhibiting externalizing behavior problems but do not meet criteria for a *DSM-IV* clinical diagnosis. As part of the intervention, parents participate in eight once-weekly sessions and receive a midweek call to check on their practice assignment and clarify class content and support practice of new skills. Although documented status is not assessed, most parents share their status during the course of the research. During the course of the intervention, the interventionist (MDR) called a parent ("Dad"[1]) who reported that his 8-year-old child was having sleep difficulties. In the process of assessing the situation, it became clear that the child was having serious stomach problems that were leading to intense pain and affecting the child's activities of daily living. Dad reported having taken his child to the free clinic, where he was told the child needed extensive medical intervention that could not be provided at the clinic and that would be costly; he was given medication that he was administering to his child, but it was reportedly not having a pain-relieving effect. Dad called the local Medicaid/Medicare office but had not received a response. He did not know how else to proceed and was concerned with his child's welfare and the family's ability to get a good night's sleep so they could function to continue trying to approach the problem the following day as well as meet other important demands (e.g., work). Dad did not speak English, and he, his spouse, and his child were all undocumented.

Going outside of the traditional approaches to treatment and setting of boundaries, the clinician contacted various local physicians and secured an appointment for an evaluation free of charge. The clinician also called the local Medicare/Medicaid office and left a message for the case worker regarding the child's urgent need for services. Dad reported having called but did not receive a return phone call. Within 12 hours, a case worker returned the call. Within 24 hours, the child had been seen by a pediatrician, and Dad had received an application for a program that would cover up to $1,000 of medical expenses for a child regardless of documented status. The visit to the pediatrician resulted in a thorough exam, an effective intervention, and a plan for preventive follow-up. Because Dad was monolingual and a suitable arrangement could not be made in such a short time, the interventionist accompanied him to the medical office visit and facilitated the communication between Dad and the pediatrician. Once the visit ended, the counselor problem-solved with Dad regarding next steps, and together they resolved that Dad would continue receiving support from the community liaison, who typically provided excellent support in these situations (but was on vacation at the time of the call).

## Discussion

In this case, the urgency of the situation dictated an immediate course of action. In a less urgent situation, a counselor can make a referral and follow-up with the family to ensure they have received the needed services. However, in an emergency situation, the welfare of the child requires immediate action (see APA, 2002, 2.02, providing services in emergencies). In this case, other reasonable alternatives were not available or feasible. The primary ethical dilemma here is between the principles of beneficence and non-maleficence (APA, 2002, Principle A) and maintaining appropriate counselor-client boundaries. The counselor made a judgment where beneficence took precedence over maintaining appropriate boundaries. Where the definition of appropriate boundaries was not entirely clear, the importance of medical intervention was decidedly so. The counselor concluded that the definition of an appropriate boundary was dictated, at least in part, by the comfort of both Dad and the counselor with the context and content of the relationship. She determined to move ahead with taking an active role in helping the family manage a difficult situation, albeit unrelated to the counseling relationship. The course of action is consistent with the social justice approach advocated by various authors (e.g., APA, 2003; Sue, 2005); the counselor used her privilege (doctoral degree, professional license, English-speaking ability, knowledge of local resources) to intercede on behalf of a family that was experiencing the effects of marginalization. A more comfortable (to the counselor) boundary was reestablished at the end of the critical incident.

## DISCUSSION QUESTIONS

1. Did the interventionist behave in accordance with standard ethical conduct in psychology (APA, ACA)?

2. Did the interventionist behave in accordance with the "Guidelines on Multicultural Education, Training, Research, Practice, and Organizational Change for Psychologists"?

3. How did the family benefit from the interventionist's actions?

4. How could they have potentially been harmed? (Please consider immediate harm as well as more conceptual issues, such as empowerment.)

5. What might have been alternative courses of action? And how appropriate or inappropriate would these alternatives be?

## NOTE

1. Details have been changed to protect the identity of the family.

## REFERENCES

Allison, D. B., Fontaine, K. R., Manson, J. E., Stevens, J., & VanItallie, T. B. (1999). Annual deaths attributable to obesity in the United States. *Journal of American Medical Association, 282,* 1530–1538.

American Counseling Association (ACA). (1997). *Definition of professional counseling.* Retrieved August 15, 2006, from http://www.counseling.org/publications

American Counseling Association (ACA). (2005). *ACA Code of Ethics.* Retrieved February 27, 2007, at http://www.counseling.org/Publications/

American Obesity Association. (2005). *Obesity in the US.* Retrieved August 18, 2006, from http://www.obesity.org/subs/fastfacts/obesity_US.shtml

American Psychological Association (APA). (2002). Ethical principles of psychologists and code of conduct. *American Psychologist, 57,* 1060–1073.

American Psychological Association (APA). (2003). Guidelines on multicultural education, training, research, practice, and organizational change for psychologists. *American Psychologist, 58,* 377–402.

Arredondo, P. (2002). Counseling individuals from marginalized and underserved groups. In P. B. Pedersen, J. G. Draguns, W. J. Lonner, & J. E. Trimble (Eds.), *Counseling across cultures (5th ed.).* Thousand Oaks, CA: Sage.

Arredondo, P., Toporek, R., Brown, S. P., Jones, J., Locke, D. C., Sanchez, J., & Stadler, H. (1996). Operationalization of the multicultural counseling competencies. *Journal of Multicultural Counseling and Development, 24,* 42–78.

Berk, M. L., & Schur, C. L. (2001). The effect of fear on access to care among undocumented Latino immigrants. *Journal of Immigrant Health, 3,* 151–156.

Berk, M. L., Schur, C. L., Chavez, L. R., & Frankel, M. (2000). Health care use among undocumented Latino immigrants. *Health Affairs, 19*(4), 51–64.

Bernal, G., & Scharrón del Río, M. R. (2001). Are empirically supported treatments valid for ethnic minorities? Toward and alternative approach for treatment research. *Cultural Diversity and Ethnic Minority Psychology, 7,* 328–342.

Bowen, D. J., Tomayasu, N., & Cauce, A. M. (1991). The triple threat: Influence of gender, race, and class on weight. *Women and Health, 17*(4), 123–143.

Carpenter, K. M., Hasin, D. S., Allison, D. B., & Faith, M. S. (2000). Relationships between obesity and DSM-IV major depressive disorder, suicide ideation, and suicide attempts: Results from a general population study. *American Journal of Public Health, 90,* 251–257.

Carr, D. (2003, February 10). Gaffes on Hispanics, from 2 well-known mouths. *New York Times,* p. C9.

Cauce, A. M., Coronado, N., & Watson, J. (1998). Conceptual, methodological, and statistical issues in culturally competent research. In M. Hernandez & M. R. Isaacs (Eds.), *Promoting cultural competence in children's mental health services: Systems of care for children's mental health* (pp. 305–329). Baltimore: Paul H. Brookes.

Centers for Disease Control and Prevention (CDC). (2006a). *BMI—body mass index: About BMI for children and teens.* Retrieved August 16, 2006, from http://www.cdc.gov/nccdphp/dnpa/bmi/childrens_BMI/about_childrens_BMI.htm

Centers for Disease Control and Prevention (CDC). (2006b). *Overweight and obesity: Defining overweight and obesity.* Retrieved August 16, 2006, from http://www.cdc.gov/nccdphp/dnpa/obesity/defining.htm

Chavez, L. R., Cornelius, W. A., & Jones, O. W. (1986). Utilization of health services by Mexican immigrant women in San Diego. *Women & Health, 11*(2), 3–20.

DeNavas-Walt, C., Proctor, B. D., & Lee, C. H. (2005). *Income, poverty, and health insurance coverage in the United States: 2004.* Washington, DC: Government Printing Office. Also available at http://www.census.gov/prod/2005pubs/p60-229.pdf

Devlin, M. J., Yanovski, S. D., & Wilson, G. T. (2000). Obesity: What mental health professionals need to know. *American Journal of Psychiatry, 157,* 854–866.

Dutton, M. A., Orloff, L. E., & Aguilar Hass, G. (2000). Characteristics of help-seeking behaviors, resources and service needs of battered immigrant Latinas. *Georgetown Journal on Poverty Law & Policy, 2,* 245–305.

Eisenman, D. P., Gelberg, L., Liu, H., & Shapiro, M. F. (2003). Mental health and health-related quality of life among adult Latino primary care patients living in the United States with previous exposure to political violence. *Journal of the American Medical Association, 290,* 627–634.

Fetzer, J. S. (2000). Economic self-interest or cultural marginality? Anti-immigration sentiment and nativist political movements in France, Germany and the USA. *Journal of Ethnic and Migration Studies, 26,* 5–23.

Fisher, C. B. (2003). *Decoding the ethics code: A practical guide for psychologists.* Thousand Oaks, CA: Sage.

Fontaine, K. R., & Bartlett, S. J. (2000). Access and use of medical care among obese persons. *Obesity Research, 8,* 403–406.

Ford, G. G. (2006). *Ethical reasoning for mental health professionals.* Thousand Oaks, CA: Sage.

Fouad, N. A., & Arredondo, P. (2006). *Becoming culturally oriented: Practical advice for psychologists and educators.* Washington, DC: American Psychological Association.

Friedman, K. E., Reichmann, S. K., Costanzo, P. R., Zelli, A., Ashmore, J. A., & Musante, G. J. (2005). Weight stigmatization and ideological beliefs: Relation to psychological functioning in obese adults. *Obesity Research, 13,* 907–916.

Fuertes, J. N., & Gretchen, D. (2001). Emerging theories of multicultural counseling. In J. G. Ponterotto, J. M. Casas, L. A. Suzuki, & C. M. Alexander (Eds.), *Handbook of multicultural counseling* (2nd ed., pp. 509–541). Thousand Oaks, CA: Sage.

Harvey, E. L., & Hill, A. J. (2001). Health professionals' views of overweight people and smokers. *International Journal of Obesity, 25,* 1253–1261.

Harvey, E. L., Summerbell, C. D., Kirk, S. F. L., & Hill, A. J. (2002). Dietitians' views of overweight and obese people and reported management practices. *Journal of Human Nutrition and Dietetics, 15,* 331–347.

hooks, b. (2000). *Feminist theory: From margin to center.* Cambridge, MA: South End Press.

Hovey, J. D., Rojas, R. S., Kain, C., & Magaña, C. (2000). Proposition 187 reexamined: Attitudes toward immigration among California voters. *Current Psychology: Developmental, Learning, Personality, Social, 19,* 159–174.

Immigration and Naturalization Service (INS). (2006). *Glossary & acronyms.* Retrieved August 15, 2006, from http://www.uscis.gov/graphics/glossary2.htm#I

Immigration and Naturalization Service (INS), United States Department of Justice. (2003). *INS releases updated estimates of U.S. undocumented resident population.* Retrieved June 13, 2006, from http://www.uscis.gov/graphics/publicaffairs/summaries/undocres.htm

Jaycox, L. H., Stein, B. D., Kataoka, S. H., Wong, M., Fink, A., Escuedero, P., et al. (2002). Violence exposure, post-traumatic stress disorder, and depressive symptoms among recent immigrant schoolchildren. *Journal of the American Academy of Child & Adolescent Psychiatry, 41,* 1104–1110.

Jones, S. J. (2003). Complex subjectivities: Class, ethnicity, and race in women's narratives of upward mobility. *Journal of Social Issues, 59,* 803–820.

Kullgren, J. T. (2003). Restrictions on undocumented immigrants' access to health services: The public health implications of welfare reform. *American Journal of Public Health, 93,* 1630–1633.

Kuppersmith, N. C., Smoot, T. M., Williams, E. D., & Cilburn, E. A. (2006). Increasing awareness of obesity as a treatable medical condition. *Journal of the Kentucky Medical Association, 104,* 141–151.

Latner, J. D., Stunkard, A. J., & Wilson, G. T. (2005). Stigmatized students: Age, sex and ethnicity effects in the stigmatization of obesity. *Obesity Research, 13,* 1226–1231.

Law, S., Hutton, M., & Chan, D. (2003). Clinical, social, and service use characteristics of Fuzhounese undocumented immigrant patients. *Psychiatric Services, 54,* 1034–1037.

Lee, Y. T., & Ottai, V. (2002). Attitudes toward U.S. immigration policy: The roles of ingroup–outgroup bias, economic concern, and obedience to law. *Journal of Social Psychology, 142,* 617–634.

Lowe, S. M., & Mascher, J. (2001). The role of sexual orientation in multicultural counseling. In J. G. Ponterotto, J. M. Casas, L. A. Suzuki, & C. M. Alexander (Eds.), *Handbook of multicultural counseling* (2nd ed., pp. 755–778). Thousand Oaks, CA: Sage.

Malhotra, S., & McElroy, S. L. (2002). Medical management of obesity associated with mental disorders. *Journal of Clinical Psychiatry, 4,* 24–32.

Marshall, G. N., Schell, T. L., Elliott, M. N., Berthold, S. M., & Chun, C. (2005). Mental health of Cambodian refugees 2 decades after resettlement in the United States. *Journal of the American Medical Association, 294,* 571–579.

Marshall, K. J., Urrutia-Rojas, X., Mas, F. S., & Coggin, C. (2005). Health status and access to health care of documented and undocumented immigrant Latino women. *Health Care for Women International, 26,* 916–936.

McElroy, S. L., Kotwal, R., Malhotra, S., Nelson, E. B., Keck, P. E., & Nemeroff, C. B. (2004). Are mood disorders and obesity related? A review for the mental health professional. *Journal of Clinical Psychiatry, 65,* 634–651.

Miranda, J., Bernal, G., Lau, A., Kohn, L., Hwang, W., & LaFromboise, T. (2005). State of the science on psychosocial interventions for ethnic minorities. *Annual Review of Clinical Psychology, 1,* 113–142.

National Center for Children in Poverty (NCCP). (2005). *Children of immigrant parents face poverty despite hard work: Increasingly excluded from federal programs to meet basic needs.* New York: Columbia University, Mailman School of Public Health.

National Center for Health Statistics. (2004). *National Health and Nutrition Examination Survey.* Retrieved August 17, 2006, from http://www.cdc.gov/nchs/about/major/nhanes/nhanes2003-2004/nhanes03_04.htm

Neal-Barnett, A. M. (2001). Being Black: A new conceptualization of acting White. In A. M. Neal-Barnett, J. Contreras, & K. Kerns (Eds.), *Forging links: African American children clinical developmental perspectives.* Westport, CT: Greenwood.

Ogbu, J. U. (1991). Minority coping responses and school experience. *Journal of Psychohistory, 18,* 433–456.

Passel, J. S. (2005). *Unauthorized migrants: Numbers and characteristics.* Washington, DC: Pew Hispanic Center.

Passel, J. S., Capps, R., & Fix, M. (2004). *Undocumented immigrants: Facts and figures.* Retrieved June 13, 2006, from http://www.urban.org/publications/1000587.html

Pew Hispanic Center. (2006, April). *Fact sheet: Estimates of the unauthorized migrant population for states based on the March 2005 CPS.* Washington, DC: Author.

Pfaffenberger, A. H. (2006). Critical issues in therapy outcome research. *Journal of Humanistic Psychology, 46,* 336–351.

Pipes, R. B., & Davenport, D. S. (1999). *Introduction to psychotherapy: Common clinical wisdom* (2nd ed.). Boston: Allyn & Bacon.

Porter, E. (2005, April 5). Illegal immigrants are bolstering Social Security with billions. *New York Times,* p. A1.

Porter, E. (2006, June 19). Here illegally, working hard, and paying taxes. *New York Times,* p. A1.

Prentice, J. C., Pebley, A. R., & Sastry, N. (2005). Immigration status and health insurance coverage: Who gains? Who loses? *American Journal of Public Health, 95,* 109–116.

Puhl, R., & Brownell, K. D. (2001). Bias, discrimination, and obesity. *Obesity Research, 9,* 788–805.

Rehm, R. S. (2003). Legal, financial, and ethical ambiguities for Mexican American families: Caring for children with chronic conditions. *Qualitative Health Research, 13,* 689–702.

Rothernberg, P. (2002). *White privilege: Essential readings on the other side of racism.* New York: Worth.

Salgado de Snyder, V. N., Cervantes, R. C., & Padilla, A. M. (1990). Gender and ethnic differences in psychosocial stress and generalized distress among Hispanics. *Sex Roles, 22,* 441–453.

Sarlio-Lahteenkorva, S., Silventoinen, K., & Lahelma, E. (2004). Relative weight and income at different levels of socioeconomic status. *American Journal of Public Health, 94,* 468–472.

Schwartz, M. B., O'Neal Chambliss, H. O., Brownell, K. D., Blair, S. N., & Billington, C. (2003). Weight bias among health professionals specializing in obesity. *Obesity Research, 11,* 1033–1039.

Schwartz, M. B., Vartanian, L. R., Nosek, B. A., & Brownell, K. D. (2006). The influence of one's own body weight on implicit and explicit anti-fat bias. *Obesity, 14,* 440–447.

Simon, G. E., Von Korff, M., Saunders, K., Miglioretti, D. L., Crane, P. K., van Belle, G., et al. (2006). Association between obesity and psychiatric disorders in the US adult population. *Archives of General Psychiatry, 63,* 824–830.

Solís, J. (2003). Re-thinking illegality as a violence against, not by Mexican immigrants, children, and youth. *Journal of Social Issues, 59,* 15–31.

Sue, D. W. (2005). Racism and the conspiracy of silence: Presidential address. *The Counseling Psychologist, 33,* 101–114.

Suro, R. (2005). *Attitudes toward immigrant and immigration policy: Surveys among Latinos in the U.S. and in Mexico.* Washington, DC: Pew Hispanic Center.

Trimble, J. E. (2000). Social psychological perspectives on changing self-identification among American Indians and Alaska Natives. In R. H. Dana (Ed.), *Handbook of cross-cultural and personality assessment* (pp. 197–222). Mahwah, NJ: Lawrence Erlbaum.

Trimble, J. E., & Dickson, R. (2005). Ethnic gloss. In C. B. Fisher & R. M. Lerner (Eds.), *Encyclopedia of applied developmental science* (Vol. 1, pp. 412–415). Thousand Oaks, CA: Sage.

Trimble, J. E., & Fisher, C. B. (2006). *The handbook of ethical research with ethnic cultural populations & communities.* Thousand Oaks, CA: Sage.

U.S. Department of Health and Human Services (USDHHS). (2001a). *Mental health: Culture, race, and ethnicity.* Washington, DC: Government Printing Office.

U.S. Department of Health and Human Services (USDHHS). (2001b). *Overweight and obesity: At a glance: The facts about overweight and obesity.* Rockville, MD: Government Printing Office.

U.S. Department of Health and Human Services (USDHHS). (2001c). *The Surgeon General's call to action to prevent and decrease overweight and obesity.* Rockville, MD: Government Printing Office.

U.S. Department of Homeland Security (USDHS). (1996). *Illegal alien resident population: Estimates of the undocumented immigrant population residing in the United States.* Retrieved June 13, 2006, from http://www.uscis.gov/graphics/shared/statistics/archives/index.htm

U.S. Department of Homeland Security (USDHS). (2006). *Yearbook of immigration statistics: 2004.* Washington, DC: U.S. Department of Homeland Security, Office of Immigration Statistics.

U.S. Department of Labor. (2006). *Foreign-born workers: Labor force characteristics in 2005.* Washington, DC: Bureau of Labor Statistics.

The World Bank. (2005). *Global monitoring report: 2005.* Washington, DC: The International Bank for Reconstructions and Development/The World Bank. Also available at http://siteresources.worldbank.org/GLOBALMONITORINGEXT/Resources/ complete.pdf

CHAPTER

14

# Cross-Cultural Gerontological Counseling

## Current Models and Common Issues

Carrie L. Hill and Susan J. Eklund

### Primary Objective

- To explain the importance of considering culture in gerontological counseling and the complex intersection of culture and aging

### Secondary Objectives

- To identify the mental health issues affecting various cultural groups
- To describe current models of gerontological counseling and critique their common principles, consideration of culture, and implications for therapeutic issues in cross-cultural gerontological counseling

PUBLIC MEDIA HAVE HIGHLIGHTED THE GROWTH OF THE OLDER POPULATION IN THE UNITED STATES. Americans older than age 65 numbered 35.9 million in 2003—a 9.5% increase since 1993. Approximately one in eight Americans is an older adult, and by the year 2030, the number of older Americans will double to 71.5 million. The most rapidly growing age group is made up of those age 85 and older, whose population is expected to increase from 4.6 million in 2002 to 9.6 million in 2030 (Administration on Aging, 2004).

Within this "graying of the population," there will be a disproportionate growth of ethnic minority elders. The percentage of minority group elderly is expected to increase from 16% in 2000 to 36% in 2050 (Federal Interagency Forum on Aging-Related Statistics, 2000). Diversity extends beyond the four groups designated by the U.S. government for purposes of research and classification (i.e., African Americans, Asian Americans, Native Americans, and Hispanics). For example, although Chinese Americans, Japanese Americans, and Korean Americans may all be classified as Asian Americans, there are differences among these subgroups that may influence the experience of old age (Morioko-Douglas & Yeo, 1990). There also are many foreign-born older persons in the United States. More than one third were born in Europe, one third came from Latin America, and one fourth were born in Asia (He, 2002).

The trend toward an aging population is worldwide. One of every 10 persons around the world is now age 60 or older, though striking differences exist between more and less developed regions. One of 5 Europeans—but only 1 of 20 Africans—is 60 years or older (United Nations, 2003). However, the older population is growing at a faster rate in several developing countries than in developed ones, pointing toward a gradual shift in the distribution of older people over time. Italy is now the world's oldest major country, with more than 18% of its population age 65 or older. Of all those age 80 or older, more than 16% are in China. By the year 2030, almost 40% of older Japanese will be age 80 or older (Kinsella & Velkoff, 2001).

The growth of the older population will increase the need for psychologists and other mental health professionals who specialize in aging. For example, a recent report by the Center for Health Workforce Studies (2005) at SUNY-Albany determined that between the years 2000 and 2010, employment opportunities for psychologists are expected to increase 64% in home health, 19% in nursing homes, and 70% in residential care. However, a shortage of psychologists—especially geropsychologists—is predicted because psychologists are substantially older than average when they enter the workforce. Thirty-four percent of doctoral-level psychologists in the United States will reach retirement age by the year 2010, but current graduation rates indicate that new psychologists will not enter the workforce at a rate that can replace those who are retiring. Furthermore, the American Psychological Association assesses that 5,000 geropsychologists will be needed by the year 2020; however, fewer than 3,000 geropsychologists are currently working in the United States (Center for Health Workforce Studies, 2005).

Clinicians who will be treating increased numbers of culturally diverse elders must learn about ethnic minority aging (Tsai & Carstensen, 1996). The American Psychological Association (2004) recognized this challenge in its "Guidelines for Psychological Practice With Older Adults" under Guideline 5: "Psychologists strive to understand diversity in the aging process, particularly how sociocultural factors such as gender, ethnicity, socioeconomic status, sexual orientation, disability status, and urban/rural residence may influence the experience and expression of health and of psychological problems in later life" (p. 242).

The purpose of this chapter is to explain the importance of considering culture in gerontological counseling and to explore the complex intersection of culture and aging. First, we discuss mental health issues affecting older members of the four major ethnic/minority groups in the United States, remaining cognizant of the dangers of overgeneralizing similarities among members of each group. A brief discussion on international aging is also included. We then describe current models of gerontological counseling and critique them in regard to common principles, consideration of culture, and implications for therapeutic issues in cross-cultural gerontological counseling.

# MENTAL HEALTH ISSUES IN A CULTURALLY DIVERSE OLDER POPULATION

## Hispanics

Elderly Hispanics are the fastest growing U.S. ethnic group, constituting 6% of all elderly in the United States (Sanchez, 1992). By the year 2050, Hispanics are expected to make up 16% of the U.S. elderly population (Federal Interagency Forum on Aging-Related Statistics, 2000).

The several cultures that make up the larger group of Hispanics in the United States, although varied, have in common a language (Spanish), a religion (Roman Catholic), and certain individual and family values (Vazquez & Clavijo, 1995). Among older Hispanics, Lacayo (1980) found that 86% identified Spanish as their preferred language, even if they could speak English. The majority of Hispanics are Mexican Americans; other groups include Puerto Ricans, Cubans, Central Americans, and South Americans.

Ethnic elders vary in their rates of mental illness (Tsai & Carstensen, 1996). Older Hispanic women, for example, have higher rates of depression, alcohol abuse, phobias, and cognitive impairment than do European American older women (Stanford & DuBois, 1992). Hispanic elders who experience greater activity limitations report higher rates of mood disorders such as depression (Abramson, Trejo, & Lai, 2002). Some research suggests that acculturated or bicultural Mexican American older adults experience less depression than do those who are less acculturated (Zamanian et al., 1992). Another study found that Hispanic older adults, compared with the general population, experience lower life satisfaction and are more likely to feel lonely (Andrews, Lyons, & Rowland, 1992).

Many assume that Hispanic elders are more often cared for by family members than are European Americans, but this belief may be stereotypical or a carryover from earlier times. Markides, Boldt, and Ray (1986) found that elderly Mexican Americans were no more likely than other older Americans to be cared for by their relatives, even though family solidarity remains important to Hispanic culture. Not surprisingly, older Hispanics report dissatisfaction with the care and attention they receive from their children (Hooyman & Kiyak, 1999).

Hispanics may use alternative or traditional health care providers, such as *curanderos* or other folk healers. Hispanics tend to underuse the mental health system and rely on themselves to solve problems (Starrett, Rogers, & Decker, 1992). Biegel, Farkas, and Song (1997) believe this underutilization stems from systemic barriers, such as lack of transportation, lack of bilingual clinicians, and insufficient outreach services. Abramson and colleagues (2002) point out that many older Hispanics believe that life circumstances are "God's will" and that only God can change them. When elderly Hispanics do seek help for mental problems, they tend to begin with their physicians, most often presenting with physical symptoms (Espino, 1990).

## African Americans

African American elders are the largest group of ethnic elders in the United States, making up 8% of older Americans; by the year 2050, this percentage will have risen to 12% (Federal Interagency Forum on Aging-Related Statistics, 2000). Functional old age occurs earlier for African Americans than for European Americans (55 vs. 65) because of higher rates of disability, lower education levels, and financial disadvantages (Jackson, 1988).

Interestingly, in the first stages of old age, both African American and Hispanic elders have earlier onsets and higher rates of severe impairment than do European Americans. However, by age 80, they have lower rates of mortality and morbidity than European Americans. This "mortality crossover effect" is sometimes attributed to selective survival of only the hardiest persons. Many Hispanic and African American elders have coped with stress and poverty throughout their lives and may find it easier to cope with negative outcomes in old age (Wing, Manton, Stallard, Haines, & Tyroles, 1985).

African American elders tend to have fewer economic resources than do older European Americans. In 1998, divorced Black women between the ages of 65 and 74 had a 47% poverty rate, one of the highest rates of any older adult subgroup (Federal Interagency Forum on Aging-Related Statistics, 2000). African American elders have a history of minimal formal education and have tended to hold low-paying jobs and suffer periods of unemployment, resulting in relatively low Social Security benefits. They tend to have more health problems than do elderly European Americans but are less likely to be seen by doctors. Older African Americans also report higher levels of psychological distress (Fillenbaum, Hughes, Heyman, George, & Blazer, 1988).

The strengths of African American families include strong family ties, high levels of economic and social support from extended family, high likelihood of family members caring for dependent older relatives, strong religious orientation, and solid respect for elders (Aschenbrenner, 1973). Elderly African Americans are less likely to reside in nursing homes than are European Americans because of the African American ethic that elders should be cared for by "blood" (Carter, 1988). However, in recent years, this strong family support system has been eroded by high levels of drug problems among adult children of many Black elders. A large number of grandparents are now full-time caregivers for their grandchildren (Tsai & Carstensen, 1996). Older African American women are four times more likely than older European American women to live with dependent relatives younger than 18 years of age (Tate, 1983).

African American elders tend to use support from friends and neighbors to a greater degree than do White elders (Taylor, 1988). Churches provide substantial material, emotional, and spiritual support to African American communities (Taylor, 1988). Religious involvement has been associated with psychological well-being among urban elderly African Americans (Frazier, Mintz, & Mobley, 2005).

## Asian Americans

Asian American elders represent 1.6% of older Americans; by 2050, this percentage will rise to 7% (Federal Interagency Forum on Aging-Related Statistics, 2000). The large group known as Asian Americans includes members of more than 20 different ethnic groups, including Chinese, Filipinos, Japanese, Koreans, and Southwest Asians (Morioko-Douglas & Yeo, 1990). Groups differ in their historical backgrounds, including their reasons for immigrating to the United States and their experiences since arriving. Most Asian American elders are relatively unacculturated to mainstream U.S. practices and reside in highly structured enclaves such as Chinatowns and Koreatowns, where their customs and traditions are maintained (Morioko-Douglas & Yeo, 1990). Among older Asian Americans, 75% speak only their native tongues.

In the mid-1800s, Chinese men were brought to the United States to provide cheap labor on railroads, on farms, and in mines in California. Most left their families behind, hoping to send for them later or to return home. However, the Chinese Exclusion Act of 1882 limited the entry of Chinese women into the United States, leaving many Chinese men to grow old alone in urban Chinatowns (Kim, 1990). Japanese immigrants, two thirds of whom were American citizens at the time, were interned in camps in the western states after the attack on Pearl Harbor in 1942. After the fall of Saigon in 1975,

Indochinese refugees began to enter the United States. Many were accompanied by their elderly parents, who have experienced difficulties adjusting to the new culture (Kim, 1990). These are just a few examples of the historical events in the lives of Asian American subgroups that contribute to their experience of aging, increase the diversity within the larger group, and influence their mental health.

Many assume that Asian Americans are well adjusted and do not need mental health services, but surveys among members of this group reveal high need (Sue, Nakamura, Chung, & Yee-Bradbury, 1994). Chinese Americans have a suicide rate three times higher than that of the total elderly population and experience more mental illness, possibly due to social and emotional isolation (Kii, 1984). Cheung (1989) identified several problems of older Chinese living in the United States, including alienation, poverty, lack of language proficiency and education, lack of access to services, immobility and transportation problems, lack of respect, and health problems.

Sue and Morishima (1982) describe the primary stressors experienced by Asian Americans as culture, conflict, minority status, and social changes. Asian cultures highly value the family and a respect for elders based on Confucianism, which emphasizes the importance of social order within families and society. In traditional Asian families, elders are authority figures—but the acculturation of many younger Asians to mainstream America has caused a breakdown of this traditional system. Some Asian American elders feel betrayed by younger relatives who have become Americanized. Yet, older Asian Americans are still more likely to live with adult children than are their European American peers (Wong & Ujimoto, 1998).

## Native Americans

Native American elderly make up 0.4% of all older Americans, and by 2050, 0.6% of older Americans will be Native American (Federal Interagency Forum on Aging-Related Statistics, 2000). Native Americans are another heterogeneous group made up of more than 500 separate tribes, including Navajo, Cherokee, Sioux, and Chippewa, as well as Eskimos and Aleuts (Hooyman & Kiyak, 1999; McCabe & Cuellar, 1994). Some 35% of Native Americans live on reservations or in other areas set aside for them, whereas others live in urban areas such as California (U.S. Bureau of the Census, 2005). Most live in impoverished situations.

Housing is poor for most Native Americans, and members of this group rank far below others in education and health (Bell, Kasschau, & Zellman, 1976). Reservation-dwelling Native Americans older than age 45 and urban dwellers older than age 55 are comparable to members of the general aging population older than age 65 (National Indian Council on Aging, 1981). Strides have been made by the Indian Health Service in the treatment of infectious diseases, but little has been done for the treatment of chronic late-life conditions. Approximately 73% of middle-aged and older Native Americans have difficulty performing basic activities of daily living (Hendricks & Hendricks, 1986). Depression levels of 10% to 30% have been reported among Native American elders (U.S. Department of Health and Human Services, 2001). Alcoholism occurs at a higher rate among Native Americans than among European Americans, although it is less of a problem in late life because the majority of alcoholics do not survive into old age (Byford, 1990).

Chovan and Chovan (1985) found that Cherokee elders use an intrapsychic mode of coping that emphasizes acceptance of circumstances and the inward focus of one's energies to maintain harmony and balance. This is in keeping with the Native American preference for collateral relations and harmony with nature that Kluckhohn and Strodtbeck (1961) report in their classic work. Harmony in interpersonal relations and noncompetitiveness are important aspects of Native American culture (Garrett, 1999).

Most urban-dwelling Native Americans are assimilated into the majority culture, while those who remain in rural areas tend to follow traditional ways that emphasize the importance of the family or clan. Relationships among clan members are paramount, and the needs of the clan come before individual needs. In general, Native Americans are accepting of the aging process, seeing it as natural and as something to be embraced. Changing values and low fertility rates are resulting in fewer younger caregivers for elderly Native Americans (Garrett, 1999).

## Aging Around the World

Social and psychological trends in aging vary around the world. For instance, suicide rates are generally higher for older men than older women across countries. However, Belgium and France have relatively high rates among older men, while Japan, Switzerland, and Russia have comparatively high rates among older women. In most countries, older men are likely to be married, while older women are more commonly widowed. Current percentages of divorced elderly are low in most countries, but this percentage is expected to increase over time (Kinsella & Velkoff, 2001).

There is a trend toward urbanization among the older population worldwide; Latin America and the Caribbean region already are highly urbanized. Still, older adults are more likely than younger adults to live in rural areas. Older women in developed countries often live alone while their male counterparts usually live with family. For example, more than half of older Danish women live by themselves; this trend is increasing rapidly in Canada as well. In developed countries, more and more elders are living in long-term care settings, despite efforts in many places to increase community- and home-based services. Rates of institutionalization in developing countries are comparatively low.

Levels of family and social support differ among developed and developing countries. Developed countries will see a sharp decrease in the number of persons available to provide elders with family and social support in the coming years. On the other hand, developing countries will see little change in social support levels over the next few decades. Part of the decline in some countries is due to lower fertility rates and, therefore, reduced family size. For instance, in 1975, 17% of older South Korean widows had no surviving son. By the year 2025, this percentage will rise to 30%. Formal home care support services are used most widely in Scandinavia and the United Kingdom (Kinsella & Velkoff, 2001).

Around the world, older adults account for a small portion of the labor force. However, levels of senior workforce participation can very greatly between countries. In New Zealand, only 10% of women between the ages of 65 and 69 still participate in the workforce, but in Rwanda, more than 73% of women in this age group are still working (Kinsella & Velkoff, 2001). Grandparents raising grandchildren is an international phenomenon that creates a different kind of work for older adults. In some countries, "skip-generation" families are common, where grandparents raise grandchildren when the middle generation moves to urban areas to find work. A study in rural Zimbabwe found that 35% of households consisted of skip-generation families (Hashimoto, 1991).

Educational advances in developed countries make it easy to assume that most older adults are now literate. Unfortunately, in many developing countries, the majority of the older population is still illiterate. In 1992, more than 80% of the elderly in Chile were literate, but less than 20% of elders in Uganda could read and write. In nearly every country, older men are more highly educated than older women (Kinsella & Velkoff, 2001). Differences in literacy and education can affect older adults' health behaviors, including those related to mental health.

# CURRENT MODELS OF GERONTOLOGICAL COUNSELING

Three models of gerontological counseling are described that we find useful when counseling culturally diverse elders. The models are distinguished from theoretical approaches (e.g., psychodynamic, cognitive-behavioral, life review) that could be used as counseling interventions within each model but do not indicate how a clinician should consider culture when counseling older adults. The models we have chosen either explicitly or implicitly allow for the consideration of culture during the gero-counseling process.

## Hays's ADRESSING Framework

Hays's (1996) model will help clinicians "(a) explore the influence of diverse cultural factors on their own identity, world view, and work with clients; and (b) consider the influence of cultural factors on their clients, particularly factors related to minority-group status, which [clinicians] of dominant cultural identities might be inclined to overlook" (p. 188). It is geared toward culturally responsive assessment, but Hays includes suggestions for establishing rapport with culturally diverse older clients, understanding their cultural identities, and ascertaining their current contexts, needs, and strengths. Because all of these tasks infiltrate the counseling process, we include Hays's framework as a model of gerontological counseling that attends to culture.

The framework is based on the American Psychological Association's (1993) "Guidelines for Providers of Psychological Services to Ethnic, Linguistic, and Culturally Diverse Populations," which list several cultural influences that clinicians must consider when providing psychological services. Hays (1996) organizes these influences into the acronym ADRESSING. The letters signify age and generational influences, disability, religion, ethnicity, social status, sexual orientation, indigenous heritage, national origin, and gender. Hays does not prioritize the influences because the "significance of cultural influences is person-specific and context-specific" (p. 188). Effective use of the framework depends on the degree to which the clinician has explored his or her own cultural identity and pinpointed areas of potential bias.

To build rapport with an older client, Hays (1996) suggests that the clinician ask himself or herself the following: "With this particular client, what are the considerations related to each of the ADRESSING factors for which I will need to think more carefully, learn more, and possibly involve a cultural liaison or consultant?" (p. 189). For example, members of older generations often prefer to be addressed by an appropriate title (e.g., Mr., Mrs., Dr.) and surname, but this preference may vary according to cultural customs. A clinician can facilitate rapport by initially using the more formal titled address and allowing the older client to suggest a desired change.

To understand an older client's cultural identity and heritage, clinicians can use the ADRESSING framework to consider cultural influences they may be prone to overlook. Hays (1996) recommends that clinicians learn about their clients' cultural influences in a variety of ways. For instance, they can consult with "cultural liaisons" about culture-specific norms and role expectations for elders, engage in community events involving culturally diverse groups, and read about cultural histories from the perspectives of members of those cultures.

Finally, clinicians can use the ADRESSING framework systematically to ascertain information about older clients' current contexts, needs, and strengths. Each cultural influence in the framework contextualizes a client's presenting problem and the choice of treatment interventions. Also, exploring with clients their coping strategies along each cultural influence can reveal multiple strengths that clinicians can incorporate into treatment planning.

## Knight's Contextual, Cohort-Based, Maturity/Specific Challenge Model

Knight's (2004) model attempts to bridge the science of gerontology and the practice of psychotherapy. It addresses the discrepancy between two schools of thought about aging. The first, the "loss-deficit" model of aging, views later life as a series of losses; depression is considered a normal response to aging. The second school of thought endorses a life span developmental approach, where normal aging is viewed more positively. Believing that each perspective has some merit but that the loss-deficit model might fuel negative views of aging, Knight developed the contextual, cohort-based, maturity/specific challenge model.

Knight's (2004) model comprises several parts. First, he suggests that the social context is important to case conceptualization and the therapeutic relationship. *Context* refers to specific environments, rules, and services for older adults. Environments include age-segregated communities, senior centers, and long-term care settings. Rules could be Medicare regulations, Older Americans Act policies, and conservatorship laws. Services might include transportation programs, meal sites, and referral services among community agencies. Knight believes that clinicians often are at a disadvantage with older clients because they are unfamiliar with these contexts. Most can relate to the context of a younger client who is living on a college campus, but they are less able to imagine what it is like for an older client to live in a nursing home.

Second, Knight (2004) distinguishes between cohort effects and developmental changes. Many differences between older and younger adults are attributed to aging when, in fact, they are due to cohort differences. A cohort is a birth year–defined group that, through socialization, developed abilities, beliefs, attitudes, and personality characteristics that will remain stable as the cohort ages and that distinguish it from other cohort groups. For instance, those who lived through the Great Depression developed habits of frugality and careful saving to avoid ever going hungry again. This is a cohort effect, not a function of aging. Sadly, clinicians might assume that older people naturally become more "stingy" or rigid as they age.

Third, Knight (2004) concludes that there is potential for continual growth toward maturity throughout the life span. By *maturity,* he means an increase in cognitive complexity, the development of expertise in work and relationships, increasing androgyny, and greater emotional complexity. He suggests that older adults may be excellent participants in counseling and show promise for therapeutic change.

The last dimension of Knight's (2004) model accounts for specific challenges of late life, such as chronic illness, disability, preparation for dying, and grieving the loss of loved ones. By using the word *specific,* Knight does not mean that these challenges occur only during later life or that they have therapeutic meaning only if older adults experience them. Rather, these challenges most commonly occur in the latter third of life. Also, elders are not immune to problems usually associated with younger populations, such as romantic conflicts and occupational concerns. Knight recommends that counseling goals and techniques should be determined by the specific challenges faced by older clients. The contextual, cohort-based, and maturity dimensions of the model can help clinicians frame the challenges and make adaptations to counseling, if necessary.

## Burlingame's Ethnogerocounseling Model

Burlingame's (1999) ethnogerocounseling model consists of three "lenses"—the *ethnic* lens, the *gero chi* lens, and the *gerocounseling* lens. By layering the lenses onto one another, clinicians can accurately and comprehensively conceptualize culturally diverse older clients and design treatment interventions.

The ethnic lens helps clinicians view themselves and their clients as ethnic beings. This lens comprises five dimensions: identity, demographics, immigration-migration experiences, cultural values, and issues. Identity encompasses "where our roots lie, where we've been, who we are now, and what we are becoming in relation to others" (Burlingame, 1999, p. 8). Demographics are statistics about the older population—specifically, minority elders—but Burlingame cautions that many population studies are flawed. Immigration-migration experiences reveal both traumas associated with immigration and migration and strengths and resources developed because of these events. Cultural values shape older clients' definitions of mental health and illness, expectations for treatment, and ideas about aging. Issues encompass all sources of pride and pain for a cultural group—particularly for a group's older members.

The gero chi lens helps clinicians think about specific processes and tasks unique to aging. *Chi* is an acronym for *circular, holistic,* and *interactive,* meaning that the dimensions of this lens are complexly related. The dimensions are the self-system, psychosocial tasks, aging tasks, and the biopsychosocial system. The self-system is the unique expression of an older individual, including self-concept, gender, and spirituality. Psychosocial tasks involve the client's progression through Erikson's (1950) eight stages of development. Although the final stage (i.e., integrity vs. despair) is often associated with later life, Burlingame (1999) believes that many elders are working on unfinished business from earlier stages. While psychosocial tasks are more existential, aging tasks are more practical and may be the issues originally brought to counseling. Examples of aging tasks are the use of medical, social, and emotional supports; adjustment to declining health; coping with financial changes; and adjustment to losses of significant others. The biopsychosocial system consists of three subsystems. The biological subsystem includes genetics, sex, current functioning, and history of illness and physical trauma. The psychological subsystem includes cognition, affect, coping skills, and personality. The sociological subsystem pertains to the broad range of relationships that affect an older person's experience, such as family, formal and informal support systems, and religious communities.

Burlingame's (1999) gerocounseling lens comprises six dimensions: the generic gerocounseling system (i.e., ethics, relationship skills, communication), the gerocounseling assessment system, the gerocounseling goal-setting system, the gerocounseling modality system, the gerocounseling intervention system, and the gerocounseling termination system.

Burlingame (1999) suggests that all three lenses must be layered onto one another if ethnogerocounseling is to be successful. The ethnic lens must be placed on top of the gero chi lens in order to view older adults as ethnic beings. The resulting conceptualizations must then be layered on top of the gerocounseling lens in order to adapt counseling in such a way that it honors older adults as ethnic beings and is tailored to individuals.

# CRITIQUE OF THE MODELS
## Common Principles

All three models consider culture to some degree. Hays (1996) and Burlingame (1999) are explicit in their recommendations, while Knight (2004) is less so. Still, he indicates that older adults raised in various sociocultural circumstances might require adaptations to counseling that go beyond adaptations based on developmental aging. The common principle is that culture is relevant to gerontological counseling with culturally diverse elders. The models also suggest that counselors examine their own views and biases if they want to counsel older adults effectively. Hays and Burlingame focus on cultural views and biases, whereas Knight concentrates more on assumptions about elders, illness and disability, and death and dying.

Each model proposes issues that culturally different older clients might bring to counseling. Hays's (1996) ADRESSING framework reveals issues along each dimension of the acronym, Knight (2004) describes specific challenges facing older adults that are commonly brought to therapy, and Burlingame (1999) recommends layering the three lenses of the model to reveal culturally relevant gerocounseling issues. Finally, all three models note the importance of context in counseling culturally different elders. Hays refers to individual contexts, whereas Knight and Burlingame include the context of the service delivery system. To make accurate, comprehensive conceptualizations of culturally diverse older clients, clinicians need to consider all contextual realms.

## Common and Uncommon Strengths and Problems

The three models share the strength of having been developed from solid knowledge bases. Hays's (1996) framework is based on guidelines provided by the American Psychological Association (1993), which gives her model an ethical nature. Knight's (2004) model synthesizes current gerontological knowledge from a variety of fields and thus is a multidisciplinary contribution. Burlingame (1999) took the most direct approach in developing her model by conducting qualitative research with culturally diverse elders, their families, and service providers to formulate her conclusions. In addition, each model provides some degree of guidance for collecting and interpreting cultural and gerontological client data, which is an important part of the counseling process.

Nevertheless, these three models share a weakness: None seems to endorse the assumption that culture is *always* relevant to gerontological counseling. Ridley, Li, and Hill (1998) argue that cultural issues should be explored within all counselor-client dyads. This includes not only when the counselor is European American and the client is not but also when both the counselor and client are of similar or different non–European American backgrounds, those in which the counselor is non–European American and the client is European American, and even those in which both the counselor and client are European American. Cultural issues are broad and not always immediately apparent. Although all three models assert that the consideration of gerontological data is always relevant to cross-cultural gerontological counseling, none of them suggests that culture is relevant to every situation.

## Common Issues in Cross-Cultural Gerontological Counseling

### Health and Illness

Approximately 80% of older adults experience at least one chronic condition (LaRue, 1992), and 12% experience functional disability (Weissert, 1983). The onset of chronic illness is often earlier among non–European American older adults, and minority elders have an increased tolerance and adaptability to illness and discomfort (American Psychological Association, 1997). In general, physical illness is a predictor of depression in older adults (Phifer & Murrell, 1986). Health issues might also present situations where health care providers (e.g., home health aides) are culturally different from the client, which can make the client uncomfortable (Hinrichsen, 2006). In light of the three models reviewed, clinicians should (a) consider how culture affects the health of their older clients, (b) explore their own reactions to chronic illness and how these reactions may affect their work with older clients, and (c) attend to contextual factors such as access to medical care and environmental motivation for the execution of medical regimens.

## Death, Dying, and Bereavement

In cross-cultural gerontological counseling, clients may be thinking about their own death, reflecting on the course of their lives, struggling with a terminal illness, or grieving for the loss of a loved one. Cultural differences may affect these issues. For example, African Americans appear to be less afraid of death than European Americans (Cicirelli, 1999), although the reasons for this phenomenon are unclear. It is easy to misinterpret positive attitudes about death as suicidal ideation, so counselors should learn about their clients' cultural beliefs about death and dying (Hinrichsen, 2006). The models suggest that counselors should (a) consider the impact of culture on their older clients' rituals and belief systems surrounding death and dying, (b) explore their own beliefs about death and dying and how these beliefs may affect their work with older clients, and (c) consider contextual factors that affect their clients' decisions about, and reactions to, death and dying.

## Social Support

Social support can come from family, friends, religious communities, or professional caregivers, among other sources. In a study of spousal caregivers of persons with dementia, Miller and Guo (2000) found that older European American male caregivers were more likely than caregivers of other race-gender combinations to receive emotional support from adult children and practical assistance from formal networks. In another study, Himes, Hogan, and Eggebeen (1996) found that minority elders were much less likely to live alone or only with their spouses than were European American elders. To adequately address social support issues, counselors should (a) explore with their clients how culture affects their access to, and utilization of, various kinds of social support; (b) examine their own assumptions about what constitutes social support to avoid a narrow conceptualization of available resources; and (c) consider broad contexts when identifying social supports and how to incorporate them into treatment planning.

## Ageism and Racism

Ageism is "arbitrarily restricting one's own or another's behavior because of age, misperceiving another or oneself because of age, or holding negative thoughts and feelings about self or other because of age" (Ponzo, 1992, p. 211). Racism is "any behavior or pattern of behavior that tends to systematically deny access to opportunities or privileges to members of one racial group while perpetuating access to opportunities and privileges to members of another racial group" (Ridley, 1995, p. 28). Regrettably, the combination of ageism and racism has not received much attention. For example, the American Psychological Association's (1993) original guidelines for the provision of psychological services to diverse populations suggest that psychologists be sensitive to issues of oppression, sexism, elitism, and racism, but ageism is not mentioned. Fortunately, the new "Guidelines on Multicultural Education, Training, Research, Practice, and Organizational Change for Psychologists" (American

Psychological Association, 2003) clearly recognize the interaction of age, race, and ethnicity and its relevance to psychological practice.

Some older adults experience a combination of ageism and racism on a regular basis, even by the mental health and medical professions (Hinrichsen, 2006). This may be a focus of counseling or may influence the context of a client's presenting issues. Counselors should be cognizant of their clients' vulnerability to ageism and racism. They also should explore their own beliefs and assumptions to prevent themselves from perpetuating ageism or racism on an unintentional or intentional basis.

## Successful Aging

Rowe and Kahn (1998) define successful aging as "low risk of disease and disease-related disability, high mental and physical function, and active engagement with life" (p. 38). This represents a turn from earlier beliefs that aging equals sickness and frailty. However, Leder (2000) cautions that the "conventional Western model of successful aging assumes that the losses that attend age should be *combated* whenever possible" (p. 37). In contrast, the *spiritual* model of aging embraces the losses of age and uses them for reflection and liberation. Leder compares the much-touted vision of an octogenarian on cross-country skis to the Native American vision of an elder as guidepost and ritual keeper. Culture affects an older adult's beliefs about what it means to age successfully. Counselors need to (a) explore the meaning of successful aging with their clients, (b) examine their own assumptions about what it means to age successfully and how these assumptions affect their counseling style, and (c) consider how contextual influences shape notions and actualizations of successful aging.

## CONCLUSION

Our purpose has been to explain the importance of considering culture in gerontological counseling. We provided an overview of (a) the mental health issues affecting various cultural groups, (b) current models of gerontological counseling that we have found useful when working with diverse older clients, and (c) common issues in cross-cultural gerontological counseling. We encourage readers to refer to the writings of Hays (1996), Knight (2004), and Burlingame (1999) for more information about their models of gerontological counseling.

Myers and Harper (2004) state that research is sorely lacking on counseling outcomes with culturally diverse older adults. Future research should focus on the efficacy and effectiveness of current models of gerontological counseling with older clients from different cultures. Information also is lacking about the incidence of mental health problems among older members of diverse populations. However, problems with accurate reporting of mental health problems and a dearth of culturally sensitive measures for elders make the acquisition of accurate information a lofty goal. Ultimately, counselors should view culturally relevant gerontological research in light of individual client differences to avoid stereotyping. It is hoped that this will increase counselors' chances of forming accurate client conceptualizations and implementing appropriate treatment interventions.

### CRITICAL INCIDENT

Mr. Hernandez is a 73-year-old Mexican American man who sought counseling upon recommendation from his family physician. Mr. Hernandez is caring for his wife, who has had Alzheimer's disease for

6 years. She is declining steadily; caregiving is becoming increasingly difficult for Mr. Hernandez to do alone. Their two children live approximately 300 miles away, and neither has invited their parents to live with them in order to provide family support. Mr. Hernandez has attended some caregiver support groups, but he has not accessed any other community resources, stating that he does not understand the programs or their eligibility requirements. Mr. Hernandez indicates that he feels "very down" but that he should not question his circumstances because these kinds of things "are in God's hands."

## Discussion

Using Knight's (2004) contextual, cohort-based, maturity/specific challenge model, many issues could be explored and clarified by the counselor. Mr. Hernandez presents with several challenges: caregiver stress, lack of social support, and feelings of sadness and hopelessness. He could be depressed; he also could already be grieving for his wife even though she is still alive, due to the way Alzheimer's disease seems to take away a person's former self.

Many contextual issues could be examined to better understand Mr. Hernandez's problems and to develop solutions. Are there deeper reasons that Mr. Hernandez does not want to access community resources? Has he experienced discrimination when dealing with government entities? How did he find the caregiver support group? Has he been able to express his feelings in this setting? Would the group leader or members be able to recommend other free services that he would feel comfortable using? Based on Mr. Hernandez's statements about God, perhaps there are friends or neighbors from his church community that could provide assistance.

In regard to cohort influences, did Mr. Hernandez grow up in a cohort that valued taking care of one's parents when they grew old? Did he take care of his own parents? What were his expectations of his own children, and how does he feel about the fact that they have not offered to help in a substantial way?

In regard to maturity, the counselor should identify and point out Mr. Hernandez's strengths, including ones he has developed since becoming a caregiver. These might include an expertise in caregiving skills, increased androgyny due to taking charge of all household chores (e.g., cooking, laundry), and Mr. Hernandez's willingness to try counseling as a means of problem solving.

Exploring Knight's (2004) dimensions of context, cohort influences, and maturity can provide culture-specific information to help shape the therapeutic goals that address the complex challenges presented by Mr. Hernandez.

## DISCUSSION QUESTIONS

1.  Describe how Hays's (1996) ADRESSING framework could be used to explore therapeutic issues and develop treatment goals with Mr. Hernandez.

2.  Describe how Burlingame's (1999) ethnogerocounseling model could be used to explore therapeutic issues and develop treatment goals with Mr. Hernandez.

3.  What common issues in cross-cultural gerontological counseling are relevant to this critical incident? Describe them in relation to Mr. Hernandez's unique cultural background.

# REFERENCES

Abramson, T. A., Trejo, L., & Lai, D. W. L. (2002). Culture and mental health: Providing appropriate services for a diverse older population. *Generations, 26*(1), 21–27.

Administration on Aging. (2004). *A profile of older Americans: 2004.* Washington, DC: U.S. Department of Health and Human Services.

American Psychological Association. (1993). Guidelines for providers of psychological services to ethnic, linguistic, and culturally diverse populations. *American Psychologist, 48,* 45–48.

American Psychological Association. (1997). *What practitioners should know about working with older adults.* Washington, DC: Author.

American Psychological Association. (2003). Guidelines on multicultural education, training, research, practice, and organizational change for psychologists. *American Psychologist, 58,* 377–402.

American Psychological Association. (2004). Guidelines for psychological practice with older adults. *American Psychologist, 59,* 236–260.

Andrews, J. W., Lyons, B., & Rowland, D. (1992). Life satisfaction and peace of mind: A comparative analysis of elderly Hispanic and other elderly Americans. In T. L. Brink (Ed.), *Hispanic aged mental health* (pp. 21–42). New York: Haworth.

Aschenbrenner, J. (1973). Extended families among Black Americans. *Journal of Comparative Family Studies, 4,* 257–268.

Bell, B., Kasschau, P., & Zellman, G. (1976). *Delivering services to elderly members of minority groups: A critical review of the literature.* Santa Monica, CA: RAND Corporation.

Biegel, D. E., Farkas, K. J., & Song, L. (1997). Barriers to the use of mental health services by African American and Hispanic elderly persons. *Journal of Gerontological Social Work, 29,* 23–44.

Burlingame, V. S. (1999). *Ethnogerocounseling: Counseling ethnic elders and their families.* New York: Springer.

Byford, F. (1990). The Native American elderly: Perspectives on alcohol, suicide, and accidents and implications for geriatric curricula content. In M. S. Harper (Ed.), *Minority aging: Essential curricula content for selected health and allied health professions* (DHHS Pub. No. HRS P-DV-90-4, pp. 129–137). Washington, DC: Government Printing Office.

Carter, J. H. (1988). Health attitudes/promotions/preventions: The Black elderly. In J. S. Jackson (Ed.), *The Black American elderly: Research on physical and psychosocial health* (pp. 292–303). New York: Springer.

Center for Health Workforce Studies. (2005). *The impact of the aging population on the health workforce in the United States.* Rensselaer, NY: School of Public Health, University at Albany.

Cheung, M. (1989). Elderly Chinese living in the United States: Assimilation or adjustment. *Social Work, 34,* 457–461.

Chovan, M. J., & Chovan, W. (1985). Stressful events and coping responses among older adults in low sociocultural groups. *Journal of Psychology, 119,* 253–260.

Cicirelli, V. G. (1999). Personality and demographic factors in older adults' fear of death. *The Gerontologist, 39,* 569–579.

Erikson, E. (1950). *Childhood and society.* New York: W. W. Norton.

Espino, D. V. (1990). Mexican-American elderly: Problems in evaluation, diagnosis, and treatment. In M. S. Harper (Ed.), *Minority aging: Essential curricula content for selected health and allied health professions* (DHHS Pub. No. HRS P-DV-90-4, pp. 453–459). Washington, DC: Government Printing Office.

Federal Interagency Forum on Aging-Related Statistics. (2000). *Older Americans 2000: Key indicators of well-being.* Washington, DC: Government Printing Office.

Fillenbaum, G. G., Hughes, D. C., Heyman, A., George, L. K., & Blazer, D. G. (1988). Relationship of health and demographic characteristics to Mini-Mental State Examination scores among community residents. *Psychological Medicine, 18,* 719–726.

Frazier, C., Mintz, L. B., & Mobley, M. (2005). A multidimensional look at religious involvement and psychological well-being among urban elderly African Americans. *Journal of Counseling Psychology, 52*(4), 583–590.

Garrett, M. T. (1999). Understanding the "medicine" of Native American traditional values: An integrative review. *Counseling and Values, 43*(2), 84–99.

Hashimoto, A. (1991). Living arrangements of the aged in seven developing countries: A preliminary analysis. *Journal of Cross-Cultural Gerontology, 6,* 359–382.

Hays, P. A. (1996). Culturally responsive assessment with diverse older clients. *Professional Psychology: Research and Practice, 27,* 188–193.

He, W. (2002). *The older foreign-born population of the United States: 2000* (U.S. Census Bureau Current Population Reports, Series P23–211). Washington, DC: Government Printing Office.

Hendricks, J., & Hendricks, C. D. (1986). *Aging in mass society: Myths and realities* (3rd ed.). Boston: Little, Brown.

Himes, C. L., Hogan, D. P., & Eggebeen, D. J. (1996). Living arrangements of minority elders. *Journal of Gerontology: Social Sciences, 51B,* S42–S48.

Hinrichsen, G. A. (2006). Why multicultural issues matter for practitioners working with older adults. *Professional Psychology: Research and Practice, 37,* 29–35.

Hooyman, N. R., & Kiyak, H. A. (1999). *Social gerontology: A multidisciplinary perspective.* Boston: Allyn & Bacon.

Jackson, J. S. (1988). Growing old in Black America: Research on aging Black populations. In J. S. Jackson (Ed.), *The Black American elderly: Research on physical and psychological health* (pp. 3–16). New York: Springer.

Kii, T. (1984). Asians. In E. B. Palmore (Ed.), *Handbook on the aged in the United States* (pp. 201–217). Westport, CT: Greenwood.

Kim, P. K. H. (1990). Asian-American families and the elderly. In M. S. Harper (Ed.), *Minority aging: Essential curricula content for selected health and allied health professions* (DHHS Pub. No. HRS P-DV-90-4, pp. 349–363). Washington, DC: Government Printing Office.

Kinsella, K., & Velkoff, V. A. (2001). *An aging world: 2001* (U.S. Census Bureau, Series P95/01–1). Washington, DC: Government Printing Office.

Kluckhohn, F. R., & Strodtbeck, F. L. (1961). *Variations in value orientation.* New York: Harper & Row.

Knight, B. G. (2004). *Psychotherapy with older adults* (3rd ed.). New York: Russell Sage.

Lacayo, C. G. (1980). *A national study to assess service needs of the Hispanic elderly: Final report.* Los Angeles: Asociación Nacional Pro Personas Mayores.

LaRue, A. (1992). *Aging and neuropsychological assessment.* New York: Plenum.

Leder, D. (2000). Aging into the spirit: From traditional wisdom to innovative programs and communities. *Generations, 23*(4), 36–41.

Markides, K. S., Boldt, J. S., & Ray, L. A. (1986). Sources of helping and intergenerational solidarity: A three generation study of Mexican Americans. *Journal of Gerontology, 41,* 506–511.

McCabe, M., & Cuellar, J. (1994). *Aging and health: American Indian/Alaska Native elders* (2nd ed., Working Paper No. 6). Palo Alto, CA: Stanford Geriatric Education Center.

Miller, B., & Guo, S. (2000). Social support for spouse caregivers of persons with dementia. *Journal of Gerontology: Social Sciences, 55B,* S163–S172.

Morioka-Douglas, N., & Yeo, G. (1990). *Aging and health: Asian/Pacific Island American elders* (Working Paper No. 3). Palo Alto, CA: Stanford Geriatric Education Center.

Myers, J. E., & Harper, M. C. (2004). Evidence-based effective practices with older adults. *Journal of Counseling and Development, 82*(2), 207–218.

National Indian Council on Aging. (1981). *American Indian elderly: A national profile.* Albuquerque, NM: Author.

Phifer, J. F., & Murrell, S. A. (1986). Etiologic factors in the onset of depressive symptoms in older adults. *Journal of Abnormal Psychology, 95,* 282–291.

Ponzo, Z. (1992). Promoting successful aging: Problems, opportunities, and counseling guidelines. *Journal of Counseling and Development, 71,* 210–213.

Ridley, C. R. (1995). *Overcoming unintentional racism in counseling and therapy: A practitioner's guide to intentional intervention.* Thousand Oaks, CA: Sage.

Ridley, C. R., Li, L. C., & Hill, C. L. (1998). Multicultural assessment: Reexamination, reconceptualization, and practical application. *The Counseling Psychologist, 26,* 827–910.

Rowe, J. W., & Kahn, R. L. (1998). *Successful aging.* New York: Pantheon.

Sanchez, C. (1992). Mental health issues: The elderly Hispanic. *Journal of Geriatric Psychiatry, 253*(1), 105–111.

Stanford, E. P., & DuBois, B. C. (1992). Gender and ethnicity patterns. In J. E. Birren, R. B. Sloane, & G. D. Cohen (Eds.), *Handbook of mental health and aging* (pp. 99–117). San Diego: Academic Press.

Starrett, R. A., Rogers, D., & Decker, J. T. (1992). The self-reliance behavior of the Hispanic elderly in comparison to their use of formal mental health helping networks. In T. L. Brink (Ed.), *Hispanic aged mental health* (pp. 157–169). New York: Haworth.

Sue, S., & Morishima, J. K. (1982). *The mental health of Asian Americans.* San Francisco: Jossey-Bass.

Sue, S., Nakamura, C. Y., Chung, R. C. Y., & Yee-Bradbury, C. (1994). Mental health research on Asian Americans. *Journal of Community Psychology, 22,* 61–67.

Tate, N. (1983). The Black aging experience. In R. M. McNeely & J. Cohen (Eds.), *Aging in minority groups* (pp. 95–106). Beverly Hills, CA: Sage.

Taylor, R. J. (1988). Aging and supportive relationships among Black Americans. In J. S. Jackson (Ed.), *The Black American elderly: Research on physical and psychosocial health* (pp. 259–281). New York: Springer.

Tsai, J. L., & Carstensen, L. L. (1996). Clinical intervention with ethnic minority elders. In L. L. Carstensen, B. A. Edelstein, & L. Dornbrand (Eds.), *The practical handbook of clinical gerontology* (pp. 76–106). Thousand Oaks, CA: Sage.

U.S. Bureau of the Census. (2005). *Statistical abstract of the United States: 2004.* Washington, DC: Government Printing Office.

U.S. Department of Health and Human Services. (2001). *Culture, race, and ethnicity: A supplement to the mental health report of the Surgeon General.* Washington, DC: Government Printing Office.

United Nations. (2003, January 15). *The ageing of the world's population.* Retrieved February 5, 2007, from http://www.un.org/esa/socdev/ageing/ageing/agewpop.htm

Vasquez, C. I., & Clavijo, A. M. (1995). The special needs of elderly minorities: A profile of Hispanics. In B. G. Knight, L. Teri, P. Wohlford, & J. Santos (Eds.), *Mental health services for older adults: Implications for training and practice in geropsychology* (pp. 93–99). Washington, DC: American Psychological Association.

Weissert, W. (1983, November). *Estimating the long-term care population.* Paper presented at the annual meeting of the Gerontological Society of America, San Francisco.

Wing, S., Manton, K. G., Stallard, E., Haines, C. G., & Tyroles, H. A. (1985). The Black/White mortality crossover: Investigation in a community-based study. *Journal of Gerontology, 40,* 78–84.

Wong, P. T. P., & Ujimoto, K. V. (1998). The elderly: Their stress, coping, and mental health. In L. C. Lee & N. W. S. Zane (Eds.), *Handbook of Asian American psychology* (pp. 165–209). Thousand Oaks, CA: Sage.

Zamanian, K., Thackery, M., Starrett, R. A., Brown, L. G., Lassman, D. K., & Blanchard, A. (1992). Acculturation and depression in Mexican-American elderly. In T. L. Brink (Ed.), *Hispanic aged mental health* (pp. 109–121). New York: Haworth.

# School Counselors

## Professional Origins in Cross-Cultural Counseling

Susanna A. Hayes and Arleen C. Lewis

---

### *Primary Objective*

- To demonstrate the importance of school counselors' awareness of, respect for, and responsiveness to the cultural worldviews of all students as they maximize educational and social opportunities in K–12 schools

### *Secondary Objective*

- To specify the functions of school counselors based on their responsibilities to serve all students, faculty, parents, and community members in accord with professional standards

---

THE CHAPTER IDENTIFIES THE EDUCATIONAL RATIONALE AND SOCIAL CONDITIONS THAT CONTRIBUTED to the emergence of school counseling in the early 20th century. The services were needed by increasing numbers of culturally diverse students who were immersed in a new educational and social context and required professional counseling support and guidance to facilitate adaptation. As centers for academic training and socialization, public schools serve all students, preparing them to recognize their talents, develop them fully, and contribute to their families and communities. The United Nations High Commissioner for Refugees (www.unhcr.ch) reported that in 2003–2004, as many as 20 million people found asylum in Australia, Western Europe, and the United States. Wars and civil insurrections create great social turmoil and dangers that force people to leave their homes (Castles,

2000). Other conditions that lead to migrations include natural disasters, famine, widespread disease, and economic hardships (Castles, 2000; Castles & Miller, 1998). Additional factors include open and porous borders, increasing transnational identities and affiliations, and the tendency for host nations to blame migrant people for social and economic problems, thereby contributing to multiple migrations (Castles, 2000). Despite great risks, high rates of migration are expected to continue throughout the 21st century.

According to Wrenn (1962), school counselors need a broad education in cultural differences and the rapid changes taking place in economics, geopolitics, and the sciences. As members of educational teams, they help students identify social and academic goals, as well as resolve problems that limit progress toward their achievement. Recognizing that students' orientation to education begins at home, which provides the foundation for subsequent training, counselors facilitate open communications with parents and demonstrate respect for their contributions to students' educational growth. Counselors advocates for culturally relevant curricular offerings, supportive relationships between students and faculty, and positive relationships among students. They facilitate open communications that respect the contributions of all constituents, including students, parents, community members, faculty and staff, and other supportive professionals. This chapter also identifies contemporary criteria for the selection and training of school counselors, including essential cross-cultural counseling skills, comprehensive counseling services, and related evaluation strategies.

## WORLD POPULATION CHANGES IN THE 21ST CENTURY: IMPACTS ON SCHOOL COUNSELORS

The beginning of the 21st century can be characterized as a time when millions of people around the globe followed ancient patterns of migration that were particularly prominent in the late 20th century (Pieterse, 2004). Social, political, and economic upheavals have forced people to leave their homelands in search of safe and hospitable places to live. A major consequence of the migrations is the growing hybridization of societies and the multicultural identities of individuals and groups (Castles, 2000). In Canada, England, France, Germany, Italy, and the United States, as well as other nations, schools enroll increasing numbers of students from culturally diverse families. These families often have pressing social and physical needs as a result of economic and social marginalization, including the inability to speak or understand the language of the majority culture. Students from economically stable families who experience major cultural transitions also need the support of school personnel to successfully pursue their goals and adapt to new environments.

While adjusting and adapting may include unconscious as well as conscious behaviors, students from differing cultures who experience genuine acceptance and inclusion at school gain confidence and feel motivated to achieve (Bruner, 1996). Most people recognize that education is an essential part of preparation for life in the host society. Facilitation of successful social relationships and the integration of culturally diverse students are a major responsibility of school counselors that is shared with teachers and administrators. Among the services counselors provide are the following: orientation sessions for students and parents, faculty mentoring and student-to-student "buddy" programs, and ongoing group guidance and discussion sessions for culturally diverse students in support of their academic progress (Ripley, 2003).

Sojourning students and their families face many physical and economic challenges to their adaptive and coping abilities when settling into a new community. Cultural and economic marginalization may be multigenerational. Those who enter a host society that is similar to their own may adjust and accommodate more easily than those who enter dissimilar communities (Castles, 2000). School personnel, particularly school counselors, can help coordinate the delivery of health care, language training, job finding, housing, and local transportation by implementing a "full-service schools" model especially for traumatized students and family members (Dryfoos, 1994).

In Australia, Canada, and the United States, children born in the host country automatically become citizens, but this is not the case in most of Europe (Castles, 2000). However, citizenship does not eliminate social discrimination. African American or Mexican American citizens in the United States may be less accepted than recent Anglo-European immigrants. Those who appear similar to the majority of the local community, even though culturally different, can blend into the mainstream (Sciarra, 2004). Similarly, aboriginal citizens of colonized nations often experience alienation for many reasons, including differing cultural values and lifeways. They often remain the poorest and least educationally advantaged members of society (Castles, 2000).

The challenges and stresses that culturally different students experience often result in physical and mental health problems (House & Kaplan, 2004). Coping with major transitions can deplete the immune system and psychoemotional resilience. School professionals, teachers, and counselors especially are often the most available source of preventative and rehabilitative services. If school professionals do not offer assistance, it is unlikely that students will receive help from overextended private or publicly funded social service agencies.

## SCHOOL COUNSELOR SERVICES FOR CULTURALLY DIVERSE STUDENTS

Professional counseling associations have emerged to support the growing number of school counselors around the globe. Some examples are the World Counselling Network (http://www.counsel ingnetwork.com), International Association for Counselling (http://www.iac-irtac.org), European Association for Counselling (http://www.eacnet.org), Canadian Counselling Association (http://www .ccacc.ca/ccacc.htm), African Counselling Association (http://www.geocities.com/ kim1122a), American School Counselor Association (http://www.schoolcounselor.org), and New Zealand Association of Counsellors (http://www.newzealand.com). At the Web site of the Canadian Counselling Association, a brief statement articulates the purpose of the association's 2,500 membership. They are dedicated to implementing policies and practices resulting in excellent counseling services that are sensitive to the needs of a pluralistic society. Within this and similar umbrella organizations are specialized counseling subgroups including school counselors. One of the largest organizations is the American School Counselor Association (ASCA), which has a specific focus of supporting the professional development of its 18,000 members worldwide. The ASCA stated that the role of school counselors is helping all students focus on social, academic, and career development for success in their student years and beyond.

A critical and universal problem that is an ongoing challenge to school counselors is the student/counselor ratio in most publicly supported schools (Sciarra, 2004). According to the National Center for Education Statistics, California, with a highly diverse total population of nearly 34,000,000, has student-to-counselor ratios of 951 to 1. Similarly high ratios exist in Minnesota (797/1), Arizona (742/1), Utah (715/1), and Illinois (708/1). The ASCA currently recommends a preferred ratio of 250/1 and indicated that, on average across the United States, the ratio is 478/1. When possible, counselors are urged to work with groups (whole class, large, small) as a service delivery mode to maximize the number of students they can effectively assist.

Like counselors of the early 20th century, professionals today need to help students prepare for and develop skills that will result in secure employment (Castles, 2000).

Frank Parsons (1909), often considered a founder of school counseling in the United States, recognized that helping students understand how to maximize their educational and future career opportunities while they were still in school was more effective than allowing them to quit school because of economic pressures to take any job that augmented their family's income. Other U.S. counselors, such as E. W. Weaver of New York and Jesse Davis in Grand Rapids, Michigan, recognized that most immigrants were struggling in a strange culture and a highly competitive job market (F. Parsons, 1909). At that time, student/counselor ratios were very high, and group approaches were seldom used (Gladding, 2003). Unfortunately, counselor services were scarce for all students, a condition that has yet to be corrected.

Parsons identified two major flaws in the U.S. education system that still persist. There were not enough schools for all eligible students, particularly in low socioeconomic neighborhoods. Consequently, schools failed to implement retention measures so students could gain basic language and math skills (F. Parsons, 1909). These problems persist around the world today, even in wealthy nations where culturally diverse and poor populations lack appropriate educational services (Kozol, 2005). As a result, cycles of poverty within some communities become a life expectation, thereby contributing to social distress and apathetic thinking and behaving.

Harvard University developed courses to train school-based vocational counselors in 1911 in response to Parsons's strong urging (Nugent, 2000). Most of those selected for training were teachers, a trend in school counseling that continues to the present. Counselors were expected to (1) encourage youth to know and understand themselves in terms of aptitudes, interests, and abilities; (2) help youth explore accurate information about careers and vocations; and (3) encourage planning for the future. Emphasis on vocational/career planning remains a common theme globally, especially in high schools (Brown, 2003; Myrick, 2003).

Eventually, counseling services were required for high school accreditation. Socioeconomic changes in the 1950s and 1960s resulted in increased single-parent households and the number of women working outside of the home. This contributed to the need for comprehensive K–12 developmental programs with counselors at all levels (Faust, 1968; Gladding, 2003; Myrick, 2003). In contrast to elementary teachers, who focus on academic instruction, evaluation, and discipline, elementary counselors encourage activities and interactions that respect socioemotional development of the whole person (Dinkmeyer & Dinkmeyer, 1984). Glasser (1998) asserted that school counselors taught problem solving, decision making, and the importance of taking responsibility for one's choices, skills that apply lifelong.

## THE COUNSELOR AS STUDENT ADVOCATE

Helping students realize that school success is a predictor of career success often requires outreach to community employers, who can be role models and mentors. The need to offer effective support for diverse students is reflected in their disproportionately high dropout rates (Bruner, 1996; Dryfoos, 1994). Recent assessments of academic achievement rates among students from low-income families around the world validate that low standards and expectations are precursors of lowered performance rates (Bertrand, 2003). Other indicators include inadequate life management skills, lack of parental support, low self-esteem, lack of involvement in school activities, and lack of cultural pride (Capuzzi & Gross, 2000).

Freedom from school regulations and opportunities to earn money are common reasons for students to leave school, where they feel unsupported and unsuccessful (Bruner, 1996; Dryfoos, 1994). Counselors who seek to ameliorate systemic practices that discourage students engage all participants in the educational process, including parents and community members (Gysbers & Henderson, 1994; Reimer, 1999). Early intervention informs students that their needs are recognized. Such responsiveness may compensate for a lack of concern from the mainstream culture as represented through school curricula and public media that often conflict with cultural norms of diverse students (Jackson, 1999; Lipka, 1998). To maintain their cultural integrity, some students leave school to decrease the pressure to conform to the norms of the mainstream (Jackson, 1999).

## Counselors and Self-Concept

In the United States, a common theme among school counselors in the 1960s was to help students develop behaviors that enhanced self-esteem and contributed to positive self-concepts. Students and educators of the era questioned the quality and purpose of life, which was focused on competition for economic power and high social status (Wrenn, 1962). Counselors applied the humanistic themes of Rogers (1961) and May (1953) to the existential questions that were common among many people around the world. Movements in support of civil rights for minority groups contributed to the rejection of "the establishment" that was considered exploitive of cultural minority groups (Faust, 1968). In the United States, the National Defense Education Act (NDEA) of 1958 and 1965 provided funds for summer institutes that recruited and trained new school counselors. They were expected to resolve intercultural and racial conflicts in schools and increase the educational benefits gained by all groups.

Despite the cultural diversity of student populations, recognition of the importance of lifestyle and value differences was not generally affirmed in school counseling practices, even into the 1980s (Lynch & Hanson, 1992). The focus remained on conventional standards of the social mainstream: high academic achievement, positive self-esteem, vocational exploration and planning, and utilization of life skills such as effective communications and problem solving. Educators and civic leaders failed to understand that members of cultural minority groups were disenfranchised and wanted to be heard and recognized as unique communities with ideals and worldviews of their own (Hackney & Wrenn, 1990; Jackson, 1999). They wanted to be included in the planning and delivery of counseling programs, including counselor selection. Adding to the problem of appropriate counseling services for all students was the underrepresentation of minority groups among professional counselors and counselor educators.

Contemporary counselors retain many conventional professional goals. However, demographic shifts, especially in the late 20th century, have increased the numbers of culturally diverse students in schools. When "minorities" become the "majority" at school, teachers and counselors observe the impact culture has on educational processes and outcomes (Carnegie Task Force, 1986; Fernandez, 1993). Broadly based collaboration with parents and community members resulted in schedules, curricular programs, and extracurricular programs that more closely conformed to local expectations of culturally diverse groups.

There are communities all over the world where cultural "minority groups" comprise a clear majority of the population (Bruner, 1996; Cornelius, 1999; Kawagley, 1995; Lipka, 1998; Reimer, 1999). When all students and faculty learn the skills of interpersonal communication with culturally different people, they are liberated from the misconception that diversity means insurmountable barriers among people (Axelson, 1993). A crucial goal is for students and faculty to realize that diversity contributes to academic and social awareness and enrichment. Essentially, cultural heterogeneity at school reflects the world as it is.

## CONTEMPORARY EMPHASIS: CULTURE AND SCHOOLING

Increased awareness of the influence culture has on learning led more schools to encourage the honoring of diverse cultural traditions at school (Campbell & Dahir, 1997; Sue & Sue, 1999). Counseling strategies, such as adult and peer mentoring, talking circles, and peer mediation that respect individual and group differences, have become increasingly common. Community members from all cultural groups can recommend school practices and policies that are culturally acceptable (Myrick, 2003; Reimer, 1999; Sue & Sue, 1999). When culturally diverse groups have been disenfranchised, they need more than a simple invitation to become engaged with school administrators and faculty. Counselors with the desire and skill to reach out and effectively communicate with parents are able to open doors to active community-school collaboration, resulting in improved holistic education of students.

Given counselor-to-student ratios, generally about 450 to 1 and higher, it is essential that counselors collaborate with other professionals in and outside of school to serve and support culturally diverse students. When students and parents realize that counselors are part of a network of helpers that extends into neighborhoods, demonstrating their concern for students' well-being, bonds with counselors are strengthened. Qualified community helpers who understand students' cultural backgrounds can also enrich curricular and extracurricular program offerings (Hackney, 1990; Myrick, 2003).

Strategically planned group counseling sessions offered by counselors allow diverse students of all ages to increase their awareness and sensitivity to cultural traditions of themselves and their peers (Corey, 2000). Surveys of students, teachers, parents, and community members can reveal interests in activities such as sharing literature, traditional stories, music, dance, sports, and traditional foods. Sponsoring programs that tap real interests increases cross-cultural and cross-generational communications (Baker, 2000; Gysbers & Henderson, 1994). Arts and crafts nights for families, talent shows, story tell-a-thons, plays, musicals, and fitness programs can encourage community and school collaboration and mutual support (Herring, 1997; Myrick, 2003). Such programs are predicated on the belief that schools can be centers of shared learning and enjoyment for the whole community.

## CHANGING SOCIETIES, CHANGING SCHOOLS

There is evidence that in addition to increased cultural diversity in communities, changing social-economic conditions of families require innovations in school counseling and guidance services (Israelashvili, 1998). Substance abuse and other high-risk behaviors require school and community interventions. Changing family structures, gender-role expectations, career options, and technological innovations challenge and reward members of all cultures (Glasser, 1985; Tyler, 1969). School personnel, especially counselors, take on guidance responsibilities that were formerly considered the family's domain (Comer, 1980; Dryfoos, 1994). Increased employment of counselors in elementary and middle schools is a direct response to changes in family life (Baker, 2000; Dinkmeyer & Dinkmeyer, 1984). Teaching students physical and psychological self-care and domestic skills, such as simple meal preparation, usually requires reinforcement at home and school. Athletic coaches or physical education instructors can teach students basic nutrition, plan indoor fitness routines, and identify benefits of avoiding high-risk behaviors that may be common among peers.

Within classrooms, teachers are highly influential as instructors of the core curriculum. Counselors support teachers, particularly when helping them develop behavior management strategies with students who may have serious behavioral problems (Glasser, 1992). If students do not understand English very well or lack the skills to complete assignments, they may feel frustrated and angry. Counselors can interview students and clarify the source(s) of their distress. Similarly, when teachers need help to prepare for conferences with parents, counselors can serve as consultants or join the discussion to facilitate communication. Working as in-school consultants who know student and community needs and expectations, counselors and teachers can develop effective classroom guidance activities that contribute to social understanding and problem-solving skills. Teamwork is especially meaningful for new teachers who need effective mentors as they develop instructional skills (Gladding, 2003).

Despite the intensity or frequency of disruptions at schools, parents expect their students to avoid disciplinary conflicts and achieve academically (Goodlad, 1984). Because few community members observe daily events at school, they may fail to recognize the constant vigilance and monitoring of students' behavior that is required just to maintain physical security (Campbell & Dahir, 1997). In addition, school personnel assume parent-like responsibilities for the socioemotional well-being of every child, thereby reinforcing the need for close school-community relationships, including consultation with various helping professionals such as social workers, school psychologists, physicians, law enforcement personnel, and community health programs.

When entering school, children take an important first step toward responsible community membership (Bronfenbrenner, 1979; Bruner, 1996; Comer, 1980). Elementary counselors help them gain self-confidence, communication skills, and social skills that are essential to forming positive relationships with teachers and peers (Sciarra, 2004). Elementary students who are socially open are eager to participate in learning activities. These are years when teacher-counselor-parent teamwork can result in effective early intervention. Middle school years are critical because students engage in deeper and broader levels of academic and personal exploration. They are expected to make responsible choices and learn to anticipate logical consequences of their behavior. High school students continue to develop personal and academic skills with increased awareness of the connection between school and the work world. Even if they drop out, they need guidance to realize their best career/vocational options (Gysbers & Henderson, 1994). School counselors can identify employers who may provide continuing education and training.

Lazarus (1989) has identified assessment strategies for counselors that relate directly to their goals as effective support personnel. They are as follows: (1) Observe and document students' social and academic behavior over time. (2) Observe and document students' affect over time. (3) Openly communicate with students in and around the school as a way to reach out informally and positively to all. (4) Ask students what they are thinking, feeling, and imagining about their life situations. (5) Listen attentively and respond to what students say. (6) Encourage students to discuss thoughts and beliefs that guide their behavior and relationships. (7) Encourage students to discuss favorable and unfavorable relationship issues. (8) Discuss and encourage preventive actions regarding drugs and substance use that influence students' feelings and behaviors. Based on the information resulting from these assessments of the student population, school counselors can identify the primary goals and objectives for their counseling program.

## Contemporary School Counselor Preparation

Graduate programs in school counseling within the United States, Canada, and most other nations are found primarily in departments of education or psychology. A typical program of study includes counseling theory and techniques, ethics, human growth and development, social and cultural foundations of individual and group behavior, development of career and vocational interests and abilities, group counseling theories and techniques, use of standardized tests and measures in schools, and organization and management of school counseling programs. Depending on accreditation standards, preservice counselors usually complete supervised practica and internships for a term, semester, or year.

The ethical standards of the ASCA require that school counselors provide services that respect individuals and their unique experience, including awareness of and respect for cultural values (ASCA, 2004a, 2004b). The ASCA (2004b) stated the following: "Professional school counselors take action to ensure that students of culturally diverse backgrounds have access to services and opportunities that promote maximum academic, personal/social and career development." Professional school counselors use a variety of strategies to increase awareness of culturally diverse persons and populations, increase sensitivity of students and parents to cultural diversity, and enhance the total school and community climate for all students.

Culturally responsive guidelines are found in the multicultural competencies for counselors and are further elaborated in Arredondo et al. (1996). Professional competencies are organized around counselor self-awareness, clarification of the worldview of culturally different clients, and culturally appropriate intervention strategies and techniques. Counselors adapt their communication skills and professional techniques to effectively serve diverse clients rather than placing the challenge of adaptation on clients.

Cultural competencies for counselors have been endorsed by the Association for Counselor Education and Supervision (ACES), a professional organization of counselor educators from many nations. The Council for Accreditation of Counseling and Related Educational Programs (CACREP) requires that school counseling training programs demonstrate that candidates acquire the knowledge and skills needed to serve diverse students (CACREP, 2001). This includes knowledge of cultural similarities and differences in family life and relationships (see Chapter 24, this volume), values and attitudes, and changes in contemporary cultures. Prospective counselors must have supervised counseling experiences with culturally diverse clients. While CACREP reviews accreditation requests by graduate programs outside of the United States, other associations are developing their own standards. For example, the Canadian Counselling Association (CCACC, 2003) has adopted accreditation and training standards for master's programs in counseling.

While a relatively small number of programs are accredited by CACREP, school counselors worldwide receive training in cultural sensitivity and diversity awareness as specified in mission statements and ethical standards of most counseling associations identified earlier in this chapter. To remain current with professional standards, all school counselors are required to have continuing education experiences that strengthen their ability to counsel diverse clients (Hobson & Kanitz, 1996).

## Contemporary School Counseling Practices

Counselor services encourage students' holistic learning and personal functioning at the highest possible levels. Included are individual and group counseling, classroom guidance, consultation, and program coordination. Appropriate dress codes, school meals, gender-role expectations, communication strategies, and respect for religious/spiritual traditions are areas that school counselors carefully monitor. The overarching principle of cultural awareness and acceptance encourages all students to have a voice and have their ideas and viewpoints respected by counselors, teachers, and peers.

# Individual Counseling

Resources for school counselors interested in cross-cultural counseling have increased significantly over the past few years and include several texts that specifically address issues for school-based professionals (Herring, 1997; Lee, 1995; Pedersen & Carey, 2003). In contrast to the more generic approach to multicultural counseling used in those texts, some educators have focused more on critical incidents that school counselors address in their work. For example, Trusty (1996) developed a model of individual counseling for dropout prevention that includes multicultural counseling. The author proposed that successful interventions include three components: the counselor examines his or her perceptions about schooling, the counselor seeks to understand the unique perspective of students, and the counselor models cultural flexibility through mediation discussions with students, parents, and school personnel.

The Center for Cross Cultural Research (CCCR) at Western Washington University produced the Online Readings in Psychology and Culture (ORPC) (http://www.ac.wwu.edu/~culture/readings.htm) that contains various examples of counselor outreach to culturally diverse clients. There is the danger that school counselors may identify so strongly with the school system that many culturally diverse students assume they cannot relate to other worldviews. When school counselors know and respect student values, they observe warning signs of alienation and take timely and appropriate measures to identify and address students' concerns.

Sojourning and immigrant students may have endured hardships they cannot or choose not to discuss with their counselors. These may include exposure to violence and the vicious brutality of open warfare; being tortured and held in captivity for long periods of time; forced abandonment of family members, home, and possessions; and exposure to physical, psychological, and emotional abuse of themselves and family members. Counselor outreach that expresses empathy and awareness of what the students and their families have endured can help students feel they can turn to the counselor when overwhelmed by symptoms of posttraumatic stress. Great care must be taken to assure these students and their parents that the counselors want to help them meet their needs and find social and physical comfort in their new home.

# Group and Classroom Guidance

Group counseling and classroom guidance also include essential components of cross-cultural sensitivity and adaptability. Group approaches offer a variety of ways to bring together students whose cultural backgrounds may conflict with the school culture and contribute to social distress or behaving contrary to school norms. While research on the efficacy of group interventions with diverse students is limited, Esquivel (1998) reviewed several programs and made the following observations. Interventions that help students enhance their personal identities, develop self-esteem, increase pride in their heritage, and develop bicultural adjustment were helpful. Diverse students succeed when they are involved in planning and designing culturally relevant group activities and become aware that their satisfaction or dissatisfaction with programs or policies may be shared by students from various cultural backgrounds.

In classroom guidance, school counselors, often in collaboration with teachers, plan and present specific lessons in the classroom rather than working with selected students in separate groups. This approach has the potential to reach all students within the school and is particularly suited for increasing intercultural sensitivity schoolwide. These sessions may include presentations by community members from various cultural backgrounds who can offer students suggestions for success at school and in careers and vocations for the future.

## CONSULTATION

Teachers, administrators, support staff, and parents all seek services of the counselor on behalf of students (R. D. Parsons & Kahn, 2005). Cultural variables influence consultation from the initial request for service to the development and execution of an action plan. Since consultation is often a triadic process, cultural differences affect each participant uniquely. Ramirez, Lepage, Kratochwill, and Duffy (1998) have addressed conceptual issues in cross-cultural consultation. They suggested that effective consultants understand particular behaviors and how they are evaluated within the client's culture(s). For school counselors, this means awareness of cultural variables that affect a client's definition of problems and acceptance of strategies that will yield culturally appropriate solutions. Careful attention to nonverbal cues as well as listening to and acting on clients' requests is essential. Asking clients for clarifications when one is unsure of the meaning of a request or statement often communicates more openness and honesty than having a ready response.

## Coordination

As liaisons between schools and community members, school counselors identify resources that are available to help resolve specific problems within a diverse student body. School counselors are in positions to develop comprehensive longitudinal perspectives on students' behavioral and academic achievement patterns. Through frequent use of needs assessments that include input from parents and community members of all cultural groups, counselors develop inclusive needs-based programs. Members of a cultural group may be in the minority (numerically) at school and have traditions that exclude open communication with school personnel, particularly when this involves speaking up at public gatherings. School counselors can seek input from members of these groups so their needs can be effectively addressed (Sue & Sue, 1999).

Experienced school counselors realize the importance of personal outreach to culturally diverse households. Mailed surveys about student counseling needs are not likely to elicit information for program development. This is particularly true if students and parents did not participate in the survey preparation or other aspects of information gathering. Culturally responsive school counselors invite parents and community members to serve as members of their advisory panel that also includes students and faculty (Myrick, 2003). A variety of activities have been found effective when encouraging participation in the planning and maintaining of effective counseling programs. These may include evening meetings preceded by potluck suppers and child care services while parents participate in discussions. Early morning breakfast meetings before parents go to work may also encourage parent input (Lewis & Hayes, 1995).

Most important, all advisers are personally welcomed to meetings, are respected and listened to, and are supported when offering suggestions for improved services. Counselor credibility and effectiveness is enhanced when parent and community input is openly received, discussed, and incorporated into counseling programs as recommended by the advisory board.

As stated above, counseling program goals and objectives are based on comprehensive needs assessments of students' academic, social, and psychological development. It is important that goals and objectives be reviewed by the representative advisers to make certain they are culturally appropriate and responsive to social and educational priorities. Counselors and their advisers are also responsible for planning and conducting program evaluations based on data that indicate if goals and objectives are met. The evaluation database may include the following:

1. counselor records of services and program events such as career fairs, college nights, guest presenters, and field trips;

2. the number and characteristics of students served;

3. the number of individual and group sessions held;

4. school retention rates, especially for groups that have high dropout levels;

5. behavioral observations in classrooms;

6. case studies;

7. pre- and postacademic and social skills assessments;

8. consultations within the school and with community agencies; and

9. constituent feedback gathered by outside interviewers.

The evaluation process and distribution of final reports are crucial ways of informing all constituents, especially culturally diverse students and parents, about counseling program effectiveness.

## ASCA National Model

To assist school counselors in developing programs that promote academic, career, and personal/social development, the ASCA has adopted a comprehensive model that includes the most recent research and updates on programs that have been found highly effective (ASCA, 2005). The National Model emphasized the importance of program planning and accountability. The four major components of the model include foundation (philosophy and mission), delivery system (how the program is implemented), management system (action plans and designated counselor responsibilities), and accountability (measurement of impact on students). The model outlines a sequence of services to all students that coincides with their developmental and educational characteristics.

The model delivery system specifies activities of school counselors according to four general categories: school guidance curriculum, individual student planning, responsive services, and system support. Guidance includes counselor-led instruction, usually in collaboration with teachers, which supports program goals. This may be whole class sessions on topics ranging from intercultural communications to personal goal setting and respectful behavior toward peers and adults at school. Group activities may target positive holistic health care, stress management, and substance abuse prevention. Parent workshops may include topics such as understanding standardized testing or strategies for discussing prevention of substance abuse with their children. Individual student planning may include individual or small-group class selection, after-school internships or job options, and career/vocational planning. Responsive services include activities designed to assist students in crisis such as grief counseling offered individually or in small groups, health consultation with medical staff, referrals to community counseling and helping agencies, and peer problem-solving sessions in response to problems such as bullying or gang activities. System support may include counselor/staff in-service training, editing counselor newsletters, and maintaining counselor Web sites.

# CONCLUSION

There is abundant historical evidence from nations around the world that family life and schooling are primary means of socializing youth. With trends toward expanded globalization, as well as changes in family composition, domestic roles, and patterns of employment, children now spend less time with family members and more time in care centers, preschools, schools, and community-based activity programs. When children enter K–12 school systems, educators assume shared and major responsibilities for their nurturance and holistic education.

School counselors, with a focus on psychosocial and academic aspects of development, are in key positions to teach, model, and reinforce positive interpersonal and cross-cultural relationship skills. The social climate of schools reflects the beliefs, expectations, and behavioral standards of those who manage and sustain the system. School counselors respect and support all members of the school community. They work closely with parents and community groups to identify the social-cultural needs of students and provide services that are culturally and educationally appropriate and effective.

As presented above, the role of the school counselor has evolved to include many functions that contribute to comprehensive school services for the ultimate benefit of students and the community. Where counselors once focused on helping students make career and vocational decisions, contemporary counselors often serve as parent and staff consultants, social-educational coordinators, classroom guidance specialists, parent educators, individual and group counselors, school-community liaisons, substance abuse and violence prevention specialists, and coordinators of emergency response teams. Each school is somewhat unique, depending on the population served and the collective resources of the system. The emphases placed on various aspects of the role also vary considerably. The profession calls for its members to successfully meet challenges that generally contribute to the network of helping professionals who support students' holistic growth and development. With effective preservice education and ongoing school outreach and collaboration with the various cultures represented in the community, school counselors contribute to cross-cultural understanding and all-inclusive multicultural education.

## CRITICAL INCIDENT

This incident is complicated due to the cultural values and lifestyle of the student and the sociocultural environment in which she and her family live. As you read the descriptive information, imagine yourself in the role of the school counselor. The setting is a high school in Dublin, and you are an Irish female who previously taught social studies for several years. "Anisa" is one of your 450 counselees whom you met briefly at a large new student orientation session.

Anisa is in ninth grade and came to Dublin 1 year ago with her father, mother, two young brothers, and her maternal grandmother, a widow. Anisa and all her family were born and raised in Islamabad, Pakistan, and are multilingual. English is the primary language spoken at home. Both mother and father are electrical engineers and are employed in the computer industry. Anisa's parents are Catholic, but her grandmother is Moslem. The parents have good incomes, are well educated, and encourage their children to study and prepare for professional careers. There are relatively few immigrant students in the high school. Most are middle-class to upper-middle-class Dubliners.

Anisa is tall, slender, and has dark hair and a dark complexion. Like her mother and grandmother, she wears a sari as her primary style of dress and usually chooses vibrant colors. Anisa speaks with a British/Pakistani accent, as does everyone in her family. Other Asian students in the school wear

"Western"-style clothing and appear to be integrated into the student population. When she has tried to be more Western in her appearance and behavior, Anisa has felt very awkward. She has a graceful posture, long hair, and striking features.

Anisa is an excellent scholar. One of the highest achieving students in her class, she excels in all areas of the curriculum. Her goal is to enter a top medical school and become a pediatrician to help the many poor children of her home city of Islamabad. Every spare minute she is reading and studying. She is very polite but remains distant with peers and teachers. When she takes time for recreation, she plays with her little brothers. Often they ride bikes or walk in a park near their home.

Recently, one of Anisa's classmates, a native Dubliner, has been attentive to her. "Joseph" talks to her in the hallways and sits near her at lunch time. Other students have observed this and teased Anisa about her new "boyfriend." Some comments are innocuous, but a few have been offensive. Anisa is very uncomfortable with this situation and has been making excuses about feeling ill and not wanting to go to school. Her grandmother lets Anisa stay home, but her parents are much less tolerant of this "avoidance technique."

One day after Joseph invited Anisa to a dance, a male student asked if Joseph might replace her family's arranged suitor. This remark was upsetting, and Anisa could not go into her class. She went to the school library, found a quiet table, and did her homework. When the librarian saw her, she questioned Anisa about missing class. Anisa simply said she did not want to go to class. The librarian went to the phone to check with the school office. Before she hung up, Anisa picked up her books and immediately left school.

The librarian called to her but was not heeded. She immediately went to the school office to report Anisa's absence. The attendance officer called Anisa's mother and reported that she had left school. Her mother agreed to find her daughter and return her to school. In less than an hour, mother and daughter were in the principal's office to discuss the situation. Anisa refused to look up or say anything. This behavior persisted for 15 minutes. When asked if she would be willing to speak with her counselor, Anisa quietly said yes, because it would be less embarrassing than being in the principal's office. After a brief phone call to the counselor, she arrived and escorted Anisa to her office for a private conversation.

## DISCUSSION QUESTIONS

1. What are some of the key elements of cultural stress that Anisa may be experiencing that are related to the differences between life in Islamabad and Dublin?

2. What are some of the possible stresses that Anisa experiences that are developmental in nature and somewhat common to high school students?

3. Is it possible that Anisa's peers and teachers regard her with their cultural stereotypes? What might some of those stereotypes be? Generally speaking, how open are middle-class to upper-middle-class Dubliners to persons from cultures other than their own?

4. Based on what you have read in the chapter, how likely do you think it would be that a student like Anisa would be referred to the counselor *before* she reached the point of discomfort she felt? What kind of services might counselors offer to facilitate cultural understanding and acceptance for both the new students and the host students?

5. If you were Anisa's counselor, what would you say and do when she walked into your office after leaving the principal's office? How likely is it that Anisa would directly identify the problems she is experiencing with her peers?

6. How or when would you want to consult with Anisa's parents? What kind of topics might you discuss with them? Would you tell Anisa that you were going to meet with her parents? Would you invite Anisa to be present at that session? Rationale?

7. Would you consult with Anisa's teachers? What topics or questions might you discuss with them? Would you tell Anisa that you were going to meet with her teachers?

8. What are some cultural factors that may influence Anisa's aloof behavior toward her peers and teachers? What cultural factors might allow her to find commonality with her peers? What cultural factors might guide Anisa's behavior toward male peers who express friendship toward her?

9. Would it be appropriate for Anisa's counselor to arrange for a weekly brief counseling session with her?

10. When might Anisa's counselor suggest possible group sessions for her? What kind of group sessions might the counselor identify as appropriate for Anisa?

# REFERENCES

American School Counselor Association (ASCA). (2004a). *Ethical standards for school counselors.* Alexandria, VA: Author.

American School Counselor Association (ASCA). (2004b). *Position statement: The professional school counselor and cultural diversity* (adopted 1988; revised 1993, 1999, and 2004). Alexandria, VA: Author. Retrieved November 7, 2005, from http://www.schoolcounselor.org/content.asp?contentid=249

American School Counselor Association (ASCA). (2005). *The ASCA national model: A framework for school counseling programs* (2nd ed.). Alexandria, VA: Author.

Arredondo, P., Toporek, R., Brown, S., Jones, J., Locke, D., Sanchez, J., et al. (1996). Operationalization of the multicultural counseling competencies. *Journal of Multicultural Counseling & Development, 24,* 42–78.

Axelson, J. A. (1993). *Counseling and development in a multicultural society.* Pacific Grove, CA: Brooks/Cole.

Baker, S. B. (2000). *School counseling for the twenty-first century* (3rd ed.). Englewood Cliffs, NJ: Prentice Hall.

Bertrand, Y. (2003). *Contemporary theories & practice in education* (2nd ed.). Madison, WI: Atwood.

Bronfenbrenner, U. (1979). *The ecology of human development.* Cambridge, MA: Harvard University Press.

Brown, D. (2003). *Career information, career counseling, and career development.* Boston: Allyn & Bacon.

Bruner, J. (1996). *The culture of education.* Cambridge, MA: Harvard University Press.

Campbell, C. A., & Dahir, C. A. (1997). *The national standards for school counseling programs.* Alexandria, VA: American School Counselor Association.

Canadian Counselling Association (CCACC). (2003). *Accreditation standards and procedures for counselor education programs at the master's level.* Retrieved November 8, 2005, from http://www.ccacc.ca/CACEP.htm

Capuzzi, D., & Gross, D. R. (Eds.). (2000). *Youth at risk: A prevention resource for counselors, teachers, and parents* (3rd ed.). Alexandria, VA: American Counseling Association.

Carnegie Task Force on Teaching as a Profession. (1986). *A nation prepared: Teachers for the 21st century.* New York: Carnegie Forum on Education.

Castles, S. (2000). *Ethnicity and globalization.* Thousand Oaks, CA: Sage.

Castles, S., & Miller, M. J. (1998). *The age of migration.* New York: Guilford.

Comer, J. P. (1980). *School power.* New York: Free Press.

Corey, G. (2000). *Theory and practice of group counseling* (5th ed.). Pacific Grove, CA: Brooks/Cole.

Cornelius, C. (1999). *Iroquois corn in a culture-based curriculum.* Albany: State University of New York.

Council for Accreditation of Counseling and Related Educational Programs (CACREP). (2001). *CACREP accreditation standards and procedures manual.* Alexandria, VA: Author.

Dinkmeyer, D., & Dinkmeyer, D. (1984). School counselors as consultants in primary prevention programs. *Personnel and Guidance Journal, 62,* 464–466.

Dryfoos, J. G. (1994). *Full-service schools.* San Francisco: Jossey-Bass.

Esquivel, G. B. (1998). Group interventions with culturally and linguistically diverse students. In K. C. Stoiber & T. R. Kratochwill (Eds.), *Handbook of group intervention for children and families* (pp. 252–267). Boston: Allyn & Bacon.

Faust, V. (1968). *History of elementary school counseling.* Boston: Houghton Mifflin.

Fernandez, J. A. (with Underwood, J.). (1993). *Tales out of school.* Boston: Little, Brown.

Gladding, S. T. (2003). *Group work: A counseling specialty* (4th ed.). Englewood Cliffs, NJ: Prentice Hall.

Glasser, W. (1985). *Control theory: A new explanation of how we control our lives.* New York: Harper & Row Perennial.

Glasser, W. (1992). *The quality school: Managing students without coercion.* New York: Harper Perennial.

Glasser, W. (1998). *Choice theory: A new psychology of personal freedom.* New York: HarperCollins.

Goodlad, J. I. (1984). *A place called school.* New York: McGraw-Hill.

Gysbers, N. C., & Henderson, P. (1994). *Developing and managing your school guidance program* (2nd ed.). Alexandria, VA: American Association for Counseling and Development.

Hackney, H. (1990). Counselor preparation for future needs. In H. Hackney (Ed.), *Changing contexts for counselor preparation in the 1990's* (pp. 77–93). Alexandria, VA: Association for Counselor Education and Supervision.

Hackney, H., & Wrenn, C. G. (1990). The contemporary counselor in a changed world. In H. Hackney (Ed.), *Changing contexts for counselor preparation in the 1990's* (pp.1–20). Alexandria, VA: Association for Counselor Education and Supervision.

Herring, R. D. (1997). *Counseling diverse ethnic youth: Synergetic strategies and interventions for school counselors.* Fort Worth, TX: Harcourt Brace College Publishers.

Hobson, S. M., & Kanitz, H. M. (1996). Multicultural counseling: An ethical issue for school counselors. *School Counselor, 43*(4), 245–255.

House, J. S., & Kaplan, G. A. (2004). The psychosocial nature of physical health. In J. S. House, F. T. Juster, R. L. Kahn, H. Schuman, & E. Singer (Eds.), *A telescope on society* (pp. 248– 270). Ann Arbor: University of Michigan Press.

Israelashvili, M. (1998). Preventive school counseling: A stress inoculation perspective. *Professional School Counseling, 1*(5), 21–25.

Jackson, R. L. (1999). *The negotiation of cultural identity.* Westport, CT: Praeger.

Kawagley, A. O. (1995). *A Yupiaq worldview.* Prospect Heights, IL: Waveland.

Kozol, J. (2005). *The shame of the nation.* New York: Crown.

Lazarus, A. A. (1989). *The practice of multimodal therapy.* Baltimore: Johns Hopkins University Press.

Lee, C. C. (1995). *Counseling for diversity: A guide for school counselors and related professionals.* Boston: Allyn & Bacon.

Lewis, A. C., & Hayes, S. A. (1995). Accountability in a culturally pluralistic school setting. In C. C. Lee (Ed.), *Counseling for diversity: A guide for school counselors and related professionals* (pp. 173–188). Boston: Allyn & Bacon.

Lipka, J. (1998). *Transforming the culture of schools.* Mahwah, MJ: Lawrence Erlbaum.

Lynch, E. W., & Hanson, M. J. (1992). *Developing cross-cultural competence.* Baltimore: Paul H. Brookes.

May, R. (1953). *Man's search for himself.* New York: W. W. Norton.

Myrick, R. D. (2003). *Developmental guidance and counseling.* Minneapolis, MN: Educational Media Corporation.

Nugent, F. A. (2000). *An introduction to the profession of counseling.* Columbus, OH: Merrill HarperCollins.

Parsons, F. (1909). *Choosing a vocation.* Boston: Houghton Mifflin.

Parsons, R. D., & Kahn, W. J. (2005). *The school counselor as consultant: An integrated model for school-based consultation.* Pacific Grove, CA: Thomson Brooks/Cole.

Pedersen, P. B., & Carey, J. C. (2003). *Multicultural counseling in schools: A practical handbook* (2nd ed.). Boston: Allyn & Bacon.

Pieterse, J. N. (2004). *Globalization and culture: Global mélange.* New York: Rowman & Littlefield.

Ramirez, S. Z., Lepage, K. M., Kratochwill, T. R., & Duffy, J. L. (1998). Multicultural issues in school-based consultation: Conceptual and research considerations. *Journal of School Psychology, 36*(4), 479–509.

Reimer, C. S. (1999). *Counseling the Inupiat Eskimo.* Westport, CT: Greenwood.

Ripley, V. V. (2003). Comprehensive school counseling program manual outline. In B. T. Erford (Ed.), *Transforming the school counseling profession* (pp. 494–498). Upper Saddle River, NJ: Merrill Prentice Hall.

Rogers, C. (1961). *On becoming a person.* Boston: Houghton Mifflin.

Sciarra, D. T. (2004). *School counseling foundations and contemporary issues.* New York: Thomson.

Sue, D. W., & Sue, D. (1999). *Counseling the culturally different: Theory and practice* (3rd ed.). New York: John Wiley.

Trusty, J. (1996). Counseling for dropout prevention: Applications from multicultural counseling. *Journal of Multicultural Counseling & Development, 24,* 105–117.

Tyler, L. E. (1969). *The work of the counselor.* Englewood Cliffs, NJ: Prentice Hall.

Wrenn, C. G. (1962). *The counselor in a changing world.* Washington, DC: American Personnel and Guidance Association.

# PART IV

## Counseling Individuals in Transitional, Traumatic, or Emergent Situations

Globalization, international migration patterns, major and tragic disruptions in the lives of millions, the displacement of millions of others by war and ethnocide (Darfur, for example), and natural disasters such as the Indonesian tsunami and Hurricane Katrina cause much grief and suffering throughout the world. In addition, rather benign and often pleasant and exciting travel for educational reasons can nevertheless create circumstances where some form of counseling is necessary. The four chapters in Part IV cover a number of important topics that often confront mental health professionals.

In Chapter 16, Nancy Arthur provides an excellent overview of a large segment, or subfield, of counseling in the educational arena that features international students. Most nations of the world accept students from different countries at various educational levels. Almost any student who is beginning a new program of study, which usually involves leaving home for the first extended time, is certain to experience enough differences in his or her life to be at least a little unsettling. When traveling to another country and culture, where the language, customs, beliefs, values, learning and performance standards, and so forth will almost certainly vary, adjustments can be severely challenging. The counselor or adviser of international students, therefore, has major professional challenges. Many professional counselors, especially in the United States and several other Western countries, are employed by colleges and universities to work in thriving components that go by such titles as the International Student Advisement Office. Counselors who work in such settings tend to have one overarching goal: to help decrease the "culture shock" the students may be experiencing and at the same time increase the students' intercultural competencies.

*Acculturation* is a general term that encompasses numerous threads of activity in research and application. Colleen Ward, the author of Chapter 17, is an authority in this field. The basic idea of acculturation, as well as its implications for theory and research, has been around for many years. Referring, as it does, to any changes that may result from first-time intercultural contact, one can easily see the importance of work in this area. An essential question that acculturation researchers ask is, "How, when, and why do people adapt to other cultures?" The ABCs of acculturation, which Ward contends constitute its three components, are Affective, Behavioral, and Cognitive. Using this convenient categorization, Ward provides a thorough overview of this domain of research. Currently, it is the "hottest" field of activity in cross-cultural psychology.

Fred Bemak and his colleague Rita Chi-Ying Chung share the honor of coauthoring two chapters in this edition of *Counseling Across Cultures,* the only authors to do so. Considering the nature of the chapters and especially their professional and physical proximity, this makes perfectly good sense. Refugees and migrants, the focus of Chapter 18, make front-page news all the time. Mental health issues and numerous political ramifications constitute highly important topics in contemporary society. They can strain resources and create heated debates that cross international borders. As this book was going to press, for example, the United States began erecting a long fence between the U.S. border with Mexico, thus making a huge statement regarding "illegal" immigration. Often lost in such events, which are usually fueled by ongoing political and economic concerns, is the mental and physical health status of those who are immigrating to improve their lives. A broad range of social issues is involved whenever refugees and migrants become a "problem" in a country.

Even more striking than chronic problems associated with refugees and migrants are acute problems associated with survivors of both human-made and natural disasters. Wars, terrorist activities, airline disasters, earthquakes, fires, tsunamis, massive floods, ethnocide, and mass killing in schools, to name just a few obvious sources of immense human grief and suffering, can stretch mental health counseling beyond their capacities to help. When the cultural component enters the picture, as it often does, effective counseling in the aftermath of tragedies and disasters poses challenges unlike any other that face the professional counselor. In Chapter 19, Bemak and Chung provide a thoughtful and useful overview of the counseling needs in such situations. The disaster cross-cultural counseling model serves as one component of their important chapter.

# Counseling International Students

Nancy Arthur

---

### Primary Objective

- To describe the common and unique aspects of counseling international students

### Secondary Objective

- To (a) outline the relationships between international students' experience of cross-cultural transitions and their counseling needs and (b) suggest ways for counselors to enhance their multicultural counseling roles with international students

---

THE OVERRIDING GOAL OF THIS CHAPTER IS TO HELP COUNSELORS EXPLORE THE COMMON AND unique aspects of counseling students from many countries and cultures around the world. The term *international student* is used to refer to "those students who study at an educational institution outside of their home country" (Arthur, 2005, p. 485). Although the terms *foreign student* and *international student* are often used interchangeably, there are negative connotations related to the term *foreign student*. Moreover, anyone can be considered to be a foreigner, depending on one's cultural point of view (Pedersen, 1991). The chapter is organized into six sections. First, a more extended introduction is presented on the numbers of international students, the problems that some of them present, and the rationale and nature of the services offered to them. Second, a focus on cross-cultural transitions provides counselors with concepts and models for appreciating the complexities of living and learning in another country. Third, a review of common transitions illustrates multiple influences on the adjustment experiences of international students. Fourth, the reentry transition is highlighted to consider relevant counseling issues for supporting international students leaving the host culture and preparing to return home. Fifth, suggestions are given for enhancing multicultural counseling roles in providing services. A case example of Peter, a 24-year-old international student from Nigeria, is woven into the discussion to highlight issues facing international students and to provide some direction for counseling. The chapter ends with a discussion about future directions for enhancing the conceptual and research literature about counseling international students.

## INTERNATIONAL STUDENTS AND COUNSELING SERVICES

At the beginning of this century, it was estimated that 1.8 million international students were enrolled in educational institutions around the world (Bohm, Davis, Meares, & Pearce, 2002). Projections for long-term growth suggest that the numbers of international students could exceed 7,000,000 by 2025 (Bohm et al., 2002). Although most of the counseling literature is directed toward international students in higher education, attention must also be paid to the growing number of adolescent students who study abroad (Kuo & Roysircar, 2006). Beyond recruitment efforts, educational institutions must provide services that support international students while living and learning in local communities.

Counselors have key roles in helping international students to integrate into local school and community environments. Counselors work with international students directly to support their learning and personal needs, as well as collaboratively with other campus personnel for an integrated approach to student services. For example, counselors work with academic staff, residence advisers, and medical personnel to better understand the common and unique issues faced by international students, as well as provide consultation and referral services. Counselors may be called upon by other members of educational settings to directly assist international students, to intervene for students, or to provide consultation about programs and policies. Counselors also need to be prepared for addressing more serious mental health issues as the stress associated with adjustment issues may exacerbate psychiatric issues and psychological problems with international students, estimated to be as high as 20% in the general population (Leong & Chou, 2002). Serious mental health crises as psychotic breaks, suicide attempts, schizophrenia, serious depression, and anxiety-phobia syndromes are also encountered within the international student population (Oropeza, Fitzgibbon, & Baron, 1991), and counselors need to be prepared for culturally sensitive assessments and intervention plans in these situations.

Counselors require a framework for delivering services that integrates an understanding of internationalization concepts and practices with multicultural counseling competencies (Arthur, 2003a). Five key areas have been suggested for counselors to enhance their responsiveness in counseling international students (Arthur, 2005):

1. Increase knowledge about emerging theories and models of cross-cultural transitions

2. Gain knowledge about the common demands faced by international students

3. Enhance multicultural competencies, including self-awareness, knowledge, and skills

4. Learn ways to be proactive about engaging international students in counseling programs and services

5. Expand counseling roles to include advocacy for addressing systemic barriers and improving institutional policies and practices that affect international students

# LEARNERS IN TRANSITION

A key characteristic of international students is that they are people in cross-cultural transition (Arthur, 2003a; Pedersen, 1991). Due to their immigration status, they are sojourners in a host country for the duration of their academic program. There are multiple reasons that lead students to pursue international education, and factors in a student's home culture have a major bearing on subsequent adjustment. The degree of voluntariness, pressures for mobility, and permanence of crossing cultures are linked to the acculturation process, referred to as the psychological changes that result from efforts to adapt during cross-cultural transition (Berry, 1997, 2001). In Peter's case, he represented the academic elite of his country and was awarded scholarships to study abroad. Other students may be less academically inclined and are motivated by travel and cultural exchange opportunities. Other mitigating factors such as parental pressure to study abroad, impending military service, or community sponsorship represent pretransition influences that can affect students' adjustment. Premigration factors and conditions in the home country can weigh heavily on students. For example, Peter was often preoccupied about family relationships at home, and he felt a tremendous sense of responsibility for academic success. Other students may perceive their sojourn as an opportunity to break away from usual constraining conditions at home and enjoy opportunities to live contrasting lifestyles.

Cross-cultural transition involves a process over time through which individuals experience a shift in personal assumptions about themselves, others, or the world around them (Schlossberg, 1984, 1992). International education is a catalyst for personal learning as students try new types of food, transportation, living arrangements, climate changes, entertainment, social relationships, and academic curriculum. However, exposure to new cultural norms can trigger dissonance about one's personal culture and require role adjustment (Ishiyama, 1995a, 1995b; Pedersen, 1991). New social and academic roles require international students to shed their typical ways of behaving in those roles, and there is immediate pressure to learn new ways of interacting. At the same time, physical distance prevents students from accessing the roles and relationships that usually provide them with sources of self-validation, social status, or social support (Ishiyama, 1995a, 1995b). When there are major disruptions to familiar roles, routines, and relationships, international students may experience loss or confusion about their personal identity. Adjustment difficulties typically arise when there are greater differences in practices between the home and host cultural environments (Pedersen, 1991).

## Culture Shock During Transitions

As part of a normal reaction during cross-cultural transition, students typically experience culture shock that manifests in psychological or physiological symptoms of stress (Oberg, 1960; Ward, Bochner, & Furnham, 2001; Winkelman, 1994). The original portrayal of culture shock outlined the stages of contact with the host culture, conflict with the host culture, and adaptation to the host culture, represented by a U-curve pattern of adjustment (Lysgaard, 1955). These three stages were elaborated in a W-curve model to represent adaptation to the upward and downward shifts in morale and to accommodate an additional stage of adjustment when people returned to their home culture (Gullahorn & Gullahorn, 1963). Research has disputed the linearity of these models and the lack of attention to individual differences (Furnham & Bochner, 1986; Leong & Chou, 2002). Recent perspectives on culture shock suggest that the stages or phases may be sequential or cyclical, depending on the individual's experience. International students may cope with some aspects of their situation effectively and struggle to manage other aspects that they perceive as overtaxing (Arthur, 2003a; Chen, 1999). Portrayals of culture shock have been quite negative, suggesting that student responses are maladaptive, as opposed to natural responses that involve cultural learning (Berry, 1997; Huxur, Mansfield, Nnazor, Schuetze, & Segawa, 1996).

Pedersen (1995) outlines four phases in a model of culture shock. During the initial tourist phase, international students are typically excited by their new discoveries and learning about cultural differences. For example, Peter was initially very enthusiastic about studying in Canada. The novelty of the experience helped Peter to frame the stress associated with cross-cultural transition in positive ways. However, in the next phase of disintegration, a turning point occured when Peter began to experience dissatisfaction about aspects of life in Canada. Peter began to perceive the local culture as a source of irritation. His morale seemed to plunge, and he attempted to cope through shutting himself off from the host culture. However, his strategy of withdrawal resulted in a crisis for Peter that was characterized by a paradox. As he was reacting negatively to his experience, Peter realized that he was dependent on interactions in the host culture for academic and personal success. When Peter made contact with a counselor, he was considering returning home, and this preoccupation was disruptive for focusing on his academic program. Counseling with Peter initially involved helping him articulate the specific aspects of the host culture that were overtaxing and to identify aspects of his transition experience that he was mastering and enjoying.

The adjustment or reorientation phase (Pedersen, 1995; Winkelman, 1994) occurred when Peter shifted from a position of cultural and personal crisis to integrating his cultural learning and appreciation for aspects of the host culture. Students typically try out new ways of coping with cultural contrasts in this phase and feel more successful about their efforts to solve problems. With some encouragement, Peter became involved in a student organization on campus that led to more social interaction, and eventually he took on a leadership role. The fourth phase of culture shock reflects a higher degree of adaptation in managing cross-cultural transition. As Peter built his sense of mastery for interacting in the host environment, he also experienced more success with and enjoyment of his academic program. The focus of counseling changed as Peter was keen to explore ways to incorporate learning about both home and host cultures in developing a bicultural identity (Helms, 1995).

## Less Stress, Better Coping

Counseling from a framework of stress and coping (Lazarus & Folkman, 1984) involves helping international students increase their capacity for managing the perceived demands of living and learning across cultures (Chen, 1999). Inadequate coping resources can have serious consequences for students' academic success and their mental health. Perceived demands such as the pace of change, academic preparation, language competencies, loss of usual support systems, and immediate demands for cultural adaptation may lead students to react in survival mode, while feeling overwhelmed with debilitating stress (Mallinckrodt & Leong, 1992; Wan, Chapman, & Biggs, 1992). Based on a transactional model of stress (Lazarus, 1990, 1993), appraisals of stress include harm (the psychological harm that has already occurred), threat (anticipation of unwelcome consequences), and challenge (positive aspects of dealing with new opportunities). In Peter's case, although he was excited about new learning opportunities, he also felt overwhelmed by all of the new changes he was encountering. His initial sense of excitement shifted to anxiety as he focused on the threat of academic and personal failure. Counseling with Peter involved helping him to identify how his existing repertoire of coping skills and resources could apply across cultures (Ryan & Twibell, 2000). Peter admitted that he missed his peer group and extended family, who gave him strong social support. Counseling involved helping Peter learn about local resources while providing some skill training about social interactions in the local context. Taxonomies developed to address life transitions (Lazarus & Folkman, 1984; Schlossberg, 1984, 1992), career transitions (Brammer & Abrego, 1992), and cross-cultural transitions (Arthur, 2000; Winkelman, 1994) are useful resources for assessing students' coping resources and for targeting skill training to meet their transition needs.

## The Process of Enculturation

The cross-cultural transition and adjustment issues faced by international students may also be understood as a process of enculturation (Popadiuk & Arthur, 2004). Ho (1995) defines enculturation as the process of "how people are actually exposed to, learn from, and are influenced by the culture to which they are exposed" (p. 5) and makes an important distinction between cultural group membership and internalized culture. Factors outside of the individual such as manner of dressing, food, customs, and organized religion are examples of external culture. In contrast, an individual's specific beliefs, attitudes, and ways of thinking are associated with internalized culture. There is a risk that counselors will stereotype international students according to their cultural group membership, which actually tells us very little about what people are experiencing during cross-cultural transitions. Instead of assuming that international students from the same cultural group have homogeneous needs, it is important for counselors to attend to individual differences and consider how students have internalized values and beliefs into their unique internalized culture. Popadiuk and Arthur (2004) provide examples to illustrate how international students from similar geographical locations in the world hold fundamentally different belief and value systems that affect their decisions and subsequent actions.

## COMMON TRANSITION ISSUES

International students face many of the issues commonly experienced in the general student population such as living away from home for the first time, course selection and registration, adjusting to a new academic environment, and making new friends (Hayes & Lin, 1994; Popadiuk & Arthur, 2004). To describe their experiences as totally separate from other students perpetuates the stereotype that international students are problem laden and that the source of their problems is internal and isolates them from other learners (Popadiuk & Arthur, 2004). Alternatively, counselors may frame adjustment issues as those common to all students, those common for anyone living in a foreign culture, and those that are unique to international learners (Furnham & Bochner, 1986; Leong & Chou, 1996).

Sandhu (1994) organizes the predominant types of concerns affecting international students into (a) interpersonal factors related to their environment and surroundings and (b) intrapersonal factors related to internal processes. Although these factors are separated, in reality there is a great deal of overlap between transition issues, and internal and external factors have reciprocal influences (Arthur, 2003a). For example, when Peter initially sought counseling, he was struggling to establish new friendships, and he lacked social supports for managing the stress associated with academic performance pressures, but he hesitated to initiate social interaction due to fears about making mistakes (Misra, Melanee, & Burant, 2003). As he gained confidence about initiating peer contact, he felt more connected to class discussions and began to feel more motivated about his academic program. To illustrate the overlapping nature of transition issues, the three domains of academic concerns, interpersonal interactions, and career planning are highlighted.

# Academic Concerns

Academic concerns are often paramount for international students (Walker, 1999). Students may feel additional pressure to succeed academically to meet the expectations of immediate and extended family or the terms of financial sponsorship from government or foreign aid. Academic concerns may also emerge due to prior academic preparation, adjusting to new instructional methodology, and workload issues. Teaching and learning methods based on constructivist and discovery methodology may be challenging for students who are used to didactic method of instruction (Barker, Child, Gallois, Jones, & Callan, 1991; Sheehan & Pearson, 1995). Most authors highlight language proficiency as the most critical factor related to the academic and social adjustment of international students (Hayes & Lin, 1994).

It should not be assumed that all international students present a deficit, as some of them may be disappointed by the standards of the host country in comparison to their prior academic preparation (Thomas & Althen, 1989). For example, Peter was initially disappointed at the lack of challenge in his academic program, and he found that the curriculum lacked global applications. He began to feel discouraged when he perceived that his expertise was not valued, and he began to question how he could transfer learning from his academic program to his home country. When his grades began to drop, he experienced intense pressure about the implications of academic failure and losing his immigration status. He perceived the consequences of expulsion from an academic program as potentially devastating. A lot of his anxiety seemed to be associated with rumination about future consequences for family relationships, employment, and loss of status.

# Social Relations

In the transition to a new country, international students often leave behind their usual social network of family and friends, and this loss can result in intense feelings of homesickness (McKinlay, Pattison, & Gross, 1996). Peter described his joy at receiving e-mail messages from friends or family back home but struggled on days when there was no news from them. He often felt lonely, and he missed holiday celebrations with family. Although he was reluctant, Peter began to realize the importance of creating new sources of social support. Peter did not have the issues associated with language proficiency that affects the social adjustment of many international students (Huxur et al., 1996; Ying & Liese, 1990). Research has suggested that confidence in using acquired language skills is a stronger predictor of individual differences in adjustment than actual language ability (Swagler & Ellis, 2003). Therefore, it is important for international students to overcome anxiety about using language skills and try out experiences in which they can gain more confidence about their abilities. In turn, greater language proficiency helps students to be flexible about the ways they communicate and adapt to alternate communication styles. This capacity for social decentering (Redmond & Bunyi, 1993) helps international students to be less concerned about social inappropriateness and allows them to focus on learning new social cues for communication. Intercultural competence influences the acculturation process and students' experience of stress (Wilton & Constantine, 2003).

Peter initially found his contacts with classmates to be problematic. Unfortunately, students in the host culture are often less motivated and unprepared to bridge cross-cultural friendships (Hayes & Lin, 1994). Negative experiences may lead international students to seek out other students who share language and other cultural similarities (Schmitt, Spears, & Branscombe, 2003; Walker, 1999). Peter agreed to participate in a program designed to facilitate international friendships. Such programs support students to go beyond superficial contacts, overcome language barriers, explore diverse values, and develop meaningful interactions (Furnham & Alibhai, 1985; Nesdale & Todd, 2000).

International students may experience dissonance about appropriate gender behavior when they are exposed to cultural contrasts that include either more liberal or more traditional attitudes (Arthur, 2005; Oropeza, et al., 1991). Research on gender differences in the experiences of international students suggests that females experience greater levels of distress (Mallinckrodt & Leong, 1992), but they also hold more liberal attitudes than males about the rights and roles of women (Gibbons, Stiles, & Shkodriani, 1991). These results suggest that females may see the advantages of living in liberal settings where women enjoy more personal rights and freedom but experience role confusion and role conflicts with family expectations for more traditional behavior. In turn, males from traditional cultures may be challenged about notions of power and male privileges when living in more liberal cultural contexts.

It was no accident that Peter preferred to talk to a female counselor. In his home culture, it would be easier for him to openly seek emotional support from his mother or a close aunt. Gender influences were also relevant to counseling when Peter discussed his efforts to make friends and begin dating. He was often confused by the behavior of local women who were far more liberal in public than he was accustomed to during interactions at home. He found it difficult to interpret their social cues and know what behavior indicated friendship versus pursuing a more intimate relationship. Peter's willingness to discuss these issues was a positive sign of a solid therapeutic relationship. At the same time, the counselor was careful to be explicit about the role of counseling and boundaries on the counseling relationship. Due to the interpersonal nature of counseling, it is important to articulate the nature of a counseling relationship to ensure that misunderstandings do not occur due to different cultural assumptions.

The social relations of international students are strongly influenced by the receptivity of members of the host educational institution and local educational institution. Unfortunately, negative stereotypes about people from nondominant racial and ethnic minority groups can be directed at international students. Experiences of discrimination and racism may be unexpected (Dei, 1992; Sandhu & Asrabadi, 1994), particularly when students move to countries such as Canada that are known for national policies on multiculturalism. Depending on the social stratification in home countries, life as an international student may represent the first time that a student has been in a minority group (Schmitt et al., 2003) or has been confronted with racist reactions from others.

Peter was dismayed at the stereotypes his instructors held about his home culture as he had never considered that he was from an "undeveloped" country. He was also alarmed when he heard his classmates refer to him as "the black guy." Peter was used to life in an upper-class family and had previously enjoyed many social privileges. The counselor supported Peter in naming these incidents as forms of racism and took seriously his observations about the lack of responsiveness by faculty to his learning needs. The counselor reviewed the campus policy on discrimination and helped Peter to develop strategies for responding to inappropriate comments from his classmates. Furthermore, the counselor helped Peter to rehearse for meeting with his academic supervisor. Consequently, Peter was invited to join a research project that was directly related to his learning goals and provided him with a new level of academic challenge.

## Career Planning

The lack of attention paid to the career planning needs of international students is surprising, considering that the choice of studying in another country is an important career decision, and many students are seeking ways to enhance employment opportunities (Shih & Brown, 2000; Singaravelu, White, & Bringaze, 2005). The career-related needs of undergraduate and graduate students differ due to the stage of specialization and focus in their career preparation (Mallinckrodt & Leong, 1992;

Shen & Herr, 2004). Arthur (2007) suggests that counselors organize career planning programs and services to assist international students in three phases of the transition process: (a) managing the cross-cultural transition of entering a new culture, (b) learning in a new cultural context, and (c) transferring international expertise to work settings in either the host or home countries.

In the first phase, international students are involved in career planning and decision making through investigating study-abroad opportunities, enrolling in higher education, selecting an academic program, and developing strategies for academic success. Counselors should not assume that the career plans of international students are well defined as these plans may not be consolidated by the individual or be realistic (Singaravelu et al., 2005).

In the second phase, international education provides students with cultural learning through exposure to new curriculum and lifestyles that may lead students to confirm their original vocational pathways or, alternatively, pose dilemmas about what options to pursue for their future (Singaravelu et al., 2005). In Peter's case, dissatisfaction with the local culture led him to question the suitability of his academic major. Career counseling interventions were useful to help Peter see that his interests and abilities were well suited for his current academic program. The focus of counseling then turned to helping Peter explore values clarification.

In the third phase, new career development issues may emerge when students approach the end of their foreign education. For example, many students decide to pursue employment in the host country and benefit from exploring the implications of such decisions and from exploring resources for job search (Shen & Herr, 2004). When international students plan to return home, they are receptive to career services for job searching and learning ways to transfer their foreign education to the local setting (Spencer-Rodgers, 2000).

These examples illustrate the necessity for international students to acquire career and life planning skills as key components of managing their cross-cultural transition (Arthur, 2007). If the main motives for studying abroad are linked to academic and employment success, then from the time of arriving in the host country, students should be preparing for their eventual return home, including their future career plans. Career counseling is an important intervention to help international students plan for their current and future career choices (Leong & Sedlacek, 1986; Shih & Brown, 2000; Yi, Lin, & Kishimoto, 2003). However, there is a need for more research to ascertain factors that influence international students' career decisions, the stability of their career choices, and what factors help them to persist in attaining their academic and career goals (Singaravelu et al., 2005).

## REENTRY TRANSITION ISSUES

Reentry refers to the reacculturation of the individual to the home culture after an extended period of exposure to another culture (Adler, 1981). The reentry transition needs to be considered within the context of the entire cross-cultural experience (LaBrack, 1993; Martin & Harrell, 1996). However, the reentry transition is different from the initial stage of transition to the host culture in three ways (Martin, 1984). First, international students expect that there will be a period of adjustment when students enter a new culture. However, they may not expect that there will be any adjustments to returning home to a familiar environment. This leaves many students and significant people in their lives unprepared for reverse culture shock (Gaw, 2000). Second, there are varying amounts of change involved between stages of cross-cultural transition (Martin & Harrell, 1996). International students are rapidly immersed into the new culture of the host country and often expect to experience dramatic change. Conversely, international students may be unprepared for the amount of change in the home culture. Students may have strong reactions about any dramatic changes or, conversely, the lack of change that has occurred during their absence. Third, the awareness of change may only surface upon the students' return (Adler, 1981). International students may only realize how much they have changed after a period of interacting with family and friends at home.

The reentry transition is considered to be more than physically relocating home; it involves the psychological process of adapting to the home culture. Research suggests that a myriad of issues may emerge during reentry transitions, including a sense of loss, employment and career mobility, continuing education, transferability of educational and language skills, resuming prior relationships, and gender-role conflict (Arthur 2003a; Brabant, Palmer, & Gramling, 1990; Pedersen, 1990). Preparation for the reentry transition benefits students through anticipatory coping and dealing with reverse culture shock (Arthur, 2003b).

Peter experienced another surge of anxiety and returned to counseling 3 weeks before returning home. Although Peter looked forward to reuniting with family and friends, he was worried about how he could continue many of the things he now enjoyed with restricted access to such opportunities at home. With prolonged exposure to the host culture, Peter had developed a sense of attachment and belonging that led to a profound sense of loss about leaving Canada. He needed to talk about how he now viewed his home culture, and counseling focused on ways for Peter to incorporate his new level of self-awareness into life at home. Reframing reentry as going to his "new home" helped him be open-minded about the impending transition.

## MULTICULTURAL COUNSELING WITH INTERNATIONAL STUDENTS

Counselors are challenged to examine their repertoire of multicultural counseling competencies for working with learners from other countries and from diverse cultural backgrounds. Counselors may have little preparation through counselor education curriculum for working with international learners and may resort to trial-and-error practices. Unfortunately, there are still various misconceptions and stereotypes about this group portrayed in the professional literature (Pedersen, 1991), and there is evidence of negative attitudes expressed by personnel who work in educational settings (Dei, 1992). As a starting point for self-awareness, counselors need to reflect about their attitudes toward working with international students from particular cultural backgrounds in order to consider how their personal beliefs may inadvertently bias professional relationships.

It is also important for counselors to be knowledgeable about the main-source countries of international students attending local schools. This knowledge is the starting place for developing general cultural understanding; however, there are variations in the experiences of students from the same country. When counselors treat international students as a homogeneous group, they risk ignoring key issues such as gender, race, religion, and history that are essential for understanding the transition experiences of individual students (Popadiuk & Arthur, 2004).

Counselors need to consider several key questions in organizing culturally responsive services for international students (Popadiuk & Arthur, 2004): (a) How do international students negotiate their transition experience when they live and learn in a foreign country that is very different from their own? (b) How are counseling services best organized to meet their transition needs? (c) How can counselors address the needs of international students, especially those from non-Western or emerging nations, in a manner that is relevant, effective, and ethical? (d) How can counselors be proactive in facilitating the positive adaptation of international students in cross-cultural transition? (e) How can counselors work collaboratively to enhance referral and service delivery? (f) How can counselors participate in strategic planning for improving the organizations and systems that affect international students?

## Improving Access and Satisfaction
## With Counseling Services

Depending on the availability of services in their home countries, many international students are unfamiliar with professional counseling. Improving access to counseling services appears to be dependent on two factors: (1) the profile that counselors build within the international student population and (2) positive relationships with academic and student support staff such as international student advisers, who are often the first points of contact for students requesting help. Counselors who participate in student orientations and who interact informally with international students are more likely to be viewed as approachable for counseling (Arthur, 2003a). Other students may be more comfortable accessing medical personnel, particularly students from cultures where stress tends to be expressed through physical symptoms, rather than through admitting incompetence or personal problems (Lin & Yi, 1997; Mallinckrodt & Leong, 1992).

The literature on utilization rates shows conflicting results, but there is some evidence that international students are less likely than local students to access counseling beyond a single session (Anderson & Myer, 1985). These results may be explained by cultural barriers to problem solving and help seeking (Brinson & Kottler, 1995; Sandhu, 1994) and by misunderstandings about the purpose of counseling (Arthur, 2003a). Counselors must be prepared to take proactive approaches to help hesitant students to access services and then to acknowledge students positively for seeking help (Hayes & Lin, 1994; Sandhu, 1994). Pretherapy orientation helps students understand the purpose of counseling and derive greater benefit from it (Leong & Chou, 2002).

Frequently, international students seek immediate solutions for crisis management and problem-solving issues associated with cross-cultural transition (Hayes & Lin, 1994). Counselors need to be able to respond to students' immediate concerns, help them to access relevant resources, and invite them to continue using counseling services as needed. Counseling style has been identified as an influential factor with clients, although caution is indicated about stereotyping international students as preferring one particular style (e.g., directive or nondirective). Preferences for counselor style may be based on cultural norms about hierarchical relationships, and students may feel more comfortable working with the counselor as an expert or authority (Mori, 2000). However, there is contrary evidence suggesting that some groups of international students prefer a nondirective style of counselor intervention (D'Rozario & Romano, 2000; Yau, Sue & Hayden, 1992). As students gain experience with the host culture, they may become more comfortable in working in more collaborative ways.

Although many international students benefit from campus and community resources to help them manage their adjustment difficulties, exclusive reliance on a problem-focused approach to counseling services is limiting. Pedersen (1991) noted that "it is important for counselors working with international students to broaden their understanding of counseling beyond narrowly defined methods and contexts" (p. 29). Multicultural counseling with international students involves taking on the role of a cultural therapist (Dei, 1992). This requires counselors to be knowledgeable about how adjustment difficulties are connected to learning in new cultural contexts. Popadiuk and Arthur (2004) argue that services for international students need to be strengthened with mandates for health promotion and illness prevention. Counselors can take leadership in designing innovative service approaches that include options such as marketing counseling services through videotapes and information delivered online, health education to international students to debunk myths about counseling and mental health issues, ongoing consultation and collaboration with international student service staff, customizing counseling by including nontraditional strategies, and facilitating positive relationships between international students and other members of the campus community (Brinson & Kottler, 1995; Popadiuk & Arthur, 2004). Group interventions are an important method of service delivery for key topics such as culture shock, skills for success, interpersonal relations, and reentry transition. The advantages of psychoeducational workshops are that information can be shared by the instructor and students can learn alternate perspectives and problem-strategies from each other. Workshops provide opportunities for international students to get to know counseling staff, informally discuss their concerns, and facilitate self-referral for future counseling needs. Counselors may be able to identify and support students who have more urgent needs for counseling (Leong & Chou, 2002).

Group interventions for international students must be designed carefully to increase attendance and relevance for international student participants (Arthur, 2003a, 2003b). Planning considerations include collaboration with other student services staff, consulting with international student leaders, carefully selecting the timing and format of group interventions to increase access by students, and considering the advantages and disadvantages of culturally similar versus culturally heterogeneous groups. Counselors who facilitate groups must be knowledgeable about the topic but also have strong facilitation skills, particularly in providing structure and support to international students, in understanding expectations and easing communication between participants. Training tools such as critical incidents, vignettes, and role-plays can be incorporated to focus the content of workshops while supporting the unique contributions of international student participants.

## Topics for Future Research

Researching the experiences of international students has made great strides, but it needs to be extended to new topics. There has been little investigation of the positive aspects of international student resiliency and of their contributions to the host environment (Popadiuk & Arthur, 2004). Aggregate research methods such as surveys result in the treatment of international students as a homogeneous group and risk misunderstandings about both the unique and common concerns associated with transition issues (Jacob & Greggo, 2001). Some researchers have chosen to do research with specific ethnic groups within the international student population, such as Asians (e.g., Kuo & Roysircar, 2006; Lin & Yi, 1997). However, counselors are cautioned lest they succumb to ethnic stereotypes on the basis in research that does not take into account levels of acculturation and thus makes subgroups of international students appear more homogeneous than they are in reality (Popadiuk & Arthur, 2004). In a review of literature on counseling international students, Leong and Chou (2002) note that attention has been concentrated on client variables, and they call for a shift in emphasis in both theory and practice to focus on therapist and counseling process variables.

## CONCLUSIONS

The literature reviewed for this chapter has emphasized the process of cross-cultural transition as a guiding framework for understanding international students' counseling needs. International students require a comprehensive approach to service delivery that takes into account pretransition factors, their experience of adjustment upon entering the host culture, new demands that surface while they live and learn in new cultural contexts, and the transition experience of leaving the host culture and returning home. Counselors have a key role in helping international students to build local support networks and acquire new coping skills. To do so, counselors are encouraged to examine emerging models of cross-cultural transitions in order to gain insight into the complexity of experiences faced by international students living and learning in a new culture and preparing to return home. Counselors are also encouraged to enhance their competencies for counseling international students through accessing current frameworks of multicultural counseling (e.g., Arredondo et al., 1996; Arthur & Collins, 2005; Sue et al., 1998), both for working individually or for improving organizational and systemic structures. At an organizational level, counselors need to be proactive through strategic planning, contributing to campus internationalization planning, campus education, and raising a positive profile about international students (Arthur, 2003a). These examples illustrate the importance of creativity and innovation in thinking about counseling and expanding counselors' roles to address the concerns of international students.

It is impossible to address all of the issues experienced by international students and all of the strategies available for designing and delivering multicultural counseling with this diverse group of learners. Further suggestions for enhancing counseling competencies for working with international students are contained in recently published books (e.g., Arthur, 2003a; Singaravelu & Pope, 2007). Finally, counselors are encouraged to share their professional experiences in counseling international students, including dilemmas and innovative practices, through contributing to the professional literature and through exchange of ideas in professional development forums.

## CRITICAL INCIDENT

### Counseling International Students

Mai was a 20-year-old female international student from China who was in the first year of a business administration program. Mai attended an orientation for international students, during which a counselor gave a presentation about culture shock and counseling services on campus. At the time, Mai was very excited to be able to study in another country, and she did not think she would experience any culture shock. However, 3 months later, she began to feel overwhelmed about her situation. She found it much more difficult to learn course material when everything was presented in English. She was often confused by the instructions given by her professors and was uncertain about their expectations. Mai would read the assigned course material until 1:00 or 2:00 a.m., but many times, her professors did not use this material in class. She was surprised to find out that other students interrupted their professors or talked at the same time. Although Mai prepared for classes, she found it hard to participate in class discussions. Mai spent any of her spare time with two other students from China. She was becoming increasingly exhausted but often found it difficult to sleep. She began experiencing severe headaches. During an appointment with a campus physician, it was suggested that Mai talk to a counselor.

Mai arrived at the counseling appointment with one of her friends and asked if they both could see the counselor. The counselor agreed, thinking that the issue might be about relationships. However, when the counselor asked Mai what she wanted to talk about, Mai said that she and her friend wanted to learn more about depression. Mai stated, "I have heard that many local students experience depression at school. We do not know what this term means but it sounds very serious. I looked on the Internet for some information but it was confusing. I am worried that the doctor I saw thinks that something is really wrong with me. Do you think that I am depressed?"

The counselor asked Mai to describe her symptoms. Indeed, many of them such as worrying, difficulty sleeping, and the resulting headaches seemed to be related to depression. However, Mai seemed very distressed about the possibility that depression might be the diagnosis. The counselor asked Mai and her friend what they thought her symptoms would mean if she had them in China. Mai said that she would talk to her family about how she was feeling and they would advise her. When the counselor asked Mai if she had consulted with her family, she looked at the floor and replied, "No, I want them to think that I am doing well here." The counselor asked Mai some more questions about her life in Canada, and they spent the rest of the hour talking about her academic program. At the end of the hour, Mai and her friend thanked the counselor for her time. Mai did not show up for a second scheduled counseling appointment.

## DISCUSSION QUESTIONS

1.  What counseling roles and activities facilitate the positive integration of international students? In what ways might these roles and activities enhance services for all students while addressing the unique needs of international students?

2.  What are some of the ways that ethical issues such as confidentiality, gift giving, and professional boundaries might become more complex when counseling international students?

3.  Discuss the advantages and disadvantages of assigning a specialist counselor versus expecting that all counselors are prepared to work with international students.

4.  If an international student expresses a desire to remain in the host country, what are the issues that may need to be explored in making such a decision?

5.  Describe how you would introduce the aims and goals of counseling to a group of international students. Furthermore, how could counselors attempt to strengthen the therapeutic alliance with individual students whose help-seeking beliefs conflict with seeking formal assistance from a counselor?

6.  What are the advantages and disadvantages of including significant others, including peers, in counseling sessions with international students? What ethical issues, including confidentiality, need to be considered when counseling international students?

7.  What are the indicators from this scenario that Mai is experiencing symptoms associated with culture shock? How could the counselor introduce this topic to normalize Mai's experience while focusing on her unique concerns?

8.  What suggestions do you have for building an effective working alliance between the counselor and Mai?

9.  Based on more thorough assessment information, the counselor believes that Mai might be experiencing depression. How can the counselor manage effective treatment given her professional knowledge about treating depression, taking into consideration Mai's cultural background?

10.  What factors might have led to Mai's decision about not attending the second counseling appointment?

11.  What are the implications of this scenario for counselors in building effective working relationships for interprofessional practice?

## REFERENCES

Adler, N. J. (1981). Re-entry: Managing cross-cultural transitions. *Group and Organizational Studies, 6,* 341–356.

Anderson, T., & Myer, T. (1985). Presenting problems, counselor contacts, and "no shows": International and American college students. *Journal of College Student Personnel, 26,* 500–503.

Arredondo, P., Toporek, B., Brown, S. P., Jones, J., Locke, D. C., Sanchez, J., et al. (1996). Operationalization of the multicultural counseling competencies. *Journal of Multicultural Counseling and Development, 24,* 42–78.

Arthur, N. (2000). Career competencies for managing cross-cultural transitions. *Canadian Journal of Counseling, 34,* 204–217.

Arthur, N. (2003a). *Counseling international students: Clients from around the world.* New York: Kluwer Plenum.

Arthur, N. (2003b). Preparing international students for the re-entry transition. *Canadian Journal of Counseling, 37*(3), 173–185.

Arthur, N. (2005). Counseling international students. In N. Arthur & S. Collins (Eds.), *Culture-infused counseling: Celebrating the Canadian mosaic* (pp. 483–509). Calgary, Canada: Counseling Concepts.

Arthur, N. (2007). International students' career development and decisions. In H. Singarvelu & M. Pope (Eds.), *Handbook for counseling international students* (pp. 37–56). Alexandria, VA: American Counseling Association.

Arthur, N., & Collins, S. (Eds.). (2005). *Culture-infused counseling: Celebrating the Canadian mosaic.* Calgary, Canada: Counseling Concepts.

Barker, M., Child, C., Gallois, C., Jones, E., & Callan, V. J. (1991). Difficulties of overseas students in social and academic situations. *Australian Journal of Psychology, 43*(2), 79–84.

Berry, J. W. (1997). Immigration, acculturation, and adaptation. *Applied Psychology: An International Review, 46*(1), 5–68.

Berry, J. W. (2001). A psychology of immigration. *Journal of Social Issues, 57,* 615–631.

Bohm, A., Davis, D., Meares, D., & Pearce, D. (2002). *Global student mobility 2025: Forecasts of the global demand for international higher education.* Sydney, NSW: IDP Education Australia.

Brabant, S., Palmer, C. E., & Gramling, R. (1990). Returning home: An empirical investigation of cross-cultural reentry. *International Journal of Intercultural Relations, 14,* 387–404.

Brammer, L., & Abrego, P. (1992). Counseling adults for career change. In H. D. Lea & Z. B. Leibowitz (Eds.), *Adult career development: Concepts, issues, and practices* (2nd ed., pp. 90–101). Alexandria, VA: National Career Development Association.

Brinson, J. A., & Kottler, J. (1995). International students in counseling: Some alternative models. *Journal of College Student Psychotherapy, 9*(3), 57–70.

Chen, C. P. (1999). Common stressors among international college students: Research and counseling implications. *Journal of College Counseling, 2,* 49–65.

D'Rozario, V., & Romano, J. L. (2000). Perceptions of counselor effectiveness: A study of two country groups. *Counseling Psychology Quarterly, 13*(1), 51–63.

Dei, G. J. (1992). *The social reality of international post-secondary students in Canada.* Ottawa: Canadian Bureau for International Education.

Furnham, A., & Alibhai, N. (1985). The friendship networks of foreign students: A replication and extension of the functional model. *International Journal of Psychology, 20,* 709–722.

Furnham, A., & Bochner, S. (1986). *Culture shock: Psychological reactions to unfamiliar environments.* London: Methuen.

Gaw, K. F. (2000). Reverse culture shock in students returning from overseas. *International Journal of Intercultural Relations, 24,* 83–104.

Gibbons, J. L., Stiles, D. A., & Shkodriani, G. M. (1991). Adolescents' attitudes toward family and gender roles: An international comparison. *Sex Roles, 25,* 625–643.

Gullahorn, J., & Gullahorn, J. (1963). An extension of the U-curve hypothesis. *Social Issues, 19,* 33–47.

Hayes, R. L., & Lin, H. (1994). Coming to America: Developing social support systems for international students. *Journal of Multicultural Counseling and Development, 22,* 7–16.

Helms, J. E. (1995). An update of Helm's White and People of Color racial identity models. In J. G. Ponterotto, J. M. Casas, L. A. Suzuki, & C. M. Alexander (Eds.), *Handbook of multicultural counseling* (pp. 181–198). Thousand Oaks, CA: Sage.

Ho, D. Y. F. (1995). Internalized culture, culturocentrism and transcendence. *The Counseling Psychologist, 23*(1), 4–24.

Huxur, G., Mansfield, E., Nnazor, R., Schuetze, H., & Segawa, M. (1996). Learning needs and adaptation problems of foreign graduate students. *Canadian Society for the Study of Higher Education, 15,* 1–16.

Ishiyama, F. I. (1995a). Culturally dislocated clients: Self-validation and cultural conflict issues and counseling implications. *Canadian Journal of Counseling, 29,* 262–275.

Ishiyama, F. I. (1995b). Use of validationgram in counseling: Exploring sources of self-validation and impact in personal transition. *Canadian Journal of Counseling, 29,* 134–146.

Jacob, E. J., & Greggo, J. W. (2001). Using counselor training and collaborative programming strategies in working with international students. *Journal of Multicultural Counseling and Development, 29,* 73–88.

Kuo, B. C. H., & Roysircar, G. (2006). An exploratory study of cross-cultural adaptation of adolescent Taiwanese unaccompanied sojourners in Canada. *International Journal of Intercultural Relations, 30*(2), 159–183.

LaBrack, B. (1993). The missing linkage: The process of integrating orientation and reentry. In R. M. Paige (Ed.), *Education for the intercultural experience* (pp. 241–280). Yarmouth, ME: Intercultural Press.

Lazarus, R. (1990). Theory-based stress measurement. *Psychological Inquiry, 1*(1), 3–13.

Lazarus, R. (1993). From psychological stress to the emotions: A history of changing outlooks. *Annual Review of Psychology, 44,* 1–21.

Lazarus, R. S., & Folkman, S. (1984). *Stress, appraisal, and coping.* New York: Springer.

Leong, F. T. L., & Chou, E. L. (1996). Counseling international students. In P. B. Pedersen, J. G. Draguns, W. J. Lonner, & J. E. Trimble (Eds.), *Counseling across cultures* (4th ed., pp. 210–242). Thousand Oaks, CA: Sage.

Leong, F. T. L., & Chou, E. L. (2002). Counseling international students and sojourners. In P. B. Pedersen, J. G. Draguns, W. J. Lonner, & J. E. Trimble (Eds.), *Counseling across cultures* (5th ed., pp. 185–207). Thousand Oaks, CA: Sage.

Leong, F. T. L., & Sedlacek, W. E. (1986). A comparison of international and U.S. student preferences for help sources. *Journal of College Student Personnel, 27,* 426–430.

Lin, J. C. G., & Yi, J. K. (1997). Asian international students' adjustment: Issues and program suggestions. *College Student Journal, 31*(4), 473–479.

Lysgaard, S. (1955). Adjustment in a foreign society: Norwegian Fulbright grantees visiting the United States. *International Social Science Bulletin, 10,* 45–51.

Mallinckrodt, B., & Leong, F. T. (1992). International graduate students, stress, and social support. *Journal of College Student Development, 33,* 71–78.

Martin, J. N. (1984). The intercultural reentry: Conceptualization and directions for future research. *International Journal of Intercultural Relations, 8,* 115–134.

Martin, J. N., & Harrell, T. (1996). Reentry training for intercultural sojourners. In D. Landis & R. S. Bhagat (Eds.). *Handbook of intercultural training* (2nd ed., pp. 307–326). Thousand Oaks, CA: Sage.

McKinlay, H. J, Pattison, H. M., & Gross, H. (1996). An exploratory investigation of the effects of a cultural orientation programme on the psychological well-being of international university students. *Higher Education, 31,* 379–395.

Misra, R., Melanee, C., & Burant, C. J. (2003). Relationships among life stress, social support, academic stressors, and reactions to stressors of international students in the United States. *International Journal of Stress Management, 10*(2), 137–157.

Mori, S. (2000). Addressing the mental health concerns of international students. *Journal of Counseling & Development, 78,* 137–144.

Nesdale, D., & Todd, P. (2000). Effect of contact on intercultural acceptance: A field study. *International Journal of Intercultural Relations, 24,* 341–360.

Oberg, K. (1960). Cultural shock: Adjustment to new cultural environments. *Practical Anthropology, 7,* 177–182.

Oropeza, B. A. C., Fitzgibbon, M., & Baron, A. J. (1991). Managing mental health crises of foreign college students. *Journal of Counseling & Development, 69,* 280–284.

Pedersen, P. (1990). Social and psychological factors of brain drain and reentry among international students: A survey of this topic. *McGill Journal of Education, 25,* 229–243.

Pedersen, P. (1991). Counseling international students. *The Counseling Psychologist, 19,* 10–58.

Pedersen, P. (1995). *The five stages of culture shock.* Westport, CT: Greenwood.

Popadiuk, N., & Arthur, N. (2004). Counseling international students in Canadian schools. *International Journal for the Advancement of Counseling, 26*(2), 125–145.

Redmond, M. V., & Bunyi, J. M. (1993). The relationship of intercultural communication competence with stress and the handling of stress as reported by international students. *International Journal of Intercultural Relations, 17,* 235–254.

Ryan, M. E., & Twibell, R. S. (2000). Concerns, values, stress, coping, health and educational outcomes of college students who studied abroad. *International Journal of Intercultural Relations, 24,* 409–435.

Sandhu, D. S. (1994). An examination of the psychological needs of students: Implications for counseling and psychotherapy. *International Journal for the Advancement of Counseling, 17,* 229–239.

Sandhu, D. S., & Asrabadi, B. R. (1994). Development of an acculturative stress scale for international students: Preliminary findings. *Psychological Reports, 75,* 435–448.

Schlossberg, N. (1984). *Counseling adults in transition: Linking practice with theory.* New York: Springer.

Schlossberg, N. (1992). Adult development theories: Ways to illuminate the adult development experience. In H. D. Lea & Z. B. Leibowitz (Eds.), *Adult career development: Concepts, issues, and practices* (2nd ed., pp. 2–16). Alexandria, VA: National Career Development Association.

Schmitt, M. T., Spears, R., & Branscombe, N. T. (2003). Constructing a minority group identity out of shared rejection: The case of international students. *European Journal of Social Psychology, 33*(1), 1–12.

Sheehan, O. T., & Pearson, F. (1995). Asian international and American students' psychosocial development. *Journal of College Student Development, 36*(6), 522–530.

Shen, Y., & Herr, E. L. (2004). Career placement concerns of international graduate students: A qualitative study. *Journal of Career Development, 31*(1), 15–29.

Shih, S., & Brown, C. (2000). Taiwanese international students: Acculturation level and vocational identity. *Journal of Career Development, 27*(1), 35–47.

Singaravelu, H., & Pope, M. (2007). *Handbook for counseling international students.* Alexandria, VA: American Counseling Association.

Singaravelu, H., White, L., & Bringaze, T. (2005). Factors influencing international students' career choice: A comparative study. *Journal of Career Development, 32*(1), 46–59.

Spencer-Rodgers, J. (2000). The vocational situation and country of orientation of international students. *Journal of Multicultural Counseling and Development, 28,* 32–49.

Sue, D. W., Carter, R. T., Casas, J. M., Fouad, N. A., Ivey, A. E., Jensen, M., et al. (1998). *Multicultural counseling competencies: Individual and organizational development.* Thousand Oaks, CA: Sage.

Swagler, M. A., & Ellis, M. V. (2003). Crossing the distance: Adjustment of Taiwanese graduate students in the United States. *Journal of Counseling Psychology, 50,* 420–437.

Thomas, K., & Althen, G. (1989). Counseling foreign students. In P. B. Pedersen, J. G. Draguns, W. J. Lonner, & J. E. Trimble (Eds.), *Counseling across cultures* (3rd ed., pp. 205–241). Honolulu: University of Hawaii Press.

Walker, J. L. (1999). *Canada first: The 1999 survey of international students.* Ottawa: Canadian Bureau for International Education.

Wan, T., Chapman, D. W., & Biggs, D. A. (1992). Academic stress of international students attending US universities. *Research in Higher Education, 33,* 607–623.

Ward, C., Bochner, S., & Furnham, A. (2001). *The psychology of culture shock* (2nd ed.). East Sussex, UK: Routledge.

Wilton, L., & Constantine, M. G. (2003). Length of residence, cultural adjustment difficulties, and psychological distress symptoms in Asian and Latin American international college students. *Journal of College Counseling, 6*(2), 177–187.

Winkelman, M. (1994). Cultural shock and adaptation. *Journal of Counseling and Development, 73,* 121–126.

Yau, T. Y., Sue, D., & Hayden, D. (1992). Counseling style preference of international students. *Journal of Counseling Psychology, 39,* 100–104.

Yi, J., Lin, G., & Kishimoto, Y. (2003). Utilization of counseling services by international students. *Journal of Instructional Psychology, 30*(4), 333–342.

Ying, Y. W., & Liese, L. H. (1990). Initial adaptation of Taiwan foreign students to the United States: The impact of prearrival variables. *American Journal of Community Psychology, 18,* 825–845.

# 17

# The ABCs of Acculturation

## Implications for Counselors

Colleen A. Ward

---

*Primary Objective*

- To provide a conceptual framework for understanding the acculturation experience and discuss its application in the context of counseling

*Secondary Objective*

- To familiarize students with empirical research on acculturating people and to highlight the importance of the sociocultural context of counseling

---

ACCULTURATION IS A WORLDWIDE PHENOMENON. ONE HUNDRED AND SEVENTY-FIVE MILLION PEOPLE now live outside of their country of origin (United Nations, 2002). But changes arising from intercultural contact are not confined to people who relocate across cultures, such as sojourners, immigrants, and refugees. Acculturation affects indigenous peoples who have been subject to involuntary colonization as well as established ethnocultural communities in multicultural societies (Berry & Sam, 1997). Intercultural contact and change are also important issues for majority groups in societies that

---

*Author's Note:* This chapter was completed during the author's tenure as James Cook Fellow in Social Science. The author would like to thank the Royal Society of New Zealand for their generous support.

are becoming increasingly culturally diverse. This chapter will consider issues confronted by acculturating people and the implications of these issues for counseling professionals.

## ACCULTURATION

Acculturation refers to the changes that result from continuous firsthand intercultural contact (Redfield, Linton, & Herskovits, 1936). Although it was first studied at the cultural level in the anthropological context and related to macro social change, it has more recently been examined at the individual level and considered by psychologists who have investigated its antecedents, correlates, and outcomes (Berry, 1997). Acculturation itself is a neutral process; the changes arising from intercultural contact may be positive or negative. For example, contact with other cultures may result in an individual developing a broader range of cultural skills, better relationships with members of other ethnocultural groups, and a stronger sense of "world-mindedness." On the other hand, intercultural contact can result in "culture shock," intergroup anxiety, and identity conflict. Unfortunately, the term *acculturation* is often misused in the psychological literature and taken to represent assimilation, the process by which nondominant or minority ethnocultural groups are assimilated into the dominant culture in a society, often shedding their cultural heritage to take on the characteristics of the contact culture.

Acculturating groups may be distinguished on at least three dimensions: mobility, permanence, and voluntariness (Berry & Sam, 1997). First, people who have made cross-cultural relocations, such as refugees, asylum seekers, immigrants, and sojourners, may be distinguished from members of sedentary groups in a society, such as native peoples and established ethnocultural communities. Second, cross-cultural travelers who resettle temporarily, such as sojourners, differ from those, such as immigrants and refugees, whose move is more permanent. Finally, those who voluntarily engage in intercultural contact (e.g., immigrants, sojourners, and ethnocultural groups) may be distinguished from those who are forced by necessity into involuntary interactions (e.g., refugees, asylum seekers, and indigenous peoples).

Marked differences in the acculturation process are known to emerge across these three dimensions. For example, groups who are involuntarily subjected to culture contact and change, such as refugees and native peoples, tend to suffer more mental health problems than voluntary sojourners and migrants (Berry, Kim, Minde, & Mok, 1987). Identity issues, changing sense of self, and shifting values appear to be less troublesome issues for short-term, compared to long-term, migrants (Ward & Kennedy, 1993). Groups who relocate across cultures are likely to experience more acute stress than sedentary populations, although both are likely to confront chronic stressors (Zheng & Berry, 1991). These distinctions will be discussed in greater detail in the following sections. The major objective of this chapter, however, is to identify themes and issues that are relevant for acculturating people in general and to offer conceptual frameworks for understanding the acculturation experience in a way that may be applied in the context of counseling and related therapeutic interventions.

## THE ABCS OF ACCULTURATION: AN OVERVIEW FOR COUNSELORS

There are three major conceptual frameworks for understanding the acculturation experience, including the problems and challenges faced by acculturating individuals and the issues that are most likely to bring them into contact with counseling professionals. The first is linked to psychological models of stress and coping and applied largely to the study of cross-cultural transition and adaptation. This model is particularly relevant to the acculturation experiences of sojourners, immigrants, and refugees and highlights the processes underlying psychological adaptation and well-being. The second model reflects a culture learning approach, which places emphasis on the social psychology of the intercultural encounter and the processes involved in learning the culture-specific skills required to thrive and survive in an intercultural context. This model underpins the sociocultural adaptation of acculturating persons and may be applied not only to short- and long-term migrants learning the skills required to operate effectively in a new cultural environment, but also to any individual or group developing intercultural competencies, including counselors who practice with multicultural clients. The third model is associated with social identification theories and is concerned with the way people perceive and think about themselves (their identity) and others (intergroup relations), including how they process information about their own group (ingroups) and other groups (outgroups). Theory and research in this area can help counselors understand and interpret conflicts arising from two or more cultural perspectives, such as identity conflict, conflict over new and old cultural values, and generational conflict in acculturating families.

The theoretical underpinnings of all three approaches have been "borrowed" from mainstream social and health psychology but applied specifically to understanding the experiences of acculturating individuals. Together, these three approaches constitute the ABCs of acculturation. *Affective* components of acculturation are highlighted in the stress and coping approach, *behavioral* elements are featured in the culture learning approach, and *cognitive* variables are emphasized in the social identity approach. While the first approach is of more direct and obvious relevance to counseling processes and will receive relatively more attention in this chapter, all three are useful for counselors who deal with acculturating clients.

## STRESS AND COPING: IT'S ALL ABOUT CHANGE

> It's an emotional adjustment to all of the changes, all of a sudden, in your routine. (A Canadian woman describing life in South America, *A portable life,* 1981)

> There were a couple of days when I woke up, I hated everything I saw. (A Canadian student in Costa Rica, *World within reach,* 1995)

The stress and coping framework conceptualizes cross-cultural transition as a series of stress-provoking life changes that draw on adjustive resources and require coping responses. This approach has been strongly influenced by Lazarus and Folkman's (1984) work on stress, appraisal, and coping, as well as earlier theory and research on life events (Holmes & Rahe, 1967). The analytical framework is broad and incorporates both characteristics of the individual and characteristics of the situation that may facilitate or impede adjustment to a new cultural milieu. Accordingly, researchers seeking to identify the factors that affect the adjustment of acculturating persons, particularly their psychological well-being and satisfaction, have examined many of the same variables as those who investigate stress and coping in other domains. These include life changes, cognitive appraisal of change, coping strategies, and social support. With respect to more culture-specific variables, cultural distance, cultural identity, and acculturation status have also been considered in sojourner, immigrant, and refugee populations (Ward, 1996).

Although the stress and coping framework may be applied to interpreting the acculturation experience of anyone who finds intercultural contact stressful, it has been particularly useful in interpreting the experiences of sojourners and new immigrants in relation to the life changes associated with relocation to a new culture. It is well known that any life changes, whether positive and desirable or negative and unwanted, evoke stress and require adjustive responses. One way of quantifying the amount of stress experienced or the extent of readjustment required has been the Social Readjustment Rating Scale (Holmes & Rahe, 1967), which is accompanied by standardized life change units (LCUs) for 43 life events. Research has indicated that recent exposure to between 200 and 300 LCUs results in a 50% risk of major illness, and over 300 is associated with an 80% risk factor. Analyses have also suggested that exposure to the life changes routinely connected with migration—such as change in living conditions, change to new line of work, change in residence, and change in social activities—exceed 300 LCUs, making new migrants vulnerable to stress-related disorders (Furnham & Bochner, 1986).

While relocation may be stressful for everyone, relocating across cultures appears particularly challenging. Young and Evans's (1997) research compared recently arrived and settled Salvadoran refugees and Anglo-Canadians in London, Ontario, Canada, and found that the former reported poorer quality of life and lower life satisfaction. Not only the changes but also the individual's appraisal of significant life events is important. Zheng and Berry (1991) examined the evaluation of potential stressors by Chinese sojourners in Canada and by Chinese and non-Chinese Canadians. Chinese sojourners tended to view language and communication, discrimination, homesickness, and loneliness as more problematic than either Chinese or non-Chinese Canadians. It is likely that the appraisal of stress is a function of cultural distance, that is, the extent of similarity-dissimilarity between the culture of origin and the culture of contact. For example, in a study of Asian and Western international students in New Zealand, Jose, Liu, and Ward (2007) found that the former reported the experience of the same recent life events more stressful than the latter.

Central to acculturation outcomes are the coping processes individuals rely on to deal with the challenges faced by living and working in a new and unfamiliar cultural context. While there are many ways to categorize coping responses, one of the most commonly used taxonomies is the distinction between problem-focused and emotion-focused strategies. Research with British expatriates in Singapore indicated that problem-focused strategies such as planning and active coping were associated with lower levels of depression, while emotion-focused strategies, including denial, venting, and disengagement, predicted more depressive symptoms. Coping with humor also predicted decrements in depression (Ward & Kennedy, 2000). Similarly, "active" coping was linked to less depression and "withdrawal" coping to greater depression in migrant Chinese adolescents in Hong Kong (Tam & Lam, 2005).

An alternative to this analysis of coping styles is the distinction of primary and secondary coping, sometimes also referred to as direct and indirect coping. Primary strategies parallel active, problem-solving responses; they are direct actions aimed at changing noxious aspects of a stress-provoking environment. Secondary strategies, however, are more cognitive than behavioral and commonly involve changing perceptions and appraisal of stressful events and situations. The efficacy of secondary strategies, particularly in collectivist cultures, has been well documented, and research on acculturative stress has also indicated that secondary strategies (acceptance and positive reinterpretation) exert a direct effect on perceived stress, which, in turn, affects psychological outcomes (Ward, Leong, & Kennedy, 1998). This is not surprising as sojourners and migrants are less likely to be able to change aspects of their new culture than to change their perceptions of it. Or, as stated by an American expatriate in Hong Kong, "You just have to smile and go with it, 'cause you are not going to change it. It's just going to be that way" (*Going international,* 1983).

What are the emotional experiences associated with culture contact and change? In the words of an expatriate from the United States in Asia, "You get a little depressive, you get a little aggressive, you maybe react wrong" (*Going international,* 1983). The emotional reactions have been discussed at great length in reference to short-term migrants, where a popular conceptualization of "culture shock" suggests that emotional reactions follow a U-curve, commencing with "entry euphoria," followed by a rapid decline in positive emotions and an eventual improvement in affect. However, even classic reviews of the phenomenon agree that the evidence for this trend is "weak, inconclusive and over-generalized" (Church, 1982, p. 542). Indeed, from a stress and coping perspective, psychological distress and negative emotions should peak on entry, when life changes are greatest and social support systems are likely to be at their lowest. This has been borne out in longitudinal studies, which have shown decrements in psychological well-being not only between predeparture and arrival in a new country (Furukawa & Shibayama, 1993) but also between entry and 4 months after arrival (Ward, Okura, Kennedy, & Kojima, 1998). This does not mean, however, that acculturation distress will typically lead to newcomers seeking psychological intervention in the early stages of transition; it may be more chronic adaptation problems that eventually precipitate help seeking.

The "entry crisis" often found in sojourners may not be observed in every acculturating group. The temporal pattern of acculturation and adjustment of refugees has been debated in light of their involuntary displacement, housing in transitory camps, and eventual resettlement in another location. While there is some suggestion that refugees experience a sense of relief upon arrival at their final destination, research has shown that the first 18 months after resettlement are still the highest risk period for psychological disorders (Chung & Kagawa-Singer, 1993).

Refugees have additional issues of premigration trauma, including a sense of loss for people and places left behind, as well as many unresolved issues connected to their forced departure.

> I feel isolated, worry about the children I left behind and my long illness—all of these make my life useless and not worth living. I am always depressed. I am worried about social fragmentations with my children and relatives back home. I have a sense of loss of my origins and purpose in life. (Iranian refugee in the United Kingdom, Duke, 1996, p. 473)

In fact, refugees are perhaps the most disadvantaged of all relocating groups as (1) they have overwhelmingly stressful premigration experiences in their country of origin; (2) migration is involuntary and motivated by "push" factors; (3) displacement is usually permanent; (4) refugees are generally underresourced with the skills required to make a successful cross-cultural transition, such as language proficiency or financial security; and (5) refugees, at least those resettled in Western nations, are likely to originate from culturally distant countries. Given this, it is not surprising that refugees exhibit more mental health problems than immigrants, sojourners, and members of the receiving society or that there is a relatively high rate of clinical problems, particularly posttraumatic stress disorder, in refugee populations (Ward, Bochner, & Furnham, 2001).

Although the stress and coping approach has been largely applied to sojourners, new immigrants, and refugees in the analysis of their reactions to acute stressors, it may be argued that it is equally applicable to indigenous peoples who have suffered chronic stressors and deprivation as individuals and communities as a consequence of contact with colonizers. Indeed, this is highlighted in Trimble and Gonzalez's chapter on counseling Native Americans (see Chapter 6, this volume), where historical trauma is seen as underpinning unresolved grief and contributing to problems such as alcoholism, suicide, homicide, domestic violence, and child abuse. This line of thinking is shared among many indigenous peoples. In 2000, Tariana Turia, the then Associate Minister of Maori Affairs, suggested at the New Zealand Psychological Society Annual Conference that the indigenous peoples suffered from "postcolonization stress disorder," contributing to psychological and social dysfunction in Maori communities.

In the main, stress and coping approaches to acculturation parallel stress and coping analyses of other life events, and as such, individuals' resources and deficits are important. Age, gender, and socioeconomic status affect adjustment outcomes, although research results are not always clear-cut. Many studies report that refugee and migrant women have a greater risk of psychological symptomatology, but this is not uniformly the case (Ward et al., 2001). In all probability, the outcomes are a function of the specific mental health indicators used in the research. Sam's (1994) study of adolescent migrants in Norway found that boys were more likely to report antisocial behaviors while girls were more likely to display depressive symptoms—findings that are consistent with intracultural gender differences in psychopathology.

With respect to age differences, Beiser et al. (1988) have suggested that adolescence and old age are high-risk periods. In the first instance, the stress of migration may be intertwined with the stress of adolescent development and identity; in the latter instance, it may be that older people have fewer psychological resources for coping with change. Education, occupational status, and income also influence the stress and coping process, and high levels of these generally function as stress-buffering factors. In contrast to the positive influences of higher socioeconomic status (SES), cultural distance has a debilitating effect on the psychological well-being of acculturating persons. The finding that psychological adjustment problems increase as culture of origin and culture of contact become more dissimilar has been consistently replicated across a range of acculturating groups (Ward et al., 2001).

Social support is one of the most important resources in coping with acculturative stress and is known to predict both psychological adjustment and physical health. Social support may arise from a variety of sources, including family, friends, and acquaintances. Stone Feinstein and Ward (1990) found that the quality of the spousal relationship was one of the most significant predictors of psychological well-being of American women sojourning in Singapore. On the other hand, marital difficulties can increase psychological distress in acculturating persons. Ataca (1996) observed that marital stressors were significantly related to psychological adaptation problems, including anxiety, depression, and psychosomatic complaints, in Turkish migrants to Canada.

Friends and acquaintances also provide sources of social support, although there is some debate as to the effectiveness of various sources. Having local friends and more frequent social contact with host nationals have been associated with a decrease in psychological problems, better life satisfaction, and better general adaptation of sojourners and immigrants (Berry et al., 1987; Furnham & Li, 1993). It is also widely recognized that host national contact facilitates culture-specific learning, also required for cross-cultural adaptation. Conational supports can likewise be very helpful to sojourners and immigrants (Berry et al., 1987). However, there is also research that suggests "cultural bubbles" can be a source of alienation and that a greater amount of time spent with conationals is associated with psychological dissatisfaction. In these instances, it is likely that conational "support" is located in cultural ghettos of dissatisfied foreigners, stifling morale and leading to more adjustment problems. This has been discussed by Adelman (1988) as a contagion effect and described by an Australian woman living in Guinea, Africa, as "depression is a very infectious thing" (*A portable life*, 1981).

Overall, research has shown that short-term migrants, including international students and expatriate businesspeople, are likely to rely both on local and "home-based" sources of social support (Ong & Ward, 2005), although the networks may serve different functions, with the former providing more instrumental support and the latter being responsible for more emotional assistance (Bochner, McLeod, & Lin, 1977; Johnson, Kristof-Brown, Van Vianen, De Pater, & Klein, 2003). Counselors should also be aware, however, that the willingness to ask for and receive social support varies across cultures, with Asians using social support less for coping with stress than European Americans (Taylor et al., 2004). This may also apply to willingness to seek assistance from professional counselors.

Finally, culture-specific knowledge and skills function as assets and equip acculturating individuals with the resources to manage the stress and coping process. Language proficiency and communication skills are particularly important and are linked to overall adjustment and general satisfaction in immigrants, refugees, and sojourners (Ward et al., 2001). Skills may be acquired through past experience or culture-specific training, both of which are associated with better psychological adaptation (Deshpande & Visweswaran, 1992; Klineberg & Hull, 1979).

## CULTURE LEARNING: ACQUIRING NEW SKILLS

In Hong Kong I gave orders to my subordinates like I were an emperor . . . in Australia, I had to be more consultative and hands-on. (A Hong Kong immigrant to Australia, Mak, 1995, p. 25)

Everything I was comfortable with in a North American suburban setting, with the shopping and schools and daily routine was drastically different in Argentina. When I set out to do my grocery shopping, which we take for granted with our big supermarkets here, as I looked around to fill up my grocery cart, the only thing I could recognize was a box of Quaker oats. Everything was packaged differently, everything had Spanish names on it, and I couldn't tell salt from icing sugar. (A Canadian woman describing life in Argentina, *A portable life,* 1981)

I behave in ways that I had never done in my country. But I do that naturally because everyone else is behaving that way. I learned naturally. I was surprised myself. (An international student in Japan, Nakashima & Tanaka, 2005, p. 10)

The culture learning perspective has its roots in social and experimental psychology and has been strongly influenced by Argyle's (1969) work on social skills and interpersonal behaviors. This approach is based on the assumption that cross-cultural problems arise because cultural novices have difficulties managing everyday social encounters. Adaptation, therefore, comes in the form of learning the culture-specific skills that are required to negotiate the new cultural milieu (Bochner, 1986). Researchers who have adopted a culture learning approach to intercultural contact and change have emphasized the significance of culture-specific variables in the adaptation process. Attention is paid to differences in intercultural communication styles, including its verbal and nonverbal components, as well as rules, conventions and norms, and their influences on intercultural effectiveness. More recently, researchers have broadened this line of inquiry in attempts to build predictive models of sociocultural adaptation with emphasis on knowledge, skills, and experience, including factors such as cultural distance and cultural identity (Ward, 1996).

Although clients may present themselves to counselors because of psychoemotional problems, it is often the case that skills deficits underpin psychological distress. For example, a new immigrant or refugee may present with symptoms of anxiety or depression, which arise from an inability to cope with the settlement process and its immediate objectives, such as obtaining a job or establishing a support network. Culture-specific skills, particularly language proficiency and communication competence, are required for these goals.

The real problem was English. I was like a deaf-mute, couldn't do shopping, talk to the milkman or go to the doctor. My husband had to take me everywhere. (An Indian immigrant to the United Kingdom, Ghuman, 1994, p. 19)

The acquisition and maintenance of culture-specific skills facilitate cross-cultural adaptation and are positively related to psychological well-being. Trower, Bryant, and Argyle (1978) linked social skills to psychological adaptation by noting that certain forms of adaptation difficulties can be exacerbated by the lack of social competence. They have also commented on the reciprocal relationship between the two domains, with social inadequacy leading to isolation and psychological disturbance as well as psychological distress affecting behavior, including an array of social skills and interactions. As stated by a Canadian in South America, "Usually you learn through experience. Your first one is a miserable one" (*A portable life,* 1981).

From a complementary perspective, communication theorists have noted the link between communication problems and anxiety, suggesting that people who lack the requisite skills avoid interacting with those of different cultural backgrounds in an effort to reduce uncertainty and anxiety (Gudykunst, 1995). There is no doubt that the social and psychological dimensions of adaptation are strongly linked (Ward & Kennedy, 1999), and recent research from the International Comparative Study of Ethno-cultural Youth, undertaken with almost 8,000 immigrant and native-born adolescents in 13 countries, suggested that sociocultural adaptation precedes psychological adaptation (Berry, Phinney, Sam, & Vedder, 2006).

Sociocultural adaptation is a construct introduced by Ward and colleagues (Searle & Ward, 1990; Ward, 1996) to refer to the ability to fit in and negotiate interactive aspects of a new cultural environment. Not surprisingly, sociocultural adaptation improves with time. A longitudinal study of Japanese students in New Zealand who were surveyed on entry and 4, 6, and 12 months later showed that sociocultural adaptation followed a learning curve, with a steep increase over the first 4 to 6 months and then a tapering off up to the end of the first year (Ward, Okura, et al., 1998). Overall, sociocultural adaptation is predicted by culture-specific knowledge, language fluency, more extensive intercultural contact, low cultural distance, and longer residence in a new culture (Ward & Kennedy, 1999).

The acquisition of culturally appropriate social skills is not only an issue for sojourners, immigrants, and refugees, as people who relocate to a new culture. It is also important for anyone living in a culturally diverse society. This includes professionals who work with people from culturally diverse backgrounds. Lack of cultural skills can affect both the professionals' effectiveness and sense of competence. For example, in a recent study of educators in New Zealand, research by Ward, Masgoret, Newton, and Crabbe (2005) indicated that teachers had positive attitudes about working with international students but lacked confidence in their skills to manage multicultural classrooms effectively. The same may be true for many counselors.

There are a variety of tools and programs available to improve intercultural effectiveness for both professionals and lay people. The critical incidents used in this book are just one technique; others include culture assimilators or intercultural sensitizers, experiential exercises, simulations, and specific training packages. Counselors may wish to take advantage of some of these tools for themselves or refer their clients for intercultural training (ICT). Research has shown that ICT leads to a range of positive outcomes, including improved intercultural skills, better job performance, decreased stress, increased self-confidence, greater enjoyment of intercultural interactions, better interpersonal relationships in culturally diverse work groups, increased world-mindedness, a decrease in negative stereotyping, and greater ease in interacting with host nationals (Brislin & Yoshida, 1994; Deshpande & Visweswaran, 1992). For further information on intercultural training, the reader may wish to consult Landis, Bennett, and Bennett's (2004) *Handbook of Intercultural Training* for an overview and sources such as Cushner and Brislin (1996), Fowler and Mumford (1995, 1999), and Hofstede, Pedersen, and Hofstede (2002) for specific techniques. Of particular relevance for counselors is Gropper's (1996) *Culture and the Clinical Encounter.*

# SOCIAL IDENTITY: LIVING IN TWO CULTURES

I have spent my whole life as a phony. I appear to be Japanese on the outside, but inside I am Korean. But I don't tell this to anyone, and I pretend to be Japanese instead . . . I started to wonder what was going on. Why was I living a double life? . . . I felt uncomfortable with other people because I kept thinking if I was honest I would tell them I am Korean. I felt constricted, like I was suffocating in my relationships with Japanese. (A woman of Korean descent in Japan, Murphy-Shigematsu, 2000, pp. 375–376)

Rather than relying on a single unifying theory to interpret acculturation, the social identity perspective is made up of a cluster of loosely related theories, models, and approaches that deal with both the individual-level analysis of ethnic and cultural identity and the group-level analysis of intergroup perceptions and relations. Phinney's (1990) work on ethnic identity, Tajfel's (1981) social identity theory, and various intergroup theories such as integrated threat theory (Stephan & Stephan, 2000) and the instrumental model of group conflict (Esses, Dovidio, Jackson, & Armstrong, 2001) are all applicable to acculturation processes; however, the most relevant perspectives for counselors are Baumeister's (1986) theory of identity crises and Berry's (1997) acculturation framework.

According to Baumeister (1986), identity conflict is an inner struggle that demands an individual to choose between two or more different identities that prescribe incompatible behaviors or commitments. The conflicted individual subjectively experiences feelings of being "torn apart" due to situational demands that prescribe different behaviors that are irreconcilable. Opposing demands are seen as leading to the betrayal of existing commitments, such as loyalty to another person, ideology, or institution.

Although support of Baumeister's (1986) model largely comes from other contexts, it is easy to see how it is relevant for acculturating persons who may be torn between two or more sets of cultural values and norms. Indeed, Baumeister argued that a major route to identity conflict involves situational circumstances demanding an individual to accept a new identity that is in conflict with the existing one. The acquisition of this new identity may result in behaviors that are inconsistent or in conflict with the individual's prior goals and values. If behaviors prescribed by the two sets of commitments became incompatible, the individual will experience distress. Peres and Yuval-David's (cited in Baumeister, 1986) work with Arab-Israelis found that due to sustained intercultural conflict, they felt neither really Israeli nor Arab; they postponed taking sides as long as possible when conflict occurred; and they often responded with hostility when forced to make a choice.

The challenges faced by sojourners, migrants, refugees, indigenous peoples, and other ethnocultural groups may be interpreted in the context of Baumeister's (1986) model where living as a member of a minority community heightens the salience of issues pertaining to identity, how people think about and perceive themselves, how they interconnect with the social and ethnic groups to which they belong, and how they relate to the larger society. Conflict may occur in a range of areas. It may start simply as defining identity for those who have multiple ethnic ancestries. For example, Trimble and Gonzalez (Chapter 6, this volume) discuss the identity question in relation to those who report their race as Indian but include non-Indian ancestry in their ethnic background and those who could, but choose not to, claim Indian ancestry. Similar issues have been highlighted in New Zealand with respect to its indigenous Maori population.

Discovering who I was, a woman of dual ethnic descent, has been an extremely traumatic journey. How could I explain to people that my dead great grandmother was in effect speaking to me, without people thinking I had "lost the plot?" I was depressed and isolated, feeling as if I was the only person in the world experiencing these types of thoughts and emotions. . . . At times I feel comfortable with being both Maori and Pakeha [a New Zealander of European descent], and then at other times I identify more strongly with being Maori and other times cannot be bothered with the ethnic politics of either side. (Gibson, 1999, pp. 1–2)

This is not to propagate a "deficiency" model of mixed-race individuals. Indeed, Ward's (2006) research with Maori-Pakeha dual-heritage adolescents demonstrated that they were not disadvantaged in terms of psychological and social adaptation in comparison with their Maori and Pakeha peers. The same can be said for dual ethnics in Hawaii and New Mexico, where there were no significant differences in psychological symptoms, anomie, and quality-of-life measures for Asian, Hispanic, Caucasian, and mixed-heritage adults (Stephan & Stephan, 1991).

For those who relocate to a new culture, as well as those who live as ethnocultural minorities in culturally diverse societies, conflicts may arise from tensions between heritage culture and "normative" culture. Conflicts also arise across generations from competing pressures of parental preferences for traditional norms and values, as well as peer group and societal demands for "modern" practices. While conflict across generations is not uncommon, Rosenthal (1984) reported greater conflict between parents and adolescents in immigrant than nonimmigrant families in Australia. Furthermore, there is some evidence that perceived differences in parents' and children's values predict identity conflict. Lin (2005) found that perceived generational differences in self-enhancement values such as achievement, power, and hedonism were related to identity conflict in Chinese adolescents and young adults whose parents did not accompany them to New Zealand. However, for adolescents and young adults with or without their parents, family cohesiveness reduced conflict.

For individuals who are members of marginalized, socially disenfranchised, and devalued groups, identity issues may be even more complicated. Retaining heritage culture implies acceptance of a negative social identity. Some respond by rejecting or denying ethnocultural heritage and "passing" as a member of the dominant or normative ethnocultural group, as illustrated in the opening quote of this section. In other instances, revitalization of ethnic consciousness and pride offers a means by which identity can be negotiated. Most individuals and groups are successful in achieving this, as evidenced, for example, by the link between ethnic identity and self-esteem found in Black, Asian, and Hispanic Americans (Phinney, 1992); Turkish migrants in the Netherlands (Verkuyten, 1990); and Vietnamese migrants in Australia (Nesdale, Rooney, & Smith, 1997).

Competing cultural pressures need not result in identity conflict. Camilleri and Malewska-Peyre (1997) have discussed coping strategies in adolescent immigrants in France who often maintain a traditional style when interacting in private at home with family members and a "modern" style when interacting with peers. Although pragmatic behavioral responses in the absence of core values change are not necessarily indicative of shifting cultural identification, what international research has consistently shown is a strong preference for bicultural identity, also known as integration, in most acculturating persons.

I do want to have two countries and two cultures. (An Asian student in New Zealand, Lewthwaite, 1996, p. 179)

I can fit into both cultures. In Indian society I behave like an Indian, here I behave like an English. I am bicultural. (A British Asian, Ghuman, 1994, p. 74)

This leads to the essence of Berry's (1997) framework of acculturation, which identifies four outcomes in response to two fundamental identity questions. Paraphrased, these are as follows: *How important is it to maintain my cultural heritage?* And *how important is it to adopt the cultural identity of my new country?* The resultant acculturation outcomes have been identified as integration (both cultural maintenance and change are important), assimilation (only adoption of a new identity is important), separation (only cultural maintenance is important), and marginalization (neither is important).

Although not without their critics (e.g., Rudmin, 2003), Berry and colleagues have produced persuasive evidence that integration is consistently the most favored acculturation response across sojourners, immigrants, refugees, and native peoples. Not only is integration preferred by acculturating groups, but it is also associated with better psychological and sociocultural adaptation in long- and short-term migrants and native peoples (Berry, 1997; Berry, Kim, Power, Young, & Bujaki, 1989). These findings have been replicated in international research, most recently and comprehensively in the International Comparative Study of Ethnocultural Youth project, which studied 32 different immigrant groups across 13 receiving nations (Berry et al., 2006).

## THE SOCIOCULTURAL CONTEXT OF COUNSELING

So far, this chapter has focused on the characteristics of acculturating persons. Although it has drawn together common themes and aspects of the acculturation experience, it has not addressed all of the important characteristics of the acculturating client. Attitudes toward counselors and counseling are also important, and these are known to vary substantially across cultures. An extensive discussion of these attitudes is beyond the scope of this chapter, but issues such as a shared understanding of distress, trauma and causes of mental health and illness, views about stigma of seeking help from a mental health professional, and cultural preferences for directive versus nondirective therapies are just some examples of cultural attitudes that will affect the therapeutic process. However, it is not only the characteristics of acculturating persons that affect the formulation and implementation of counseling strategies. Tatar (1998) has identified two additional core factors: the multicultural competencies of the counselor and the sociocultural context.

The multicultural competencies of the counselor are the focus of this book. Multiculturalism has become the "fourth force" in counseling, and this book addresses the application of multicultural perspectives to the counseling process. This includes awareness of key issues: that entry into the counseling system is affected by cultural conceptions of mental health, that culture-sensitive empathy and rapport are important in establishing a working alliance, that culture-specific modes of counseling work better with some cultural groups, and that aspects of the acculturation experience can influence receptiveness toward counseling (Sue & Sundberg, 1996).

Despite awareness of these issues, counselors are not uniformly effective in multicultural interventions. In Tatar's (1998) research, four intercultural counseling approaches were identified with respect to immigrant students, but these can be extended to work with other acculturating persons. The first and most widespread strategy, counselor as "culturally encapsulated assimilator," was the least reflective of multicultural effectiveness. In this approach, counselors were trapped in the culturally dominant way of thinking that advocated rapid assimilation "in the students' best interests." Tatar comments that the assimilative approach supports a cultural deficiency model, building on the premise that the dominant culture is also the superior one. The second approach identified was counselor as "self-facilitator," with emphasis placed on the individuality of each student, rather than seeing a migrant as a member of a labeled group. Tatar describes this method as involving the counselor as an active influence, working with not only the student but also with relevant others in recognition and acceptance of the client as undergoing a developmental transition in a multicultural society. The third approach was labeled counselor as "specialist," where the counselor's personal or professional expertise was used to devise innovative strategies for client needs. Although this often achieved positive outcomes, a challenge when working with allied professionals was to avoid ethnic stereotyping of certain client groups. Finally, there were counselors as "translators," where the counselor served as a bridge between two cultures, not only assisting migrants to operate effectively in their new environment but also educating local students about other cultures and what can be learned from them.

The final factor identified by Tatar (1998), pertaining to the broader social context, is often overlooked and deserves further consideration. Important questions include the following: What is the nature of the sociocultural context? What are the attitudes held by counselors and the wider society? Are pervading assumptions about cultural diversity implicitly assimilationist, or is integration welcomed? Are members of minority groups competing on a level playing field, or are they subjected to blatant or subtle discrimination? Unfortunately, as the focus in this chapter has been on the characteristics of the acculturating person, one may be tempted to adopt the implicit and prevailing ideology that it is the responsibility of the immigrant, refugee, sojourner, native person, or member of an ethnocultural minority to adapt and "fit into" the wider society. But in reality, the acculturation process is a two-way street.

Take, for example, the issue of discrimination. Seven of 10 second-generation adolescent migrants in France report being deeply affected by discrimination (Malewska-Peyre, 1982). More than 80% of Korean migrants in Canada have acknowledged experiencing discrimination (Noh & Kaspar, 2003). A recent survey by the New Zealand Immigration Service indicated that one in five immigrants reported the experience of discrimination and that this occurred most frequently in work-related areas (New Zealand Immigration Service, 2004). Perceived discrimination has been related to a variety of negative outcomes, including increased stress; lowered self-esteem and group esteem; impaired health; antisocial behaviors, such as drug use and delinquency; identity conflict; and poorer work adjustment and job satisfaction (Ward et al., 2001). Should our efforts, then, be predominantly channelled into assisting acculturating people to deal with discrimination, or should we be working toward improving intercultural relations more broadly? In reality, this is not an either/or question. It does, however, highlight the point that the sociocultural context can often be the source of psychological distress and a reason to lead an acculturating person to seek counseling services.

## CONCLUSION

This chapter has identified generic themes and issues for acculturating persons and provided three conceptual frameworks for interpreting and understanding their experiences. It has also discussed similarities and differences in the acculturation process of indigenous peoples, sojourners, immigrants, refugees, and ethnocultural groups. The sociocultural context of the counseling process has received special attention, and along these lines, counselors are challenged to consider culture contact and change from a broad perspective and acknowledge the social and political influences on and outcomes of the counseling process.

## CRITICAL INCIDENT

Marianna, a recently qualified counselor from the United States, has accompanied her husband to Malaysia, where he has been posted for 3 years on an international assignment. Marianna has joined a counseling practice in Kuala Lumpur that specializes in providing services to the expatriate community but also accepts local clients on request. Marianna has been working in this practice for 6 months.

Lakshmi d/o Rajah, a 20-year-old student at a local university, has come to Marianna on the recommendation of one of her expatriate professors.

Lakshmi is a Hindu and lives with her extended family of her father, mother, older brother, younger brother, younger sister, and paternal grandmother. Her father is a well-respected professional in the local community, her mother is a homemaker, her elder brother has recently completed his university studies in law and has joined a small practice, and her younger siblings are still at school. Lakshmi's family is largely traditional, although the parents and children are English speaking, and the parents expect that the children will complete university degrees.

In the counseling session, Lakshmi is very forthcoming about her current "problem." In fact, she first sought to discuss the issue with her Australian professor, who recommended that Lakshmi see a professional counselor. The presenting issue is this: Lakshmi's father had promised her in marriage to the son of a well-known Malaysian Indian family when she was a small girl. It is expected that the wedding will take place next year after Lakshmi finishes her university degree. Lakshmi is close to her family and wants to please her father, but she does not want an arranged marriage. Furthermore, she has become emotionally, though not sexually, involved with a classmate, a young Indian man who would like to pursue a relationship with her. Lakshmi is not sure what to do and is experiencing increasing anxiety over the situation. This is affecting her studies.

Lakshmi asks Marianna for help in dealing with this conflict. She is particularly interested in receiving concrete suggestions as to how this issue might be resolved. How should Marianna respond?

## DISCUSSION QUESTIONS

Imagine you are Marianna and discuss the following questions.

1. How does this incident illustrate acculturation? Who are the acculturating persons?

2. How would you feel about Lakshmi's issues? How might these feelings influence your intervention? Would those influences be appropriate?

3. What role do cultural values and traditions play in this scenario? How might they influence your understanding or management of this case?

4. How might you approach working with this client? Would you work with her as an individual? Would you involve family members? If so, who and how?

5. Would you approach the case in the same way if Lakshmi and her family were resident in the United States as opposed to Malaysia? How and why?

6. How would you respond to Lakshmi's request for explicit directives in dealing with the issues? Why?

# REFERENCES

Adelman, M. B. (1988). Cross-cultural adjustment: A theoretical perspective on social support. *International Journal of Intercultural Relations, 12,* 183–205.

Argyle, M. (1969). *Social interaction.* London: Methuen.

Ataca, B. (1996, August). *Psychological and sociocultural adaptation of Turkish immigrants, Canadians and Turks.* Paper presented at the XIII Congress of the International Association for Cross-Cultural Psychology, Montreal, Canada.

Baumeister, R. F. (1986). *Identity: Cultural change and the struggle for self.* New York: Oxford University Press.

Beiser, M., Barwick, C., Berry, J. W., da Costa, G., Fantino, A., Ganesan, S., et al. (1988). *Mental health issues affecting immigrants and refugees.* Ottawa: Health and Welfare Canada.

Berry, J. W. (1997). Immigration, acculturation and adaptation. *Applied Psychology: An International Review, 46,* 5–34.

Berry, J. W., Kim, U., Minde, T., & Mok, D. (1987). Comparative studies of acculturative stress. *International Migration Review, 21,* 491–511.

Berry, J. W., Kim, U., Power, S., Young, M., & Bujaki, M. (1989). Acculturation attitudes in plural societies. *Applied Psychology, 38,* 185–206.

Berry, J. W., Phinney, J., Sam, D. L., & Vedder, P. (Eds.). (2006). *Immigrant youth in cultural transition: Acculturation, identity and adaptation across national contexts.* Mahwah, NJ: Lawrence Erlbaum.

Berry, J. W., & Sam, D. (1997). Acculturation and adaptation. In J. W. Berry, M. H. Segall, & C. Kagitçibasi (Eds.), *Handbook of cross-cultural psychology: Vol. 3. Social behavior and applications* (pp. 291–326). Boston: Allyn & Bacon.

Bochner, S. (1986). Coping with unfamiliar cultures: Adjustment or culture learning? *Australian Journal of Psychology, 38,* 347–358.

Bochner, S., McLeod, B. M., & Lin, A. (1977). Friendship patterns of overseas students: A functional model. *International Journal of Psychology, 12,* 277–297.

Brislin, R., & Yoshida, T. (1994). *Intercultural communication training: An introduction.* Thousand Oaks, CA: Sage.

Camilleri, C., & Malewska-Peyre, H. (1997). Socialization and identity strategies. In J. W. Berry, P. Dasen, & T. S. Saraswathi (Eds.), *Handbook of cross-cultural psychology: Vol. 2. Basic processes and human development* (pp. 41–67). Boston: Allyn & Bacon.

Chung, R. C. Y., & Kagawa-Singer, M. (1993). Predictors of psychological distress among Southeast Asian refugees. *Social Science and Medicine, 36,* 631–639.

Church, A. T. (1982). Sojourner adjustment. *Psychological Bulletin, 91,* 540–572.

Cushner, K., & Brislin, R. (1996). *Intercultural interactions: A practical guide* (2nd ed.). Thousand Oaks, CA: Sage.

Deshpande, S. P., & Viswesvaran, C. (1992). Is cross-cultural training of expatriate managers effective? A meta-analysis. *International Journal of Intercultural Relations, 16,* 295–310.

Duke, K. (1996). The resettlement of refugees in the UK: Main findings from an interview study. *New Community, 22*(3), 461–478.

Esses, V., Dovidio, J., Jackson, L., & Armstrong, T. (2001). The immigration dilemma: The role of perceived group competition, ethnic prejudice, and national identity. *Journal of Social Issues, 57,* 389–412.

Fowler, S., & Mumford, M. G. (Eds.). (1995). *Intercultural sourcebook: Cross-cultural training methods* (Vol. 1). Yarmouth, ME: Intercultural Press.

Fowler, S., & Mumford, M. G. (Eds.). (1999). *Intercultural sourcebook: Cross-cultural training methods* (Vol. 2). Yarmouth, ME: Intercultural Press.

Furnham, S., & Bochner, S. (1986). *Culture shock: Psychological reactions to unfamiliar environments.* London: Methuen.

Furnham, A., & Li, Y. H. (1993). The psychological adjustment of the Chinese community in Britain: A study of two generations. *British Journal of Psychiatry, 162,* 109–113.

Furukawa, T., & Shibayama, T. (1993). Predicting maladjustment of exchange students in different cultures: A prospective study. *Social Psychiatry and Psychiatric Epidemiology, 28,* 142–146.

Ghuman, P. A. S. (1994). *Coping with two cultures.* Clevedon, UK: Multilingual Matters.

Gibson, K. (1999). Maori women and dual ethnicity: Non-congruence, "passing" and real Maori. In N. Robertson (Ed.), *Maori and psychology: Research and practice* (pp. 1–4). Hamilton, New Zealand: University of Waikato, Maori Health Research Unit.

*Going international: Beyond culture shock.* (1983). San Francisco: Copeland Griggs.

Gropper, R. C. (1996). *Culture and the clinical encounter.* Yarmouth, ME: Intercultural Press.

Gudykunst, W. B. (1995). Anxiety/uncertainty management (AUM) theory. In R. L. Wiseman (Ed.), *Intercultural communication theory* (pp. 8–58). Thousand Oaks, CA: Sage.

Hofstede, G. J., Pedersen, P. B., & Hofstede, G. (2002). *Exploring culture: Exercises, stories and synthetic cultures.* Yarmouth, ME: Intercultural Press.

Holmes, T. S., & Rahe, T. H. (1967). The Social Readjustment Rating Scale. *Journal of Psychosomatic Research, 11,* 213–218.

Johnson, E. C., Kristof-Brown, A. J., Van Vianen, A. E. M., De Pater, I. E., & Klein, M. R. (2003). Expatriate social ties: Personality antecedents and consequences for adjustment. *International Journal of Selection and Assessment, 11*(4), 277–288.

Jose, P., Liu, J., & Ward, C. (2005, April). *Stress and adaptation among local and international students in New Zealand.* Paper presented at the Sixth Biennial Conference of the Asian Association of Social Psychology, Wellington, New Zealand.

Jose, P., Ward, C., & Liu, J. H. (2007). Cross-cultural adaptation of Asian and Western international students in New Zealand. In J. H. Liu, C. Ward, A. B. I. Bernardo, M. Karasawa & R. Fischer (Eds.)., *Casting the individual in societal and cultural contexts: Social and societal psychology for Asia and the Pacific* (pp. 205–224). Seoul: Kyoyook-Kwahak-Sa Publishing.

Klineberg, O., & Hull, W. F. (1979). *At a foreign university: An international study of adaptation and coping.* New York: Praeger.

Landis, D., Bennett, J. M., & Bennett, M. J. (Eds.). (2004). *Handbook of intercultural training* (3rd ed.). Thousand Oaks, CA: Sage.

Lazarus, R. F., & Folkman, S. (1984). *Stress, coping and appraisal.* New York: Springer.

Lewthwaite, M. (1996). A study of international students: Perspectives on cross-cultural adaptation. *International Journal for the Advancement of Counseling, 19,* 167–185.

Lin, E.-Y. (2005, April). *Predictors of Chinese students' identity conflict.* Paper presented at the Sixth Biennial Conference of the Asian Association of Social Psychology, Wellington, New Zealand.

Mak, A. (1995, Winter). Occupational concerns and well-being of skilled Hong Kong immigrants in Australia. *Australian Journal of Career Development,* pp. 24–28.

Malewska-Peyre, H. (1982). L'expérience du racisme et de la xénophobie chez jeunes immigrés [Young immigrants' experience of racism and xenophobia]. In H. Malewska-Peyre (Ed.), *Crise d'identité et déviance chez jeunes immigrés* (pp. 53–73). Paris: La Documentation Française.

Murphy-Shigematsu, S. (2000). Cultural psychiatry and minority identities in Japan: A constructivist narrative approach to therapy. *Psychiatry, 63,* 371–384.

Nakashima, M., & Tanaka, T. (2005, April). *Formation of personal relations and social skills in international students in Japan.* Paper presented at the Sixth Biennial Conference of the Asian Association of Social Psychology, Wellington, New Zealand.

Nesdale, D., Rooney, R., & Smith, L. (1997). Migrant ethnic identity and psychological distress. *Journal of Cross-Cultural Psychology, 28,* 569–588.

New Zealand Immigration Service. (2004). *Migrants' experiences of New Zealand: Pilot survey report.* Wellington: New Zealand Immigration Service.

Noh, S., & Kaspar, V. (2003). Perceived discrimination and depression: Moderating effects of coping, acculturation and ethnic support. *American Journal of Public Health, 93,* 232–238.

Ong, A. K.-J., & Ward, C. (2005). The construction and validation of a social support measure for sojourners: The Index of Sojourner Social Support. *Journal of Cross-Cultural Psychology, 36,* 637–661.

Phinney, J. (1990). Ethnic identity in adolescents and adults: Review of research. *Psychological Bulletin, 108,* 499–514.

Phinney, J. (1992). The Multigroup Ethnic Identity Measure: A new scale for use with diverse groups. *Journal of Adolescent Research, 7,* 156–176.

*A portable life.* (1981). Montreal: Instructional Communication Centre, McGill University.

Redfield, R., Linton, R., & Herskovits, M. J. (1936). Memorandum for the study of acculturation. *American Anthropologist, 38,* 149–152.

Rosenthal, D. (1984). Intergenerational conflict and culture: A study of immigrant and non-immigrant adolescents and their parents. *Genetic Psychology Monographs, 109,* 53–75.

Rudmin, F. W. (2003). Critical history of the acculturation psychology of assimilation, separation, integration and marginalization. *General Review of Psychology, 7,* 3–37.

Sam, D. (1994). The psychological adjustment of young immigrants in Norway. *Scandinavian Journal of Psychology, 35,* 240–253.

Searle, W., & Ward, C. (1990). The prediction of psychological and sociocultural adjustment during cross-cultural transitions. *International Journal of Intercultural Relations, 14,* 449–464.

Stephan, W. G., & Stephan, C. W. (1991). Intermarriage: Effects on personality, adjustment and intergroup relations in two samples of students. *Journal of Marriage and the Family, 53,* 241–250.

Stephan, W. G., & Stephan, C. W. (2000). An integrated threat theory of prejudice. In S. Oskamp (Ed.), *Reducing prejudice and discrimination* (pp. 23–46). Hillsdale, NJ: Lawrence Erlbaum.

Stone Feinstein, B. E., & Ward, C. (1990). Loneliness and psychological adjustment of sojourners: New perspectives on culture shock. In D. M. Keats, D. Munro, & L. Mann (Eds.), *Heterogeneity in cross-cultural psychology* (pp. 537–547). Lisse, The Netherlands: Swets & Zeitlinger.

Sue, D., & Sundberg, N. D. (1996). Research and research hypotheses about effectiveness in intercultural counseling. In P. B. Pedersen, J. G. Draguns, W. J. Lonner, & J. E. Trimble (Eds.), *Counseling across cultures* (4th ed., pp. 323–352). Thousand Oaks, CA: Sage.

Tajfel, H. (1981). *Human groups and social categories.* Cambridge: Cambridge University Press.

Tam, V. C.-W., & Lam, R. S.-Y. (2005). Stress and coping among migrant and local-born adolescents in Hong Kong. *Youth and Society, 36*(3), 312–332.

Tatar, M. (1998). Counseling immigrants: School contexts and emerging strategies. *British Journal of Guidance and Counseling, 26,* 337–352.

Taylor, S. E., Sherman, D. K., Kim, H. S., Jarcho, J., Takagi, K., & Dunagan, M. S. (2004). Culture and social support: Who seeks it and why? *Journal of Personality and Social Psychology, 87*(3), 354–362.

Trower, P., Bryant, B., & Argyle, M. (1978). *Social skills and mental health.* London: Methuen.

United Nations. (2002). *World immigration report.* New York: Author.

Verkuyten, M. (1990). Self-esteem and the evaluation of ethnic identity among Turkish and Dutch adolescents in the Netherlands. *Journal of Social Psychology, 130,* 285–297.

Ward, C. (1996). Acculturation. In D. Landis & R. Bhagat (Eds.), *Handbook of intercultural training* (2nd ed., pp. 124–147). Thousand Oaks, CA: Sage.

Ward, C. (2006). Acculturation, identity and adaptation in dual heritage adolescents. *International Journal of Intercultural Relations, 30,* 243–259.

Ward, C., Bochner, S., & Furnham, A. (2001). *The psychology of culture shock.* London: Routledge.

Ward, C., & Kennedy, A. (1993). Acculturation and cross-cultural adaptation of British residents in Hong Kong. *Journal of Social Psychology, 133,* 395–397.

Ward, C., & Kennedy, A. (1999). The measurement of socio-cultural adaptation. *International Journal of Intercultural Relations, 23,* 659–677.

Ward, C., & Kennedy, A. (2000). Coping with cross-cultural transition. *Journal of Cross-Cultural Psychology, 32*(5), 636–642.

Ward, C., Leong, C.-H., & Kennedy, A. (1998, April). *Self construals, stress, coping and adjustment during cross-cultural transition.* Paper presented at the Annual Conference of the Society of Australasian Social Psychologists, Christchurch, New Zealand.

Ward, C., Masgoret, A.-M., Newton, J., & Crabbe, D. (2005). Teachers' attitudes toward and interactions with international students. In C. Ward (Ed.), *Interactions with international students* (pp. 43–85). Wellington: CACR & Education New Zealand.

Ward, C., Okura, Y., Kennedy, A., & Kojima, T. (1998). The U-curve on trial: A longitudinal study of psychological and sociocultural adjustment during cross-cultural transition. *International Journal of Intercultural Relations, 22,* 277–291.

*World within reach: Culture shock.* (1995). Kingston, Ontario, Canada: International Centre, Queen's University.

Young, M., & Evans, D. R., (1997). The well-being of Salvadoran refugees. *International Journal of Psychology, 32*(5), 289–300.

Zheng, X., & Berry, J. W. (1991). Psychological adaptation of Chinese sojourners in Canada. *International Journal of Psychology, 26,* 451–470.

# Counseling Refugees and Migrants

Fred Bemak and Rita Chi-Ying Chung

---

### Primary Objective

- To assist mental health practitioners in understanding and providing effective multicultural counseling and psychotherapy with refugees and migrants by providing a model of treatment and psychotherapy (Multilevel Model of Psychotherapy)

### Secondary Objectives

- To provide an understanding of the sociopolitical and historical context of mental health for refugees and migrants
- To provide an awareness and understanding of the importance of premigration trauma on postmigration adjustment
- To sensitize mental health practitioners regarding the impact of acculturation, cultural belief systems, and associated adjustment issues that affect the psychological well-being of refugees and migrants

---

WITH GLOBALIZATION, THE ADVANCEMENT IN TECHNOLOGY, AND THE ACCESSIBILITY TO INTERNATIONAL and national travel, there has been a rapid increase of migrants worldwide and therefore the need to discuss culturally responsive counseling with this population. Before we begin this discussion, it is important to distinguish between the different migrant populations. The term *migrants* encompasses a variety of different groups. The major difference is between those who were involuntarily *forced from* versus voluntarily *chose to* migrate to another country. The former group is known as refugees, who left their home countries due to war, political instability, regional and national conflicts, genocide, social and economic upheaval, poverty, and natural disasters (United Nations, 1995) compared to immigrants who made the decision to migrate. Although refugees experience a more difficult adaptation since they flee from their home country by being forced out or impelled by fear, both refugees and immigrants encounter similar challenges during postmigration. Given these commonalities, the term *migrants* will be used when addressing both groups in this chapter. The chapter will begin with a brief description of refugees and immigrants, present relevant demographics and salient issues encountered by migrants, and then discuss the challenges facing migrant populations as a foundation of understanding the migrant experience. Issues related to providing cultural responsive mental health services will also be discussed, which will lay the groundwork for presenting the Multilevel Model of Psychotherapy, Social Justice, and Human Rights with migrant populations.

## Migration Demographics

In the past 40 years, the number of global migrants has risen dramatically so that in 2000, there were approximately 175 million international migrants (International Organization for Migration, 2005), which comprise 2.9% of the world population. Approximately 70,000 refugees have resettled in the United States each year for the past decade (Geltman & Cochran, 2005), complementing the large number of immigrants, which generated a total of 946,142 migrants in 2004 (Rytina, 2005). Also significant is the emergence of undocumented migration as a universal phenomenon throughout the developed world as a result of tighter immigration restrictions (Massey & Capoferro, 2004). In the United States, an estimated 7 million illegal immigrant workers, who will not be entitled to benefits, provide subsidies of $7 billion annually, generating $56 billion in earnings in 2002 (approx. 1.5% of the total reported national wages), which in turn produces $6.4 billion in Social Security taxes that will never be claimed (Porter, 2005). Estimates are that Mexico has the largest number of unauthorized immigrants with 4.8 million in 2000 (U.S. Immigration and Naturalization Service, 2003). Also contributing to illegal migration is human smuggling and trafficking, which has become a highly profitable business for organized crime (Chung, 2005).

## The Impact of Migration

Migrants have significant impact on countries to which they relocate. Their presence raises policy issues for host countries that relate to social and economic factors, such as employment, housing, educational access and support, health care, and so on; they also reflect immigration policies in host countries, as well as possibly reduce unemployment and fill the need for unskilled labor. International policies influence the migration experience so that forced or voluntary migration, previous occupation and work experience, education, politics, historical relationship between the country of resettlement and country of origin, and demand for certain types of labor will all significantly affect the postmigration experience. Host countries vary markedly with regards to policies, programs, and the reception of migrants. Typically, there are three domains—legal and political, cultural, and socioeconomic (Freeman, 2004)—that constitute loosely connected regulations and policies for incorporating migrants into the fabric of existing society. Resettlement is complicated by having identifies and affiliations in the country of origin and country of resettlement, resulting in political, personal, economic, and social relationships in more than one country (Vertovec, 2004). These issues are further complicated by the availability of modern technology and the accessibility of international travel. Essentially, modern-day migration transcends traditional boundaries and may generate confusion about political, personal, social, and cultural identity.

# THE REFUGEE EXPERIENCE

In the 21st century, refugee migration is prevalent due to political instability, regional and national conflicts, war, genocide, social and economic upheaval, poverty, natural disasters, deportation, and growing populations (Bemak, Chung, & Pedersen, 2003). Expenditures by Western nations to determine the refugee status of asylum seekers are 10 times the amount that the United Nations High Commission for Refugees (UNHCR) spends on protecting refugees (Mills, 2005). Similar to previous years, the majority of refugees in the world today are women, children, and handicapped people who often lack the mental, physical, and economic resources to survive under harsh conditions (Bemak et al., 2003). The majority of refugees come from developing countries. Given that refugees' relocation is not a self-determined but rather an escape from intolerable and chaotic conditions, the migration process is extremely difficult and frequently dangerous, resulting in loss of family, identity, community, and culture; a downgrade in socioeconomic employment and status; the difficulty of having to learn a language; dramatic shifts in social, familial, and gender roles; and acculturation, adjustment, and adaptation problems in the new country (e.g., Bemak et al., 2003; Brody, 1994; Chung, Bemak, & Kagawa-Singer, 1998; Chung & Kagawa-Singer, 1993). These problems have brought about serious mental health issues for this population.

## Premigration Trauma

Premigration experiences are an important part of refugee adjustment. To understand the refugee experience, mental health professionals must be aware of and understand premigration experiences that are often stressful or traumatic (Bemak et al., 2003). Many refugees have been subjected to the atrocities of war and living in refugee camps, where they experienced and witnessed torture and killing, atrocities, incarceration, starvation, rape and sexual abuse, physical beatings, and injuries. Furthermore, those who managed to escape to refugee camps faced problems of overcrowding, poor nutrition and sanitary conditions, poor medical care, continued violence, and issues of safety that oftentimes compounded already existing psychological problems. Therefore, it is not surprising that numerous studies have found that refugees are more prone to psychological problems than are other populations (e.g., Bemak et al., 2003; Chung et al., 1998; Hauff & Vaglum, 1995; Marsella, Friedman, & Spain, 1993).

Mollica, Wyshak, and Lavelle (1987) categorized four major types of trauma: (a) deprivation (e.g., food and shelter), (b) physical injury and torture, (c) incarceration and reeducation camps, and (d) witnessing torture and killing. In addition, refugees have experienced loss, through death or separation, of their nuclear and extended families and communities and countries. Due to premigration trauma, refugees are at risk for developing serious mental health problems that include depression, anxiety, posttraumatic stress disorder (PTSD), and a host of other psychological difficulties and have been found to experience higher rates of incidence of psychopathology compared to the general U.S. population (e.g., Kinzie, 1993; Marsella et al., 1993; Vickers, 2005). For example, it was estimated that in a clinical refugee population (those who sought traditional Western mental health services), PTSD is 50% or higher, and depressive disorders were 42% to 89% higher than in the general population (e.g., Hauff & Vaglum, 1995; Van Velsen, Gorst-Unsworth, & Turner, 1996). In more extreme situations, it was found that depression ranged from 15% to 80% (e.g., Carlson & Rosser-Hogan, 1991; Pernice & Brook, 1994).

Some subgroups within the refugee population are at higher risk for developing serious mental health disorders. Older refugees are one such group who may experience more difficulties in adjusting to a new environment, while single men (younger than 21 years old) may also be at risk because of their lack of familial and social support (Bemak et al., 2003). Unaccompanied minors or children and adolescents with no adult family members during resettlement are another vulnerable group. Refugee women and girls are also susceptible to mental health problems, in part because of incidences of rape and sexual abuse that occurred before migration (Chung & Bemak, 2002b; Chung et al., 1998), as well as the percentage of refugee women who are widowed when their husbands are killed during war. For example, Cambodian refugee women who experienced genocide had significant difficulties in postmigration adjustment (Chung, 2001), similar to women from Rwanda and Somalia.

The process of acculturation and adjustment takes place within the context of these mental health concerns. In its broadest sense, acculturation is defined as a changing process that facilitates adaptation to another culture (Berry, 1986). Acculturation for refugees may pose intense and complex clinical challenges for psychotherapists given their involuntary flight and associated premigration trauma experiences. It is therefore critical for mental health professionals to take into account the premigration experiences and understand how the premigration events can compound and play a major influence on postmigration adjustment and adaptation.

The next section discusses the challenges that all migrant populations have encountered and presents major themes related to contemporary issues in counseling this population. Although some of the constructs are similar to other cross-cultural counseling situations, the cultural dynamics and the historical and sociopolitical background of migrant populations present their own unique characteristics that are traceable to respective cultures of origin and cultures of resettlement. These differences must be clearly understood and incorporated into therapeutic relationships at multiple levels, including individual, family, group, and community. This section includes (a) cultural belief systems, (b) utilization of mainstream mental health services, (c) acculturation and mental health, (d) psychosocial adjustment and adaptations, and (e) the Multilevel Model of Psychotherapy, Social Justice, and Human Rights with migrants.

## Cultural Belief Systems

Historically, Western models of psychotherapy have been based on a worldview that emphasizes individual psychotherapy as a means to enhance optimal independent functioning, coping abilities, and adaptation. This is in direct contrast to the cultural context for migrants who have often come from collectivistic cultures that focus on interpersonal relationships and social networks and may have a holistic approach to mental health. In collectivistic cultures, personal identity is defined by family, community, and social networks rather than on the basis of individual accomplishments and needs, generating an emphasis on interdependence. Paradoxically, being individually oriented and independent may be perceived by many migrant groups as contrary to their cultural beliefs and norms. As a result, standard clinical interventions in the United States are frequently in conflict with fundamental migrant belief and value systems. Understanding and providing mental health interventions for problems within a culturally relevant framework for migrants may be a complicated and difficult process.

The psychotherapist and the migrant client may have different perceptions of both the problem and effective intervention strategies. For example, refugees from Asia or Africa may believe in animism or spirits as the cause of emotional imbalance and may be visualizing and hearing deceased relatives. Traditional Western psychotherapists attribute these symptoms to psychosis and employ counseling techniques and medication that focus on the symptomatology (the "hallucination") to treat the underlying psychosis. Indigenous healing methods would approach the same symptoms from a different cultural framework and incorporate the concept of the deceased relative and spirit as an important and relevant personal and spiritual communication that may contribute to the stabilization of the individual and possibly the entire family.

The need to understand and validate the client's conceptualization of problems within the context of culture has been greatly emphasized (e.g., Kleinman, Eisenberg, & Good, 1978). Thus, the cultural conceptualization of mental illness encompasses the symptom manifestation (Chung & Kagawa-Singer, 1993), help-seeking behavior (Chung & Lin, 1994), and expectations of treatment and outcome. For example, refugees from Africa who come from a culture where deceased ancestors continue to provide wisdom and guidance for the living may present symptoms of pain in the head or insomnia that may be explained as upsetting the ancestral spirits. Therefore, they tend to seek help from individuals who respect and honor their cultural belief system, such as traditional healers who can assist in communicating with the ancestors to establish the cause of the problem and subsequent solution. Similar complaints and symptoms are found across cultures. However, they may appear in different patterns and be attributed to a different causation (e.g., Kirmayer, 1989; Phillips & Draguns, 1969), making it important for the therapist to be aware, understand, and accept the impact of culture and the complexity of the cultural construction of mental illness/mental health as it relates to migrant clients. Therapists must be knowledgeable and aware and should develop and employ culturally sensitive therapeutic interventions and skills (Kagawa-Singer & Chung, 1994; Pedersen, 2000) while also maintaining an awareness of cross-cultural errors in underdiagnosis or overdiagnosis of symptomatology. These problems arise due to lack of awareness, understanding, and acceptance of the influence and impact of culture on mental health. It is critical to bring diagnosis and intervention in line with the migrants' cultural belief system, values, and healing practices. To that end, therapists should acknowledge and confirm the clients' cultural conceptualization of their problems.

## Utilization of Mainstream Mental Health Services

Although there is a need for mental health services for migrants, several factors contribute to a historical reluctance to seek help from mainstream mental health services. First, mainstream mental health services in resettlement countries may be the last choice of treatment by migrants. Consistent with cultural belief systems and practices, migrant groups may explore traditional healing methods such as indigenous healers, elders, families, friends, and religious leaders. Only after failing to locate or receive help from these customary support networks do migrants seek out mainstream mental health professionals, so that the choice is by default. The situation is further complicated because by the time migrants finally access a psychotherapist, the problem has grown more severe and therefore may enter mainstream services with more serious symptoms. In fact, more than 75% of people in the world use complementary or alternative treatments (Micozzi, 1996). A second reason is the cultural insensitivity of mainstream services. The lack of cultural responsiveness by mainstream services has been found to account for low utilization, high dropout rates, and premature termination by clients (Sue, Fujino, Hu, Takeuchi, & Zane, 1991). This may relate to mainstream services being unable to accommodate cultural differences with regard to such issues as time or language and not understanding the impact of behaviors such as voice tone, speaking volume, and nonverbal communication. For example, direct eye contact, shaking hands with a member of the opposite sex, or touching is offensive in some cultures. Thus, service systems are created that are often viewed as "insensitive." If migrants do overcome the obstacles and actually go to a mainstream mental health facility, they may encounter "offensive" receptionists, staff, or professionals that may trigger recollections of encounters with negative authority figures. The result of such encounters is to accentuate the cultural gap and heighten the migrants' negative reaction to mental health services.

Third, there is the problem of language. Not knowing the language of the host country may be an obstacle to receiving psychotherapy since many mental health services do not have translators. Even when bilingual translators are available, there may still be skill deficiencies that cause problems in trying to move beyond literal translations in order to understand more subtle yet essential issues, such as the context of person within culture. Bilingual translators can assist in interpreting innuendoes of tonal changes, the meaning of nonverbal behavior, and a cultural framework that provides a context for social relationships and definition of self. It should be mentioned that although children sometimes act as translators for families, this is not necessarily an effective method of communication given difficulties translating the actual context of the conversation or the lack of verbatim translations (Bemak et al., 2003). Furthermore, family dynamics change if children are used as translators in traditional hierarchical families. Thus, translators must not only be carefully trained but also be able to establish a well-defined partnership with clinical professionals, which is crucial for effectively overcoming language and cultural barriers. A promising technique is to invite clients to name important feelings or issues in their first language (Draguns, 1998). The fourth reason for low utilization of mainstream mental health services is inaccessibility (Bemak et al., 2003). Clinics and private offices are frequently located in areas that may be difficult to reach and are perceived as culturally alien. Public transportation systems may be complicated, difficult to use, and time-consuming. Furthermore, particularly in urban areas, the community-based mental health facilities may be located in poorer sections that migrants perceive as unsafe.

## Acculturation and Mental Health

A classic study by Odegaard (1932) provided a foundation for understanding the relationship of migration and mental illness for migrant populations. Initially, such studies involved examining psychiatric hospital admission rates of immigrants and found them disproportionate (e.g., Eitinger, 1960; Mezey, 1960). The study of acculturation generally considers models of acculturation (which comprise assimilation, integration or biculturalism, rejection, and deculturation), social indicators, stress, and adaptation. Researchers (e.g., Berry, 1986; Szapocznik & Kurtines, 1980) have concluded that biculturalism or integration produced healthier acculturation outcomes. Migrants may experience cultural shock with a sense of helplessness and disorientation since their arrival into countries of resettlement introduces them to new cultures and reference groups that are frequently more individualistic than collectivistic (Bemak & Greenberg, 1994). Movement from a sociocentric society to an egocentric society may present difficulties for the migrant (Bhugra, 2004). Individual and cultural differences also play an important role along with one's ability to integrate their culture of origin with the culture of relocation. Successful acculturation is also influenced by important factors such as an individual's desire and willingness to adapt, his or her ability to identify with a new reference group, acceptance of the host culture's norms and values, support by social and family networks, and resolution of past psychological trauma. For refugees, the acculturation process is compounded by premigration experiences that link with psychosocial maladjustment and may hinder the adaptation process.

## Psychosocial Adjustment and Adaptation

Implicit in the discussion of acculturation is the issue of psychosocial adjustment. The first 1 to 2 years of resettlement is a crucial period when migrants attempt to meet basic needs such as housing and employment (Tayabas & Pok, 1983). Bemak (1989) outlined a three-phase development model of acculturation affecting psychosocial adjustment. The first phase is a period of security and safety when migrants attempt to use existing skills to master the new environment and achieve psychological safety. Successful completion of the first phase will usher in the second phase, where skills from the culture of origin and the new culture are integrated in the process of acculturation. The third phase follows successful adaptation and is highlighted by a growing sense of future. In this developmental model, it is only after a basic mastery of culture and language and a sense of psychological safety that migrants begin to contemplate and plan for realistic and attainable future goals and to implement strategies for achieving these objectives. Therefore, migrant adaptation in the resettlement country includes learning new coping skills and new behavioral and communication patterns. Oftentimes, this proves to be a challenge especially if migrants are accustomed to act in a certain manner such as "acting dumb" (remaining numb and unresponsive) as a survival skill to cope with psychological, physical, and sexual trauma. These survival strategies in the resettlement country may appear to be strange and inappropriate.

Another important factor in refugee adaptation to a new country relates to the marked ambivalence about relocation, unlike their immigrant counterpart who made the choice to migrate. The refugee experience is characterized by the loss of control over decision making with regard to essential questions in one's life such as geographic location, job opportunities, and social networks. Furthermore, there may be resentment on the part of the refugee toward the host country. For example, some refugees in Africa, Asia, and Latin America have felt abandoned by countries that they believed were protecting them from the atrocities of war, even though they may relocate to these countries at a later time. These feelings may contribute to an uneven adaptation process.

Survivor's guilt is another common problem that has been associated with refugees (Bemak et al., 2003) and may have implications for other migrant groups. Many refugees are haunted by feelings of guilt focused on escaping from dangerous conditions in their home country where they left behind family, friends, and loved ones. Awareness that the people who remained in the country of origin are alive and not ill or suffering may partially relieve survivor's guilt, while knowledge about them living in unpleasant conditions generates added emotional stress. If migrants have little or no information, they may be plagued by feelings of intense stress and guilt. There is a cycle of pain and sadness so that the migrant's happiness, success, and well-being may correlate with intensified feelings of hurt and associated guilt.

## Language Barriers

Language plays an important role in migrant adjustment. English as a second language (ESL) programs in the United States offer language training yet fall short of attending to issues that emerge with cultural language acquisition. Learning a new language may symbolize abandoning one's homeland and may be a catalyst for feelings of cultural identity loss. An example of this was the El Salvadorian migrant who struggled with learning English. In a painful moment, she explained in Spanish, "To learn English is to forget my country. I don't want to lose myself and speak English!" Another example was the Cambodian adolescent whose mother had been executed during mass genocide under the Khmer Rouge regime. One night after migrating to North America, the mother angrily appeared to the adolescent in a dream, exhorting her to "stop speaking English. You must speak Khmer! Remember you are Cambodian!" Experiencing the frustration of trying to learn a new language may also bring back memories of "better times and easier communication" with neighbors, friends, and family. The struggle with language may exacerbate emotional problems and frustrations in understanding the new environment and contribute to culture shock. ESL classes may also create feelings of helplessness and cause regressive behavior similar to earlier developmental years when, as a child, one was learning to master his or her environment and may evoke questions about self-worth, as well as cause a loss in social status and feelings of inadequacy and low self-esteem.

Furthermore, learning the language of the new culture may stimulate a redefinition of family relationships, causing dysfunction, conflicts, role confusion, and subsequent painful social restructuring. One example of this is the child who has acquired language skills more quickly than the adults in the family, thereby causing a reversal of roles. The adults become dependent on the child for cultural and language translation. This is a particularly confusing issue for highly structured matriarchal or patriarchal families where the ensuing role confusion may affect aspects of the established family patterns. An example was an Ethiopian wife who studied ESL classes at night, which required her to leave home in the evenings and fall short on fulfilling her traditional household duties. As she became more proficient in the new language, she identified with the customs and practices of the new culture. She acquired a greater sense of independence and rejected her traditional role as a wife, which, in turn, triggered marital disequilibrium and conflict.

## Education and Employment

Many migrants face not only social readjustment problems but also difficulties in finding employment that matches their training and education. Migrants with higher levels of education have more difficulties gaining legal immigration status to the United States than those with lower levels of schooling (Feliciano, 2005). Educational qualifications from countries of origin are often not transferable in resettlement countries, while jobs held in countries of origin may not be applicable to the skills needed in a more technologically advanced society. Subsequently, the migrant is oftentimes forced to "begin again" or "start from scratch." This search and struggle for gainful employment may result in a decrease in status, poor self-esteem, and feelings of hopelessness. Downward occupational mobility may be especially painful for migrants who had achieved professional status in their country of origin and encounter barriers to licensure and credentialing in addition to the usual fluctuations of a competitive employment market. Changes in familial and gender roles add to already strained family situations. Unemployment or underemployment of men commonly forces wives to work. Such changes in gender roles produce a conflict between the values of their culture of origin and those of the host country (Chung et al., 1998). Ironically, whereas men may experience a downward socioeconomic status, women from developing countries may experience upward socioeconomic mobility.

## Changes in Family Dynamics

Relocation may dramatically affect the family. One example is when migrants face new rules regarding traditional childrearing practices, discipline, and punishment that are contradictory and illegal in the resettlement country. New rules guiding behavior, such as childrearing, may create confusion and adjustment difficulties within the migrant family. Uncertainty is further exacerbated when families find children acculturating faster than adults, which potentially creates conflict regarding prevailing practices such as dating, marriage, parties, curfews, and school extracurricular activities, transforming formally well-established norms to become items for negotiation rather than clear norms dictated by parents. Thus, adaptation to the host culture brings with it the potential for a decrease in adherence to traditional values, which, in turn, promotes the loss of authority for adults and triggers intergenerational conflicts. Migrant children and adolescents witness the transformation of their parents from previously autonomous and culturally competent caretakers to depressed, overwhelmed, and dependent individuals. Confidence in parents is often undermined as they grapple with the new language and are disoriented and confused about new customs. Changing family dynamics may create intense anxiety for the parents as they experience a loss of authority and control.

## Education

Migrant children and adolescents often face problems in schools and may be prone to extreme risk for truancy and dropout (Goldberg, 1999). The norms regulating classroom and school behavior are different from the home country, the ongoing social and extracurricular activities are not easily accessible for newly enrolled migrants, and expectations for academic and personal growth may not fit with family-determined goals and worldviews. Furthermore, the expectations for academic success, as traditionally defined in Western resettlement countries with an emphasis on scores, grades, early course and vocation choices, and rankings, may be contradictory to cultural norms for migrant students (Bemak & Chung, 2003). For example, the 10th-grade Somalian child is expected to meet with a school counselor to define class selections that will have a significant impact on his or her life's vocation. To some degree, this career-defining moment is based on previous grades and perceived ability of the student to succeed in more demanding classes. Choosing a future career through academic courses at the age of 15 is quite different from school in Somalia, where school attendance past a certain age was uncommon, and classes taken in 10th grade were not regarded a road map for future vocations.

Problems in schools may relate to the status of being a foreigner. Different language, dress, ways of socially interacting, habits, and foods may elicit prejudicial responses from peers and staff. Migrant children may become targets of physical and emotional abuse, verbal harassment, assault, or robbery. Furthermore, there is a longstanding history of school personnel and other mental health professionals being confused and misdiagnosing aggressive behavior that has been documented with migrant children who have been exposed to sustained trauma. Van der Kolk (1987) stated that "traumatized children have trouble modulating aggression. They tend to act destructively against others or themselves" (p. 16). Similar patterns have been found with other migrant populations (Bemak & Chung, 2003; Boothby, 1994). For more in-depth description of issues related to migrants and school, see Bemak and Chung (2003).

## DISCRIMINATION AND RACISM AS BARRIERS IN PSYCHOSOCIAL ADJUSTMENT

In addition to the above psychosocial adjustment issues, migrants often encounter negative attitudes and behaviors in the resettlement country that result in discrimination. These behaviors have been identified as a natural by-product of the Western focus on individualism (Pedersen, 2000) and may be manifested overtly or covertly. An example of this is the anti-Arab sentiment since the attacks on September 11, 2001, that has been displayed in Australia, France, the United Kingdom, and the United States in the form of hate crimes, riots, and beatings. This type of racism has an impact on the adjustment of migrants. The degree and overt nature of racist behavior may be correlated with antagonism toward a perceived enemy such as Iraq and Arabs in general, as well as the economic health of the resettlement country that defines jobs, resource availability, policies, and practices that characterize community and social behaviors toward culturally different newcomers. Concerns about immigration policies and the changing demographics of communities may precipitate hostility and prejudice, blaming migrants for unemployment or underemployment. We have coined the term *political countertransference* to capture this type of negative reaction toward migrants (Chung, 2005).

## MULTILEVEL MODEL OF PSYCHOTHERAPY (MLM), SOCIAL JUSTICE, AND HUMAN RIGHTS WITH MIGRANT POPULATIONS

Psychotherapy and counseling with migrants require unique skills, understanding, and sensitivity to the history, psychological realities, and deeply rooted trauma and loss associated with migration. Training and supervision have rarely addressed multiculturalism, social justice, and human rights themes that incorporate migrant experiences. Therefore, it is essential to reconceptualize effective clinical interventions. This is especially important when working within a Western-based verbal psychotherapeutic framework that relies on trust, reciprocal understanding, and open and free communication that are strained when cultural barriers exist (Draguns, 1998). Given the complexity of the migrant experience, numerous issues need to be carefully considered when providing clinical interventions. It is with the understanding of the distinctness of migrant experience that we propose the Multilevel Model (MLM) of Psychotherapy, Social Justice, and Human Rights for migrant populations. A more thorough exposition with case study applications is contained in Bemak et al. (2003).

The MLM incorporates the multicultural guidelines (American Psychological Association, 2003), and psychotherapists working with migrant populations must take into account the complexity of the migrant's historical background, past and present stressors, the acculturation process, psychosocial issues in adaptation, and cultural influences on the conceptualization of mental illness and cultural belief systems and worldviews. Within the MLM context, mental health professionals should be able to culturally adapt individual, family, and group counseling skills and techniques to migrant populations. These culturally adapted interventions are based on a comprehensive understanding, awareness, and acceptance of the cultural, sociopolitical, and historical background of the migrant clients, as well as the ability to experience and communicate empathy across cultures (Chung & Bemak, 2002a). Fundamental in employing the MLM is personal awareness and understanding of the ethnic/racial identity process for migrant clients, as well as insight into their own identity (Helms, 1995) and the interaction of that identity with the migrant client. Lack of awareness about these issues frequently leads to misdiagnoses, premature termination by the client, and even harmful treatment.

Unlike traditional mental health precepts that were originally rooted in psychodynamic constructs for cognitive and affective processes with a particular focus on prevention of emotional distress, the MLM provides a psychoeducational model that includes cognitive, affective, and behavioral interventions inclusive of cultural foundations and their relation to community and social processes. The MLM includes the following five phases:

Level 1: Mental health education

Level 2: Individual, group, and/or family psychotherapy

Level 3: Cultural empowerment

Level 4: Indigenous healing

Level 5: Social justice/human rights

The five levels are interrelated and may be implemented concurrently. Although each level can be viewed as separate, their interrelationship is essential for attaining the goals of psychotherapy. It is important to note that there is no fixed sequence to implementing the MLM levels, allowing them to be used simultaneously or independently. Emphasis and utilization of any one level or a combination of levels is determined by the psychotherapist. The MLM does not require additional resources or funding; rather, it represents a reconceptualization and diversification of the role of the psychotherapist as a helper.

Level 1, mental health education, focuses on educating client(s) about mainstream mental health practices and interventions. Migrants may not be aware of the types of services available or expectations for how to behave as a client. Basic procedures such as intake assessments, professional and interpersonal dynamics in the counseling process, the interpreter's role, time boundaries, and any use of medication may be strange concepts for migrants. Thus, Level 1 informs the individual, family, or group about the process of psychotherapy and the mental health encounter, explaining respective roles and expectations. Although Level 1 is always introduced at the beginning of any mental health intervention, it may be reintroduced at any point in the psychotherapeutic process if clarification is needed and expectations need to be redefined.

Level 2 is based on more traditional Western individual, group, and family therapy interventions while incorporating an understanding of cultural norms and practices in healing. Traditional techniques rooted in Western psychodynamic practices are alien to many migrants, resulting in the need to be more directive and active during psychotherapy with some groups (Kinzie, 1985). Specific therapeutic techniques have been identified that are effective in working with migrants. Draguns (1996) identified salient issues in cross-cultural therapy with PTSD, including the interpretation of actions, feelings, and experiences; quality and nature of verbal interactions between client and psychotherapist; role of verbal communication; role expectations for professional and client; interrelationship of somatic and physical symptoms with psychological distress; the use of metaphor, imagery, myth, ritual, and storytelling; and the nature of the relationship between client and psychotherapist. Cognitive-behavioral interventions have also been recognized as helpful with migrants (Bemak & Greenberg, 1994; Hodes & Tolmac, 2005), as has existential counseling (Parthasarthi, Durgamba, & Murthy, 2004). De Silva (1985) noted the compatibility of cognitive-behavioral therapy with Buddhist tenets, and Comas-Diaz (1985) identified a number of linkages with Hispanic cultures. Beiser (1987) explained how cognitive-behavioral interventions with Southeast Asian refugees helped reorient them to the present and away from a painful preoccupation with past memories and uncertain futures. Storytelling and projective drawing helped children to regain control over traumatic events they had experienced (Pynoos & Eth, 1984), while Charles (1986) used cultural characteristics to provide counseling in his work with Haitian refugees who held strong moral values (e.g., honesty) as beneficial. Bemak and Timm (1994) showed how dreamwork was important in the therapeutic intervention with a Cambodian refugee. Other techniques that may be employed in individual counseling include gestalt interventions, relaxation, role-playing, and psychodrama.

Mental health professionals must also consider the migrant's background as it relates to current psychological functioning. Many refugees were politically forced to migrate. Forcible and frequently dangerous intrusions into personal lives and behaviors by governments and authority figures led to fear and distrust. Daily survival required a hypersensitivity about the motives of those seeking personal information. Entering the office of the mental health professional and being asked personal questions may be experienced as highly threatening and inappropriate. Since counseling requires self-disclosure and intimate social interaction, the psychotherapist must be very careful in establishing trust with the immigrant and refugee client. This must be done while keeping in mind the impact of the client's personal experience on his or her worldview and the therapeutic relationship. For example, a Bosnian student hid and watched several men beat and rape her mother, yet was powerless to intervene, knowing that she would face the same fate if she attempted to protest the rapists' actions. When she first met a psychotherapist, her affect was blunted, she was reluctant to express any feelings or opinions, and she was highly mistrustful.

It is our belief that group psychotherapy is critical in fostering interdependence and healing and facilitating acculturation of migrants. Even though it has not yet been a prominent mode of therapeutic intervention with migrants, it is viewed as a key element in the MLM. Therapeutic factors in group work that are applicable for migrants are universality, altruism, corrective emotional experiences (Yalom & Leszcz, 2005), and love (Bemak & Epp, 1996). Ehntholt, Smith, and Yule (2005) discussed the benefit of refugee children sharing the common experience of a traumatic event in group counseling, while Urlic (2005) purported the same for adults. Others have also extolled the merits of group therapy with migrants (e.g., Friedman & Jaranson, 1994; Kinzie et al., 1988). The emphasis on group psychotherapy is highlighted in Level 2, with the use of the group format expanded upon in Level 1, where psychoeducational information sessions are incorporated, and Level 3, where groups meet to discuss cultural empowerment.

The strong family bonds and the demands on migrant families to adapt hold the promise of making family therapy the intervention of choice for addressing systemic problems. Therefore, MLM also embodies family counseling as a major therapeutic intervention. Little has been written until recently about family therapy with this population. Bemak (1989) and Szapocznik and Cohen (1986) have made a start by describing the roots, experiences, and subsequent family system problems in the course of acculturation. Professionals who provide family counseling must have a clear understanding and substantial knowledge about the background and traditional relationships of families in specific cultures of origin.

MLM's Level 3, cultural empowerment, helps the migrant gain a sense of environmental mastery. Many professionals find themselves faced with migrant clients whose motivation is to understand and effectively adapt to the world around them, rather than delving into psychological problems. The frustration of not understanding how systems work or not knowing how to access services or get assistance with problems related to education, finances, health, or employment may be a predominant concern that must first be resolved before other issues can be explored. Thus, mental health professionals must be attuned to the challenges of adapting to a new culture and provide case management–type assistance that will empower the migrant. In MLM, the psychotherapist is not expected to actually become the client's case manager. Rather, the psychotherapist becomes a "cultural systems information guide," assisting the migrant with relevant information about how the cultural system works and what the client can do to resolve associated problems. The need for the therapist to function in this capacity may extend over a prolonged period, with the longer term goal aimed at the development of skills to deal with multifaceted aspects of the system in the new culture, which in turn creates the conditions for cultural mastery and empowerment (Bemak, 1989).

One aspect of cultural empowerment in the MLM relates to experiences of discrimination and racism that migrants may encounter in the resettlement country. Some migrants come from racially homogeneous cultures with no exposure to racial, ethnic, or cultural diversity or experience as an ethnocultural minority. Furthermore, there may be an upsurge of hostility to migrants by individuals, local communities, states, and the federal government that correlates with economic and political trends and may result in scapegoating. It is important for psychotherapists to understand and appreciate the effects of individual and institutional racism and discrimination and explore coping strategies, skills, and deeper psychological problems related to these hostile acts as part of Level 3.

Level 4 of the MLM, indigenous healing, is the part of the model that combines Western traditional and nontraditional healing methodologies. The World Health Organization (1992) described how an integration of indigenous healing with Western traditional healing practices resulted in more effective therapeutic outcomes. Still, indigenous practices that are successful addressing mental health problems in the culture of origin are all too often disregarded by the Western mental health professional. There is a need for a professional openness to non-Western culturally bound healing to support and enhance the psychotherapeutic process. Simultaneously, the psychotherapist must be mindful that not all indigenous workers are legitimate healers, nor are all indigenous healing practices effective or relevant. Assessing the capabilities of indigenous workers and incorporating them in "treatment partnerships" offers a rich integration of healing practices from the cultures of origin and resettlement. In addition, if communities are highly spiritual in nature, religious leaders may play an important role in the therapeutic process.

An example of cooperative treatment is a Vietnamese male young adolescent who was having problems with anger. Since the adolescent was a practicing Buddhist, the psychotherapist referred him to a Buddhist monk to supplement the counseling. The adolescent spent weekend retreats with the monk and maintained his weekly sessions with the therapist. In therapy, the adolescent described how the monk would sit with him, relate stories about people and anger that were relevant to his situation, and sometimes laugh with him about his problem. He shared how helpful this time and attention were for him. Simultaneously, he became more open and trusting with the psychotherapist, expressing appreciation for understanding "his" culture. The psychotherapist and monk maintained contact, working together to help the adolescent. Therapists, therefore, must be willing to make a referral to an indigenous healer while being receptive to such interventions. It is also essential for mental health professionals to have access to healers and/or community elders to work in conjunction with them in the treatment process (Hiegel, 1994). By working cooperatively with traditional healers, the psychotherapist is also acknowledging an awareness, understanding, and acceptance of clients' cultural belief systems, resulting in achieved credibility.

Level 5, social justice and human rights, addresses social injustices and potential human rights violations encountered by migrant populations in resettlement countries. Similar to the other MLM levels, Level 5 is not a discrete level but is infused throughout the various MLM levels. This level requires the psychotherapists to assume a social advocacy role emphasizing basic human rights that contribute to psychological problems for clients. In Level 5, psychotherapists are both proactive and active rather than only reactive to social injustices and human rights violations that clients encounter. In daily encounters, as discussed previously, migrants can experience social injustices through an unequal access of resources, services, or opportunities; discrimination in health, housing, and employment; and/or unfair treatment in the legal and education systems. The premise of MLM Level 5 is that migrant clients' (similar to all human beings) mental health is not solely an intrapsychic issue and that environmental variables affect an individual's mental health. By not addressing outside variables, the psychotherapist is merely "Band-Aiding" the situation. For example, talking with the client regarding how to cope with discrimination in the workplace without discussing strategies on how to prevent or intervene is not addressing the core root of the discriminatory behavior that may likely continue as an ongoing problem. Examples of the type of social justice work that psychotherapists could do may include educating clients about their rights; assisting clients, their families, and communities to fight for equal treatment and access to resources and opportunity; changing policy and legislation by writing to legislators; and educating helping professionals regarding migrants' experiences and cultural influences. The work on social justice and human rights is an integral component of the MLM and important to effectively address the mental health issues of migrant clients.

# CONCLUSION

Counseling and psychotherapy with migrants is complex. To effectively assist the migrant in attaining a sense of mental health and well-being, we have developed the MLM of psychotherapy, social justice, and human rights, a five-level intervention approach that integrates Western psychotherapy with indigenous healing methods, cultural empowerment, psychoeducational training, and social justice/human rights. The MLM takes into account cultural belief systems, acculturation, psychosocial adaptation, and the influence of resettlement policy on mental health, providing a holistic framework that conceptualizes an integrated strategy to meet the multifarious needs of the migrant population.

## CRITICAL INCIDENT

This section provides four brief descriptions of possible migrant mental health problems. The descriptions will be followed by an analysis of how to apply the MLM.

Zewditu came to Chicago from rural Sudan. Her husband and brothers disappeared when they were captured by soldiers and taken away to fight in the war. Zewditu was incarcerated and repeatedly raped and tortured. She remarried but has difficulty with her new husband. She is afraid to go to sleep at night and is very distrustful of men in authority.

Eduardo is an 18-year-old Guatemalan who migrated to Boston with his family. Many members of his family were killed in the civil war, and he blames the White people in America for their deaths. He easily loses his temper, especially when challenged by Whites, causing his family to worry he might hurt someone and get in trouble.

Hung is a 67-year-old Vietnamese man who lives in California. He is very depressed because his two daughters seem to be "too American," not caring for him or showing proper respect to him in front of his peers. He is so embarrassed that he has recently stopped going out, refusing to leave his home.

Najwa is a 16-year-old Iraqi girl who came to St. Louis with her family 2 years ago. Although she seems to have come to terms with the war atrocities she witnessed in Iraq, she has been the target of repeated incidents of discrimination and racism in her high school and community. As a result, she is quite often absent from school and for the first time failing classes.

### Applying the MLM Model

None of the four individuals described above knew about Western counseling. Therefore, using the MLM Level 1 (mental health education) would help to familiarize each of the migrants with clear expectations. Level 2 (individual, group, and/or family psychotherapy) requires careful analysis of how and where to bring in the family and broader social system, given that all four clients come from collectivistic cultures. Creative techniques in counseling that were underscored by cultural appropriateness could be used here and include storytelling, narrative therapy, role-playing, or psychodrama. Level 3 (cultural empowerment) would emphasize helping clients and their families master their new culture and focus on strategies and skills that would address challenges they might face during postmigration (e.g., access to health care, securing a license to drive, problems with heating bills, housing assistance, etc.). In Hung's situation, this may include forming partnerships with community leaders in educating the Vietnamese community on issues of acculturation and intergenerational conflict. Indigenous healing is Level 4 of the MLM and would involve linking with appropriate and recognized healers in the respective communities of the four clients. For example, in Zewditu's situation, counselors could work in partnership with traditional healers in the community to assist Zewditu in coping with her experiences of rape, hence helping her to work through her distrust of all men and developing a healthier relationship with her husband. Finally, Level 5 (social justice/human rights) involves working with the four clients to ascertain their human rights. For example, Eduardo has a right to challenge inappropriate confrontations by Whites and would need to learn about his rights, while Najwa may have recourse to do something about the experience as the recipient of discrimination and prejudice. It is important to note that the MLM five levels are interchangeable and not introduced in any specific order or sequence.

## DISCUSSION QUESTIONS

1. Discuss the impact of premigration trauma on refugee mental health and the relationship between premigration trauma and postmigration adjustment.

2. How does culture affect refugee mental health, and how do expectations for treatment outcomes affect psychological interventions with refugees?

3. Are standard American diagnoses in the *DSM-IV* applicable with refugee populations?

4. What are the various reasons for the underutilization of mainstream mental health services by refugees?

5. Discuss models of acculturation that contribute to psychological adjustment and well-being for refugees. What factors contribute to successful refugee acculturation?

6. How can you creatively adapt the Western model of psychotherapy (e.g., MLM Level 2) to effectively work with refugees, and why is cultural empowerment an essential component of the MLM model?

7. Why would the mental health practitioner collaborate with indigenous healers? How can healers be incorporated into mainstream practice? What are some of the objections against collaborating with healers in providing mental health services to refugees?

# REFERENCES

American Psychological Association. (2003). Guidelines on multicultural education, training, research, practice and organizational change for psychologist. *American Psychologist, 58,* 377–402.

Beiser, M. (1987). Changing time perspective and mental health among Southeast Asian refugees. *Culture, Medicine, and Psychiatry, 11,* 437–464.

Bemak, F. (1989). Cross-cultural family therapy with Southeast Asian refugees. *Journal of Strategic and Systemic Therapies, 8,* 22–27.

Bemak, F., & Chung, R. C.-Y. (2003). Multicultural counseling with immigrant students in schools. In P. Pedersen & J. Carey (Eds.), *Multicultural counseling in schools* (2nd ed., pp. 84–101). Needham Heights, MA: Allyn & Bacon.

Bemak, F., Chung, R. C.-Y., & Pedersen, P. (2003). *Counseling refugees: A psychosocial cultural approach to innovative multicultural interventions.* Westport, CT: Greenwood.

Bemak, F., & Epp, L. (1996). The 12th curative factor: Love as an agent of healing in group psychotherapy. *Journal of Specialists in Group Work, 21*(2), 118–127.

Bemak, F., & Greenberg, B. (1994). Southeast Asian refugee adolescents: Implications for counseling. *Journal of Multicultural Counseling and Development, 22*(4), 115–124.

Bemak, F., & Timm, J. (1994). Case study of an adolescent Cambodian refugee: A clinical, developmental and cultural perspective. *International Journal of the Advancement of Counseling, 17,* 47–58.

Berry, J. W. (1986). The acculturation process and refugee behavior. In C. L. Williams & J. Westermeyer (Eds.), *Refugee mental health in resettlement countries* (pp. 25–37). Washington, DC: Hemisphere.

Bhugra, D. (2004). Migration and mental health. *Acta Psychiatica Scandinavica, 109,* 243–258.

Boothby, N. (1994). Trauma and violence among refugee children. In A. J. Marsella, T. Bornemann, S. Ekblad, & J. Orley (Eds.), *Amidst peril and pain: The mental health and well-being of the world's refugees* (pp. 239–259). Washington, DC: American Psychological Association.

Brody, E. (1994). The mental health and well-being of refugees: Issues and directions. In A. J. Marsella, T. Bornemann, S. Ekblad, & J. Orley (Eds.), *Amidst peril and pain: The mental health and well-being of the world's refugees* (pp. 57–68). Washington, DC: American Psychological Association.

Carlson, E. B., & Rosser-Hogan, R. (1991). Trauma experiences, posttraumatic stress, dissociation and depression in Cambodian refugees. *American Journal of Psychiatry, 148,* 1548–1551.

Charles, C. (1986). Mental health services for Haitians. In H. P. Lefley & P. B. Pedersen (Eds.), *Cross-cultural training for mental health professionals* (pp. 183–198). Springfield, IL: Charles C Thomas.

Chung, R. C.-Y. (2001). Psychosocial adjustment of Cambodian refugee women: Implications for mental health counseling. *Journal of Mental Health Counseling, 23*(2), 115–126.

Chung, R. C.-Y. (2005). Women, humans rights and counseling: Crossing international boundaries. *Journal of Counseling and Development, 83,* 262–268.

Chung, R. C.-Y., & Bemak, F. (2002a). The relationship between culture and empathy in cross cultural counseling. *Journal of Counseling and Development, 80,* 154–159.

Chung, R. C.-Y., & Bemak, F. (2002b). Revisiting the California Southeast Asian mental health needs assessment data: An examination of refugee ethnic and gender differences. *Journal of Counseling and Development, 80*(1), 111–119.

Chung, R. C.-Y., Bemak, F., & Kagawa-Singer, M. (1998). Gender differences in psychological distress among Southeast Asian refugees. *Journal of Nervous and Mental Disease, 186*(2), 112–119.

Chung, R. C.-Y., & Kagawa-Singer, M. (1993). Predictors of psychological distress among Southeast Asian refugees. *Social Science and Medicine, 36*(5), 631–639.

Chung, R. C.-Y., & Lin, K. M. (1994). Helpseeking behavior among Southeast Asian refugees. *Journal of Community Psychology, 22,* 109–120.

Comas-Diaz, L. (1985). Cognitive and behavioral group therapy with Puerto Rican women: A comparison of group themes. *Hispanic Journal of Behavioral Sciences, 7,* 273–283.

De Silva, P. (1985). Buddhism and modern behavioral strategies for the control of unwanted intrusive cognitions. *The Psychological Record, 35,* 437–443.

Draguns, J. G. (1996). Ethnocultural considerations in the treatment of PTSD: Therapy and service delivery. In A. J. Marsella, M. J. Friedman, E. T. Gerrity, & R. M. Scurfield (Eds.), *Ethnocultural aspects of posttraumatic stress disorder* (pp. 459–482). Washington, DC: American Psychological Association.

Draguns, J. G. (1998). Transcultural psychology and the delivery of clinical psychological services. In S. Cullari (Ed.), *Foundations of clinical psychology* (pp. 375–402). Boston: Allyn & Bacon.

Ehntholt, K. A., Smith, P. A., & Yule, W. (2005). School-based cognitive-behavioural therapy group intervention for refugee children who have experienced war-related trauma. *Clinical Child Psychology & Psychiatry, 10,* 235–250.

Eitinger, L. (1960). The symptomatology of mental disease among refugees in Norway. *Journal of Mental Science, 106,* 315–326.

Feliciano, C. (2005). Educational selectivity in US immigration: How do immigrants compare to those left behind. *Demography, 42,* 131–154.

Freeman, G. P. (2004). Immigrant incorporation in western democracies. *The International Migration Review, 38,* 945–970.

Friedman, M., & Jaranson, J. (1994). The applicability of the posttraumatic stress disorder concepts to refugees. In A. J. Marsella, T. Bornemann, S. Ekblad, & J. Orley (Eds.), *Amidst peril and pain: The mental health and well-being of the world's refugees* (pp. 207–228). Washington, DC: American Psychological Association.

Geltman, P. L., & Cochran, J. (2005). A private-sector preferred provider network model for public health screening for newly arrived resettled refugees. *American Journal of Public Health, 95*(2), 196–200.

Goldberg, M. E. (1999). Truancy and dropout rates among Cambodian students: Results from a comprehensive high school. *Social Work in Education, 21*(1), 49–63.

Hauff, E., & Vaglum, P. (1995). Organized violence and the stress of exile: Predictors of mental health in a community cohort of Vietnamese refugees three years after resettlement. *British Journal of Psychiatry, 166,* 360–367.

Helms, J. E. (1995). An update of Helms' white and people of color racial identity models. In J. G. Ponterotto, J. M. Casas, L. A. Suzuki, & C. M. Alexander (Eds.), *Handbook of multicultural counseling* (pp. 199–217). Thousand Oaks, CA: Sage.

Hiegel, J. P. (1994). Use of indigenous concepts and healers in the care of refugees: Some experiences from the Thai border camps. In A. J. Marsella, T. Bornemann, S. Ekblad, & J. Orley (Eds.), *Amidst peril and pain: The mental health and well-being of the world's refugees* (pp. 293–310). Washington, DC: American Psychological Association.

Hodes, M., & Tolmac, J. (2005). Severely impaired young refugees. *Clinical Child Psychology & Psychiatry, 10*(2), 251–261.

International Organization for Migration. (2005). International migration data and statistics. *World Migration: Costs and Benefits of International Migration (Section 3).* Retrieved November 12, 2005, from http://www.iom.int

Kagawa-Singer, M., & Chung, R. C.-Y. (1994). A paradigm for culturally based care in ethnic minority populations. *Journal of Community Psychology, 22,* 192–208.

Kinzie, J. D. (1985). Overview of clinical issues in the treatment of Southeast Asian refugees. In T. C. Owan (Ed.), *Southeast Asian mental health: Treatment, prevention, services, training, and research* (pp.113–135). Washington, DC: National Institute of Mental Health.

Kinzie, J. D. (1993). Posttraumatic effects and their treatment among Southeast Asian refugees. In J. Wilson & B. Raphael (Eds.), *International handbook of traumatic stress syndromes* (pp. 311–320). New York: Plenum.

Kinzie, J. D., Leung, P., Bui, A., Ben, R., Keopraseuth, K. O., Riley, C., et al. (1988). Group therapy with Southeast Asian refugees. *Community Mental Health Journal, 3*(2), 157–166.

Kirmayer, L. J. (1989). Cultural variation in the response to psychiatric disorders and emotional distress. *Social Science & Medicine, 28*(3), 327–339.

Kleinman, A., Eisenberg, L., & Good, B. (1978). Culture, illness and care. *Annals of Internal Medicine, 88,* 251–258.

Marsella, A. J., Friedman, M., & Spain, H. (1993). Ethnocultural aspects of PTSD. In J. Oldham, M. Riba, & A. Tasman (Eds.), *Review of psychiatry* (Vol. 12, pp. 157–181). Washington, DC: American Psychiatric Press.

Massey, D. S., & Capoferro, C. (2004). Measuring undocumented migration. *The International Migration Review, 38,* 1075–1102.

Mezey, A. (1960). Personal background, emigration and mental health in Hungarian refugees. *Journal of Mental Science, 106,* 618–627.

Micozzi, M. S. (1996). *Fundamentals of complementary and alternative medicine.* New York: Churchill Livingstone.

Mills, K. (2005). The refugees convention 50 years on: Globalization and international law. *Human Rights Quarterly, 27,* 725–730.

Mollica, R. F., Wyshak, G., & Lavelle, J. (1987). The psychosocial impact of war trauma and torture on Southeast Asian refugees. *American Journal of Psychiatry, 144*(12), 1567–1572.

Odegaard, O. (1932). Emigration and insanity: A study of mental disease among the Norwegian born population of Minnesota. *Acta Psychiatrica et Neurologica Supplement, 4,* 1–206.

Parthasarthi, M. S., Durgamba, V. K., & Murthy, N. S. (2004). Counselling migrant families in Southern India. *International Journal for the Advancement of Counselling, 26,* 363–367.

Pedersen, P. (2000). *A handbook for developing multicultural awareness* (3rd ed.). Alexandria, VA: American Association for Counseling and Development.

Pernice, R., & Brook, J. (1994). Relationship of migrant status (refugee or immigrant) to mental health. *International Journal of Social Psychiatry, 40,* 177–188.

Phillips, L., & Draguns, J. (1969). Some issues in intercultural research on psychopathology. In W. Caudill & T. Y. Lin (Eds.), *Mental health research in Asian and the Pacific* (pp. 21–32). Honolulu, HI: East-West Center Press.

Porter, E. (2005). Not on the radar: Illegal immigrants are bolstering social security. *Generations, 29,* 100–103.

Pynoos, R., & Eth, S. (1984). Children traumatized by witnessing acts of personal violence: Homicide, rape or suicide behavior. In S. Eth & R. Pynoos (Eds.), *Post-traumatic stress disorder in children* (pp. 17–44). Washington, DC: American Psychiatric Press.

Rytina, N. F. (2005). U.S. legal permanent residents: 2004. In *Office of Immigration Statistics annual flow report.* Retrieved November 27, 2005, from http://uscis.gov/graphics/shared/statistics/publications

Sue, S., Fujino, D., Hu, L., Takeuchi, D., & Zane, N. (1991). Community mental health services for ethnic minority groups: A test of cultural responsive hypothesis. *Journal of Consulting and Clinical Psychology, 59*(4), 533–540.

Szapocznik, J., & Cohen, R. E. (1986). Mental health care for rapidly changing environments: Emergency relief to unaccompanied youths of the 1980 Cuba refugee wave. In C. L. Williams & J. Westermeyer (Eds.), *Refugee mental health in resettlement countries* (pp. 141–156). New York: Hemisphere.

Szapocznik, J., & Kurtines, W. (1980). Acculturation, biculturalism, and adjustment among Cuban-Americans. In A. M. Padilla (Ed.), *Recent advances in acculturation research: Theory, models, and some new findings* (pp. 914–931). Boulder, CO: Westview.

Tayabas, T., & Pok, T. (1983). The arrival of the Southeast Asian refugees in America: An overview. In *Bridging cultures: Southeast Asian refugees in America* (pp. 3–14). Los Angeles: Special Services for Groups-Asian American Community Mental Health Training.

United Nations. (1995). *Notes for speakers: Social development.* New York: Department of Public Information, United Nations.

Urlic, I. (2005). Recognizing inner and outer realities as a process: On some countertransferential issues of the group conductor. *Group Analysis, 38,* 249–263.

U.S. Immigration and Naturalization Service. (2003). *Estimates of the unauthorized immigrant population residing in the United States: 1990 to 2000.* Retrieved November 27, 2005, from http://uscis.gov/graphics/shared/statistics/publications

Van der Kolk, B. A. (1987). *Psychological trauma.* Washington, DC: American Psychiatric Press.

Van Velsen, C., Gorst-Unsworth, C., & Turner, S. (1996). Survivors of torture and organized violence: Demography and diagnosis. *Journal of Traumatic Stress, 9,* 181–193.

Vertovec, S. (2004). Migrant transnationalism and modes of transformation. *The International Migration Review, 38,* 970–1002.

Vickers, B. (2005). Cognitive model of the maintenance and treatment of post-traumatic stress disorder applied to children and adolescents. *Clinical Child Psychology & Psychiatry, 10,* 217–234.

World Health Organization. (1992). *Refugee mental health: Draft manual for field testing.* Geneva, Switzerland: Author.

Yalom, I., & Leszcz, M. (2005). *The theory and practice of group psychotherapy* (5th ed.). New York: Basic Books.

CHAPTER

# 19

# Counseling Disaster Survivors

## Implications for Cross-Cultural Mental Health

Fred Bemak and Rita Chi-Ying Chung

---

### Primary Objective

- To assist mental health practitioners in understanding and providing cross-culturally responsive counseling in disaster situations by providing an intervention model (the Disaster Cross-Cultural Counseling Model)

### Secondary Objectives

- To provide an overview of emergency relief disaster counseling
- To examine cross-cultural considerations in providing counseling to disaster survivors
- To become familiar with guidelines for implementing the Disaster Cross-Cultural Counseling Model

---

IN RECENT YEARS, THE WORLD HAS FACED NUMEROUS NATURAL AND HUMAN-INDUCED DISASTERS THAT have caused serious disruption and displacement of hundreds of thousands of people. These events consisted of the attacks on September 11, 2001; the tsunami in South Asia; hurricanes such as Katrina and Rita in the United States and the Caribbean; earthquakes in China, Japan, Afghanistan, and Pakistan; and conflict in Darfur. For example, there has been an ongoing conflict in the Darfur region of western Sudan since February 2003 where approximately 300,000 have lost their lives. There has been systemic and wide-scale ethnic cleansing, murder, rape, torture, and enslavement (Amnesty International, 2006), resulting in significant death, destruction, family disruption, and migration. These and other disasters have displaced and dislodged people from multiple cultures, races, ethnicities, and socioeconomic classes, requiring an immediate humanitarian aid in the form of basic shelter, food, housing, sanitation, water, security, and medical services.

In addition to meeting the core basic needs, there are significant psychological issues encountered by survivors of disasters as they attempt to rebuild and reconstruct their lives, demanding a critical mental health response. These mental health issues can be far-reaching and may be needed even years after the disaster had occurred. The scale, magnitude, and quantity of the global disasters across different cultures necessitate a different type of response for different times that is culturally sensitive and responsive, particularly given the voluminous need for mental health assistance from diverse cultural groups and the reality of limited resources.

This chapter examines the growing contemporary need for culturally responsive mental health interventions with disaster survivors. The chapter begins with a brief overview of emergency relief counseling, followed by a presentation of the Disaster Cross-Cultural Counseling Model (DCCC). The DCCC is a cross-cultural model that incorporates a holistic approach examining issues within an ecological, sociological, cultural, economic, political, and psychological context of social justice and equity as a core aspect of disaster counseling. Sixteen key issues in culturally responsive disaster counseling that are applicable using the DCCC model in different types of disasters will be presented. The chapter concludes with a description of five case study critical incidents exploring the implementation of the DCCC and the impact of race, ethnicity, and class on mental health disaster counseling. The term *survivors* will be used throughout the chapter rather than *victims*.

## OVERVIEW OF EMERGENCY RELIEF DISASTER COUNSELING

Given the degree of devastation that results from a disaster, it is evident that survivors will experience a multitude of psychological problems, including posttraumatic stress disorder (PTSD), anxiety, and depressive symptoms, such as sadness, hopelessness, feelings of being overwhelmed, and the lack of emotional and physical energy (Dudley-Grant, Mendez, & Zinn, 2000; Norris, Perilla, & Murphy, 2001). Symptoms may vary for each individual and manifest in different ways. Some also experience sleep disturbances that are oftentimes accompanied by nightmares that are fraught with the images of the disaster; anxiety about relocating and one's current living circumstances, which are often temporary and crowded; a need to talk about one's personal experience related to the disaster; concerns about feeling part of the community and its recovery; fear and anxiety about personal and physical safety and those of loved ones; grief over loss of loved ones and pets; and profound losses of valued and meaningful possessions. Disasters, such as hurricanes, can provoke anxiety in individuals that may be triggered by changes in the weather and the recurring fear of being vulnerable to environmental forces beyond one's control. There may also be difficulties in concentrating and completing tasks and dealing with demands of being self-reliant and strong (Dudley-Grant et al., 2000), with a heightened sense of guardedness and anxiety about whether one's life could return to a normal routine. Some may feel that they have been overlooked or ignored by media and federal agencies, such as the case in the Mississippi Gulf Coast after Hurricane Katrina where survivors felt that the media concentrated primarily on New Orleans during and after the hurricane.

Studies (e.g., Jones, Frary, Cunningham, Weddle, & Kaiser, 2001; Pfefferbaum, 1997) have found that the degree of PTSD experienced by disaster survivors is influenced by multiple variables. These variables are divided into three general categories: (1) individual characteristics, such as age, gender, race/ethnic, trait anxiety, history of mental illness, developmental level, family characteristics, cultural factors, attribution style, and coping strategies; (2) the emotional experience and response during and after the event (e.g., positive vs. negative); and (3) the severity of physical damage to property, injury to or death of loved ones and/or friends, and the level of exposure of the individual to the event.

Ethnic, racial, and cultural differences in PTSD have also been found. One of the first studies that compared two communities after a disaster from two different countries (California, USA, and Chile) found that the Chileans reported more PTSD symptoms than their Californian counterparts (Durkin, 1993). Other studies found that African Americans and White females were more likely to exhibit PTSD and comorbid symptoms when compared to White males (March, Amaya-Jackson, Terry, & Constanzo, 1997). Results differ when comparing children across ethnic and racial groups, with White children more susceptible to distress than African Americans (Jones et al., 2001). It was suggested that these results were attributed to factors such as acculturation, socioeconomic status, and coping strategies.

## THE DISASTER CROSS-CULTURAL COUNSELING (DCCC) MODEL

In the days, weeks, months, and sometimes years after a disaster, the common types of problems encountered by survivors are related to day-to-day living. Issues such as transportation; not being able to locate a missing loved one; the loss or death of family, friends, and pets; unemployment; loss of child care; inadequate temporary housing accommodations; filling prescriptions; and loss of medicine, eyeglasses, hearing aids, and so on all contribute to psychological problems. These problems are exacerbated by the loss of legal papers and important documents, including birth certificates and medical, school, and employment records, thus impeding the following: applying for medical, health, and financial benefits; proving citizenship; applying for housing; securing loans; and accessing social services and other types of assistance.

Mental health professionals must emphasize daily challenges in disaster work rather than immediately delving into deeper psychological issues. We would suggest a three-phase DCCC model, based on Bemak's (1989) psychosocial adjustment developmental model for refugees. For each phase of the DCCC, culturally responsive interventions are employed. In Phase I, counselors and psychologists assist disaster survivors to use existing skills to master the new environment and feel psychologically safe. During Phase II, there is an integration of formerly used skills with newly developed skills to handle the postdisaster situation, followed by Phase III, where there is stabilization and mastery over the postdisaster circumstances that are accompanied by increasingly successful adaptation. During Phase III, there is a growing sense of hope about the future and the ability for the disaster survivors to examine future goals and directions for themselves and their loved ones. It is important that mental health professionals are clear about the continuum of postdisaster adjustment within the culturally responsive framework of the DCCC. In summary, the DCCC begins with an initial priority of basic survival, life, and safety needs that facilitates stabilization and an equilibrium that allows coping and adaptation. This, in turn, leads to the ability to integrate past and present and build toward future goals and directions.

Given the degree of devastation, survivors often become disorganized in their planning and thinking. They are overwhelmed and may become unproductively overactive. Mental health professionals can assist survivors in the DCCC Phrase II by guiding survivors through problem solving and assist with prioritizing and focusing on specific goals and action, keeping in mind the cultural context. Identifying and selecting one immediate problem that is relatively solvable provides a beginning step that assists in bringing back a sense of control and confidence in survivors. It is also important to assess survivors' functioning and coping and identify issues such as PTSD and suicidal ideation, while at the same time evaluating available resources and social support networks.

## Implementing the DCCC

Cross-cultural disaster counseling requires culturally sensitive interventions that involve cross-cultural empathy (Chung & Bemak, 2002), guiding and encouraging clients to tell their stories and share their feelings, and active listening whereby the mental health professional is open and receptive to clients' painful stories and disaster experiences. This can be done in relief centers, shelters, schools, mental health facilities, or other private or public facilities. It is important to skillfully coalesce active listening without judgment, intervention, or interpretation (Dudley-Grant et al., 2000). This allows for silence and interventions that facilitate the telling of one's story. Concurrently, it is important to attend to nonverbal cues that may elicit deeper feelings and be able to unobtrusively reflect on feelings, thereby encouraging emotional expression, consistent with prior research that links catharsis to healing (Bemak & Young, 1998). This is of utmost importance in cross-cultural communication where there may exist inherent distrust by clients to self-disclose to a mental health professional from a different racial or ethnic background.

Some examples of helpful interventions include the following: "these are normal reactions to a disaster," "it is understandable that you feel this way," "you are not going crazy," "it wasn't your fault," "you did the best you could," and "things may never be the same, but they will get better and you'll feel better" (Substance Abuse Mental Health Services Administration [SAMHSA], 2006), which normalize reactions to the disaster. It is critical to note that the impulse by mental health professionals to try to "fix" the survivors' painful situation or "make" survivors feel better may in fact backfire and result in feelings of being discounted, misunderstood, or further alienated. Common errors in disaster counseling include interventions such as the following: "it could have been worse," "you can always get another pet/car/home," "it's best if you just stay busy," "I know just how you feel," or "you need to get on with your life" (SAMHSA, 2006). When statements such as these are made in cross-cultural counseling situations, they may be construed as patronizing or insensitive.

Disaster survivors may experience PTSD. The American Counseling Association (2005) has suggested 10 ways to recognize PTSD: reexperiencing the event through vivid memories or flashbacks; feeling "emotionally numb"; feeling overwhelmed by what would normally be considered everyday situations and diminished interest in performing normal tasks or pursuing usual interests; crying uncontrollably; isolating oneself from family and friends and avoiding social situations; relying increasingly on alcohol or drugs to get through the day; feeling extremely moody, irritable, angry, suspicious, or frightened; having difficulty falling or staying asleep, sleeping too much, and experiencing nightmares; feeling guilty about surviving the event or being unable to solve the problem, change the event, or prevent disaster; and feeling fear and a sense of doom about the future. In disasters, the depth of these reactions has the potential to create highly charged interpersonal dynamics in cross-cultural settings. In our experience, given the heightened sensitivity during a disaster and associated feelings and high levels of vulnerability, interventions create the strong possibility to promote a significant cross-cultural interpersonal connection based on a shared humanity, or they may promote a greater divide between mental health professionals and clients when differences are accentuated. It is a moment of intervention that requires maximal cross-cultural sensitivity and awareness, especially in times of acute distress, fear, and anxiety.

In addition, mental health professionals need to know the suicide warning signs. If a client is threatening or hinting at hurting or killing himself or herself; looking for or seeking access to firearms, pills, or other items that could be harmful; talking or writing about death, dying, or suicide; expressing feelings of hopelessness; or sharing feelings of rage or uncontrolled anger, all of these could be signs of suicide or potential violence. Other indications may include seeking revenge, acting reckless or engaging in unseemly risks, expressing feelings of being trapped with no escape, increasing the use of alcohol or drugs, withdrawing from friends and family, feeling overly anxious and agitated, sleeping too much or too little, having dramatic mood changes, and losing a sense of purpose to live (SAMHSA, 2006). Again, during a time of susceptibility and defenselessness, cross-cultural issues have the potential to become accentuated and require the mental health professional to be culturally competent.

Group work is also an ideal intervention for disaster survivors and must be facilitated within a multicultural framework (Bemak & Chung, 2004). Groups provide a commonly felt bond of universality. Sharing their disaster story with others who have encountered the same or similar experiences can be reassuring for those who believe that their experience was unusual or unique (Ehntholt, Smith, & Yule, 2005). This format provides opportunities to explore loss and reminisce about "before," to observe a variety of coping strategies, to view others at various stages in the resolution of trauma, and to gain satisfaction (altruism) by helping others. Thus, groups can serve as a forum for survivors to vent their feelings and problem-solve issues related to the disaster experience (Peuler, 1998) and offer a forum for people to quickly identify those with greater psychological need (Gillis, 1993).

Brief psychotherapy with youth, focusing on trauma and grief, up to 3 years after a disaster event has also been found to be effective (Goenjian, Karayan, & Pynoos, 1997). Since avoidance is a common reaction to a major disaster for children, behavioral techniques have been found to be effective. Play therapy, anxiety management techniques, and projective techniques, such as play, art, drawing, relaxation, storytelling, educating children about common posttrauma symptoms, desensitization, and other behavioral techniques, have all been found helpful with this population (Deblinger, McLeer, & Henry, 1990; Pfefferbaum, 1997). Workshops have also been found to be beneficial in helping survivors understand postdisaster stress management and develop coping strategies. Interventions should reflect developmental capabilities of survivors (Pynoos & Nader, 1993). In addition, it is important that survivors of all ages are educated about the possibility of retraumatization and the possible need for additional mental health support. Given that the DCCC is a culturally responsive model, it can be implemented in school- and community-based prevention and intervention programs that have the potential to promote normalcy and reduce stigma for children and parents.

## Cultural Considerations

It is essential that mental health professionals doing postdisaster work using the DCCC have an understanding and sensitivity to the relevant cultural norms and expectations of the cultural groups with whom they are working (Marsella, Friedman, & Gerrity, 1996). Since disasters affect a great number of ethnically and racially diverse individuals and communities, different interventions may be required to address their unique ways of coping with postdisaster stress. Their desires may also consist of the need for and pursuit of more formalized mental health support. Simultaneously, a cultural sense of honor and pride, religious and spiritual orientation and belief systems, and ways of handling and dealing with grief and loss are significantly different across cultures. Similarly, communication across cultures also presents the challenge to go beyond language and respond to nuances of specific words, phrases, slogans, proverbs, and colloquialisms, which take on particular importance at times of high levels of stress. Well-intentioned attempts to help without considering cultural factors may create misunderstanding and be interpreted as meddling or interference or even as political attempts to exert influence and/or control. Related to these needs for cross-cultural sensitivity, mental health professionals must also be aware of, understand, and acknowledge the historical and sociopolitical background of survivors from ethnic, racial, and oppressed populations that may contribute to cultural mistrust.

According to Doherty (1999), a major goal in counseling and psychotherapy has historically been to bring about a degree of conformity to the norms of the dominant majority group. When doing cross-cultural disaster work, the aim to link stability with the dominant group raises serious questions about respect for the norms and culture of diverse groups. Working from a framework of the dominant culture has the potential to alienate and further traumatize the survivors, with the potential to convert survivors to victims. In the DCCC model, mental health professionals must take into account the normative lifestyle and culture of the various affected groups when helping individuals accommodate and stabilize during postdisaster.

Given the lack of resources and services, another factor that we witnessed during our recent trip to the Mississippi Gulf Coast to work with Katrina survivors was anger and resentment directed at other racial and ethnic groups. We observed numerous displays of anger and resentment between Black, Latino, White, and Vietnamese survivors that flared up in parking lots, supermarket lines, rental car agencies, and disaster relief centers. The racial tensions manifested in direct ways through verbal encounters and sometimes physical assault. Tensions were high, and racism was more overtly expressed than usual. Although the values and attitudes themselves may already have been present, the actual expression was more open with the potential for greater and more direct hostilities. We would suggest that mental health professionals using the DCCC model must be aware and openly and constructively address racial and ethnic tensions in disaster situations where there may be potential conflicts over access to resources and services.

Another factor that is important to consider when working with the DCCC model is how a counselor or psychotherapist enters a disaster site. Mental health teams dispatched to disaster sites can at times be an overwhelming presence. Carrying the assumption that "you need us" without being sensitive to the cultural values regarding Western-based counseling brings with it the danger that the mental health professionals may quickly become unwelcome. The openness of the community to disaster counseling may coincide with the usage of culturally appropriate rituals in responding to grief and loss and making sense of the disaster experience. For example, in Mississippi, many people spoke about God and the Devil as the forces behind the disaster and the postdisaster healing. To negate this framework for understanding Katrina and the future would have challenged a cultural belief system and diminished trust and credibility with clients. Thus, it is important to not impose on clients a "one-size-fits-all" rationale for what happened or inflict a belief system for how they should grieve or mourn, which, however well intentioned, may cause more harm than good. Using the DCCC, it is imperative to harbor respect and understanding for the cultural beliefs and rituals of those affected by the disaster.

## Cultural Differences in Dealing With Loss and Grief

Different cultures have dissimilar beliefs and understanding about the origin and nature of life and death. This is manifested in rituals and practices associated with honoring major life transitions and events, culturally sanctioned manners in which to express one's feelings during major life transitions, the perceived social implications and appropriateness of those feelings, techniques for dealing with feelings that cannot be directly expressed, and expectations from family and community (Rosenblatt, 1993). Historical studies have shown how individuals in Western culture have mourned differently over time (Kohn & Levav, 1990; Newnes, 1991). Cross-cultural studies show variety in cultural responses to death, manner of mourning, and nature of internalization of loss. Rather than being process oriented, mourning is seen as an adaptive response to specific tasks required by the losses that must be dealt with, regardless of the individual or historical backgrounds (Hagman, 1995), and must be addressed with cultural sensitivity.

For example, White Americans report thinking significantly more about grief, religious feelings, and death than the Japanese (Asai & Barnlund, 1998). In Japan, ancestor worship is ritualized and supported by the belief that the living maintain their bonds with the dead. This approach provides a resolution by survivors that is linked with the journey of rebirth for the deceased, providing emotional benefits and an ongoing relationship based on continued balance and harmony with the deceased (Goss & Klass, 1997). Rubin (1990) compared mourning behaviors in the United States with those in an Israeli kibbutz. The finding suggested that in a dense social network such as a small- or medium-sized kibbutz, mourning is part of a wider circle of family, friends, neighbors, and coworkers and that the funerals in the United States may force loose social networks to generate an image of social support.

## GUIDELINES FOR IMPLEMENTING THE DISASTER CROSS-CULTURAL COUNSELING MODEL

Using the DCCC requires cross-cultural sensitivity, awareness, knowledge, and skills, as defined by the American Psychological Association's (2003) multicultural guidelines. Along the lines of the multicultural frameworks that define the general field of counseling and psychology, specific recommendations are applicable to disaster recovery. The following are 16 guidelines for effectively implementing the DCCC in postdisaster counseling.

1. Understand the context of the disaster event within a culturally relevant framework. Is the disaster considered a work of nature, a spiritual or religious occurrence, the wrath of God, a message from a higher being, punishment from ancestors, and so on? Understanding, appreciating, and accepting the meaning of the event for survivors helps to effectively shape culturally responsive interventions that are embedded in the inherent cultural and individual worldviews.

2. Mental health professionals must be highly sensitive to language barriers and make sure not to neglect survivors because of language differences (Bemak, Chung, & Pedersen, 2003). It is essential that psychologists and counselors consult with members of the local community to assist with translation as needed (Hobfoll et al., 1991). Simultaneously, it is important to carefully discuss confidentiality and mutually define with bilingual translators their comfort and ability to maintain privacy regarding other survivors within their ethnic community who may be clients.

3. The focus of initial contact with survivors is on fundamental survival needs within a cultural context. It is essential to begin by helping survivors deal with meeting the basic needs for food, water, clothing, physical health, safe, and shelter. To discuss psychological health is premature when there are fears and anxiety about these basic needs. Basic survival must also be considered within the framework of the larger culture. For example, many Hurricane Katrina survivors of color felt marginalized and believed that those with greater socioeconomic status and those who were White had better access to resources and service systems. This type of reaction by minority groups within majority cultures creates important dynamics that are essential to address within the therapeutic context and may elicit feelings and subsequent expressions of anger, rage, depression, sadness, hopelessness, and despair.

4. As mental health professionals engage in cross-cultural counseling with diverse populations, it is important to be aware of perceived issues of cultural mistrust (Coleman, Wampold, & Casali, 1995).

Distrust of the counselor or therapist may create barriers in the therapeutic relationship that hinder openness and discussion about the deep-rooted pain and anguish caused by a disaster. Along with knowing about cultural mistrust, one must also maintain an awareness of feelings of racism, prejudice, and discrimination that may be experienced by the survivor group and become apparent in transference reactions during the therapeutic encounter.

5. Mental health professionals must incorporate advocacy into their work when they witness unfair or unequal treatment related to services and resources (Bemak & Chung, 2005). This oftentimes is related to cultural diversity and covert discrimination or inattention to basic needs and rights. Collaboration with survivors is particularly important since they may feel vulnerable and helpless and lack the skills and ability to challenge inept or unresponsive systems, particularly after a disaster. Forming these partnerships requires bonding and alliances to co-advocate along with survivors to get basic services. Needless to say, this type of alliance and co-advocacy are not typically part of traditional psychotherapy.

6. Mental health professionals must move out of traditional roles and be proactive in establishing linkages with other service providers, agencies, and officials. This is critical in fostering credibility and trustworthiness as mental health providers. Furthermore, having contacts with individuals who provide support services such as housing, clothing, food, and so on is a key to meeting basic needs. For example, working in the Gulf Coast following Hurricane Katrina, it was critical that we linked with physicians who were providing medical treatment, federal government officials who were distributing housing vouchers, food and clothing distributors, insurance company agents, religious leaders, and established community leaders from various ethnic groups.

7. It is important to work from a larger ecological context (Bemak & Conyne, 2004) so we as mental health professionals can provide support within this larger family and community context. Waxler-Morrison, Anderson, and Richardson (1990) identified questions that help facilitate the context of health and culture, asking about how survivors reconstruct their lives and relationships, meet their community obligations, and maximize their satisfaction in relationships. It is essential to ask these types of questions and understand the relationship of social and collectivistic values combines with the larger ecology of each individual.

8. DCCC also necessitates the psychoeducational information approach when appropriate. Dissemination of relevant information can be helpful in facilitating psychological healing, especially knowing that for the first few months of postdisaster, there are significant behavioral and psychological difficulties such as sleeping or eating problems. Important information can also be given as it relates to race relations, given intensified feelings after disasters that may be displaced onto different cultural groups that may dissipate over time with psychoeducational groups and group interventions. There should be a caution here to not rely solely on education as a means for postdisaster healing but rather to integrate psychoeducational interventions as part of a broader intervention strategy that incorporates attention to culture.

9. In any disaster, it is important to designate a lead team member who can be the liaison with regional, state, national, international, and nongovernmental organization officials (Aguilera & Planchon, 1995). This is a key component of working with the DCCC model and was evident in Mississippi working with Katrina survivors when the first author was the lead contact attending meetings with state and regional mental health officials, Federal Emergency Management Agency (FEMA) and SAMHSA representatives, and regional community leaders.

10. Employing the DCCC model uses some of the training pedagogy that has been established for mental health professionals. Current disaster counseling requires licensed professionals who could commit for 2-week time periods, which, in the case of Hurricane Katrina, left many survivors without counseling support. In the DCCC model, we require a licensed professional who will provide supervision for unlicensed professionals or graduate students. In addition, the DCCC allows for 1-week intensive time commitments. This significantly expands the human resource pool and provides excellent training under supervision, similar to a practicum or internship experience. It was tragic after Hurricane Katrina when there were tremendous mental health needs, yet restrictions on licensure requirements, and 2-week minimum commitments made it difficult for mental health workers to offer their services. Subsequently, when we took 14 advanced graduate students to work on the Gulf Coast, we saw almost 600 survivors within a 1-week period. There were daily 2- to 3-hour supervision and debriefing evening sessions and constant cell phone backup contact during the workdays with all 14 students for any emergencies.

11. Implementing the DCCC model requires building disaster response capacity building among local mental health professionals to ensure long-term sustainability. A combination of training and supervising local professionals and paraprofessionals (in regions where there are few or no professionals) to provide counseling support is key to working toward longer term capacity building.

12. The focus of the DCCC is on strengths and coping strategies (Doherty, 1999), not on psychopathology. Disasters create devastating situations that generate strong and sometimes dysfunctional survival strategies. A premise for the DCCC model is to understand the context for coping strategies rather than view them as pathological.

13. The DCCC model strongly promotes the use of natural support systems in disaster relief work. It is critical that mental health workers have a clear understanding of the nuclear and extended family and community relationships within a cultural context and work with groups of survivors accordingly.

14. Using the DCCC model, there is a focus on group, family, and community work that underscores the need for human connection and belonging that is critical postdisaster. Thus, we encourage group interventions wherever possible to promote a sense of universality and common bonds. Drawing on the experiences of others has shown great benefit and is recommended for disaster counseling work (Paton, 1996).

15. Mental health professionals must approach their work with clients with a maximum level of psychological self-awareness, as well as social, cultural, and political self-awareness. The mental health professional's awareness of these different levels intersects with the survivor's sharply heightened worldviews following a disaster.

16. The 15 guidelines for using the DCCC model thus far have focused on working with survivors. It is also important to acknowledge and accept that mental health professionals working in disaster relief will also need "self-care." Our feelings as mental health professionals may be greatly accentuated working with people in postdisaster crisis. Therefore, we must be ready to deal with the strong and pronounced countertransference issues and pain associated with doing intensive work, especially when emphasizing cross-cultural counseling. It is therefore important that mental health professionals ensure that they receive support and supervision. Professionals must take time to debrief with other professionals on-site and have support networks available via cell phones and other means.

# CONCLUSION

As the world experiences global warming and climate changes, it is inevitable that natural disasters will occur. Often, those who have the least help and assistance during postdisaster are impoverished and come from culturally diverse ethnic and racial groups. The DCCC proposes a model of culturally responsive postdisaster counseling and guidelines for implementation that are derived from the multicultural guidelines. The DCCC addresses culturally sensitive counseling in a postdisaster situation that requires mental health professionals to be flexible, creative, and aware of their own stereotypes, biases, and privilege when working with cross-cultural disaster survivors.

## CRITICAL INCIDENT

The five critical incidents are taken from real-life situations experienced during work in Mississippi after Hurricane Katrina. The critical incidents describe the implementation of the DCCC model through a series of case studies that portray pre- and postdisaster life circumstances and the psychological well-being of various survivors. Each of the vignettes describes DCCC-based cross-cultural mental health interventions following Hurricane Katrina. The critical incidents were coauthored with 14 individuals[1] who were part of the Counselors Without Borders Project team providing counseling in Mississippi. To fully understand the context of the critical incidents, this section will begin with a brief description of the disaster relief centers, the setting where the mental health disaster counseling took place, followed by the five critical incidents. All clients' names used are fictitious to maintain confidentiality.

## Disaster Relief Centers

The disaster relief centers (DRCs) in the United States are set up by local and federal government officials to provide assistance for disaster survivors. All resources such as food, water, and clothing are free. In our experience with Hurricane Katrina, the DRCs located in higher socioeconomic status (SES) areas have more resources and assistance, such as medical care and clothing, as compared to the low-SES areas, where there might only be food and water. The DRCs may be housed in large buildings such as a school gymnasium, a warehouse, or a large tent. All around the DRC facilities are tables for various types of assistance—for example, debris removal, financial aid, applying for a trailer, other accommodations (i.e., shelters, hotels, etc.), medical assistance, and so on. In front of each table are rows of chairs for people to sit as they wait their turn, similar to an open-spaced waiting room. All the case studies took place at the DRC where survivors were seeking assistance.

## Case Study 1

Mr. Tran is a 40-year-old Vietnamese who lost his apartment and belongings in Hurricane Katrina after living in Mississippi for 21 years. For the past 3 months, Mr. Tran and his daughters (ages 10 and 14) were living in a tent. FEMA workers had serious concerns about Mr. Tran and his children living in a tent with temperatures dropping below 30 degrees. However, Mr. Tran refused to move to a shelter. Given the concerns, a FEMA worker asked a counselor to speak with Mr. Tran. The counselor learned in an hour session that Mr. Tran was afraid to move to the shelter, believing that it was not only dangerous but that he and his children could be separated. He felt they could handle the cold with the blue FEMA tarp he had placed over the tent for warmth, safety, and protection from the rain. Mr. Tran also told the counselor about how several other Vietnamese friends in adjacent tents had created a tent community and had become an extended family. They all shared one car to go to the DRC for food and clothing and to do errands, and they spoke daily about their predicament after the storm. He was proud of his tent home and thought it was a secure place and supportive community for both himself and his children.

As the counselor probed further, she learned about Mr. Tran's flight during the Vietnam War and his witnessing of human atrocities, as well as his 3-year refugee camp experience in Malaysia. Living in the tent with his children brought back memories of Malaysia and gave him a sense of safety, especially since he felt there was no imminent danger. In fact, his children were both attending school and had a set routine with friends and their studies, which was another reason why he resisted moving to a shelter. Also, they had all become closer as a result of their tent experience and his older daughter's new role in the family helping to prepare group meals for their tent community.

The counselor heard clearly about Mr. Tran's pride in being a hard worker and acquiring material possessions, such as a television, and his subsequent devastation when an insurance inspector, after surveying the hurricane damage, told Mr. Tran that he had nothing worthy of an insurance claim. Mr. Tran was highly distraught about the decision and kept mentally repeating the inspector's comment that he had nothing. The counselor was highly supportive of Mr. Tran, carefully listening to his story, acknowledging his history and its link to his current life in a tent community, being aware and respecting cross-cultural differences and countertransference, and showing respect for cultural values that were inherent in the Vietnamese community.

## Case Study 2

Rosa, a Latina in her 30s, was at the DRC with her 8-month-old daughter. The counselor noticed them sitting alone waiting for a housing official, so she walked over to see how they were doing. When the counselor said "Hello," the response from Rosa was "No English." The counselor, being White American without Spanish language skills except for a few broken phrases, attempted to get an interpreter but was told that the interpreter would not be available for 1 hour. Rosa's eyes were wide, she seemed scared, and her speech was fast. The counselor used one of the few phrases she knew in Spanish, *bonito bambino* (beautiful baby), in an attempt to connect and make Rosa feel less afraid. Rosa smiled and repeated what was said, correcting the counselor's Spanish and causing both of them to laugh. Rosa thanked the counselor for saying her daughter was beautiful. The counselor then began playing with the child and gave nonverbal support to Rosa by smiling and making eye contact. Rosa pointed to her daughter and said, "*ocho*" (8 months old). As they waited for the interpreter, the counselor and Rosa worked on a housing application, filling out the paperwork, with the counselor using words like *nombre* and *telefono*. Rosa would smile and answer slowly, teaching the counselor the numbers in Spanish using her fingers. When the counselor was able to repeat the numbers, Rosa would become excited. Sometimes during the hour, Rosa and the counselor sat together in silence. The hour was profound, with Rosa's anxiety and fear being reduced and a human connection created that transcended language and culture. Rosa profusely thanked the counselor when she left a few hours later. This demonstrates the cross-cultural connection one can make despite language barriers and that assisting survivors with basic needs, such as filling out a form for housing, is just as important as working on deeper psychological issues.

## Case Study 3

At a crowded DRC, Maggie, an elderly White woman, was trying to secure a trailer since Katrina had destroyed her house. The destruction had left behind a pile of what had once been Maggie's life, which included her furniture, pictures, walls, and the roof that had once offered shelter and protection from the rain and wind for her and her late husband. After the disaster, Maggie moved into a crowded home with her daughter Sue, who was a heavy drinker and verbally abused Maggie; Sue's boyfriend; and three children. Their fighting and arguments escalated weekly until finally Sue ordered her mother to leave. Being kicked out of her daughter's home, Maggie found herself alone (her husband had died 6 months before of a heart attack) and pleading her case to FEMA to get a trailer.

Maggie was distraught, and the FEMA worker was at a loss about what to do or say as Maggie, deeply sobbing, poured out her fears of being totally alone. The FEMA worker hurriedly found a counselor to help out. The counselor, Djimie, a Sudanese woman of Moslem faith wearing a traditional *hijab,* readily agreed to help. Djimie approached Maggie and introduced herself. Maggie was visibly surprised by Djimie's appearance and dress, yet as Djimie sat down and asked Maggie what was causing the tears, Maggie looked Djimie in the eyes and started sharing about the destruction of her home and loss of family and very quickly took out a stack of photos, pointing tearfully to family members, her deceased husband, and her abusive daughter. Djimie reached out and took Maggie's hand as she talked. Although recounting the details was very painful for Maggie, she was deeply concerned about her daughter, explaining to Djimie about her strong Christian beliefs in the importance for a child to respect and care for one's parents. Maggie tearfully reflected on the vicious cycle that might be perpetuated, with her granddaughter eventually abusing her own mother, and was deeply pained by the thought. She held tightly to Djimie's hand, crying.

The African counselor of Moslem faith and the devout Christian White woman continued to hold hands, talking about family, neighbors, current friends, loss, and faith. Sharing deep spiritual beliefs and the value of family loyalty and respect, Djimie could identify and relate to Maggie. As they talked, Maggie's voice became lighter, and her face brightened, remembering her kind neighbors. "They gave up a bed in their home for me and gave me gifts to cheer me up." Djimie chimed in, "So you're not alone?" Maggie responded thoughtfully, "No, I'm not alone." This seemed to be a turning point in their encounter as Maggie talked about a nephew in Atlanta and other friends who had supported her. Djimie reflected her identification with the loss of family, friends, and community as they spoke. Soon the FEMA worker returned and helped Maggie fill out the housing application. Upon completing the form, Maggie smiled and hugged Djimie, profusely thanking her, and walked out of the DRC. Finding the threads of commonality and transcending the cultural, religious, and ethnic differences was essential in the encounter. Although these two individuals came from dramatically different backgrounds, there was a core of cross-cultural counseling skills that created a human experience in a time of great crisis for the client.

## Case Study 4

Pearlington, Mississippi, is a rural community with residents who are either on fixed incomes or living below the poverty level, and although it was located in the eye of the hurricane, it was one of the last areas to have a DRC, leaving many residents without basic necessities such as food and clothing for more than 2 months. Community residents attempted to help one another as best they could, but patience wore thin. Thus, even as people came together to help each other, tensions mounted, and racial tensions began to creep back into the everyday occurrences. When asked about the increased racial tensions in Pearlington, one man said, "Yep—things are finally getting back to normal around here."

A situation occurred that illustrated this dynamic. In an effort to support each other and survive, an older Black couple (PJ and Natasha) and a White man (Dave) were neighbors who helped one another in the aftermath of the hurricane. PJ and Natasha lost their home, so in an effort to be helpful, Dave signed the papers to his van over to the couple so they could use the van as shelter until they were able to secure a trailer from FEMA. One morning, PJ and Natasha's 32-year-old daughter, Kelicia, drove the van to the DRC's food supply center. Everything was free, and the rule was to take only what you needed. Dave became angry seeing Kelicia put many items into the van and accused her of abusing the honor code policy to only take needed supplies. Kelicia became defensive and made a comment about Dave being White. This enraged Dave, who grabbed an axe from his bag and ran toward the van, proceeding to smash the van's windows and doors, sending shattered glass everywhere. Kelicia stood next to the van screaming, crying, and ranting, saying, "White people always done me wrong," "I can't trust White people," "My Mama is gonna blame me for what he done," and "Jesus is the only one who never cheats me!" Security officers and the military quickly apprehended Dave and removed him from the site. Having heard the glass shatter and seeing groups clustering, counselors came over to see what had happened. Many White people had gathered together in a group and were defending Dave and confronting Kelicia about taking too many goods at the center and not leaving enough for other people. Similarly, African Americans were also standing in a group and talking about how it was fine what Kelicia took and that Whites always got special treatment.

Seeing this volatile situation, a White male counselor (Pete) in his late 40s walked over to Kelicia to see if he could help. In front of the gathering crowds, he reached out his hand and encouraged her to sit down. At first she ignored him and continued screaming, crying, yelling, and pacing. Pete remained by her, talking and attempting to engage her until Kelicia finally slumped down onto a nearby bench, tearfully repeating, "White people always done me wrong," and "I can't trust White people." Seeing an opportunity to get closer, Pete sat down next to her, picked up her cap and handed it to her, and calmly assured her that it was not her fault and she did not cause the incident. Sitting next to her, he listened to her, allowed her to vent, and spoke to her in a calm, soothing voice, validating her feelings and brushing off the racial comments she made that were directed at people "like him." Kelicia continued to assert that she mistrusted White people, while Pete continued to quietly talk with her. Eventually, she was able to calm down enough to talk with Pete, who by then invited one of the local Black clergy who knew Kelicia to join them. The three of them developed a plan to tell Kelicia's parents about what happened and to find alternative shelter for the family. As Kelicia continued to make plans, Pete cleaned out the broken glass from the van.

Repercussions from this confrontation resounded through the rest of the day at Pearlington. Pete spoke with many people upset by the scene from both the Black and White communities and listened to strong opinions from both sides, largely divided along racial lines, with Whites supporting Dave's confrontation with Kelicia and expressing their belief that the Blacks are *always taking all the goods,* while Blacks believed that Whites *always got special treatment.* This situation demonstrates multiple and complex issues that emerge in the aftermath of a disaster (e.g., high levels of stress facing residents; the associated anger, mistrust, and fear; potential volatility in race relations in a disaster situation; socioeconomic issues in an impoverished community; and use of the DCCC interventions in the midst of a racially charged event). The counselor's reaction in this situation was helpful in addressing the immediate needs and feelings of the woman, validating her feelings, and maintaining his support for her despite her racially charged comments that were also directed at him. Throughout the crisis, the counselor did not personalize Kelicia's statements and remained calm and grounded, helping her to feel heard and thus de-escalate the situation. He quickly expanded her support system by connecting her with a leading clergyman in the Black community, respecting her distrust of Whites yet maintaining a role in supporting her. He followed through after the situation and calmed down Kelicia by personally cleaning out the glass from the van, going far beyond the traditional counseling-by-talking-only role; he then continued to speak with and listen to both African American and White perspectives about the incident, helping to further diffuse the situation.

## Case Study 5

Disaster survivors frequently do not have contact with individuals from cultural and ethnic backgrounds other than their own. This was also true after Hurricane Katrina. This case study describes a unique opportunity to facilitate counseling between different racial and ethnic groups who have a shared experience of a disaster. In the DRC situated in a low-SES area, a White middle-aged man (John) and his mother (Judith), in her 70s, were waiting for clothes and food. Sandy, a White female counselor in her

30s, sat next to John and Judith, and they immediately began talking. John and his mother were animatedly describing the hurricane and how they lost their home and all of their possessions. They explained how they were living in temporary hotel accommodations and would be forced to leave in 2 weeks. As they spoke, a clear sense of hope and optimism was increasingly apparent, and Sandy was struck by their resilience.

As they were taking, an African American woman (Jamila) in her 40s sat down on the empty seat next to Sandy. As everyone shifted one seat closer to the food and clothing room, Sandy kneeled down in front of John and Judith and told Jamila that she was welcome to take the vacant seat. Sandy asked Jamila in an empathetic way how she was doing. As Jamila began to tell her hurricane story, John and Judith were intensely listening. Noticing their interest, Sandy asked John and Judith if they could relate to Jamila's feelings of loss. "Yes, of course, we had the exact same thing," Judith replied. A look of understanding and compassion emanated from Jamila's eyes, and the three of them noticed and acknowledged each other for the first time. They started sharing with each other their experiences, losses, and pain as Sandy facilitated the exchange. The commonality of experiences between individuals from two distinct cultures had been facilitated for people who had no contact with "other folks," as they each explained.

As the three individuals were talking, an Asian woman (Anh) in her 30s was walking close by, looking confused and lost. Anh needed to see a doctor, but in the place where the doctor typically sat was a sign saying "Doctor Not Here." Anh was being ignored and dismissed as she asked people around her in broken English what to do. Sandy asked Anh if she could help. Anh looking highly distressed and responded in broken English, "Need doctor...where go?" Sandy turned to the threesome who were continuing to commiserate with each other and asked, "Can you help this woman? She's looking for a doctor and he's not here right now. Do you know of another doctor in the area that could help?" John told Anh about a doctor in the area, and with the help of his mother and Jamila, they described the office location. As they were helping Anh, her voice became animated, her eyes showed gratitude, and the threesome offering help leaned forward, trying to explain the directions to the doctor's office. Clearly, this was an act of kindness in a difficult moment. Anh, with great appreciation, hugged each of them very tightly, saying, "Thank you" and walked away, leaving John, Judith, and Jamila to continue a lively conversation about the hurricane and their respective predicaments.

Sandy helped bring three different cultures together that would not likely meet or interact with each other. The ability of the counselor to facilitate a cross-cultural interaction required a clear sense of historical and current racial issues specific to the region, an awareness of her own biases and prejudices, and communication skills that would be received across racial and ethnic lines. The intervention was further enhanced by promoting an act of altruism in providing assistance to Anh, who, without language skills, found three helpful people coming to her rescue. Each person walked away with a feeling of comfort and connection that transcended traditional cultural barriers.

## DISCUSSION QUESTIONS

1.  What are some of the psychological problems that may occur as a result of a disaster?

2.  Many disaster survivors experience posttraumatic stress disorder (PTSD). What variables contribute to the degree of PTSD that is faced by disaster survivors?

3.  Discuss how acculturation, socioeconomic status, and coping strategies may contribute to cross-cultural issues in disaster counseling.

4.  Describe the three phases of the Disaster Cross-Cultural Counseling Model (DCCC).

5.  What are five ways to recognize PTSD?

6. Discuss three key cultural considerations when using the DCCC model.

7. How might a mental health professional working with disaster survivors handle language barriers?

8. How can one deal with cultural mistrust in a disaster counseling situation?

9. Discuss the benefits of group counseling in disaster interventions.

## NOTE

1. The contributing authors on the critical incidents case studies are as follows: Kelly Badger, Lori Birmingham, Stacy Hurley, Delia Cordero, Karen Croushorn, Sarah Evans, Melissa Keylor, Sue Manchen, Fatima Mekki, Kerry McNamara, Neva Ortuno, Adam Shane, Nikki Zawakzki, and Marla Zometsky.

## REFERENCES

Aguilera, D. M., & Planchon, L. A. (1995). The American Psychological Association California Psychological Association Disaster Response Project: Lessons from the past, guidelines for the future. *Professional Psychology: Research & Practice, 26,* 550–557.

American Counseling Association. (2005). *Crisis fact sheet: 10 ways to recognize post-traumatic stress disorder.* Retrieved November 13, 2005, from http://www.counseling.org/PressRoom/PressReleases.aspx

American Psychological Association (APA). (2003). Guidelines on multicultural education, training, research, practice and organizational change for psychologists. *American Psychologist, 58,* 377–402.

Amnesty International. (2006). *Sudan: Human rights concerns.* Retrieved June 15, 2006, from www.amnestyusa .org/countries/sudan/index.do

Asai, A., & Barnlund, D. C. (1998). Boundaries of the unconscious private, and public self in Japanese and Americans: A cross-cultural comparison. *International Journal of Intercultural Relations, 22,* 431–452.

Bemak, F. (1989). Cross-cultural family therapy with Southeast Asian refugees. *Journal of Strategic and Systemic Therapies, 8,* 22–27.

Bemak, F., & Chung, R. C.-Y. (2004). Teaching multicultural group counseling: Perspectives for a new era. *Journal for Specialists in Group Work, 29,* 31–41.

Bemak, F., & Chung, R. C.-Y. (2005). Advocacy as a critical role for school counselors: Working towards equity and social justice. *Professional School Counseling, 83,* 196–202.

Bemak, F., Chung, R. C.-Y., & Pedersen, P. (2003). *Counseling refugees: A psychosocial cultural approach to innovative multicultural interventions.* Westport, CT: Greenwood.

Bemak, F., & Conyne, R. (2004). Ecological group work. In R. K. Conyne & E. P. Cook (Eds.), *Ecological counseling: An innovative approach to conceptualizing person-environment interaction* (pp. 195–217). Alexandria, VA: American Counseling Association.

Bemak, F., & Young, M. (1998). The role of catharsis in group psychotherapy. *International Journal of Action Methods, 50,* 166–184.

Chung, R. C.-Y., & Bemak, F. (2002). The relationship of culture and empathy in cross-cultural counseling. *Journal of Counseling and Development, 80,* 154–159.

Coleman, H. L. K., Wampold, B. E., & Casali, S. L. (1995). Ethnic minorities' ratings of ethnically similar and European-American counselors: A meta-analysis. *Journal of Counseling Psychology, 42,* 55–64.

Deblinger, E., McLeer, S. V., & Henry, D. (1990). Cognitive behavioral treatment for sexually abused children suffering post-traumatic stress: Preliminary findings. *Journal of the American Academy of Child Adolescent Psychiatry, 29,* 747–752.

Doherty, G. W. (1999). Cross-cultural counseling in disaster settings. *Australasian Journal of Trauma Studies, 3,* 113–210.

Dudley-Grant, G. R., Mendez, G. I., & Zinn, J. (2000). Strategies for anticipating and preventing psychological trauma of hurricanes through community education. *Professional Psychology Research & Practice, 31*(4), 387–392.

Durkin, M. (1993). Major depression and posttraumatic stress disorder following the Coalinga (California) and Chile earthquakes: A cross-cultural comparison. In R. Allen (Ed.), *Handbook of disaster interventions* (pp. 405–420). Corte Madera, CA: Select Press.

Ehntholt, K. A., Smith, P. A., & Yule, W. (2005). School-based cognitive-behavioural therapy group intervention for refugee children who have experienced war-related trauma. *Clinical Child Psychology and Psychiatry, 10*(2), 235–250.

Gillis, H. M. (1993). Individual and small-group psychotherapy for children involved in trauma and disaster. In C. F. Saylor (Ed.), *Children and disasters* (pp. 165–186). New York: Plenum.

Goenjian, A. K., Karayan, I., & Pynoos, R. S. (1997). Outcome of psychotherapy among early adolescents after trauma. *American Journal of Psychiatry, 15,* 536–542.

Goss, R. E., & Klass, D. (1997). Tibetan Buddhism and the resolution of grief: The Bardo-thodo for the dying and the grieving. *Death Studies, 21,* 377–395.

Hagman, G. (1995). Mourning: A review and reconsideration. *International Journal of Psycho Analysis, 76,* 909–925.

Hobfoll, S. E., Spielberger, C. D., Breznitz, S., Figley, C., Folkman, S., Lepper-Green, B., et al. (1991). War-related stress: Addressing the stress of war and other traumatic events. *American Psychologist, 46,* 848–855.

Jones, R. T., Frary, R., Cunningham, P., Weddle, J. D., & Kaiser, L. (2001). The psychological effects of Hurricane Andrew on ethnic minority and Caucasian children and adolescents: A case study. *Cultural Diversity and Ethnic Minority Psychology, 7*(1), 103–108.

Kohn, R., & Levav, I. (1990). Bereavement in disaster: An overview of the research. *International Journal of Mental Health, 19,* 61–76.

March, J. S., Amaya-Jackson, L., Terry, R., & Constanzo, P. (1997). Posttraumatic symptomatology in children and adolescents after an industrial fire. *Journal of the Academy of Child and Adolescent Psychiatry, 36,* 1080–1088.

Marsella, A. J., Friedman, M. J., & Gerrity, E. T. (1996). *Ethnocultural aspects of posttraumatic stress disorder: Issues, research, and clinical applications.* Washington, DC: American Psychological Association.

Newnes, C. (1991). Death, dying, and society. *Changes: An International Journal of Psychology and Psychotherapy, 17,* 177–180.

Norris, F. H., Perilla, J. L., & Murphy, A. D. (2001). Postdisaster stress in the United States and Mexico: A cross-cultural test of the multicriterion conceptual model of posttraumatic stress disorder. *Journal of Abnormal Psychology, 110,* 53–63.

Paton, D. (1996). Responding to international needs: Critical occupations as disaster relief agencies. In D. Paton & J. M. Violanti (Eds.), *Traumatic stress in critical occupations: Recognition, consequences and treatment* (pp. 139–172). Springfield, IL: Charles C Thomas.

Peuler, J. N. (1998). Community outreach after emergencies. In M. H. Lystad (Ed.), *Mental health response to mass emergencies: Theory and practice* (pp. 239–261). New York: Brunner/Mazel.

Pfefferbaum, B. (1997). Posttraumatic stress disorder in children: A review of the past 10 years. *Journal of the American Academy of Child and Adolescent Psychiatry, 36*(11), 1503–1511.

Pynoos, R. S., & Nader, K. (1993). Issues in the treatment of posttraumatic stress in children and adolescents. In J. P. Wilson & B. Raphael (Eds.), *International handbook of traumatic stress syndromes* (pp. 535–637). New York: Plenum.

Rosenblatt, P. C. (1993). Cross-cultural variation in the experience, expression, and understanding of grief. In D. P. Irish & K. F. Lundquist (Eds.), *Ethnic variations in dying, death, and grief: Diversity in universality* (pp. 13–19). Washington, DC: Taylor & Francis.

Rubin, N. (1990). Social networks and mourning: A comparative approach. *Omega: Journal of Death and Dying, 21,* 113–127.

Substance Abuse Mental Health Services Administration (SAMHSA). (2006). *National Mental Health Information Center.* Retrieved November 13, 2006, from www.mentalhealth.samhsa.gov/publications/allpubs/KEN-01–0096/default.asp

Waxler-Morrison, N., Anderson, J. M., & Richardson, E. (Eds.). (1990). *Cross-cultural caring: A handbook for health professionals.* Vancouver: UBC Press.

# PART V

## Counseling in the Context of Some Common Culture-Mediated Circumstances

At first glance, the five chapters in this, the final section of the book, appear strikingly hetero-geneous. Yet, there is a characteristic that they share: All of them are novel, in topics introduced, services described, and conceptualizations offered. Thus, Chapter 20 addresses the counsel-ing issues in coming to grips with spirituality in its various cultural contexts of manifestation. Proceeding from the metaphor of many rivers flowing into the sea, this chapter's authors recognize the universality of the human quest for ultimate meaning, even though the paths toward this elusive goal are embedded in the traditions, practices, and beliefs of various and distinct cultures. The following questions are designed to simulate further thought and discussion on this chapter:

1.  How may a client's membership in a church, temple, or mosque intersect with pressures to assimilate into the "mainstream" U.S. culture?

2.  For feminist counselors, women's spirituality is an important issue. How does this value clash with the client's worldview, as presented in Chapter 20?

3.  Is counseling a "valueless" endeavor? If it is not, how can counselors deal with clients' values that may be considered harmful, cause distress or pain, and/or inhibit personal growth?

4.  What are some examples of healthy and unhealthy spirituality? Is it possible that the client is engaging in a *spiritual bypass* in such a situation?

5.  Professional ethicists regard reparative or conversion therapy for the purpose of changing a person's sexual orientation to be unethical because it can result in harm to a person. What alterna-tive interventions may be offered that are respectful of cultural and religious differences and yet embrace psychological and sexual well-being?

Chapter 21 shifts readers' attention from the spirit to the body. Its author's central point is that socioeconomic and ethnic factors influence a person's access to health-related information and thus affect both health promotion and health maintenance.

Patient-centered consultation is introduced, and its integration into multicultural counseling is promoted. The following questions and topics may help readers in dealing with health issues and concerns of their counselees:

1.  Describe four pathways by means of which social status may influence a person's health, and give an example of each of these four pathways.

2.  How would you try to prevent poor health by changing the characteristics of each pathway in order to make it more health promoting?

3.  What is patient-centered care? How does it improve a person's health?

4.  How has counseling been used to alter sedentary lifestyles and to what effect?

5.  Discuss the benefits of and the problems with the new World Health Organization (WHO) definition of health.

Chapter 22 breaks new ground in going beyond the consideration of the well-known concept of cultural empathy. In this connection, cultural confrontation is introduced as an important microskill for exploring counselees' relationship to their culture or cultures. Cultural confrontation enables individuals to identify incongruities within the messages emitted by their culture. The authors of this chapter consider cultural confrontation as a counterweight to two widespread tendencies in counseling—namely, the underestimation of clients' distinctive cultural values and their uncritical and undifferentiated acceptance. The following five questions help to elaborate this novel and provocative concept:

1. Why is cultural sensitivity an inadequate construct for demonstrating multicultural counseling competence?

2. What are the essential features of cultural confrontation?

3. Does cultural confrontation imply a harsh or even brutal bringing to awareness those features of the culture that the counselee has been reluctant or resistant to face?

4. In what ways is cultural confrontation a skill of advanced cultural empathy?

5. Why is it important for counselors to go beyond a blanket acceptance of cultural differences in values and not to underestimate the distinctiveness of their counselees' cultural values?

The central feature of Chapter 23 is a recently formulated model for assessing and conceptualizing alcohol and substance abuse in distinctive ethnocultural milieus and for implementing culturally sensitive interventions. Discussion topics for this chapter are organized around the critical incident presented by the authors, as follows:

1. What are some of the specific events that led to the client's not returning to counseling?

2. Describe how the events in the interview were structured by culture and identify the specific cultural issues that may have led to the impasse. These issues might include linguistic, sociolinguistic, value-related, and symbolic factors as described in this chapter, as well as levels of acculturative strategy or previous exposure to "Western" approaches to treatment.

Chapter 24 is focused on the role of the family in multicultural counseling. Based on the results of a major recent multinational research project, this chapter is relevant to a host of issues in multicultural counseling encounters at individual, group, and family levels. The following questions may help close the gap between the research findings and the counseling practices: There are different types of nuclear and extended family systems (e.g., stem, joint, and fully extended).

1. How might the dynamics of counseling change as a function of clients being from these different family systems?

2. In your view, will the traditional types of families in non-Western cultures eventually evolve into the nuclear, divorced, and one-parent family systems now prevalent in North America and northern Europe? Present arguments on both sides of this issue and explore the impact of this possible evolution on counseling practices and its rationale.

3. What are the similarities and differences in family networks, roles, and psychological variables, as found in the recent study of 27 nations by Gorgias et al.?

A number of chapters in this book present much information on various ethnocultural groups, especially in Part II. Select any one of these chapters and identify problems and issues that may surface in the context of family counseling. Also comment on issues and problems that one may expect to see in family counseling with gay and lesbian couples (Chapter 12), elderly family members (Chapter 14), or when family counseling is focused on religious or spiritual issues (Chapter 20).

# Spirituality in Counseling Across Cultures

## Many Rivers to the Sea

Mary A. Fukuyama, Todd Sevig, and Johanna Soet

---

### Primary Objective

- To provide an overview of how spirituality, religious beliefs, and the transpersonal are relevant to cross-cultural counseling

### Secondary Objectives

- To clarify the meanings of spirituality, religion, and the transpersonal as they relate to mental health, illness, and healing
- To examine universal and culture-specific approaches to understanding spirituality and cultural worldviews
- To understand dimensions of counseling competencies in integrating spirituality into cross-cultural counseling

---

*People hunger for experiential answers to the ultimate questions. They seek something that can be sensed in the heart as well as known in the mind.*

May (1982, p. 8)

T he relationship of spirituality, religion, and the transpersonal to mental health is complex and challenging. Although it is too large to grasp in its completeness, it is too important to ignore or deny when considering the fundamentals of cross-cultural counseling. Spiritual and religious beliefs are embedded in culture. Despite the mental health field's wavering on this topic, the question is no longer whether or not to include spirituality and religion in counseling but, rather, *how?*

Recently, mental health professionals began to explore the interface of spirituality in counseling with renewed vigor. This chapter focuses on how spirituality may be integrated into cross-cultural counseling by taking a multicultural perspective. The chapter has the following main goals: (a) to provide an overview of the importance of spirituality to multicultural counseling and psychotherapy, (b) to examine how spirituality is expressed through different cultural worldviews, and (c) to discuss implications and make recommendations for counselors who wish to integrate spirituality into cross-cultural counseling. The terms *multicultural* and *cross-cultural* will be used interchangeably throughout the chapter and refer to cultural differences and similarities based on membership in broadly and inclusively defined identity groups, such as gender, race, ethnicity, sexual orientation, age, national origin, physical abilities, religion, and class.

The contents of this chapter are built on several assumptions:

- Spiritual and religious beliefs and practices are common to humanity and are connected to health, sickness, and healing in most cultures of the world.

- There is growing interest in and acknowledgment of the importance of spirituality in society at large, as well as within the profession of psychology, counseling, and other mental health professions in particular, visible through increased publications and conference programming.

- Although it is not possible for counselors to be experts on all religious or spiritual beliefs, it is possible to have a basic understanding of how religion and spirituality affect people's lives, counseling issues, and the counseling process.

- Spirituality and religious beliefs and practices have the potential to aid counselors in becoming more aware of diversity and therefore more effective and sensitive in cross-cultural encounters (Fukuyama & Sevig, 1999).

- All people have multiple identities, including spiritual and religious affiliations. When describing multicultural or cross-cultural counseling, some identities may be more or less salient, illustrating the importance of cultural context.

This chapter is divided into three sections. In the first section, a brief overview of the history of addressing spirituality in counseling is presented. A confluence of various movements within psychology and counseling has shaped a contemporary view of spiritual, religious, and transpersonal dimensions, and these movements and accompanying definitions are discussed. In the second section, the inclusion of spirituality within cultural worldviews is presented from both universal and culture-specific perspectives, including Asian, indigenous, and women's spiritual worldviews. Spirituality has a "natural home" within multiculturalism, and counselors who aspire to be multiculturally competent are invited to become familiar with diverse spiritual and religious languages, beliefs, and practices. In the third section, the implications of integrating spirituality into cross-cultural counseling are considered. Topics such as counseling content and process, spiritual competencies, and appropriateness of referral to religious and spiritual resources are discussed.

## Brief Overview

From a historical perspective, psychology in general, and counseling in particular, has had an *ebb-and-flow* relationship with spirituality. Recently, there has been a reawakening in multiple fields of research and practice. Some of the manifestations can be found in areas such as addictions recovery, wellness, holistic health, and transpersonal growth and development, and some have been in psychotherapy in general (Kelly, 1995; Richards & Bergin, 1997; Scotton, Chinen, & Battista, 1996; Shafranske, 1996). A relatively independent approach, *mindfulness,* has recently gained wide attention. Mindfulness is based on Eastern meditation practices and encourages the user to pay attention in the present in a nonjudgmental manner. Mindfulness and meditation has found its way into the fields of psychology, psychiatry, and medicine (Kabat-Zinn, 1990). In addition, authors have looked at the role spirituality can play specifically in multicultural counseling (Fukuyama & Sevig, 1999; Richards & Bergin, 2000).

Concurrent with the evolution of consciousness on these issues in psychology and counseling, the multicultural movement has recognized the importance of spirituality cross-culturally and within cultures. Most cultural traditions are holistic and consider mind, body, and spirit as one. In addition, most peoples of the world are spiritually oriented. This holistic approach to life is in contrast to the secular culture in the United States, which is compartmentalized through professional specialties, separateness, and emphasis on individualism (Myers, 1988). Multicultural counselors and psychologists are currently wrestling with the impact of the awareness of how these multiple worldviews affect individuals' mental health.

Within the American Counseling Association, the Association for Spiritual, Ethical, and Religious Values in Counseling (ASERVIC) has developed guidelines for spiritual competencies in counseling (available online at www.aservic.org). Nine main points were developed through a series of meetings, a national summit, and counselor input and are summarized below.

To be competent to help clients address the spiritual dimension of their lives, a counselor needs to be able to articulate religious, spiritual, and/or transpersonal beliefs, practices, and development over the life span. To this end, counselors are asked

- to explain connections, similarities, and differences between religion, spirituality, and the transpersonal;
- to describe·beliefs and practices in a cultural context;
- to engage and articulate one's self-exploration of personal beliefs;
- to explain various models of spiritual development across the life span;
- to demonstrate sensitivity to and acceptance of a variety of spiritual expressions from the client;
- to identify the limits of one's understanding of a client's expression and demonstrate appropriate referral skills;
- to assess the relevance of the spiritual domains in the client's therapeutic issues;
- to be sensitive and respectful of the spiritual themes in the counseling process as befits each client's expressed preference; and
- to use a client's spiritual beliefs in the pursuit of the client's therapeutic goals as befits the client's expressed preference (Burke, cited in Miller, 1999).

Cashwell and Young (2005) edited a book in which each chapter is devoted to one of the nine competencies mentioned above. This book aimed to fill the gap between understanding the importance of including spirituality and putting this knowledge into action. One chapter is specifically on understanding religion and spirituality in a cultural context (Fukuyama, Siahpoush, & Sevig, 2005), and other chapters include at least some aspect of multiculturalism.

In order to proceed with this discourse, definitions and parameters on the constructs of spirituality, religion, and the transpersonal as related to counseling will be considered next.

*Spirituality* is a concept that is ever present in human life and yet, paradoxically, remains difficult to put into words in the traditional sense of definitions. However, some of the dimensions that have been identified in the counseling literature range from esoteric mysticism to matters of everyday living.

Hill and colleagues (2000) suggested that spirituality includes thoughts, feelings, experiences, and behaviors that arise from a search for the sacred, that is, those things that are holy, "set apart," transcendent, and of ultimate value to a person. Spirituality includes a relationship with transcendence and certain spiritual values, including meaning and purpose in life, a sense of mission and goals, helping others, and striving toward making the world better (Elkins, Hedstrom, Hughes, Leaf, & Saunders, 1988). Kelly (1995) emphasized that boundaries are important in any definition or discussion of religion and spirituality. He suggested that spirituality and religion are, at a minimum, grounded in a reality that is clearly outside of the boundaries of the empirical, perceived, and material world.

Religion has been defined as "the means and methods (e.g., rituals or prescribed behaviors) of the search that receive validation and support from within an identifiable group of people" (Hill et al., 2000, p. 66). Albanese (cited in Kelly, 1995) described religion as having an "extraordinary" dimension that is centered on "otherness," "transcendence," and moving beyond everyday culture and a second dimension of "ordinary" that is centered on everyday life, culture, and norms. Although some people consider themselves to be spiritual without being religious, by definition, religion assumes spirituality because spirituality is its most central function (Pargament, 1999).

The transpersonal was a concept developed from humanistic psychology, whose theorists have asserted that psychology is also about the study of the soul (Elkins, 1995). Contributors such as Carl Jung, Abraham Maslow, Rollo May, and James Hillman have suggested that spirituality and the search for meaning is at the center of human existence. Definitions of transpersonal psychology and psychotherapy derive from both psychological and spiritual sources. According to Cortright (1997), "Transpersonal psychology can be understood as the melding of the wisdom of the world's spiritual traditions with the learning of modern psychology" (p. 8).

## SPIRITUALITY AND WORLDVIEWS

*God is unity, but God always works in variety.*

Ralph Waldo Emerson

In this section, both universal and cultural specific perspectives on spirituality, mental health, and healing will be offered. In cross-cultural psychological research and scholarship, the *etic* (cultural universal) and *emic* (cultural specific) perspectives both afford insights about the human condition and the diverse ways in which people survive in the world. Both approaches are helpful in understanding cross-cultural healing and helping (Fukuyama, 1990; Locke, 1990). An investigation of world religions illuminates common themes (Beversluis, 2000). Universal perspectives will be drawn from the works of Huston Smith, professor emeritus of world religions. Cultural specific examples, reflective of the authors' interests, will be explored through examining Asian, indigenous, and women's spiritual worldviews. It is hoped that counselors will become familiar with diverse spiritual and religious languages, beliefs, and practices in order to understand the role of spirituality in healing.

## Universal Perspectives

Huston Smith (cited in Cortright, 1997) has described a conceptual framework for understanding the universal qualities of spirituality and the commonalties that exist across all religions. This framework provides common ground for understanding a variety of multicultural expressions found in both organized religion and in diverse spiritual paths. Based on the idea of a "perennial philosophy," Smith and colleagues extracted universally agreed-upon concepts about the nature of spirituality from the major world religions. The framework defines the nature of God or Higher Power from both Western and Eastern perspectives and describes different levels of identity and existence. The *concept of God* taken from world religions' perspectives is that God is both personal and impersonal (Smith, 1992). Both Eastern and Western religions include the personal and impersonal. What differentiates them is a matter of emphasis. From a Western perspective, God is a Personal Divine, as found in monotheism in the major three Middle Eastern religions, Judaism, Christianity, and Islam. The personal God is known by many names and is contextualized in culture. For example, in the Hebrew tradition, even though G-d is so unfathomable the Name cannot be spoken, G-d is also as intimate as the love between newlyweds.

From a Christian perspective, God's love was manifested in the life of Jesus, who calls people into loving one another responsibly and provides a source of salvation to humanity. The Islamic tradition shares its origins with Hebrew and Christian traditions. Muslims believe that the Prophet Muhammad was the last messenger of God, but Abraham, Moses, and Jesus are recognized as important historical figures. Central beliefs include the unity of God and all things, the recognition of Muhammad as the prophet, the innate goodness of human beings, the importance of a community of faith, and the importance of living a devout and righteous life to achieve peace and harmony (Altareb, 1996).

In contrast, in the Eastern traditions, God is known as the Impersonal Divine, or nondual in nature. Nonduality refers to the unity or completeness of reality despite differences or polarities. A spiritual goal is to merge the individual into the Impersonal Divine, and this is accomplished through spiritual practices such as meditation, karma yoga, and devotion. As the individual becomes aware of normal human conditioning and develops an observer self, a connection with his or her nondual nature (or unity) of reality becomes possible.

In the Hindu worldview, the impersonal God gives rise to the personal God, and both are present everywhere. In this way, Hinduism values both the personal and impersonal equally, and God is depicted with several faces as well as seen as a unified force. Another way of expressing this concept is to say that God is both *immanent* (personal and present) and *transcendent* (impersonal and beyond our understanding). For many people, it is easier to develop a devotional relationship with an anthropomorphic God because it is difficult to relate to an abstract impersonal being (Shumsky, 1996).

In addition, there are four levels or dimensions of human identity that include body, mind, soul (the "final locus of individuality"), and spirit (the atman that is Brahman/Buddha-nature) (Cortright, 1997, p. 28). Finally, Smith identified four levels or dimensions of existence: (1) The terrestrial plane is observed and measured by the five senses; (2) the intermediate plane refers to psychic, subtle energies, the domain of spirits (e.g., entities), and unconscious archetypes (e.g., Jung); (3) the celestial plane contains the Personal Divine, theistic-relational traditions, God, and Divine beings; and (4) the infinite plane is depicted by the Impersonal Divine, Oneness, and Divine Unity and is without form and beyond all distinctions.

In the remainder of this section, the worldviews and spiritualities of selected cultural groups will be described to expand the reader's awareness of different ways of conceptualizing spirituality and its role in mental health; they are expressions of Asian, indigenous, and women's spiritualities. We selected these specific worldviews to be illustrative but certainly not inclusive of all possible worldviews. It is through presenting a variety of perspectives that the reader is encouraged to seek further knowledge of different spiritual worldviews.

## Cultural-Specific Perspectives

*Asian Worldview.* Most East Asian cultures are influenced by Buddhism, Confucianism, and Taoism, which emphasize such traits as silence, nonconfrontation, moderation in behavior, self-control, patience, humility, and simplicity (Sheu & Fukuyama, 2007). Other Asian cultural values also include filial piety, respect for authority and elders, well-defined social roles and expectations, fatalism, conformity to norms, and the centrality of family relationships and responsibilities (Kim, Atkinson, & Yang, 1999). These cultural values continue to influence Asian American cultures in the United States, even as immigrants and children of immigrants assimilate and/or acculturate into U.S. mainstream culture. Asian Americans participate in diverse faith systems, and their religious/spiritual experiences may be an amalgam of Eastern and Western beliefs and values.

However, religion and spirituality are central to the Asian American experience (Ano, Mathew, & Fukuyama, in press). The Pilot National Asian American Political Survey (PNAAPS), a comprehensive survey of Asian American religious and political attitudes, attempted to clarify the religious and political affiliations of Asian Americans in the United States in 2001–2002. According to the results of this survey, the vast majority (72%) of Asian Americans identified with a religious tradition. More specifically, respondents replied that they were the following: Christian (including Catholicism), 46%; Buddhist, 15%; Hindu, 6%; Muslim, 2%; "other" religious affiliations, 3%; "none," 19%; refused, 8%; and "not sure," 1% (Lien & Carnes, 2004). Other examples of the importance of religion to Asian Americans include the following trends: About two thirds of Asian Americans report that religion plays a very important role in their lives, the largest pan–Asian American movement is religious, Asian Americans more readily identify with a religion than a political party, the largest Asian American college and university student organizations are religious, and many Asians come to the United States seeking religious freedom (T. Carnes & Yang, 2004).

Religious beliefs offer ways "to make meaning" of suffering. Eastern religious or spiritual beliefs offer explanations about life-death issues, such as karma and reincarnation. For example, central to the Hindu belief system are the concepts of *atman,* the soul in all beings; *samsara,* the continuous flow of birth, death, and rebirth as the atman transmigrates; *dharma,* devotion or duty; and *karma,* the belief that all actions have consequences that result in either a "good" rebirth or a "bad" rebirth (Firth, 2005).

Clients often struggle to find meaning in the midst of suffering and try to understand why "bad things happen" to them. A simplistic approach to karma is to presume that one has done something bad in a previous life for which he or she is now being punished. A more complex way of viewing karma is to distill one's actions as contributing toward good (or evil) and that opportunities arise continuously to contribute positively or negatively toward past, present, and future existences. Following this line of reasoning, reincarnation and rebirth are described through the following metaphor. "The successive existences in a series of rebirths are not like the pearls in a pearl necklace, held together by a string, the 'soul,' which passes through all the pearls; rather they are like dice piled one on top of the other. Each die is separate, but it supports the one above it, with which it is functionally connected. Between the dice there is no identity, but conditionality" (Schuman, cited in Rinpoche, 1992, p. 91).

Mental and physical illness may be attributed to spiritual causes. The concept of spirit possession and soul loss was thought to be related to illnesses in Asian cultures (Das, 1987). Such patients were treated with exorcism, magic, or shaman rituals to retrieve lost parts of self (Fadiman, 1997; Moodley & West, 2005). The shaman journey to find lost parts of self is similar to doing inner child work from a Western psychotherapy perspective. The goal is to bring these parts of the self in contact with each other so the individual is no longer disassociated (Ingerman, 1991).

Asian American immigrants face challenges of coping with multiple cultural adjustments. For Asian American immigrants who deal with prejudice, racism, and discrimination, religion may provide a sense of refuge. The ethnic church may provide social support and buffer pressures to assimilate. T. Carnes and Yang (2004) noted that some Asian Christians, particularly Koreans, actually immigrate to the United States as a means of seeking validation for their religious identity. Many immigrant families struggle with differing levels of acculturation, including the first-generation immigrant, the 1.5 generation (composed of individuals born in Asia and raised in the United States from latent childhood), and second and third generations born in the United States. Some adult children of immigrants may choose a religious tradition that departs from their parents. In such instances, intergenerational conflicts may arise.

When does participation in religion empower people, and when does it co-opt them? Busto (1996) raised a controversial point in his discussion of the connection between Asian American college students, the model minority stereotype, and Christian evangelism on college campuses. He observed that Asian Americans are overrepresented in campus evangelical para-church groups and said that "Asian American evangelicals also appear to be stereotyped as God's whiz kids—exemplars of evangelical piety and action—to which other evangelicals should aspire" (p. 140). Clearly, the Asian American experience with organized religion is mixed. For some Asian Americans, evangelical Christianity may be seen as unwelcome assimilation and, for others, an important safety net. Thus, it is important to assess the meaning and both positive and negative expressions of religion and spirituality for Asian clients.

*Indigenous Earth-Based Worldview.* Earth-based spirituality may be found in various spiritual, religious, and political movements. Native American traditions (M. T. Garrett & Wilbur, 1999), paganism (Starhawk, 1999), deep ecology, and eco-feminism share a common focus on nature, the earth, environmental concerns, and living in balance with natural forces. A spirituality of geographical place has come into direct conflict with colonization and private enterprise, such as is the case of the indigenous peoples in the Americas. The history of cultural genocide has included direct attacks on indigenous forms of spiritual practice, beliefs, and customs. In addition, paganism, which literally means *country dweller,* has been persecuted historically by institutionalized religion, for example, through witch hunts. Such disruptions and violence directed against earth-based religions are cause for believers to be cautious in sharing their spiritual beliefs with others. In addition, the tendency within the popular culture to exoticize Native American spirituality and to culturally appropriate spiritual practices for profit (such as the sweat lodge or peace pipes) are reasons why indigenous peoples may be cautious about sharing their practices (LaDue, 1994; Trimble & Thurman, 2002).

Nevertheless, an earth-based worldview is one that warrants understanding from the mental health profession. The indigenous tribes in North America are diverse, scattered, and constitute more than 550 federally recognized nations. It is presumptuous to assume that spirituality is a homogeneous phenomenon among Native peoples. Nevertheless, several common values and dimensions have been described, including the principals of "medicine, harmony, relation, and vision" (M. T. Garrett & Wilbur, 1999). Qualities of humility, respect for all, awareness of beauty in everyday life, acceptance, living in harmony with nature, caretaking, realizing the connection of all living things, respect for elders, and living one's life purpose are valued. Symbolically, the circle represents life processes (circular, cycles), and it promotes the most sacred dimensions of life. "The components of the Circle of Life—spirit, nature, body, and mind—constitute the Four Directions represented in this wheel. The Circle of Life symbolizes the innumerable circles that surround us, that exist within us, and of which we are all a part. It shows us the sacred relationship we have to all living things—to life itself" (J. T. Garrett & Garrett, 1994, p. 139). From this perspective, illness or mental problems happen as a result of loss of harmony with these life processes or being "out of step with the universe" (M. T. Garrett & Wilbur, 1999, p. 198).

According to Natalie Curtis (1968), "The English word *medicine* has come to be applied to what the Lakota Indian calls *wakan. Wakan* means both mystery and holiness as well as strength, and is used by the Lakota to designate all that is sacred, mysterious, spiritual, or supernatural. The Supreme Being of the Lakota is called *Wakan-Tanka.* In English this name is commonly rendered 'The Great Spirit,' but it would be translated more correctly as 'The Great Holy-Mystery'" (p. 32). Healing plants, herbs, manipulation, and sweat baths are curative agents. The Holy Men/Women (healers) are prophets, soothsayers, moral leaders, and healers in their tribes. The Indian concept of healing is through divine power, and the healing agents may be through a supernatural charm. The act of cure is usually accomplished with song, ceremony, and prayer.

Mental health professionals who are non-Native are advised to develop sensitivities to Native values and beliefs and to refrain from adapting Native healing practices without tribal sanction and training. However, creative interventions, including the arts, music, poetry, and other nonverbal means, such as dreamwork and guided imagery, are culturally congruent with Native healing practices (Dufrene & Coleman, 1994; Herring, 1997; Trimble & Thurman, 2002). Native Americans offer a model for spirituality that is congruent with holistic health, ecology, and community building, which are all important issues. The earth-based spirituality brings an important message to the collective consciousness. The ultimate question is, How can non-Natives learn from and appreciate indigenous spirituality without corrupting it or perpetuating the cultural genocide that has been part of official government policies for centuries?

*Women's Spirituality.* The work of several authors considers the potential impact of gender on spiritual development. Most women's spiritual development takes place within patriarchal cultural and religious systems. S. R. Anderson and Hopkins (1991) state

> Throughout history women have learned about spiritual realization from men. Male guides and male interpreters—priests, rabbis, ministers, Zen masters, yogis, and countless other male teachers have defined what spirituality is and how it is to be developed and experienced in our lives. In almost all accounts of the sacred, both language and story have been the expressions of men conveyed in male imagery. (p. 7)

Western women as an oppressed group have few current institutional or cultural images that reflect feminine spirituality or religious figures. Therefore, they are faced with acceptance of current patriarchal religious systems, trying to connect with the relatively few female figures (e.g., the Virgin Mary) or developing their own path. Carol Christ (1997) argues that this current lack of feminine cultural/spiritual role models is not historically the norm, nor is it true for all religions. Goddess worship and goddess figures were an integral part of spiritual practice for many cultures in early history and continue in some cultures today. For example, Shakti is a powerful goddess in the Hindu religion that is related to death and rebirth—the cycle of life. There has been a resurgence of interest in Goddess worship in Western cultures as well. Christ describes this "Rebirth of the Goddess" as finding

> a compelling image of female power, a vision of the deep connection of all beings in the web of life and a call to create peace on earth. The return of the Goddess inspires us to hope that we can heal the deep rifts between women and men, between "man" and nature, and between "God" and the world, that have shaped our western view of reality for too long. (p. xiii)

This renewed interest in Goddess worship is one way in which both women and men may find connection or expression of feminine or woman-centered spirituality. Other people may find a different path. Traditional and nontraditional religious women's circles, Wicca, and Paganism or Neo-paganism have all been part of the women's spirituality movement (R. D. Carnes & Craig, 1998).

Although the predominant Western metaphor used for spiritual development is that of the *journey,* S. R. Anderson and Hopkins (1991) argue this concept is based on male hero myths and the idea of needing to leave home to mature fully. Joseph Campbell describes how, in almost every culture, the hero myth involves a man severing old bonds and moving "his spiritual center of gravity" from family to some unknown territory (from S. R. Anderson & Hopkins, 1991 p. 46). Parks (2000) has written extensively on the spiritual development of men and women. She has taken into account groundbreaking work such as Carol Gilligan's (1993) *In a Different Voice,* which expanded the concept of moral development to include the primacy of connection for women. Parks describes the experience of developing faith as involving both journeying and abiding. Her description of the young adult process of "venturing and dwelling" (p. 52) echoes that described by authors on the subject of women's spiritual development. For example, Anderson and Hopkins state that the concept of "leaving home" to develop spiritually may often be a much more literal process for men than for women. Women's transformations may happen while remaining connected to hearth and home or, at least, with a less severe disconnection.

Carol Christ (1995) describes women's spiritual development as involving the process of experiencing *nothingness, awakening, insight,* and *new naming.* The experience of nothingness may be common to both men and women, but it springs from different sources. Christ describes how, when a woman rejects the self-hating and misogynistic messages of the culture, she experiences a feeling of nothingness and questions the meaning of her life. This questioning can lead to an awakening and insight into her grounding in the powers of self and being. This awakening may be a body or community-centered event for a woman. New naming happens when women give words and form to their experience. This process has the potential for radically altering spiritual discourse. As poet Muriel Rukeyser describes, "What would happen if one woman told the truth about her life? The world would split open" (qtd. in Christ, 1995, p. 24).

As an example of this truth telling, Reilly (1995) describes *The Woman's Bible,* created in 1898 by a group of women led by Elizabeth Cady Stanton. They provided interpretation of the Bible and highlight inconsistencies or biases that are evident in organized religion's choices. For example, there are two accounts in Genesis of the creation of humans, one in which man and woman are created at the same time and one that states that woman was created with Adam's rib. Unfortunately for women, the second account has been favored throughout Judeo-Christian history. This led biblical scholars to create the myth of Lilith, the assertive and sexually self-possessed first mate of Adam. Lilith has been used in Jewish and Christian culture as an example of the fallen woman, the sexual predator, the evil seductress, and is described as unnatural and unfeminine. People have different names for this forgotten and misrepresented aspect of women's spirituality. Christ (1997) talks about the "Goddess," Estes (1992) about "Wild Woman," and Reilly (1995) about "Lilith," but they all possess something not found in most descriptions of women in Western culture: the power to define themselves.

Finally, gender may interact with other factors such as race or ethnicity to create other unique developmental paths for women. For example, Watts (2003) suggests that spirituality offers African American college women a way to (a) cope with racism and prejudice, (b) resist the negative cultural images of being Black and female, and (c) develop an integrated identity. The poet Ntozake Shange speaks to the double burden of being a woman and Black in a society defined by White men. In defiance of this, she proclaims, "I found god in myself . . . & I loved her fiercely" (qtd. in Christ, 1995, p. 97). The work of all these authors illustrates how the spiritual development of women may be influenced by a myriad of factors that differentiate the process from men's spiritual development.

The intersection of ethnicity, culture, gender, and religion offers complex interactions that require focus and study, not quick assumptions. For the counselor who aspires to be cross-culturally sensitive to spiritual beliefs and practices, it is suggested that he or she become exposed to diverse belief systems and then decide the extent to which he or she can effectively relate to such beliefs. This section has offered a modest sampling of spiritualities found in diverse cultural worldviews. The issue of spiritual competencies will be addressed in the next section.

## IMPLICATIONS FOR CROSS-CULTURAL COUNSELING

In this section, various implications of integrating spirituality in counseling across cultures are presented and discussed. Following a multicultural learning model of engaging *awareness, knowledge, skills, passion,* and *action* cross-culturally (Fukuyama & Sevig, 1999), counselors can develop multicultural and spiritual competencies. Included will be counseling content and process issues, counseling interventions, spiritual competencies, and appropriateness of referral to religious and spiritual resources.

*Content.* Certain counseling issues include spirituality as a more or less direct component, while other issues are related indirectly. For example, most clients regard death and dying as having a spiritual or religious component. Factors such as the meaning of life, the meaning of death, what happens after death, and terminal illness are examples of issues that involve a very direct connection with religious and spiritual domains. Other counseling issues may include spirituality, depending on the person's development or particular history. For example, a career counseling client may be questioning, *What is the meaning of my life* or *what is my calling in life?*

Religious and spiritual beliefs and practices may be expressed in both functional and dysfunctional ways, and the counselor is encouraged to discern with the client which ways spirituality is part of the problem and/or part of the solution (Fukuyama & Sevig, 1999). In some instances, people may have religious wounds or use spirituality to *bypass* necessary psychological growth (Cashwell, Myers, & Shurts, 2004).

*Process.* A main part of the counseling process has been the relationship; this relationship has been described as central to therapy by various investigators (Bordin, 1968; Gelso & Carter, 1985; Kelly, 1995). Kelly (1995) extended this to include the role of spirituality in the counseling relationship. He noted that spirituality can inform the relationship and make it more meaningful and deep for both counselor and client. Taking this a step further, when multicultural factors are added to the complexity, the process becomes more human and real for both counselor and client.

On a spiritual level, it is possible for counselors to incorporate values such as connectedness of all beings, compassion, forgiveness, and respect with the goal of affirming human dignity and diversity as a vital part of existence. Kelly (1995) described how spirituality represents an active process of personal and relational humanness. "Spirituality entails not only an awareness of human potential and creativity in personal depth, but also a sense of fundamental human relatedness within a larger sphere of universal connectedness and transcendent meaning" (p. 89).

It is important to note that within multicultural counseling, the counselor needs to be able to recognize and address multiple social identities. To enhance the full potential of both counselor and client, spirituality in its purest form can aid in this process. By including all of who the client is and all of who the counselor is, the counseling enterprise can strive toward fulfilling the "potential" described by Kelly (1995).

Other process issues include variables such as consciousness, being present in the counseling situation, and communicating core counseling conditions. However, certain issues contraindicate pursuing a more overt spiritual exploration, such as active psychosis with spiritual language, cases of spiritual or religious abuse, or when the client is overly stressed or preoccupied with religious or spiritual topics. Finally, counselors need to be keenly aware of their own transference issues with regard to spirituality and religion in order not to impose beliefs or values onto clients.

*Counseling Interventions.* Various interventions in therapy use spirituality to guide and inform counseling practice across cultures. It is important to understand how spiritual and religious beliefs influence the problem (both cause and cure) before engaging in a spiritual intervention. Multicultural literature has provided a framework of cross-cultural counseling that uses an intentional focus on understanding the client's spiritual background and identity (Shimabukuro, Daniels, & D'Andrea, 1999). Therefore, in clinical assessments, it would be important to assess the clinical issue of focus as well as a client's spiritual beliefs and practices that might be influencing the issue. This assessment is helpful for diagnostic purposes and can also lead to a deeper examination of how spirituality is or is not playing a role. This exploration phase also helps the client feel fully understood and gives directions for possible interventions.

After the assessment, decisions made about interventions come into play. When deciding with a client how best to intervene, a classification from Faiver, O'Brien, and Ingersoll (2000) is helpful. They outline five categories of spiritual interventions: (1) in session versus out of session, (2) religious versus spiritual, (3) denominational versus ecumenical, (4) transcendent versus nontranscendent, and (5) affective, behavioral, cognitive, and interpersonal. The authors list a number of specific interventions within these five categories. Other examples of spiritual counseling interventions include taking a spiritual history and using a spiritual genogram (Dunn & Dawes, 1999; Frame, 2000), using nontraditional techniques for creativity in emotional expression (Frame, Williams, & Green, 1999), and utilizing visualization or focusing techniques (Hinterkopf, 1997). The degree to which counselors will incorporate spiritual techniques will depend on such factors as counselor spiritual beliefs, theoretical orientation and style, employment setting, and training and supervision.

*Competencies.* Frame (2003) outlined the following as important steps in attaining a degree of competency in working with spiritual issues: (1) self-awareness, (2) knowledge of otherness in learning about differences, (3) skill acquisition, (4) assessing barriers, and (5) willingness to learn. R. G. Anderson (2004) outlined similar areas for chaplains who want to become more culturally sensitive: (1) capacity to know and explain one's own spiritual/cultural groundedness; (2) the capacity to learn about others and "otherness"; (3) the capacity to demonstrate multispiritual/multicultural attitudes, knowledge, and skills; (4) the capacity to identify relational barriers and one's own limitations; and (5) the capacity to demonstrate respect and a willingness to learn.

In addition to examining spiritual competencies, professional mental health workers are also encouraged to adopt and operationalize multicultural competencies (American Psychological Association, 2003; Arredondo et al., 1996). Both areas of competency development are compatible and complementary to one another, and it is recommended that training programs incorporate both simultaneously.

*Referrals.* Within the multicultural competencies guidelines, practitioners are encouraged to collaborate and refer when appropriate to indigenous healers and religious or spiritual resources. Counselors need to know their comfort zone and their limits with respect to religious and spiritual processes. Developing boundaries on this work is appropriate and desirable, especially due to the personal and powerful nature of spiritual experiences. Although this may seem antithetical to learning and growing as a practitioner, it is not. Counselors often grow along with the clients with whom they are working; however, what is always central is the client's need for help. This is why the competencies for spiritual issues instruct the counselor to know oneself and understand when to refer to a religious/spiritual practitioner. If a counselor starts to feel that she or he is learning but not providing the help that is sought, then it is time to consult and/or refer.

When connecting with a religious professional (rabbi, minister, shaman, imam, priest, etc.) for either consultation or when making a referral, it is helpful to know about this professional ahead of time. This will avoid the possibility of retraumatizing the client if he or she has had a negative religious experience in the past.

## CONCLUSION

A discussion of recommendations for the future development of this area and research and training concerns are addressed in this conclusion. This chapter had the goal of introducing the reader to theory and the practice of incorporating spirituality into counseling across cultures. Several examples of cultural groups and accompanying worldviews were included in discussions of health, illness, and healing processes related both in general and specific to counseling. The reader is invited to find other cultural expressions of mental health and mental illness with the goal of adding toward a framework of incorporating spirituality into counseling across cultures.

We reflect here on a number of current and future developments in this specific part of multicultural counseling. As noted in the introduction, there has been a recent awareness and—indeed, more than awareness—a blossoming of work on spirituality in the past 5 years. In fact, some authors have suggested that spirituality is becoming a fifth force in counseling (Stanard, Sandhu, & Painter, 2000). As the field continues to grow in knowledge of both processes and content areas that lend themselves directly to spiritual issues, a number of considerations will need to be addressed.

*Research.* Both quantitative and qualitative research efforts are needed to explicate the complexities of religion, spirituality, and the transpersonal in multicultural counseling. Traditional quantitative studies are more likely to be found in measuring correlates of religion and health (Koenig, 1997) or studies in the psychology of religion or social psychology. A review of the quantitative measures used to measure transpersonal and spiritual constructs indicated that few studies cross-validate the various instruments currently available in the literature (Friedman & MacDonald, 2002). Given the complexity of spirituality, the authors recommended that research studies should incorporate multidimensional measures of constructs.

Another area of research that could prove useful in this area is to engage in process research. We recommend drawing on methodologies of process research with a specific focus on spiritual issues in cross-cultural counseling. For example, during the mid-1980s in the field of counseling psychology, process research emerged and expanded (see Borgen, 1992). This research methodology and accompanying assumptions include taking into account the many counselor and client variables in the counseling dyad that contribute to the process, embracing multiple realities of both counselor and client, emphasizing the notion that human behavior should be studied holistically, and resisting a paradigm of overly simple cause-and-effect relationships (Borgen, 1992). These research emphases lend themselves well to the study of spirituality and cross-cultural counseling.

*Training and Professional Development.* It is recommended that students and professionals alike engage in training, coursework, supervision, and/or continuing education workshops on this topic. Training in this area requires a balance of personal exploration, experiential learning, didactic understanding, and skill building (Sevig & Etzkorn, 2001). Although counselors typically seek strategies and advice about interventions, we suggest that personal awareness is a prerequisite to doing this work. As mentioned, many counselors and psychologists have transference issues that may be triggered when engaging with religious, spiritual, and transpersonal phenomena.

Finally, we would like to end this chapter by expanding the landscape of spirituality in cross-cultural counseling. This could include some nontraditional approaches within the traditional boundaries of counseling. Examples include integrating cognitive behavioral work and religious counseling, working collaboratively with pastoral counselors, and helping clients to integrate day-to-day religious or spiritual practices in conjunction with traditional psychological counseling. We recommend that the path to integration of mind, body, and spirit is holistic and inclusive of diversity at many levels.

## CRITICAL INCIDENT

### The Case of Cherie

Cherie (fictitious name) is a 24-year-old Asian American (Korean, 1.5 generation, immigrant) woman who is a graduate student in business. She has come to the university counseling center for help with issues of depression stemming from her struggles with her sexuality. She is from a fundamentalist nondenominational Christian background, which she continues to practice. She is concerned that she might be bisexual or lesbian and is disturbed by these thoughts and feelings. Although she is lonely and wishes for companionship, she does not feel that she can allow herself any intimacy other than a heterosexual relationship. She believes that her homosexual tendencies are punishment as bad karma or, in Christian terms, her "cross to bear." She has not disclosed any of these thoughts to her parents, friends, or church community and feels anxious about coming to therapy but feels desperate for help. She wishes that she could be converted to "normal heterosexuality."

This is a complicated case study involving multiple social identities, including ethnicity, gender, and religion. Immigrant ethnic churches provide a sense of belongingness and an opportunity to hold positions of power, and they tend to be religiously conservative. Religious principles influence and are mutually influenced by traditional Asian cultural values, such as hierarchy of authority, family, and filial piety. Ethnic churches also preserve culture and transmit culture to the next generation.

Numerous issues arose in working with this client, influenced by culture and religion of the counselor and the supervisor. The counselor was a 34-year-old Caucasian Jewish woman who had converted to her faith about 8 years earlier and who practiced feminist therapy. She was currently married with two children and identified as bisexual. The supervisor was a 55-year-old Latina who practiced Catholicism. However, she was open about her disagreements with the church on a number of issues, including women's rights and homosexuality. She identified as heterosexual and was divorced with two grown children in their 20s.

The counselor met with this client weekly for 4 months. During this time, she sought supervision on multiple occasions to process her reactions to the client's perceptions of herself and of the world that clashed with the counselor's feminist, religious, and personal values. With her supervisor, she explored feeling angry at a society that had given her client these messages. She also identified her own reactions to a fundamentalist Christian faith that related to her experiences growing up in a religiously conservative community. A key tension that the counselor and supervisor struggled with was how to support the client without imposing the counselor's worldviews on her, especially when the client's worldviews were causing her distress. The counselor tried a number of interventions, including introducing alternative religious interpretations to the client's. This was often met with quoting of scriptures by the client in support of her belief system. The counselor realized that she could not match the client's knowledge or adequately address the client's religious beliefs. However, she was hesitant to send her to speak to clergy within the client's religion, which might reinforce the condemning attitudes of her sexual orientation that were causing the client's depression.

## DISCUSSION QUESTIONS

1. How might the client's church membership intersect with pressures to assimilate into U.S. mainstream culture?

2. For the feminist counselor, women's spirituality was an important issue. How does this value potentially clash with the client's worldview as presented?

3. Is counseling a "valueless" endeavor? If not, how do counselors deal with clients' values that may be seen as harmful, causing distress or pain or inhibiting their growth?

4. What are examples of healthy and unhealthy spirituality? Is it possible that the client is engaging in a *spiritual bypass* in this situation?

5. Professional ethics state that reparative or conversion therapy to "change someone's sexual orientation" is unethical because it can harm the client. What other interventions may be offered that are respectful of cultural and religious differences and yet embrace psychological well-being and healthy sexuality?

6. What are your reactions to this case study?

## REFERENCES

Altareb, B. Y. (1996). Islamic spirituality in America: A middle path to unity. *Counseling and Values, 41,* 29–38.

American Psychological Association. (2003). Guidelines on multicultural education, training, research, practice, and organizational change for psychologists. *American Psychologist, 58,* 377–402.

Anderson, R. G. (2004). The search for spiritual/cultural competency in chaplaincy practice: Five steps that mark the path. In R. G. Anderson & M. A. Fukuyama (Eds.), *Ministry in the spiritual and cultural diversity of health care: Increasing the competency of chaplains* (pp. 1–24). Binghamton, NY: Haworth Pastoral Press.

Anderson, S. R., & Hopkins, P. (1991). *The feminine face of God: The unfolding of the sacred in women.* New York: Bantam.

Ano, G., Mathew, E., & Fukuyama, M. (in press). Religion and spirituality. In A. Alvarez & N. Tiwari (Eds.), *Asian American psychology: Current perspectives.* Mahwah, NJ: Lawrence Erlbaum.

Arredondo, P., Toporek, R., Brown, S., Jones, J., Locke, D. C., Sanchez, J., et al. (1996). Operationalization of the multicultural counseling competencies. *Journal of Multicultural Counseling & Development, 24,* 42–78.

Beversluis, J. (Ed.). (2000). *Sourcebook of the world's religions: An interfaith guide to religion and spirituality.* Novato, CA: New World Library.

Bordin, E. S. (1968). *Psychological counseling* (2nd ed.). New York: Meredith Corporation.

Borgen, F. H. (1992). Expanding scientific paradigms. In S. D. Brown & R. W. Lent (Eds.), *Handbook of counseling psychology* (2nd ed., pp. 111–139). New York: John Wiley.

Busto, R. V. (1996). The Gospel according to the model minority? Hazarding an interpretation of Asian American Evangelical college students. *Amerasia Journal, 22*(1), 133–147.

Carnes, R. D., & Craig, S. (1998). *Sacred circles: A guide to creating your own women's spirituality group.* San Francisco: HarperCollins.

Carnes, T., & Yang, F. (2004). *Asian American religions: The making and remaking of borders and boundaries.* New York: New York University Press.

Cashwell, C. S., Myers, J. E., & Shurts, W. M. (2004). Using the developmental counseling and therapy model to work with a client in spiritual bypass: Some preliminary considerations. *Journal of Counseling & Development, 82,* 403–409.

Cashwell, C. S., & Young, J. S. (2005). *Integrating spirituality and religion into counseling: A guide to competent practice.* Alexandria, VA: American Counseling Association.

Christ, C. (1995). *Diving deep and surfacing: Women writers on spiritual quest* (3rd ed.). Boston: Beacon.

Christ, C. (1997). *Rebirth of the Goddess: Finding meaning in feminist spirituality.* New York: Routledge.

Cortright, B. (1997). *Psychotherapy and spirit: Theory and practice in transpersonal psychotherapy.* Albany: State University of New York Press.

Curtis, N. (Ed.). (1968). *The Indians' book: Songs and legends of the American Indians.* New York: Dover.

Das, A. K. (1987). Indigenous models of therapy in traditional Asian societies. *Journal of Multicultural Counseling & Development, 15,* 25–37.

Dufrene, P. M., & Coleman, V. D. (1994). Art and healing for Native American Indians. *Journal of Multicultural Counseling and Development, 22,* 145–152.

Dunn, A. B., & Dawes, S. J. (1999). Spirituality-focused genograms: Keys to uncovering spiritual resources in African American families. *Journal of Multicultural Counseling and Development, 27,* 240–254.

Elkins, D. (1995). Psychotherapy and spirituality: Toward a theory of the soul. *Journal of Humanistic Psychology, 35*(2), 78–98.

Elkins, D. N., Hedstrom, L. J., Hughes, L. L., Leaf, J. A., & Saunders, C. (1988). Toward a humanistic-phenomenological spirituality: Definition, description, and measurement. *Journal of Humanistic Psychology, 28(4),* 5–18.

Estes, C. P. (1992). *Women who run with the wolves: Myths and stories of the wild woman archetype.* New York: Ballantine.

Fadiman, A. (1997). *The spirit catches you and you fall down.* New York: Farrar, Straus & Giroux.

Faiver, C. M., O'Brien, E. M., & Ingersoll, R. E. (2000). Religion, guilt, and mental health. *Journal of Counseling & Development, 78,* 155–161.

Firth, S. (2005). End-of-life: A Hindu view. *The Lancet, 366,* 682–686.

Frame, M. W. (2000). The spiritual genogram in family therapy. *Journal of Marital and Family Therapy, 26*(2), 211–216.

Frame, M. W. (2003). *Integrating religion and spirituality into counseling: A comprehensive approach.* Pacific Grove, CA: Brooks/Cole.

Frame, M. W., Williams, C. B., & Green, E. L. (1999). Balm in Gilead: Spiritual dimensions in counseling African American women. *Journal of Multicultural Counseling and Development, 27,* 182–192.

Friedman, H. L., & MacDonald, D. A. (2002). *Approaches to transpersonal measurement and assessment.* San Francisco: The Transpersonal Institute.

Fukuyama, M. A. (1990). Taking a universal approach to multicultural counseling. *Counselor Education and Supervision, 30,* 6–17.

Fukuyama, M. A., & Sevig, T. D. (1999). *Integrating spirituality into multicultural counseling*. Thousand Oaks, CA: Sage.

Fukuyama, M., Siahpoush, F., & Sevig, T. D. (2005). Religion and spirituality in a cultural context. In C. Cashwell & J. S. Young (Eds.), *Integrating spirituality and religion into counseling: A guide to competent practice* (pp. 123–142). Alexandria, VA: American Counseling Association.

Garrett, J. T., & Garrett, M. W. (1994). The path of good medicine: Understanding and counseling Native American Indians. *Journal of Multicultural Counseling and Development, 27,* 134–144.

Garrett, M. T., & Wilbur, M. P. (1999). Does the worm live in the ground? Reflections on Native American spirituality. *Journal of Multicultural Counseling and Development, 27,* 193–206.

Gelso, C. J., & Carter, J. (1985). The relationship in counseling: Components, consequences, and theoretical antecedents. *The Counseling Psychologist, 13*(2), 155–243.

Gilligan, C. (1993). *In a different voice: Psychological theory and women's development*. Cambridge, MA: Harvard University Press.

Herring, R. D. (1997). The creative arts: An avenue to wellness among Native American Indians. *Journal of Humanistic Education and Development, 36,* 104–113.

Hill, P. C., Pargament, K. I., Hood, R. W., McCullough, M. E., Swyers, J. P., Larson, D. B., et al. (2000). Conceptualizing religion and spirituality: Points of commonality, points of departure. *Journal for the Theory of Social Behavior, 30*(1), 50–77.

Hinterkopf, E. (1997). *Integrating spirituality in counseling: A manual for using the experiential focusing method*. Alexandria, VA: American Counseling Association.

Ingerman, S. (1991). *Soul retrieval: Mending the fragmented self*. New York: Harper San Francisco.

Kabat-Zinn, J. (1990). *Full catastrophe living: Using the wisdom of your body and mind to face stress, pain, and illness*. New York: Delta.

Kelly, E. W., Jr. (1995). *Spirituality and religion in counseling and psychotherapy: Diversity in theory and practice*. Alexandria, VA: American Counseling Association.

Kim, B. S. K., Atkinson, D. R., & Yang, P. H. (1999). The Asian values scale: Development, factor analysis, validation, and reliability. *Journal of Counseling Psychology, 46,* 342–352.

Koenig, H. G. (1997). *Is religion good for you health? The effects of religion on physical and mental health*. New York: Hawthorn Pastoral Press.

LaDue, R. A. (1994). Coyote returns: Twenty sweats does not an Indian expert make. *Women & Therapy, 15*(1), 93–111.

Lien, P., & Carnes, T. (2004). The religious demography of Asian American boundary crossing. In T. Carnes & F. Yang (Eds.), *Asian American religions: The making and remaking of borders and boundaries* (pp. 38–51). New York: New York University Press.

Locke, D. (1990). A not so provincial view of multicultural counseling. *Counselor Education and Supervision, 30,* 18–25.

May, G. (1982). *Will & spirit: A contemplative psychology*. New York: Harper & Row.

Miller, G. (1999). The development of the spiritual focus in counseling and counselor education. *Journal of Counseling & Development, 77,* 498–501.

Moodley, R., & West, W. (Eds.). (2005). *Integrating traditional healing practices into counseling and psychotherapy*. Thousand Oaks, CA: Sage.

Myers, L. J. (1988). *Understanding an Afrocentric world view: Introduction to an optimal psychology*. Dubuque, IA: Kendall/Hunt.

Pargament, K. I. (1999). The psychology of religion and spirituality? Yes and no. *International Journal for the Psychology of Religion, 9*(1), 3–16.

Parks, S. D. (2000). *Big questions, worthy dreams: Mentoring young adults in their search for meaning, purpose and faith*. San Francisco: Jossey-Bass.

Reilly, P. L. (1995). *A God who looks like me: Discovering a woman-affirming spirituality*. New York: Ballantine.

Richards, P. S., & Bergin, A. E. (1997). *A spiritual strategy for counseling and psychotherapy*. Washington, DC: American Psychological Association.

Richards, P. S., & Bergin, A. E. (Eds.). (2000). *Handbook of psychotherapy and religious diversity*. Washington, DC: American Psychological Association.

Rinpoche, S. (1992). *The Tibetan book of living and dying.* New York: HarperCollins.

Scotton, B. W., Chinen, A. B., & Battista, J. R. (1996). *Textbook of transpersonal psychiatry and psychology.* New York: Basic Books.

Sevig, T. D., & Etzkorn, J. (2001). Transformative training: A year-long multicultural counseling seminar for graduate students. *Journal of Multicultural Counseling and Development, 29,* 57–72.

Shafranske, E. P. (Ed.). (1996). *Religion and the clinical practice of psychology.* Washington, DC: American Psychological Association.

Sheu, H. B., & Fukuyama, M. A. (2007). Counseling international students from East Asia. In H. D. Singaravelu & M. Pope (Eds.), *Handbook for counseling international students* (pp. 173–193). Alexandria, VA: American Counseling Association.

Shimabukuro, K. P., Daniels, J., & D'Andrea, M. (1999). Addressing spiritual issues from a cultural perspective: The case of the grieving Filipino boy. *Journal of Multicultural Counseling & Development, 27,* 221–239.

Shumsky, S. G. (1996). *Divine revelation.* New York: Simon & Schuster.

Smith, H. (1992). *The world's religions.* New York: Harper San Francisco.

Stanard, R. P., Sandhu, D. S., & Painter, L. C. (2000). Assessment of spirituality in counseling. *Journal of Counseling & Development, 78,* 204–210.

Starhawk. (1999). *The spiral dance: A rebirth of the ancient religion of the great Goddess.* New York: Harper San Francisco.

Trimble, J., & Thurman, P. (2002). Ethnocultural considerations and strategies for providing counseling services for Native American Indians. In P. Pedersen, J. Draguns, W. Lonner, & J. Trimble (Eds.), *Counseling across cultures* (5th ed., pp. 53–91). Thousand Oaks, CA: Sage.

Watts, S. K. (2003). Come to the river: Using spirituality to cope, resist and develop identity. *New Directions for Student Services, 104,* 29–40.

# 21

# Health Psychology in Multiethnic Perspective

Frances E. Aboud

---

## *Primary Objective*

- To identify associations between physical and mental/social health and evaluate how health providers can counsel behavior change

## *Secondary Objectives*

- To understand how and why socioeconomic status (SES) and ethnicity cause illness and inadequate health behaviors
- To outline the current concept of "patient-centered consultation" in medical practice and its application to cross-cultural counseling

---

THE HEALTH OF INDIVIDUALS HAS BEEN DEFINED BY THE WORLD HEALTH ORGANIZATION IN TERMS OF physical, mental, and social well-being and not simply the absence of disease. This definition has at least two components that are of great significance to counselors. One is that health is seen as a continuum, ranging from illness to well-being, with growth toward the positive end of the spectrum being as important as recovery from the disease end. Most people are somewhere in between the extremes, striving toward well-being. The second component is the explicit recognition of the importance of mental and social health, as well as its potential impact on physical health, and vice versa.

The notion of health as a continuum is central to the philosophy of a counselor, who accepts his or her client's current position on the continuum and his or her desire to move forward. The research reviewed here therefore includes the perspective of people who are more as well as less healthy. Counseling skills are as important to health care providers who are giving bad news of a cancer diagnosis as they are to a genetic counselor discussing the future probabilities of contracting a disease or a school counselor coordinating the efforts of a troubled child, parent, and teacher. Health education and promotion efforts are important when counseling for cancer screening as well as for exercise and diet. It is now generally accepted that patient education and counseling on health-promoting and health-compromising behaviors are both clinically effective and cost-effective (Fielding, 1999).

The interconnections among physical, mental, and social health are a matter for empirical examination. Consequently, the major theme running throughout this chapter concerns how and why the three components of well-being connect. The simple answer, of course, is that they are all parts of the same person. However, we know of people whose physical illness has not harmed the quality of their mental or social life. For example, as a group, men with prostate cancer have a higher quality of life, according to their own reports of physical, social, and psychological functioning, than might be expected of someone who has cancer (J. A. Clark, Rieker, Propert, & Talcott, 1999). Yet few people recognize how pervasive is the impact of pain (Skevington, 1998) or depression (Bonicatto, Dew, Zaratiegui, Lorenzo, & Pecina, 2001) on all domains of one's life. These discrepancies are important to keep in mind while reviewing the evidence for generally strong connections. The significance for counselors is in being able to identify the nature of the problem as physical, mental, social, or more than one and selecting the best route to address the problem. So, even if the problem is physical deterioration as a result of overusing alcohol, with implications for family and job functioning, or an apparently more constrained problem such as pain or asthma, touching on all components of well-being in the counseling encounter might prove efficacious.

## PHYSICAL HEALTH AND SOCIAL MARKERS

A number of indicators of health and illness are collected by health centers and survey groups in the United States and elsewhere. By examining physical health in relation to socioeconomic status, ethnicity, gender, and age, researchers have identified lower SES groups, minority ethnic groups, and the young as in special need of proactive services. The evidence is, of course, much more complex than this simple conclusion and depends on the type of health problem being addressed.

Race and ethnicity in the United States are usually grouped according to White (non-Hispanic), Black (African American), Hispanic, Native American, and Asian American in health studies (Williams & Collins, 1995). Categories are used with simplicity in mind when collecting and analyzing health statistics (because all of these groupings are heterogeneous in terms of their actual background). The newly introduced category of "mixed background" is yet to be evaluated. Krieger, Williams, and Moss (1997) also point out that minority ethnic groups tend to have lower income and occupation and fewer economic assets to be used in an emergency than Whites, despite having the same educational level. While studies attempt to isolate the effects of ethnicity by statistically controlling for SES, the careful reader will be aware that for many minorities, one's ethnicity has a powerful effect on the socioeconomic constraints and opportunities one meets throughout life. If ethnicity by itself accounts for little of the variation in health, after controlling for SES, this is most likely because ethnicity and SES are closely connected. As might be expected, the impact of SES and ethnicity on health is less due to biological vulnerability than to social inequality.

*Mortality.* The "social gradient" in mortality is now a robust finding generally acknowledged by North American and European health professionals. It refers to the fact that both SES and ethnicity, separately or together, are strongly related to one's chances of dying prematurely (for reviews, see Adler et al., 1994; Krieger et al., 1997; Lillie-Blanton & Laveist, 1996; Macintyre, 1997; Williams & Collins, 1995). The gradient appears to characterize a series of steps—with every increment in income, occupation, and education, one's chances of not dying prematurely are increased. This means that over a 10-year period, men and women between 25 and 64 years with 8 years of schooling are more likely to die than those with a college education.

Several points could be made about the gradient (see reviews cited above). One is that the gradient may by steeper for men than for women. Another is that the steps may be steeper at the lower SES end than the upper end, implying that small increments in income and education for those at the lower end show larger differences in survival than do such increments at the upper end. Third, over the past 40 years, premature mortality has generally declined, but less so for people at the lower end of the SES scale. Not everyone has benefited equally from recent medical advances.

There is a similar mortality gradient for ethnic differences (Kaufman, Long, Liao, Cooper, & McGee, 1998; Lillie-Blanton, Parsons, Gayle, & Dievler, 1996; Williams & Collins, 1995). African Americans, in particular, have a higher premature death rate, largely due to three causes: infant mortality, cardiovascular disease (heart attack and stroke), and cancer. The case of infant mortality will be described shortly; however, higher cardiovascular disease is often attributed to hypertension due to the stresses of racism (R. Clark, Anderson, Clark, & Williams, 1999), and cancer deaths have been attributed to delayed treatment and inadequate screening (Gilliland, Hunt, & Key, 1998).

Ethnic differences in infant mortality show that twice as many Black infants die compared to White infants (Luke, Williams, Minogue, & Keith, 1993). This has been traced to more of the former being either low birth weight or premature. Yet medical advances are such that underweight and premature infants need not die or even be significantly delayed beyond the early years. Childhood mortality shows the same ethnic discrepancy: twice as high for Black children between 1 and 4 years and only slightly lower for those between 5 and 14 years (Singh & Yu, 1996). For example, for every 100,000 infants born between 1989 and 1991, 42 White preschool children died, whereas 63 American Indian and 80 Black children died. Among school-aged children ages 5 to 14 years, the rates were 23, 28.6, and 28.6, respectively. Hispanic and Asian (and Pacific Islander) children have mortality rates similar to or lower than White children, though there is national variation within these groups. The leading cause of death in children, accounting for some 40% of deaths, is unintentional injuries resulting from car accidents and violence.

*Physical and Mental Illness.* SES and ethnic disparities in illness and disability have also been well documented both for physical (e.g., Adler et al., 1994; Krieger et al., 1997; Lillie-Blanton et al., 1996; Ren, Amick, & Williams, 1999; Williams & Collins, 1995) and psychological illness (e.g., Kessler, Mickelson, & Williams, 1999). The latest evidence comes from a report of three adult data sets—two American and one British—finding that health, as measured by signs of cardiovascular disease, depression, and self-ratings of overall health, was significantly worse with each step down in SES (Marmot, Ryff, Bumpass, Shipley, & Marks, 1997). Furthermore, most categories of chronic disease show higher rates among less educated adults (Adler et al., 1994).

Mental illness is the same; both lifetime and 12-month combinations of depression, anxiety, and substance abuse are more likely to be present in those ages 18 to 54 years with lower education (Kessler, Foster, Saunders, & Stang, 1995; World Health Organization [WHO] International Consortium in Psychiatric Epidemiology, 2000). For example, in the WHO study, 17% of Americans were identified with high levels of anxiety in the past 12 months, 10.7% with depression, and 11.5% with substance abuse problems, and 12% had more than one of these problems. Compared to those with college education, those who did not complete high school were almost four times more likely to have a combination of these mental illnesses. Conduct disorder and substance abuse were the two problems most likely to lead to early school dropout (Kessler et al., 1995), especially among men. Regardless of whether one looks at education, income, or employment, at each step down in the SES ladder, there are more people with mental health problems.

Ethnic inequalities in physical health are also very wide (see Lillie-Blanton et al., 1996). Black Americans experience more chronic illness and more restrictions in daily activities due to ill health than White Americans (Ferraro, Farmer, & Wybraniec, 1997). Special attention has often been paid to cardiovascular disease such as hypertension (high blood pressure). Black men and women are more likely to have hypertension than White men and women at each level of SES. We will see shortly how the experience of racial discrimination in daily life may contribute to this problem. Diabetes is also much more common among Black and Asian adults than Whites, leading to more rapid decline in kidney function (e.g., Krop et al., 1999). Cancer outcomes are also significantly worse for minority ethnic groups than for others (Meyerowitz, Richardson, Hudson, & Leedham, 1998).

Mental illness indicators are usually taken from self-reports of symptoms experienced in the past month or year, symptoms indicative of depression, anxiety, and perhaps substance abuse. In large national samples, Black adults did not experience more depression or anxiety than White adults (e.g., Kessler et al., 1995; Kessler et al., 1999; Ren et al., 1999). This is also the case for substance abuse, where even in the peak years of young adulthood, Black men and women are less likely to abuse alcohol (Holden, Moncher, & Schinke, 1990). However, when present in young minority men, it tends to have a greater impact on school, family, and job functioning, leading to school dropout and unemployment.

In summary, there appear to be social inequalities in mortality and physical illness whereby those with lower education, income, and occupation are more likely to die prematurely and suffer from certain diseases such as heart and respiratory problems than those at a slightly higher SES, all the way up the SES scale. Black and Native Americans in comparison with Whites have higher infant and child mortality, more chronic illness, and worse outcomes for certain diseases such as hypertension, diabetes, and cancer. While mental illness also appears to be more common among those with lower SES, it does not appear to be more common among ethnic minority groups.

## PATHWAYS FROM SES-ETHNICITY TO HEALTH

To understand these social inequalities in health, we review the major pathways studied. Many analysts have attempted to explain ethnic differences in terms of SES because minorities are disproportionately represented in lower SES groups. This simply means that the pathways from minority ethnic status to poor health (e.g., through unhealthy work environment or difficulties accessing health care) are similar to the pathways from low income and education to health. However, ethnicity may have a unique contribution to make in explaining why at each SES level, Black Americans show higher levels of illness and death than White Americans.

Researchers have been searching for the pathways from social status to health (Macintyre, 1997). They fall into several categories: (a) the physical environment (e.g., crowding, toxicity), (b) the social environment (e.g., single-parent family, less control over job demands, values), (c) health behaviors (e.g., smoking, drinking, diet, exercise), and (d) access to and use of medical information, treatments, and preventive services. There seems to be strong evidence that health deteriorates after working many years in a manual job or living in crowded, polluted conditions or lacking quality, free health services. Education and medical care are two important pathways to elaborate here.

The developmental course of poor and minority children indicates that health behaviors may constrain their educational careers and, thereby, their adult occupation and income (Evans, 2004). A full review of the SES differences in mortality, chronic illness, symptoms of acute illness, injuries, and self-rated health found large differences among children younger than 10 years, which receded during the adolescent years, only to reappear in young adulthood (Goodman, 1999; West, 1997). West (1997) suggests that a leveling effect takes place when adolescents move away from a solely parental and neighborhood influence to the diverse influences of a large high school, along with peer and behavioral choices made by the adolescents themselves (e.g., to hang around with those who smoke and drink). A large study in Finland supports this hypothesis (Karvonen, Rimpela, & Rimpela, 1999). Regardless of parental occupation, the adolescents' own educational status at 16 and 18 years (e.g., drop out or remain in school and achievement) showed a stronger association with smoking, alcohol abuse, lack of physical exercise, and high-fat diet. In fact, among adolescents whose family origins were lower SES, those who remained in school and had high achievement showed better health behaviors. So, adolescents have the opportunity to diverge from their parents' SES by making choices as to who their peer reference group will be, how achievement oriented they will be, and how much drinking, smoking, and sexual activity they will engage in.

Educational attainment is not only useful as a proxy for adult SES but also a strong determinant of adult health behaviors. This has been studied extensively in developing nations of the world, where a mother's level of education significantly affects whether her children survive childhood (Grosse & Auffrey, 1989). One of the reasons why education translates into health and long life concerns the ability to seek and make good use of current health care information and services. This is true also in industrialized countries such as the United States, where researchers found that good health followed from "health literacy and numeracy" skills (Baker, Parker, Williams, Clark, & Nurss, 1997). Although schooling and health literacy were moderately related, the actual ability to read and understand health care materials was a stronger determinant of health.

Medical care might also be poorer for low SES and minority families. African Americans say they are least likely to experience discrimination in medical settings than in other situations (Ren et al., 1999). Still, they may be viewed by their physicians as less likely to comply with medical advice, less likely to receive social support for complying, and more likely to engage in substance abuse than White patients, despite evidence to the contrary from these particular patients (van Ryn & Burke, 2000). Whether or not this places constraints on the information or decision making shared with minority patients is not clear, though it did translate into less time spent with the patient (see also Blackhall, Murphy, Frank, Michel, & Azen, 1995). Many minority people delay seeking professional help for symptoms that might indicate serious physical diseases such as cancer, hypertension, and diabetes. While lack of medical insurance is an obvious explanation, minority people, particularly less affluent ones, might dislike the stereotypic judgments and the blame they receive when they enter the health care system.

Although the health care system may be the least discriminatory of all public domains, the prevalence and impact of racial/ethnic discrimination in other walks of life could affect health. Within the category of social-environmental conditions that lead from SES and ethnicity to illness is racial discrimination. Like acculturative stress, which refers to the external and internal demands placed on people who seek a comfortable compromise between potentially conflictual cultures in their lives, being a target of racism may be stressful (R. Clark, Anderson, et al., 1999). Reasonable ways of reacting to unfair treatment and prejudice include frustration, anger, and depression; these emotions may be detrimental to one's physical and mental health. For example, frustration and anger could lead to heightened blood pressure and subsequently hypertension, a more prevalent illness among African Americans (e.g., Gump, Matthews, & Raikkonen, 1999). And while we found no evidence for minorities having more mental illness than Whites, feelings of powerlessness, sadness, hopelessness, and shame could become a basis for depressed affect.

Only recently have people created instruments to measure the experience of being a target of racism, assess its prevalence, and examine its consequences for health. One such measure, called the Perceived Racism Scale, was developed by McNeilly et al. (1996). Forty-three items are used to assess the frequency of exposure to racist incidents (e.g., Racial jokes or harassment are directed to me at work. I am often ignored or not taken seriously by my boss.). Emotional responses (e.g., angry, frustrated, sad, ashamed) and coping reactions (e.g., I work harder to prove them wrong. I deal with it by ignoring it.) are also assessed. Such measures are only now being used in health-related research. More commonly used are one or two questions about exposure: Have you ever experienced unfair treatment, been prevented from doing something, or been made to feel inferior because of race at school, getting a job, at work, getting medical care, in a public setting . . . ? (Kessler et al., 1999; Ren et al., 1999). Data from large national surveys found that 60% to 90% of Black Americans and 10% to 20% of White Americans had experienced discrimination due to their race at some point in their lives; the figures were 52% and 24%, respectively, for discrimination due to SES (Ren et al., 1999). While Black Americans did not have worse psychological distress or depression, those who had frequent exposure to racial and SES discrimination had higher levels of psychological distress, anxiety, and depression (Jackson et al., 1996; Kessler et al., 1999; Ren et al., 1999). The "racism as stressor" hypothesis is a promising new pathway to be explored. Results have at first been somewhat surprising, in that while Black Americans appear to have more exposure to discrimination, they may be less vulnerable to emotional consequences because parents teach their youngsters how to cope but are more vulnerable to cardiovascular problems (Harrell, Hall, & Taliaferro, 2003). Unexpectedly high levels of perceived discrimination were reported by White Americans, by men, and by better educated Black Americans. Also, the day-to-day variety of racism may be more detrimental to mental health than the lifetime variety (Kessler et al., 1999).

The next section moves from the group-level evidence to the individual person who seeks health care. In many ways, ethnic minority patients are excluded from participating in and taking responsibility for their medical care.

## BENEFITS OF AND BARRIERS TO PATIENT-CENTERED CARE

Being excluded from full participation in medical decision making is detrimental to your health. The goal of patient-centered care is full participation. It has many benefits for both the health provider (e.g., counselor, nurse, physician) and the client or patient. Yet, it is largely an ideal waiting to be reached because of the many barriers to be overcome. In the traditional consultation, the health professional takes charge, and the patient follows and abides. However, most health professionals now agree that the synchronized participation of both the health provider and the patient is preferable. Full participation means that people who seek care to improve their health are partners in the process of identifying and managing the problem. What does it mean to be a *partner*? Like a dance partner, it requires sensitivity to one's partner's moves almost before they occur, the potential for variations in who takes the lead, and a large amount of creativity within a set framework. So, in a patient-centered consultation, patients must be treated as partners in the dialogue and their participation encouraged. Easier said than done!

How is a patient-centered consultation conducted? Mead and Bower (2000, 2002) observed many interactions between providers and patients and derived the following criteria:

1. *Sharing power and responsibility.* This entails eliciting each person's knowledge and understanding of the problem, as well as its management, and responding appropriately to them. Providers ask patients about the problem, how they feel about it, whether they feel more comfortable with one management strategy over another, and how they are coping. Patients likewise seek explanations and options from the provider and take responsibility for following whatever they have agreed to do to improve their own health.

2. *Therapeutic alliance.* This means that the provider and patient work to develop a relationship based on trust and respect for the purpose of arriving at commonly agreed therapeutic goals for the patient. Each listens to the other's opinion, and together they negotiate an agreed strategy to manage the problem.

3. *Patient as a person.* The provider in particular, but also the patient, must recognize the patient's emotional reaction to the illness, which might be fear of death, fear of stigma, loss of confidence, identity loss, and grief. They both must recognize the patient's limits in terms of information about the problem and ability to fully carry out the required treatment.

4. *Provider as a person.* This is parallel to the patient as a person. The provider may not be sensitive or responsive to the patient's state of mind and may hold false stereotypes of the patient and his or her capacity to recover. So patients need to be assertive in these cases to make their feelings and capacities known. The provider also has limits to his or her expertise, and for some health problems, there simply is no quick fix.

5. *Biopsychosocial perspective.* This refers to the understanding that physical problems also have psychological and social implications. Given that one third of people who visit a family physician have psychosocial problems, communication about the patients' personal experiences is necessary to understand the full problem. One or two open-ended questions on the part of the provider are usually sufficient to facilitate discussion on the psychological and social components of the problem (e.g., How's life at home? How's life at work?).

These are indeed laudable goals for medical consultations. They elevate the status of a patient from a passive dependent to an active partner. Furthermore, partnership with patients leads to health benefits. Patients who experience patient-centered consultations feel more enabled to cope with their problem; they are also more satisfied and likely to return for health care. More important, they tend to adhere to the treatment decisions worked out during the consultation, and their health status improves as a result. It is not difficult to understand why the above criteria lead to better adherence. People who are trusted act in a trustworthy manner; people who share in the decision to take a certain medication or alter their diet are more likely to feel responsible for following through on those decisions.

Despite the obvious benefits, there are many barriers to full provider-patient partnership. Both patients and health providers (e.g., counselors, nurses, physicians) have reasons for limiting a patient's full participation. Among providers, the first and simplest explanation is that their training, expertise, and experience give them a head start in identifying the problem and proposing a solution. Most people would agree that is why they seek the help of a professional—to get the best advice and help in solving their problem. However, it is now recognized that physician training and expertise is limited in the domain of psychosocial skills necessary for patient-centered care. Most medical schools are now actively training the next generation of doctors to be more sensitive, responsive, and inclusive. The specific verbal and nonverbal behaviors are well known, such as asking open-ended questions, presenting information about the problem and the alternative treatment options, and facilitating the patient's participation (Mead & Bower, 2002; Roter, 2000). They are not entirely the same behaviors as used by psychological counselors because the goal is to take action to remedy a health problem rather than for patients to understand themselves and set their own goals. So although medical expertise is the essence of what is sought in a medical encounter, health providers are now expected to be informative, facilitative, responsive, and participatory (Paasche-Orlow & Roter, 2003). Stereotypes are another barrier. Health providers, either from personal experience or from reading the research, know that patients from certain SES and ethnic groups are more or less likely to adhere to the treatment plan, come back for follow-up visits, get the support of their family to change their diet or study habits, and emotionally cope with the stress of screening for cancer. Even when the research findings are valid, they never explain everyone's situation; in fact, they rarely account for even half the people. To treat people as if they fit the statistic, without giving them the opportunity to disconfirm it, is an unwarranted generalization and constitutes stereotyping.

Patients also have characteristics that limit their full participation in making shared decisions and expressing themselves fully. Many have low levels of health literacy. They fail to grasp the seriousness of their condition despite simple explanations, some pregnant women and patients undergoing surgery cannot read brochures or booklets handed out to them, or they cannot follow instructions on a bottle of medication (Baker et al., 1997). The social and educational system needs to teach students about health so they can understand their own and that of the family they care for. Patients are being taught how to ask more questions to elicit explanations from their doctor about their illness, its causes, and the treatment options. Most people want to share their symptoms and feelings with their doctor, but not everyone wants to share in the decision of which treatment to follow. Many prefer to leave this up to the provider. However, when fully informed, patients have the freedom to accept or reject the offered treatment. Freedom to choose carries with it responsibility for the choice. Shouldering that responsibility is not easy for patients. Emotionally coping with illness or the fear of illness is also difficult, so many people would rather deny it. We all possess that limitation to some extent. So the patient-centered approach also places a greater burden on patients to become informed, involved, and responsible.

A great deal of emphasis is now being placed on health providers to accommodate patients from diverse cultures, many of whom speak a nonshared language. Cross-cultural competence concerns the skills and attitudes of the health provider in understanding the patients' beliefs about health and illness and how symptoms are experienced and expressed. We might expect that cross-cultural competence in a medical consultation would affect the less technical communications, particularly the ones having to do with patient-centered care. This is so; doctors who understand the cultural beliefs of their patients are better at eliciting and responding to patients' concerns and giving them a feeling of control (Fernandez et al., 2004). A more serious factor is the language discrepancy between provider and patient, particularly Spanish-speaking patients in consultation with English-speaking providers (see Flores, 2005, for a review). As of the year 2000, there were more than 20 million Americans with limited English proficiency, two thirds of whom were Spanish speaking. Not only do patients with limited English proficiency speak much less to their provider, but providers are also less responsive (Rivadeneyra, Elderkin-Thompson, Cohen Silver, & Waitzkin, 2000). Patients leave feeling misunderstood and not understanding their diagnosis or the treatment plan. Their impression of the provider is that he or she was not friendly, concerned, or respectful. Patients are dissatisfied with the service and unlikely to return. This means that, when ill, they do not seek help until their situation is so bad as to require expensive care and hospitalization. Worse, the potential for serious clinical errors is immense and has been documented (Flores et al., 2003).

The use of informal translators, such as nurses or family members, also contributes heavily to the error rate. One study found that half of the consultations had only minor nonserious translation errors, but the other half had serious errors (Elderkin-Thompson, Cohen Silver, & Waitzkin, 2001). The major error is omission, meaning that the interpreter fails to translate something said by the patient or the complete instruction of the provider. For example, informal interpreters are more likely to omit information to patients about side effects of medication, as well as omit information to doctors for an accurate diagnosis.

The following is a case of a woman who initially complains of numbness in her limbs and constant tiredness, taken from Elderkin-Thompson et al. (2001). However, the nurse interpreter talks about numbness and swelling. Here is part of the later communication, which perpetuates and adds to the confusion.

| | |
|---|---|
| *Doctor:* | Does she have any other problem? |
| *Interpreter:* | Do you have any other problems? Your feet? |
| *Patient:* | Yes, my feet, they went two or three times. I fell day before yesterday in the street and I couldn't get up. |
| *Interpreter:* | Do you feel weak? |
| *Patient:* | Yes, tired, I'm tired. Everything I hold makes me tired. |
| *Interpreter:* | When she gets tired and she falls down on the floor. Three days ago it was the third time. |
| *Doctor:* | She fell down? Did she pass out? |
| *Interpreter:* | Um hmm. |
| *Doctor:* | She passed out? She doesn't remember anything? |
| *Interpreter:* | She doesn't know. |

Only when the interpreter subsequently asked the patient, "When you fall, did you lose memory?" was the error corrected because the patient said, "No, no, no, nothing like that." The lack of accurate translation here led to the mistaken connection between feet, falling, and fainting, when in fact the woman was low on thyroid. However, the reference to numbness and feet misdirected the doctor's problem solving into other fruitless diagnoses.

Patients with trained as opposed to untrained medical interpreters during the consultation are more likely to be satisfied with their care; they return for follow-up appointments, get their prescriptions filled, and use preventive screening services (Flores, 2005). The obvious conclusion is that greater use of trained interpreters would improve patient adherence, prevention, health outcomes, and satisfaction, as well as lower health costs.

# COUNSELING FOR THE PROMOTION OF HEALTH

Education and counseling are now recognized as effective methods for changing health behaviors and thereby promoting health and preventing deterioration due to illness (Mullen et al., 1997). Three points made earlier reinforce the idea that counseling must become an important method of change in health. One is that people generally are able to report accurately their health status using a range of privately accessible yet appropriate information, such as current symptoms and pain, body size, health behaviors, and daily functioning. Strategies to improve their health can therefore be discussed and negotiated with their full participation. Second, social inequalities in health demonstrate how environmental, social, and psychological factors interfere with healthy development long before one is sick enough to seek medical help. It therefore becomes important to reach people from all social groups and ages in a manner that is responsive to their needs. Third, educational and counseling strategies are the only way to help people take responsibility for maintaining and improving their health once they leave the clinic.

There are many areas in which counseling is used to help people make wise and informed decisions about their health. These include screening for diseases such as cancer, testing for genetic predispositions, encouraging adherence to HIV and tuberculosis medication, promoting safer sex, and changing the so-called lifestyle health behaviors associated with diet, exercise, tobacco, and alcohol. We often naively assume that once informed about the detrimental effects of their behavior, people will change. But they do not. Good intentions are not always translated into behavior. Adopting new behaviors is impeded by old habits. So, personal counseling is needed to help people rearrange their lifestyle.

The promotion of healthy exercise and diet is one example of an area where counseling is used to reduce cardiovascular disease and the consequences of diabetes during the productive adult years. Surprisingly, half of strokes and heart attacks occur among those younger than 65 years. People at most risk for cardiovascular events are those with hypertension, diabetes, and excess weight. Thus, diet and exercise are the two health behaviors to be changed. Rather than simply enforcing proper diet and activity on those with the highest risk, community prevention efforts are being directed to the general population (Egan & Lackland, 1998). Because food preferences are usually acquired early in the home and are strongly influenced by ethnicity and education (Devine, Wolfe, Frongillo, & Bisogni, 1999), school-based programs for children and adolescents solicit cooperation from parents and teachers to improve lunches and physical education at school (e.g., Nader et al., 1999). The goal is to instill healthy eating and activity habits that will carry on into adulthood.

However, of greatest concern now is the sedentary lifestyle of 60% of the American adult population who are apparently not active enough to acquire any cardiovascular benefits. Attempts were made first to encourage physicians to counsel their patients on physical activity, yet such advice was either not given or went unheeded. Programs are now being conducted to encourage physical activity more directly by offering programs through communities and clinics to sedentary adults. They are based on two behavioral change models: One states that there are different motivations operating at each stage on the route to change, and the second states that certain social and cognitive processes help to increase the new behaviors. The Activity Counseling Trial set the same target for everyone—namely, 30 minutes of moderate-intensity physical activity, such as brisk walking, 5 or more days a week or 3 or more days of vigorous activity. None met the target at the start. Some people received advice from their physician and a health educator who helped them set goals; others received this plus 15 regular telephone counseling sessions to solve current and future barriers to meeting goals, provide reinforcement, and offer social support for maintaining activity (Writing Group for the Activity Counseling Trial Research Group, 2001). Two years later, women and men showed improved respiratory fitness in terms of lung capacity. Close to 30% also met the target for physical activity each week. Although individual counseling is considered labor intensive and not cost-effective, there seems to be an awareness of the fact that, unless worksites arrange for exercise, people need help changing their daily schedule to fit in 30 minutes of exercise a day. From a public health perspective, the benefits are immense in terms of a healthier population with better physical and mental well-being. This offers hope that others will create and evaluate innovative health programs to improve health literacy and health behaviors.

# CONCLUSIONS

A review of the evidence suggests strongly that ethnic inequalities, along with SES inequalities, are associated with higher infant mortality rates, more premature mortality, and more physical illness for certain minority groups. While there does not seem to be more psychological illness among ethnic minorities, the social and occupational consequences of physical or mental problems are more severe for minorities. The adolescent years were identified as one important turning point, where an individual's choice of peers, health behaviors, and educational goals can affect his or her future social status and health. People often seek care and counseling in order to discuss the social and psychological domains of their life, the part that is rarely included in a medical encounter. That is, both patients and nonpatients seek counseling on how to manage their lives for maximum health. This includes counseling on physical exercise and diet as well as genetic counseling and screening for disease.

## CRITICAL INCIDENT

A woman in her 50s comes in to see a counselor, complaining of weakness and shortness of breath. In the course of the consultation, she complains that her husband has recently shown less interest in her, and her children are growing away from the home. She recently went to a doctor complaining that she was dying from cancer. Although the doctor could not find anything, she suggested a mammogram. The woman is afraid that her family is going to leave her just when she needs them—when she is dying of cancer. The health counselor decides to probe for reasons why the woman has jumped to the conclusion that she is dying but will not go for a mammogram to confirm whether she has cancer.

C: What is your problem? What is bothering you?

W: My family is leaving me. They don't come home like usual. They stay out late.

C: That must worry you. Why do you think this is happening?

W: This is my life. What can I do! They don't listen to me any more!

C: When did this start to happen?

W: When I found out that my friend has breast cancer. I was so upset, I couldn't listen to her whole story. She told me it came from being hit on her body.

C: That must be difficult for her, and it's good of you to give her support.

W: But no one will give me support when I get cancer! I may even have it now. My heart is sick and my stomach is sick. I can't sleep at night.

This case demonstrates why some women, particularly Latinas of Mexican origin, are less likely than others to seek screening for cancer. It is not simply due to low SES, though that is a part. Some women also believe that cancer comes from being hit and receiving a bruise, or from God; they believe it is fatal, so preventive and treatment services are useless. Their only coping mechanism is to claim that they are not susceptible. However, this particular lady experiences a convergence of events that together undercut her coping strategy. She now worries that the mammogram will find cancer, her appearance will be ruined, her husband will no longer love her, and her children will abandon her. Life has become unbearable whether she goes or does not go for the mammogram. The goal of counseling from a health psychology perspective is to encourage her to go for screening and to take responsibility for the course of her life and behavior. An interesting paper by Borrayo (2004) examines how Latina women can be persuaded to attend cancer screening by providing information about cancer screening in an entertaining manner, within a familiar psychosocial context, that allows the woman to feel she is sharing the decision with her family and will thereby continue to provide for the needs of her family. The elements were used to help develop a video called Where's Maria? but they are equally relevant to those counseling women.

## DISCUSSION QUESTIONS

1.  What is the counselor's approach during this session? What aspects are useful and not useful, and how would you continue the session from here?

2.  How would you counsel someone from another ethnic group (e.g., Asian, Black, White, Muslim) presenting with a similar problem?

3.  What goals would you help this woman set for herself, and how would you help her achieve the goals?

# REFERENCES

Adler, N. E., Boyce, T., Chesney, M., Cohen, S., Kaher, R. L., & Syme, S. L. (1994). Socioeconomic status and health: The challenge of the gradient. *American Psychologist, 49,* 15–24.

Baker, D. W., Parker, R. M., Williams, M. V., Clark, W. S., & Nurss, J. (1997). The relationship of patient reading ability to self-reported health and use of health services. *American Journal of Public Health, 87,* 1027–1030.

Blackhall, L. J., Murphy, S. T., Frank, G., Michel, V., & Azen, S. (1995). Ethnicity and attitudes toward patient autonomy. *Journal of the American Medical Association, 13,* 820–826.

Bonicatto, S. C., Dew, M. A., Zaratiegui, R., Lorenzo, L., & Pecina, P. (2001). Adult outpatients with depression: Worse quality of life than in other chronic medical diseases in Argentina. *Social Science & Medicine, 52,* 911–919.

Borrayo, E. A. (2004). Where's Maria? A video to increase awareness about breast cancer and mammography screening among low-literacy Latinas. *Preventive Medicine, 39,* 99–110.

Clark, J. A., Rieker, P., Propert, K. J., & Talcott, J. A. (1999). Changes in quality of life following treatment for early prostate cancer. *Urology, 53,* 161–168.

Clark, R., Anderson, N. B., Clark, V. R., & Williams, D. R. (1999). Racism as a stressor for African Americans: A biopsychosocial model. *American Psychologist, 54,* 805–816.

Devine, C. M., Wolfe, W. S., Frongillo, E. A., & Bisogni, C. A. (1999). Life-course events and experiences: Association with fruit and vegetable consumption in 3 ethnic groups. *Journal of the American Dietetic Association, 99,* 309–314.

Egan, B. M., & Lackland, D. T. (1998). Strategies for cardiovascular disease prevention: Importance of public and community health programs. *Ethnicity & Disease, 8,* 228–239.

Elderkin-Thompson, V., Cohen Silver, R., & Waitzkin, H. (2001). When nurses double as interpreters: A study of Spanish-speaking patients in a US primary care setting. *Social Science & Medicine, 52,* 1343–1358.

Evans, G. W. (2004). The environment of childhood poverty. *American Psychologist, 59,* 77–92.

Fernandez, A., Schillinger, D., Grumbach, K., Rosenthal, A., Stewart, A. L., Wang, F., et al. (2004). Physician language ability and cultural competence: An exploratory study of communication with Spanish-speaking patients. *Journal of General Internal Medicine, 19,* 167–174.

Ferraro, K. F., Farmer, M. M., & Wybraniec, J. A. (1997). Health trajectories: Long-term dynamics among Black and White adults. *Journal of Health & Social Behavior, 38,* 38–54.

Fielding, J. E. (1999). Public health in the twentieth century: Advances and challenges. *Annual Review of Public Health, 20,* xiii–xxx.

Flores, G. (2005). The impact of medical interpreter services on the quality of health care: A systematic review. *Medical Care Research & Review, 62,* 255–299.

Flores, G., Laws, M. B., Mayo, S. J., Zuckerman, B., Abreu, M., Medina, L., & Hardt, E. J. (2003). Errors in medical interpretation and their potential clinical consequences in pediatric encounters. *Pediatrics, 111,* 6–14.

Gilliland, F. D., Hunt, W. C., & Key, C. R. (1998). Trends in the survival of American Indian, Hispanic, and Non-Hispanic White cancer patients in New Mexico and Arizona, 1969–1994. *Cancer, 82,* 1769–1783.

Goodman, E. (1999). The role of socioeconomic status gradients in explaining differences in US adolescents' health. *American Journal of Public Health, 89,* 1522–1528.

Grosse, R. N., & Auffrey, C. (1989). Literacy and health status in developing countries. *Annual Review of Public Health, 10,* 281–297.

Gump, B. B., Matthews, K. A., & Raikkonen, K. (1999). Modeling relationships among socioeconomic status, hostility, cardiovascular reactivity, and left ventricular mass in African American and White children. *Health Psychology, 18,* 140–150.

Harrell, J. P., Hall, S., & Taliaferro, J. (2003). Physiological responses to racism and discrimination: An assessment of the evidence. *American Journal of Public Health, 93,* 243–248.

Holden, G. W., Moncher, M. S., & Schinke, S. P. (1990). Substance abuse. In A. S. Bellack, M. Hersen, & A. E. Kazdin (Eds.), *International handbook of behavior modification and therapy* (2nd ed., pp. 869–880). New York: Plenum.

Jackson, J. S., Brown, T. N., Williams, D. R., Torres, M., Sellers, S. L., & Brown, K. (1996). Racism and the physical & mental health status of African Americans: A thirteen year national panel study. *Ethnicity & Disease, 6,* 132–147.

Karvonen, S., Rimpela, A. H., & Rimpela, M. K. (1999). Social mobility and healthy related behaviors in young people. *Journal of Epidemiology & Community Health, 53,* 211–217.

Kaufman, J. S., Long, A. E., Liao, Y., Cooper, R. S., & McGee, D. L. (1998). The relation between income and mortality in U.S. Blacks and Whites. *Epidemiology, 9,* 147–155.

Kessler, R. C., Foster, C. L., Saunders, W. B., & Stang, P. E. (1995). Social consequences of psychiatric disorders: I. Educational attainment. *American Journal of Psychiatry, 152,* 1026–1032.

Kessler, R. C., Mickelson, K. D., & Williams, D. R. (1999). The prevalence, distribution, and mental health correlates of perceived discrimination in the United States. *Journal of Health & Social Behavior, 40,* 208–230.

Krieger, N., Williams, D. R., & Moss, N. E. (1997). Measuring social class in US public health research: Concepts, methodologies, and guidelines. *Annual Review of Public Health, 18,* 341–378.

Krop, J. S., Coresh, J., Chambless, L. E., Shahar, E., Watson, R. L., Szklo, M., et al. (1999). A community-based study of explanatory factors for the excess risk for early renal function decline in Blacks vs Whites with diabetes: The atherosclerosis risk in communities study. *Archives of Internal Medicine, 159,* 1777–1783.

Lillie-Blanton, M., & Laveist, T. (1996). Race/ethnicity, the social environment, and health. *Social Science & Medicine, 43,* 83–91.

Lillie-Blanton, M., Parsons, P. E., Gayle, H., & Dievler, A. (1996). Racial differences in health: Not just black and white, but shades of gray. *Annual Review of Public Health, 17,* 411–448.

Luke, B., Williams, C., Minogue, J., & Keith, L. (1993). The changing pattern of infant mortality in the US: The role of prenatal factors and their obstetrical implications. *International Journal of Gynaecology & Obstetrics, 40,* 1999–1212.

Macintyre, S. (1997). The Black Report and beyond: What are the issues? *Social Science and Medicine, 44,* 723–745.

Marmot, M., Ryff, C. D., Bumpass, L. L., Shipley, M., & Marks, N. F. (1997). Social inequalities in health: Next questions and converging evidence. *Social Science & Medicine, 44,* 901–910.

McNeilly, M. D., Anderson, N. B., Armstead, C. A., Clark, R., Carbett, M., Robinson, E. L., et al. (1996). The Perceived Racism Scale: A multidimensional assessment of the experience of White racism among African Americans. *Ethnicity & Disease, 6,* 154–166.

Mead, N., & Bower, P. (2000). Patient-centredness: A conceptual framework and review of the empirical literature. *Social Science & Medicine, 51,* 1087–1110.

Mead, N., & Bower, P. (2002). Patient-centred consultations and outcomes in primary care: A review of the literature. *Patient Education and Counseling, 48,* 51–61.

Meyerowitz, B. E., Richardson, J., Hudson, S., & Leedham, B. (1998). Ethnicity and cancer outcomes: Behavioral and psychosocial considerations. *Psychological Bulletin, 123,* 47–70.

Mullen, P. D., Simons-Morton, D. G., Ramirez, G., Frankowski, R. F., Green, L. W., & Mains, D. A. (1997). A meta-analysis of trials evaluating patient education and counseling for three groups of preventive health behaviors. *Patient Education & Counseling, 32,* 157–173.

Nader, P. R., Stone, E. J., Lythe, L. A., Perry, C. L., Osganian, S. K., Kelder, S., et al. (1999). Three-year maintenance of improved diet and physical activity: The CATCH cohort. Child and Adolescent Trial for Cardiovascular Health. *Archives of Pediatrics & Adolescent Medicine, 153,* 695–704.

Paasche-Orlow, M., & Roter, D. (2003). The communication patterns of internal medicine and family practice physicians. *Journal of the American Board of Family Practice, 16,* 485–493.

Ren, X. S., Amick, B. C., & Williams, D. R. (1999). Racial/ethnic disparities in health: The interplay between discrimination and socioeconomic status. *Ethnicity & Disease, 9,* 151–165.

Rivadeneyra, R., Elderkin-Thompson, V., Cohen Silver, R., & Waitzkin, H. (2000). Patient centeredness in medical encounters requiring an interpreter. *American Journal of Medicine, 108,* 470–474.

Roter, D. (2000). The enduring and evolving nature of the patient-physician relationship. *Patient Education and Counseling, 39,* 5–15.

Singh, G. K., & Yu, S. M. (1996). US childhood mortality, 1950 through 1993: Trends and socioeconomic differentials. *American Journal of Public Health, 86,* 505–512.

Skevington, S. M. (1998). Investigating the relationship between pain and discomfort and quality of life, using the WHOQOL. *Pain, 76,* 395–406.

van Ryn, M., & Burke, J. (2000). The effect of patient race and socio-economic status on physicians' perceptions of patients. *Social Science & Medicine, 50,* 813–828.

West, P. (1997). Health inequalities in the early years: Is there equalisation in youth? *Social Science & Medicine, 44,* 833–858.

Williams, D. R., & Collins, C. (1995). U.S. socioeconomic and racial differences in health: Patterns and explanations. *Annual Review of Sociology, 21,* 349–386.

World Health Organization (WHO) International Consortium in Psychiatric Epidemiology. (2000). Cross-national comparisons of the prevalences and correlates of mental disorders. *Bulletin of the World Health Organization, 78,* 413–425.

Writing Group for the Activity Counseling Trial Research Group. (2001). Effects of physical activity counseling in primary care. *Journal of the American Medical Association, 286,* 677–687.

# Cultural Confrontation

## A Skill of Advanced Cultural Empathy

Charles R. Ridley, Lanaya L. Ethington, and P. Paul Heppner

### Primary Objective

- To explain the concept of cultural confrontation and demonstrate how counselors can apply this therapeutic microskill practically in multicultural counseling

### Secondary Objectives

- To demonstrate how an underestimation and/or an uncritical acceptance of clients' cultural values and belief systems can undermine therapeutic change
- To illustrate that psychological problems, distress, and dysfunction can be a manifestation of cultural impasses or extreme and rigid adherence to an individual's cultural values
- To explain how cultural confrontation is a demonstration of advanced cultural empathy
- To provide examples of cultural confrontation used in actual practice

*As a little girl I remember watching the wisps of smoke curl from my father's cigarettes. I would delight in the whole process, the lighting of the match, the two quick shakes of his hand, the sound of his first breath taking in the tobacco. On special occasions, my father would take me on walks in grassy areas, pointing out our role in the world and how we had the responsibility to take care of it. At different times of the year, he would break his cigarette and make an offering to our ancestors on those walks. I remember always wondering when it would be my turn to do the same. It was the 1970's and the warnings of the dangers of smoking were not as prevalent as they are now. My father a Lakota man, born and raised on the reservation, taught me to honor tobacco but his dependence on nicotine played a significant role in his life span only reaching 56 years.*

McCloskey (2007)

AS THE MENTAL HEALTH PROFESSIONS HAVE SOUGHT TO ENSURE THAT PRACTITIONERS ARE CULTURALLY competent and sensitive, they have inadvertently overlooked a critical aspect of multicultural counseling competence. Often they assume that counselors should accept without question clients' cultural values. In their thinking, uncritical acceptance reflects an unbiased approach to counseling, especially as it pertains to clients whose cultural backgrounds are radically different from their own. The assumption of automatic acceptance is both implicit and, in our opinion, invalid, consequently rendering many practitioners of the profession incompetent instead of demonstrating the competence to which they aspire. Although it is imperative to identify, understand, and respect clients' cultural values, it is equally imperative for practitioners to critically examine cultural impasses and values to determine how they manifest themselves in clients' psychological distress. We maintain that in some cases, rigid and extreme adherence to cultural values not only is dysfunctional but also creates a great deal of psychological distress. We suggest that examination of clients' cultural impasses and at times cultural confrontation are essential competencies under the larger domain of multicultural counseling competence.

## THE PROBLEM IN PERSPECTIVE

The call for multicultural counseling competence and sensitivity is replete in the counseling and applied psychological literature. For instance, the American Psychological Association (APA) published guidelines on multicultural education, training, research, practice, and organizational change for psychologists (APA, 2003). The document underscores the importance the profession places on these considerations. In particular, Guideline 2 calls for psychologists to recognize the importance of multicultural sensitivity when interacting with culturally different individuals (APA, 2003). This call to the practice of psychology has implications for training because recognizing that multicultural issues are an important component of counseling and applied psychology implies that training in multicultural issues is necessary (Toporek, Liu, & Pope-Davis, 2003).

We too recognize the importance of multicultural counseling competence and the concomitant training required to achieve this end. Given the history of racism and oppression in mental health delivery systems (Ridley, 2005), the emphasis on cultural competence and sensitivity is not only long overdue but essential. We are concerned, however, that discussions in the literature of cultural competence and sensitivity have a tacit flaw: They almost suggest or imply that mental health professionals uncritically accept differences in clients' cultural values. In fact, counselors and psychologists frequently are urged to respect cultural, racial, and ethnic differences in counseling. We certainly agree that clients always are worthy of the counselors' respect. However, all too often, *respect* is synonymous with an *uncritical acceptance,* regardless of the physical and psychological impact. Consider the language in the APA guidelines on multicultural education, training, research, practice, and organizational change. The document calls for the following:

respect and inclusiveness for the national heritage of all cultural groups, recognition of cultural contexts as defining forces for individuals' and groups' lived experiences, and the role of external forces such as historical, economic, and sociopolitical events. (APA, 2003, p. 382)

Similarly, a principle of Locke's (1998) model of multicultural understanding is the treatment of culturally diverse group members with dignity, respect, and responsibility. Hanna, Bemak, and Chi-Ying Chung's (1999) counselor wisdom paradigm calls for counselors to be extremely tolerant and accepting. One of the tasks of Ramirez's (1999) multicultural model of psychotherapy is to provide a nonjudgmental, positive, and accepting atmosphere devoid of conformity or assimilation pressures. While we recognize these principles, tasks, and guidelines as not only very important but essential to multicultural counseling, we want to make explicit the current absence of the examination of cultural binds or impasses, and especially cultural confrontation, as important components of multicultural counseling.

## CONCEPTUAL TENETS UNDERLYING CULTURAL CONFRONTATION

We propose that cultural confrontation is a microskill of the larger domain of multicultural counseling competence. Our proposal is based on five tenets, and we now discuss these tenets.

1. *The superordinate goal of psychotherapy is to facilitate change toward resolving clients' psychological distress.* The goal is consistent with the needs of clients who typically seek counseling because they are unable to resolve stressful problems in their lives (e.g., Heppner, Cooper, Mulholland, & Wei, 2001; Heppner, Witty, & Dixon, 2004). Most clients do not enter therapy because they want their lives to remain the same; indeed, the overarching aim of psychotherapy is to facilitate changes that are beneficial to the client. On this issue, a general principle of the APA Code of Ethics is *beneficence:* doing what is best for our clients (APA, 2002). As such, it is important for therapists to identify key processes that lead to change in counseling (Warwar & Greenburg, 2000). This is not to suggest that therapeutic change is always easy or devoid of psychological pain. Often just the opposite is true. For example, becoming congruent in Rogerian therapy involves the self-concept and self-experience becoming more similar. This requires clients to face themselves in the proverbial psychological mirror, which is a prelude to self-actualizing and becoming fully functioning persons. The process necessarily evokes psychological pain, which Rogers labels as anxiety. But the superordinate goal to which therapists aspire is therapeutic change, which is attainable only through the facilitation of such a painful process.

Ridley (2005) suggests that psychological presentations always are contextualized in culture; therefore, therapeutic change always has a cultural manifestation. That is, although the *process* of facilitating therapeutic change is the superordinate goal of therapy, the *content* of the change will vary across cultural contexts. This occurs at both the idiographic and nomothetic levels of culture because counselors must be aware of the importance of within-group and between-group differences in cultural values. For example, a member of a minority group consciously and unconsciously may adhere to a broad array of values, some of which may be endorsed by his or her cultural group and others that are more representative of the dominant culture. Moreover, all clients have idiographic values that are a product of their individualized experiences; they have nomothetic values that represent their shared histories and identities as members of groups. Counselors need to be aware of how the cultural values of their clients manifest themselves as part of the change process. Furthermore, counselors need to skillfully incorporate cultural considerations into the basic design of counseling interventions (Ridley, Mendoza, Kanitz, Angermeier, & Zenk, 1994).

2. *Conflicting cultural values, and subsequently behaviors and lifestyle choices, may create psychological distress.* Frequently, the behaviors and lifestyle choices resulting in the psychological distress are both unnecessary and self-defeating. Unfortunately, many individuals are so focused on their psychological distress that they overlook the real source of their problems. Furthermore, some self-defeating behaviors may be more obvious than others, but the psychological pain and concomitant self-defeating consequences experienced as a result of the behaviors may not be easily discerned. For example, self-defeating behavior that is manifested as clients provoking others to engage in physical fights is more easily observed than cognitive processes such as overgeneralization, selective abstraction, or dichotomous thinking. Consider the African American client who has had the unfortunate experiences of being the victim of racial profiling and racial slurs. As we would expect, these experiences are traumatic. However, the client then overgeneralizes these experiences to every encounter with Whites, never testing reality to determine if these new encounters might be different. The overgeneralization leads the client to conclude erroneously that all Whites are racist. Played out in therapy, the client presents as guarded and nondisclosing, making it difficult to achieve any therapeutic gain. Understandably, the psychological pain that accompanies the self-defeating behavior is as real as the behavior itself and therefore necessitates clinical attention. Peck (1978) made this astute observation: "The difficulty we have in accepting responsibility for our behavior lies in the desire to avoid the pain of the consequences of that behavior" (p. 42).

3. *Individuals exhibit dysfunctional behavior in all cultures, and recorded history indicates its existence across time.* The need to understand and treat psychological disorders is universal. Archaeological and anthropological evidence makes this clear. Unfortunately, it is common to take a pseudoetic view of mental health—superimposing one's cultural values on other cultures and interpreting the mental health status of individuals through culturally constricted lenses (e.g., Triandis, Malpass, & Davidson, 1973). Nevertheless, the universality of human dysfunction and the recognition that dysfunction is culturally contextualized suggest that culture is implicated in psychological presentations. Consider people from individualistic cultures that take rugged individualism to an extreme: Some of them are so obsessed with their achievements that they compromise their psychological and physical health.

4. *Mental health professionals facilitate therapeutic change by recognizing and addressing self-defeating behavior, especially those related to cultural conflicts.* Although there are many aspects of the therapeutic change process, therapists certainly may help clients become aware of the motivations and consequences of self-defeating behaviors. As suggested previously, many clients are not cognizant that their choices—let alone the reasons why they choose their behaviors—are inherently self-defeating. Other clients recognize their behaviors as self-defeating but lack the motivation to change. Their resistance to change hinges on secondary gains—the psychological benefits they derive from remaining in a dysfunctional state. Keeping in mind that the superordinate goal of psychotherapy is to facilitate therapeutic change to resolve the clients' stressful problems (Heppner et al., 2001), therapists need to recognize the various factors that contribute to the behaviors and, for the purpose of this chapter, especially cultural conflicts and impasses.

5. *In addition to recognizing cultural conflicts and impasses, mental health professionals must supportively challenge cultural specific self-defeating behaviors.* If counselors do not accept this challenge, they inadvertently may undermine therapeutic process and outcome. When clients' cultural values manifest themselves through cultural conflicts, impasses, and self-defeating behaviors, multiculturally competent counselors must have the skills to identify this information to promote therapeutic

change. The need may not be apparent to clients because of their identification with a particular culture. Nevertheless, it is in this context that therapists may engage sensitively in cultural examination and, if necessary, challenge to help clients become cognizant of the reasons underlying their distress and the resulting self-defeating behaviors.

# CULTURAL CONFRONTATION AND PROFESSIONAL ETHICS

The general principles of the APA Code of Ethics are nonhierarchical, and psychologists must strive to act in accordance with all of the principles (Fisher, 2003). Principle E of the Code of Ethics calls for psychologists to "respect the dignity and worth of all people" and to "respect cultural, individual, and role differences, including those based on age, gender, gender identity, race, ethnicity, culture, national origin, religion, sexual orientation, disability, language, and socioeconomic status" (APA, 2002, p. 1063). Psychologists concomitantly are bound to Principle A, which articulates that psychologists strive to do good by promoting the welfare of others and strive to do no harm (APA, 2002). The American Counseling Association (ACA) Code of Ethics has similar admonitions. The preamble states, "Association members recognize diversity and embrace a cross-cultural approach in support of the worth, dignity, potential, and uniqueness of people within their social and cultural contexts" (ACA, 2006, p. 235).

Serving the best interests of clients and respecting cultural differences does not mean that ethical professionals overlook or minimize cultural conflicts. Mental health professionals have an ethical responsibility to help clients examine cultural conflicts, impasses, and values that create physical and psychological distress. Professionals failing to recognize cultural conflicts and impasses, as well as failing to address culturally influenced behaviors that are inherently self-defeating, are not helpful, nor are they acting in an ethically appropriate manner (Ridley, Liddle, Hill, & Li, 2001).

Along similar lines, competent professionals must be aware of their own biases and cultural values to ensure they are not engaging in unintentional racism and/or oppression (Thompson & Neville, 1999). According to Ridley (2005), racism is any behavior or pattern of behavior that tends to systematically deny access, opportunities, or privileges to members of one racial group while allowing members of another racial group to enjoy those opportunities or privileges. Ridley considered unintentional racism to be the most insidious form of racial victimization because unintentional racists are unaware of the harmful consequences of their behavior. Mental health professionals may avoid cultural confrontation as a show of respect for their clients. This behavior may be well intentioned and seem responsible on the surface. But inaction is an important element in the victimization of minority clients: It inadvertently reinforces clients' dysfunctional patterns along with its attending psychological pain. We should note that some mental health professionals are so frightened of doing the wrong thing that they refuse to do or say anything when issues of race or culture arise. In so doing, they actually perpetuate the problem they seek to avoid by refusing to act.

# RELEVANT CONSTRUCTS

The definition of cultural confrontation hinges on the definition of two relevant constructs—multicultural counseling competence and confrontation. We take the position that cultural confrontation is one among many components of multicultural counseling competence. Furthermore, it is a specific application of confrontation, a widely used microskill of counseling. Understanding both constructs is essential to defining cultural confrontation.

## Multicultural Counseling Competence

A number of conceptualizations of multicultural counseling competence appear in the literature. We elect to use the definition posited by Ridley (2005). He defines the construct as the beneficial incorporation of cultural data in counseling to facilitate therapeutic change. *Culture* is broadly construed to include the full range of human experience that may play a critical role in issues presented to counselors, including knowing how one is perceived by others. By using a broad definition of culture, "multicultural" counseling can be extrapolated to all counseling relationships. Indeed, it is difficult to imagine counseling relationships where culture does not play any role. It is the charge of therapists to recognize cultural data as such and to sensitively incorporate the data into their counseling interventions in ways that are most beneficial for the clients.

In addition, Ridley and Mollen (in press) differentiate competence from competency, suggesting that multicultural counseling competence consists of an array of competencies, each of which is composed of a cluster of microskills. Cultural confrontation is a microskill that is necessary to obtain multicultural counseling competence. Of course, many competencies and microskills contribute to multicultural counseling competence. Many of these have been discussed in the literature, such as knowledge, skills, and attitudes related to counseling multicultural clients.

## Confrontation

Confrontation is one among a number of microskills developed to help counselors intervene intentionally to facilitate the process of counseling. According to Ivey and Ivey (2007), confrontation is the "ability to identify incongruity, discrepancies, or mixed messages in behavior, thought, feelings, or meanings" (p. 261). Confrontation is both a powerful and complex microskill. It is powerful in that it is facilitating clients who are stuck at impasses to move intentionally toward self-enhancing behaviors and lifestyle choices. It is complex in that it involves several steps. Finally, the confrontation is not aggression toward clients but an assertive intervention to facilitate change. Along these lines, Ivey and Ivey (2007) provide this explanation:

> Confrontation is *not* a harsh challenge. Think of it, rather, as a more gentle skill that involves listening to the client carefully and respectfully and then seeking to help the client examine self or situation more fully. Confrontation is not "going against" the client; it is "going with" the client; seeking clarification and the possibility of a new resolution of difficulties. Think of confrontation as a *supportive challenge.* (p. 263)

The essence of confrontation is to assist clients in considering how they disregard the inconsistencies and cultural impasses that result in their dysfunctional patterns. Before clients realistically can problem-solve and face the many and difficult challenges of living, they must become self-aware and resolve their incongruities and discrepancies. The failure to resolve personal incongruities and discrepancies entails a fundamental inability to achieve therapeutic change.

## DEFINITION OF CULTURAL CONFRONTATION

Cultural confrontation, as previously mentioned, is both a component of multicultural counseling competence and a special application of the microskill confrontation. We define *cultural confrontation* as the identification and clarification of a discrepancy between a client's adherence to or exaggeration of a cultural value and the resulting self-defeating consequences. Like any confrontation in counseling, the goals of this intervention are to move the client beyond the impasse, achieve resolution, and adopt self-enhancing behaviors. This microskill consists of two phases: critical examination and supportive challenge.

## Critical Examination

The purpose of this phase is to determine whether a challenge of the client's cultural values is necessary. Counselors should be open to the possibility that any client needs to be challenged, but they should not assume this is necessary with every client. This assumption is no more valid than overlooking any client's pattern of dysfunction. Values associated with cultural conflicts and impasses may contribute to self-defeating behavior and psychological distress in one client but not another client. Therefore, the rationale for challenging clients is an established causal connection between their cultural values and self-defeating behavior. In some cases, a critical examination will reveal no connection. Here, further challenging of the client is not necessary. In other cases, a critical examination will reveal a causal connection between clients' cultural values and their self-defeating behavior. The counselor has no choice but to challenge clients concerning the discrepancies and inconsistencies in their psychological presentations.

## Supportive Challenge

The purpose of the supportive challenge is twofold: (a) to clarify for clients the causal connection between their cultural values and the self-defeating consequences and (b) to seek resolution of clients' discrepancies and impasses. In regards to the clarification, counselors should realize that most clients are unaware of the connection and that the pattern provides a psychological benefit even though it is self-defeating. In regards to the resolution, counselors should realize that helping clients to move beyond their discrepancies and surmount their impasses is a major undertaking. This requires considerable skill, patience, and willingness to work with intense emotions. After all, the discrepancies and impasses are well entrenched in the clients' experiences, and they do not easily go away. Ultimately, the goal of a challenge is to assist the client in facing reality, solving problems effectively, and making sound lifestyle choices.

## CULTURAL CONFRONTATION AS ADVANCED CULTURAL EMPATHY

Empathy has been considered for many years to be an integral component to counseling and psychotherapy, although no complete agreement on the definition of empathy exists in the literature. Most definitions of empathy describe how an individual attempts to perceive, conceptualize, or understand how another person experiences the world (Ridley & Lingle, 1996; Warwar & Greenburg, 2000). Cultural empathy is a special case of empathy, and it has been defined as the learned ability of counselors to accurately understand the self-experience of clients from other cultures (Ridley & Lingle, 1996; Ridley & Udipi, 2002). Drawing on the work of Rogers (1959, 1961), the self-experience is a composite picture of a person's psychological world or frame of reference, consisting of emotions, attitudes, values, and perceptions. As he explains, it is "all that is going on within the envelope of the human organism at any given moment" (Rogers, 1959, p. 197) and "the experiencing of experience" (Rogers,

1961, p. 76). Counselors' understanding of the self-experience is informed by their interpretation of clients' cultural data. Cultural empathy consists of two major processes: cultural empathic understanding and cultural empathic responsiveness. Cultural empathic understanding is the process through which counselors perceive the self-experience—the composite picture of the client's psychological world. The key is that counselors' perceptions of clients should be as accurate as possible. Cultural empathic responsiveness is the process through which counselors communicate to clients their understanding of the clients' self-experience. The key is that the communication not only demonstrates an accurate understanding of clients but also demonstrates an attitude of concern and respect.

Egan (1998) distinguishes basic empathy from advanced empathy, and this distinction is especially useful in conceptualizing cultural confrontation as advanced cultural empathy. Basic empathy "involves *listening* to clients, *understanding* them and their concerns to the degree that this is possible, and *communicating* this understanding to them so that they might *understand themselves* more fully and *act* on their understanding (Egan, 1998, p. 81). Cultural empathy is the ability of counselors to understand their clients' internal frame of reference, particularly as it pertains to culture. Thus, basic cultural empathy may be considered a counselor's ability to understand the cultural components that are part of their clients' self-experience *and* that are currently part of their clients' self-awareness. Counselors who respond to the cultural components that clients incorporate into their self-awareness are practicing basic cultural empathy.

Ridley and Udipi (2002, pp. 320–321) provide a helpful vignette of a counselor's use of basic-level cultural empathy.

*Client:*    When I get down on myself, I question whether my parents thought about the impact of a mixed marriage on their children. As a biracial individual, I struggle with knowing where I belong. Sometimes I feel like I belong to both races, and sometimes I do not feel like I am either Black or White. Relatives on both sides of the family are nice to me, but I wonder if they are pretending.

*Counselor:*    You want to be certain about your place in the world, and it matters that those who are close to you accept you as you are. Yet it is not always clear to you that by being biracial you have a place or, if you do, that is acceptable. You want to find an answer so you can be up on yourself.

In the above example, the counselor is effective in both understanding and communicating that understanding of the client's self-experience. The counselor uses different words than the client but reflects the essence of what the client is saying. For instance, the client never uses the words *place in the world* or *acceptable,* but having a place and acceptance are core themes embedded in the client's words. This demonstration of basic cultural empathy indicates that the counselor accurately perceives and, therefore, understands and consequently communicates personal themes of which the client is aware. But the counselor does not communicate any new insights of which the client may be unaware.

Egan (2002) describes advanced empathy as a communication skill that highlights deeper messages to clients. He suggests that advanced empathy is demonstrated when counselors assist clients in taking implicit aspects of their self-experience (what is implied by what they say) and making them explicit. Here counselors identify themes in which their clients are unaware, making connections they may be overlooking (Egan, 2002). Essentially, advanced empathy is the ability of counselors to help clients get in touch with aspects of their self-experience that currently are not part of their self-awareness. Counselors use advanced cultural empathy to help their clients realize cultural components that are part of their self-experience but were previously not part of their self-awareness.

Consider again the previous vignette. Now notice how the counselor builds on that material and moves beyond basic empathy to advanced empathy.

*Counselor:* You want to be certain about your place in the world, and it matters that those who are close to you accept you as you are. Yet it is not clear to you that by being biracial you have a place or, if you do, that is acceptable. You want to find an answer so you can be up on yourself. But based on what you just said and some earlier comments you made, I wonder if you really believe that it is possible for you ever to be up on yourself. That is because you are afraid that you might never find your place. Furthermore, the anger you have toward your parents for not considering the impact of their decision leaves you with a feeling of hopelessness.

In the above example, the counselor provides some fresh insights into the client's self-experience. The client is unaware of some deep feelings and attitudes. However, it takes the attentive listening of the counselor to "hear" what the client is saying between the lines. The counselor brings to the client's awareness his uncertainty of ever being happy, his fear of never finding his place in the word, and his anger toward his parents. Of course, the counselor must be careful to neither misunderstand the client nor put words in the client's mouth. A misinterpretation not only would contradict the purpose of advanced empathy but could also misdirect the course of therapy.

Cultural confrontation is a skill integral to practicing advanced cultural empathy. Cultural confrontation allows counselors to assist clients in accessing conflicts of which they may not be aware but are nevertheless real and negatively affecting their functioning. Counselors must first use basic cultural empathy to conceptualize the cultural components of their clients' presentation from the clients' point of view. Then they must use advanced cultural empathy to explore implicit cultural messages that may contribute to psychological distress. Cultural confrontation is used to facilitate therapeutic change because it seeks to make accessible parts of a client's self-experience that were previously inaccessible. This may result in necessary psychological pain that clients experience as they become more congruent. Using the skill of cultural confrontation is dependent on the counselor's ability to recognize how culture contributes to their clients' presenting concerns.

## GUIDELINES TO CULTURAL CONFRONTATION

The practical question pertaining to cultural confrontation is this: How do mental health practitioners examine cultural values and challenge clients concerning their self-defeating behaviors related to cultural conflicts? Embedded in the above question is another question: How do mental health professionals employ cultural confrontation in a way that results in positive therapeutic outcomes? We recognize that such an intervention is demanding, and for some professionals, it is daunting. Nevertheless, we reiterate that by avoiding this intervention, the therapist is abdicating an often powerful tool to promote change, thereby decreasing the likelihood of favorable counseling outcomes. To answer the aforementioned questions, we provide seven guidelines to assist professionals in the process of cultural confrontation. We present these guidelines as representing important elements or ingredients in the process of cultural confrontation and recognize that the order of our presentation oversimplifies the complex and nonlinear process of counseling.

1. *Accept cultural confrontation as an essential microskill of multicultural competence.* Many counselors have fears and apprehensions about confronting any client. The intervention forces them out of their comfort zone. Moreover, in light of the tremendous emphasis in the literature and training programs on respecting clients' cultural values, it is understandable how some counselors would find it particularly difficult to consider this microskill as an intervention they personally would employ. Counselor-trainees, in particular, often experience anxiety (Gross, 2005), and they may especially be prone to forego confronting culturally diverse clients. Nevertheless, counselors should remind themselves of the importance of this intervention and commit themselves to engage in cultural confrontation despite their fears and anxieties. The last thing counselors should do is avoid cultural confrontation.

2. *Establish a strong working alliance with clients in general, but it is especially important to have a strong working alliance before engaging in a cultural confrontation.* A working alliance is facilitative of therapeutic change. It has been cited as an integral part of counseling in general (Bachelor & Horvath, 1999) and multicultural counseling in particular (Roysircar, Hubbell, & Gard, 2003). A critical element of the working alliance in multicultural counseling is cultural empathy. In addition, counselors need to move from basic to advanced cultural empathy before engaging in cultural confrontation. Advanced cultural empathy allows counselors to recognize how cultural components contribute to their clients' psychological distress, even though the clients themselves may not have this awareness.

3. *Time the cultural confrontation.* Like any intervention, timing is everything. Counselors should not confront their clients prematurely, nor should they postpone confrontation when it is an appropriate time to confront. Both actions are counterproductive. On one hand, Ridley (1984) explained the importance of not prematurely confronting African American clients, some of whom overgeneralize their experiences of racism:

> The new role of the therapist is to facilitate the client's ability to discriminate sociopsychological cues. Generalizing to all Whites or all situations is no longer a desirable response. A sensitized therapist would confront and encourage discussion of the cultural paranoia during the early phases of treatment. Without such confrontation, the potential benefits of therapy and future interracial experiences could be restricted. (p. 1240)

On the other hand, Knox, Burkard, Johnson, Suzuki, and Ponterotto (2003) demonstrated the consequences of avoiding racial issues in counseling. They reported that White psychologists normally did not address race with racially different clients, and they did so because of their feelings of discomfort. These psychologists' within-therapy behavior, however, contradicted their perception, for they believed that discussions of race in therapy had positive effects.

4. *Anticipate client resistance to cultural confrontation.* Resistance is clients' attempts to interfere with the process of constructive change (Ridley, 2005). Underlying resistance are psychological processes in the clients intended to protect themselves from emotional pain. Resistance can be reflected in a wide range of behaviors, some of which are obvious, others of which are less so. For instance, some resistance is active, such as a client arguing with a counselor about the counselor's interpretation of the self-defeating behavior. Other resistance is passive, such as a client faking cooperation with the therapist by making *counseling-correct* statements to cover up unresolved issues. The best measure counselors can take to try to prevent resistance is establishing a strong therapeutic alliance. In the context of the alliance, clients are more likely to feel safe and less vulnerable in facing their discrepancies and inconsistencies. However, even the best attempts to prevent resistance are not always successful. Here counselors should sensitively name the resistance and then help clients to realize how it serves to maintain their self-defeating behavior and interfere with their progress in counseling.

5. *Affirm clients' cultures.* Obviously, counselors should never denigrate a client's culture. This requirement holds true even when counselors ascertain a connection between clients' cultural values and their self-defeating behavior. We know that culture plays a major role in shaping identity, values, and behaviors. Therefore, to dismiss or downplay the important role of culture is to undermine clients at the core of their psychological experience. Based on this premise, helping clients to examine the cultural context of their distress, including cultural confrontation, does not imply that their cultural values are bad or unimportant. Instead, the intervention of cultural confrontation takes into account that cultural values affect clients' cognition, affect/mood, and behaviors at many different levels. At the same time, the premise implies that it is harmful for counselors to promote cultural confrontation disrespectfully or prematurely. Clients are more likely to terminate therapy prematurely, or it may significantly damage the therapeutic relationship.

6. *Assist clients in understanding the causal connection of the pattern of behavior to their psychological consequences.* Unless clients understand the nature of the connection, they are unlikely to accept it as a valid hypothesis. Actually, the causal connection entails two levels: the connection of the cultural values of the client to the self-defeating pattern and the connection of the self-defeating pattern to the psychological consequences. It is essential for clients to understand both levels of connection.

Within the context of cultural empathy and a strong working alliance, another critical component is for counselors to be able to help clients examine the cultural context of their distress. Many clients are so focused on the symptoms they are experiencing that they fail to see them in the context of their lifestyles or cultures. If counselors can help clients make the link between their cultural values, behaviors, and psychological pain, therapeutic change is more likely to occur. For example, a male client from an individualist culture may engage not only in independent but even isolationist behaviors due to an idiographic combination of cultural values of supporting oneself, achieving individual merit, and having a strong sense of shame associated with asking for help. On the other hand, an overemphasis on saving face and interpersonal harmony for a female incest survivor from a collectivistic culture may result in very high levels of psychological distress and a number of self-defeating behaviors later in her life. Moreover, behavioral dysfunction may result from an overemphasis of a particular cultural value. Here a client's self-defeating behavior is extreme even for members of the client's culture, as in the case of clients who are so individualistic in cultural orientation that they develop a narcissistic personality disorder or so collectivistic in cultural orientation that they develop a dependent personality disorder. Neither is healthy.

Based on the work of Ridley, Li, and Hill (1998), the following suggestions may be useful in establishing the connections between cultural values and self-defeating behavior and between self-defeating behaviors and psychological consequences.

- Determine if clients' cultural values reflect in self-enhancing behaviors. If these cannot be determined, there is a strong possibility that the cultural values reflect in self-defeating behaviors.

- Determine whether clients' behaviors represent extremes even for members of their culture.

- Consider whether behaviors that appear outwardly as assets could be insidiously self-defeating and behaviors that appear outwardly as deficits could be assets.

- Explore clients' interpretations of their psychological presentations.

- Recognize your biases to avoid misinterpretation of clients' psychological presentation.

7. *Help clients change their behavior and make new lifestyle choices.* It is one thing for clients to understand and come to terms with the sources of their dysfunctional patterns. It is another thing for

them to actually change their behavior. In addition to anticipating resistance to change, counselors ought to realize that only part of the equation of change is stopping self-defeating behavior. The other part is teaching clients new behaviors that are self-enhancing. To help clients change their behavior, counselors may draw upon any number of theoretical orientations and employ a variety of strategies. Critical to the change process is the naming of a specific behavioral pattern to be acquired. The ultimate test of the effectiveness of counselors' critical examination and supportive challenge is whether clients retain appreciation for their cultures while choosing lifestyle practices that are self-enhancing.

## CASE EXAMPLE

We use a case example to demonstrate cultural confrontation in action. Rocio Rosales, a doctoral candidate in counseling psychology at the University of Missouri–Columbia, provides this material based on her counseling experiences. She discusses not only the issues related to cultural confrontation with a Latina client but also the issues that this raises for her as a Latina therapist.

> In my development as a counselor, I have struggled to remain true to myself both as a counselor and as a Mexican American. Through this process, I have integrated my cultural beliefs into my work and found a balance that remains authentic to my clients and me. Although I recognize the value of confronting client's cultural values that lead to dysfunctional behavior and distress, I must acknowledge the distress that this confrontation has caused for me as a racial/ethnic minority counselor.
>
> In my training, I have struggled most with incorporating a new role within my Mexican cultural values when counseling some clients. The most difficult piece of this work has been in challenging some clients; I had to push myself to be more vocal, direct, and at times confrontational—communication styles that are not practical to my culture. Challenging clients is in stark contrast to my cultural values of *personalismo* (personalism) and *respeto* (respect). I had to learn how to reconcile the communication style of my culture with the communication style needed for conducting effective therapy.
>
> In addition to the discomfort and internal struggle I felt in incorporating a new role within my cultural values for the benefit of my therapeutic work with some clients, this struggle has magnified when working with a client who is of the same ethnic background as me. Something about challenging clients on values that I hold so dear in my heart cannot help but make me feel as though I may be betraying my cultural heritage. These values are at the core of my culture and ones that I take pride in; thus, questioning these values, I feel as though I am being disloyal. Nonetheless, through my counseling work, I recognize that pride and inflexibility in these values may hinder positive change for my clients if I am not flexible in balancing my cultural values with counseling values.
>
> Through providing an example of my work with a Latina client, I hope to illustrate the benefit of finding a balance between and within cultural values. Alicia was a 20-year-old Latina college student that presented with depressive symptoms. Through further exploration, Alicia confided that she felt a tremendous amount of guilt in going to college, far from family. This was especially difficult because of the Latino cultural value of *familismo* (familism), which explained her distress in pursuing a college education away from her family.
>
> Her family history compounded her feelings of guilt as her family continually called her to come home because of difficult times. Alicia felt guilty in not being able to go home because she would fall behind in her schoolwork, but was also not able to concentrate on her studies if she would stay because of the importance of family. Alicia wanted to be with her family, but the stressful home environment also increased her distress. It became clear that in our work, we would have to address her cultural value of *familismo* and examine its fit with her to decrease her distress. In doing so, being authentic and transparent while discussing this cultural value was important to our examination of *familismo*. Through these discussions, Alicia came to realize that while family is important, the best way to help

her family was to take care of herself. Toward the end of our work and through processing conflicting cultural values and emotions, Alicia felt that she could balance her family's needs along with her own needs. Through this processing, Alicia felt that she could let go of her guilt because she also recognized the importance of her own needs.

This case was extremely difficult because I could identify with Alicia's love for her family and placing her family's needs before her own. After each session, I had to process with my peers because I could not help but feel that I was being an impostor in questioning her on values that I also believed. How much more betrayal can that imply? Needless to say, this was a difficult process for me as well as for my client. However, through seeing Alicia's progress and through my own reflection, I have felt less betrayal and more prepared and equipped to help future clients on similar issues.

Through this process, I feel as though I have successfully bridged two worlds and remained true to myself as a counselor and as Mexican American. I believe that the nature of counseling, in providing a safe space and through *confianza* (trust), allowed my client and me to explore and challenge certain aspects of her cultural values in a particular situation or context. It is my hope that in sharing what we explored in *confianza,* confronting cultural values to fit her needs, other counselors may learn that while this process is difficult, it also can be a healing experience for clients.

Based on this case material, here is a vignette of how cultural confrontation might be employed.

*Counselor:* Alicia, you have talked at length about the importance of your family. I can identify with your feelings since *familismo* is so much a part of our culture. We really are fortunate to have this heritage. Nevertheless, your tone suggests to me something else that concerns me: You feel as though you are at fault for not being with your family to help with the problems. After hearing your story, I want to raise an idea for you to think about. Family is a good thing, and you are experiencing guilt both about not being there for your family and not helping to solve the problems at home. In addition, your depression and distress are not good for your physical and emotional health. Is it possible that you are considering only the importance of family in the short term as opposed to looking at the long-term consequences if you do well in school? Is it also not possible to support your family without being at home and solving the problems? Believe me, I have struggled with the same issues. Perhaps, the best way you can help your family is by standing up to the pressure, not allowing your relatives or yourself to put you on a guilt trip, and completing your education now so that you can actually take better care of your family in the future. In addition, you can help your family by supporting them, through listening, without feeling the pressure to solve the family problems. In doing these things, you really can be an asset to your family.

This case poignantly depicts the struggle counselors may have in helping their clients to examine not only the role and function of traditional values in their lives but also the parallel struggle of clients' psychological presentations, which jar counselors to reflect on and clarify their own cultural beliefs. The myriad of thoughts and feelings that arise from cultural confrontation may be daunting for any counselor, which thereby emphasizes the need for counselors to consult with colleagues and supervisors who are multiculturally competent. In the vignette, the counselor displays basic cultural empathy by reflecting on the value the client attaches to family and advanced cultural empathy by insightfully noting the client's deep sense of responsibility for the family problems and future welfare. Finally, the counselor challenges the client's approach to family, pointing out the inherent conflicts between the short- and long-term consequences and between supporting and solving problems.

# CONCLUSION

In the quest to make multiculturalism integral to professional counseling, the profession inadvertently has overlooked important presuppositions that underlie its interventions. By overlooking these pre-suppositions, practitioners of the profession sometimes are unhelpful or even harmful rather than therapeutic in their counseling—a practice that contradicts their intentions to be helpful. One of these presuppositions is that the cultural values of clients should be accepted uncritically. We maintain that counselors' respect of clients' cultural values should not be equated with their uncritical acceptance. Indeed, the failure to critically examine clients' cultural values and subsequently confront their cultural values that result in self-defeating behavior and lifestyle choices reflects incompetence in mul-ticultural counseling, resulting most likely in unfavorable treatment outcomes. Therefore, we explained the microskill of cultural confrontation and provided guidance to assist professionals in implement-ing this intervention.

## CRITICAL INCIDENT

### A South Korean Student

The following incident, written by Dr. Dong-gwi Lee (Yonsei University, Korea), nicely illustrates the complexities inherent in an array of cultural values. In addition, it demonstrates the need for cultural competence in examining and confronting a client's cultural values.

According to Yonhap News ("Suicide," 2006) in South Korea, on March 21, 2006, a 20-year-old Korean college student committed suicide by throwing himself on the track of an approaching subway train in Seoul. A witness reported that the student was anxiously staring at the track and suddenly jumped off on it the moment he saw the train approaching closely. Based on the police report, the student was ranked at the top of the list when matriculating into the Engineering School of one of the most prestigious universities in Korea but recently took a leave because of a drastic drop in his grades, presumably due to his heavy involvement in extracurricular activi-ties. The report added that the student seemed to suffer from frequent altercations with his parents on account of his poor grades, resulting in isolating himself from any social contact for a month. The night before his suicide, it was reported that the student received a harsh reprimand from his parents due to his recent decision to take a leave without having consulted with them.

This sad story offers points of discussion for counselors in the United States working with Asian and Asian American adolescents in terms of (a) how some East Asian values seem to have influ-enced the student's decision of killing himself and (b) the unique challenges counselors may encounter when serving Asian clients with similar presenting issues. The student's psychological turmoil may be likely conceptualized by his struggles with some traditional Asian values, such as saving face for one's family as well as filial piety (Kim, Atkinson, & Yang, 1999; Kwan, 2000). This student was likely feeling shameful and/or guilty about his "poor grades"; grades tend to be highly valued in Korean culture and a reflection of family success. The student's "poor grades" disappointed his parents, and thus resulted in a "harsh reprimand." Not surprisingly, such emotional turmoil may have been a big blow to his self-esteem as his reputation in his family drastically changed from being a "TOP" student to probably being a "trouble maker." It also seems noteworthy that the student was facing an important task of developing his identity and his life values and preferences, as implied by his strong engagement in extracurricular activities. Unfortunately, it seemed to be too much of a burden to handle both demands (i.e., saving family face and meeting personal needs). The student needed help to resolve this situation. Unfortunately again, traditional Asian values of saving face for one's family often preclude Asians from pursuing professional counseling. More specifically, in Korea, seeking professional help, especially for a male, can indicate a sign of weakness. Moreover, divulging family discord to people other than members of the family is typically discouraged because of the potential to lose face for the family. In essence, the student seems to have been in a very stressful cultural and personal impasse. The student seems to have chosen to withdraw from social contact to avoid confrontation; however, this aggravated his situation by limiting his resources in dealing with the stress. It appears that his suicide resulted from the interplay among his fear of losing family face, lack of family support, and fragile self-esteem coupled with escalated loneliness and helplessness. In short, sometimes a combination of overemphasizing traditional Asian values of filial piety and saving face as well as expectations for Korean males can combine to create difficult emotional dilemmas.

My observations as a supervisor for American counselor trainees who have not been frequently exposed to cultures other than their own suggest that the majority of them could be categorized into two categories: (a) *overacceptance of cultural differences,* which refers to an individual's simple acceptance of cultures different from their own with no reflections or questions attached (e.g., I have to just accept others' cultures of which I am totally ignorant), or (b) *underestimation of cultural differences,* which is a belief about the universality across cultures (e.g., human beings have more similarities than differences). Note similar distinctions were made by other scholars (e.g., color consciousness vs. color blindness, Ridley, 2005; "*alpha bias,* the tendency to exaggerate differences" [vs.] "*beta bias,* emphasizes similarity at the expense of attention to group differences," Gelso & Fassinger, 1992, p. 290); however, these terms were not directly applied to populations other than Americans. In short, counselors who lack multicultural competence can make two mistakes: (a) overacceptance of the client's culture and (b) underestimation of cultural differences. In both cases, the client's culture is not fully incorporated into the conceptualization of the client's presenting problems, nor is it a focus of the intervention strategies. In working with the student in the story, a novice counselor could make the mistake of not fully discussing the Asian cultural influence and its toll on the student's psychological health given the counselor's simple acceptance of Asian cultures at the surface level. If a counselor trainee overlooks cultural differences, the counselor overlooks the power of cultural issues.

## Discussion

In the example above, the student might have benefited from an examination of the cultural context of his situation, perhaps increasing his awareness and the consequences of his interpretations and expectations of his personal and cultural values. In essence, the counselor could facilitate a respectful process of exploring his values and assumptions about his values (which could even involve various levels of confrontation) to help the client move toward a values clarification and purposeful decision making. But if a counselor trainee is overaccepting of cultural differences, she or he is likely to not only accept the cultural values but also even ignore the stressful impact of the cultural values. Because the counselor accepts the client's cultural values, the counselor has difficulty accurately conceptualizing the client's presenting problem and is often devoid of the client's cultural context. Moreover, the counselor typically does not conceptualize addressing the cultural values as part of counseling and even attempts to work around the cultural impasse. In essence, because the counselor lacks such multicultural counseling competencies, the counselor avoids intervening with cultural dilemmas and discussing the client's cultural values, which can result in ineffective or even harmful counseling experiences for the client.

1.  Imagine you were the counselor of the 20-year-old man discussed above, and after much discussion with him, you found the need to engage in cultural confrontation. Write a brief description of how you might have engaged this man in a cultural confrontation.

2.  Further imagine that the client reacted defensively to your cultural confrontation and clearly appeared to be angry with you. How would you (a) respond to his reaction, which likely may have been resistance on his part, and (b) manage the working alliance with this client?

# REFERENCES

American Counseling Association (ACA). (2006). ACA Code of Ethics. *Journal of Counseling and Development, 84,* 235–253.

American Psychological Association (APA). (2002). Ethical principles of psychologists and code of conduct. *American Psychologist, 57,* 1060–1073.

American Psychological Association (APA). (2003). Guidelines on multicultural education, training, research, practice, and organizational change for psychologists. *American Psychologist, 58*(5), 377–402.

Bachelor, A., & Horvath, A. (1999). The therapeutic relationship. In M. A. Hubble, B. L. Duncan., & S. D. Miller (Eds.), *The heart and soul of change: What works in therapy* (pp. 133–178). Washington, DC: American Psychological Association.

Egan, G. (1998). *The skilled helper: A problem-management approach to helping* (6th ed.). Pacific Grove, CA: Brooks/Cole.

Egan, G. (2002). *The skilled helper: A problem-management and opportunity-development approach to helping* (7th ed.). Pacific Grove, CA: Brooks/Cole.

Fisher, C. B. (2003). *Decoding the ethics code: A practical guide for psychologists.* Thousand Oaks, CA: Sage.

Gelso, C. J., & Fassinger, R. E. (1992). Personality, development, and counseling psychology: Depth, ambivalence, and actualization [APA Centennial Feature]. *Journal of Counseling Psychology, 39,* 275–298.

Gross, S. M. (2005). Student perspectives on clinical and counseling psychology practica. *Professional Psychology: Research and Practice, 36,* 299–306.

Hanna, F. J., Bemak, F., & Chi-Ying Chung, R. (1999). Toward a new paradigm for multicultural counseling. *Journal of Counseling and Development, 77,* 125–134.

Heppner, P. P., Cooper, C. C., Mulholland, A. M., & Wei, M. F. (2001). A brief, multidimensional, problem-solving based psychotherapy outcome measure. *Journal of Counseling Psychology, 48,* 330–343.

Heppner, P. P., Witty, T. E., & Dixon, W. A. (2004). Problem-solving appraisal and human adjustment: A review of 20 years of research utilizing the Problem Solving Inventory. *The Counseling Psychologist, 32,* 344–428.

Ivey, A. E., & Ivey, B. I. (2007). *Intentional interviewing and counseling: Facilitating client development in a multicultural society* (6th ed.). Pacific Grove, CA: Brooks/Cole.

Kim, B. S. K., Atkinson, B. R., & Yang, P. H. (1999). The Asian Values Scale: Development, factor analysis, validation, and reliability. *Journal of Counseling Psychology, 46,* 342–352.

Knox, S., Burkard, A. W., Johnson, A. J., Suzuki, L. A., & Ponterotto, J. G. (2003). African American and European American therapists' experiences of addressing race in cross-racial psychotherapy dyads. *Journal of Counseling Psychology, 4,* 466–481.

Kwan, K.-L. K. (2000). Counseling Chinese people: Perspectives of filial piety. *Asian Journal of Counseling, 7,* 23–41.

Locke, D. C. (1998). *Increasing multicultural understanding* (2nd ed.). Thousand Oaks, CA: Sage.

McCloskey, C. (2007). *The relationship between cultural identification, emotion regulation, mental health and tobacco use of Native Americans.* Dissertation proposal, University of Missouri–Columbia.

Peck, M. S. (1978). *The road less traveled: A new psychology of love, traditional values and spiritual growth.* New York: Touchstone/Simon & Schuster.

Ramirez, M., III. (1999). *Multicultural psychotherapy: An approach to individual and cultural differences* (2nd ed.). Boston: Allyn & Bacon.

Ridley, C. R. (1984). Clinical treatment of the nondisclosing Black client: A therapeutic paradox. *American Psychologist, 39,* 1234–1244.

Ridley, C. R. (2005). *Overcoming unintentional racism in counseling and therapy: A practitioner's guide to intentional intervention* (2nd ed.). Thousand Oaks, CA: Sage.

Ridley, C. R., Li, L. C., & Hill, C. L. (1998). Multicultural assessment: Reexamination, reconceptualization, and practical application. *The Counseling Psychologist, 26,* 827–910.

Ridley, C. R., Liddle, M. C., Hill, C. L., & Li, L. C. (2001). Ethical decision making in multicultural counseling. In J. G. Ponterotto, J. M. Casas, L. A. Suzuki, & C. M. Alexander (Eds.), *Handbook of multicultural counseling* (2nd ed., pp. 165–188). Thousand Oaks, CA: Sage.

Ridley, C. R., & Lingle, D. W. (1996). Cultural empathy in multicultural counseling: A multidimensional process model. In P. B. Pedersen, J. G. Draguns, W. J. Lonner, & J. E. Trimble (Eds.), *Counseling across cultures* (4th ed., pp. 27–46). Thousand Oaks, CA: Sage.

Ridley, C. R., Mendoza, D. W., Kanitz, B. E., Angermeier, L., & Zenk, R. (1994). Cultural sensitivity in multicultural counseling: A perpetual schema model. *Journal of Counseling Psychology, 41,* 125–136.

Ridley, C. R., & Mollen, D. (in press). *Redefining multicultural counseling competence: Bridging theory into meaningful practice.* Thousand Oaks, CA: Sage.

Ridley, C. R., & Udipi, S. (2002). Putting cultural empathy into practice. In P. B. Pedersen, J. G. Draguns, W. J. Lonner, & J. E. Trimble (Eds.), *Counseling across cultures* (5th ed., pp. 317–333). Thousand Oaks, CA: Sage.

Rogers, C. R. (1959). A theory of therapy, personality and interpersonal relationships as developed in the client-centered framework. In S. Koch (Ed.), *Psychology: A study of science: Formulations of the person and the social context* (pp. 184–256). New York: McGraw-Hill.

Rogers, C. R. (1961). *On becoming a person.* Boston: Houghton Mifflin.

Roysircar, G., Hubbell, R., & Gard, G. (2003). Multicultural research on counselor and client variables. In D. B. Pope-Davis, H. L. K. Coleman, W. M. Liu, & R. L. Toporek (Eds.), *Handbook of multicultural counseling competencies in counseling & psychology* (pp. 247–266). Thousand Oaks, CA: Sage.

Suicide of a Korean college student. (2006, March). *JoongAng Daily.* Retrieved March 22, 2006, from http://news .joins.com/society/200603/22/20060322201831077230003300310.html [in Korean]

Thompson, C. E., & Neville, H. A. (1999). Racism, mental health, and mental health practice. *The Counseling Psychologist, 27,* 155–223.

Toporek, R. L., Liu, W. M., & Pope-Davis, D. B. (2003). Assessing multicultural competence of the training environment. In D. B. Pope-Davis, H. L. K. Coleman, W. M. Liu, & R. L. Toporek (Eds.), *Handbook of multicultural competencies in counseling and psychology* (pp. 183–190). Thousand Oaks, CA: Sage.

Triandis, H. C., Malpass, R. S., & Davidson, A. R. (1973). Psychology and culture. *Annual Review of Psychology, 24,* 355–378.

Warwar, S., & Greenburg, L. S. (2000). Advances in theories of change and counseling. In S. D. Brown & R. W. Lent (Eds.), *Handbook of counseling psychology* (3rd ed., pp. 310–345). New York: John Wiley.

CHAPTER

23

# Drug and Alcohol Abuse in Cross-Cultural Counseling

Gerald V. Mohatt, James Allen, and Lisa Rey Thomas

---

## Primary Objective

- To identify and describe essential definitional issues in cross-cultural counseling with substance-abusing clients

## Secondary Objectives

- To identify and describe key components of a cultural model for assessment and case conceptualization
- To identify and describe essential factors for culturally appropriate treatment and after-care planning

---

*Authors' Note*: Preparation of this chapter was supported by grants from the National Center for Research Resources (P20 RR016430, Gerald V. Mohatt, Principle Investigator [PI]), the National Institute of Alcohol Abuse and Alcoholism Grants 1 R21 AA015541 (Gerald V. Mohatt, PI, and James Allen, Co-Investigator) and 1 R21 AA016098–01 (James Allen, PI; Gerald Mohatt and John Gonzalez, Co-Investigators), and the National Center for Minority Health and Health Disparities Grants 1R24 MD001626 (Gerald V. Mohatt, PI; James Allen and John Gonzalez, Co-Investigators) and 1R24 MD001764–01 (Dennis Donovan, PI, and Lisa R. Thomas, Co-Investigator). Additional funding for research that informed this chapter came from the support of the National Institute of Alcohol and Alcohol Abuse and the National Center for Minority Health and Health Disparities Grant 1R01 AA11446–012A2 (Gerald Mohatt, PI; James Allen and Kelly Hazel, Co-Investigators).

Fists clenched, body tense, and once again in the locked ward at the Veterans Administration (VA) hospital, Stanley whispers, "I can't stand it, the voices, the sounds, the smells." Then he lapsed into silence. Speech came in short bursts: "I don't want to be here. What good is another shrink?" I asked him to tell me about what he felt. No words came. He moved back and became more motionless as I spoke. Little eye contact whenever I began to talk made me feel unsure about what he was feeling. Was he listening? Has he already given up on our work, I wondered? More silence and one-word answers to questions pushed me to talk longer and to ask more questions. He finally spoke, "Give me some medicine, Doc. That'll stop them."

"I can see about that," I reply.

"That one medicine I don't like much. It makes me sick, real sick," he whispered.

The story above is of Stanley Eagle Jones, a 58-year-old divorced, Northern Plains American Indian male. Stanley has received medical, mental health, and substance abuse treatment services from the VA since his discharge from the military, following three tours in Vietnam. He is currently treated for a number of chronic medical conditions, including hypertension, chronic obstructive pulmonary disease, diabetes, and cardiac disease. Stanley has also received treatment for depression and posttraumatic stress disorder (PTSD), as well as for alcohol and other drug abuse problems. Medications prescribed to him have been a cocktail of mood stabilizers to calm down his hypervigilance and hyperarousal, as well as alpha antagonists focused on his reexperiencing trauma and autonomic hyperarousal, both significant PTSD symptoms. In the past, Stanley has also been on a selective serotonin reuptake inhibitor (SSRI) for the anxiety that is part of his depression. Stanley reacted negatively to a medication change to an antipsychotic medication, Seroquel, by indicating that it made him "sick." When asked what *sick* meant, he said it made him nauseous and "too slowed down." Stanley has received inpatient psychiatric treatment at least two times per year in the past five years for suicidal and homicidal thoughts and for medication management. Currently, the psychiatrist is trying to adjust his medication to stabilize his mood, while also controlling his disorganized thoughts and agitation and reducing the medication side effects. While in inpatient treatment, he has required a code response for severe agitation numerous times and was in restrained isolation once. Although he has requested a Native therapist over the years, this has never been available to him. He generally takes medications for brief periods. When his symptoms are reduced and he "feels better," he discontinues their use.

Stanley reported to the emergency room agitated and in severe distress, and he requested that he be admitted to the inpatient psychiatric ward. He reported that he was experiencing severe flashbacks, suicidal and homicidal thoughts, and urges to drink. He stated that he had been taking his medications as prescribed and that he had not consumed any alcohol for the past week. He felt like curling up and sleeping for hours. "Maybe, if I just go to sleep, I will get better and I can tough it out," he says in his usual monotone. Stanley received the medication that he requested but now says that he does not like how it makes him feel. He says that he feels sick the next day after the new meds. It reminds him of something that he has avoided and did not like. He says that he does not know much about the long-term drug or alcohol effects, but he does realize that alcohol is powerful. "It has a big spirit that is very hungry," he tells me, when I ask him what he thinks about his hopeful plans to stay sober.

"Hungry?" I ask.

"Really," he replies with a short giggle and a quick, penetrating look directly at me. I realize I must learn more about this man if I will ever understand how to help him.

The notes help a bit: Stanley grew up in a rural town adjacent to his tribal reservation. He does not speak but understands his tribal language. His English is accented with the dialect of the reservation. He reported a history of neglect and abuse by his alcoholic parents. Stanley has had problems with his alcohol use since his return from Vietnam. Over the years, he has used marijuana and, more recently, methamphetamine and oxycontin. He decided he did not like the effects of meth and oxy on his friends, so he stopped using them five years ago on his own, but he continues to use marijuana, though alcohol is his preferred drug of use. In the past two years, Stanley noted that his drinking was increasingly feeling out of control. He is divorced and is estranged from one of his two sons but close to the other. In addition, he is caring for his ill father and his grandmother, to whom he states he is now close. Stanley's sister was recently killed in a motor vehicle accident, and Stanley is now caring for her son, his 14-year-old nephew, as well. Stanley states that his nephew is currently experimenting with alcohol and other drugs and that he has also reported suicidal thoughts and exhibited suicidal behaviors. Stanley notes that his drinking over the past year has prevented him from "being on top of things" with his nephew and ill father. He indicates that he drinks some muscatel with friends or, if they have enough money, will buy cases of beer. They will do this about every month at the beginning of the month, when the monthly checks arrive. They drink what they have available with their friends until it is gone. Currently, Stanley states that his commitment to caring for his father, nephew, and grandmother is the only reason he has not completed a suicide at this time.

The above case defines a set of challenges for the counselor who will treat Stanley and his substance abuse problem. These issues are in some ways universal, in that they surface in most cross-cultural alcohol and drug counseling cases. They include co-occurring mental illness with substance abuse, complex medical problems, how to go about a culturally appropriate assessment of a substance abuse problem, the challenges to establishing and maintaining a cross-cultural therapeutic relationship with a substance-abusing person, and how to develop individualized, culturally grounded, and culture-specific strategies for effective interventions.

Drug and alcohol abuse, as well as its associated negative consequences, is critical to consider in cross-cultural counseling. Like Stanley, a client may present with substance abuse as the primary concern. Or instead, substance abuse may be only one of many issues that a client presents with (e.g., marital and other family problems, daily living problems, health problems) or may not be perceived by the client as important at all, relative to other presenting problems. Approaches to treating substance abuse are well documented and include a variety of different "evidence-based" approaches (for reviews, see Donovan & Marlatt, 2005; Longabaugh et al., 2005; Marlatt & Donovan, 2005). However, empirical support for the usefulness, appropriateness, and effectiveness of current evidence-based practices for diverse populations remains minimal. One recent review identified 43 different interventions possessing at least some evidence of being effective for treating substance abuse. Out of these 43 interventions, five have been tested with African Americans, two with Hispanics/Latinos/Latinas, and none have been tested with Asian/Pacific Islanders, American Indians/Alaska Natives, or gay/lesbian/bisexual/transgendered populations (Alcohol & Drug Abuse Institute, 2006). Given this current status, it is critical that strategies developed in cross-cultural counseling for mental health concerns inform our approaches in working with ethnically and culturally diverse clients with substance abuse problems.

As there are a number of counseling and therapeutic strategies for substance abuse from which counselors can draw, but few possessing any empirical support with diverse populations, we will present a methodology to adapt methods that appear to us as promising in their potential to fit within a cultural model for treatment. We begin our discussion with definitional issues in culture and how culture shapes our work with a client. This will be followed by a discussion of a cultural model for assessment and case conceptualization, and with a presentation of cultural factors in treatment and aftercare planning. This chapter then concludes with a general discussion of some of the cultural considerations important in substance abuse counseling with people from African, Hispanic, Asian, and American Indian ethnic, racial, and cultural backgrounds.

## Cultural Frames for Alcohol and Drug Abuse Counseling: A Point of Departure

For the purposes of this chapter, our working definition of culture comes from Geertz (1973):

> The concept of culture I espouse . . . is essentially a *semiotic* one. Believing, with Max Weber, that man is an animal suspended in *webs of significance* he himself has spun, I take culture to be those webs. . . . It is public because meaning . . . *systems of meaning* are necessarily the collective property of a group. (pp. 4–5)

This definition stresses that culture is a *shared meaning system,* one that regulates the web of behavior. For us, four aspects of culture are critical to the counseling process: *linguistic, sociolinguistic, values,* and *symbolic.* Each of these aspects has a specific role in the counseling relationship, as well as in understanding important cultural factors in drug and alcohol abuse and the recovery from abuse.

## Linguistics, Sociolinguistics, Values, and Symbolic Meaning

Linguistic differences are critical to understand the person sitting across from us in a counseling relationship. He or she may speak a different language and therefore may be unable to confidently explain his or her experience to another who speaks a different language or dialect. The counselor will have great difficulty in understanding the client unless he or she understands this person through his or her first language. To understand the person's experience, which is essential for developing a therapeutic alliance, we may need to work with an interpreter who will become, inevitably, a co-counselor. This is particularly the case in refugee counseling.

As complex as language differences are, so too are many of the differences in English-language dialectic. How will Stanley talk to us? What sense will we make of the words and their meaning in his dialect? We must know the words he chooses to express emotions in his dialect. What did Stanley mean by "sick, really sick?" Though he stated he wanted medication, within his dialectic, the meaning of *medication* may also refer to the experience of being hung over. Does wanting his "medication" also mean that he has in fact recently used alcohol? His language tells us that "medication" may have a deep physical and emotional significance for him, something that he "needs" but is also ambivalent about. What is clear is that we must gain access to an understanding of the client's meanings, as embedded in his language and dialect.

Sociolinguistics describes the social language of nonverbal behavior (e.g., eye gaze, nodding) as well as the verbal sequencing of speech (e.g., pace, pause time). Attributions are often based within this level of culture. For many African Americans, a person may expect a rapidity of nuanced speaking that allows one to form a sense of interactional rhythm, while for many Native Americans, a person may expect slower paced speech and longer pauses to establish this same interactional rhythm. This rhythm between client and counselor is critical for a sense of comfort and for the development of trust that the client will be understood (Erickson, 1975). Nonverbal expressions can also serve as a source of data that allows the counselor to make assessments about the client and how counseling is progressing. Stanley's intake counselor wondered why Stanley seemed so agitated but had such a monotonic verbal presentation and avoided eye contact. Stanley's counselor concluded that this sociolinguistic aspect of the interaction was a sign of depression. However, an alternative explanation regarding this eye contact is that the alternation of averted gaze with a direct gaze instead signified the working out of a culturally based interactional rhythm that will become the heart of a comfortable, trusting relationship.

Values are significant aspects of culture. Many American Indian groups are collectivist in nature (Herring, 1999; Triandis, 1988; Trimble, 1987). Stanley presents a number of values-focused issues for the counselor to address and to integrate into therapy using a strengths-based perspective. For example, Stanley is a caretaker for his family. How might we see this? Is this codependence, or is this an expression of his culturally defined role responsibilities as a member of his family? Without a cultural assessment and understanding of values, one cannot accurately assess Stanley's life situation in order to begin to work effectively with him in counseling. If this caretaker role is a culturally sanctioned role responsibility, we will want to nurture and support it and to avoid labeling and pathologizing it. Other values issues abound in Stanley's case. Stanley also stated he wanted to "sleep," but he should "tough it out." This may show a sense of ambivalence toward tribal values that are gender bound. Is he, as a man, expected to "go it on his own?" Stanley also places a high value on immediate relief with "medications" without side effects, but "medicine" is also something that he may experience through traditional ceremonies; therefore, this type of "medicine" may also be something Stanley expects from other healing situations.

Finally, culture relates to the symbolic order, the deep cultural meanings and *explanatory models* (Kleinman, 1988) for illness and health held by the client. Stanley presents three very interesting examples of the symbolic. The first example relates to voices and what voices mean to Stanley. Stanley wants to silence the voices and what they are saying to him. A careful history of Stanley's background and cultural orientation—what the voices are saying, when they began, and how they began—can help properly identify if these voices are potential culturally based symbols related to spirituality, alcohol-produced delirium experiences, or, at the most extreme spectrum, the manifestation of a psychotic process. Richard Two Dogs, an Oglala medicine man (personal communication, 2003), indicated during the case discussion of a young American Indian man that voices are always real, must be considered as such, and always come from either the spiritual world or the person's own unconscious. In his view, we must learn from where the voices come and also make sense of what they are saying with the person.

Second, Stanley tells us that alcohol is a spirit, a hungry one. He marks this by shifting his eye gaze from averted to direct while speaking this. Learning the cultural meaning system behind this explanation of the power of alcohol will allow the counselor to think symbolically about how Stanley can identify and confront this spirit of alcohol respectfully, so that he can control it, remove it from his life, or continue to live with it but no longer feed it.

Third, Stanley simultaneously wants and does not want medicine. He has a trust in medicine that may come both from his experience within the Western medical system and the experience of the medicine he has received in traditional ceremonies. His ambivalence appears to have to do with the particular side effects of one of the medications he has been prescribed, which remind him of a hangover. His openness to Western medications, while at the same time going to a local medicine man, indicates that Stanley mixes indigenous and Euro-American belief systems. We must understand Stanley's experience with medicine and its meaning to ensure that he receives medications he will continue to use.

We have now provided a case example, our understanding of culture, and a sense of how this cultural framework is structured and informs our understanding of this case. For the counselor to use this framework in counseling, he or she must next have a methodology that situates the client within his or her culture. Clearly, Stanley is a complex person possessing many aspects of his indigenous culture along with a number of influences from Euro-American culture. Planning the counseling intervention will require an equally sophisticated assessment approach that links culture both to an understanding of Stanley's problems and to treatment.

# MULTICULTURAL SUBSTANCE ABUSE ASSESSMENT

Substance abuse assessment is most effective when practiced using models that systematically bring cultural knowledge into the assessment process. This can be achieved when assessment is conducted using a culturally congruent, collaborative, and strengths-based approach that includes the input of a collateral information source. Drug and alcohol abuse assessment should explore history and consequences of use, acculturation status, levels of identity, motivation for change, and personal assets, all of which include important cultural elements (Trimble, 1987). Multicultural substance abuse assessment identifies cultural factors that will be important to a positive counseling outcome.

Each of the four aspects of culture essential to cultural competency in multicultural substance abuse counseling—linguistics, sociolinguistics, values, and symbolic meaning—is also critical in the assessment interviewing process. Knowledge of how interpersonal interactions are sociolinguistically patterned within the cultural group of the person being assessed, the meaning of nonverbal cues within the culture, and nuances of local dialect and linguistic conventions are all examples of culturally competent interviewing skills in assessment that are crucial to the establishment of trust, which is the first step in obtaining a detailed history and understanding of the person.

## A Collaborative Approach to Multicultural Substance Abuse Assessment

A collaborative approach to assessment can be particularly helpful in multicultural substance abuse assessment. In the case of cross-cultural assessment, the assessor is often from a different cultural background. The power differential between minority clients and majority or high-status counselors replicates the historical and institutional context of racism and oppression experienced by the client and his or her ethnic group. This alone may produce distrust between counselor and client. One goal of a collaborative assessment approach is empowerment of the individual through the assessment process. In providing an opportunity for the client to achieve a sense of control and self-direction in the assessment process, it can provide an antidote to the sense of disempowerment that such contexts have created in the past and instead enhance self-efficacy. In collaborative assessment, the person is invited to frame his or her own assessment questions regarding use and misuse of drugs and alcohol and to provide input and reflection on the interpretation of the meaning of assessment results, as well as the use of these results. The person develops alongside with the assessor a description of the assessment findings. The person may even assist in modifying an initial assessment finding to improve its accuracy. Clear procedures are laid out for respectfully dealing with instances where a client and the counselor disagree on the meaning of a behavior or the consequences of substance use.

## Cultural Assessment of Use and Consequences

Multicultural substance abuse assessment is a comprehensive exploration of the person's history and consequences of use, motivation for change, acculturation status, and personal assets. The importance of a thorough psychosocial history in substance abuse assessment cannot be overemphasized.

It is crucial to develop the ability to explore with the person his or her social history; important life events, especially traumatic experiences; and any history of mental health problems, within an atmosphere of trust. Genograms may be useful in assisting the client in identifying important family relationships as well as patterns of substance abuse within a kinship network (Witko, 2006). In addition, more specialized elements of history taking are needed related to the person's lifelong use of substances. This should include an assessment of initiation into and patterns of early use, as well as past and present quantity and frequency of use. It is important to be aware of cultural factors in quantity and frequency of use. For example, within some cultures, such as some American Indian and Alaska Native groups, drinking style is often characterized by binge use (May & Gossage, 2001).

Alcohol and drug use assessment instruments can be of help in assessing the severity of a substance abuse problem. Two measures that have been used or adapted for use with multicultural groups are the Drinker's Inventory of Consequences (DrInC; Miller, Tonigan, & Longabaugh, 1995) and the Alcohol Use Disorders Identification Test (AUDIT; Conigrave, Hall, & Saunders, 1995). The AUDIT was developed by the World Health Organization, has been used globally, and examines quantity, frequency, alcohol-related problems, and signs of alcohol dependence. The DrInC is a widely used measure of adverse drinking consequences developed for Project MATCH, a multisite alcohol treatment matching study that included Hispanic and African American samples. The DrInC, as a measure of consequences, avoids confounding drinking style with more severe, long-term alcohol dependence and is available in a short form and in long and short forms to assess drug use consequences.

## Acculturation Status Assessment

An important place to begin in multicultural substance abuse assessment, as in all multicultural assessment, is with an assessment of acculturation status and racial, ethnic, or cultural self-identification (Dana, 2005; Trimble, 1996, 2003). In this assessment, our focus is at the individual level of analysis. Berry (2002) provides one useful way of understanding cultural contact status in terms of *integration* or *biculturalism, assimilation, separation,* or *marginalization.* From the perspective of a person from the nondominant group, *assimilation* occurs when an individual no longer wishes to maintain his or her cultural identity, *separation* occurs when the individual maintains his or her cultural identity, *integration* or *biculturalism* occurs when an individual maintains his or her original culture and seeks to participate in the more dominant cultural network, and *marginalization* occurs when there is little interest in cultural maintenance or participation in the dominant culture. Assessment of acculturation status can help in our understanding of Stanley's strengths, identifying assets that can be mobilized in counseling, and can inform an appropriate balance between culturally specific approaches and more conventional treatment choices.

Two cautions in thinking about acculturation are important. First, though there has been a significant effort in the research to understand cultural identification as a protective factor from substance abuse, no direct relationship has emerged. The relationship appears to be much more complex (Oetting, Donnermeyer, Trimble, & Beauvais, 1998; Trimble & Mahoney, 2002; Whitbeck, Hoyt, McMorris, Chen, & Stubben, 2001). Second, we firmly believe working with a person in counseling, emphasizing an understanding of cultural identity, can be enormously beneficial in the long-term recovery from substance abuse problems. However, our experience has been that very early in the recovery process, counseling work directly exploring identity issues may be premature and may even interfere with the process of learning and using critical skills necessary to cope with the immediate feelings of craving and the triggers for relapse into substance abuse.

# Collateral Assessment

Because denial and minimization can be part of the problem in substance abuse, collateral assessment is important. A collateral can be a significant other, a relative, or a concerned friend; for Stanley, it is a fellow member of the Akicita Society. The Akicita, or Warrior Society, is an American Indian veterans group common to many Plains Indians reservations that honors and supports veterans. This additional source of information provides a cross-check on the veracity of the assessment information provided by the person; in the case of Stanley, the collateral also provided a rich source of cultural knowledge regarding the identity, cultural factors in substance use, and, in particular, some of the culturally based strengths that can motivate the person to change. The collateral offered this new information about Stanley:

> Stanley rarely leaves the reservation area except to shop or drink in the border towns. It is clear he is uncomfortable when around non-Native people and he therefore avoids and rarely interacts with them; this is why he has always requested a Native counselor. Though he does not speak his tribal language, he understands it and use words in isolation. He knows many of the old stories and helps Elders when he is not drinking. Though Stanley is not an outgoing person, he makes it a point to go to pow-wows and other community gatherings, and as a member of his local Akicita Society, dances at pow-wows. When asked how he views himself, he describes himself through his home reservation.

On the basis of these observations, the acculturative status concept of *separation* helps us in our cultural understanding of Stanley's strengths and of his predicament.

# Strengths-Based Assessment

Following an examination of acculturation and self-identification status, a culturally informed, strengths-based substance abuse assessment focuses on the identification of assets that a treatment approach might access. Across cultures, assessment across three general areas can guide the counselor in identifying these assets: *behavioral control* and *prosocial commitment, mood stability,* and *psychocultural factors.* Behavioral undercontrol (Sher & Trull, 1994), which includes impulsivity, sensation seeking, and, at the extreme, antisocial characteristics, enhances substance abuse risk. Though Stanley experiences periods of severe distress that include the extremes of homicidal and suicidal feelings, he thus far has been able to not act out impulsively on these feelings. Instead, in these situations, he attempts to withdraw and shut himself down ("curling up and sleeping for hours"). In addition, outside of a few misdemeanor alcohol-related conduct infractions, Stanley does not have a history of legal difficulties, and he displays a significant degree of commitment to family members. This suggests one of Stanley's strengths is his ability for behavioral control.

A second behavioral pattern to assess in multicultural substance abuse assessment is mood stability. Degree of uncomfortable anxiety and depression, often termed *negative affectivity,* increases risk of using substances for relief from discomfort (Conger, 1956; Sher, 1987). Stanley endures a significant degree of psychological pain related to traumatic memory, flashbacks, and depression, and this highlights the important consideration of co-occurring disorder in substance abuse assessment. Like many other individuals with alcohol and drug disorders, Stanley has a co-occurring mental health disorder. The counselor's assessment in this area identified, in the text-revised fourth edition of the *Diagnostic and Statistical Manual of Mental Disorders* (*DSM-IV-TR;* American Psychiatric Association, 2000), posttraumatic stress disorder, dysthymia, and recurrent major depressive episodes.

However, the counselor went beyond this diagnosis and also completed a *DSM* cultural formulation. This cultural formulation linked his alcohol problems with combat trauma (for an example of a cultural formulation for a Southern Plains veteran with alcohol problems and PTSD, see Manson, 1996) and with the symbolic referent of the hungry spirit of alcohol. This cultural formulation tied Stanley's problems to a cultural explanatory model specific to his tribe.

An assessment of psychocultural factors is probably the most important area for multicultural substance abuse treatment planning. These include such things as community and cultural norms for consumption, peer influences, and the types of prosocial cultural role expectations and practices that are incompatible with drug and alcohol abuse. Stanley's collateral informant shared the following additional information on psychocultural factors:

> Most of Stanley's friends use alcohol excessively and have alcohol problems; however, several of the members of the veterans society have quit drinking entirely, and they have encouraged Stanley to do the same. Stanley wants to seek doctoring in a ceremony, but realizes drinking makes him put it off. He views his drinking and his drug use as in conflict with the Elders' teachings, so when he is not sober, he does not go to ceremonies or help Elders, and he realizes his drinking is in conflict with his strong desire to some day in the future be of service to his reservation community as an Elder himself. There have also been several occasions when his nephew or father has needed Stanley, but he has been too drunk to be of use to them. After Stanley sobered up, he felt quite shameful about this.

A clear strength coming out of Stanley's cultural background is his commitment to his tribal cultural values of extended family and kin. Stanley's strong desire to contribute in traditional ceremonies, along with his sense of duty as guardian and protector of his extended family, motivates Stanley to gain control over his life; Stanley takes very seriously his culturally sanctioned role responsibilities as a guardian and protector to his nephew, ill father, and grandmother, as well as a man who someday in the not too distant future may be called upon to become an Elder himself. These are examples of the types of psychocultural factors that can either maintain or facilitate recovery from substance abuse.

## Motivation to Change

An additional area to consider in substance abuse assessment is the person's current level of motivation for change. Stanley completed the DrInC assessment of consequences along with his counselor as part of one of their first interviews. As they began this interview, Stanley said that he had been aware of a problem with his drinking for sometime, but he was unsure about his ability to change anything about it. Together, the two reviewed the long list of life consequences from alcohol in Stanley's life. This proved a key moment in the assessment and the entire counseling process. As Stanley looked at his answers and his score on the DrInC, he visibly winced when told he experienced a level of consequences from drinking at a similar intensity to people admitted to inpatient treatment. Stanley seemed surprised when the counselor, rather than making him feel this was something shameful, instead invited Stanley together with the counselor to try to make sense of this in terms of what it meant in Stanley's life. Stanley spoke. His emotions rose, he looked the counselor in the eye, and he simply said, "Something has got to change. I am feeding this spirit!"

Assessment was carefully paced and slowly built trust along the way; it was made clear to Stanley that only Stanley was the expert about Stanley. Instead of leaving Stanley feeling shamed about the disarray of his current life, the assessment process proved therapeutic.

# FROM ASSESSMENT TO COUNSELING

In terms of allowing Stanley to move along in his readiness to change away from his addictive disorders, individuals can be understood to move from Stage 1—*Precontemplation,* or not yet considering change, to *Contemplation,* an awareness of the problem and ambivalence, to *Determination* to change, then *Action* to change, and finally *Maintenance* of sustained change, with occasional *Relapse,* involving a return to Stage 1 (DiClemente & Prochaska, 1998). The counselor, during the previous session, assessed Stanley as moving into Stage 3—Determination.

Stanley's counselor proposed a complementary therapeutic approach for recovery. This included work with his counselor to enhance his motivation to stop his use of alcohol and substances, using a culturally adapted motivational enhancement therapy approach (Miller, Zweben, DiClemente, & Rychtarik, 1992). As part of their review of the assessment, the counselor also discussed a referral to a respected local medicine man, who would work with Stanley to prepare him to take part in a purification ritual for stopping drinking. In addition, the counselor referred Stanley to an Alcoholics Anonymous (AA) group in his reservation community, following Stanley's own request for this, given his interest in additional support and his desire for a sponsor who was a local fellow veteran in the Akicita Society. Finally, Stanley agreed to continue to see his counselor and to continue to work with his psychiatrist on his medications. Each of these elements is part of a multimodal system of care that mixes indigenous and Western treatments, patterned by the cultural and the recently completed assessment. Next, we briefly describe key elements in this mix.

## Motivational Enhancement Therapy

The counselor chose the motivational enhancement therapy (MET) approach because of its cross-cultural use; its congruence with the assessment approach taken, including the use of the DrInC; its flexibility for cultural adaptation; and its fit with the work of Marlatt and Donovan (2005) on mindfulness training as part of relapse prevention later in the counseling process. Our experience with indigenous groups points to a number of factors critical in selecting a counseling approach with culturally diverse individuals. No one set of factors applies to all groups, but there are certain qualities that we have found important in our clinical and research experience with American Indians and Alaska Natives. First, clients often desire a practical, problem-solving approach (LaFromboise, Trimble, & Mohatt, 1990). Second, they expect to make rapid progress and experience relief analogous to their experience with healing ceremonies (Mohatt, 1988). Third, depending on their acculturational status, they prefer to combine and integrate Western and indigenous approaches (LaFromboise et al., 1990). Fourth, the approach needs to enhance efficacy, particularly in the form of communal mastery (Hobfoll, Jackson, Hobfoll, Pierce, & Young, 2002). Fifth, although clients want their clinician to be open to working with healers and other healing modalities, they expect that the counselor will commit to work on this material with them in counseling, rather than to simply refer them to other people for this work (Mohatt, 1988). This last factor is consistent with face-to-face, kinship-based cultural values that emphasize a personal and consistent relationship. The following are recommendations for a brief counseling approach that comes out of these considerations, recognizing that no two clients are alike, new information may arise in the process, and changes in the person's life circumstances will always require a flexibility in any approach.

## Session 1: Feedback

For Stanley, the foundation of empathy was achieved during the assessment process. If the system places him with a new counselor, the counselor will need to achieve this same relationship. Our recommendation is to have the same person complete the assessment and continue as the counselor to preserve continuity and established trust. One focus during the assessment feedback session was ensuring that the sociolinguistics, environment of the sessions, and feedback information provided are consistent with Stanley's views and explanatory models about his substance abuse problem, as well as reflected his sense of himself. This serves to enhance his sense of efficacy. At each point in this session, Stanley guided the process, received the feedback from the clinician, and decided on the next step. At the end of the feedback session, the final summary worked out by the clinician and Stanley led him to choose a set of treatment modalities that included counseling, AA, continued work with the psychiatrist on a medication regime, and use of a traditional healer.

Therefore, the first session of MET will recapitulate this assessment summary and provide additional feedback to enhance his sense of determination, to solidify the stage of change in which he is at present, and to encourage him to move to into the next phase of change, action. The counselor should let Stanley direct much of this process, allowing him to further educate the counselor about who Stanley is and what he learned during the assessment process. In closing this session, the counselor should finalize the specific set of modalities that Stanley chose (e.g., AA, psychiatrist, etc.). The counselor might ask during this ending for Stanley to choose some symbolic item that represents to him the work of the assessment and his commitment to change, such as an oral recording, a stone, a piece of sage, a photograph, or a written contract. This will then allow the counselor to move seamlessly into the second session devoted to values clarification.

It is critical at this and at every stage of Stanley's process for the counselor to consider how to integrate his or her work into the traditional ceremonies Stanley is attending by using an integrative strategy. For example, Stanley is attending a purification lodge on the reservation to request help and healing. The counselor can encourage Stanley to present the feedback plan within the ceremony at the lodge and to request assistance in developing a plan based on this assessment. He can also be encouraged to bring the symbolic item from counseling to the purification lodge, in order to present it with his verbal prayer.

## Session 2: Values Clarification

In the second session, the counselor and Stanley will begin to create a plan based on his values, with the goal of enhancing his motivation to move toward action and to foster and maintain those motivational strategies inherent in his cultural life. For Stanley, many of these assets are focused on his family and his cultural role as a caretaker. The session should provide him with opportunities to reflect on how he feels when he is able to care for his family, as well as how his decisions influence his relationships and roles within his family and affect his family and tribal community. Stanley can be invited to consider how he will begin to experience, when he is sober, his family moving toward a life that is safe and protected, as well as himself becoming helpful to the next generation. Mindfulness exercises, allowing him to feel within his body and his thoughts this sensation of helpfulness and how service to the next generation can replace this addiction, can be taught in the session. He may choose to make these experiences concrete by writing statements on a card, such as, "When I sit with my nephew and share stories of our past, he wants me to continue. I can't do this unless I am well and sober. Accomplishing this makes me feel like I am doing what an uncle is supposed to do in our culture."

Another motivational source that represents a culture-based asset is Stanley's involvement with the traditional Akicita Society. His veteran status is a point of pride. His ability to embrace this value in action can also be placed on a written card: "When I am involved with the society, I help my fellow veterans and receive help from them that makes me realize how important it is to deal with my PTSD. I can heal and help others."

Finally, Stanley has embraced attending traditional ceremonies. This would be a good time to review with him what he is learning and what he is being advised to do (e.g., have other ceremonies for healing, review his thoughts regarding his goals toward healing). For example, he might be thinking of promising to complete a Sun Dance to help his family. Exploring the meanings he is making out of his immersion in ceremonial life can help Stanley choose ways to become further involved with these cultural practices that can help sustain his sobriety.

At the end of this session, the counselor should review how Stanley feels about each value that he has articulated. Is it consistent with his desires? Will it support him toward the changes that he wants—to live a "clean" life committed to his family and community? Again, at the end of this session, he should be encouraged to summarize his ideas regarding his most important values for maintaining sobriety and to present them in the next purification lodge he attends, during which he can again ask for help in achieving them.

## Sessions 3 and 4: Recapitulation and a Plan for Change

The first two sessions provide a base for spending the next two sessions to recapitulate the work that Stanley and his counselor have done and to craft this work into a long-term plan for sobriety with specific goals. We suggest a minimum of four sessions for Stanley, as most Northern Plains American Indian ceremonies are in multiples of four (e.g., Sun Dance, Vision Quest, and healing ceremony for a serious illness). It is important when working with other ethnically and culturally diverse clients to orient formal therapy plans similarly within elements of the clients' cultural framework.

At this stage, the counselor should discuss with Stanley the possibility of having a special traditional ceremony at the end of their sessions in which the counselor attends the ceremony to copresent the change plan and ask for assistance for all of those involved in the plan (e.g., the family, the AA group, professionals, healers, and Stanley). The counselor's attendance would recapitulate the integrative nature of the process that is at the foundation of this cross-cultural work. Finally, we recommend for American Indian and Alaska Native clients that a follow-up session is scheduled for a later date. This session is more than simply a "booster" session. Within the cultural context, the follow-up session has meaning in that it communicates to Stanley the sense that this is a relationship that he can count on and that the counselor is willing to continue to assist. For other cultures, it is important to analyze whether the person may prefer a level of autonomy that is less interdependent.

## Treatment Framework Synopsis

Because this vignette focuses on counseling, we have not described in detail each of the other treatment modalities and cultural considerations for them (e.g., AA, psychiatric consultation, etc.). Each of these must be addressed during the counseling process, consistently reviewing with Stanley important elements outside counseling, such as how he is doing in AA, how he is doing with the psychiatrist, or in his role in the Akicita Society. In Stanley's substance use counseling, the counselor actively works with a mixture of traditional and Western approaches that constitute a system of care for Stanley. Therefore, we recommend the counselor consider facilitating a meeting between Stanley, the medicine man, the psychiatrist, the AA sponsor, family members such as his father and grandmother, and the counselor to discuss ways to collaborate and integrate (Herring, 1999; Trimble & Thurman, 2002). Such communication would allow the key members of the treatment team to receive direction from Stanley and his family, identify areas that might present problems with integration, and discuss openly the cultural framework of the therapeutic process.

# CULTURAL FACTORS IN SUBSTANCE ABUSE COUNSELING

We have emphasized assessing and understanding the within-group variability in substance use patterns and assets useful to recovery among ethnocultural groups. Thus far, we have used a case study with an American Indian man to elaborate key concepts. In the remaining discussion, we describe selected strengths common to many members of other selected ethnocultural groups that provide examples of the types of assets that can be mobilized in recovery. Though our discussion here focuses on groups in the United States, elements of the discussion are relevant to immigrant groups globally and provide a model for beginning to think of assets within a specific cultural context. In addition, we acknowledge the risk in providing these examples of stereotyping members from cultural groups, particularly when presenting groupings that often constitute an *ethnic gloss* (Trimble, 1995). Tremendous variability exists within ethnocultural groups, and none of these examples applies to all members of a group. However, each counselor's approach to substance abuse treatment with a client with whom she or he does not share the same culture can incorporate many of the conceptual structures that we have presented. First, we recommend the use of the cultural formulation in the *DSM-IV-TR* to guide case conceptualization, diagnosis, and treatment planning. Second, careful attention to the initial matching of counselor ethnicity was important in our example because of Stanley's expressed requests. This may or may not be critical to working with other ethnocultural clients but deserves careful consideration. Third, attending to linguistics, sociolinguistics, values, and symbolic meaning of the client is important for all ethnocultural clients. Fourth, a strengths-based assessment of acculturation, significant family relationships, and motivation to change would be appropriate for use with clients from most ethnocultural groups. Fifth, blending traditional healing practices of each particular client with more conventional treatment approaches may be beneficial for all ethnocultural clients. We briefly describe each of four cultural groups below: African American, Hispanic, Asian American, and American Indian/Alaska Native.

## African American

Substance abuse remains a serious problem for many African Americans. However, recent surveys suggest that drug use prevalence rates are decreasing for younger African Americans (Johnson, O'Malley, & Bachman, 1996). At the symbolic level, spirituality has played an important historical role for African Americans as they endured slavery and racism in the United States. This role for spirituality, along with the important role for church, continues to this day. Afrocentric identity, or nigrescence (White & Parnham, 1990), also emphasizes a collectivism focusing on a concern for the welfare of the whole group and for relationships with the community. Values associated with spirituality, church, and a collectivist concern all provide important assets that can be potentially mobilized in an African American person's recovery from substance abuse.

## Hispanic

The general term of *Hispanic* refers to many disparate groups that vary enormously in their substance use patterns. For example, heroin is a main drug of use for several generations among certain families in East Los Angeles who identify with the *pachuco* or *cholo* lifestyle (Moore, 1990), as well as the most frequent illicit drug of abuse for people of Mexican descent in a study of substance abuse treatment admissions (Rouse, 1995). Similar to Native Americans, the client may be steeped in the culture of healing that uses various types of traditional healing systems such as the *curandero*. A careful assessment of the cultural specific explanatory model for substance abuse must take into account such systems. Potential assets in substance abuse counseling include the values of *respeto,* deference to elders and others of higher social ranking; *personalismo,* attention to wishes of others; and *confianza,* the development of strong interpersonal relationships based on trust.

## Asian American

Although this is perhaps the most diverse ethnocultural group in the United States, data on patterns of use for this group are limited. Existing data often combine disparate Asian subgroups possessing quite different languages, religions, and histories (Yu & Whitehead, 1997). In contrast to the model minority stereotype, more recent data suggest that recent Japanese immigrants, along with Chinese American individuals who are at higher levels of assimilation to the host culture, exhibit high levels of alcohol use, while the less assimilated members of many subgroups of Asian Americans are heavy cigarette smokers (Myers, Kagawa-Singer, Kumanyika, Lex, & Markides, 1995). Although it is difficult to generalize about a pan-Asian values set, many Asian Americans are influenced by values emphasizing the importance of (a) family as the central social unit and the avoidance of behavior that brings shame to the family, (b) a social hierarchy of respect to elders and those of higher social rank, and (c) personal and emotional restraint. Recognition of these values as assets, as well as adaptation of conventional substance abuse counseling approaches to accommodate them as strengths, can facilitate the recovery process from substance abuse for many Asian Americans. Explanatory models that reflect the symbolic understanding of disease and the use of traditional healers are important, particularly for many of the new Asian immigrants such as the Hmong (Fadiman, 1997).

## American Indians and Alaska Natives

In the case study discussion, we illustrated an integrated, complementary approach to assessment and counseling structured by indigenous culture-specific treatments that use traditional healers, ceremonial life, collaborative assessment, and a cultural adaptation of the MET. Additional culture-specific treatments include cultural or spirit camp immersion experiences that accentuate traditional values and spirituality. Other modern forms of treatment have been culturally adapted. A good example is the talking circle, which is a form of group counseling that was derived by analyzing how healing ceremonies are structured. Mindfulness training and meditation have been adapted for use with adolescents to resonate with the cultural-spiritual systems of indigenous groups. Each of these treatments focuses on a treatment that provides the linguistic and sociolinguistic context that is comfortable and is structured by indigenous values and resonates with the explanatory models that symbolically make sense within the culture.

## SUMMARY: CULTURAL FACTORS IN MULTICULTURAL SUBSTANCE ABUSE COUNSELING

Table 23.1 provides an overview of the principles of multicultural substance abuse counseling that guided our work in the case presented and organized our discussion in this chapter. The principles emphasize the importance of considering the high rates of the comorbidity of substance abuse with other disorders in substance abuse counseling. They also emphasize the social context, including a consideration of the acculturation status of the individual, an appreciation of cultural norms not only in terms of risk

| TABLE 23.1 | Guiding Principles for Cross-Cultural Drug and Alcohol Abuse Counseling |
|---|---|
| Comorbidity | Comorbidity with psychological disorders is the norm in substance abuse disorders |
| Social Context | Acculturation status: Link substance abuse assessment to the personal and community cultural context: |
| | Linguistic and sociolinguistic factors |
| | Values |
| | Symbolic system |
| Cultural Norms | Understand the cultural norms: |
| | Patterns of substance use |
| | Risk and protective factors |
| Spirituality | Explore cultural understandings of the role of spirituality in recovery |
| Cross-Cultural Counseling Process | Work within the cultural, sociolinguistic, and social interactional framework in counseling and the person's explanatory models using the following: |
| | A collaborative substance abuse assessment approach |
| | Cultural adaptations to substance abuse counseling approaches (e.g., 12 step, motivational interviewing, relapse prevention) |
| | Culture-specific intervention and healing approaches |

but also as providing protection from substance abuse and assets, attention to cultural understandings of spirituality and its role in the recovery process, and the central importance of fitting the substance abuse counseling process to culture understandings and the culturally based system of care for the individual. By way of summary, we conclude with four recommendations for structuring multicultural substance abuse counseling driven by the guiding principles described in Table 23.1.

1. Establishing a relationship of trust is essential for effective multicultural substance abuse counseling and is best initiated by assessment, intake, and counseling processes that are collaborative in nature. This also requires cultural competence on the part of the person completing the assessment and doing counseling. Professionals of the same ethnicity can often establish trust most effectively, provided they have the requisite cultural competency. When it is not possible to find a counselor of the same ethnicity, the counselor must possess cultural competency with the person's ethnocultural group.

2. Training and supervision of the counselor should provide continued development in an understanding of cultural factors at the linguistic and sociolinguistic levels, as well as how values, explanatory models, and symbolic systems can structure each part of the process of understanding and helping the client.

3. Complementary therapeutic approaches that use resources from within the community can be crucial elements for effective treatment. These resources include traditional healers and ceremonies, Elders as role models and as potential natural helpers, and significant others in the extended family system. These comprise cultural resources and assets with influence to initiate change or to maintain gains and help prevent relapse.

4. Substance abuse often is comorbid with various psychiatric disorders, including depression, anxiety, and PTSD and complex PTSD (Herman, 1995). The impact has major repercussions within the extended family and community systems within the culture. This requires an integrated approach to treatment that does not separate services by agencies or by Western versus traditional healing approaches. In multicultural substance abuse, the counselor must understand the counseling process as it fits within a system of care of complementary therapeutics that includes community resources and professionals. Counseling cannot be separate but must be actively linked with traditional healing practices, other resources, and other professionals in the system of care, and the system of care in multicultural substance abuse treatment should be client and family directed.

In summary, cultural factors structure the patterns and the meaning of substance use and abuse, the person's expectations for the substance abuse counseling process, and several of the important factors within and throughout the course of recovery. Throughout, we have emphasized an approach that highlights the strengths and assets within various cultural traditions that can be mobilized in the recovery from substance abuse. A deeper understanding of the role of culture in the substance abuse counseling process can allow the counselor to form relationships that empower the client to initiate, maintain, and solidify change.

## CRITICAL INCIDENT

### Drug and Alcohol Abuse in Cross-Cultural Counseling

Stanley had gone out of state to visit his adult son. While there, he began to experience an increase in PTSD symptoms and increasing urges to drink. He presented to the local VA clinic and asked to see a mental health counselor. Before meeting with Stanley, the young male therapist quickly reviewed Stanley's electronic record and noted that he had been treated for substance abuse in the past. Following clinic protocol, the therapist did a brief intake to determine the level of Stanley's distress, the most pressing issues, and a brief treatment plan.

The therapist asked Stanley to briefly describe why he was seeking services that day. Stanley, not meeting the therapist's eyes, replied, "I don't know." The therapist, believing that Stanley was avoiding eye contact because he was trying to hide something, asked, "I see from your records that you are a recovering alcoholic. Have you been drinking or using drugs?" Stanley did not reply. "Have you been going to your AA meetings? We have them here at the clinic, you know." Stanley replied, "They wouldn't understand me here" and withdrew further into his chair. The therapist, concerned, stated, "We won't be able to help you with your mental health issues if you're in denial and won't go to AA meetings. This is your problem and you're responsible for addressing it. Others can't help you until you help yourself." Stanley said "okay" and just listened until the session was over and left. He did not return for his follow-up appointment.

## DISCUSSION QUESTIONS

1. What are some of the specific events that led to the client not returning to counseling?

2. Describe how the events in the interview were structured by culture: Point out the specific cultural issues that may have led to impasse. These might include elements described in the chapter related to the levels of

linguistics, sociolinguistics, values, and symbolic factors, as well the levels of acculturation strategy or previous exposure to "Western" approaches to treatment.

3. What are some alternative ways that the counselor could have interacted with Stanley, and how could they have changed the outcome?

4. Create a critical incident for a person from a culture different than your own around the issue of a potential relapse into substance abuse. Describe how inattention or attention to key cultural factors could lead to a problematic outcome or could result in a more successful therapeutic event.

## REFERENCES

Alcohol & Drug Abuse Institute. (2006). *Evidence-based practices for treating substance use disorders: Matrix of interventions.* Joint project of the University of the Washington Alcohol & Drug Abuse Institute and the Northwest Frontier Addiction Technology Transfer Center, with funding from the Washington State Division of Alcohol and Substance Abuse. Retrieved April 1, 2006, from http://adai.washington.edu/ebp/ matrix.pdf

American Psychiatric Association. (2000). *Diagnostic and statistical manual of mental disorders* (4th ed., text revision). Washington, DC: Author.

Berry, J. W. (2002). Conceptual approaches to acculturation. In K. M. Chun, P. B. Organista, & G. Marín (Eds.), *Acculturation: Advances in theory, measurement, and applied research* (pp. 17–37). Washington, DC: American Psychological Association.

Conger, J. J. (1956). Reinforcement theory and the dynamics of alcoholism. *Quarterly Journal of Studies on Alcohol, 17,* 296–305.

Conigrave, K. M., Hall, W. D., & Saunders, J. B. (1995). AUDIT questionnaire: Choosing a cut-off score. *Addiction, 90,* 1349–1356.

Dana, R. H. (2005). *Multicultural assessment: Principles, applications, and examples.* Hillsdale, NJ: Lawrence Erlbaum.

DiClemente, C. C., & Prochaska, J. O. (1998). Toward a comprehensive, transtheoretical model of change: Stages of change and addictive behaviors. In W. R. Miller & N. Heather (Eds.), *Treating addictive behaviors* (2nd ed., pp. 3–24). New York: Plenum.

Donovan, D. M., & Marlatt, G. A. (Eds.). (2005). *Assessment of addictive behaviors* (2nd ed.). New York: Guilford.

Erickson, F. (1975). Gatekeeping and the melting pot: Interaction in counseling encounters. *Harvard Educational Review, 45,* 44–69.

Fadiman, A. (1997). *When the spirit catches you and you fall down.* New York: Farrar, Strauss & Giroux.

Geertz, C. (1973). *The interpretation of cultures.* New York: Basic Books.

Herman, J. L. (1995). Complex PTSD: A syndrome in survivors of prolonged and repeated trauma. In G. S. Everly & J. M. Lating (Eds.), *Psychotraumatology: Key papers and core concepts in post-traumatic stress* (pp. 87–100). New York: Plenum.

Herring, R. (1999). Helping Native American Indian and Alaska Native male youth. In A. M. Horne & M. S. Kiselica (Eds.), *Handbook of counseling boys and adolescent males: A practitioner's guide* (pp. 117–136). Thousand Oaks, CA: Sage.

Hobfoll, S. E., Jackson, A., Hobfoll, I., Pierce, C. A., & Young, S. (2002). The impact of communal-mastery versus self-mastery on emotional outcomes during stressful conditions: A prospective study of Native American women. *American Journal of Community Psychology, 30,* 853–871.

Johnson, L. D., O'Malley, P. M., & Bachman, J. C. (1996). *National survey results on drug use from the Monitoring the Future Study, 1975–1994: Vol. 2. College students and young adults.* Rockville, MD: National Institute on Drug Abuse.

Kleinman, A. (1988). *Rethinking psychiatry: From cultural category to personal experience.* New York: Free Press.

LaFromboise, T., Trimble, J., & Mohatt, G. V. (1990). Counseling intervention and American Indian tradition: An integrative approach. *The Counseling Psychologist, 18,* 628–654.

Longabaugh, R., Donovan, D. M., Karno, M. P., McCrady, B. S., Morgenstern, J., & Tonigan, S. (2005). Active ingredients: How and why evidence-based alcohol behavioral treatment interventions work. *Alcohol: Clinical & Experimental Research, 29,* 235–247.

Manson, S. M. (1996). The wounded spirit: A cultural formulation of post-traumatic stress disorder. *Culture, Medicine and Psychiatry, 20,* 489–498.

Marlatt, G. A., & Donovan, D. M. (Eds.). (2005). *Relapse prevention: Maintenance strategies in the treatment of addictive behaviors* (2nd ed.). New York: Guilford.

May, P. A., & Gossage, J. P. (2001). New data on the epidemiology of adult drinking and substance use among American Indians of the Northern states: Male and female data on prevalence, patterns, and consequences. *American Indian and Alaska Native Mental Health Research, 10*(2), 1–26.

Miller, W. R., Tonigan, J. S., & Longabaugh, R. (1995). *The Drinker Inventory of Consequences (DrInC): An instrument for assessing adverse consequences of alcohol abuse* (Project MATCH Monograph Series, NIH Pub. No. 95–3911, Vol. 4). Rockville, MD: U.S. Department of Health and Human Services, Public Health Service, National Institutes of Health, National Institute on Alcohol Abuse and Alcoholism.

Miller, W. R., Zweben, A., DiClemente, C. C., & Rychtarik, R. G. (1992). *Motivational enhancement therapy manual: A clinical tool for therapists treating individuals with alcohol abuse and dependence* (Project MATCH Monograph Series, Vol. 2). Rockville MD: U.S. Department of Health and Human Services, National Institute of Alcohol Abuse and Alcoholism.

Mohatt, G. V. (1988). Psychological method and spiritual power in cross-cultural psychotherapy. *Journal of Contemplative Psychotherapy, 5,* 85–115.

Moore, J. (1990). Mexican American women addicts: The influence of family background. In R. Glick & J. Moore (Eds.), *Drugs in Hispanic communities* (pp. 127–153). New Brunswick, NJ: Rutgers University Press.

Myers, H. F., Kagawa-Singer, M., Kumanyika, S. K., Lex, B. W., & Markides, K. S. (1995). Behavioral risk factors related to chronic diseases in ethnic minorities. *Health Psychology, 14,* 613–621.

Oetting, E. R., Donnermeyer, J. F., Trimble, J. E., & Beauvais, F. (1998). Primary socialization theory: Culture, ethnicity, and cultural identification: The links between culture and substance use: IV. *Substance Use & Misuse, 33,* 2075–2107.

Rouse, B. A. (1995). *Substance abuse and mental health sourcebook* (DHHS Pub. No. (SMA) 95–3064). Washington, DC: Government Printing Office.

Sher, K. (1987). Stress response dampening. In H. T. Blane & K. E. Leonard (Eds.), *Psychological theories of drinking and alcoholism.* New York: Guilford.

Sher, K., & Trull, T. (1994). Personality and disinhibitory psychology: Alcoholism and antisocial personality disorder. *Journal of Abnormal Psychology, 103,* 91–102.

Triandis, H. C. (1988). The self and social behavior in differing cultural contexts. *Psychological Review, 98*(3), 506–521.

Trimble, J. E. (1987). Self-understanding and perceived alienation among American Indians. *Journal of Community Psychology, 15,* 316–333.

Trimble, J. E. (1995). Toward an understanding of ethnicity and ethnic identity, and their relationship with drug use research. In G. Botvin, S. Schinke, & M. A. Orlandi (Eds.), *Drug abuse prevention with multiethnic youth* (pp. 3–27). Thousand Oaks, CA: Sage.

Trimble, J. E. (1996). Acculturation, ethnic identification, and the evaluation process. In A. Bayer, F. Brisbane, & A. Ramirez (Eds.), *Advanced methodological issues in culturally competent evaluation for substance abuse prevention* (CSAP Cultural Competence Series 6, pp. 13–61). Rockville, MD: Office for Substance Abuse Prevention, Division of Community Prevention and Training, U.S. Department of Health and Human Services.

Trimble, J. E. (2003). Introduction: Social change and acculturation. In K. Chun, P. B. Organista, & G. Marin (Eds.), *Acculturation: Advances in theory, measurement, and applied research* (pp. 3–13). Washington, DC: American Psychological Association.

Trimble, J. E., & Mahoney, E. (2002). Gender and ethnic differences in adolescent self-esteem: A Rasch measurement model analysis. In P. D. Mail, S. Heurtin-Roberts, S. E. Martin, & J. Howard (Eds.), *Alcohol use among American Indians and Alaska Natives: Multiple perspectives on a complex problem* (National Institute on Alcohol Abuse and Alcoholism Research Monograph No. 37, pp. 211–240). Bethesda, MD: National Institute on Alcohol Abuse and Alcoholism.

Trimble, J. E., & Thurman, P. (2002). Ethnocultural considerations and strategies for providing counseling services for Native American Indians. In P. Pedersen, J. Draguns, W. Lonner, & J. Trimble (Eds.), *Counseling across cultures* (5th ed., pp. 53–91). Thousand Oaks, CA: Sage.

Whitbeck, L. B., Hoyt, D. R., McMorris, B. J, Chen, X., & Stubben, J. D. (2001). Perceived discrimination and early substance abuse among American Indian children. *Journal of Health and Social Behavior, 42,* 405–423.

White, J. L., & Parnham, T. A. (1990). *The psychology of Blacks: An African-American perspective.* Englewood Cliffs, NJ: Prentice Hall.

Witko, T. M. (2006). A framework for working with American Indian parents. In T. M. Witko (Ed.), *Mental health care for urban Indians* (pp. 155–171). Washington, DC: American Psychological Association.

Yu, E. S., & Whitehead, J. (1997). Task Group I: Epidemiology of minority health. *Journal of Gender, Culture, & Health, 2,* 101–112.

# Family and Counseling With Ethnic Groups

## James Georgas

---

### Primary Objective

- To provide an overview of contemporary structures and functions of families in various cultures and ethnic groups and why they are important in cross-cultural counseling

### Secondary Objective

- To point out ways in which families of different cultures adapt to different stages of acculturation

---

CHANGES IN THE FAMILY DURING THE PAST 100 YEARS HAVE BEEN THE GREATEST IN THE HISTORY OF THE world. Most are familiar with changes in North America and northern Europe, with the increase of nuclear families and the decrease of extended families and, during the past 20 or more years, with the increase of unmarried families, divorced families, unmarried mothers, and homosexual families. However, nuclear families have also been increasing in countries throughout the world. Many family sociologists, cultural anthropologists, and psychologists assume that, based on modernization and globalization theories, family types in the majority world will inevitable converge, sooner or later, to the family types of Western societies. However, this is still an open question according to current research on family in cultures throughout the world. Family types and functioning and human behavior are shaped within the context of cultural institutions, norms, values, language, history, and traditions.

The increasing numbers of immigrants in many countries throughout the world necessitate that counselors become sensitive to cultural features of ethnic groups, particularly to differences in family functioning in different cultures. Counselors are trained in counseling techniques but often employ the values of their societies in their interactions with clients. For example, an important psychological difference between cultures is that Western societies employ individualist values, while in many countries throughout the world, collectivist values are important, particularly family values. Counseling people from different ethnic groups requires knowledge of family systems in different cultures. In the United States and northern Europe, the high percentages of nuclear families, one-parent families, and divorced families reflect changes during the past few decades in the structure of the family. In the majority world, whose population represents nearly 90% of the world, extended families predominate.

The first section of the chapter begins with the definition of family. The concepts of structure and function of family will follow. The different family types and their predominance in different cultures are described. This is followed by how the ecological and social features of societies shape different types of families, with different structures, functions, and psychological features.

The second section discusses the important concept of family change in the Western world and in the majority world.

The third section analyzes the different acculturation strategies of ethnic groups to a host society. The concept of assimilation of ethnic groups to a host society, the "melting pot," is not an accurate picture of the different ways in which people adapt to their new society.

The following section describes how family networks, roles, and psychological characteristics differ and are similar across cultures. Personality traits, emotional closeness with the members of nuclear and extended families, family values, and general values are psychological characteristics particularly relevant to counseling people from different ethnic groups.

The fifth section discusses the relationships between cultures, social institutions, families, and psychological characteristics. In counseling individuals from different ethnic groups, it is necessary to understand the complex relationships of the individual and the family within their culture, which are not always similar to those of Western societies.

The sixth section discusses the psychological consequences related to the decrease of the traditional extended family systems and the increase of nuclear family systems. The last section presents conclusions.

# FAMILY SYSTEMS
## Family Definitions

Most definitions of family stem from sociology and cultural anthropology. The term *family* is often perceived by sociologists and psychologists in the United States, Canada, and northern Europe as synonymous with *nuclear family,* that is, mother, father, and children. But this perception reflects to a certain degree cultural values of Western societies about family. In the majority world, *family* very likely connotes grandparents, aunts, uncles, and cousins, from both sides of the parents, and even unrelated persons close to the family.

Two concepts, *structure* and *function,* are important in the definition of family. Structure refers to the number of members of the family and to the familial positions such as parent, child, grandparent, uncles and aunts, and other kin, while function refers to ways in which families satisfy their physical and psychological needs and meet survival and maintenance needs (Smith, 1995, p. 9).

A definition of family that for decades has served as a point of reference for cultural anthropology is that of P. M. Murdock (1949): "The family is a social group characterized by common residence, economic cooperation, and reproduction. It includes adults of both sexes, at least two of whom maintain a socially approved sexual relationship, and one or more children, own or adopted, of the sexually cohabiting adults" (p. 2). A second aspect of the definition of family has to do with its functions as a social institution. Murdock defined the functions of the family as sexual, reproduction, socialization, and economic. Murdock also concluded that the nuclear family was a universal human social grouping, either as the sole prevailing form of the family or as the basic nucleus from which more complex familial forms are compounded.

A more recent definition of family challenges P. M. Murdock's (1949) definition in view of recent increases in the United States, Canada, and northern Europe of one-parent families, either divorced, adoptive, unmarried, or widowed mothers, and same-sex families. The family sociologist Popenoe (1988) defines family as follows: (a) The minimal family composition is one adult and one dependent person, (b) the parents do not have to be of both sexes, and (c) the couple does not have to be married. Popenoe's definition differs from Murdock in that the nucleus constituting a family is one adult and one dependent person, the parents can be of the same sex, and the couple does not have to be married. In addition, although Popenoe agrees with procreation as a family function, he modifies Murdock's functions as socialization of children, sexual regulation, economic cooperation, and provision of care, affection, and companionship.

Families satisfy their physical and psychological needs in order to maintain the family and to survive as a group. For example, families universally must provide shelter for themselves—a house—either a permanent edifice or a temporary abode such as a tent or an igloo. They maintain the home, clean and repair it, add rooms, and so on. Families engage in some type of work to provide sustenance and other family needs. This work might be farming, fishing, hunting, herding, gathering of berries, working in a store or a factory, owning a small business, working as a nurse or computer specialist, and so on. The family provides food for its members—that is, buying food at the market or raising crops, gathering roots, herding animals, fishing, and also cooking, cleaning the utensils, storing food, and so forth. The family provides, mends, and cleans clothes. They raise and educate the children, teach them the traditions of the community, and maintain contacts with kin. The parents provide emotional warmth and comfort to the child and to each other. The family participates in the marriage of the sons and daughters. These are some of the major functions of the family that are universal across all cultures in the world but vary according to how these functions are manifested in a culture.

# Family Types

Most cultural anthropologists (Ember & Ember, 2002; Levinson & Malone, 1980) agree that a universal characteristic of families in small societies throughout the world is the emphasis on genealogical relationships. In most cultures, the genealogical relationship is based on "blood," but it may also be based on adoption, as in present-day Western societies and also in the past, as in Japan, in which the father could disinherit his son and adopt a young man who seemed more worthy.

Family types can be classified as two-generation and three- or more generation families.

## Two-Generation Families

The *nuclear* family consists of mother, father, and their children, biological or adopted. Recent developments in Europe and North America would lead to adding homosexual parents with children to this category.

The *one-parent* family is also a two-generation family, consisting of the child and the divorced parent, unmarried parent (usually the mother), or the widow or widower.

## Three- or More Generation Families

Extended families consist of at least three generations: the maternal and paternal grandparents; the wife/mother, husband/father, and their children; and the aunts, siblings, cousins, nieces, and other kin of the mother and father as well as unrelated persons. Each type of extended family varies considerably according to the culture.

Extended families can be *polygamous* (multiple wives or husbands) or *monogamous* (one father and one mother). Polygamous families are further separated into *polygynous* (one father and two or more wives/mothers) and *polyandrous* (one wife/mother and two or more husbands/fathers). It is interesting to note that polygynous families were the norm in 83% of small preindustrial societies (G. P. Murdock, 1967), in contrast with monogamous families in 16% of societies and polyandrous in 0.5%. In contrast to stereotypes, the actual number of polygynous families in Islamic nations today is very small (e.g., almost 90% of husbands in Qatar, Kuwait, United Arab Emirates, Oman, Bahrain, and Saudi Arabia have only one wife). The low percentage of polygynous families at the present time is due to the reluctance of young women in these countries to enter into such a union.

The terms *patriarchal* and *matriarchal* refer to the authority structure of the family. The patriarch or matriarch is head of the family, controls the family property and finances, makes the important decisions, and is responsible for the protection and welfare of the entire family. For example, the authority structure of Elizabeth, Queen of the United Kingdom, is matriarchal.

## Main Extended Family Types

*Patrilineal* and *matrilineal* families are at least three generational. The *monogamous* variation can potentially consist of the grandparents, the married sons, the grandchildren, and the grandfather's or grandmother's siblings, nieces, grand-nieces, and, in many cases, other kin. The *polygynous* variation consists of the multiple wives and their children and their kin. In Africa, the mother's brother raises the children and supports her sister, while the father keeps a distance.

The *stem* extended family lives together under the authority of the grandfather-patriarch. The distinctive aspect of the stem family is that the oldest son inherits the family property, and the stem continues through his first son. The other sons and daughters either remain, if unmarried, or leave the household upon marriage. In the past, the stem family was found in England, southern France, Austria, southern Germany, and other societies, such as Japan.

The *joint* family differs from the stem family in that all the sons share the inheritance and work together. Joint extended families are characteristic in Europe, India, and East Asia.

The *fully extended* family, the *zadruga* in the Balkans countries of Croatia, Bosnia, Serbia, Montenegro, Albania, and Bulgaria, has a structure similar to that of the joint family, but with the difference that cousins and other kin are also included as members of the family.

# Kinship

Kinship has been the heart and soul of cultural anthropology's study of the family since the 19th century. Kinship refers to rules of descent, postmarital residence, marriage, and divorce.

## Rules of Descent

Rules of descent refer to relationships with paternal and maternal kin. They are differentiated according to two types of kin. *Consanguineal* kin are relatives related through blood, while *affinal* kin (in-laws) are relatives through marriage. *Lineal* relationships are biological relationships (e.g., grandparents, parents, and grandchildren). *Collateral* relationships are those with uncles and aunts, cousins, and nephews and nieces. These are critical concepts in different cultures because they also are related to the types of relationships and obligations toward lineal, collateral, and affinal kin; to lines of descent; to residence; to inheritance of property; and to gender and family roles, economic activities, religious activities, childaring practices, and even political behavior.

These aspects of organization center on strict sets of rules with kin, many of them as ritualized behaviors. Societies with specific rules for kin are usually hierarchical in structure and related to how power is distributed between males and females, as well as across generations.

## Postmarital Residence

Patterns of marital residence, according to Ember and Ember (2002), are as follows:

- *Patrilocal* is residence with or near the father's patrilineal kinsmen, the most prevalent residence pattern throughout the world with approximately 67% of societies.

- *Matrilocal* is residence with or near the wife's matrilineal kinsmen (15% of all societies).

- *Bilocal* is residence with or near the parents of the husband or the wife (7%).

- *Avunculocal* refers to residence with or near the maternal uncle or other male matrilineal kinsmen of the husband (4%).

- *Neolocal* means residence apart from the parents or relatives of both spouses. This is characteristic of nuclear family residence in northern Europe and North America but accounts for only 5% of families worldwide.

## Marriage and Divorce

In most societies, marriage is arranged between the families rather than as a result of romantic love. Many societies have norms as to whom one is permitted to marry (*endogamy*) and restrictions regarding whom one cannot marry (*exogamy*). An example of exogamy is incest, which is nearly universal. In India and Pakistan, endogamy means that marriage is usually restricted to the same caste, the same village, the same religion, and the same race. These social norms are not as restrictive in North America and Europe, although marriage to someone of another racial or ethnic group or religion, or with a spouse of a different level of education or social status, may not be approved in some groups. Marriage with someone with the same family name was disapproved in China. In some societies, marriage is not permitted with first cousins or with the son or daughter of a godparent. In other societies, such as Saudi Arabia, cross-cousin marriage is highly desirable. Marriage to one's cousin, preferably the son or daughter of the paternal brother (uncle), reflects a continuation of close family bonds and the preservation of the family property. In other societies, if a husband dies, the wife must marry the brother. The decision of a young couple to marry on the basis of love, with or without the consent of the parents, occurs in a minority of the world societies, particularly North America and Europe.

Divorce is socially disapproved in all societies. Societies differ in the degree to which divorce is controlled and by which institutions. Divorce is directly controlled by the family in some societies, while in others, there is indirect control by social institutions and by the dominant religion. For example, Catholicism does not permit divorce except under highly unusual situations requiring a special dispensation. The Christian Orthodox Church permits three marriages. Islamic law, the *sharia,* permits divorces, but divorce has legal and social consequences for the husband. Since the married daughter inherits property from the father, she retains this property in her name after marriage, and the husband has no legal claim to it after divorce.

## Determinants of Family Types

An important question studied primarily by anthropologists, but also by sociologists, is the ecological and social determinants of family types in different cultures. Subsistence, or means of obtaining food, based on ecological features of the physical environment (e.g., climate, flora, fauna, and terrain), appears to be related to different types of family structure and function as well as settlement patterns. People who live in areas where the land is fertile grow crops in order to subsist. Herding of animals also takes place in areas where land is fertile but even in mountains, savannahs, or the desert. Some societies subsist by fishing, others by hunting, and others by gathering. In today's industrial and postindustrial societies such as the United States, Canada, and Europe, the means of subsistence are provided by working in industry or in commerce, by owning a small business such as a restaurant, by being a government employee, and so forth.

Agricultural societies tend to have a permanent base, as well as land and houses near kin, usually part of a town or small community. Subsistence farming, the norm in the majority of countries throughout the world, requires the cooperation of members of the family and kin to cultivate crops.

Hunting or gathering as a means of subsistence requires moving from area to area. Many hunting and gathering societies do not have a permanent home but temporary huts or shelters. Mobility means that the small nuclear family is more adaptable for survival under these ecological restraints.

In modern industrial society, where people are hired to provide services or to work in industry, where money is the means of exchange, and where people live in urban areas and apartments or houses are expensive, the nuclear family is functional.

Blumberg and Winch (1972) found that the nuclear family is typical in small hunting and gathering societies as well as in urban areas in industrial societies, while the extended family is found in settled, intensive agricultural societies. This is called the *curvilinear* hypothesis. Nimkoff and Middleton (1960) found evidence that highly differentiated social stratification is found in extended families. Children in agricultural and pastoral societies are taught to be responsible, compliant, and obedient and to respect their elders and hierarchy. Less stratification was found in nuclear families in hunting and gathering societies, where children tend to be self-reliant, independent, and achievement oriented and the family is less stratified. A good hunter of any age is respected for his or her competence in killing game, which is different from agricultural societies in which hierarchy and age are criteria for respect.

A variety of family types is usually found within polyethnic societies. For example, small family businesses thrive in urban areas in the United States, Canada, and Europe, particularly among recent immigrant families and established ethnic groups. Ethnic family businesses in Britain are a means of reducing labor costs but also a means of continuing the patriarchal family structure and function in an urban setting. The children help the family in the business, and this is also a way for the parents to look after the children while they work. The Chinese in Britain have restaurants and take-away businesses; Greeks, Turks, and Cypriots are involved in catering and the manufacturing of clothes; and other ethnic groups, such as Indians and Pakistanis, are involved in similar small businesses. The presence of family-organized small businesses is typical in the United States.

Thus, small family-owned businesses are a means of autonomous economic activity and also a means of continuing a modified extended family structure and function in an urban setting to replace their reliance on agricultural subsistence in their native country. That is, the attitudes and values related to the autonomy and independence of farmers can be adapted to the operation of a small family business, as an alternative to the prospect of losing autonomy in economic activity as an employee in a large business in an urban setting.

## FAMILY CHANGE

The analysis of family change began in France in the 19th century. Auguste Comte viewed changes in the family as a product of the French Revolution. The rejection of the hierarchical and autocratic relations between the aristocracy and the citizens led to an egalitarian climate in the family and a rejection of the patriarchal authority of the father. This was accompanied by the migration of sons and daughters to large cities and the formation of nuclear families. Theories of family change were promulgated by many sociologists during the 19th century. These theories supported two viewpoints on family change: (1) The family system is declining, with terms being used such as *crisis, breakdown, dissolution, disintegration, marginalization,* and *fragmentation,* or (2) changes in family have positive and adaptive elements.

The most influential theory of family change in the 20th century was that of sociologist Talcott Parsons (1943, 1949, 1965). According to Parsons, family has two main functions: *instrumental,* related to survival, and *expressive,* related to the maintenance of morale and cooperation. Parsons theorized that migration to the large cities from the agricultural communities and the increasing industrialization of the United States during the first decades of the 20th century resulted in the geographical isolation of the nuclear family from its extended family network, which resulted in their psychological isolation. Its reduction in size resulted in loss of its productive, political, and religious functions. The nuclear family became primarily a unit of residence and consumption. Its financial and educative functions are dependent on the state, and its major remaining function is the socialization of children and the psychological equilibrium of the parents. The nuclear family parents, who have chosen each other freely based on love, are isolated from their kin and share rational and pragmatic values.

Parsons did not perceive changes from the extended family to the nuclear family system as reflecting the decline of the family but as a positive adaptation to social change. The nuclear family, composed of the working father, the housewife mother, and the children, was characterized by an increase in psychological aspects of the companionship between mother and father and greater emphasis on the psychological aspects of the socialization of the children. These changes were partly reflections of the autonomy of the nuclear family from the extended family due to their living apart from the extended family, their independent economic activity, and their reliance on the state for education of the children, employment, health, and other provisions granted by the society.

However, studies of social networks in North America and northern Europe in the past 40 years have indicated that the nuclear family is not as psychologically isolated from its kin or as autonomous to the degree assumed by Parsons and other family sociologists. Nuclear families, even in industrial countries, have networks with grandparents, siblings, and other kin. The question is the degree of contact, communication, and psychological bonds with members of their extended families, even in present-day United States.

How much has the family changed in Asia, Africa, Europe, the Americas, and Oceania? Family types have changed most radically in North America and northern Europe, but changes in the family have occurred throughout the world at different rates and in different forms. Many of the rules, practices, and family types have changed in recent years, while others have remained unchanged. In a changing world in which small societies have been exposed to television, the Internet, increased economic changes, technology, and tourism, the structure and function of the family have been changing, just as these societies have also been changing.

A critical question raised by modernization theory and globalization is the following (Huntington, 1996; Inkeles, 1998): Will the traditional types of families in these cultures eventually evolve into the nuclear family, divorced family, and one-parent family systems of North America and northern Europe? Or do cultural features of each society continue to play a role in maintaining aspects of their traditional family structure and function and also in shaping changes in family types? Let us analyze more closely issues related to this important issue.

Because of economic changes, the traditional family systems of small societies are no longer totally dependent on subsistence systems such as hunting, gathering, or even agriculture. The number of nuclear families is increasing in urban areas in most developing societies, young people are increasingly choosing their spouses rather than having to submit to arranged marriages, women are entering the workforce, traditional family roles have changed, and the father no longer has absolute power in the family. There is a trend toward more families becoming structurally nuclear, even in small societies. But it may be misleading to conclude that families throughout the world are "becoming . . . nuclear" functionally in the sense of the North American and northern European nuclear family. Even though the numbers of nuclear families are increasing in most societies, they still maintain very close relations with their kin. In urban areas in many societies, nuclear families of the married sons and daughters live in the same building or very near the grandparents. There is an economic explanation for this. In the richest nations of world (e.g., the United States and Canada, northern Europe, Japan, and South Korea), a high economic level for the past four or five decades has permitted young people to work and also rent an apartment or obtain a mortgage to buy a house. In the rest of the world, wages of young people are not high enough for them to secure an independent abode. So nuclear families live near the grandparents. In Japan and South Korea, for example, where economic circumstances permit a married son to acquire a separate home, the married son and the wife still maintain very close relationships with the grandparents and continue to adhere to values such as respecting the grandparents. Even working wives with higher education take pains in maintaining many traditional family values in these countries.

Securing an independent home represents a basic psychological need for privacy, whether the home is thousands of miles away from the parents or in the apartment next door. Thus, a separate residence does not necessarily mean psychological isolation from kin relationships. Geographical proximity and psychological distance are not the same. A separate domicile of the nuclear family members, either next door or far away, is geographical separation but does not necessarily imply psychological separation from the kin.

Another change is in the power of the father in the family. With the increase of educated and working mothers in many societies throughout the world, the mother has gained economic power, as have working children, while the absolute authority of the father has lessened. In Mongolia, studies have found that children in urban areas side with the mother because she not only works and brings in money but also cooks and cares for the house and them.

Thus, modernization and globalization would predict that the morphological change of traditional types of families to the nuclear and one-parent family structure and function as in North America and Western Europe, bulldozed by an economic engine, is just a matter of time. On the other hand, there is support for the argument that various paths lead to different forms of family structure and function, influenced by economic growth but also shaped by longstanding cultural traditions. The answer is not yet in to these predictions. It is also a question of whether the centrifugal forces of economic and institutional changes, which tend to weaken emotional ties among family members, are more powerful than the centripetal psychological forces that establish emotional bonds among people, particularly among family members. Psychology, particularly cross-cultural psychology, can play a critical role in attempting to find answers to this dilemma.

## ACCULTURATION OF ETHNIC GROUPS

Acculturation is an important concept related to the processes of cultural change and psychological change when cultural groups and individuals from each culture come into contact (Berry, 2006; Ward, Chapter 17 [this volume]). The concept of acculturation has been used in the analysis of how immigrants change when adapting to their receiving society, such as in the United States, Canada, and many countries throughout the world. Acculturation also refers to how ethnic groups relate to each other and change in multicultural societies. The waves of economic migrants and the resultant cultural diversity present a challenge to the cultural identity of a number of European countries at the present time. In other countries with a history of different cultures, such as in the Balkans and Eastern Europe, conflicts between ethnic groups have resulted in revolutions and wars.

That is, acculturation has two facets. One facet is how individual members of ethnic groups, whether migrants, refugees, indigenous peoples, or even tourists, acculturate to a new society, but also how members of the dominant society acculturate to the members of the ethnic groups. A second facet is acculturation at the cultural level of each society. Ethnic groups bring to the new society features of the heritage of their culture, but the host society also acculturates, changing features of its society to accommodate features of the ethnic culture. This mutual change of cultural patterns of both cultures is very complex and may take many decades to occur. The degree to which a dominant society acculturates to ethnic groups is closely related to its social institutions, and societies historically have differed widely in this respect. For example, the United States and Canada have historically welcomed immigrants from countries throughout the world, but many other countries did not and do not. Ethnic groups bring their religion, language, music, foods, and so on and adapt certain features to those of the host society. But the host society also adopts many of the cultural features of the ethnic groups.

Of particular interest to the theme of this chapter is how individuals and ethnic groups acculturate to the receiving society and the policy of societies regulating the acculturation of ethnic groups. It has long been assumed that immigrants acculturate to societies through the process of *assimilation,* such as the traditional immigration "melting pot" policy of the United States. However, Berry (1980) has indicated that individuals and ethnic groups actually acculturate in different ways and not only through assimilation. Berry proposes four types of "acculturation strategies" composed of attitudes and behaviors of individuals and ethnic groups. These attitudes and behaviors can be directed toward combinations of (1) the receiving or dominant society and (2) the individual's ethnic group. Berry describes four possible acculturation strategies formed by the orientations toward one's ethnic group and toward the host society or other ethnic groups. These orientations refer to (1) the preference for maintaining one's heritage, culture, and identity or its rejection and (2) the preference for contact with and participation in the host society and/or other ethnic groups or its rejection.

## Acculturation Strategies

- The *assimilation* acculturation strategy is a combination of attitudes toward not maintaining one's cultural heritage and preferring interactions with members of the dominant and other ethnic groups. This is the "melting pot" type of acculturation strategy—that is, seeking to adapt completely to the identity, culture, and norms of the dominant culture and shedding the identity and culture of one's ethnic group.

- *Separation* is the antithetic acculturation strategy in which attitudes are toward maintaining one's cultural heritage, maintaining contact and interaction only with members of one's ethnic group, and declining contacts with the dominant culture. Separation strategy is often characterized by individuals or ethnic groups not learning the language of the dominant culture, with close relationships only with people of their own ethnic group, and other attitudes, values, and behaviors that indicate their rejection of the dominant culture.

- *Integration* is the acculturation strategy in which individuals and ethnic groups maintain aspects of their cultural identity and heritage but also seek interaction and contact with the dominant culture.

- *Marginalization* is the lack of interest in maintaining one's cultural heritage but also the lack of interest in interactions with others.

In a study by Berry, Phinney, Sam, and Vedder (2006) with 5,000 immigrant youth from 13 countries, integration was by far the most frequent acculturation strategy, followed in descending order of choice by separation, assimilation, and marginalization.

The above analysis of acculturation strategies is from the perspective of the individual or ethnic group. However, as discussed above, acculturation is a two-way process; societies also acculturate to ethnic groups. Berry (2006) describes the analogous types of acculturation strategies of individuals and societies. The acculturation strategy of *integration* at the individual or ethnic group level corresponds to a *multicultural* strategy or policy of a society. These societies attempt to recognize and accept the rights of all ethnic groups. *Assimilation* corresponds at the societal level to the *melting pot* policy in which individuals are encouraged to adopt fully the identity and culture of the society. *Separation* at the individual or ethnic group level corresponds to *segregation* at the societal level. Segregation refers to the laws and policy of the dominant society toward ethnic groups who may not be afforded equal status, opportunities for education, access to work, or other rights. *Marginalization* is a stricter policy of *segregation* of certain ethnic groups.

The relevance of family types to acculturation strategies of individuals and ethnic groups, but also of societies toward ethnic groups, is an important issue in this chapter. There is a diversity of family types across cultures, and part of the cultural heritage that immigrants bring with them is the type of family structure and function of their society. This includes the values associated with family and family roles in their culture (e.g., the father, whose word is law, is the patriarch of the family; the mother's role is in the home; and the sons and daughters must conform to the father's demands).

An important aspect of counseling individuals from ethnic groups is the counselor's assumptions and values about the family. First, just the word *family* may have a different denotation as well as connotation when asked by the counselor and responded to by the client. The counselor in, for example, the United States may assume that when asking the about the client's family, the client will also assume that the term *family* denotes "nuclear family." The counselor might also assume that "nuclear family" is associated with democratic and equal relationships between parents and children, the equality of mother and father in financial and other matters, considerable freedom and independence of teenagers, teaching children to make their own decisions, and expectations that adult children after high school or college will support themselves economically and live in a separate household.

On the other hand, in response to the counselor's question about family, the ethnic client might very reasonably assume that "family" refers to one's very extended family; to the father's autocratic values in which there are hierarchical relationships of grandfather, father, mother, sons, and daughters; to expectations that the children and the mother obey the decisions of the father and grandfather; to maintaining close relationships and "not rocking the boat" with grandparents, aunts, and uncles on both sides of the family; of showing respect to kin; and so on.

Thus, the counselor should attempt to probe the family type and relationships of the client with his or her family. This, of course, is the normal procedure of any counselor. But, in working with ethnic individuals, this procedure requires that the counselor is conscious of his or her knowledge, individualistic values, and assumptions regarding the "American family" and seeks to understand the relationships of the family in the ethnic group. This procedure is not simple if one adds to this process the variables discussed above (e.g., the ethnic group, the family types of the ethnic group, the acculturation strategy of the client, whether the parents or the family are first generation or second generation, the length of residence of the client and family in the country, etc.).

## FAMILY NETWORKS, ROLES, AND PSYCHOLOGICAL VARIABLES ACROSS CULTURES

The emphasis of the chapter up to now has been on differences—differences between cultures, differences in family types, differences between ethnic groups, and differences in acculturation strategies of individuals and ethnic groups and the policies of societies toward ethnic groups. Yes, there are differences in family characteristics across cultures. But there are also similarities in family characteristics across cultures.

A study of family characteristics was based on 27 countries throughout the world (Georgas, Berry, van de Vijver, Kagitçibasi, & Poortinga, 2006): United States, Canada, Mexico, Brazil, Chile, the Netherlands, France, Germany, Britain, Greece, Bulgaria, Turkey, Cyprus, Spain, Algeria, Saudi Arabia, Nigeria, Ghana, Ukraine, Georgia, Iran, Pakistan, India, China, Japan, Mongolia, South Korea, and Indonesia. The analyses were based on social characteristics of each country: socioeconomic level, percentage of the population engaged in agriculture, highest monthly temperature, educational status, and dominant religion. The family variables were family roles of the mother, father, grandmother, grandfather, aunts and uncles, and 20-year-old and 10-year-old males and females, as well as family networks. The psychological variables were emotional bonds with members of the nuclear family and kin, personality traits, family values, and personal values.

# DIFFERENCES ACROSS CULTURES
## Socioeconomic Level of Countries

Countries differed most on family and psychological variables according to their socioeconomic level (affluence, percentage of the population engaged in agriculture, educational structure; see Table 24.1).

Values appear to be the most important psychological variable differentiating countries with high and low affluence levels, particularly agricultural societies and the societies of North America and northern Europe. Low-socioeconomic, primarily agricultural countries have higher hierarchical family values (Georgas et al., 2006) as compared to high-socioeconomic countries. These hierarchical values are characteristic of agricultural countries in which the father has the social power, and the mother and girls have less power than the father and boys (the father should handle money, the father is the breadwinner, the mother accepts the father's decisions, the father is head of family, the mother's place is at home, and the mother should be the go-between). Although these family values are strongly related to the socioeconomic level of countries, note that even countries at the medium socioeconomic level (such as Greece, Bulgaria, and others) that were recently agricultural cultures strongly reject these hierarchical roles related primarily to the autocratic power of the father in agricultural extended families.

The personal values (Schwartz, 1994) of embeddedness (honor elders, national security, respect for tradition, social order, family security, reciprocate favors), hierarchy (authority, social power, wealth), and harmony (unity with nature, environment protection, world of beauty) show the same profile. It appears that with increasing socioeconomic level of the country, better educational facilities and opportunity for work are created for both males and females. Increased knowledge and the opportunity to earn money apart from the family lead young people to reject the authoritarian role and power of the father.

Relationships with family and kin values (children respect grandparents, honor family's reputation, parents teach behavior to children, children take care of old parents, children should obey parents,

**TABLE 24.1** Clusters of Countries Based on Socioeconomic Level

| High | Medium | Low |
|---|---|---|
| United States | Greece | Indonesia |
| Canada | Saudi Arabia | Pakistan |
| Germany | Ukraine | India |
| Japan | Mexico | Algeria |
| France | Bulgaria | Ghana |
| The Netherlands | Chile | Nigeria |
| United Kingdom | Cyprus | |
| Hong Kong | Brazil | |
| South Korea | Turkey | |
| Spain | Iran | |
| | Georgia | |

problems are solved within family, children should help with the housework, good relationships should be maintained with relatives) are correlated with the socioeconomic level of countries but to a lesser degree than the hierarchical role values and the personal values of Schwartz (1994).

The expressive and instrumental family roles are less correlated than values with the socioeconomic level of countries (see Table 24.2). These family roles resemble Parsons's (1943, 1949) and also Durkheim's (1888, 1892/1921) roles. Both mothers and fathers have somewhat higher expressive roles in low-socioeconomic countries than in high-socioeconomic countries (Figures 24.1 and 24.2). Fathers and mothers in higher affluent countries tend to share the financial roles more than in low- and medium-socioeconomic countries, in which fathers are more involved in financial matters than mothers. Mothers in affluent societies have about the same or more power in the family than fathers, while the opposite is observed in medium- and low-affluence societies.

The personality traits of agreeableness (understanding, sympathetic, considerate, quarrelsome, deceitful, rude) and conscientiousness (organized, reliable, responsible, careless, lazy, disorderly) are also in the same direction, with higher means in low-affluence than in high-affluence countries, but with very low correlations.

Family networks are measures of the degree of relationships of family and kin. As found in many studies in high-affluence countries, kin and family live further apart. However, the correlation with frequency of visits and telephone calls is not linear. Medium-affluence countries visit and telephone more frequently family and kin than both high- and low-affluence countries. It appears that young people move away from the family home, presumably to get a better education and to find work in urban areas. But it seems that contact with family and kin is maintained to a large degree, even in high-affluence countries.

**TABLE 24.2**  Family Roles of Mothers and Fathers

| Expressive | Financial | Child Care |
| --- | --- | --- |
| Keeps pleasant environment | Manages finances | Takes kids to school |
| Provides emotional support for kids | Contributes finances | Does housework |
| Provides emotional support for spouse | Gives pocket money | Helps kids with housework |
| Keeps family united | Supports kids' career | Plays with children |
| Emotionally supports grandparents | Does the shopping | |
| Preserves relations relatives | Resolves disputes | |
| Conveys traditions | | |
| Protects the family | | |
| Supports grandparents | | |
| Conveys religion | | |
| Teaches manners | | |
| Takes care of grandparents | | |

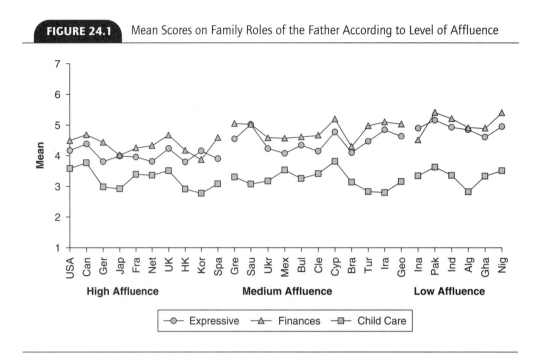

**FIGURE 24.1** Mean Scores on Family Roles of the Father According to Level of Affluence

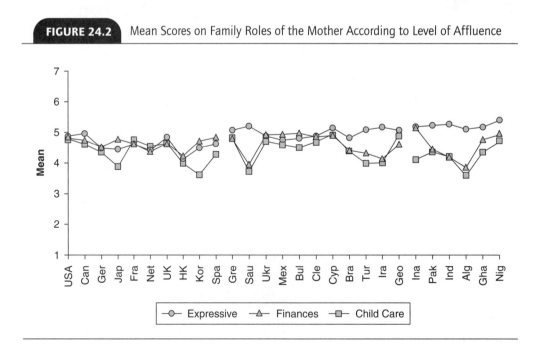

**FIGURE 24.2** Mean Scores on Family Roles of the Mother According to Level of Affluence

## Religious Denominations Across Countries

Religious denominations of countries are also a significant source of variation, although less so than the socioeconomic index. Only a few relationships were found.

Muslim fathers and mothers had the highest scores on expressive/emotional roles, followed by the Orthodox, Protestant, and Catholic countries. Muslim fathers had the highest means on financial roles, with the same order of religions. Christian Orthodox mothers had the highest means on the child care role, and Muslim mothers had the lowest. Orthodox countries had the highest means on visits with and telephone calls to family and kin.

## Similarities Across Countries

Emotional bonds with members of the nuclear and extended family were not related to the socioeconomic level of countries and, more important, did not differ across countries; this was a very robust universal finding, stronger with the nuclear family than with the extended family in all countries. Support was not found for the erosion of emotional ties to the nuclear family in Western societies, nor was emotional closeness to members of the family closer in countries with extended family systems. In addition, another universal finding was that emotional bonds were closest with the mother, second with siblings, and third with the father in all countries (Georgas et al., 2001; Georgas et al., 2006). Some might have expected that in the conjugal family in the United States, Canada, and northern Europe, young adult respondents might feel emotionally closer to the father than to their siblings.

Other universal findings were as follows: Expressive roles were higher than instrumental roles for all family positions across countries, whatever the socioeconomic level of the country; mothers scored higher than fathers on expressive roles and child care roles across countries, again whatever the socioeconomic level; fathers scored higher than mothers on the financial role, except in high-affluence countries; the financial role of mothers was not related to the socioeconomic level of countries, nor was the child care role of fathers; mothers across all countries performed more housework (cleaning, cooking, washing) than fathers; and older children played a more important role in maintaining family functions, with higher scores on both expressive and instrumental roles.

## Family and Social Institutions

The primary focus of the chapter has been on the family and the ethnic group. We have employed the term *ethnic group* up to now in an undifferentiated manner, usually as an ethnic group in a multicultural society or as a nation. Let us now look at the interrelationship between family and social institutions.

We often perceive family, particularly in North American and European societies, as an autonomous unit—that is, just the family itself and not in context with the state. However, from the perspective of cultural anthropology and family sociology, family is a social institution nested within the larger context of the state. That is, the individual is a member of a nuclear family. The nuclear family is nested within an extended family network. The extended family is nested within a group of extended families or kin called the clan, with relationships based on blood, through marriage, and through mutually beneficial relationships. Clans are nested within a larger group that may be loosely related through a common religion or ethnic origin or geographical region of the ethnic group. The clans may be antagonistic or in a state of truce, or they may form an alliance against a common ethnic enemy or the state.

The large nation-state was created throughout history, such as the Chinese empire, the Athenian empire, the Hellenistic empire under Alexander, the Roman empire, the Ottoman empire, Japan, the British empire, the Russian empire, the United States in the 18th century, and, in the 19th and 20th centuries, the European countries, India, and the Islamic countries. Almost all empires and nation-states governed various ethnic groups, most of which were subservient to the central government and without rights.

For most people throughout the world, central government was a powerful, distant, unfriendly institution whose only contact with their community was to collect taxes and to impose unwanted laws. The means of subsistence, for survival, protection against one's enemies, and psychological sustenance, were met by nuclear family, the extended family, and the clan. In most societies throughout the world, communities were composed of extended families, tied together through blood relationships, marriage, and the clan.

These nation-states or empires centralized power through social institutions regulating political, judicial, educational, religious, and other functions. The regulation of the social institutions was through edicts of the autocrat or monarch that were often arbitrary—for example, French monarch Louis XIV's declaration of *"l'etat c'est moi"* (I am the state). In today's democratic societies, laws regulating social institutions are based on equality of all citizens, protection of individual rights, and the protection of these rights through the courts.

In many autocratic regimes in countries throughout the world and even in some democracies at the present time, laws are perceived by many ethnic groups as unjust and as not granting the same rights as the dominant ethnic group. In these ethnic communities, all issues were decided by the leader or elders of the community without formal laws and with a history of tradition. But most important, these community elders were "family" in the sense described above. Under these circumstances, there was no ethical conflict between obeying the law of the state and loyalty to the "family" or community. Family loyalty was to the extended family and the clan and not to the state because the family and the clan were the basis for survival, protection, and development. In many societies throughout the world, when times are difficult, when your livelihood is threatened, when there are economic problems, and when there are health problems, the vital question is this: Whom do you trust and rely on, your extended family or the state?

## PSYCHOLOGICAL CONSEQUENCES OF CHANGES IN FAMILY SYSTEMS

What are the psychological consequences of the decrease of the traditional extended family systems and the increase of nuclear family systems? Are they weakening kin relations and the autonomy of the nuclear family in the United States, as Parsons theorized? One study (Georgas et al., 2006) suggested that family networks do not differ much between high-affluence and low-affluence countries, except for living further apart. Living arrangements in cultures throughout history, even in the United States, Canada, and northern Europe, were such that families often lived and slept together in one room. A separate room for each sibling is relatively recent in many cultures. With increasing affluence of many societies, newly married couples purchase or rent a separate house, often through aid from their parents. From a psychological viewpoint, individuality is a basic psychological phenomenon that does not exist only in Western societies. Agricultural societies control the social expression of individuality, whether through values, laws, or traditions. However, certain psychological needs of the individual may be universal and transcend the institutions, values, and traditions of societies. That is, increased affluence leads to changes in societies and social institutions. Some psychological variables also change, particularly attitudes, values, and behavior. However, how much other psychological variables change in relation to societal change, particularly those related to personality and bonds with people, is still an open question.

One of these is the need for psychological privacy, even in extended family systems. From a psychological point of view, we would speculate that a separate household might represent the need for privacy of the young couple and some degree of psychological separation from the parents, particularly the wife of the husband from the mother-in-law and the father-in-law.

Although emotional bonds with extended family members are not as close as with members of the nuclear family, interestingly enough, they do not differ much in countries with different socioeconomic levels throughout the world. Many believe that in cultures with clans and closely bound extended family systems, all the members of extended families and kin live harmoniously and are cooperative and happy. Cooperation in extended family systems, particularly in agricultural societies, is necessary for subsistence. However, in these societies, issues such as land rights and use, inheritance, and other matters require a delicate equilibrium between members of the extended family to avoid disputes that lead to open conflicts and are detrimental to the family, clan, or community.

Relationships between family members and kin are regulated through societal values, particularly in agricultural communities, dictating how one *should* behave toward family and kin. The findings of Georgas et al. (2006) suggest that family values are related to the socioeconomic level of the country and that they are still in effect in primarily agricultural countries but less so in more affluent countries. It also appears that values related to hierarchical relationships within the family, as well as hierarchical values in general, are the most important indicators of family change. Young people appear to increasingly reject the authoritarian model of the father, who makes all the decisions in the family, and the role of the submissive and conforming mother and children. On the other hand, family values related to maintaining relationships with family members and kin have changed much less than hierarchical roles within the nuclear family.

The role of the mother as primary caretaker in the family appears to have been subject to change to a far lesser extent than that of the father as authority figure and breadwinner in all societies. Another indicator of family change is the increased power of the mother in the family. The mother's engagement in the workforce, her higher level of education, and her economic contribution to the nuclear family have resulted in a lessening of authority of the father in many former agricultural societies. The mother has become at least as or more powerful than the father in affluent societies. Much of the family power may have shifted down in affluent countries and is now shared among parents and children, who enjoy more autonomy than in traditional family contexts.

## CONCLUSIONS

One conclusion stemming from this study is that while families are changing in different cultures throughout the world, the findings with the psychological variables suggest that close emotional relationships remain with members of the nuclear family, and communication with kin is still frequent, even in affluent Western societies.

That changes in the economy of countries, from subsistence level to industrial, service, and postindustrial economies, result in social changes and in changes in the family is not a matter of contention. The issue is whether these changes, driven by an economic engine, result in convergence of the same types of family structure and function as found in Western societies and have been predicted by modernization and globalization theories.

Cultural diffusion has been an inexorable process throughout the history of mankind. Egyptian culture influenced Greek culture, Greek culture influenced Roman culture, Roman culture influenced European culture, and so on. Geographical contiguity and contact between cultures have been the primary elements in cultural diffusion. In today's world, television, cinema, the Web, trade, and tourism are means of cultural diffusion beyond geographical contiguity. However, the critical question of cultural diffusion as related to modernization and globalization processes is whether there are limits to the degree of cultural diffusion. Will there be absolute homogenization of cultures throughout the world—one language, one religion, one food, and so forth? Will the national and cultural identity of individuals wither away?

Intercultural contacts or socioeconomic development do not necessarily or inevitably lead to the homogenization of all aspects of cultures throughout the world or of the behavior of individuals. Psychological universals, such as emotional bonds with the family and kin, the patterning of emotional bonds with members of the nuclear family, and the different gender differences in child care and housework, do not appear to reflect globalization processes as much as basic similarities in psychological processes of individuals across cultures.

In conclusion, the counselor should be aware of a number of variables when working with ethnic groups. One variable is that the family type is related to the context of the society. Another is that the term *family* in most ethnic groups connotes the extended family and not the nuclear or one-person family. A third is that values, including family values, are the most important psychological variables differentiating societies. In addition, the most important family value has to do with the authoritarian power of the father in agricultural societies. A fourth is that although there are differences in family roles in different societies, there are also many similarities of fathers' and mothers' family roles. And, finally, it appears that many psychological processes such as emotional closeness with the nuclear family and kin do not differ very much across cultures.

## CRITICAL INCIDENT

### Georgas

A Western-trained counseling psychologist had occasion to counsel a client from Saudi Arabia. After the client presented his problem and symptoms, his training taught him to inquire about the history of the problem and then about the relationships the client had with his family. The client described his father, then his mother, then his brothers and sisters. The counselor dutifully noted the information and was ready to inquire further about his relationships with them. But the client continued, describing the other wives of his father and his half-brothers and sisters. He continued, delineating his numerous uncles and aunts and his cousins on the side of his father, his mother, and the other wives of his father. The client went further, describing the family network of his grandfather (only the father of his father), his other sons and daughters, and so on. The counselor withdrew into a state of shock and then limited his inquiries to the history of the symptoms, without attempting to tie them to the relationships with the family. It was the counselor's first introduction to the fact that there are extended families and that many more relatives influence and shape psychological development than just one's father, mother, and siblings, as he had been trained. It also made him aware that the majority of families throughout the world are polygamous and not monogamous, as in Europe and North America.

The counselor's training in the United States emphasized the relationships of the individual to her or his nuclear family. Discussions of cases such as this can create confusion and intense discussions when confronted with the degree of attachment of mothers and fathers to the grandparents and other members of the extended family. Why should there be such close emotional attachments to the members of the extended family? Why did grandparents, aunts and uncles, and brothers and sisters continually interfere with issues of the nuclear family? One of the values of the nuclear family in Western societies is that grandparents should not interfere in the lives of their married children. Wasn't this interference an indication of the pathology of the extended family? Eventually, discussions will help work through these issues, especially if one realizes that the family, including the extended family, is an important and positive element in the psychological development of the child. It can also be a factor in the development of psychopathology. The basic lesson is that relationships of the individual with the extended family cannot be ignored. This learning experience was chronologically parallel with the development of family therapy during the 1960s.

As discussed in the chapter, there are different perceptions and connotations of "family" by counselors in the United States, Canada, and northern Europe as compared to most of the rest of the world. In Western countries, the term *family* is usually associated with *nuclear family,* that is, mother, father, and children, living in a house apart from grandparents, aunts, and uncles, who come together only during Thanksgiving or Christmas and New Year. This perception reflects, to a large degree, cultural values of Western societies about family. The nuclear family is associated with behaviors and values of Western societies, such as the following: The father should be friends with his children; children should speak up and be heard; the equality of the mother and father in financial matters, making decisions together, works; teenagers should be granted considerable freedom; children should be taught to make their own decisions; after high school or college, the children will "leave the nest," find a job, and be independent; and (grand)parents should not interfere in the lives of their married children.

Therefore, consider the following when involved with professional counseling:

- In most countries throughout the world, *family* connotes the extended family, that is, grandparents, aunts, uncles, cousins, and even unrelated persons close to the family.

- Counselors should be aware of the differences in family structure and function of different ethnic groups, and most are. But an important aspect of counseling individuals from ethnic groups is the assumptions and values about the family of the client. That is, the typical procedure of any counselor is to seek information about the type of family and relationships of the client with his or her family. But, in working with ethnic individuals, this procedure requires the counselor to be aware of how one's knowledge, individualistic values, and assumptions regarding the "nuclear family" may influence the client.

- No matter how well trained, no matter how objective and nonjudgmental, a counselor always has a personal "microtheory" of different approaches to understanding, communication, and counseling clients. And these personal assumptions of the counselor influence the client, directly or indirectly, through verbal and nonverbal cues. Also, the common nucleus in these different approaches to counseling about problems in interpersonal relationships is the assumption of the self-development, individuality, and independence of the client. This, after all, is a basic tenet of counseling and of psychology.

- A counselor in North America or northern Europe is aware of the dynamics of interpersonal behavior in nuclear families and how to aid the individual to clarify her or his relationship with members of the nuclear family. However, one's microtheory of the relationship between the individual and her or his nuclear family does not necessarily extend to extended family relationships of recent immigrant families and of the different types of acculturation strategies of these families.

1.   There are different types of nuclear and extended family systems (e.g., stem, joint, fully extended). What might be the potential ecological and social determinants of these different family types?

2.   What are some possible explanations of why ethnic individuals in multicultural countries such as the United States, Canada, or Australia choose to open a restaurant, cleaners, or other small business rather than work in an office or factory?

3.   Provide an analysis of your family network—that is, your father's and mother's parents (your grandparents), their brothers and sisters (your uncles and aunts), your siblings, and your first cousins. How far do they live from you, how frequently and when do you visit them, and how frequently do you telephone them? With which do you have the closest relationships or emotional bonds?

4.   Will the traditional types of families in non-Western cultures eventually evolve into the nuclear family, divorced family, and one-parent family systems of North America and northern Europe? Present arguments on both sides of this issue.

5.   It has long been assumed that immigrants acculturate to societies through the process of *assimilation*, such as in the United States, whose traditional immigration policy has been "the melting pot." What are the four types of acculturation strategies of immigrants according to Berry's theory? Which has been found to be most common? Explain why, according to the psychological theory of identity formation.

6.   What are the major differences in family networks, family roles, and psychological variables across cultures, as found in a recent study of 27 nations by Georgas et al. (2006)?

7.   What are the major similarities or universals in family roles and psychological variables across cultures, as found in a recent study of 27 nations by Georgas et al. (2006)?

8.   One conclusion stemming from Georgas et al. (2006) is that while families are changing in different cultures throughout the world, the findings with the psychological variables suggest that close emotional relationships remain with members of the nuclear family, and communication with kin is still frequent, even in affluent Western societies. Discuss.

# REFERENCES

Berry, J. W. (1980). Acculturation as varieties of adaptation. In A. Padilla (Ed.), *Acculturation: Theory, models and findings* (pp. 9–25). Boulder, CO: Westview.

Berry, J. W. (2006). Acculturation: Living successfully in two cultures. *International Journal of Intercultural Relations, 29,* 697–712.

Berry, J. W., Phinney, J. S., Sam, D. L., & Vedder, P. (2006). *Immigrant youth in cultural transition: Acculturation, identity, and adaptation across national contexts.* Mahwah, NJ: Lawrence Erlbaum.

Blumberg, R. L., & Winch, R. F. (1972). Societal complexity and familial complexity: Evidence for the curvilinear hypothesis. *American Journal of Sociology, 77,* 898–920.

Durkheim, E. (1888). Introduction a la sociologie de la famille [Introduction to the sociology of the family]. *Annales De la Faculte des Lettres de Bordeaux, 10.*

Durkheim, E. (1921). La famille conjugale [The conjugal family]. *Revue Philosophique de la France et de l'Etranger, 90,* 1–14. (Original work published 1892)

Ember, C. R., & Ember, M. (2002). *Cultural anthropology* (10th ed.). Upper Saddle River, NJ: Prentice Hall.

Georgas, J., Berry, J. W., van de Vijver, F. J. R., Kagitçibasi, C., & Poortinga, Y. H. (2006). *Families across cultures: A 30-nation psychological study.* Cambridge, UK: Cambridge University Press.

Georgas, J., Mylonas, K., Bafiti, T., Christakopoulou, S., Poortinga, Y. H., Kagitçibasi, Ç., et al. (2001). Functional relationships in the nuclear and extended family: A 16 culture study. *International Journal of Psychology, 36,* 289–300.

Huntington, S. P. (1996). *The clash of civilizations and the remaking of world order.* New York: Simon & Schuster.

Inkeles, A. (1998). *One world emerging? Convergence and divergence in industrial societies.* Boulder, CO: Westview.

Levinson, D., & Malone, M. J. (1980). *Toward explaining human culture.* New Haven, CT: HRAF Press.

Murdock, G. P. (1967). *Ethnographic atlas.* Pittsburgh, PA: HRAF Press.

Murdock, P. M. (1949). *Social structure.* New York: Free Press.

Nimkoff, M. F., & Middleton, R. (1960). Types of family and types of economy. *American Journal of Sociology, 66,* 215–225.

Parsons, T. (1943). The kinship system of the contemporary United States. *American Anthropologist, 45,* 22–38.

Parsons, T. (1949). The social structure of the family. In R. N. Anshen (Ed.), *The family: Its functions and destiny* (pp. 33–58). New York: Harper.

Parsons, T. (1965). The normal American family. In S. M. Farber (Ed.), *Man and civilization: The family's search for survival* (pp. 34–36). New York: McGraw-Hill.

Popenoe, D. (1988). *Disturbing the nest: Family changes and decline in modern societies.* New York: Aldine De Gruyter.

Schwartz, S. H. (1994). Beyond individualism-collectivism: New cultural dimensions of values. In U. Kim, H. C. Triandis, C. Kagitçibasi, S.-C. Choi, & G. Yoon (Eds.), *Individualism and collectivism: Theory, method, and applications* (pp. 85–119). Thousand Oaks, CA: Sage.

Smith, S. (1995). Family theory and multicultural family studies. In B. Ingoldsby & S. Smith (Eds.), *Families in multicultural perspective* (pp. 5–35). New York: Guilford.

# Index

# About the Editors

**Juris G. Draguns** was born in Latvia, completed primary schooling in his native country, graduated from high school in Germany, and obtained his undergraduate degree in the United States. His PhD in clinical psychology is from the University of Rochester. In 1997, he retired from Pennsylvania State University as Professor Emeritus of Psychology. He has taught and lectured, in five languages, at the University of Mainz in Germany; Lund University in Sweden; East-West Center in Hawaii; Flinders University of South Australia; National Taiwan University in Taipei, University of the Americas–Puebla in Cholula, Mexico; and University of Latvia and Baltic Russian Institute, both in Riga. He continues to pursue his interests in cross-cultural research on psychotherapy and counseling and other topics. He is recipient of the American Psychological Association's Award for Contributions to the International Advancement of Psychology and of an honorary doctoral degree from the University of Latvia and is President of the Society for Cross-Cultural Research.

**Walter J. Lonner** has been dedicated to cross-cultural psychological research since the mid-1960s. He is Founding and Special Issues Editor of the *Journal of Cross-Cultural Psychology,* which was inaugurated in 1970. A charter member, past president, and Honorary Fellow of the International Association for Cross-Cultural Psychology (IACCP), he has been involved with about forty books concerning various facets of cross-cultural psychological research and its applications. In 2006 IACCP inaugurated a Distinguished Invited Lecturer Series in his name to honor his contributions and continuing dedication to the field. In 2007 the Center for Cross-Cultural Research at Western Washington University followed suit and inaugurated a similar series. He has had sabbatical leaves in Germany, Mexico, and New Zealand and has attended conferences and delivered papers in more than 30 countries. A former Fulbright scholar (Germany, 1984–1985), he is Professor Emeritus of Psychology at Western Washington University, where he co-founded the Center for Cross-Cultural Research in 1969. Most importantly, prior to his retirement in 2001 for nearly 35 years he taught his favorite course, Psychology and Culture, more than 100 times.

**Paul B. Pedersen** is a Visiting Professor in the Department of Psychology at the University of Hawaii and Professor Emeritus from Syracuse University. He has taught at the University of Minnesota, Syracuse University, University of Alabama at Birmingham, and for 6 years at universities in Taiwan, Malaysia, and Indonesia. He was also on the Summer School Faculty at Harvard University, 1984–1988, and the University of Pittsburgh—Semester at Sea voyage around the world, spring 1992. International experience includes numerous consulting experiences in Asia, Australia, Africa, South America, and Europe and a Senior Fulbright award teaching at

National Taiwan University, 1999–2000. He has authored, coauthored, or edited 40 books, 99 articles, and 72 chapters on aspects of multicultural counseling and international communication. He is a Fellow in Divisions 9, 17, 45, and 52 of the American Psychological Association. For more information and a complete curriculum vitae, contact http//:soeweb.syr.edu/chs/Pedersen.

**Joseph E. Trimble,** PhD (University of Oklahoma, Institute of Group Relations), formerly a Fellow at Harvard University's Radcliffe Institute for Advanced Study, is Professor of Psychology at Western Washington University, a Senior Scholar at the Tri-Ethnic Center for Prevention Research at Colorado State University, and a Research Associate for the National Center for American Indian and Alaska Native Mental Health Research at the University of Colorado Health Sciences Center. He has held offices in the International Association for Cross-Cultural Psychology and the American Psychological Association. He holds Fellow status in three divisions in the APA (Divisions 9, 27, and 45). He is past President of the Society for the Psychological Study of Ethnic Minority Issues (Division 45 of the APA) and a Council member for the Society for the Psychological Study of Social Issues (Division 9 of the APA Association). He has generated more than 100 publications on cross-cultural and ethnic topics in psychology, including 16 edited, coedited, and coauthored books; one of his coedited books, the *Handbook of Racial and Ethnic Minority Psychology,* was selected as *CHOICE* Magazine's Outstanding Academic Titles for 2004. His most recent book, with Celia B. Fisher, is titled *The Handbook of Ethical Research With Ethnocultural Populations and Communities.* The majority of his articles, book chapters, and books focus on the role of culture and ethnicity in psychology, with an emphasis on American Indian and Alaska Native populations. In the past decade, though, he expanded his interests to include writing and research on ethnic and racial identity, cultural measurement equivalence, spirituality, and ethics, as well as contributing to the growth of ethnic psychology. He has received numerous excellence in teaching and mentoring awards for his work in the field of ethnic and cultural psychology, including the Excellence in Teaching Award and the Paul J. Olscamp Faculty Research Award from Western Washington University; APA's Division 45 Lifetime Achievement Award; the Janet E. Helms Award for Mentoring and Scholarship in Professional Psychology at Teachers College, Columbia University; the Washington State Psychological Association Distinguished Psychologist Award for 2002; the Peace and Social Justice Award from APA's Division 48; and the Distinguished Elder Award in 2007 from the National Multicultural Summit and Conference. Also, he was the O'Brien Visiting Fellow at Scripps College in 2007.

# About the Contributors

**Frances E. Aboud** is Professor of Psychology at McGill University in Montreal. She has been conducting research on ethnic identity and prejudice for the past 30 years. In addition to her publication in social psychology and child development journals, she is the author of *Children and Prejudice* (1988). She has also taught courses in and studied issues related to health psychology, particularly as they apply to problems of developing countries. After her experience in Ethiopia as a member of the McGill-Ethiopia Community Health Project, she published *Health Psychology in Global Perspective* (1998). More recently, as a scientist associated with the Centre for Health and Population Research (ICDDR,B) in Bangladesh, she has given courses and conducted research on early childhood education and feeding in rural Bangladesh. She is currently Senior Editor of Health Psychology for the international journal *Social Science and Medicine.*

**James Allen** is Professor of Psychology at the University of Alaska Fairbanks and, recently, a Fulbright scholar at the Psychosocial Centre for Refugees, University of Oslo. His interests are in cultural, clinical, and community psychology. His research focuses on cross-cultural measurement development and adaptation, acculturation and human rights issues with indigenous people and refugees, and participatory research methodologies with tribal communities. His recent work focuses on protective and recovery factors with Alaska Natives, as well as the development and implementation of culturally based prevention and treatment services for Alaska Native youth.

**Nancy Arthur** is Professor in the Division of Applied Psychology and a Canada Research Chair in professional education at the University of Calgary, Calgary, Alberta, Canada. Her teaching and research interests include multicultural counseling and career development. She authored the book *Counselling International Students: Clients From Around the World.* Her coedited book with Sandra Collins, *Culture-Infused Counselling: Celebrating the Canadian Mosaic,* received the Canadian Counselling Association Book Award in 2006. She is currently coediting a book with Paul Pedersen on case incidents in counseling for international transitions that involves collaboration with authors from 12 different countries.

**Fred Bemak** is Professor in the Counseling and Development Program and the Director and cofounder of the Diversity Research and Action Center at George Mason University. His research focuses on cross-counseling counseling, social justice, youth and families at risk, and refugee and immigrant psychosocial adjustment. He has provided training and consultation in 30 countries, as well as throughout the United States, and is a former Fulbright Scholar, Kellogg Foundation International Fellow, and World Rehabilitation Fund International Fellow. He has authored numerous publications in his areas of research, including a coauthored book with Rita

Chi-Ying Chung and Paul Pedersen on the psychosocial adjustment of refugees. He is currently working with Rita Chi-Ying Chung on a book on social justice and multiculturalism.

**J. Manuel Casas** is Professor in the Counseling, Clinical, and School Psychology Department at the University of California, Santa Barbara. He has published extensively (more than 130 publications) and serves on numerous editorial boards. He is the coauthor of the *Handbook of Racial/Ethnic Minority Counseling Research* and is one of the editors of both editions of the *Handbook of Multicultural Counseling*. His recent research has focused on Hispanic families and children who are at risk for experiencing educational and psychosocial problems, including drug and alcohol abuse. His research emphasizes the resiliency factors that can help Hispanic families avoid or overcome such problems. Together with his colleagues, he has brought numerous research grants to the campus and the community. He is a consultant to several private and governmental agencies and organizations.

**Ana Mari Cauce** is Executive Vice Provost and Earl T. Carlson Professor of Psychology at the University of Washington, where she previously served as Chair of the Department of Psychology and Chair of American Ethnic Studies. She is interested in the development of ethnic minority youth and at-risk youth more generally. She is recipient of numerous awards, including the University of Washington's Distinguished Teaching Award, as well as Distinguished Contribution Awards from the American Psychological Association for excellence in research on minority groups and families and from the Society for Community Research and Action for her work with at-risk youth and families.

**Doris Chang** is Assistant Professor of Psychology at the New School for Social Research. She completed postdoctoral training at the Department of Social Medicine, Harvard Medical School in clinically relevant medical anthropology. Grounded in an interdisciplinary framework, her research and clinical interests include cross-cultural issues in diagnosis and mental health treatment, the cultural contexts of domestic violence and service delivery in Asian immigrant communities, and social change and mental health care in the People's Republic of China. In 2006, she received the Early Career Award for Distinguished Contributions from the Asian American Psychological Association.

**Rita Chi-Ying Chung** is Professor in the Counseling and Development Program, George Mason University. Her research focuses on social justice and multiculturalism in the areas of psychosocial adjustment of refugees and immigrants, interethnic group relations and racial stereotypes, and trafficking of Asian girls. She has lived and worked in the Pacific Rim, Asia, and Latin America. She was the former Chair of the American Counseling Association (ACA) Human Rights Committee and the ACA International Committee; currently, she is an Executive Council Member of the International Association for Counselling. She has coauthored with Fred Bemak and Paul Pedersen on a book about the psychosocial adjustment of refugees and is currently working with Fred Bemak on a book on social justice and multiculturalism.

**Tuere Binta Cross** graduated with a BA in psychology from Mount Holyoke College and completed her master's degree in social work from New York University. Her work and internship experience include counseling at-risk families, working in specialized foster care, and practicing psychoanalytic psychotherapy at the Training Institute for Mental Health in New York City. Her future plans involve obtaining a certificate in analysis and eventually opening a clinical practice.

**William E. Cross Jr.** received his doctorate in social psychology from Princeton University. He is the author of *Shades of Black* (1991), a frequently cited text on Black identity. Currently, he coordinates the doctoral program in social-personality psychology at the Graduate Center for the City University of New York.

**Marwan Dwairy** is Associate Professor of Psychology at Emek Yezreel College and Oranim College. He is a licensed expert and supervisor in three areas: educational, medical, and developmental psychology. In addition, he is a licensed clinical psychologist. In 1978, he established Israel's first psychological services center for Arabs in Nazareth, Israel. He continues to serve in this capacity as a supervisor in different psychological centers. He has developed and standardized several psychological tests for Arabs. He served as a professor in several universities: graduate program at Nova Southeastern University in Florida; Haifa University, Israel; and Technion, Israel. He is a reviewer for several journals, and he served on the editorial board of *Clinical Psychology Review* and edited a special issue (December 1999) for that journal devoted to cross-cultural psychotherapy in the Middle East. He has published several books and articles on cross-cultural psychology and mental health among Arabs, in which he presented his models and theories concerning culturally sensitive psychology.

**Susan J. Eklund** is Professor Emerita in the Department of Counseling and Educational Psychology at Indiana University, Bloomington. She also holds emerita status as Byron Root Professor of Aging, Director of the Center on Aging and Aged, and Associate Dean of the Faculties. Her research interests include cognitive function and mental health issues in aging as well as influences of culture on the experience of aging.

**Lanaya L. Ethington** is a doctoral student in the Counseling Psychology program at Indiana University in Bloomington. She received a BA in Spanish and psychology from the University of Michigan and an MA in intercultural studies from Dublin City University. Her research interests include multicultural counseling, multicultural consultation, and career development.

**Mary A. Fukuyama** has worked at the University of Florida Counseling Center for the past 25 years as a counseling psychologist, supervisor, and trainer. She is a clinical professor and teaches courses on spirituality and multicultural counseling for the Department of Counselor Education and also the Counseling Psychology Program. She is an active member of the University of Florida's Center for Spirituality and Health, and her research interests include a qualitative study on "multicultural expressions" of spirituality. She coauthored, with Todd Sevig, *Integrating Spirituality Into Multicultural Counseling.*

**Elizabeth M. P. Gama** completed her doctoral studies at the University of Minnesota and was a university professor in Brazil, where she taught for many years. An accomplished researcher, she has published many articles and presented papers at national and international meetings. Her interest in women's issues started in graduate school and has continued in many of the articles she has written since then. Currently, she lives in Brazil, where she is Managing Director and Senior Consultant of Develop, a human management consulting firm, and has been providing selection and development assessment and coaching to managers and executives.

**James Georgas** is Professor Emeritus of Psychology at the University of Athens, Athens, Greece. He is President of the International Association for Cross-Cultural Psychology; Member of the Executive Committee, International Union of Psychological Science; Member of the Board of Directors, International Association of Applied Psychology; Member of the Aristotle Prize Committee, European Federation of Psychologists Associations; and Member of the Scholarship Committee, Alexander

S. Onassis Public Benefit Foundation. A recent publication is *Families Across Culture: A 30 Nation Psychological Study* (2006).

**John Gonzalez** is Assistant Professor of Psychology at the University of Alaska Fairbanks. He is a member of the White Earth Ojibwe Nation in Northern Minnesota and a graduate of the Indians into Psychology Doctoral Education (INPSYDE) program at the University of North Dakota. His interests are in the areas of mental health issues for indigenous people and ethnic minorities, with an emphasis on understanding ethnic and cultural identity factors to increase prevention programs. His work is guided by his life experience of growing up on the reservation, and he hopes to be able to give back to his people someday.

**Ingrid Grieger** currently is Director of the Counseling Center at Iona College in New Rochelle, New York, and Adjunct Professor of Counseling at Fordham University's Graduate School of Education. She has strong clinical, teaching, and research interests in women's issues in counseling, as well as in multicultural counseling, multicultural organizational development, and mental health and wellness issues for college student populations. A frequent presenter and writer regarding these topics, she has authored chapters in the *Handbook on Counseling Women,* the *Handbook of Multicultural Counseling* (2nd ed.), and the *Handbook of Multicultural Assessment: Clinical, Psychological, and Educational Applications* (3rd ed.).

**Sunny S. Hansen** is Professor Emerita in the Counseling and Student Personnel Psychology Program in the College of Education and Human Development at the University of Minnesota, where she earned her doctorate She has taught and advised students in career development, gender issues, and multicultural counseling for many years. She was creator of the BORN FREE program to expand options and reduce stereotyping of both genders. BORN FREE currently is being updated with an international component and should be on a Web site by 2007. Her research interests are in gender-role socialization, career guidance across cultures, and career development of women. She is a Fellow of the American Psychological Association (APA), American Counseling Association (ACA), and the National Career Development Association (NCDA). She has lectured and conducted workshops in all states and 35 countries. In 2006, she was honored as one of 100 distinguished alumni of the College of Education in its centennial year. Her most recent book, now under revision, is *Integrative Life Planning,* a holistic model of career development.

**Amy K. Harkins** received her doctorate in counseling psychology from Arizona State University in 2005. She earned her BA in psychology at the University of Vermont and an MA from the Counseling and Student Personnel Psychology Program at the University of Minnesota. Currently, she is a geropsychology postdoctoral resident with Deer Oaks, a behavioral health organization in Texas. Her primary research and practice interests have focused on multicultural issues within the framework of positive psychology.

**Susanna A. Hayes** is Associate Professor Emeritus in the Department of Psychology at Western Washington University. During her career, her primary teaching responsibilities were in the master's-level School Counseling and Mental Health Counseling programs. For eight years, she was a teacher and counselor on the Colville Indian Reservation in Eastern Washington. She also worked with inner-city schools in Saginaw, Michigan, for three years. For three months early in 2007, she taught in Rome, Italy, for Loyola University of Chicago in its Study Abroad program.

**P. Paul Heppner** currently is Professor at the University of Missouri–Columbia and one of the founders and codirectors of the Center for Multicultural Research, Training, and Consultation. He has received numerous MU and national awards, including three Fulbright awards. He has been an active researcher with more than 120 publications and more than 200 presentations at national conferences, and he has been an invited speaker in 12 countries. He has served on several editorial boards, as well as the Editor of *The Counseling Psychologist.* He has a long list of professional service, including serving as President of the Society of Counseling Psychology.

**Carrie L. Hill** earned her doctorate in counseling psychology with a minor in gerontology from Indiana University–Bloomington in 2001. She has spent more than 10 years working for agencies in the health, human service, and senior markets, and currently she is owner of Blooming Hill Writing Services. She is the Southern Regional Representative to the Executive Board of the Utah Gerontological Society and serves as Editor of its newsletter. She has published more than a dozen journal articles and book chapters on subjects related to gerontology, multicultural issues, and psychology.

**Farah A. Ibrahim** is Professor at the University of Colorado Denver and Health Sciences Center. A fellow of the American Psychological Association and a licensed psychologist, she has served as the elected president of Counselors for Social Justice (2002–2003), a national division of the American Counseling Association. Her research and teaching has focused on cultural issues in counseling. She developed the Cultural Identity Checklist and, with Harris Kahn, the Scale to Assess Worldview. She has served on several counseling psychology and counseling journal editorial boards and currently serves as the book review editor and a reviewer for the *International Journal for the Advancement of Counseling.* She consults nationally on issues of cultural competence with organizations, colleges, universities, and public schools.

**Szu-Hui Lee** following her internship at McLean Hospital/Harvard Medical School stayed on to become a clinical postdoctoral fellow at the Obsessive Compulsive Disorder Institute, a residential treatment facility for patients with severe and refractory obsessive-compulsive disorder. Her interests include multidisciplinary mental health treatment and service delivery as well as education/prevention and training within the cross-cultural context. Her research has focused on the correlates between culturally salient factors and psychological well-being of people of color broadly and Asian/Asian Americans specifically. She is actively involved with the Asian American Psychological Association and American Psychological Association.

**Frederick T. L. Leong** is Professor of Psychology at Michigan State University (MSU) in the I-O and Clinical Psychology Programs. Prior to MSU, he was on the faculty at Southern Illinois University (1988–1991), The Ohio State University (1991–2003), and the University of Tennessee (2003–2006). He has authored or coauthored more than 100 articles in various counseling and psychology journals and 50 book chapters; he has also edited or coedited six books. He is a Fellow of the American Psychological Association (Divisions 1, 2, 17, 45, and 52) and the Association for Psychological Science. He is a Charter Fellow of the Asian American Psychological Association. He was the recipient of the 1998 Distinguished Contributions Award from the Asian American Psychological Association and the 1999 John Holland Award from the APA Division of Counseling Psychology. His major research interests are in cultural and personality factors in career development and work adjustment, occupational stress, culture and mental health (particularly with Asians and Asian Americans), and cross-cultural psychotherapy. He is the immediate past President of both the Asian American Psychological Association and the Division of Counseling Psychology of the International Association of Applied Psychology. Currently, he is President of Division 45 of the APA (Society for the Psychological Study of Ethnic Minority Issues). His latest project is the *Sage Encyclopedia of Counseling,* for which he is the Editor-in-Chief.

**Arleen C. Lewis** is Professor of Psychology and Director of the MEd School Counseling Program at Western Washington University in Bellingham, WA, where she has been a member of the faculty since 1987. She was previously Associate Professor of Counselor Education at the University of Arkansas in Fayetteville.

**Charlea T. McNeal** is Research Associate with the Anxiety Disorders Program in the Department of Psychiatry at the University of Michigan. She obtained her doctoral degree in social psychology and master's degree in social work at the University of Michigan in 1999 and completed a postdoctoral fellowship with the Family Research Consortium—III under the tutelage of Vonnie McLoyd. She is also a licensed social worker. Her clinical, teaching, and research interests center on mental health in interpersonal contexts, with an emphasis on family processes in racial ethnic minorities, especially African American couples.

**Gerald V. Mohatt** is Professor of Psychology and Director of the Center for Alaska Native Health Research at the University of Alaska Fairbanks. Throughout his career, he has focused on building new settings in rural areas to increase opportunity for rural indigenous groups. His current work is to establish a permanent center to do interdisciplinary research on health disparities of Alaska Natives. He was raised in rural Iowa. He has two sons, their two partners, and a granddaughter. He has worked with American Indian, Canadian First Nations, and Alaska Natives since 1968.

**Joseph G. Ponterotto** currently is Professor of Education in the counseling programs at Fordham University's Graduate School of Education. His primary research and teaching interests are in the areas of multiculturalism and research design. He coedited the April 2005 special issue of the *Journal of Counseling Psychology on Qualitative Research Methods* with Beth Haverkamp and Sue Morrow. His most recent book is *Preventing Prejudice: A Guide for Counselors, Educators, and Parents* (2nd ed., 2006), coauthored with Shawn Utsey and Paul Pedersen.

**Mark Pope** is Professor of Counseling and Family Therapy and Chair of that same division at the University of Missouri–Saint Louis. He is past President of the American Counseling Association, the National Career Development Association, and the Association for Gay, Lesbian, and Bisexual Issues in Counseling, and he is the Editor of *The Career Development Quarterly.* He previously served as the Director of Psychological Services for the Native American AIDS Project in San Francisco. His research interests include multicultural career counseling, psychological assessment, history of and public policy issues in counseling and psychology, gay/lesbian issues, Native American issues, and violence in schools.

**Jason Duque Raley** is Assistant Professor at the University of California, Santa Barbara. He received his doctoral training in Stanford University's Graduate School of Education in the area of Language, Literacy, and Culture. His current work explores the relationship among culture, learning, and social interaction, as well as the epistemology and practice of qualitative research. As codirector of the Center for the Study of Teacher Learning in Practice, he focuses on the contribution of contemporary learning theories to the understanding of teaching and learning in schools. Recent publications examine the nature of peer relations among Mexican American youth, the role of ethnicity in school experience, and the way people in diverse groups negotiate and accomplish "safe spaces" for learning.

**Charles R. Ridley** is Professor and Codirector of Training of the doctoral program in Counseling Psychology at Indiana University in Bloomington. He also is a former Associate Dean of Research and the University Graduate School at that institution. He is a Fellow in Divisions 17 and 45 of the American Psychological Association. His various scholarly interests include multicultural counseling, training, and assessment; organizational consultation; the use of religious resources in psychotherapy; and therapeutic change. His book, *Overcoming Unintentional Racism in Counseling and Therapy: A Practitioner's Guide to Intervention,* was the recipient of the Gus Meyers Center Award for Human Rights.

**Melanie M. Domenech Rodríguez** is Associate Professor of Psychology at Utah State University. Currently, she is evaluating the effectiveness of a Parent Management Training–Oregon intervention, culturally adapted for use with Spanish-speaking Latinos, to prevent the escalation of externalizing behavior problems into clinical syndromes. The research is supported by a K01 grant from the National Institute of Mental Health. She also has ongoing collaboration with researchers in Mexico City and Monterrey. She is a licensed psychologist. She completed her doctoral degree at Colorado State University in 1999 and a postdoctoral fellowship with the Family Research Consortium—III. She was born and raised in Puerto Rico and lives in Logan, Utah, with her spouse and two daughters.

**Todd Sevig** is Director of Counseling & Psychological Services at the University of Michigan, Ann Arbor. He has focused his career on the delivery of mental health services to university students in various capacities, including peer programming/counseling, multicultural training and counseling, and administration. He has also worked in the Program on Intergroup Relations at the University of Michigan and focused on areas such as White awareness, intergroup dialogue, and social justice. He is coauthor, with Mary Fukuyama, of *Integrating Spirituality Into Multicultural Counseling.* He is the son of a Lutheran minister and a musician and was raised in northern Minnesota and Iowa. He is married to Sharon Vaughters and has two children, Mara and Joseph. Recent areas of research interest include spirituality in counseling, bi/multiracial identity development, and changing trends in college student mental health.

**Johanna Soet** is the Director of the Sexual Assault Prevention and Awareness Center at the University of Michigan. She is a counseling psychologist who has focused on issues that disproportionately affect women, sexuality, multicultural competency, and spirituality. Her current work includes addressing sexual violence on college campuses, the role of men in the antiviolence movement, and researching and attending to college student mental health needs. She is also an advocate for Jewish student concerns and works to address Christian privilege in the academic setting. She shares her home with two young sons, three cats, and a guinea pig.

**Lisa Rey Thomas** received her doctorate from the University of Washington in clinical psychology. Following her internship at the Veterans Administration Puget Sound Health Care System, she became a postdoctoral fellow at the Alcohol and Drug Abuse Institute (ADAI), University of Washington. She is currently a Research Scientist at ADAI and coinvestigator on an NCMHD-funded Community-Based Participatory Research project with a local reservation tribal community. She is committed to reducing health disparities, increasing access to effective and culturally appropriate services, and promoting good health in underserved communities, with a particular focus on mental health and substance abuse issues in American Indian and Alaska Native communities. She serves on numerous committees and task groups, including the American Psychological Association's Committee on Ethnic Minority Affairs (chair-elect, 2006).

**Ivory Achebe Toldson** is Assistant Professor in Counseling Psychology at Howard University and Senior Research Analyst for the Congressional Black Caucus Foundation. He received his doctorate in counseling psychology from Temple University and the Du Bois Fellowship from the U.S. Department of Justice. His clinical experiences include serving as a correctional and forensic psychology intern at the U.S. Penitentiary and the clinical director of the Manhood Training Village, a residential group home for adolescents in state custody. His primary areas of research include Black men in the criminal justice system, social justice in counseling and education, culturally responsive counseling, substance abuse treatment, and counseling in urban diverse communities.

**Melba J. T. Vasquez** is a psychologist in independent practice in Austin, Texas. She is coauthor, with Ken Pope, of the books *Ethics in Psychotherapy & Counseling: A Practical Guide* (3rd ed., 2007) and *How to Survive and Thrive as a Therapist: Information, Ideas and Resources for Psychologists in Practice* (2005). She served as President of the Texas Psychological Association, past President of APA Divisions 35 (Society of Psychology of Women) and 17 (Society of Counseling Psychology), and as the first Latina member-at-large of the APA Board of Directors. She is a Fellow of the APA and holds the Diplomate of the American Board of Professional Psychology. She is a cofounder of APA Division 45, Society for the Psychological Study of Ethnic Minority Issues, and of the National Multicultural Conference and Summit.

**Clemmont E. Vontress**, a licensed psychologist, is one of the country's best-known authorities on cross-cultural counseling. He also is recognized for his articles, chapters, and books on existential counseling and traditional healing. He has made several field trips to West Africa to study methods used by folk healers to treat patients complaining of physical, psychological, social, and spiritual problems. He also has studied and written about ethnopsychiatry, an approach used in France for counseling immigrants from developing countries. Professor Emeritus of Counseling at George Washington University, where he worked for 28 years, he has been a Visiting Professor at the Johns Hopkins University, Atlanta University, Kuwait University, Howard University, and other institutions. A consultant to numerous organizations in this country and abroad, he has traveled widely in the United States, the Middle East, Africa, Europe, and the Caribbean. His interest in finding effective approaches for counseling culturally different clients began when he was in graduate school. His book, *Counseling Negroes* (1971), was the first one to call attention to the impact of culture and race on counseling Blacks in the United States. Since that time, he has written more than a hundred articles, chapters, and books on cross-cultural counseling, traditional healing, and existential counseling and psychotherapy.

**Colleen A. Ward** is Professor of Psychology and Director of the Center for Applied Cross-Cultural Research at Victoria University of Wellington, New Zealand. She has held teaching and research appointments at the University of the West Indies, Trinidad; Science University of Malaysia; National University of Singapore; and University of Canterbury, New Zealand. She is currently President of the Asian Association of Social Psychology and holds the James Cook Fellowship in Social Science in New Zealand. Her major research interests are in the area of acculturation, and she is coauthor (with Stephen Bochner and Adrian Furnham) of *The Psychology of Culture Shock*.